THE
RUGBY
ANNUAL

FIRST EDITION

THE
RUGBY
ANNUAL

FIRST EDITION

Editor: Bill Mitchell
Associate Editor: Nigel Starmer-Smith

PELHAM BOOKS

Contents

Opposite title page David Pickering (Wales) is not puffing and blowing; he is just trying to escape from Eric Champ (France).

First published in Great Britain in 1986 by
Pelham Books
27 Wrights Lane
Kensington
London W8 5DZ

Copyright © Sackville Design Group Ltd, 1986

Designed and produced by Sackville Design Group Ltd
78 Margaret Street, London W1N 7HB
Art director: Joyce Chester
In-house editor: Lorraine Jerram

British Library Cataloguing in Publication Data

The Rugby Annual.—1985-86 –
  1. Rugby football—Periodicals
  796.33'3'05   GV944.8

ISBN 0-7207-1701-9

Typeset in Times New Roman by MacSet Ltd, Wembley and by Sackville Design Group Ltd
Origination by Anglia Reproductions, Witham
Printed and bound in Great Britain by Hazell Watson and Viney Limited, Aylesbury

Message from the RFU   7
by Air Commodore R. H. G. Weighill, CBE, DFC
Editorial Preface   8
by Bill Mitchell
Foreword   9
by Nigel Starmer-Smith
Review of the Season, 1985-86   10
Diary of the 1985-86 Season   17

FEATURES
The Springboks Crushed   26
by Willie John McBride
The Best Fifteens, 1977-86   29
Goal-kicking Forwards: a Dying Breed?   34
Professionalism: the End of the Game as We Know It?   36
The State of the Five Nations: Our Best Fifteen   37
How the North Beat the All-Blacks   40
by Bill Beaumont
The Commentator's Lot   42
by Nigel Starmer-Smith
Flying Scots Triumph Over Sassenachs   44
by John Rutherford
1985-86, Experimentation and Learning   47
by Tricia Moore
The International Board Centenary: a Great Congress   50
'The Man with the Whistle'   52
by Clive Norling
England's Full House   55
by Steve Smith
Klynger, Tacklinger og Scoring: Rugby in Denmark   58
by Robin D. S. Allan
Grand Slam at Colombes   60
by J. P. R. Williams
The World Cup, 1987   62

INTERNATIONALS
Five Nations Championship   74
Other Internationals   83

TOURS
Scotland Tour of Canada 88
Ireland Tour of Japan 91
England Tour of New Zealand 92
France Tour of Argentina 97
United States Tour of Japan 97
Cardinal Newman Club Tour of Europe 97
Fiji Tour of Wales and Ireland 98
New Zealand Tour of Argentina 102
Japan Tour of France 103
Australia 18 Group Tour 103
New Zealand Combined Services 104
Queensland Tour of England, Ireland and 104
Wales
Scotland Tour of Spain and France 105
England 'B' in Italy 105

ENGLAND 106
John Player Special Cup 110
County Cups 113
Thorn EMI County Championship 114
Thorn EMI Divisional Championship 118
Oxford and Cambridge 119
Universities Athletic Union 124
British Polytechnics Sports Association 124
Hospitals Challenge Cup 125
Inter-Services Championship 126
The Barbarians 127
Middlesex Seven-a-Side Tournament 128
Schools 130
English Clubs 131

SCOTLAND
Review of the Season 140
by Bill McLaren
Schweppes Scottish National Leagues 143
Scottish Border Sevens Tournaments 145
Scottish Inter-District Championship 146
Cup Results 146
Schools 146
Scottish Clubs 147

IRELAND
Review of the Season 152
by Sean Diffley
Irish Roll of Honour, 1985-86 154
by Frank Byford
Irish Inter-Provincial Championship 155
Leinster Senior League 155
Irish Clubs 155

WALES 160
Schweppes Welsh Challenge Cup 164
Welsh Cup Finals 165
Welsh Clubs 166

FRANCE 170
The French Championship 172
The French Cup 173

AUSTRALIA 174
New South Wales International Sevens 175

NEW ZEALAND 176
Hong Kong International Sevens 178

SOUTH AFRICA 179

RECORDS
Major Tours Summary 182
Results of International Matches 186
International Records 199
International Referees 205
International Caps 208
Record Cap-Holders 234

1986-87 239

Acknowledgements 240

Message from the RFU

by Air Commodore R. H. G. Weighill, CBE, DFC

I am honoured to have been asked to write a message from the RFU as a preface to this first edition of *The Rugby Annual*.

In my thirteen years as Secretary of the RFU I have seen vast changes in every facet of the game. Many of the changes in the laws have enhanced the game; and certainly those aimed at safety have been most successful. However, some of the other changes have not been so successful, and I welcome the news that the International Rugby Football Board is to put these right and that there are to be no further changes at least for a number of years.

Competition in the game has never been more healthy than at present, with the County Cup Competition, the John Player Special Cup and the Thorn EMI County and Divisional Championships exciting great interest and enthusiasm. However, the competitive spirit can also breed a ruthlessness and sometimes violence that are not acceptable, and I cannot stress too strongly that there is no place in Rugby for the cheat and the thug and they must be scrupulously weeded out.

I would like to think, as I once did, that 'It is only a game', but Rugby is now big business and we need all the money we can get if we are to survive and thrive in a world where every other sport is competing for the interest and support of the public.

It is our proud boast that Rugby is the last stronghold of amateurism amongst the major spectator sports and long may it be so. However, we must appreciate that the pressures on top players are enormous and, if they are to remain truly amateur and continue to play for their countries and give so much pleasure to Rugby followers everywhere, they will need staunch support and a sympathetic understanding of their problems.

A book like *The Rugby Annual* is an invaluable addition to the bookshelves of all Rugby followers, and some of the features and articles will provoke spirited discussion in club bars wherever Rugby is played.

I have enjoyed my time as Secretary of the RFU enormously and take this opportunity to thank the countless unsung honorary administrators of the game throughout the world at every level for their support, their devotion to the game and, most valuable of all, their friendship.

Paul Thorburn (Wales) celebrates victory over Scotland in Cardiff and his own part - two massive kicks and fifteen points!

Editorial Preface

by Bill Mitchell

When, back in September 1985, Sackville asked me if I would like to edit a new Rugby book I accepted with alacrity, because it seemed to be an admirable opportunity to offer the Rugby readers something new, which could be added to their libraries. As far as I was – and still am – concerned there cannot be too many books on the game.

Now, about a year later and after a great deal of hard work by several very conscientious people, the results of those efforts appear and we are sure you will thoroughly enjoy this addition to Rugby's literature. Because many people have put in long hours with the work on this book it is only right – and my pleasure – to pay tributes where they are due to everyone who has made this possible.

At the very beginning right through to the crossing of the final 't's and dotting of the ultimate 'i's Melanie Faldo and Stuart Williams have been a great help and inspiration and they have been given the firm backing of the Managing Director of Sackville Design Group, Al Rockall, and Heather Thomas, who have both given regular encouragement and advice. At Pelham Books there has been the experience and guidance of Dick Douglas-Boyd, whose knowledge is always invaluable.

It is necessary only to look at the contributors – Nigel Starmer-Smith (the Associate Editor), Bill McLaren, Clive Norling, Sean Diffley and many others – to see how well we have been supported from outside the offices. The five most memorable matches read like a Rugby 'Hall of Fame'; we have certainly looked for quality.

Although the unsung heroes and heroines of this publication seek no public honour for themselves, it is important to any editor to acknowledge the good work, good temper and general pleasantness of those who do the 'hard slogging'. They should and must be given their share of the credit, so we all salute the efforts of Joyce Chester, Lorraine Jerram, Stephen Rogala-Kaluski, Philip Evans, Lloyd Raworth, Yvonne Carmouche and Jackylyn McCalla. All played a full part – and more – and to them we are eternally grateful.

Enjoy this venture! We are sure that you will find it stimulating.

Foreword

by Nigel Starmer-Smith, editor, 'Rugby World & Post'

The development of Rugby Union Football at so many different levels, from Mini-Rugby to Golden Oldies via the club, regional and International game, together with its expansion in worldwide terms and the advent of a first-ever World Rugby Cup, has exposed the need for greater documentation and an authoritative handbook both to inform and entertain.

It is hoped that in our attempt to fulfil this need, initially through the magazine of world Rugby, *Rugby World & Post*, and now through this new and exciting annual compendium of the sport, *The Rugby Annual*, we have gone a long way towards satisfying that demand .

In this book you will find comprehensive coverage of all events of significance at home and abroad, with in-depth detail and analysis of subjects as wide-ranging as the Five Nations Championship and Women's Rugby. Here, too, you can read and reflect upon the views of many famous names from the world of Rugby such as Willie John McBride, J. P. R. Williams, John Rutherford and Steve Smith, together with many of *Rugby World & Post*'s regular contributors including Bill McLaren, Bill Beaumont and Clive Norling. And, of course, we pride ourselves on the quality of the photographic material used to illustrate important Rugby action.

The Rugby Annual seeks to present facts and figures in a thoroughly readable way. It does not differentiate between countries where the calculation of International caps is concerned, assessing records on the basis that if a cap has been awarded it counts as the same whether it is against an International Board country or not. Also included are numerous features of special interest to followers of the game and nothing of importance has been omitted, particularly the fact that the next months could be amongst the most difficult the administrators of the sport have encountered. There is no point in sweeping under the carpet details of potential perils; the game is presented as it is today – mostly good, but with a few problems that have to be faced and, we hope, overcome.

At a time when Rugby is faced with new challenges and is developing in new directions all the time, I am sure that this book will help you to savour events of the recent past with enjoyment and enrich those still to come, notably the World Cup in 1987. A very significant Rugby year is over and all the signs are that an even more momentous one beckons.

All books are produced essentially for the reader's enjoyment and I have no doubts that this one will satisfy the most stringent of demands.

Review of the Season, 1985-86

Introduction

Whilst no-one could claim that the season just ended was in any way a vintage one, it was nevertheless good; and this was partly due to the fact that it was in many ways a period for looking forward rather than taking backward glances. The impending World Cup is one reason for this, but it has also been a good season for the arrival of new faces – and perhaps new heroes. In fact, the worst feature of the season was the period of shocking weather that disrupted competitions and caused massive reorganizations of fixtures, which meant that even in Scotland senior games of importance were being played right up until the end of April.

International Board

Until the fixtures for the season were published few people knew that the IB was becoming a centenarian like many famous clubs. Early in April there was a congress of representatives from fifty four Rugby-playing countries, which was a most stimulating occasion for all who attended and must have brought forward the day when this great game will be played widely by an even larger number of nations at really high-class levels. The World Cup in 1987 in Australasia may be the first test of this concept.

There will be problems for the future because of the increasing number of countries becoming involved, many of whom will not be satisfied with a situation in which they have no voice or voting power in the organization of the game. So in due course, once those outside the 'big eight' have been given Associate Member status, it would be fair for them to be represented on the main board by elected delegates from their number. The exact number of delegates would be a matter for decision by the IB.

Five Nations Championship

Any season in Europe is dominated by the Five Nations Championship, especially when there are no touring teams from the southern hemisphere to

Phil Davies (Wales) passes to his scrum-half, Robert Jones. England beat Wales at Twickenham for only the tenth time in forty years.

take away the limelight. This was not an outstanding campaign, and turned out to be somewhat frustrating because at the end of it there was no outright Champion. France and Scotland shared the title.

That France were the best team could not be questioned, but a lack of discipline at Murrayfield against a greatly changed Scottish team cost them the title. On a pleasant afternoon in January the French committed too many silly infringements in easy kicking positions for Gavin Hastings, who scored all of his side's eighteen points. On the same day England beat Wales at Twickenham for only the tenth time in forty years and they looked the most likely challengers for the title, a situation that had not changed two weeks later when Ireland lost in Paris and Scotland were a little unlucky to lose in Cardiff. This left England as the only unbeaten country.

This situation changed a fortnight later, when the Murrayfield disaster took place and Scotland may well have given the season's best International performance. Wales won in Dublin the same afternoon, so the title remained wide open. By the fourth round of matches it looked possible that the championship would be shared by three countries – England, Scotland and France. England, having beaten Ireland, were in with a theoretical chance in Paris; however, they suffered their expected defeat against the French, who had won in Cardiff in that fourth series of matches, and thus saw the end of their title-sharing aspirations.

That French game against England had started an hour before Scotland's game in Dublin, where the Irish played their best Rugby of the season, but still lost to Scotland by a single point; Michael Kiernan missed a late penalty and the lucky visitors escaped for their share of the title.

Subsequently, both Champions met Romania and both won with Scotland perhaps giving the more convincing performance with their victory in Bucharest; so was that title 'dead heat' so unjust after all? If the French were in fact the best it was not by such a wide margin. Of the others, Wales needed to find some new forwards as a matter of some urgency, England needed a different tactical approach allied to more athleticism, and Ireland looked for more 'beef' up front to provide good ball for their talented backs plus some luck.

Exciting New Faces

It is a boring season indeed that produces no new faces worthy of mention. This recent campaign did not fail us and several excellent prospects made their International debuts; others with few caps before became established stars.

France give us a good start in this respect by providing Lafond, a full-back playing for the moment on the wing, that exciting new prop Marocco and Champ, a dashing flanker.

Scotland's contribution to the list of new faces is really prolific with the outstanding Hastings brothers (Gavin and Scott), Matt Duncan, that strong-running wing, David Sole, a prop whose season was cut short by an unnecessary injury, and Finlay Calder, twin brother of Jim (who had earlier gained a fistful of caps). Add to that list the 'White Shark', John Jeffrey, and it can be seen why the game was so exciting north of Hadrian's Wall.

Wales may have had a moderate season, but Jonathan Davies really made a great advance and became a real personality, whilst his scrum-half partner for Wales, Robert Jones, had a fine first International season as did the young centre, John Devereux. Later, Paul Moriarty played well as a newly-capped flanker.

In International terms England produced only one outstanding new prospect in their giant no. 8, Dean Richards, who made a most successful debut against Ireland at Twickenham. On the club scene there were, however, several players who might do well if given the chance, and we may yet see great things from Richard Moon, the Nottingham scrum-half. Redman of Bath, who has two caps so far, is also a fine prospect.

Ireland awarded few new caps during the season and of those who did appear for the first time Keyes did not have an opportunity to make his mark because of injury. The Ulster full-back, Rainey, may be another to watch for the future.

One of the most exciting players of all is currently qualified for a country that has not yet played a full International match in Europe. He is the Canadian schoolboy from Harrow, Gary Rees, who was outstanding for Wasps in the John Player final at Twickenham. He has three possible options for representative honours (Canada, Wales and England) and it will be interesting to see which choice he makes. But he is an excellent player already and Harrow School had a remarkable season as a result of having him available.

These were satisfying days for those who look for new heroes and personalities.

Outstanding Teams

Without good club sides there are no really good players and as always there were plenty of successful clubs. Some did as expected and had good results, but there were other teams that broke existing monopolies.

The four best teams in France reached the semi-finals of the Championship and they were Agen, Graulhet, Toulon and Toulouse. All played splendid Rugby and also provided plenty of talent for the French selectors to consider.

Britain's outstanding club side was probably Pontypool from Gwent; the club is greatly criticized for allegedly playing nine-man or ten-man Rugby, but the club's wing men would deny this and try-scoring statistics would seem to back their judgment. Cardiff and Newport, the Schweppes finalists, were other good teams, but the most gratifying advance was made by Glamorgan Wanderers, who had an excellent season and finished in second place to Pontypool in both the main Welsh Merit Tables; Neath will also testify to their prowess since they lost to the Wanderers in the Schweppes Cup at the Gnoll.

Ireland had an outstanding club side in Shannon, who won the Munster Cup and enjoyed an unbeaten season (only one draw appeared in their record). Lansdowne, winners of the Leinster Cup and League, were another noteworthy Irish club side.

Scotland's two best sides were Hawick and Kelso, who shared the main honours. Hawick were once again the winners of the Schweppes National League First Division, but Kelso had the ample consolation of beating them for the Border League title. Both clubs performed extremely well in Sevens tournaments when at full strength.

England had several good clubs with the best probably being Bath, winners of the John Player Special Cup, Gloucester, who won the John Smith Merit Table A title, Wasps, who played well despite losing the final of the John Player Cup and did well in the Merit Tables, Nottingham and Leicester. Wasps deserve credit for the fact that they always endeavoured to play enterprising and open Rugby.

Youths, Schools and Juniors

One of the delights of the season was to attend the *Rugby World & Post* Annual Dinner, when various awards were made for the leading clubs at Youth, Schoolboy and Junior levels and four teams received awards on that occasion. This reflected great credit not only on the teams but also on the coaches, who selflessly spent hours – and days – working with them. The winners included St Brendan's Sixth Form College from Bristol, a team from Newton-le-Willows in Lancashire and Bangor Under-Sixteens. Harrow School, for their outstanding record (one hundred per cent for the first time in their history), received the fourth award, which was another feather in the cap not only of Gary Rees, but also of that great former England flanker, Roger Uttley.

The Australian 19 Group tourists, who did not receive an award, nevertheless made yet another faultless tour of Europe, which ended with a comprehensive triumph over England at Twickenham. Those who saw the French Youth side beat both

Pontypool RFC, Schweppes Welsh Challenge Cup winners in 1983, pose before the final against Swansea. Since then Pontypool,

Britain's outstanding club team, have won the Western Mail Merit Table for three successive seasons.

Trevor Ringland (Ireland) escapes from Dean Richards' tackle to score for Ireland.

Wales and England will shudder at the thought of future contests at full International level if that side was a reliable guide to future results. They were awesome to watch.

With so many dedicated coaches in every country the game is in good hands and we await results with keen interest.

Referees

These gentlemen all too often take the blame from certain scribes when a team that is expected to win does not do so. Some criticisms one reads are based on ignorance, bias and, on occasions, pure malice; the referee must accept this even though he knows that the strictures come from people who have the benefit of being able to study TV 'play-backs' and other visual evidence after the event, which they have been able to observe from the comfort of the press-box. There are in fact one or two journalists who specialize in criticizing referees, but on the whole most of the others are fair and objective as are those who cover matches on television and radio.

Nevertheless, referees need words of encouragement since they do a difficult job to the best of their ability and we deplore unjust criticism, because among other things it encourages certain players to believe that the authority of officials is there to be flouted. Whether one likes it or not, someone must be in charge.

There are indeed several very good referees and we have seen good displays from, amongst others, Clive Norling, who is possibly the best there is, Bob Francis of New Zealand, D. I. H. Burnett of Ireland, J. B. Anderson of Scotland, the Liverpool man, Fred Howard, and Francis Palmade of France, who handled many matches superbly well, including the match between Ireland and Scotland in Dublin in March, which (sad to say) was his last International. We salute all these gentlemen and the others who give up their Saturday afternoons to officiate at all levels.

Of course, they do make mistakes, but has anyone thought how difficult it is to spot every forward pass and every other infringement? However, it might be possible in the future to expand the powers of touch judges to assist referees over such matters

Paul Thorburn (Wales) is tackled by Eric Bonneval (France) in one of the outstanding matches of the Five Nations Championship.

as offsides and forward passes, but that is for the authorities to decide.

Outstanding Matches

There were several fine performances during the season and great matches outside the Five Nations Championship, where excellent entertainment was provided by several games notably Wales and Scotland, France and Ireland, Scotland and England, England and Ireland, Wales and France, France and England and Ireland and Scotland.

In addition to those matches, there were three memorable games at Twickenham starting with the Varsity Match in December won by Oxford for the first time since 1979 against a talented and, possibly, unlucky Cambridge team. Anyone who saw the match will remember the courageous second-half defensive work of Oxford, particularly the wing, Vessey, who made some marvellous cover tackles. Another memorable display came from the Southern Hemisphere team against the Five Nations, when the virtuosity of Kirwan, Botha, Gerber and Du Plessis thrilled the crowd.

Another game to provide superb entertainment was the John Player Special final, and Wasps with their blistering start did much to make the match such great fun to watch.

Any one of these matches could be nominated as 'Match of the Season'.

'Rugby World & Post' Awards

Earlier the dinner given by *Rugby.World & Post* was mentioned in connection with awards to Youth, School and Junior teams, but at the same dinner the magazine's annual 'Player of the Year' award was presented. There were six nominees, only British Isles players being eligible. There had been a large poll of readers.

The six started with Peter Winterbottom from England and this was well deserved for a flanker who had suffered more than his fair share of injuries in recent seasons and had made a brave return to the game. In that Murrayfield disaster he was one of the few English players who maintained his form in a badly beaten team, and in other games he could always be relied on to play his heart out.

From Ireland came Brendan Mullin, who always looked a very good player in a side that was either being consistently outplayed or was right out of

Wales v. France: Jonathan Davies (Wales), voted 'Player of the Year' by 'Rugby World & Post', receives this pass from Bleddyn Bowen and is about to set up another exciting attack.

luck. He scored a good try at Twickenham and it will be interesting to see how Oxford University perform with him and the New Zealand All-Black David Kirk in their team this coming season.

The main nominee from Wales was Jonathan Davies, whom we have already mentioned elsewhere in this feature. If he keeps his form and fitness he could join any Rugby 'Hall of Fame' alongside fellow-countrymen such as Cliff Morgan, Barry John and Phil Bennett. Can more be said?

Scotland had three nominees in Colin Deans, their inspiring hooker and captain, John Jeffrey (the 'White Shark), who was possibly the outstanding flanker of the season, and Gavin Hastings, who in his debut season scored fifty two Five Nations points and then added another twenty one in the match against Romania.

In keeping with the theme of future prospects the winner was Jonathan Davies, who was a good choice and not simply because he has become such a fine entertainer. His speech of acceptance was as good as any made on such an occasion.

Other Outstanding Players

Since we have placed some emphasis on new men in the game – Deans was the only 'old-stager' nominated for a *Rugby World & Post* award – it would be only right to record that many established players continued to adorn the scene.

Probably the best player in the Five Nations tournament was Philippe Sella of France, whose compatriots Serge Blanco, Pierre Berbizier, Garuet and Dubroca also did very well. But Sella, for us, was the top man in Europe this season.

In a poor pack Jeff Whitefoot from Wales still contrived to look a fine exponent of the skill of playing at loosehead-prop, whilst in England John Carleton played wonderfully well for his club Orrell as a centre and might well have been recalled to the International team with benefit to that side. In Bristol many will say with some justification that Alan Morley remains a great wing; he seems to go on forever.

The recall of Tony Ward to the Ireland team for their final match was not only an occasion of nostalgia; he still looked a very good player and it seemed a pity that he had been away from the International scene for so long. Also for Ireland both Trevor Ringland and Nigel Carr looked fine players even in a struggling team.

The Scottish team was still able to rely upon that great half-back pairing of John Rutherford and Roy Laidlaw, who set up a world record for an

Man with problems! Ces Blazey (New Zealand), the new President of the IRB, has some difficult problems to face over the next twelve months.

International half-back pair and played as well as ever. Milne, Paxton and Beattie were the other players to shine.

Other Personalities

The season saw the retirement of Air Commodore R. H. G. Weighill from the post of Secretary to the RFU and tribute is paid to him elsewhere in the book; he as always graced the scene with efficiency and dignity. The new Secretary of the RFU is to be Mr Dudley E. Wood from Surrey and we all wish him well. In New Zealand Ces Blazey was about to stand down as supremo of their RFU and Danie Craven in South Africa, who has been their 'Mr Rugby' for so long, was as energetic as ever in a difficult position in which he could not be expected to go on forever.

International Caps

What is or is not a full International match? The announcement by Wales that they are to award full caps for their matches at the close of this season in Fiji, Tonga and Western Samoa raises some problems. In the past only games between IB countries have generally been recognized in this country as being full Internationals, but the case for extending the awarding of caps officially for matches involving Argentina and Romania has become overwhelming and these games are now mostly given recognition as such.

For the World Cup all matches must logically be recognized as being of full International status, but during the Fiji tour this past season there was an anomaly in that Ireland, who almost lost to the visitors, did not award caps, whereas Wales, who won easily, did so. France's matches against Japan are a grey area, but are not usually recognized as being of full status and only their FIRA games against Romania are given that honour nowadays by them, which is a consistent and logical policy. Japan are due to tour England and Scotland early in the new season and at the moment their matches seem unlikely to be accorded full status.

Outside the World Cup, one could argue that caps should only be awarded for games involving countries that are seen to be of genuine International standards, and that means the 'top ten', i.e. the IB countries plus Argentina and Romania. To award caps for matches against other countries, who seem to fall short in ability of the required standards, would seem to cheapen the honour of being 'capped' for a country. This is obviously a difficult area and should not discourage the developing nations of Rugby, whose time and recognition will come when they are good enough.

We must, of course, accept the Welsh RU's decision about their South Pacific tour, but we hope that countries will standardize the system in the very near future.

Epilogue

In these days when people may be just a little bit cynical about life in general it is a great pleasure to be associated with such a fine activity as Rugby Football, which is on the whole a relaxing game to watch, played by pleasant people, watched by civilized spectators (who are usually prepared to discuss events in a rational manner), administered by dedicated and friendly people and covered by members of the press who are amongst the most respected in the profession. It is a socially pleasant and stimulating sport.

In such circumstances is there a better way of spending a Saturday afternoon than by watching a game of Rugby? It is a rhetorical question.

Diary of the 1985-86 Season

September

1st: The season starts. At Headingley, a match in aid of the Bradford Fire Appeal sees the Yorkshire President's XV lose to an International XV (14-36). Fourteen International caps appear in the Duchess of Beaufort's XV at Bristol, but the home club wins (52-14). Harlequins win their own Sevens by beating Kelso in a thrilling final (20-18), whilst Melrose win in Selkirk.

2nd: Neath, winners at Torquay Athletic on Sunday, fail to make it a Devon double and lose at Plymouth Albion (20-14).

3rd: Gloucester comfortably win a South-West Merit Table match in Exeter (13-36).

4th: Richmond's first John Smith Merit Table match at home ends badly. Saracens are too good (13-3).

7th: The first full programme brings a large victory for Wasps over Maesteg (39-9), whilst Saracens (22-10 home winners over Headingley) and Bristol (31-10 at home to Northampton) maintain good starts. Nottingham win at home to Moseley (17-12), but Waterloo thrash Richmond at Blundellsands (55-7) and Coventry lose at home to Newport (27-13). Glamorgan Wanderers are surprise winners away at Aberavon (16-10). Are Bedford and Gloucester in for torrid seasons? Results against Leicester at home (Bedford lose 6-52) and at Swansea (Gloucester lose 44-3) are ominous.

11th: Maesteg shock Llanelli at Stradey Park (28-6). Bristol are routed at Cardiff (28-0) as are Cross Keys at Swansea (45-4). Bath win at home against the touring Alberta Province from Canada (36-10).

14th: The headlines come from the Memorial Ground, Bristol, where the home club and Newport are in disgrace after a brawl results in the referee, George Crawford, walking off the field in the first half; a local referee takes over and Bristol win (21-14). At Twickenham, London Welsh in a Centenary match lose to a strong, but scrappy, Barbarians team (24-27). Other matches see Cardiff scrape home against Neath (30-27) and Harlequins win at Northampton (24-21). Wasps win at Richmond (13-7) and Swansea at Moseley (25-10), but at Leicester the visit of Bath brings a massive defeat for the home side (15-40)

16th: The RFU are to seek reports from the two clubs and the referee, George Crawford, before acting on the latter's voluntary exit from the field at Bristol.

17th: Llanelli's bad start to the season continues at Tredegar, where they lose (20-14).

18th: Gloucester's weak form continues as they lose at Glamorgan Wanderers (13-6). Newport lose at Rodney Parade against Pontypool (15-16), whilst Bridgend beat Munster at the Brewery Field (26-9).

21st: In John Smith Merit Table matches results follow form with Bath in Table A overwhelming Moseley at home (50-10); London Scottish win (15-12) in the same section against Headingley. London Welsh lose at home against Leicester (15-38) and, at Bedford, Nottingham win (52-10). Harlequins lose at home to Llanelli (16-28), whilst the visit of Saracens to Bridgend is won (17-9) by the home team. Rosslyn Park win well at home to Gosforth (24-12) and in a Welsh tussle Neath beat Newport (22-9). Cardiff's win at Coventry is hard-earned (22-13), whilst Bristol are not disgraced despite losing away to Swansea (22-11).

22nd: A glorious autumn afternoon at the Old Deer Park is beautifully organized by London Welsh and there is excellent entertainment. The semi-finals involve Llanelli and Public Schools Wanderers, and Bridgend and Leicester, with the final producing an overwhelming win for the scratch team, who beat 'The Tigers' (38-6). The French fly-half, J.-P. Lescarboura, has a broken leg (sustained whilst playing for Dax against Tulle).

25th: Bath draw at Newport (16-16), whilst the poor form of London Welsh continues as they lose a London Merit Table match at home to Metropolitan Police (12-16). The good run of Glamorgan Wanderers comes to an end as they lose at home to Pontypridd (6-16). Llanelli have a fine home win over Bridgend (36-16).

28th: There are more John Smith Merit Table matches with visiting teams winning in every case. In Table A, Leicester win against Harlequins (19-9) and Wasps win at Headingley (35-17). Elsewhere, Richmond advance in the John Player Cup against London Irish (21-14) and other first round winners are Wakefield, Lichfield (a shock win at Nuneaton 23-19), Bedford (very narrowly at Evesham, 13-9), Saracens, Gloucester (87-3 at home to Exeter University) and Broughton Park among others. On the club scene Coventry win against Sale (11-0) and Bath win at Llanelli (15-18). Newport win at home to Swansea (17-16).

October

1st: In club matches Neath lose at home to Newbridge (21-22). Northampton beat Fylde at home (40-11) and Penarth make a game of it at home against Aberavon (3-8).

2nd: In Welsh matches Pontypool beat Swansea (23-10) and Cardiff win at Pontypridd (32-3). Gloucester at Kingsholm beat Llanelli (27-12)

3rd: The Fijians have arrived in Wales for their ten-match tour.

4th: In Merit Table matches there is a win in John Smith A for Sale against Moseley (21-16) at Brooklands. In club matches Bath lose their unbeaten record at Aberavon (16-15), Harlequins lose at home to Swansea (15-24), Leicester comfortably turn back Coventry (42-16), Maesteg narrowly fail to halt Pontypool at home (13-14) and Cardiff win at Newport (13-7). Yorkshire fail to beat visitors Ulster (18-24), whilst the Schweppes

Scottish National Leagues start with a shock for Gala, who lose away to Edinburgh Academicals (11-6).

9th: The Fijian tour starts at Cross Keys, where the home club is celebrating its Centenary Season; the visitors win (26-12) against gallant opposition. Cardiff are thrashed at home by Bridgend (7-16), whilst also in Wales, Ebbw Vale easily dispose of Aberavon (28-6).

11th: Bristol are severely reprimanded for their part in the George Crawford 'walk-off' and are warned about their future conduct by the RFU, who have referred the Newport part of the incident to the Welsh Rugby Union.

12th: The Fijians continue in Wales and are badly thrashed by Cardiff (31-15). In John Smith Merit Table matches Wasps do well at Bristol to win (15-12), whilst Harlequins score eight tries against Gloucester at Twickenham (43-6). Bath win unconvincingly against Liverpool (26-12), while, in Wales, there are wins for Bridgend over London Welsh (18-12), Aberavon at Maesteg (20-12), Pontypool over Bedford (53-0) and Swansea at home to Llanelli (17-15).

15th: In the Midlands Division of the Thorn EMI County Championship Leicestershire beat Warwickshire (25-13), whilst Notts, Lincs & Derbys win away against North Midlands (10-6). In Wales, Bridgend win narrowly at Tredegar (10-9).

16th: Swansea lose to Fiji (14-23), who record their second win. The Thorn EMI County Championship continues with victories in the North for Yorkshire away to Lancashire (26-24). Also in the North, Cumbria beat Cheshire at Aspatria (15-12) and Durham beat Northumberland for the first time in sixteen years (12-3 away). There are also three London matches with Middlesex beating Kent (17-3), whilst Sussex fight back to beat Hampshire (9-6) and Surrey struggle before beating Hertfordshire at Roehampton (20-9).

18th: The RFU announce that the New Merit Table C has been approved. For the moment there will be no promotion to Merit Table B.

19th: Bad luck for Fiji as they lose by a single point in Dublin to Ireland (16-15). Bath win comfortably against Bristol (26-7). London Welsh win for the first time against Llanelli (19-18) at the Old Deer Park. Leicester win at Northampton (14-6), Nottingham at Waterloo (15-6) and West Hartlepool at home to Sale (20-10). In Wales, Aberavon beat Moseley (13-9), whilst Abertillery give Pontypool a hard time at home (18-26).

20th: France 'B' beat Wales 'B' in Sainte Foy la Grande (30-13).

22nd: Newport beat the Barbarians at Rodney Parade (38-29).

23rd: The Fijians lose in Belfast to Ulster (23-9). In the Thorn EMI County Championship there are wins for Eastern Counties away to Hampshire (12-9), North Midlands (the Group winners in their area) at home to East Midlands (24-12) and Warwickshire at home to Staffordshire (37-16). Club matches see Bath win at home against Cardiff (16-13), whilst there are wins in Wales for Abertillery at home to Aberavon (18-6), Llanelli overwhelmingly at home to Bristol (58-10), Pontypool

away to Newbridge (29-13) and Swansea at home to Bridgend (32-13).

26th: Fiji narrowly win against Connacht (7-6). There are no John Player Cup second round surprises, but Bedford are overwhelmed by Broughton Park to go out of the competition (10-27). In club matches in England, Harlequins lose heavily at home to Cardiff (16-38), Rosslyn Park win again (at Headingley, 6-3), Leicester win at home against Swansea (18-10), London Welsh are outplayed at home by Neath (31-10), Moseley beat Coventry at the Reddings (14-13), Northampton beat Oxford University (27-10) and Bath win at US Portsmouth (29-13). In Wales, Bridgend beat Aberavon at home (17-15), Llanelli beat Cambridge University at Stradey Park (39-8), Newbridge beat the visiting Maesteg (25-12), Newport beat Glamorgan Wanderers at Rodney Parade (20-18), and Pontypool win for the fifteenth consecutive time (by 32-18 away to South Wales Police). The three unbeaten teams in the Scottish First Division all win well – Watsonians at Edinburgh Academicals (49-0), Hawick at home to Preston Lodge (33-3) and Boroughmuir away to Kilmarnock (13-9).

28th: The draw is made for the third round of the John Player Special Cup in England and it is a most intriguing affair including London Scottish v. Sale, Coventry v. Leicester, Gosforth v. Northampton and Gloucester v. Bristol! All matches bar one are due to be played on Saturday, 25th January 1986.

29th: Neath beat the much improved Glamorgan Wanderers at the Gnoll (20-3). The Executive Director for the 1987 World Cup is based in Wellington, New Zealand, and is a recently retired District Court Judge, Sir Desmond Sullivan.

30th: Fiji win again in Wales beating Newport (7-6), but have lock Savai sent off and suspended for six weeks; his tour is over. In the Thorn EMI County Championship there is a shock for Middlesex beaten at Sudbury by Surrey (16-10). In the London Group, Kent win away to Herts at Croxley Green (32-21) whilst, in Group B, Eastern Counties beat Sussex at Cambridge (20-7). In the North, there are wins for Lancashire away to Cheshire (44-6), Yorkshire at home to Northumberland (31-6) and Gloucester (13-0), Bath beat Maesteg (30-9), Bridgend win at home against Cross Keys (16-4), Cardiff beat Newbridge (41-15) at home and Ebbw Vale lose at home to Swansea (12-9).

November

2nd: Honours are shared by Neath and Gloucester, who remove the perfect records of Pontypool and Rosslyn Park (20-3 away and 25-6 at home respectively). In England, the Fijians win for a fifth time beating London Welsh (22-9); at last Bedford win (against Oxford University 3-0); Cambridge lose away to London Scottish (16-14), Bristol beat Bridgend at home (19-15), Harlequins lose to London Irish at Stoop (9-13), Leicester fall at home to Cardiff (15-20), Moseley at home beat Newport (18-0) and Northampton beat Aberavon (9-3). In Wales,

Paul Thorburn (Wales) is tackled by S. Laulau (Fiji) as Bob Ackerman (Wales) closes in to provide support, Cardiff, 9th November.

Llanelli dismiss Leinster (37-3), Maesteg lose at home to Nottingham (35-12), Newbridge lose at home to Bath (23-15), Pontypridd at home beat Abertillery (24-10), South Wales Police beat Richmond in Bridgend (18-12) and Swansea rout Blackheath (24-12) at home. Scotland's First Division leaders all win – Boroughmuir, Hawick and Watsonians.

5th: Llanelli beat Fiji at Stradey Park (31-28) after being behind (25-0) after thirty minutes.

6th: The Midlands final of the County Championship is between Leicestershire (home winners over Notts, Lincs & Derbys 26-9) and Warwickshire (winners at Moseley against North Midlands 46-4) on 20th November. Oxford University lose at Cardiff (44-7), Pontypool are extended at Cross Keys (18-9), Newport lose at home to Pontypridd (14-12) and Gloucester beat South Wales Police at Kingsholm (15-14).

8th: The WRU announces a crackdown on violence including the banning of dismissed players from Internationals; Newport are censured for September's fiasco at Bristol. Wales award full caps against Fiji. Neath at home beat Bridgend (16-0) and Cardiff at Arms Park edge out Ebbw Vale (13-12).

9th: Wales easily beat Fiji in Cardiff (40-3); the visitors win five and lose five on tour. Elsewhere in the County Championship the North sees Durham surprise Yorkshire (19-11 at Hartlepool), Cheshire beat Northumberland at Birkenhead Park (17-14) and Lancashire oust Cumbria at Carlisle, where visiting England lock, Steve Bainbridge,

is sent off for fighting. The opening South-West Division matches bring wins for Gloucestershire over Cornwall at Lydney (13-9) and Somerset against Devon at Weston-super-Mare (19-7). In the London Division Hampshire win at last beating Sussex at Trojans RFC (13-6). In club matches Gloucester win a John Smith Table A match against Bath at Kingsholm (15-11). Oxford University win at Blackheath (7-6), but Cambridge lose at home to Leicester (9-31). Rosslyn Park win their last game against Newport at home (7-4), but London Welsh lose again (at Moseley, 36-13). Richmond lose at home to Harlequins (7-11) and Wasps sting visiting Saracens (48-6). In Scotland the unbeaten Championship records of Boroughmuir (at home to West of Scotland 8-13) and Watsonians (9-15 at home to Gala) disappear; Hawick (14-10 at home to Heriot's) alone have full points. Ulster continue winning, beating Munster in Belfast (23-3); Connacht shock Leinster in Dublin (9-6).

11th: Llanelli and Swansea draw in splendid fashion at Stradey Park (15-15).

12th: Leicester win a John Smith Table A match at Nottingham (15-9).

13th: The London Division Group A ends. Kent shock Surrey at Askeans (23-6) and qualify for National semi-finals of the Championship ahead of Middlesex, who beat Herts (13-10), and Surrey on points difference.

16th: The County Championship brings expected wins in the North for leaders, Durham, at home to Cheshire (26-0), Lancashire away to Northumberland (38-3) and

Yorkshire at home to Cumbria (28-10). In the South West, Cornwall beat Devon (21-3) and Gloucestershire defeat Somerset (23-10) – both home wins! Amongst the clubs the John Smith Merit Table matches bring rewards for Gosforth in Table A at Headingley (12-6) and Leicester at home to Wasps (19-6); Nottingham at Beeston beat Sale (23-6). Elsewhere, Blackheath lose again, to Cambridge University at Rectory Field (15-0). Coventry lose at home to Bath (16-22), London Welsh at home to Bristol (16-29), Oxford University at home to Harlequins (9-16), Richmond lose to London Scottish (17-25) and the Rosslyn Park unbeaten home record goes against Moseley (6-10). Cup Day in Wales produces only two senior losers in the 'Schweppes' – Pontypridd (4-0 at Dunvant) and Tredegar (6-12 at home to Swansea University). Hawick are shocked in Scotland by Kilmarnock away (25-12), so Stewart's-Melville go top on points difference (they beat Preston Lodge at Inverleith 44-6). Other joint leaders are Hawick and Kelso.

18th: Schweppes announce discontinuation at the season's end of the Scottish National Leagues sponsorship.

19th: Penarth's winning run ends at home with a defeat by Neath (40-3).

20th: Stanley's XV, with French centre Charvet brilliant, beat Oxford University at Iffley Road (40-18). Warwickshire reach the national semi-finals of the County Championship beating Leicestershire at Leicester (26-3) in the Midland final. Pontypridd lose at home to Pontypool (7-12).

23rd: The last two national semi-finalists of the County Championship emerge. Up North, Lancashire beat Durham (25-9) at Waterloo and win on points difference from Durham and Yorkshire, who defeat Cheshire at Morley (34-12). Northumberland beat Cumbria at Gosforth (10-4), so Cheshire are last! In the South West, Gloucestershire beat Devon (25-6 at Exeter) to win the top group and qualify with Lancashire; Cornwall beat Somerset at Redruth (22-3). In a John Smith Merit Table A match Moseley win at home against Leicester (7-6). From Old Deer Park there is bad news: Newport and London Welsh draw (15-15), but three players are dismissed – Young and Perry (Newport) and Llewelyn (Welsh). Bristol beat South Wales Police (25-14) at home, Cambridge University lose at home to Harlequins (13-26), as do Oxford University at home to London Scottish (3-31). Gloucester beat London Irish at Kingsholm (44-3). In Wales, Aberavon lose at home to Pontypool (25-7), Llanelli win at Stradey Park against Cardiff (13-3) and Neath thrash Blackheath at home (19-6). Stewart's-Melville still top the Schweppes First Division in Scotland on points difference from Hawick and Kelso. In Ireland, Ulster beat Connacht at Galway (16-6) and Leinster defeat Munster at Cork (15-6).

25th: In the draw for the semi-finals of the Thorn EMI County Championship Kent are at home to Gloucestershire, and Warwickshire entertain Lancashire on 8th March 1986.

26th: Llanelli win at Pontarddulais in the outstanding Schweppes Welsh Cup first round match (37-12).

27th: It seems likely that Terry Holmes will 'go North' with Bradford Northern. Cardiff beat Maesteg at home (15-3), Swansea win at Pontypridd (20-19) and Pontypool crush Abertillery at home (35-3). Cambridge University rally late to beat Steele-Bodger's XV (19-18).

30th: In Wales, Cardiff thrash South Wales Police at home (38-6), but have Robert Norster sent off for fighting; he misses Wales's Internationals. Aberavon beat Bristol at home (25-11), Bridgend lose at home to leaders, Pontypool, (7-15), and Newport beat Llanelli at home (7-6). Elsewhere Bath lose at home to Neath (7-13), Cambridge University lose at home to Northampton (16-24), London Irish lose at home to London Scottish (10-14), London Welsh lose at home to Harlequins (4-19) and Rosslyn Park defeat visiting Abertillery (13-9). In Scotland in District Championship matches (both at Murrayfield) Edinburgh defeat North & Midlands (29-12) and South edge out Glasgow (19-16).

December

2nd: South Africa calls off the 1986 Lions Tour.

4th: Save & Prosper Group have agreed to sponsor ground improvements at Twickenham for the next three years. Bridgend beat Pontypridd (23-14) at home and Newport win (27-7) at Ebbw Vale.

6th: The new Wales coach in succession to John Bevan, who resigned owing to ill-health, is to be Tony Gray (ex-London Welsh) from North Wales.

7th: The English Divisional Championship starts with wins for London over the South & South-West at the Stoop Memorial Ground (22-3), whilst Midlands beat the North at Nottingham (28-15). Scotland 'B' beat Italy 'B' unconvincingly in Glasgow (9-0) and, in Ireland, Ulster beat Leinster in Dublin (19-13) to take the provincial title, whilst Munster beat Connacht at Cork (16-9). In English John Smith Merit Table action, London Scottish win away in Table A against weakened Bath (10-8) with Gloucester successful at Leicester (15-9) and Moseley winning at home to Headingley (36-10).

8th: At l'Aquila, the Italians beat a young Romanian team (19-3).

10th: Oxford break the Cambridge victory sequence at Twickenham (7-6) in a thriller.

11th: In Wales, Pontypool win a tour match at Llanelli (10-3), whilst Glamorgan Wanderers beat Bridgend at Ely (8-7); Maesteg thrash Penarth at home (28-10) and Abertillery win at home against a struggling Swansea side (18-12).

14th: The English Divisional Championships continue with wins for London against the North at Otley (7-3) and for Midlands away to South & South-West at Gloucer (19-9). In English Merit Table matches unbeaten records go with London Scottish losing at home in Table A to Wasps (22-16); Bristol win at home against Moseley (22-6). In the Scottish Inter-District Championship, both visiting teams win – South against Edinburgh (10-3) and Anglo-Scots against North & Midlands (28-6). In club matches Leicester win at Blackheath (16-12),

Harlequins at home to Bedford (27-7), Saracens at home to Nottingham (23-14) and Waterloo at home to Sale (16-12). Of the Welsh teams, Pontypool win at Nuneaton (32-3), Aberavon are successful at home against Newport (12-7), Bridgend surprise Neath (19-12) at home and Cardiff beat visiting London Welsh (22-17).

16th: Anglo-Scots beat Glasgow (17-13) at Hillhead in the Scottish Inter-District Competition.

19th: Steve Bainbridge, sent off in a Thorn EMI County Championship match, will not be picked for England this season by RFU decree.

21st: Midlands are the Thorn EMI Division Champions. They beat London at Northampton (12-3). South & South-West are last, having lost at Bristol to the North (28-17). In John Smith Merit Table matches there are Table A wins for Harlequins at Bath (16-7), Sale at Headingley (12-9), Leicester at home to Bristol (30-25) and Nottingham at home to Gosforth, previously unbeaten (23-9). Coventry beat Gloucester (17-13) at home and Northampton win away to Wasps (16-3). In Scotland, Glasgow beat North & Midlands at Robert Gordon's (30-10) and the Anglo-Scots are beaten at home (Richmond) by Edinburgh (23-9). In the Schweppes Welsh Cup Newbridge lose at home to Neath Athletic (10-3).

26th: Boxing Day results include wins in England in club games for Sale at Broughton Park (13-9), Coventry at home to Moseley (19-3) and Saracens at Northampton (18-12). In Wales, Cardiff edge out Pontypridd at home (10-4), Llanelli avenge a defeat by London Welsh (35-10

at home), Neath do the same to Aberavon (32-8), Pontypool rout Cross Keys at home (46-0) and Swansea yield at home to Glamorgan Wanderers (7-10).

28th: The weather is the winner today. Barbarians win at Leicester at last (19-16) and the Murrayfield Blanket allows three matches to be played there; French Schoolboys beat Scotland (13-6), whilst the Inter-District title goes again to the South, who beat Anglo-Scots (16-13). In the other game Edinburgh beat Glasgow (10-7).

January

1st: A good start for Simon Halliday (Bath) and Graham Robbins (Coventry), who win their first England caps against Wales on 18th January at Twickenham. Nigel Melville (Wasps) is captain. A dismissal at Llanelli on New Year's Eve means no Welsh caps this season for Richard Moriarty (Swansea). In the John Smith Merit Table A Gloucester win at home against Moseley (8-3). In Wales, Cardiff thrash Bath (30-12). In Scotland there are away wins for Hawick at Heriot's (11-10) and for Kilmarnock in the 'Derby' at Ayr (10-7).

4th: The Irish senior team at Lansdowne Road wins their trial (21-12) and the team is as expected for the first Five Nations match, against France in Paris on 1st February. Scotland's selectors have faces like the red shirts of the winning trial team, who beat the senior team (Blues) at Murrayfield (41-10). In England two John Smith Merit Table A matches beat the elements and

Oxford v. Cambridge: Coll MacDonald (Oxford) receives this scoring pass from Neil Macdonald, his captain, to go over for the game's only try. Oxford win (7-6) after five successive defeats.

Leicester win at home their 'away' game against Headingley (23-7). London Scottish fail to repel visiting Gloucester (13-37). In Wales, Swansea lose at Aberavon (18-9).

5th: Queensland Tourists at Blackheath beat Kent (32-9).

8th: Queensland fail in unfriendly conditions at Wasps RFC and lose to Middlesex (14-4). Llanelli thrash visiting Abertillery (34-0) and Pontypridd win at home against Lydney (13-4). The touring Australian Schools beat Munster easily in Limerick (25-0). Scotland select their team against France, who have themselves made changes through injuries, and choose six new caps including the Hastings brothers (Gavin and Scott) – the first time since 1891 that brothers have made their debuts together. Other new caps are Duncan (West of Scotland), Sole (Bath) Finlay Calder (Stewart's-Melville, and twin of omitted Jim) and Jeremy Campbell-Lamerton (son of the 1966 Lions captain in New Zealand).

10th: The Welsh team to meet England at Twickenham on 18th January is announced with three new caps under Pickering (Llanelli) as captain. They are Devereux (Bridgend) at centre, R. Jones (Swansea) at scrum-half and D. Waters (Newport).

11th: Queensland lose in Dublin to Leinster (15-12). In English John Smith Merit Table matches London Scottish win Table A against Gosforth at home (21-6). In English club matches there are wins for Coventry at home to Bristol (21-13), Gloucester at home to Leicester (15-10), Harlequins at Blackheath (33-6), London Welsh at home to Bath (26-9), Nottingham at Rosslyn Park (28-16) and Sale at home to Bedford (17-7). The Scottish Schweppes League resumes with Hawick staying top after edging out Kelso (13-9); other winners are Edinburgh Academicals, Selkirk, Heriot's, Watsonians and West of Scotland. In Wales, Cardiff are shocked at Aberavon (24-3), Pontypool beat Pontypridd at home (38-3) and Swansea beat Newport at home (22-19).

13th: The French lose Gallion and Champ for the match at Murrayfield on Saturday, 18th. The replacements are Berbizier and Erbani.

14th: Queensland end an Ulster unbeaten record of seventeen matches with a narrow win in Belfast (6-4); Ulster's Matthews is injured and out of Ireland's team in Paris on 1st February. The Schweppes WRU Cup Second Round is completed with Maesteg's win (17-6) at Cilfynydd.

15th: In Wales, home winners are Aberavon (18-10) against South Wales Police and Llanelli (39-4) against Glamorgan Wanderers.

17th: Moseley beat Saracens at home (21-10), and, in Wales, Tredegar beat Abertillery at home (13-9). The new Secretary of the RFU in succession to Air Commodore R.H.G. Weighill is to be a Surrey man, Dudley E. Wood.

18th: International day! Two try-less teams win at home with Scotland (six penalty-goals by Gavin Hastings) beating France (two tries) at Murrayfield (18-17) and England (six penalty-goals and one drop – all by Andrew) edging out Wales at Twickenham (21-18). Queensland

beat Munster at Cork (24-15) and Gloucester at Kingsholm win a John Smith Merit Table A match against Wasps (25-13). Cardiff win at London Welsh (19-3), Rosslyn Park beat South Wales Police (28-22) at home (two sent off by Roger Quittenton) and Waterloo at home beat Headingley (25-3).

21st: Queensland end the British Isles section of their tour by beating Llanelli in the Carwyn James Memorial Match (13-12).

22nd: Scotland drop Campbell-Lamerton from their team to meet Wales in Cardiff on 1st February; his replacement is I.A.M. Paxton (Selkirk).

24th: Wales make no changes in the team to meet Scotland in Cardiff on 1st February.

25th: Cup day in Wales and England produces few surprises. The 'Big One' in Wales's Schweppes Cup brings a home victory for Llanelli over Pontypool (27-6), but Neath are shocked at home by Glamorgan Wanderers (12-9). All minor teams go out and other survivors are Aberavon, Bridgend, Maesteg, Cardiff, Newport and Swansea. In England's John Player Cup two matches are postponed and the shock is Wakefield's win (23-19) at Rosslyn Park. With no other shocks, those to advance are Camborne, Leicester, Gloucester, Harlequins, Lichfield, London Scottish, London Welsh, Nottingham, Bath (by a 16-16 draw at Orrell), Saracens, Wasps and Moseley. The Scottish programme is frosted off.

26th: Blackheath win at Richmond in the John Player Cup (12-7). Glamorgan Wanderers' reward for beating Neath is an away 'Derby' at Cardiff. The rest of the draw pairs Llanelli with Aberavon, Newport with Swansea and Maesteg with Bridgend (home teams first).

27th: The John Player Cup draw (fourth round) brings few 'big' matches, but Moseley and Bath should be tough.

29th: The Australian Schools win a twelfth time by thrashing England at Twickenham (29-6)

31st: England are unchanged for the visit to Murrayfield apart from a replacement change – Simpson (Sale) for Simmons (Wasps) as hooker. Overnight, three John Smith Merit Table mathes are played in England bringing Table A wins for Gloucester at home to Bristol (21-6) and Wasps at Moseley (12-6). In Table B, Bedford beat visiting London Welsh (16-13). At club levels Bath thrash Rosslyn Park (35-5 at home), Penarth at home shock Swansea (26-9), Neath beat visiting West of Scotland (16-8), Cross Keys do the same to Melrose (24-22) and Pontypool inflict a heavy defeat on Ayr (33-4).

February

1st: Wales beat Scotland at Cardiff (22-15) after being outplayed for long periods and being outscored in tries (1-3). France convincingly beat Ireland in Paris (29-9) with a three-nil try-count. In John Smith Merit Table A matches, Leicester beat London Scottish (24-0) at home, whilst the John Player Cup Round Three is completed with Broughton Park beating Vale of Lune at home (12-6) and Northampton advancing by drawing at Gosforth (6-6). Metropolitan Police at home beat Harlequins for the first time (22-17), and Richmond lose at home to Headingley (0-8).

3rd: The England 'physio', Don Gatherer, resigns.

4th: Newport win at Bridgend (20-16)

5th: Aberavon win at Pontypridd (23-6). Scotland are unchanged for the Calcutta Cup match at Murrayfield on 15th February, when Ireland drop Phil Orr and Jim McCoy plus Anderson in the pack and bring in P. Kennedy (London Irish), D. Fitzgerald (Lansdowne) and B. McCall (London Irish).

7th: Paul Moriarty (Swansea) plays at Lansdowne Road, Dublin, for Wales v. Ireland replacing Brown (Pontypool); he is a new cap.

8th: Britain freezes and play is limited. In the John Player Special Cup (England) only three results appear – Harlequins and Bath (both away) beat Lichfield (23-6) and Moseley (22-4) respectively with London Welsh edging out visiting Camborne (12-9). Leicester beat Northampton at home (25-15) and, in Wales, Llanelli at home beat Ebbw Vale (24-22) and Neath win at Swansea (11-3). The Scottish Schweppes matches are reduced to two with away wins for Heriot's and Stewart's-Melville.

9th: David Sole (Bath), injured at Moseley, gives way to A. K. Brewster (Stewart's-Melville) at loosehead-prop in Scotland's team for the Calcutta Cup match next Saturday.

10th: Nigel Carr (Ards) fills Ireland's flanker vacancy in Dublin on Saturday against Wales.

12th: Rory Underwood fails a fitness test. His place on the England wing goes to M. Harrison (Wakefield). Llanelli (at home) beat Newport (27-12).

13th: Ireland lose lock, B. W. McCall; his replacement against Wales is J. Holland (Wanderers).

15th: Joy for Scotland and Wales! The Scots score a record victory for the series over England at Murrayfield (33-6) and Wales succeed in Dublin against Ireland (19-12). The weather decimates the club scene; Glamorgan Wanderers win at Plymouth Albion (41-13), South Wales Police beat Tredegar at home (16-3) and Wasps win at Torquay Athletic (37-3).

19th: Tony Ward (Greystones) is restored to the Irish squad for Twickenham; Dean is injured.

21st: Wales are unchanged for their Cardiff 'showdown' with France on 1st March. Steve Smith resigns as coach to England's youth team owing to work commitments.

22nd: Another victory for the weatherman! The John Player Special Cup programme in England disappears, whilst in Wales one Schweppes match is played, at Llanelli, where the holders are eliminated by Aberavon (11-10). Also in Wales, Rosslyn Park come away from ailing Neath winning (23-20).

23rd: Ireland make three changes for Twickenham on 1st March. K. D. Crossan (Instonians), R. Keyes (a new cap from Cork Constitution) and B. W. McCall (London Irish) replace Finn, the injured Dean and Holland respectively.

24th: England make six changes (one positional) from the team routed at Murrayfield. Harrison switches to the right wing to the exclusion of Smith and out go Salmon,

Halliday, Rendall, Hall (injured) and Robbins; in come Simms, Clough (a new cap, from Cambridge University), Chilcott, Rees and Dean Richards (another new cap, from Leicester). France drop Chadebech and Estève for Cardiff on 1st March; in come D. Charvet and E. Bonneval, both of Toulouse.

25th: Scotland's Leagues will be sponsored next season (for nine years) by McEwan's.

28th: Both International matches scheduled for 1st March are on! There will be a late change in each match with Morrow (Bangor) replacing Kearney for Ireland at Twickenham and Mark Titley (Swansea) expected to replace the unwell Lewis for Wales in Cardiff.

March

1st: France end the Championship hopes of Wales at Cardiff (23-15) and England beat Ireland at Twickenham (25-20); eleven tries are scored in the two games and the title remains undecided. Nottingham win at Headingley in the John Smith Merit Table A.

2nd: Scotland 'B' beat France 'B' in Villefranche-sur-Saône (12-10).

4th: Llanelli draw at Cardiff (16-16), but Pontypool lose at Neath (16-12).

5th: Barbarians thrash East Midlands at Northampton (35-6). Aberavon beat Abertillery (22-3). England (for Paris) and Scotland (for Dublin) are unchanged, but Ireland bring back Phil Orr, for a fiftieth cap, and W. Anderson (Dungannon) for Kennedy and Spillane.

8th: Bath are the first to reach the John Player semi-finals beating London Welsh away (18-10); into the quarter-finals go Nottingham, London Scottish and Gloucester against home victims Wakefield (26-7), Northampton (11-6) and Saracens (13-6) respectively. The Schweppes Welsh semi-finals are complete with home wins for Cardiff over Glamorgan Wanderers (21-12) and Newport over Swansea (10-4); Bridgend score the only try at Maesteg where they draw (9-9). The County Champions final (Thorn EMI) features Kent and Warwickshire, the visiting losers being Gloucestershire (16-3) and Lancashire (19-15). Royal Navy beat The Army at Twickenham (13-3) and, in John Smith Merit Table A, Wasps win at Sale (20-9). Schweppes Scottish winners are Watsonians, Gala, Heriot's FP, Hawick, Kelso, Edinburgh Academicals and Stewart's-Melville, who still lead Division 1 with Hawick having games in hand.

9th: Leicester win at Broughton Park in the John Player Special Cup fourth round (46-6).

10th: The semi-finals draw for the John Player Special Cup is made with many 'either/ors', but Gloucester and Bath are kept apart.

12th: Loughborough retain the UAU title (14-0 v. Nottingham at Twickenham), with Leeds winning the Polytechnics Cup (15-12 v. Kingston at Sunbury) and The London surprisingly the Hospitals Cup (10-6 v. St Mary's at Richmond). Duncan (Scotland) and Keyes (Ireland) miss the Dublin match on Saturday through injury and are replaced by K. Robertson (Melrose) and Tony Ward (Greystones).

15th: The Five Nations Championship is shared as France comfortably beat England in Paris (29-10), but Scotland, the co-winners, luckily win in Dublin against Ireland (10-9). In John Smith Merit Table matches in England, Nottingham thrash visiting London Scottish in Section A (30-6).

17th: The British Lions party for the IB Centenary matches is selected under the captaincy of Colin Deans (Scotland); the party includes in total six players each from Scotland and Ireland with five from Wales and four from England.

19th: Matt Duncan (West of Scotland) returns for his country's match in Bucharest against Romania on 29th March replacing Keith Robertson. Ebbw Vale beat Llanelli (19-16).

20th: Scotland's twenty six-man party for a tour of Spain and France in May is to be led by Gary Callander (Kelso); seven uncapped players are included.

21st: Wales will tour Fiji, Tonga and Western Samoa in summer 1986.

22nd: The Welsh Schweppes Cup produces two finalists – Cardiff (winners over Bridgend 17-9) and Newport (beating Aberavon 15-6). The John Player in England stutters on with London Scottish home winners over Gloucester (12-8) and Leicester away winners against Harlequins (15-7) reaching the semi-finals; Wasps win at Blackheath (24-12) to reach the last eight. Hawick virtually clinch the Scottish Schweppes First Division by winning away to Stewart's-Melville (16-6).

24th: The Barbarians choose seven new men for their Easter tour of South Wales.

28th: Wasps draw at Nottingham in the John Player Cup but reach the semi-finals on a two-one try-count. Penarth lose the final match against the Barbarians (15-39).

29th: Scotland finish their season's Internationals with a victory over Romania in Bucharest (33-18). Gavin Hastings scores another twenty one points. Barbarians win at Cardiff (24-19). In a John Smith Merit Table match Gloucester (Table A leaders) beat visiting Headingley (14-7). In Wales, Leicester win at Neath (15-11), London Welsh lose at Aberavon (36-9) and Harlequins at Swansea (29-19). Bath win well at Bristol (10-3).

31st: Routs in Wales for Barbarians at Swansea (48-13), Leicester at Pontypool (39-6) and London Welsh at Newport (48-16). Llanelli are shocked at Moseley (43-4) but Bedford surprise Northampton away (22-16).

April

1st: Hawick beat Boroughmuir (21-3).

2nd: Bridgend thrash visiting Cardiff (30-3). John Rutherford (Selkirk) replaces the injured B. Bowen in the Lions team for the IB Centenary matches.

5th: Bath, the holders, and Wasps reach the John Player Special Cup final (Twickenham, 26th April) at the

Ireland v. Scotland: 'It's unbelievable!' Phil Orr (Ireland) seems to say in despair as he has just seen Michael Kiernan, his colleague, miss a vital penalty near the end of the game.

expense of Leicester (10-6 away) and London Scottish (11-3 at home) respectively. In John Smith Merit Table games, Bristol win away to Harlequins in Section A (20-6). Cardiff at home overwhelm Bedford (68-28), Aberavon win at Llanelli (16-12) and Pontypool beat Newport at home (14-12). The RAF are the Inter-Services Champions again after beating The Army at Twickenham (16-13).

6th: New Zealand win the Hong Kong Sevens beating French Barbarians in the final (32-10). Devon & Cornwall beat Spain at Torquay (30-6).

7th: Mike Rafter is to be the new coach of Bristol.

8th: Bob Norster (Cardiff) and Richard Moriarty (Swansea), after bans from the Five Nations matches, are in the Wales touring party for Fiji, Tonga and Western Samoa. David Pickering (Llanelli) is captain.

9th: A poor England Under-23 team beats Spain at Twickenham (15-10); Barnes (five penalties) scores all the points and Spain the only try! Wasps win away at London Welsh (19-12) in the London Merit Table meaning no John Player Cup campaign next season for 'The Welsh'. Newport beat Pontypridd away (34-0) but lose prop Alun Williams, who was sent off with the home team's Mike Hughes. Hawick clinch the Schweppes Scottish First Division at Selkirk (26-3), making it nine wins in thirteen seasons! Jonathan Davies (Neath) is out of the British Lions team for Cardiff on 16th April and is replaced by Malcolm Dacey (Swansea). Rosslyn Park win their own Sturges Sevens beating Cambridge University in the final (34-4).

12th: Warwickshire win the Thorn EMI County Championship at Twickenham beating Kent (16-6). France beat Romania in Lille (25-13). The Melrose Sevens are won by Kelso, who beat Racing Club de France in the final (22-16).

13th: The *Mail on Sunday* reports that an unofficial New Zealand team, with nearly all the leading players included, will tour South Africa immediately after the IB celebration matches. Richmond beat London Welsh in the final of the Oxfordshire Sevens (20-6).

16th: The Rest of the World beat the British Lions at rain-swept Cardiff Arms Park (15-7).

17th: D. G. Lenihan (Ireland) will captain the Five Nations against the Southern Hemisphere on Saturday 19th April at Twickenham; the opposition is led by Andy Dalton (New Zealand). Melrose escape relegation from Division 1 of the Schweppes Scottish League beating Edinburgh Academicals at home (16-4). Preston Lodge go down.

18th: England's Youths lose at the Old Deer Park to France Juniors (35-6).

19th: At Twickenham the Five Nations are overwhelmed by three nations – the IB Overseas XV (alias New Zealand, Australia and South Africa); the score – 32-13. Great Britain's Ladies lose unluckily to France at Richmond (8-14). Bath turn away Llanelli (19-10), Coventry do the same to Pontypool (16-12), Moseley likewise to Bridgend (20-6), Leicester to Gosforth (56-15) and Maesteg to Bristol (19-16). Cardiff lose at Neath (22-12). In John

Smith Table A, Leicester beat back Gosforth (56-15), whilst Gloucester win at Sale (29-15) to stay on top. Transvaal lose to a visiting World XV (24-17).

20th: Graham Price (Pontypool), sent off at Coventry yesterday (his first ever dismissal), will miss the rest of the season.

21st: Kelso beat Hawick in a vital Border League match (12-6) at home; the Greens must now win their last two games to share the title.

23rd: The IB order South Africa to cancel the unofficial New Zealand Rugby tour. The team beat the Junior Springboks at Johannesburg (22-21).

26th: A beautiful day produces good finals at Twickenham and Cardiff with Bath winning the 'John Player' against gallant Wasps (25-17) and Cardiff beating brave Newport (28-21); seven tries adorn each match. Orrell win at Saracens (10-3) and lead John Smith Merit Table B. Northern Transvaal lose to the visiting New Zealand 'Cavaliers' (10-9). The Jed-Forest Sevens are won by Kelso who beat Melrose in the final (28-10).

30th: Melrose beat Hawick at home (18-9); Kelso are Border League Champions. The New Zealand 'Cavaliers' beat Orange Free State (31-9). In Wales, Cardiff beat visiting Pontypool (27-19), Newport and Newbridge draw at Rodney Parade (15-15), Glamorgan Wanderers win at Pontypridd (17-7) – the Wanderers reach 1,000 points for the season – and South Wales Police turn back Maesteg (21-16).

May

1st: Scotland's tourists beat Spain in Barcelona (39-17).

3rd: The excellent Harlequins win the Middlesex Sevens beating Nottingham (losing finalists again) in the final (18-10). In John Smith Merit Table matches, Bristol win at Nottingham in Table A (25-16), whilst Gosforth beat back Moseley (10-6) but are relegated along with Headingley. In Table B, Coventry thrash Orrell at home (31-6); both are promoted, Orrell as Champions. Transvaal beat the New Zealand 'Cavaliers' (24-19). Bath beat Gloucester at home (22-9) and Pontypool rout Newbridge (34-12).

4th: The Scotland touring team lose in France to Côte Basque (40-19); the location was Bayonne.

5th: The New Zealand 'Cavaliers' win in Cape Town against Western Province (25-16). Newport win at Abertillery (52-6) and Neath at home to Pontypridd (36-10).

6th: Scotland's tourists draw at Tarbes with a Regional Selection (16-16).

7th: Ebbw Vale are winners at home to Bridgend (16-10). Alan Morley (Bristol) is to retire at the end of his club's tour of Canada this month. England 'B' beat their Italian counterparts in Catania (27-14).

10th: Italy and England 'B' draw in Rome (15-15). South Africa win the first unofficial Test against the New Zealand 'Cavaliers' (21-15). The French Barbarians beat the Scotland touring team (32-19) in Agen.

11th: Agen and Toulouse will contest the French Championship final in Paris on 24th May.

The Springboks Crushed

Willie John McBride describes his most memorable match

Willie John McBride is a gentle giant who played in eighty full International matches, sixty three of them for his native Ireland and a record seventeen for the British Isles, whom he led on a tour of South Africa in 1974. It was for him and everyone connected with the tour a most strenuous experience in every way; it was also the first time in modern years that a Lions team went through an entire tour unbeaten, and much of the credit for this was due to his magnificent leadership.

The Springboks were not merely beaten; they were annihilated! It is not surprising, therefore, that the greatest memories of his career come from that tour, and from the Second Test in particular. Willie John recalls:

Willie John McBride (Ballymena and Ireland), captain of the invincible Lions in South Africa, 1974.

'This was not just a simple matter of being asked to lead a team on a tour. The tour in this case was a most controversial one to South Africa and there was considerable pressure on us to call it off; but once the Home Unions had decided to go it was up to us to make a success of it. However, it was not an easy decision for me to take; but I decided to go because I thought that it was right to maintain sporting links with South Africa.

That was not my only problem though, because at the time of the tour there was a workers' strike in Northern Ireland, and once I was on tour I heard nothing from my wife for several weeks. Eventually she moved to England for a brief spell and we were able to make contact with each other again, but it had been a very difficult time for all involved. To add to these problems, the government of the day opposed the tour, so once we had left we were on our own; but we had the consolation of knowing that everyone who had come on that tour had done so willingly and was determined to make it a success. Early on we had a talk amongst all the members of the party and it was absolutely clear that they were all one hundred per cent loyal to the team and to me as captain. Throughout the tour, they were to respond magnificently to every challenge, all thirty in the party.

It was fortunate that we had a good winning start, so our first real problem was to select a team for the First Test in Cape Town. It is important not to make a mistake at this stage of a tour, since an immediately settled Test team is vital to the success of a series.

That First Test saw us off to a very good start to the series as we won in Cape Town in damp conditions (12-3). Everything went right even though it was a tough game in which no tries were scored.

We made no changes for the Second Test two weeks later in Pretoria at the Loftus Versveld Stadium. This was to be for all of us the vital match and I remember saying to the team before the game, "This is the most important match of my life. It is the most important match of the tour. We must win it!" It was crucial because victory would mean that the series could not be lost. We knew it was likely to be far harder than the Cape Town match since we would be back playing on a very hard pitch; we would also be playing at 5,000 feet

Willie John McBride gives support to Mervyn Davies (no. 8) and Gordon Brown as the tourists clinch the series.

above sea level and that would mean the likelihood of breathing difficulties.

I felt confident that even those who would not be playing would care as much about the outcome as those who were actually on the field.

Normally before a game we would not leave the hotel until we actually made our way to the ground, and the same happened this time. We usually went by coach and on the way we would sing. The trip to Loftus Versveld was a short one, but Billy Steele, the Scottish wing, started us singing "Flower of Scotland" and we were still singing as we reached the stadium. No-one left the coach until we had finished. I knew then that the spirit in the team was so good that we couldn't fail to win. For the record, here is the line-up:

South Africa: I. McCallum *(Western Province)*; G. Germishuys *(Orange Free State)*, P. Whipp *(Western Province)*, J. Snyman *(Orange Free State)*, C. Pope *(Western Province)*; G. Bosch *(Transvaal)*, P. Bayvel *(Transvaal)*; N. Bezuidenhout *(Northern Transvaal)*, J. Fredrickson *(Transvaal)*, J. H. F. Marais *(Eastern Province) (captain)*, J. Ellis *(South West Africa)*, J. Williams *(Northern Transvaal)*, K. de Klerk *(Transvaal)*, D. MacDonald *(Western Province)*, M. du Plessis *(Western Province)*. *Replacements:* D. Snyman *(Western Province)* for McCallum; L. Vogel *(Orange Free State)* for Snyman

British Isles: J. P. R. Williams *(Wales)*; W. C. C. Steele *(Scotland)*, R. Milliken *(Ireland)*, I. R. McGeechan *(Scotland)*, J. J. Williams *(Wales)*; P. Bennett *(Wales)*, G. O. Edwards *(Wales)*; J. McLauchlan *(Scotland)*, R. Windsor *(Wales)*, F. E. Cotton *(England)*, R. M. Uttley *(England)*, W. J. McBride *(Ireland) (captain)*, G. L. Brown *(Scotland)*, J. F. Slattery *(Ireland)*, T. M. Davies *(Wales)*

Referee: C. de Bruyn *(Transvaal)*

As I said, it was the team spirit that made me sure that we would win, and we did. We scored five tries through J. J. Williams (who scored twice), Phil Bennett, Gordon Brown and Milliken (a fellow

Skipper Willie John McBride of the Lions grabs for the ball with Chris Ralston of England in support during the Final Test at Ellis Park, Johannesburg.

Irishman). Phil Bennett had one penalty and a conversion and Ian McGeechan dropped a goal. For South Africa, Bosch dropped a goal and had two penalties. The final score was a massive twenty eight points to nine.

The determination of the team was probably best demonstrated by Phil Bennett, who caught a South African stud as he crossed for his try. It resulted in a nasty gash and the medical officer advised him to retire. I asked him to stay on if he could and he replied without hesitation, "I'm not going off!" He got up and converted his try!

After the match the fifteen who had not played rushed into the dressing-room to offer their congratulations, such was the unity of the team. The sequel to that victory came as we relaxed in the Kruger National Park a day later and poor Phil Bennett could not walk properly, so I carried him round!

We won the Third Test almost as easily (26-9) at Port Elizabeth and after that game our team applauded the other fifteen in the stand as we left the field. The Final Test in Johannesburg was drawn (13-13), although we scored two tries to their one and thought we had won with another, but it had been a great tour.

It would have been impossible to have picked another thirty players with the same loyalty and who had reached the peak of their careers at the same time, and it was wonderful to lead such a magnificent bunch of men, who, first choices and the others alike, blended as a perfect team. That Second Test was decisive.'

Willie John McBride is now a successful banker, having retired in 1975 from International Rugby. There can have been few better or more popular captains. He is still remembered with great affection by all who have been associated with him.

The Best Fifteens, 1977-86

Any publication worth its salt must take the plunge at some time. In this case, we may provoke a few arguments by selecting our best fifteens from 1977 to the present for each of the Five Nations. The criteria are as consistent as they can be and are fairly simple. To be selected a player should still have been at his best when the decade started and we have tried to avoid picking players out of their recognized positions, although there are a few exceptions to this rule of thumb. Replacements have been chosen for their versatility where it would seem to be appropriate. We also give reasons for our choices.

John Carleton, holder of twenty six England caps, selected for the best England XV of the decade.

England

England's best period came from 1977 until 1982, since which time only five matches out of twenty two have been won. In 1980 the Grand Slam was achieved and it is logical that Bill Beaumont's team of that year should form the bulk of the selected fifteen with the amiable Lancastrian as skipper. Most of the choices are virtually automatic, starting at full-back where 'Dusty' Hare, for all his limitations in terms of speed, but not as far as commitment is concerned, has no real rival. The two wings Carleton and Slemen also cannot be disputed and it is difficult to make a case against two highly effective centres that year in Dodge and Woodward. It is also difficult to argue against John Horton and Steve Smith as half-backs. Similarly, the forwards virtually select themselves for the main fifteen, with a front-row of Cotton, Wheeler and Blakeway and Bill Beaumont and Colclough at lock. Only the back-row selection might provoke argument, but we go for Uttley and Neary on the flanks with John Scott at no. 8. It would be a very useful side and only the selection of the replacements could really be criticized – if at all!

The English team
15 W. H. Hare *(Nottingham, Leicester)*
14 J. Carleton *(Orrell)*
13 C. R. Woodward *(Leicester)*
12 P. W. Dodge *(Leicester)*
11 M. A. C. Slemen *(Liverpool)*
10 J. P. Horton *(Bath)*
9 S. J. Smith *(Sale)*
1 F. E. Cotton *(Coventry, Sale)*
2 P. J. Wheeler *(Leicester)*
3 P. J. Blakeway *(Gloucester)*
4 W. B. Beaumont *(Fylde) (captain)*
5 M. J. Colclough *(Angoulême, Wasps, Swansea)*
6 R. M. Uttley *(Gosforth)*
7 A. Neary *(Broughton Park)*
8 J. P. Scott *(Rosslyn Park, Cardiff)*
Replacements
16 G. H. Davies *(Cambridge University, Coventry, Wasps)*
17 L. Cusworth *(Leicester)*
18 N. D. Melville *(Wasps)*
19 G. S. Pearce *(Northampton)*
20 S. E. Brain *(Coventry)*
21 P. J. Winterbottom *(Headingley)*

Scotland

During the 1970s Scotland had a very patchy record, although some brilliant individuals appeared in the dark-blue jersey. But apart from a pause in 1985 the present decade has been one of distinction for the Scots, who have seen some of their greatest-ever players emerge. For a country which traditionally has a lack of strength in depth, there has been a remarkable array of outstanding talent; in only a few cases has selection been easy.

Amongst the backs there is a choice at full-back of three very good players – Andy Irvine, Peter Dods and Gavin Hastings. Irvine is selected because of the large number of appearances made by him and the fact that he is the world record points scorer in International matches, but Hastings could overtake him in future years. Amongst the backs there is, perhaps, a shortage of talent on the wings and an abundance amongst the centres. At right-wing-three-quarter we feel that there is no other choice than the admirable Keith Robertson, who is better as a centre but gained many caps there. A case could also be made to pick another person, Bruce Hay, out of position on the left, but Roger Baird has played exceptionally well of late and his lack of representative tries for Scotland is more than offset by his general all-round ability. Hay

Andy Irvine (Heriot's FP, Scotland and British Lions) in action against Wales at Murrayfield in 1977.

would be a very worthy replacement. There have been many fine centres, but McGeechan and Renwick may well have been the best of all, although David Johnston must run them both close and is another worthy replacement. No problems exist at half-back where Rutherford and Laidlaw have broken all International partnership records. Rutherford is probably the best fly-half ever to play for Scotland and many would make a similar claim for Laidlaw at the base of the scrum. As the latter's replacement there is a choice between the

The Scottish team
15 A. R. Irvine *(Heriot's FP)*
14 K. W. Robertson *(Melrose)*
13 I. R. McGeechan *(Headingley)*
12 J. M. Renwick *(Hawick)*
11 G. R. T. Baird *(Kelso)*
10 J. Y. Rutherford *(Selkirk)*
 9 R. J. Laidlaw *(Jed-Forest)*
 1 J. Aitken *(Gala) (captain)*
 2 C. T. Deans *(Hawick)*
 3 I. G. Milne *(Heriot's FP, Harlequins)*
 4 A. J. Tomes *(Hawick)*
 5 A. J. Campbell *(Hawick)*
 6 J. Jeffrey *(Kelso)*
 7 D. G. Leslie *(Dundee HSFP, West of Scotland, Gala)*
 8 I. A. M. Paxton *(Selkirk)*

Replacements
16 N. A. Rowan *(Boroughmuir)*
17 G. J. Callander *(Kelso)*
18 J. R. Beattie *(Glasgow Academicals, Heriot's FP)*
19 A. J. M. Lawson *(London Scottish, Edinburgh Wanderers)*
20 D. I. Johnston *(Watsonians)*
21 B. H. Hay *(Boroughmuir)*

British Lion, Douglas Morgan, and Alan Lawson, with the latter marginally preferred.

For the pack, the Grand Slam team would seem to be the best source of selection, as those 1984 heroes were a rarity among Scots since 1946 – they were winners! So the front-row should be Jim Aitken (the captain), Colin Deans (Scotland's greatest-ever hooker) and Iain Milne (possibly the greatest-ever tighthead). At lock there are four candidates in Alastair McHarg, Bill Cuthbertson, Alan Tomes and Alister Campbell. Campbell has the unusual distinction for a Scot of having played both in a Grand Slam and Championship-sharing team, whilst Tomes was an essential part of that famous 1984 team; so we choose the two Hawick men. Back-row stars have also been plentiful with two very good no. 8's in Iain Paxton and John Beattie and such marvellous flankers as David Leslie, the Calder twins and John Jeffrey. With some reluctance the twins are omitted. In selecting the replacements we are left with choices from people with very few caps – so consistent have been the incumbents – for the front-row, but neither Callander nor Rowan in the front-row would let anyone down, whilst if we finally pluck up our courage and pick Paxton as the senior no. 8 we can look no further than John Beattie for the third forward replacement; he did a fine job as a lock when asked to replace Cuthbertson in the 1984 Calcutta Cup match.

Both in 1984 and 1986, the junior team in the Scotland trial thrashed the seniors and this could happen if a mythical 'Rest' team were to be selected from the remaining talent, but we will not examine that possibility here.

Ireland
Selected by Sean Diffley

Selecting a team to represent Ireland from the last ten seasons is made difficult by the memory of some of the country's all-time great players who left the scene before this period started. Nevertheless, the choice available in this period is good.

The full-back choice rests between Hugo MacNeill, Rodney O'Donnell and Tony Ensor, and with his successful British Lions connections MacNeill gets the vote. The wings produced two outstanding candidates for the right with Trevor Ringland winning the vote over Tom Grace, but, on the left, Keith Crossan is an automatic choice, as is Mike Gibson for one of the centre spots; the other choice there is the exciting Brendan Mullin over David Irwin and Mike Kiernan, who is selected as a replacement.

Ollie Campbell and John Robbie virtually select themselves for the half-back position with Tony Ward and Patterson as the replacements. Similarly, selection of the pack causes little difficulty; the only arguments likely to arise are over the selection of Philip Matthews at the expense of John O'Driscoll and of Fergus Slattery over Nigel Carr. Replacements, too, cause few problems of choice with Whelan at hooker, Declan Fitzgerald at prop and John O'Driscoll to cover the other positions. Ciaran Fitzgerald is the automatic choice for the captaincy with his fine track record.

Mike Gibson, winner of a record eighty one caps. The match is Wales v. Ireland on 15th January 1977.

The Irish team

15 H. P. MacNeill (*Dublin University, Blackrock College, Oxford University, London Irish*)
14 T. M. Ringland (*Queen's University, Belfast, Ballymena*)
13 C. M. H. Gibson (*Cambridge University, North of Ireland*)
12 B. J. Mullin (*Dublin University*)
11 K. D. Crossan (*Instonians*)
10 S. O. Campbell (*Old Belvedere*)
9 J. C. Robbie (*Dublin University, Cambridge University, Greystones*)
1 P. A. Orr (*Old Wesley*)
2 C. F. Fitzgerald (*St Mary's College*) (*captain*)
3 G. A. J. McLoughlin (*Shannon*)
4 D. G. Lenihan (*Cork Constitution*)
5 M. I. Keane (*Lansdowne*)
6 J. F. Slattery (*UC Dublin, Blackrock College*)
7 P. M. Matthews (*Ards*)
8 W. P. Duggan (*Blackrock College*)

Replacements
16 P. C. Whelan (*Garryowen*)
17 D. C. Fitzgerald (*Lansdowne*)
18 J. B. O'Driscoll (*London Irish, Manchester*)
19 C. S. Patterson (*Instonians*)
20 A. J. P. Ward (*Garryowen, St Mary's College, Greystones*)
21 M. J. Kiernan (*Lansdowne, Dolphin*)

Wales

The period as far as Wales is concerned is very much a story of two phases: four seasons of resounding success followed by six of mediocrity, so any Welsh selection must concentrate for its choices on the earlier days, when many outstanding players were still playing. The 1980s must also be largely ignored, since nothing has been won during that time, whereas the 1970s produced three Grand Slams, two in the period under review. The Welsh choices will look like a collection from 'The Hall of Fame', which will cause feelings of nostalgia for all Welshmen nowadays.

At full-back there is only one candidate, the great J. P. R. Williams; and for the two wings one need look no further than the two all-time greats,

Welsh outside-half, Phil Bennett, kicks during the British Lions match against Natal in Durban on 20th July 1974.

Gerald Davies and J. J. Williams. Selection of centres is less easy, but there are three fine candidates in Steve Fenwick, Ray Gravell and D. S. Richards of Swansea with our vote going to the first two with the latter, who has probably been a better fly-half, as a replacement. At half-back there are again two automatic choices in Phil Bennett and Gareth Edwards, with the injury-prone Terry Holmes as a replacement at scrum-half. The other choice for a replacement is not easy, but G. Evans (Maesteg) was a fine all-round back who probably deserved more caps than he received and he is preferred to Gareth Davies of Cardiff.

The forwards were playing at their best in the 1970s and there are some very good candidates for selection with the choice of the front-row settling on that very formidable Pontypool trio of Faulkner, Windsor and Graham Price; as replacement hooker we suggest Phillips of Cardiff with Ian Stephens of Bridgend for prop. In the second row there would seem to be three good candidates in Allan Martin, Geoff Wheel and Bob Norster; Wheel is chosen for his general strength and ability in the mauls with Martin preferred to Norster because of his bonus as a place-kicker. In the back-row we suggest Derek Quinnell and Terry Cobner as flankers with Jeff Squire at no. 8; the replacements at forward would be completed by the inclusion of Norster. It would be a great and exciting side particularly behind the scrum. The captain? Terry Cobner.

The Welsh team
15 J. P. R. Williams *(London Welsh, Bridgend)*
14 T. G. R. Davies *(Cardiff)*
13 S. P. Fenwick *(Bridgend)*
12 R. W. R. Gravell *(Llanelli)*
11 J. J. Williams *(Llanelli)*
10 P. Bennett *(Llanelli)*
 9 G. O. Edwards *(Cardiff)*
 1 A. G. Faulkner *(Pontypool)*
 2 R. W. Windsor *(Pontypool)*
 3 G. Price *(Pontypool)*
 4 A. J. Martin *(Aberavon)*
 5 G. A. D. Wheel *(Swansea)*
 6 T. J. Cobner *(Pontypool) (captain)*
 7 D. L. Quinnell *(Llanelli)*
 8 J. Squire *(Newport, Pontypool)*

Replacements
16 G. Evans *(Maesteg)*
17 D. S. Richards *(Swansea)*
18 T. D. Holmes *(Cardiff)*
19 I. Stephens *(Bridgend)*
20 A. J. Phillips *(Cardiff)*
21 R. L. Norster *(Cardiff)*

France

For France, the last decade has been a period of great success with two Grand Slams and two other seasons when there was a share of the title. Also, in 1984 the coveted Grand Slam was missed at the last hurdle after a memorable match at Murrayfield and in two seasons, 1977 and 1985, no tries were conceded. The French have in fact not only been an outstandingly attractive side, but they have also been excellent in defence. Team selection in such circumstances has not been easy owing to the abundance of outstanding players, but nevertheless we are sure that our final choice will meet with qualified approval.

At full-back there can only be one choice, Serge Blanco, and the three-quarters (despite the many brilliant players) have produced four really outstanding men in the wings Averous and Estève and the centres Sella and Codorniou. In time, Charvet and Bonneval may contradict these assessments, but for the moment they remain very difficult to challenge. At scrum-half there have been two really outstanding players with Gallion being our preferred selection to Berbizier, but at fly-half it has not been so easy. Romeu passed his best as the decade began, leaving Lescarboura, who is adequate but not outstanding, as our first choice followed by the efficient Laporte, who merits a place as a replacement.

The selection of the pack is also not easy but we suggest a front-row of Dospital, Dintrans and Paparemborde, which leaves the excellent Marocco and Garuet as spectators as we select Dubroca to cover all three positions as a replacement. The best two locks have probably been Haget and Condom, which explains why the line-out has not always been a fertile source of possession. Rives (our captain) and Erbani were outstanding flankers among many and Joinel has played right through the decade, making him a model choice for no. 8. The two remaining forward replacements we suggest are Lorieux and the versatile Rodriguez, who can play almost anywhere in the pack including prop. But if all twenty one players were to be shut away on a desert island for a few weeks, thus depriving us of their availability, we could undoubtedly choose a side of almost equal ability from the others who represented France in the decade! Discipline has been the main problem, otherwise they might win everything.

Coq au vin? Jean-Pierre Rives, France's charismatic captain, celebrates victory at the Parc des Princes against Scotland, 1983.

The French team
15 S. Blanco *(Biarritz)*
14 J.-L. Averous *(La Voulte)*
13 P. Sella *(Agen)*
12 D. Codorniou *(Narbonne)*
11 P. Estève *(Narbonne)*
10 J.-P. Lescarboura *(Dax)*
 9 J. Gallion *(Toulon)*
 1 P. Dospital *(Bayonne)*
 2 P. Dintrans *(Tarbes)*
 3 R. Paparemborde *(Pau)*
 4 F. Haget *(Agen, Biarritz)*
 5 J. Condom *(Boucau)*
 6 J.-P. Rives *(Toulouse, RCF) (captain)*
 7 D. Erbani *(Agen)*
 8 J.-L. Joinel *(Brive)*
Replacements
16 D. Dubroca *(Agen)*
17 L. Rodriguez *(Mont-de-Marsan)*
18 A. Lorieux *(Grenoble)*
19 P. Berbizier *(Agen)*
20 G. Laporte *(Graulhet)*
21 J. M. Aguirre *(Bagnères)*

Goal-kicking Forwards: a Dying Breed?

Who was the last forward you saw taking place-kicks in an International match? Twenty years ago or even in the mid 1970s such a question would have been unthinkable, but now it would not be the easiest of questions to include in a quiz programme. At a recent function this was discussed with some colleagues and there were some very interesting answers, which required some good memories for correct replies.

It is thought that Allan Martin (Aberavon) was the last forward to take goal-kicks in International matches and he last played for Wales in 1981 against Ireland and France. The giant lock was – and still is for Penarth – a very good line-out specialist whilst he was also useful for long-range kicks, Phil Bennett and Gareth Davies (amongst others) being the regular place-kickers for Wales for medium-range efforts. Before Martin, Wales did not often use forwards for place-kickers, but in 1947 W. E.

Allan Martin (Aberavon and Wales), one of an endangered species? Where have all those goal-kicking forwards gone?

Tamplin of Cardiff did win a game in Paris by scoring with a massive penalty-kick – the game's only score. And who can forget John Taylor's kick at Murrayfield in 1971? A match-winner!

Before Martin, Scotland had the eccentric but highly effective boot of Peter Brown (Gala) who made his last appearance for Scotland in 1973. Brown made twenty seven appearances in total, but it was in 1971 that he made some of his most famous kicks starting with a conversion attempt in Paris, which spiralled off his right boot in a crazy fashion from touch before clearing the cross-bar. Later in the same season in injury time he had a slightly easier kick to bring Scotland victory at Twickenham for the first time since 1938. He calmly plonked the ball down, then turned his back on it and swung round to convert comfortably. A year later at Murrayfield he put over more penalty-goals and scored a try as the Calcutta Cup remained North of the Border for another year. Before Peter Brown, Scotland's most notable place-kicking forward was H. M. Inglis (Edinburgh Academicals), who gained seven caps in 1951 and 1952.

England's most recent forward-kicker was the huge lock from Northampton and the Royal Air Force, P. J. Larter, who won twenty four caps for England between 1967 and 1973 and also played a Test in South Africa with the British Lions team of 1968. Another claim to fame was his appearance for England with the side that won in Johannesburg in 1973 (18-9), but Sam Doble was the kicking hero that day. Another England kicking forward was D. St G. Hazell (Bristol), who played in the four Championship matches of 1955 as a prop and kicked three penalty-goals during that campaign with his left boot. G. W. Hastings (Gloucester), capped thirteen times as a prop between 1955 and 1958, was another good kicker.

For Ireland, kicking forwards have been thin on the ground and it is thought that Dr J. Murphy-O'Connor (Bective Rangers) in his only match for them at Twickenham in 1954 was the last to score as a forward – he was a no.8 and was injured during the match after scoring Ireland's only points from a penalty. D. McKibbin (Instonians), a large prop, was another goal-kicking forward with a very short run-up; he played eight times in 1951 and 1952.

French kicking forwards have also been a rarity but Jean Prat (Lourdes), their no. 8 and outstanding captain of the fifties, not only took place-kicks but also was an expert drop-kicker; he had two successful efforts at Twickenham in France's victory of 1955 (16-9) and he played thirty eight times for his country.

Elsewhere, New Zealand have rarely looked beyond their full-backs – Bob Scott, Don Clarke, Fergie McCormick, Joe Karam, Alan Hewson, etc. – and the only major deviation from this pattern was the use of the lethal left boot of Ron Jarden, a left-wing-three-quarter, but the Springboks did produce two effective locks, who could kick well. Who of that generation will forget the massive Okey Geffin (Transvaal), who played in only seven Internationals, but in one of these (the First Test against the 1949 All-Blacks in Johannesburg) he kicked five penalty-goals to give his side victory against opposition, which scored the only try? (When did we hear that complaint before?) His boot during the 1951-52 tour of Britain landed seven conversions against Scotland at Murrayfield when the South Africans scored nine tries and won by 44 points to nil ('And lucky to score nil' as one Scottish wag put it!). During that same tour Hennie Muller, the vice-captain and no. 8, also took kicks at goal. F. C. H. Du Preez (Northern Transvaal), who played a record thirty eight times for the 'Boks', was also an effective long-range kicker from 1960 until 1971.

For the Wallabies R. E. McMaster (Queensland)

The clenched teeth tell it all. John Taylor (London Welsh and Wales) sends another vital kick on its way.

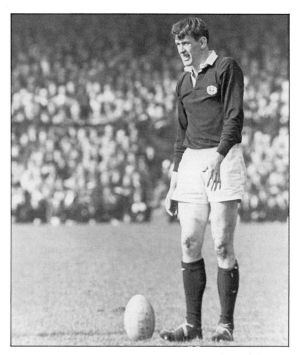

Peter Brown (Gala and Scotland) takes his usual perfunctory look at the target before landing one of his numerous goals.

was possibly the only genuine kicking forward since they, like the All-Blacks, have tended to use backs to take their kicks. He gained seven caps in the late 1940s.

In other spheres there have been successful place-kickers, and the winning points for London Counties, the only team to lower the colours of the 1951-52 Springboks, came from Alan Grimsdell, a lock with a strong left foot. In the University match, a prop, J. G. M. Webster, landed a left-footed penalty-goal from touch in 1980 for the Dark Blues; that was the last successful kick by a forward in the fixture, and Mallett of Oxford, a no. 8, was also successful with a very eccentric effort the previous year. Other kicking forwards in the fixture have been Currie and Gould (Oxford) and Loveday and Harvey of Cambridge. Gould took over in 1965 from Bob Hiller, whilst Harvey scored the last ever goal from a mark in the fixture – in 1964.

So, as Allan Martin plays out his career with Penarth does he reflect that he is the last of a dying breed? Perhaps, ruefully, he does. Or has he realised the fact at all? In an era when forwards are far more athletic than before, it is an irony that the art of place-kicking seems to have been abandoned. It is also ironic that Alastair McHarg did not include place-kicking in his otherwise all-embracing repertoire.

Professionalism: the End of the Game as We Know It?

Professionalism is a concept alien to the majority of players and followers of Rugby Union. The traditional, and indeed widespread, view is that the establishment of a professional status in the sport could only result in undesirable elements being introduced. Such a view is normally justified by drawing comparisons with developments in sports such as soccer, cricket and tennis, where playing the game for its own sake now seems to take second place to financial gain; sportsmanship, too, is often absent. There is a strong feeling that Rugby should remain an amateur sport, but international developments look set to determine otherwise.

When late in 1985 the South African Union announced that, for the time being at least, there would be no invitation to the British Isles to visit the Republic there was much relief amongst many followers of sporting matters in these islands. The greatest of the celebrations probably came from Edinburgh, which was due to host the Commonwealth Games in 1986 and wanted as few defections as possible. This move by South Africa, in addition to the legal actions that prevented an All-Blacks tour of the Republic in 1985, saved the 'Friendly Games'.

After the initial euphoria, a further cold and hard look at the situation is most important. Politics play an important role in modern sport and can influence the choice of a country's sporting opponents, especially in the case of South Africa. Although some attempts are being made by their sports administrators to liberalize sports, they are still not acceptable to the rest of the world who deplore the system of apartheid practised in South Africa. While this political system is in operation, it seems that any attempts to produce a multi-racial sporting society will be ignored by the governments and sporting bodies of other states.

In the light of present international opinion, the South Africans may feel justified in creating their own international sporting events, as is happening to some extent at the moment with the recent tour by New Zealand. Meanwhile, other countries are cancelling tours to South Africa because the selection of players for national sides depends not only on their ability but also on whether they have sporting links with South Africa. It would not be surprising, therefore, if South Africa was to hit back by creating an International professional circus. This has already happened in cricket, and it subsequently brought about a lowering of standards in the sport in Australia where the move began.

Amongst white South Africans, especially the Afrikaners, Rugby Union is at least as much a religion as it is in South Wales. If they are denied access to the International scene they may devise their own alternative, and since there is said to be plenty of ready cash it would be relatively easy for them to set up an International circus, attracting class players with attractive financial offers. Since this is a distinct possibility, with professionalism looming large on the horizon, we can only guess at the, possibly disastrous, effects that this move might have on the game as we know it.

The implementation of a circus would probably run as follows: If the money really is available, an alternative World Cup would probably take place in South Africa with twenty or thirty of the players from the leading countries taking part. They would then be banned from playing Rugby Union again in their own countries. Worse still, once the South African season came to an end, they would most likely move to the British Isles and continue their activities there with no shortage of people wanting to join the bandwagon. Thus the game would have effectively turned professional without a preventative shot having been fired. Whether it would be a bad thing or not is another matter, but who can expect avid Rugby players and followers to let it happen without, in resignation, deciding to accept this new concept of their favourite sport?

So, the Commonwealth Games may well have been saved, but at what cost to Rugby Union amongst other sports? Imposing bans on South Africa and on the players associated with sport in that country may have far-reaching repercussions throughout the game and bring about a new movement towards professionalism.

Philippe Sella (Agen and France) breaks away against Scotland. He was the outstanding player in the Five Nations Championship.

The State of the Five Nations: Our Best Fifteen

Although a team was chosen for the IB Centenary celebration matches, the selectors had to leave out several players who were, for a number of reasons, unavailable. No harm can be done if we suggest our own Five Nations XV for this season based on the form we have seen. Players have not been selected out of their normal positions.

Full-backs

Six players have appeared in the full programme including Stuart Barnes, who deputized twice for Huw Davies of England, once briefly and once at greater length. Of the number, three – Blanco (France), Thorburn (Wales) and Gavin Hastings (Scotland) – were outstanding, and cases for the inclusion of all of them could be made. However, Blanco is an exceptional performer amongst other great players, even if he may have lost some of his speed (through, it is alleged, giving up smoking), and he must gain the vote.

Wing-three-quarters

In making this selection we omit players who do not specialize in the positions in question. This rules out Lafond, who is really a full-back and who would be on the replacement bench. There are some other excellent candidates and, had he not missed the match in Dublin, Duncan (Scotland) might have been a very strong contender. As it is, the right-wing position must go to the strong-running Ringland (Ireland), who scored three tries in the competition for an unsuccessful team. On the left, there are various candidates and Underwood (England), Bonneval (France) and Baird (Scotland) all have strong claims; Crossan (Ireland) was injured for much of the season and did not see a great deal of the ball. Nor, for that matter, did Underwood, but it is thought that in a good team he would prosper and he has the track record to back this assumption, so he is selected ahead of the other admirable candidates.

Centre-three-quarters

The competition has produced an embarrassment of riches with only England having failed to produce any candidates for selection, largely because the four players fielded (plus John Palmer, a replacement) seldom saw enough of the ball for any judgments to be made. Ireland, Scotland and Wales fielded the same pair in all four matches and France made only the one change, the brilliant Charvet for the far from incompetent Chadebech. The other French centre, Sella, was the tournament's outstanding player and is an automatic choice, leaving several candidates for the other position. But we want to win the match against our hypothetical opponents and need a specialist place-kicker in the side in addition to Blanco, who is not a first choice for France. Bowen is a good possibility from Wales, but again he is not a first choice kicker for his country. Michael Kiernan has a good record for Ireland, if we forgive his temporary lapses against Scotland; he is also a fine player in his own right and is thus selected to partner Sella. This is hard luck on Devereux (Wales), Bowen (Wales), Scott Hastings (Scotland), Johnston (Scotland), Brendan Mullin (Ireland) and Charvet, but centre play has been of a high standard and we cannot find room for everyone.

Half-backs

The Irish selections have been unsuccessful owing to injuries (three fly-halves were used) and loss of form in the case of Bradley at scrum-half; and England's pair, Andrew and Melville, have not been at their best. Melville would seem to be jinxed by injuries and anyone who has been replaced in three of his nine appearances would be too much of a risk. His replacement for England, Hill, is a fine scrum-half, but he must convince everyone that he can behave himself properly on the field before he merits serious consideration. The three remaining scrum-halves all had excellent campaigns, but Robert Jones (Wales) showed his inexperience against the French, when he missed at least one vital tackle. Berbizier (France) and Roy Laidlaw (Scotland) were the only two scrum-halves to score tries during the competition. Since Laidlaw not only made a comeback to International Rugby after being effectively written off a year ago but his try, an individual effort of genius against Ireland, won Scotland a share of the title, so he earns the vote against the admirable Frenchman, who is the replacement. The only two fly-halves in serious

Colin Deans (Scotland) tries to hand off Jérôme Gallion (France). Deans has now played forty four times as hooker for Scotland.

contention, if we exclude Laporte on the grounds of advancing years, are Jonathan Davies (Wales) and Rutherford (Scotland). The latter has the superior defensive qualities, but Davies has, whenever the opportunity presented itself and on occasions when there have only been half-chances, looked a very good player. With the right support he could be devastating; so he is selected.

Hookers

Colin Deans (Scotland) has been outstanding both as a hooker and as captain of his country and gains the vote ahead of Dubroca (France), who is not a specialist although his efforts in an emergency have been most praiseworthy. As a consolation, he is chosen as the replacement to cover all the front-row positions. The others – Brain (England), Fitzgerald (Ireland's captain) and James (Wales) – are good players but fall short of the standards set by the other two.

Prop Forwards

This has been a weakness of every country except France and Scotland, whose David Sole would have been in contention had he not been injured after two matches. His fellow countryman, Iain Milne, is a strong candidate for the tighthead position. Phil Orr (Ireland) was dropped for part of the campaign and may have lost some of his form, whilst neither pair from Wales or England, who used two looseheads, was convincing. The French pair (Marocco at loosehead and Garuet at tighthead) were far and away the best and therefore win selection.

Locks

With Robert Norster (Wales) ruled out, this was not a vintage season and selection is not easy. The French line-out tactics reflect their own lack of confidence in the ageing Haget and Condom, whilst Scotland used a no. 8 in Paxton to partner the admirable Campbell. The Welsh pair were not a success and England's Colclough and Dooley were badly outplayed at Murrayfield and in Paris. Ireland have probably the best of the bunch in Lenihan, whom we select along with Dooley, who has the potential to improve his mobility and scrummaging to add to his fine line-out work. McCall (Ireland) would be selected as a replacement.

Flankers

Neither England nor Wales were satisfactory in this respect even though the players they selected did have potential. Ireland's Nigel Carr missed

The 'White Shark', John Jeffrey (Scotland). His pursuer is Jonathan Davies (Wales).

much of the season through injury and the best performers were the exciting Champ (France) and Jeffrey (Scotland) plus the less spectacular Erbani (France) and Finlay Calder (Scotland). Champ and Jeffrey are younger, which is a none too convincing reason for giving them the votes.

No. 8

There were only two real candidates for this position. Dean Richards (England) is discounted on the grounds of inexperience, and Iain Paxton (Scotland) is selected as a replacement because he played three times as a lock. This leaves Joinel (France) and Beattie (Scotland). The latter is younger and probably more mobile and is thus selected.

So the team selected for our mythical match is:

15 S. Blanco *(France)*
14 T. M. Ringland *(Ireland)*
13 P. Sella *(France)*
12 M. J. Kiernan *(Ireland)*
11 R. R. Underwood *(England)*
10 J. Davies *(Wales)*
 9 R. J. Laidlaw *(Scotland)*
 1 P. Marocco *(France)*
 2 C. T. Deans *(Scotland) (captain)*
 3 J.-P. Garuet *(France)*
 4 D. G. Lenihan *(Ireland)*
 5 W. A. Dooley *(England)*
 6 J. Jeffrey *(Scotland)*
 7 E. Champ *(France)*
 8 J. R. Beattie *(Scotland)*

Replacements
16 D. Dubroca *(France)*
17 B. W. McCall *(Ireland)*
18 I. A. M. Paxton *(Scotland)*
19 P. Berbizier *(France)*
20 J. Y. Rutherford *(Scotland)*
21 J.-B. Lafond *(France)*

The opinions expressed here are personal and it is appreciated that with only one Welsh player in the selected squad Welsh supporters might well complain. But this has been a bad period for a nation that has not figured in the Championship reckoning in this decade. The Welsh strengths are in positions where others are, perhaps, slightly stronger. England suffered the consequences of two bad defeats, at Murrayfield and in Paris, and Ireland's good showing is based on the fact that certain players have played extremely well in difficult circumstances. Scotland only failed to play well in Dublin (and still won luckily), so six selections do not flatter their efforts, whilst some would have advocated the choice of the whole French team *en bloc*. On reflection, however, this would not really have produced the strongest possible team even if it had been a temptation. France's problem is that some of their players are over thirty, or will be by next season, and will thus, sooner rather than later, lose pace and be compelled to bow out.

How the North Beat the All-Blacks

Bill Beaumont describes his most memorable match

Bill Beaumont is the most capped English Rugby captain. He led his country on twenty one occasions and also played on thirty four occasions for England from 1975 until 1982, when he was advised to retire on medical grounds owing to head injuries. He was a player respected and liked by everyone from every Rugby-playing country and he created his own large slice of history by leading England to her last Grand Slam triumph in 1980.

A logical choice, perhaps, would be his country's superb victory over Scotland at Murrayfield in 1980 when that Grand Slam was clinched. However, Bill has chosen a different triumph.

'My most memorable match, of many, took place at Otley on 17th November 1979 when I had the pleasure of captaining Northern Division against the All-Blacks, who were on a tour of England and Scotland at the time.

It was a murky and very windy afternoon and, not for the first time, the All-Blacks had arrived unbeaten. We in the North fancied our chances, as the bulk of our team came from the North-West side that had toured South Africa that year and we had built up some good teamwork and spirit on that trip, with the help of Des Seabrook, our very good coach. So, unlike many other sides that are selected to meet touring teams, we knew a lot about each other and we had a plan of action.

Never before have I felt so confident about a match and I thought to myself: "This is the day!" For the record, the teams lined up like this:

Northern Division: K. O'Brien *(Broughton Park)*; J. Carleton *(Orrell)*, A. Wright *(Sale)*, A. M. Bond *(Sale)*, M. A. C. Slemen *(Liverpool)*; A. G. B. Old *(Sheffield)*, S. J. Smith *(Sale)*; F. E. Cotton *(Sale)*, A. Simpson *(Sale)*, C. White *(Gosforth)*, R. M. Uttley *(Wasps)*, W. B. Beaumont *(Fylde)* (captain), J. P. Sydall *(Waterloo)*, A. Neary *(Broughton Park)*, P. J. Dixon *(Gosforth)*

New Zealand: R. Wilson; S. Wilson, M. Taylor, G. Cunningham, B. Fraser; E. Dunn, M. Donaldson; J. Speirs, A. Dalton, B. Johnstone, G. Mourie *(captain)*, A. Haden, J. Fleming, K. Stewart, M. Mexted. *Replacement:* P. Sloane for Dalton, 54 minutes

Referee: A. M. Hosie *(Scotland)*

Anyone reading that New Zealand line-up will realize the huge task we faced, but, as I have said, I have never felt so confident as I did then. They had great back-row players, but so had we with Roger Uttley, Peter Dixon and Tony Neary and on that

The ever-popular Bill Beaumont, captain of Northern Division, England and the British Lions during his 'annus mirabilis', which started in November 1979 and ended with the captaincy of the British Lions.

windy November afternoon we in effect played them at their own game.

It all depended really on the first half, when we played against the gale and turned round with a nine point lead thanks to a try by Steve Smith, which was converted by Alan Old, who also kicked a penalty-goal. But the most important thing was that we had been beating their great back-row and had stopped them from playing. Since they were the basis of all New Zealand's attacks this meant that their talented backs had very few chances, and Smith's try for us was a fine effort.

Of course, with the wind in our favour we had a much easier passage after half-time (if there are ever any easier passages against teams from New Zealand) and we added tries by Bond, who went over twice, and Alan Old himself. All this resulted from our back-row's ability to 'tie-in' their All-

Northern Division v. New Zealand, 17th November 1979: The All-Blacks cannot stop this try by Sale's Tony Bond for the Northern Division. Taylor and Dunn look on helplessly and Andy Haden (no.4) arrives too late.

Black counterparts, and the rest of the pack did its job well, too, so that we had plenty of possession.

As always, the All-Blacks never gave up and they managed a try in reply by Stu Wilson, which Richard Wilson successfully converted; he also kicked a penalty-goal. But the final score in our favour was twenty one points to nine and a try-count in our favour of four-one. It was a great afternoon and one I will never forget.

The national selectors could not very well pick the same team selected by Mike Weston and Des Seabrook from this game to play in the Twickenham International a week later, when we lost by a single point (9-10). But the tactics of that match formed the basis of England's play during the Five Nations Championship that followed, with the English back-row playing a very important role particularly in our wins over Ireland at Twickenham and against Scotland at Murrayfield, when John Carleton was free to score a hat-trick of tries.

It was a great season for me, but that match at Otley in November that really started it all off was the one I shall remember best of all. It was also one of the best sides I ever led, if not the best. All but three of them played for England and, of those three, Kevin O'Brien has won three caps for Ireland and is still a reliable full-back for Lancashire. Wright was close to honours and Simpson has toured with England and has also been on the bench more times than he can remember without being called upon to replace anyone; perhaps his time will come. I hope so.'

Bill Beaumont was England's captain a record number of times and his caps won as a lock (thirty four) are also a record for the position. His ultimate great moment that season came when he was carried shoulder high off the field at Murrayfield to generous home applause after that Grand Slam and Calcutta Cup win. He remains a popular figure and can regularly be seen and heard on television, giving expert assessments of the game.

The Commentator's Lot

by Nigel Starmer-Smith

The trouble with being a commentator is that, in truth, you cannot win! In most other professions you are not exposed to the same widespread belief that it is a job that almost anybody could do just as well, probably better, if only the opportunity were to come their way. Maybe they have a point. But at least if you are a neurological surgeon, a nuclear physicist or even a dentist there are few people outside the profession who would have the audacity to suggest that if they were given the tools of the trade they could step right in and show you how it should be done. Furthermore, whilst the surgeon may be rewarded with the acknowledgement by ten patients out of ten that his efforts with the scalpel and forceps were entirely to their satisfaction, the sporting commentator starts out with the basic premise that he can never hope to satisfy his entire audience. Some may dislike his accent, his style or his tendency to over- or under-dramatize, to talk too much or too little, to provide a surfeit of explanatory detail and interpretation for the expert or to leave the uninitiated bewildered by a spectacle that they can make neither head nor tail of. In sum, everyone, it seems, is a would-be commentator, and inevitably only a very few people will ever appreciate that it is a rather more demanding task than it may appear to be at first glance.

The principal function of the commentator must be to identify the players; and the gist of the critics' argument runs something like this: what could be more straightforward, thirty players in two teams in different strips numbered one to fifteen, and all that is required is to match the appropriate name to the number? Yes, in theory, but it is seldom appreciated that perched high up in the upper stand rafters or maybe down at ground level, most of the time the players are running towards you with their numbers of course on their backs! Even when they can be clearly observed you may find yourself at the Recreation Ground, Bath, where the right-wing is no. 15 and centre no. 14 in deference to an old superstition that does not allow them to wear a no. 13 jersey. Similarly, at Bristol, where no. 1 (traditionally prop forward) is in fact letter I, scrum-half, since letters not numbers adorn the players at the Memorial Ground. Add to that confusing recollections of the days when Coventry numbered backwards 15 to 1, or the first sighting of the touring Japanese, Maoris or Tongans. With due respect to my brethren from those far-flung Rugby centres, there can be slight problems of instant recognition of the huddle of Rugby players of seemingly identical physical characteristics – eptitomized by the unforgettable quartet of Maori forwards Colin Cooper, Scott Crichton, Paul Koteka and Billy Bush, each a giant of similar dimensions, dark-skinned, all with medium-length, jet black hair and all sporting beards and bandit moustaches!

So it is that you learn – often at brief acquaintance with a newly-arrived team, or maybe a junior club side in a cup match – to mark and inwardly digest individual characteristics that help you to become name-perfect in quick time. Red hair, an unusual gait, a balding patch, a moustache, sleeves rolled up – all these idiosyncracies can be manna from heaven for the Rugby commentator who has to make instant identification during the play, and who has to be familiar with not just thirty players, but twelve replacements, three match officials together with sundry doctors, physios and trainers. And remember, there is no time for a fleeting glance down at a programme to check a number seven against the player's name. Rest assured that, by the time that is achieved, the ball will have passed through a further four pairs of hands and a try scored. There is an unwritten law that applies to that situation.

So with the assimilation of names and physical characteristics completed and the pronunciation (with welcome advice gained from the appropriate Embassy or High Commission in the case of touring sides) of Geldenhuys, Polutele Tu'ihalamaka, Nobuyuki Veyama or Adolfo Soares Gache successfully learned, the problems are over. Or are they? At ground level, your view of the action may be obscured by other players blocking out those who are closest to the ball or, by contrast, at the furthest extremity of the stadium, in Rugby's equivalent to the theatre hall 'Gods' at Parc des Princes, for instance, or the Boet Erasmus Stadium, Port Elizabeth, you may well be over 100 yards from the playing surface and the players more akin to swarming ants than mighty seventeen-stone forwards or sylph-like wing-three-quarters.

And all the time through your headphones run the TV director's comments and instructions, as

Nigel Starmer-Smith, TV's presenter of 'Rugby Special' and commentator on the big matches, ready for the afternoon's action.

necessary information is passed on to the four, six or eight cameramen covering the match: 'Number 2, give a close-up of Jonathan Davies; 3, I want a wide-angle of the crowd; Nigel, talk through a replay of that try.' Other information relayed involves clues as to a shot that may be coming up on the screen, or a specific instruction to be followed. While all this is going on, of course, you endeavour to convey a controlled and accurate commentary to the viewer.

The mention of replays raises the issue of another interesting challenge for the commentator in all matches outside the Internationals. It is desirable at points in the game to replay visually, and with comment, exciting moments, sequences or try-scoring passages. So the director will request the verbal replay to go with pictures. The only problem is that there is no visual replay to guide you through; that is 'painted in' afterwards on edited matches. So the commentator has to recreate the passage of play in his mind and talk through it as if actually seeing it again. And since you are never sure when a try is about to be scored, it can be a fascinating mental exercise. No doubt those with videos can enjoy the opportunity of spotting and rechecking any errors without appreciating that the commentary – not the commentator – was blind!

Included in this unintended apologia there could be thrown in for good measure the exceptional hurdles that often confront the commentator, like adverse and unforeseen weather conditions: striving to stay alive, for example, beneath camera-cover tarpaulins while an amazing horizontal torrent of sleet froze on our faces during the nightmarish experience (for the commentators) of the 3rd Lions Test in Dunedin in 1983; and trying desperately to make some sensible observations when thick fog descended on Bristol during the county semi-final between Gloucestershire and Surrey. And who was it that contrived to say: 'It looks as though the Gloucestershire backs are going forwards, so the chances are that the Surrey forwards are going back. In fact it looks as though both teams are going backwards and forwards'?

More pertinently, though, there is the obvious difficulty of interpreting the referee's decision instantly and at a distance and with the myriad complexities of the law to consider. You will find Rugby commentators are sympathetic to the problems of the man in the middle.

Finally, I would return to the unanswerable question that confronts the man behind the microphone – 'Who is his audience?' Is he to pitch his commentary at the Rugby expert, coach or player, or at the casual viewer who just happened to switch on the television and may be watching the sport for the first time? Or is there a majority of listeners who come somewhere between those two extremes? I hope so, for somewhere in that middle area the description of play will, if not delight, at least satisfy requirements. But in no way can you please everybody.

But if the Rugby commentator craves indulgence, do not feel sorry for him. For his is the enjoyment of being there, of witnessing first-hand the thrills of the cup tie in Southend or the Test match at Eden Park and all the excitement and fun that Rugby uniquely supplies both on and off the field. It is almost as good as playing!

Flying Scots Triumph Over Sassenachs

John Rutherford describes his most memorable match

John Young Rutherford is recognized by the majority of Scotsmen as being the greatest fly-half ever to have played for his country, and the editor of this book considers it a personal privilege to have seen this great, and modest, man in action. Older generations may make claims on behalf of Herbert Waddell and Wilson Shaw, who were undoubtedly marvellous players. But John Rutherford is a fly-half in the modern context; he is the complete footballer – a fine handler of the ball, excellent passer and kicker, superb tackler and masterly tactician, with speedy reactions to openings.

John has played for Scotland at a time when the

John Rutherford (Selkirk), Scotland's best-ever fly-half and most capped player in that position with thirty seven appearances.

country's fortunes have on the whole been good, and he has many happy memories of matches in a dark-blue jersey. Let him tell his own story:

'In my career at International level, there have been three matches that stand out. First, there was that marvellous win at Cardiff in 1982, when we scored five tries and thirty four points against Wales in a fine open game on a spring afternoon. I am tempted to nominate that one as my most memorable match. The next great occasion was that Grand Slam match against France, but I did not really enjoy that one very much; there was too much tension because there was far too much at stake. I did, however, enjoy the celebrations afterwards; that was great fun!

But the most memorable occasion for me was the match this year at Murrayfield against England, which we won by thirty three points to six; in the process we broke a number of records and also played a really good game.

In a way, the media were responsible for our performance that afternoon, since we were constantly being told that England were favourites, not only to thrash us, but also to take the Triple Crown, even the Grand Slam. The argument was that they had beaten Wales at Twickenham with a very good performance by their forwards, and Wales had beaten us. We felt we were unlucky that afternoon in Cardiff, so the press forecasts angered us and we were determined to show them up.

So we were, for a variety of reasons, more fired-up than usual for this match. We lined up like this:

Scotland: A. G. Hastings *(Cambridge University, London Scottish)*; M. D. F. Duncan *(West of Scotland)*, S. Hastings *(Watsonians)*, D. I. Johnston *(Watsonians)*, G. R. T. Baird *(Kelso)*; J. Y. Rutherford *(Selkirk)*, R. J. Laidlaw *(Jed-Forest)*; A. K. Brewster *(Stewart's-Melville FP)*, C. T. Deans *(Hawick) (captain)*, I. G. Milne *(Harlequins)*, J. Jeffrey *(Kelso)*, I. A. M. Paxton *(Selkirk)*, A. J. Campbell *(Hawick)*, F. Calder *(Stewart's-Melville FP)*, J. R. Beattie *(Glasgow Academicals)*

England: G. H. Davies *(Wasps)*; S. T. Smith *(Wasps)*, J. L. B. Salmon *(Harlequins)*, S. J. Halliday *(Bath)*, M. Harrison *(Wakefield)*; C. R. Andrew *(Nottingham)*, N. D. Melville *(Wasps) (captain)*; P. A. G. Rendall *(Wasps)*, S. E. Brain *(Coventry)*, P. J. Winterbottom *(Headingley)*, W. A. Dooley *(Preston Grasshoppers)*, M. J. Colclough *(Swansea)*, J. P. Hall *(Bath)*, G. L. Robbins *(Coventry)*. *Replacements:* N. C. Redman *(Bath)* for Hall, in the second half; S. Barnes *(Bath)* for Davies, 4 minutes from time

Referee: B. C. Francis *(New Zealand)*

Before the match, we took very seriously the stories about the England pack and we were quite concerned about the dangers that were lurking there. Our own scrummaging would be a problem since we would be outweighed by almost a stone a man. We also had a problem with the line-out, where Dooley and Colclough had done so well against Wales. In the scrums, however, we held our own at the very first, which was our own put-in near the England '22', and from then onwards we continued to do so. We had expected to be pushed back through a lack of weight and we had gone for speed in the pack to compensate; in fact, five of the pack were really back-row men, but the policy paid off.

The line-outs were the other problem, and we decided beforehand to counter this by calling as many four-man line-outs as possible; that also worked well. So, after some early fisticuffs, which soon died down when eveyone on both sides decided to play Rugby, we began to look good and by half-time we had a lead (12-6). This might have been a different story had Rob Andrew kicked a few more goals, but he didn't and Gavin Hastings

did! Also, we could point to two near-misses for tries by Matt Duncan and Roger Baird, who was stopped by a tackle that brought a penalty, and another success for Gavin Hastings. In a good half for us, Paxton and Beattie had done well in the line-outs, better than expected, and we had held on well in the scrums.

So we started the second half with an uneasy lead, and it made me anxious when we spent nearly twenty minutes of pressure without having anything to show for it. England only broke out once, but Harrison's run was halted by a fine tackle by Finlay Calder. Then I tried a break, but was tackled; from the ruck, Roy Laidlaw passed to Gavin Hastings who drew the cover and sent in Matt Duncan for a try in the corner. When Gavin also converted from touch I felt much better and began to think that it would be enough; England were not likely to recover from that, especially at Murrayfield. Then Gavin Hastings went on to add another penalty-

Roy Laidlaw (Scotland) sets up another attack as he breaks away from Nigel Melville with almost his whole team in support.

goal and we could afford to relax. Our fast forwards had shaken English confidence.

England obviously thought that they had lost, and a very loose pass from Colclough was snapped up by our back-row. I joined in support, received a pass and had men outside me, but I saw an opening, really a kind of tunnel, and knew I could score, which I did. Gavin Hastings again converted. There were only a few minutes left and I would have settled for that. I would, in fact, have settled for 21-6, but we hadn't finished.

Colclough again made a mistake and Roger Baird snapped up the ball as he had done at Cardiff four years ago; he made another run like the one in Wales, and when he was checked he had plenty of forward support. John Beattie kept the move going and the ball reached me with Scott Hastings close by; I passed to him and it seemed as if we had a whole team overlapping. Scott went over for our

John Rutherford beats the despairing tackle of Graham Robbins to score Scotland's second try. Rob Andrew looks resigned.

best try and his brother, Gavin, kicked his eighth goal of the game for a final score of 33-6. Speed and athleticism had beaten strength.

It was a match where, happily for us, everything we planned came off and where our worst fears before the game came to nothing. It was my most memorable match.'

John Rutherford is Scotland's most capped fly-half with thirty seven appearances; he also played once for the British Lions against New Zealand in 1983. With Roy Laidlaw, he has established a world record for a pairing at half-back in Internationals (thirty). He has never been dropped by Scotland, and the two half-backs have been key men in Scotland's two best seasons since the Second World War – the Grand Slam year of 1984 and the season just ended.

For those of us who remember the bad days of the early 1950s it is nice to become accustomed to regular victories, and we can only hope that John Rutherford and Roy Laidlaw keep healthy until the World Cup, their big target.

1985-86, Experimentation and Learning

by Tricia Moore, Press Officer, the Women's Rugby Football Union

No sport will ever succeed until it has established secure roots, so perhaps the Women's Rugby Football Union's greatest achievement last season was successfully to encourage the growth of their game. In 1983, when the WRFU was formed, there were only twelve member teams, whereas at the end of the 1985-86 season there were at least forty sides regularly playing fixtures. Significant in this growth has been a shift towards the formation of club sides. In 1983 all but one side were based at universities and colleges while students now make up only fifty per cent of the teams. Clubs lend a stability to the game that the three-yearly turnover of players at universities cannot match, so the trend is an important factor in securing a future for women's Rugby. Among these new club sides, two stand out as marking the beginning of what will hopefully become another trend; Wasps and Pontypool were the first women's teams to be based at first-class men's clubs.

The WRFU can be justly proud of its achievements; women's Rugby is now guaranteed stability, depth and a secure future. The grass roots level of the sport is very healthy. But what about the other end of the scale; has enough attention been paid to encouraging the game at a higher competitive level? Initial indications would suggest not.

In December 1985, a touring side from the United States came to Britain and totally outclassed all the opposition it encountered. Wivern WRFC, a US national side in everything other than name, were a team of athletes (boasting an Olympic standard hurdler and a champion weight-lifter) and they easily defeated Britain's first regional sides, beating the North (44-0), the Midlands (44-0) and the South (20-0). The Americans performed a great PR exercise on behalf of women's Rugby, displaying impressive ball-handling and running skills, but they left the British feeling a little demoralized by the ease of their victories.

It did not augur well for Britain's first full International, against France on 19th April at Richmond Athletic Ground. Predictions were pessimistic but, to the credit of both the players and the coaches, these misgivings proved unfounded. The French did eventually win (14-8) but Great Britain fiercely contested the match (going 8-4 up at half-time after Wasps fly-half Karen Almond scored two

Tricia Moore (Finchley WRFC and Great Britain), Press Officer for the Women's RFU, plays a strong game in the pack.

impressive tries) and gave a good account of themselves. The game proved conclusively that Britain can compete in the international arena.

However, the significance of this match was not confined to the field; the International probably brought more recognition to the game than any other single event. The Rugby press attended in numbers and publicly acknowledged the feasibility of the women's game. The ensuing reports were almost unanimously encouraging and positive, describing the game purely in Rugby terms. After years of appearing on women's and feature pages, this major transition onto the sports pages marked a real step forward for women's Rugby.

Last season's forays into International Rugby exposed one fundamental weakness in the British game – the lack of a regular, consistently high standard of competition. The regional teams were in no way ready for the US onslaught, and the Great Britain team had to play their first International with little more preparation than the regular round of friendly club games, and some hard squad training sessions. Unlike the home side, both the United States and France have national championships and regular regional fixtures; the more talented players in both countries are challenged and stretched by first-class competitive games. It is feasible that the British lost against France because they found it hard to sustain the fast, high standard of Rugby necessary to defeat a French side whose members play representative, regional and national Rugby on a regular basis.

Currently, the only competitive edge in women's Rugby is provided by one-day tournaments. These tournaments have become a tradition of women's Rugby in this country as early administrative problems meant they were in effect the only form of national competition. Last season the Rugby Travel/WRFU tournament in November was the largest such tournament held in Britain, with 500 players in attendance. As with other such tournaments, the day was a great social occasion as well as an exciting festival of exhibition Rugby. Women participating in their first tournament rubbed shoulders with well-established, experienced players. The day drew to an unsatisfactory conclusion with Wasps squeezing past Finchley on penalty-goals after a drawn final. The Loughborough tournament, the oldest tournament in women's Rugby, was held in March and was a similar sort of occasion with most of the same teams present. Finchley once more lost in the final, with the host side winning 4-0.

However, at a time when emphasis should have been shifting away from short-game tournaments, a proliferation of new tournaments emerged. This form of competition is not intrinsically harmful to the game, but it is potentially damaging if played at the expense of full-length games. Tournament Rugby requires totally different game plans, and develops players in a way that is not always compatible with the full-length game. Indeed, games of seven-minute halves tend to undermine the skills and stamina needed in full games (which are currently thirty minutes each way). With some teams playing four consecutive tournaments, the shortened version of the game jeopardized the development of proper Rugby for a substantial part of a season that had always been severely interrupted by the weather.

The solution probably lies not in reducing the number of tournaments held, but in encouraging teams to attend a maximum of two per season. By placing a regional bias on each tournament, more teams would be given the opportunity to compete, and the same twelve sides would not attend most tournaments as they do now. This would simultaneously eliminate the current problem of trying to establish which tournament produces the 'British Champion'.

Full-length games were always played as 'friendlies' until last season when the Rugby Travel Merit Table was introduced to lend some purpose to these fixtures. This was partially successful and gave credence to sides, like the winners Finchley, who prefer to play full-length games than compete in tournaments. However, the Merit Table is not the full answer. Problems peculiar to women's Rugby led the WRFU to establish laws that were at once flexible enough to allow all sides to take part, and open to abuse. There was nothing to stop

teams playing members of other clubs, cancelling fixtures or refusing to play superior sides for fear of defeat. The vast majority of teams played by the spirit of the competition but no national championship with these types of loophole will maintain credibility forever.

Tournaments were ineffective, the Merit Table was not the complete solution, and it became evident towards the end of last season that competition in women's Rugby needed complete reorganization. To the credit of the WRFU they are attempting to do just that this season, by introducing a full-length game National Championship. There will be four regional leagues, played on preordained Sundays, to produce a winner and a runner-up to compete in the national play-offs. Organization at the early stages will be devolved to newly elected regional bodies, who will have responsibility for appointing selectors to choose a regional team to play regular fixtures (along the lines of last year's men's div-isional championship). Rules, which will prevent players from representing more than one club and will penalize clubs that cancel fixtures with an immediate forfeit of points, have been negotiated.

The 1985-86 season has surely laid the groundwork for the continued growth of women's Rugby, both in terms of participation and standard of performance. As Carol Isherwood, Secretary of the WRFU, commented, 'We have achieved so much in the past two years, it is sometimes hard to believe that the WRFU has been in existence for such a short time. At our first meeting in December 1983 we could not have predicted quadrupling our membership or playing an International. It was hard work, but I think we have now established the right balance between encouraging new women to play and helping experienced players to improve.' Women's Rugby has forged ahead in the last two seasons and with the new National Championships the French had better watch out next year!

Debbie McLaren, Great Britain's only Scottish player, tries to avoid three French tacklers (April 1986). The other British player is Karen Almond (Wasps).

Left *The Great Britain Ladies team against France on 19th April 1986 at Richmond.*

The International Board Centenary: a Great Congress

By now, most people know that this year the International Rugby Board celebrated its centenary. During the week beginning Monday, 14th April 1986, there was a congress of fifty six Rugby-playing countries, which was held at Heythrop Park in Oxfordshire. As people also probably know, there are actually only eight members of the IB – the Five Nations, Australia, New Zealand and South Africa.

The IB was in fact founded in Ireland in 1886 by Ireland, Scotland and Wales, each with three votes. England remained aloof, but joined in 1890, taking six votes to two each for the other three. This imbalance was partly redressed in 1911, when England's powers were reduced to four votes; and there was no further change until 1948, when England's share of the voting was further reduced to two with Australia, New Zealand and South Africa joining the Board with their own power of a single vote each, which was increased to parity with the others in 1958. Twenty years later (as recently as 1978) France joined the élite with the same voting powers. That is the brief history of the Board.

This year the situation remained unaltered after the meeting of the fifty four nations, who were all offered Associate Membership. This should satisfy them for the moment, but countries such as the United States will not be happy with this situation for long. One can appreciate their dislike of a state of affairs in which they do not have any real say in the administration of a major sport. However, for

the moment it would seem to be for the best, since it would be difficult to discriminate against all the other nations by admitting just one new member to the Board, particularly as that member's playing capabilities are not as good as two other non-members (only associates) in Romania and Argentina, who are now recognized as full International countries. FIFA is a good example of a body where the smaller nations have an influence far above their abilities and organization. However, it is highly desirable that some form of associate membership should be encouraged and it may also be a good idea, if it has not already been adopted unknown to us, for the same associate members to have, say, two votes as a block in the future.

Meanwhile, the meeting had numerous good effects. Many countries became in effect new friends, with International matches being organized between likely and highly unlikely potential opponents. This is something that should be encouraged, since, whilst we for the moment would like to maintain the status quo, we would like to see a general improvement in international standards so that all countries can eventually play all other countries on merit and eventually, also on merit, earn IB votes, with full membership.

A thoroughly happy week ended in a somewhat embarrassing situation for two full members when it became clear that unknown to two delegations – those of New Zealand and South Africa – an unauthorized team from the former was about to start a tour of the latter without formal permission. A separate IB members' meeting demanded that the tour should be called off forthwith, but no-one believed that any halt would actually be called.

This left both Dr Danie Craven of South Africa and Ces Blazey of New Zealand in a dilemma and only time would tell how greatly this would affect not only the domestic scenes in the two countries involved, but also world Rugby as a whole. Would some thirty one New Zealanders at the top level be suspended from all Rugby in New Zealand? If they were to be suspended, for how long would the ban prevail? We feel that any drastic action could ruin amateur Rugby as we know it and possibly put an end to plans for a World Cup.

That same separate IB meeting of the members also decided a few important administrative and legal points. Of the latter, the controversial maul law was modified so that referees must no longer

whistle when a player goes to ground; now if the ball is available play can continue.

Other points included a limitation of all tours to thirteen matches; Australia tour England and Scotland in 1988 and New Zealand go to Wales and Ireland in 1989. Also, payment for books, newspaper, television and radio work was authorized for ex-players, provided that they have made a statutory declaration that they have stopped playing. The same applies to coaches and referees, but people already disciplined for former 'offences'

International Board 1986

Rugby Football Union
A. E. Agar, J. MacG. K. Kendall-Carpenter

Scottish Rugby Union
W. L. Connon, G. K. Smith

Irish Rugby Football Union
H. R. McKibbin, CBE, A. R. Dawson

Welsh Rugby Union
G. J. Treharne, K. A. Rowlands

Australian Rugby Football Union
Dr I. R. Vanderfield, OBE, R. V. Turnbull

New Zealand Rugby Football Union
C. A. Blazey, OBE, ED (*Chairman*), R. C. Stuart, OBE

South African Rugby Board
Dr D. H. Craven, Prof. F. C. Eloff

French Rugby Federation
A. Ferrasse, A. Martin

Honorary Secretary of Board
J. G. M. Hart

Centenary Congress Organizing Committee
A. E. Agar (*Chairman*), G. Burrell, A. R. Dawson,
J. G. M. Hart, U. G. Godfrey, G. Treharne,
R. H. G. Weighill, R. Williams

---

will not have their penalties rescinded and this leaves such admirable people as Fran Cotton, Bill Beaumont, Mike Davis and Gareth Edwards still out in the cold.

Air Commodore R. H. G. Weighill will be the new Honorary Secretary to the IB, in succession to John Hart, with temporary offices at Whitton Road, Twickenham. One of his early tasks will involve an IB meeting in October 1986 to discuss amateurism. To some that might seem like an unimportant meeting, but by then there could be a desperate struggle to ensure the survival of the sport. We do hope that it will not be as bad as that and we certainly wish the new Secretary well. These same sentiments go out to the whole Board.

Five Nations v. Overseas Unions, 19th April 1986: Trevor Ringland (Five Nations) avoids this tackle by Naas Botha (Overseas Unions) to score his side's second try and improve the score line.

'The Man with the Whistle'

by Clive Norling

In the early days of Rugby, the two opposing captains were responsible for ruling on any infringements of the few laws that were in existence at that time. The growth of the game led to two umpires with flags controlling the game (the forerunners of the modern touch judges) and eventually to the appointment of a single referee to take charge of the thirty players. I doubt very much if the referee of the early 1900s envisaged the pressures and demands that are now placed on the 1980s 'man with the whistle'. The game has become faster, the laws more complex; the media coverage of the game via TV, radio and the press has become more intense; and the attitudes of the players, coaches and spectators have changed.

So with all these increased pressures how do you produce a Rugby referee who will remain cool, calm and collected on the International field, when everyone around him is in an emotional state? Perhaps a detailed explanation of my career might offer an insight into the life of an International referee.

Due to a back injury in 1967, I turned my attention to refereeing; perhaps I was lucky being Welsh because in Wales there is a clear-cut process that enables the ordinary player or spectator to pick up the whistle and become an efficient referee. In June each year, the Welsh Rugby Union holds its referees' course in Cardiff at the National Sports Centre. The week before the course, the aspiring referees must attend regional law courses throughout Wales. At these meetings, the Senior or International referees, who later lecture in Cardiff, explain the meaning and interpretations of the laws. Then at the weekend, all the new referees gather in Cardiff for the practical course which is run under the guidance of Malcolm Lewis, WRU Assistant Coaching Organizer, and Sam Williams, the Senior Referees Advisor. Also in attendance are the Welsh International referees to talk on, and demonstrate, the art of refereeing. All aspects of the referee's job are covered, from the type of kit required, controlling the game, and even first aid, to how to write a disciplinary report. At the end of the course all the aspiring referees are encouraged to join their local team to get fit for the start of the season in September, and they will then be expected to sit the WRU referees' examination in December. The examination is in two parts: a written paper (1½ hours) and, if successful, an oral examination with a senior advisor. If they pass both parts of the examination, they are appointed as a qualified WRU referee.

I qualified in December 1968, and then joined the Hampshire Referees Society for five years whilst I was in college in Portsmouth. I returned to Wales in 1974, and as a qualified WRU referee applied to be placed on the WRU Referees List. I was accepted and placed in Grade 2. There are different grades of referee from probationer up to International referee. When controlling a game in Wales, the referee is assessed by the two teams involved, who mark a card out of 100. Depending upon his marks, a referee will either be promoted or demoted at the end of each season. The competent referee will make his way up the ladder through club games, until he reaches the top as an exchange referee. This means that he is now capable of handling games in other countries, and, when he referees in those countries, they will send reports back to Wales on how he performed. I reached exchange grade in 1976 and refereed in Scotland, Gala v. Jordanhill, and also in Ireland, Blackrock College v. CIYMS. Hopefully, good reports will mean the referee is eventually placed on the International Panel, the pinnacle of any referee's career. I was very fortunate in being made an International referee in 1977. Every season, each country nominates three officials as International referees, and with the acceptance of independent referees for Internationals in all countries, the referee has a chance to see the world.

When I became an International referee I found the pressures started to grow. I felt that I should be fitter and have a better knowledge of the laws than the average referee. I started my fitness training with my club, Neath Athletic, in June and, linked with rounds of golf, squash and cricket, aimed to be superfit at the start of the season. Nowadays with International matches in February and March, and cup finals in April, I try not to peak too early in the season. Pre-season in August is taken up with club trials, seven-a-side tournaments at Cwmtawe, Aberaeron and Newport, and a programme of general fitness training.

My first meeting with my fellow referees from

England v. Ireland at Twickenham, 1st March 1986: Top referee, Clive Norling, signals a penalty.

and spectators. Currently, the International Board appears to change laws without having seen the intended changes being put into practice. I feel that at these IB meetings players, coaches and referees should join the administrators for one week so that intended changes could be experimented with by players in trial games, and the coaches and referees could constructively comment on the laws. Hopefully this will happen in future years for the betterment of the game.

This annual meeting in London is only one of very many referees' meetings and conferences that I attend during the season. As an International referee there is a great demand for you to appear at these meetings to give your views and the benefit of your experiences to other referees. During the season it is not unusual for me to attend at least one referees' meeting per week. Also, invitations come from Rugby clubs to speak at dinners, sports forums and presentation evenings, and further invitations from other bodies such as Rotary, Round Table and OAP's mean that the referee's calendar can become pretty full even without games to referee!

The pressure really begins to build up after Christmas with the start of the Five Nations Championship. There is a referees' rota for all International games, with different countries responsible for appointing their referees to a particular game. Last season, the Welsh Rugby Union had to appoint a referee for the England v. Ireland game and also the France v. England match. Nowadays an International is just like any other game for me to referee. About six years ago, the IB brought in the ruling that the referee and the two touch judges should be from the same country, and so when I go to referee a Five Nations game I take my fellow Welsh Panel referees with me to act as touch judges. The evening before an International is spent either at the theatre or having a meal together. On the day of the game I never eat lunch but I make sure that I eat a good breakfast. In other countries, you are looked after by the local referees' society, who normally transport you to and from the game.

Once at the ground, a quick pitch inspection is followed by a joke session in the referees' changing-room. I have been very fortunate in having some great characters as fellow Welsh officials, and the atmosphere is always lighthearted before the game. We have a quick talk about how we will work together as referee and touch judges, and how we will communicate on the field. Now that touch judges can assist the referee at International level by signalling for acts of foul play, it is important that the referee and touch judges are on the same

other countries came in December 1977, when we met at the East India Club, London. This is now a regular annual meeting to discuss interpretations of law. Interpretation is a major problem in the refereeing world because Welsh referees do not always see eye to eye with English or Irish referees let alone Australian or New Zealand referees. This is why I firmly believe that there is a need to simplify the laws so that not only referees understand them, but, more importantly, the players wavelength. The touch judge has the power to send a player off the field for an act of foul play he sees but the referee misses, so it is vitally important that there is consistent interpretation amongst the match officials.

I apply the same laws to International players as I do to club players. It is important for all referees to set standards early in the game so that the players know exactly what is expected of them in that particular match. The quicker the referee and the players understand each other, the better the game tends to turn out. In an International game the pace is faster than any other game the referee is likely to handle, and he must learn to react and make his decisions more quickly otherwise he is left behind by the players. The eighty minutes soon pass and the referee is blowing the final whistle before he realizes what has happened!

After the game, it is back to the hotel for drinks and the banquet with the players. The pressmen are eager to talk about any controversial incidents, and the referee must be on his guard as to what he tells the press. 'Rugby Special' will be showing highlights of the game, and any mistakes by the referee will soon be spotted by millions of viewers. The media is just an added pressure, one which the modern referee has to learn to live with. He will be criticized, but he will also be praised and as a referee you must learn to accept both with a smile.

It is nowadays unusual for an International referee to control more than one International per season, so you must hope and pray that you have your best game of the season in that International, and not your worst. When a player has an off day he has fourteen team-mates to help him through the game; when the referee has an off day there is no-one to help him, and referees are often judged on one game.

Once the International is over, it is back to the bread and butter of club matches, youth and school games in the mud and the rain; and on cold days it is often difficult to find a touch judge! Not all the games I referee are Internationals, far from it; the vast majority of matches are ordinary, everyday fixtures, but the players will still be expecting an International performance from the referee. And inevitably at the end of the game, someone is bound to say, 'Call yourself a referee, Norling, you don't even know the meaning of the word!'

Referee Clive Norling observes some 'play' as does Ciaran Fitzgerald (Irish captain) on the left. The whistle soon went.

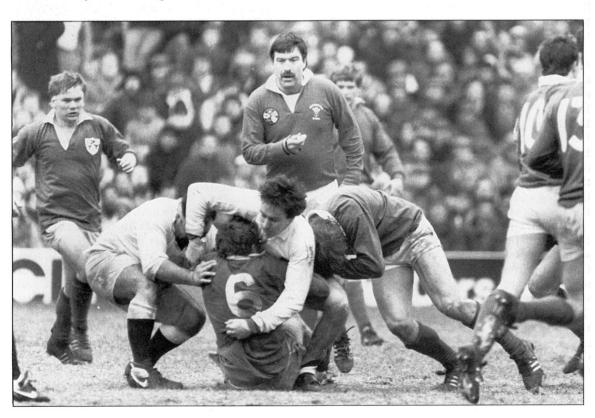

England's Full House

Steve Smith describes his most memorable match

Steve Smith was England's scrum-half on twenty eight occasions. He won his first cap in 1973 against Ireland in Dublin and he made his last appearance in 1983 in the Calcutta Cup match at Twickenham. He was also twice called up by the British Lions to replace injured tourists – in South Africa in 1980 and New Zealand in 1983 – but he was not selected for any Tests.

His International career has been a tale of appearances followed by spells out of favour, which he has cheerfully accepted, no doubt hoping that his big day would one day come – and eventually it did! That day was in March 1980.

'To be an England player in the 1970s was a frustrating experience, because the team went through a very hard time. There were some great Welsh teams around at that time and when they were not winning Grand Slams and Triple Crowns the French were on top, so it was left to England to dispute the 'Second Division title' with Ireland and Scotland and occasionally we did not even win that! We did have many good players, but somehow they never managed to be a really good team.

When the 1979-80 season started there was at least a different situation, because we had been on a tour of South Africa for the North-West and that experience had been a very tough one for us. From that tour a good Lancashire side was built up and Lancashire players formed a large part of the team from the North of England, which beat the All-Blacks at Otley in November 1979. The All-Blacks did beat England narrowly at Twickenham, but the basis for a strong England team was there with the Leicester lads to provide strength to add to those players from Lancashire and the North.

Also, many good players, who had failed so far to win any titles, were still there and playing well, so all that was needed was a good start to the Championship. We started well by beating Ireland at Twickenham (21-9) and followed this with a victory over France in Paris (17-13). Wales came to Twickenham and lost an astonishing match (9-8) thanks to the boot of 'Dusty' Hare, so Murrayfield and Scotland stood in the way of the Triple Crown, Grand Slam and Championship. This was probably the last chance for most of us to achieve all that.

We did have a good team and it is nonsense to say that we were merely a side that relied on a

Steve Smith (Sale and England), the extrovert scrum-half of England's Grand Slam side of 1980.

strong scrummaging pack for our success. Some of those forwards were really good footballers, especially Fran Cotton, Peter Wheeler, Bill Beaumont (the captain) and John Scott, who was the most inexperienced player in the team. We also had great flankers in 'Nero' and Roger Uttley. Behind the scrum we had John Horton, a most underrated fly-half, whose excellent kicking was well appreciated by our forwards, who felt that he took a great deal of weight off their problems. Then there were two good centres in 'Dodgy' and Clive Woodward with wings in John Carleton and Mike Slemen, who were as good as any then playing. 'Dusty', apart from being a safe kicker and prolific points

John Carleton (Orrell and England) runs in unopposed for his third try against Scotland at Murrayfield on 15th March 1980 – Grand Slam for England!

Right *Steve Smith's try for England! Rutherford's tackle is evaded as 'Dusty' Hare, England full-back, runs up in support.*

scorer, was a fine attacking full-back. So we had it all there and for once it seemed that the selectors had got it right.

For that Calcutta Cup match we were well prepared and our stay at the Peebles Hydro in that beautiful countryside did us a lot of good before the big day. The night before, we told ourselves that this was it! We were in the best possible shape to take on Scotland. Also, we were pleased to see a French referee appointed, as this would mean an open game. For the record, the teams lined up like this:

Scotland: A. R. Irvine *(Heriot's FP) (captain)*; K. W. Robertson *(Melrose)*, J. M. Renwick *(Hawick)*, D. I. Johnston *(Watsonians)*, B. W. Hay *(Boroughmuir)*; J. Y. Rutherford *(Selkirk)*, R. J. Laidlaw *(Jed-Forest)*; J. N. Burnett *(Heriot's FP)*, K. G. Lawrie *(Gala)*, N. A. Rowan *(Boroughmuir)*, M. A. Biggar *(London Scottish)*, A. J. Tomes *(Hawick)*, D. Gray *(West of Scotland)*, D. G. Leslie *(West of Scotland)*, J. R. Beattie *(Glasgow Academicals)*. *Replacement:* J. S. Gossman *(West of Scotland)* for Hay during second half

England: W. H. Hare *(Leicester)*; J. Carleton *(Orrell)*, C. R. Woodward *(Leicester)*, P. W. Dodge *(Leicester)*, M. A. C. Slemen *(Liverpool)*; J. P. Horton *(Bath)*, S. J. Smith *(Sale)*; F.

E. Cotton *(Coventry, Sale)*, P. J. Wheeler *(Leicester)*, P. J. Blakeway *(Gloucester)*, A. Neary *(Broughton Park)*, W. B Beaumont *(Fylde) (captain)*, M. J. Colclough *(Angoulême)*, R. M. Uttley *(Wasps)*, J. P. Scott *(Rosslyn Park, Cardiff)*
Referee: J.-P. Bonnet *(France)*

We had the benefit of a terrific start and, after a blank early period, we scored three marvellous tries. First, a splendid run by Clive Woodward completely bamboozled the Scottish defence and he put over John Carleton; then, after I had done some inter-passing with the forwards, we went to the blind side and Clive again ran well to send Mike Slemen for the second. That was followed by some intense forward pressure and with all their pack 'sucked in' we won possession. I saw Bruce Hay coming to tackle me, but I was able to take it and pass to John Carleton who had simply to dive over. 'Dusty' converted two of the tries and we led 16-0. By half-time, Andy Irvine and 'Dusty' had swapped penalties and we still had a sixteen-point lead.

For once we felt quite relaxed, which is not good

for an International, and we quickly increased our lead after half-time when I was able to combine with the forwards; we seemed to go open one moment, then blind, then open again, but it ended up with me scoring our fourth try! Scotland managed to reply with another Andy Irvine penalty and 'Dusty' had one more for us, before John Carleton went over for our last try when a sliced kick by 'Dodgy' bounced badly for Gossman, the replacement, and perfectly for John, who scored a hat trick as a result.

To make it a perfect match for everyone, Scotland fought back near the end and scored tries by Tomes and Rutherford, which were both converted by Andy Irvine; so, in the final minutes, when we were very tired, we were a bit desperate to hold on to our lead. But we won well and that was the Grand Slam and everything else won too. A great occasion!

That evening I celebrated with my father, mother and sister, who had all been at the match. My father had followed my career since I was twelve years old and it was nice to have them there on my big day. Later on there was a dance at the North British Hotel and several of us were able to have some more enjoyment!

It was a great win by a great side and we enjoyed giving our loyal English supporters, of whom there are very many after all, something to cheer about. We had a great reception.'

Steve Smith went on to lead England when Bill Beaumont was forced to retire in 1982 with a bad head injury. A narrow defeat at Twickenham against Ireland and a drawn match at Murrayfield, when Andy Irvine's last kick of the match from a long way out rescued the Scots, prevented another Grand Slam from a very useful side.

Steve was an underrated player, but those who played with him rated his work very highly indeed. He was 'Mr Reliable' personified and, in addition to his accurate passing, was a very shrewd kicker and sound defender. He deserved more caps than he won, although he would be the last person to complain about that.

Klynger, Tacklinger og Scoring: Rugby in Denmark

by Robin D. S. Allan, Lecturer in Danish, University College London

It may be surprising for many to learn that Denmark, a country which one nowadays has come primarily to associate with soccer, in fact possesses a thriving Rugby Union Association. Not only can this Association – Dansk Rugby Union – boast an impressive programme of national divisional matches at various levels, but it is also involved in several international fixtures each year.

The history of Rugby in Denmark goes back to 1931. In that year, James White, an English journalist, and a Dane called Noel Jørgensen, who had played some Rugby in England, formed København Rugby Klub (Copenhagen Rugby Club). Unfortunately, adverse press reaction appears to have been instrumental in causing the failure of this first Danish venture into the sport. In 1933 some Danish soldiers at Roskilde took up the game, yet this attempt also failed to produce any lasting result. However, one of these soldiers, Eigil Hemmert Lund, never lost his interest in Rugby, and in 1949, when he joined the Copenhagen Police Force, he managed to form a police team – Politiets Rugby Klub. James White, who had returned to Denmark, and Frederick Leismann from the British Embassy assisted this new venture, and a fixture with a team from Stockholm in Sweden was arranged. The Swedes had been playing Rugby since 1933, and it was perhaps no surprise that they won the match, but only by the margin 8-0. A second club was also formed in this year consisting of young Danish soldiers who had served with the British Army during the war. In 1950 a third club, and the first civilian club, was founded with the name Speed, and Dansk Rugby Union came into being, with Eigil Hemmert Lund as its first president. With this, the future of Rugby in Denmark was now assured.

Another match against Sweden was arranged, this time the first 'official International', which Sweden won 14-0. The following year, Sweden again defeated the Danes, this time 30-3. Even though in these early years of Danish Rugby there were not many Danish teams, quite a number of international fixtures took place. In 1953, for example, teams from West Germany (Victoria Hannover), England (Workington RFC) and Spain (Barcelona Union Club) visited Denmark. Also in this year, the first national Cup Competition took place, with Speed as the winners.

The number of Danish clubs gradually began to grow, as indeed did the competence of the players, and in 1963 Denmark recorded its first win over Sweden, beating them 6-0. In 1971, Dansk Rugby Union achieved official recognition in Danish sporting circles and was incorporated as a member of Dansk Idræts Forbund, the Danish Sports Federation. Today, Rugby is played in Denmark by some 2,000 people, a not inconsiderable number given the size of the nation's population. At senior level there is a First Division consisting of six teams from around the country, together with an 'additional' team called Exiles (ex-patriot Britons who play in Denmark but not actually as part of the league tournament), and a Second Division, which is divided into an Eastern and a Western Sector, each of which has four teams. At intermediate and junior levels, there are also similar divisional structures. Indeed, the junior level of the game is an area to which Dansk Rugby Union is devoting a lot of energy, since this is naturally where the future of the sport in Denmark lies.

The present Danish First Division Champions are Lynet, and they have held this position now for six years in a row. So far this season they have been performing well, and would appear to have a good chance of taking the Championship for a seventh year. Not only have Lynet been dominant in the First Division Championship in recent years, but they have also produced good performances in the Cup Competition: they have been finalists in 1982, 1983, 1984 and 1985. In 1982 they defeated CSR/Nanok, who then took their revenge by defeating them in 1983; in 1984 Lynet regained the trophy by beating Exiles and finally in 1985 they retained it by scoring yet another victory over CSR.

Lynet took part in the Thames International Rugby Tournament of 1985, where they produced a most creditable performance. Their 'host club' was Dartfordians RUFC, against whom they played their first match, losing 9-0. In their second match, against Llanidloes RC, they notched up their first victory of the tournament, defeating the Welsh

Above *Bernard White, coach and manager of the Danish national team.* Right *Danish schoolboys show courage and enthusiasm; attention to youth is the reason why the Danes look forward to the future with confidence.*

side 16-10. After the introductory rounds, Lynet took part in the Plate Cup Competition. In their first match, they drew 4-4 with Gannets, and then went on to defeat Benfica from Portugal 12-6. In the semi-final against Lausanne, Switzerland, they won 4-0, and they then went on to meet Gravesend in the final. By all accounts, this must have been an exciting match to watch, for, after some five minutes, the Danish 'underdogs' had managed to gain a lead of 17-0. They successfully managed to stave off the attacks which Gravesend then mounted, and 17-0 remained the scoreline at the final whistle; Lynet thereby won the Plate Cup for 1985. In the whole tournament, their overall position was 5th, and Lynet had reason to feel very satisfied indeed with their performance.

Internationally, Denmark has remained as active in Rugby terms as it was at the time of the game's introduction. In the last three seasons it has played in seven 'friendlies' against the national squads from West Germany, Holland, Belgium, Sweden and Norway. Unfortunately, the only country they managed to defeat in this period was their Scandinavian neighbours Norway (28-12). The present coach/manager of the Danish international side is in fact an Englishman, Bernard White, who is a lecturer in Physical Education at Leeds Polytechnic,

and who visits Denmark regularly to train and lead the team. In a recent article in Dansk Rugby Union's quarterly magazine *Rugby nyt*, White reveals his pleasure at his involvement with the Danish team, which has now spanned more than ten years, and expresses his optimism over the future of Danish Rugby, both nationally and internationally. Regrettably, Denmark recently withdrew its participation from the FIRA tournament for financial reasons, but its international involvement in Rugby is still as strong as ever, and in May 1986 it has fixtures against the international squads of Belgium and Switzerland.

It is to be hoped that Rugby will continue to flourish in Denmark, both at club level and internationally. Given the right conditions for growth at home, and suitable encouragement from abroad, there is no real reason why Danish Rugby in future years might not be able to look forward to achieving those heights which Danish soccer has reached.

Much of the information for this contribution was kindly provided by John Frimann of Dansk Rugby Union. For further information about Rugby in Denmark, contact: Dansk Rugby Union, Idrættens Hus, Brøndby Stadion 20, 2605 Brøndby, Denmark. Tel: 02-45 55 55 ext. 338

Grand Slam at Colombes

J. P. R. Williams describes his most memorable match

J. P. R. Williams holds the record for the greatest number of caps won in International matches by a full-back with fifty four appearances for Wales and another eight for the British Lions. He also played once for Wales as a flanker. By general consent he was probably the greatest full-back of all time with his immaculate fielding of the ball, powerful running and lethal tackling.

With so many matches played at the top level of the sport he has numerous happy memories, since his career coincided with some of the greatest Welsh and British Lions teams that ever graced the game. It is interesting to note, therefore, that his best memory is of a match that took place when he was still a medical student at St Mary's Hospital, Paddington.

'The year was 1971. The opponents were France and it was to be the last International match at the famous Stade Colombes. Both sides were unbeaten and this was the match to decide the Grand Slam.

Two years previously in 1969 we had been in a

J. P. R. Williams – fifty five caps for Wales and eight British Lions appearances – possibly the world's greatest-ever full-back.

similar position but had only achieved a draw (8-8). We had then embarked on a full Welsh tour to New Zealand, Australia and Fiji, and in spite of being European Champions we were heavily defeated by an excellent All-Black team in both Test matches.

The 1971 British Lions tour of New Zealand and Australia was due to commence in the May following this Grand Slam match in Paris. Wales had won all their other matches fairly easily that season and therefore came to France as Triple Crown winners.

We were under tremendous pressure from the beginning of the match and I remember one particular attack where I had to pull off a last-ditch tackle against the right-wing Roger Bourgarel. I did not realize at the time how important this tackle was to turn out. Not only did it prevent him from scoring, but it paved the way for an interception later on in that first half. France were leading 5-0 when another attack by them looked certain to produce a score. Again Bourgarel was coming towards me and yet I could sense that he was not going to try to get around me on this occasion. Out of the corner of my eye I could see our flanker John Taylor covering, and in a split second I decided to do something that I very rarely did during my first-class Rugby career – I went for an interception. The interception came off and I suddenly found myself haring out of my own 25-yard-line with not a Frenchman in sight.

Being only twenty two years of age at the time it did not seem such a long way to the try-line! However, on reaching the opposing 25-yard-line, two of the French three-quarters were coming across field to cut me off. Out of the corner of my eye I saw Gareth Edwards supporting. I veered inside off my left foot at that moment, checking the two defending Frenchmen, and threw a pass to my left to Gareth who was storming up the left touch-line. Gareth scored in the corner, and, in spite of the missed conversion, I think that this was a great psychological lift for our side as we turned almost inevitable points for the French into three points for our team. The half-time whistle blew shortly after this and the difference in our morale at that point was quite incredible.

We turned around the second half convinced

that we had withstood all the pressure that France could throw at us and so it proved. Barry John had pulled off a rare tackle on the French no. 8, Dauga, sustaining a broken nose. However, Barry soon scored a delightful try and in spite of some nerve-racking moments we ran out worthy winners by 9 points to 5.

We all knew that there was great significance in this win. We had beaten an excellent French side and we had withstood tremendous pressure. I am convinced that this was the foundation of the success of the 1971 Lions Tour in New Zealand. We had a fantastic belief in ourselves after this match and the nucleus of the British Lions team selected for New Zealand were Welsh. Such names as Barry John, Gareth Edwards, Gerald Davies, John

J. P. R. in action for Wales in 1971. His interception created the Grand Slam winning try.

Dawes, John Bevan, Mervyn Davies and John Taylor were destined to go into the record books as great Welsh and British Lions players. Of course, there were many other great players from the other countries including Mike Gibson, Willie John McBride, Gordon Brown and Peter Dixon.

Interestingly, the first Test in New Zealand was a little similar to the Wales v. France game in Paris the previous March. New Zealand had us under intense pressure for most of the game. Our defence held out and eventually we scored a try by Ian McLaughlan from a charged-down clearance kick by one of the All-Black three-quarters.

I think that both these matches showed how solid defence can be turned into attack, and how out of intense pressure a vital score can develop. As captain of the Grand Slam team in 1971 John Dawes was the automatic choice for captain of the British Lions team to New Zealand. He was to prove an outstanding captain and much underrated centre-three-quarter.

There have been many memorable matches during my career but I believe that this match against France in Paris in 1971 laid the foundations of the continued success of Wales and the British Lions in 1970s.'

For the record the teams that famous day in Colombes lined up like this:

France: P. Villepreux *(Toulouse)*; R. Bourgarel *(Toulouse)*, R. Bertranne *(Bagnères)*, J.-P. Lux *(Tyrosse)*, J. Cantoni *(Béziers)*; J.-L. Berot *(Toulouse)*, M. Barrau *(Beaumont)*; J. Iraçabal *(Bayonne)*, R. Bénésis *(Narbonne)*, M. Lasserre *(Agen)*, B. Dauga *(Mont-de-Marsan)*, C. Spanghero *(Narbonne)*, W. Spanghero *(Narbonne)*, J.-P. Biemouret *(Agen)*, C. Carrère *(Toulon)* *(captain)*

Wales: J. P. R. Williams *(London Welsh)*; T. G. R. Davies *(London Welsh)*, S. J. Dawes *(London Welsh)* *(captain)*, A. J. Lewis *(Ebbw Vale)*, J. C. Bevan *(Cardiff)*; B. John *(Cardiff)*, G. O. Edwards *(Cardiff)*; D. B. Llewelyn *(Llanelli)*, J. Young *(Harrogate)*, D. Williams *(Ebbw Vale)*, W. D. Morris *(Neath)*, W. D. Thomas *(Llanelli)*, M. G. Roberts *(London Welsh)*, J. Taylor *(London Welsh)*, T. M. Davies *(London Welsh)*

Referee: J. Young *(Scotland)*

J. P. R.'s magnificent career was to last another ten seasons at the top level and he was, apart from the season he mentions here, a key man in the unbeaten Lions' tour of South Africa in 1974, whilst he played in two more Welsh Grand Slam teams (those of 1976 and 1978). He never gave less than one hundred per cent; opponents probably thought he did even more than that!

Having qualified as a doctor, he now practises sports medicine at his clinic in Bridgend, where he is giving even more to the game than he has already offered.

The World Cup, 1987

Once it was known that there would be a World Cup in Australia and New Zealand in May and June 1987, speculation was aroused as to who would be the selected finalists and who would be the ultimate winners. Later we will try to analyze each group and work out the likely final outcome.

First, however, we will briefly touch on the issues involved. For example, is a World Cup a 'good thing' for the game? To that question there can be no answer until after the competition has been completed, when we will be able to decide whether:

1 The event has advanced the arrival of professionalism in the game or not.

2 Such an event has brought an increase in sportsmanship or, conversely, an increase in violence with the stakes so high.

3 It has helped the cause of the weaker countries, thus spreading the playing of the game to more countries.

4 It can have played any part in improving International goodwill.

5 The British Isles has now become a 'second-rate' Rugby-playing area.

6 The best nation has actually won the event.

However, it is possible to forecast possible outcomes. In the case of Question No. 1, professionalism may well take over long before the tournament takes place, since the absence of South Africa who would have been certain semi-finalists at the very least, might mean by then that a professional circus is already established, with the result that not only would the best players in the world be absent for good, but also (Question 6) the best nation may not emerge as the 'World Champions'

Trophy Draw for the 1987 World Cup

First Round	Venue	Date	Second Round	Venue	Date
Pool 1			**Game A**		
England v. Australia	Sydney	23rd May	Winners of Pool 1	Sydney	7th June
Japan v. United States	Brisbane	24th May	v. runners-up of Pool 2		
England v. Japan	Sydney	30th May	AUSTRALIA		
Australia v. United States	Brisbane	31st May	IRELAND		
England v. United States	Sydney	3rd June			
Australia v. Japan	Sydney	3rd June			
Pool 2			**Game B**		
Canada v. Tonga	Napier	24th May	Winners of Pool 2	Brisbane	8th June
Ireland v. Wales	Wellington	25th May	v. runners-up of Pool 1		
Tonga v. Wales	Palmerston North	29th May	WALES		
Canada v. Ireland	Dunedin	30th May	ENGLAND		
Tonga v. Ireland	Brisbane	3rd June			
Wales v. Canada	Invercargill	3rd June			
Pool 3			**Game C**		
New Zealand v. Italy	Auckland	22nd May	Winners of Pool 3	Christchurch	6th June
Argentina v. Fiji	Hamilton	24th May	v. runners-up of Pool 4		
New Zealand v. Fiji	Christchurch	27th May	N. ZEALAND		
Argentina v. Italy	Christchurch	28th May	SCOTLAND		
Italy v. Fiji	Dunedin	31st May			
New Zealand v. Argentina	Wellington	1st June			
Pool 4			**Game D**		
France v. Scotland	Christchurch	23rd May	Winners of Pool 4	Auckland	7th June
Romania v. Zimbabwe	Auckland	23rd May	v. runners-up of Pool 3		
Romania v. France	Wellington	28th May	FRANCE		
Scotland v. Zimbabwe	Wellington	30th May	FIJI		
Scotland v. Romania	Dunedin	2nd June			
France v. Zimbabwe	Auckland	2nd June			

One could still see countries like Italy, Zimbabwe, Japan, Tonga, Fiji, Canada and the United States struggling to make any impression on the other, stronger, countries but their task would become a little easier and there might be a few surprises. If the stronger nations are able to turn out their best teams some heavy defeats may be suffered by the weaker seven countries and this may not prove beneficial to the future of the Game in those places, when one remembers that other sports have their adherents in those countries. That would seem to take care of Question 3.

This leaves three questions to answer and No. 5 is very much in the lap of the gods. If there is no professional circus in South Africa it should be possible for one of the home countries to do well, with England and Wales potentially the best equipped nations involved. If there is a circus, things could go drastically wrong for the British Isles teams, but Australia and New Zealand would also suffer badly.

Questions 2 and 4 are also difficult to answer, but the example of other international sporting events, such as the Olympic Games and soccer's World Cup, are not encouraging. Goodwill and decent behaviour are not always present at these major competitions and it could be reasonable to assume that the Rugby World Cup will follow the same pattern, given the high stakes involved and the intense competition. The World Cup is very much an unknown quantity in all respects and we can only hope that the concept of Rugby Football as an honest and sporting amateur game remains intact.

As a footnote, we should perhaps point out that all the forecasts could be thrown into total confusion if New Zealand players are disciplined for an unofficial tour of South Africa in 1986.

The table below shows the dates and venues for the matches in the 1987 World Cup in full detail. The reader can follow his/her team around the Antipodes and fill in the results.

Semi-finals	Venue	Date	Final	Venue	Date
Winners of Game A v. winners of Game D	Sydney	13th June	Match between the winners of the two semi-finals	Auckland	20th June
AUSTRALIA			AUTRALIA		
FRANCE			N.ZEALAND		
			World champions		
			N.ZEALAND		
Winners of Game C v. winners of Game B	Brisbane	14th June			
ENGLAND					
N. ZEALAND					

First Round Prospects and Forecast

Pool One

In theory, Australia and England are the strongest teams here and they meet in the first match on 23rd May 1987 in Brisbane. The winners will probably win the pool and go through to a Second Round match against the runners-up of Pool 2, which could mean a match against Ireland in Sydney. The runners-up of this pool would then expect to face Wales in Brisbane. With the very best will in the world one cannot forecast any surprises, although the United States might, with a physically powerful team, give either of the two favourites a good game. Japan's recent form seems to have deteriorated badly and they will need miracles merely to provide close matches. Our pool forecast is: 1. Australia; 2. England; 3. United States; 4. Japan.

Pool Two

Wales and Ireland meet in the pool's second match (but they will be making their own debuts) in Palmerston North; this game should decide the opposition to Australia and England in the Second Round and we forecast that Wales will have to fly across to Brisbane to face England, with Ireland, who will be in Brisbane by then, having to make a shortish trip to Sydney to face the Wallabies. Again, it seems most unlikely that either Canada or Tonga will upset this prediction, and their opening pool match should really decide who will finish third and fourth in the pool. Our forecast for this grouping is: 1. Wales; 2. Ireland; 3. Tonga; 4. Canada.

We plump for Wales to beat Ireland only because they have a better record overall in matches between the two countries. By next year the scene may well have changed. We think that Tonga may prove too strong for Canada, but again this forecast is not made with any conviction. The arrangement of venues means some tiring travelling in this pool.

Pool Three

Again, it should not be difficult to reach a correct forecast of the ultimate result of this pool unless other considerations, such as a circus, decimate New Zealand's power. If the All-Blacks are at full strength, playing at home, they should win the pool with Argentina second, although here at least Fiji might have something to say to the contrary. They make their debut in the pool's second match against the Pumas and that, for neutrals, might be a game well worth the admission fee since a Second Round place may depend on it. Up to now, Italy's International form has been moderate and it is improbable that they will travel well, a criticism that has not ever been directed towards the Pumas, who we believe will go through to the Second Round to meet the winners of Pool Four in Auckland. Could this be France? New Zealand, we confidently predict (barring accidental circumstances), will meet the Pool Four runners-up (and we hope they will be Scotland) in Christchurch. Our none too confident forecast of the Pool Three final placings is: 1. New Zealand; 2. Argentina; 3. Fiji; 4. Italy.

Pool Four

This is by far the most difficult pool to forecast with only Zimbabwe appearing to have no chance. In normal circumstances one would predict a pool win for France, whose teams have usually done well on tour and have won Tests in all the major countries of the southern hemisphere. Romania have no form guide in this direction, while Scotland have never won a Test in New Zealand, although they have done so in Australia and, a long time ago, in Argentina. For purely sentimental reasons we think that Scotland may qualify, but please do not castigate us with unseemly scorn if Romania in fact do so. Also, one cannot rule out the possibility that France will finish third in the pool, but that is a remote prospect. France play the Scots in the pool's first game and this might well prove decisive both in a playing and a psychological sense. So, our timorous pool forecast is: 1. France; 2. Scotland; 3. Romania; 4. Zimbabwe.

Second Round

If our forecasts have been correct – and we would have earned champagne dinners if they are – the round will read as follows:

Game A: Australia v. Ireland
Game B: Wales v. England
Game C: New Zealand v. Scotland
Game D: France v. Argentina

Australia should be favoured to win the first of these quarter-finals, but it may not be easy since they have yet to win a home Test against Ireland, having lost all three matches played against them at home. It could be tricky for them, but we nevertheless must stick our necks out – so we forecast an Australian advance.

Wales in recent seasons have done very well against England and should win. But it should be mentioned that the English team will have done less travelling than their opponents and might just be awkward enough to win. However, we still predict a Welsh win.

New Zealand in Christchurch must be overwhelming favourites to beat the Scots, who would do well to keep the score down. This forecast is almost a 'banker'. Scotland have never beaten the All-Blacks and such an upset here is unlikely (to say the least).

So, we come to the last of the quarter-finals and it could be very tough, as the Pumas have beaten the French recently in a Test. But the French might prove to be the better travellers, as we have already said, and with no great confidence we predict their passage to the semi-finals.

So our semi-finalists (if you have not already worked it out) are Australia, Wales, New Zealand and France. If we have selected three correctly we hope for another champagne dinner.

Semi-finals

The waters become more dangerous for us, but if we have been correct the two matches will be as follows:

Australia v. France
New Zealand v. Wales

The French record in Australia is excellent, but even so they have won only two Tests out of five played there with one draw; however, two of the losses happened in 1981 when the French suffered badly through injuries. But the World Cup will be special and at home the Wallabies must be favoured and they receive our vote.

In the other semi-final the only advantage Wales will have over the All-Blacks, whom they have not beaten since 1953, will be that they will have had longer to acclimatize, but New Zealand usually plan their campaigns well and they also have physical advantages allied to superior forward techniques. They must be given our vote.

The final: Australia v. New Zealand
Third place match: France v. Wales

The Final

This is scheduled for Auckland on Saturday, 20th June 1987, and it could be an All-Antipodean affair. The record of New Zealand in these encounters is vastly superior, with the All-Blacks by the end of the 1985 season in the southern hemisphere having won fifty six times against only nineteen Wallaby victories and four draws. At home, they should become first holders of 'The William Webb Ellis

Trophy' and that is the result we predict. But we are not offering to eat trilby hats if we are wrong. Please only write in to congratulate us if we are correct!

World champions: New Zealand

Runners-up: Australia

Third place: France

Earlier in this section we forecast the outcome of the World Cup. This was based more on historical form than on current performances, since, as Ireland regularly demonstrate, today's Grand Slam heroes can be tomorrow's wooden-spoonists. We can nevertheless make some observations on the countries taking part.

Pool 1

England
Headquarters: The Rugby Football Union, Twickenham, TW2 7RQ, Middlesex, England
Secretary elect: Dudley E. Wood

If recent form is any guide, England have little chance of advancing beyond the quarter-finals, but it would be a mistake to write them off completely. From time to time the country with the largest total number of players manages to find a superb team, as happened in 1957 and 1980 when nothing could stop them.

Their mediocre record abroad might also be reason to write England off, but again we should remember three excellent performances in the victories against the Springboks in South Africa in 1972 (after a Five Nations whitewash) and in New Zealand in 1973. The victory in the series in Argentina in 1981 was also no mean achievement, so it would be foolhardy to give them no chance. But how could they do it?

Behind the scrum this past season the play has been very poor, with Rob Andrew losing form after his points-scoring feat against Wales. It is therefore hard to assess the players outside him, but Jamie Salmon is highly rated in New Zealand (he was actually picked to play for the All-Blacks) and the three other centres chosen are all players with good potential – Halliday, Clough and Simms. There are also three very useful wings in the shape of Underwood ('Underused' as he has been dubbed), Harrison and Simon Smith, but finding an adequate full-back may be a problem as Huw Davies has so far failed to impress as a successor to Hare. Barnes might be a possibility, although he may be needed at fly-half instead, whilst the doubts about the fitness of Melville make it important that Richard Hill of Bath should be given every encouragement to advance.

After the game against Wales at Twickenham this year most critics were prepared to back England for the Triple Crown at the very least, so much had they dominated in every phase of that forward battle. Scotland, meanwhile, went to Cardiff and also showed up the Welsh pack but not to the extent that anyone could have expected the disaster that was to befall the English forwards at Murrayfield. The sheer athleticism of the home eight left a general outcry for similar selections for the England team. In the two remaining matches Ireland were beaten thanks to a good, but still none too athletic display by the pack and the defeat in Paris at least reflected no discredit on the same players.

But to win a World Cup the England side will need to become really mobile to match the All-Blacks, France, Australia and, yes, Scotland. This means that at least one of the locks must be something more than a mere good scrummager or line-out expert. The back-row, or any combination of several useful players, should be good enough and by the end of next season Chilcott, Brain and Pearce, if they escape injuries, should have enough international experience to stand up to the best.

For England it is a question of finding the right blend and correct tactics for the kind of opposition they are going to meet and some people may yet be surprised by them.

Japan

Secretary: S. Konno, c/o Sanshin Enterprises Company Ltd, Ichibancho Central Building, 22-1, Ichibancho, Choyoda-Ku, Tokyo 102, Japan

It is very hard to see Japan making any impression and they may well be more than satisfied with one victory, over the United States. Since their close match against Wales a few seasons ago their form has not improved. The tour to France late in 1985, when all matches were lost by heavy margins, including both Tests by margins of more than fifty points, will have done little to increase confidence. In fact, one of their best players, Hirao, was playing on the wing for Richmond at the time, having been left out of the national side.

A lack of forward physique will always be a bad handicap and some Japanese teams have shown ingenuity to overcome this by various clever mauling ploys, but they will need some new and more committed players plus their old guile to have any chance of escaping from the Antipodes with honour.

Australia

Headquarters: Rugby Union House, Crane Place, Sydney, New South Wales, Australia
Secretary: John D. Dedrick

Australia, playing most of their matches at home, will start justly as one of the favourites for the World Cup, as they have proved in recent seasons to be a team without any weaknesses. Or is that true? Certainly there should be no defections to any form of professional Rugby until after the event, so they will have their best men of the most recent past available, with Mark Ella being the notable exception.

That is the major weakness of the side and Michael Lynagh, who is a very fine player, does not seem to possess the genius of Ella, with his clever running and generally superb tactics. How badly will he be missed? Elsewhere among the backs there are several very good players starting with Gould at full-back, with two fine wings in Campese and Moon (plus Grigg as a more than useful deputy); the centres could be Slack and Black (or Lane, perhaps), and Farr-Jones is a fine scrum-half. But will that Ella spark be missed?

Forwards have always been a problem with Australian teams, but in the Grand Slam tour of 1984 in Britain the Argentinian, Rodriguez, made

David Campese, Australia's brilliant and rapid wing, will be one of the big personalities of the World Cup.

a big difference as a tighthead-prop, whilst Cutler made sure that plenty of line-out ball was won. If both of them are still there and fit along with the sturdy hooker, Tom Lawton, there will be a good basis for possession already built in, with the likelihood that the usual athletic and efficient back-row of Poidevin, Codey and Tuynman will have, if anything, improved. They could turn out a very good side again and there are plenty of good young players continually emerging to keep even those stars on their toes.

Australia should do very well, but the absence of Mark Ella will leave a niggling doubt in many minds.

United States

Secretary of the United States Rugby Football Union: R. Jones, 3923 S. E. 21st Place, Cape Coral, Florida 33904, USA

Like Japan the United States will not be expected to do particularly well in the first World Cup, but a lack of physique will not be one of their problems since they will have no problems in finding men of the right size to compete. The real problem will be a lack of expertise and an absence of players with any real experience of even world-class club competition let alone international contacts. Until Rugby Union becomes a sport popular enough to rival their own American Football they will probably always struggle.

A possible guide to their prospects of at least winning a match can be taken from the fact that they did tour Japan in 1985 and won the International series. They may well have to be satisfied with that in Australia.

Tom Smith (United States), 'Player of the Tournament' in the 1986 Hong Kong International Sevens.

Pool 2

Wales

Headquarters: The Welsh Rugby Union, National Ground, Cardiff Arms Park, Westgate Street, Cardiff CF1 1JL, Wales
Secretary: Ray Williams

The 1980s have so far been a barren period for Wales after the consistent successes of the previous decade and it is easy to see where the problems now lie – at forward. Of those presently available for the men in red there is only one who was considered good enough to be selected for the British Lions team for the IB Celebration match in Cardiff and he was the prop, Whitefoot. Two other forwards were under disciplinary bans from International play and one of them, the lock Norster, was badly missed. However, the other, Richard Moriarty, is a player whose best position is the subject of argument and he has rarely done himself

justice in Welsh colours ; perhaps he should be a lock along with Norster. Paul Moriarty looks as if he could be a good flanker at International level, which means that Wales desperately need to find four new men for the pack, although in the right company the hooker, Billy James, may yet reach the required standard. At tighthead the promising Stuart Evans from Neath, when free of injury, could be the answer, which means that the search should be on for another no. 8 and a flanker. Lyn Jones of Neath could be the first of those people, whilst Pickering, if he can recover form, confidence and fitness could just keep his place, but it might be a good idea to give the captaincy to someone else.

That 'someone else' might be Jonathan Davies, the one player of the past season who has consistently shown flair and class at outside-half; with Robert Jones (a year advanced in experience) as his partner, the half-back problem seems to have been solved in advance. Devereux and Bowen have been widely acclaimed as centres, but Malcolm Dacey of Swansea could find a berth there at the expense of one of them. There are plenty of good wings with Hadley, Titley and Lewis all good players and the likes of Cardiff's Glasson to challenge, whilst Thorburn has only to maintain his form to be the first choice at full-back. So behind the scrum Wales have no apparent problems, provided that the forwards can give them the ball quickly enough. Some attention should be paid to the tackling, which has let them down on a few occassions recently.

Any forecast of a World Cup must take a Welsh challenge seriously, at least to reach a respectable rating. But without the improvements (with greater athleticism amongst the forwards being essential) mentioned the Welsh could struggle to satisfy their supporters and admirers.

Ireland

Headquarters: The Irish Rugby Football Union, 62 Lansdowne Road, Dublin 4, Ireland
Secretary: R. Fitz-Gerald

Ireland will start the new season as something of an unknown quantity, since a Championship success in the Five Nations in 1985 has been followed by a blank 1986 campaign. The main weakness has been a lack of forward power, which meant that France and England gave them a very hard time indeed; in one case (at Twickenham) they conceded two pushover tries and a penalty-try, which was the result of backward momentum.

For the home game against Scotland a temporary repair job was carried out, but from now onwards they may have to continue without the very estimable services of Phil Orr and Ciaran Fitzgerald, whose places could be returned to Paul Kennedy and Harry Harbison. This will also mean a change of captaincy – but to whom? In a small country like Ireland there is a shortage of top-class talent and they do remarkably well in spite of it, but how they will actually be able to counter the problems of heavier and, in many cases, more mobile opponents is something that will trouble their selectors considerably. Will they be able to do so with the others who will still be available – McCall, Fitzgerald (the tighthead prop), Lenihan, Carr, Anderson (or Spillane) and Morrow (or Matthews, if fit)? They will probably be best served by looking for a mobile blend and hoping that the talent in training will do the trick.

However, that pack did provide a good supply of ball in the match against Scotland, mainly through the excellent Lenihan in the line-outs, and this proved to any doubters that outside the scrum there is some excellent talent with a very good full-back in MacNeill, two excellent wings (Ringland and Crossan) and fine centres in Mullin and Kiernan. At half-back, Keyes and Dean are very useful contenders for the fly-half position with Tony Ward there to take over with his own form of genius, if the selectors are prepared to take a chance with him again. At scrum-half Bradley had a very mediocre season and it might be time for Ulster's Brady to take over. But those backs, if given the ball, can wreak havoc on any defence.

Ireland could reasonably be expected to reach the last eight, but whether they go any further is in the lap of the gods. They are usually such an entertaining side that their supporters, and aficionados of the game, would hope that they do even better than that.

Canada

Headquarters: (through) The Executive Director, Canadian Rugby Union, 333 River Road, Vanier, Ontario, K1L 8B9 Canada

Canada will do well to win a single match at the World Cup and much depends on the kind of team they are able to select. British Columbia beat the visiting Scotland tourists in 1985 and the bulk of the team must presumably come from that source. In 1983 there was a tour of England that had mixed results, although a brave showing was produced against England at Twickenham, when behind the scrum there were useful performers in the full-back, Wyatt, and the half-back pairing of MacMillan and MacLean, all three from British Columbia. Two props, Dukelow and Breen, from the same province, also did well and there was a useful back-row in Cvitak, Russell and Godziek, all from Ontario. Locks capable of winning good line-out ball may be a problem, but Canada can at least be guaranteed to put up a good show and, if they can have some time training together, they should improve on their sad results during the Australian tour of 1985.

Tonga

Secretary: Viliami H. Petelo, P O Box 369, Nuku' Alofa, Tonga

The only form guide for Tonga's prospects comes from the local tournament with Western Samoa and Fiji, which usually shows the latter in the best light, and from the recent Hong Kong Sevens when they did reach the quarter-finals. But Sevens are a different proposition from the fifteen-a-side game where large forwards are a necessity if good ball is to be won; this could be their main problem.

The country did visit Britain in the autumn of 1974, when a good start to the tour was followed by some very heavy defeats. There was also evidence of indiscipline and this must be watched at an important competition like the World Cup, where referees will be instructed to be very firm so as to avoid the kind of scenes that make the round-ball version of the World Cup an occasion where good-will on an international level is generally totally absent.

Pool 3

New Zealand

Headquarters: Ground Floor, Huddart Parker Building, Post Office Square (P O Box 2172), Wellington, 728-168, New Zealand
Secretary: B. R. Usmar

In any competition in which New Zealand are involved they will start as favourites and this situation is reinforced by the fact that they are drawn at home and may only need to cross the Tasman Sea for one match – a semi-final. However, the location of the tournament is not the only reason why they will be highly fancied to win. They also just happen to have very good players at their disposal. There are no apparent weaknesses and, where they are likely to meet superiors in certain aspects of tactics, they have an inborn ability to improvise and play to their strengths.

Their traditional strengths lie in their immensely powerful packs, able efficiently to obtain possession and make the best use of it more often than not through forward drives with the ball-carrier always being supported by large and mobile athletes. This is still very much the case, although the old idea that the backs are merely there to make up the numbers is now out-dated; they also have fine mid-field men and wings.

So who are the men likely to wear the All-Black jerseys at the inaugural World Cup? The most recent selection at full-back has been Crowley, who is usually a reliable place-kicker and sound defender and who can also time his attacking forays well. The wings in the party could be Kirwan, Craig Green and Clamp; all three are very capable. In the centre one would expect to see Steve Pokere, Warwick Taylor, Victor Simpson and, perhaps, Bill Osborne in the party and again we observe an awesome array of talent there. Grant Fox and Wayne Smith are both very competent first five-eighths and if David Kirk is unavailable from Oxford University the choice at scrum-half could involve

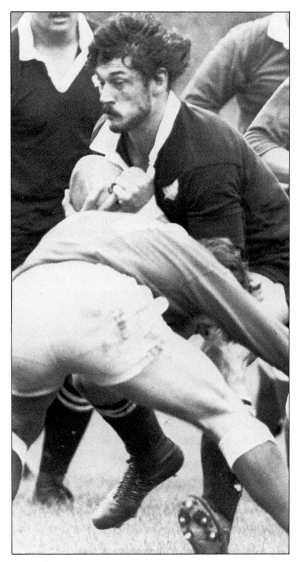

Murray Mexted (New Zealand) in action in 1980. Will he be adding to his collection of caps?

the brilliant veteran Dave Loveridge and Donald. If there is a plentiful supply of the ball any combination of those players will make good use of it.

The pack should present a formidable challenge to all opponents. It is a sobering thought that they have two such marvellous no. 8's as Murray Mexted and Wayne Shelford; and even if Andy Haden is now somewhat elderly as a lock his potential replacements are all excellent – Gary Whetton, Murray Pierce and Albert Anderson. There is no lack of flankers with Hobbs and Shaw probably the best available, and in the front-row they have such stalwarts as McGratton, McDowell, Gary Knight,

John Ashworth and Scott Crichton as props with two superb hookers in Andy Dalton, the possible captain, and Hika Reid.

Recent International Sevens tournaments have also shown that such people as Botica, Brook-Cowden and Zinzan Brooke must also be in contention for places, so the future of New Zealand Rugby is in good hands.

So, are there any weaknesses? If there are, it can be guaranteed that the coaches will be able to conceal them effectively, particularly at home. However, a lesson in caution can be learnt from the 1950 Soccer World Cup, which was held in Brazil and saw the home country, who were very hot favourites, lose their final match against Uruguay and with it the World Cup. Surprises can happen as England players from that era will also testify, however unwillingly – they lost to the United States in that event!

Argentina

Headquarters: UAR, Pacheco de Melo 2120, Buenos Aires, Argentina

If New Zealand are favourites in this pool then Argentina will be expected to be the other qualifiers for the last eight on the basis of consistent form for many years, which means that the team is now recognized as being of senior International status and all IB countries award caps for matches against them. Their recent form has been most impressive with a drawn series in 1985 against France and one lost and one drawn against New Zealand. All the matches were in Buenos Aires.

The big question will concern the team's ability to travel well, but in this respect history is in their favour. Since 1973 Ireland, Scotland, Wales and England have all been visited with only the Irish gaining a clear-cut victory against them; against England a well-merited draw was achieved at Twickenham, although in return contests in Buenos Aires in 1981 the visitors managed a draw and victory. A tour of Australia in 1983 produced a win in the first Test and defeat somewhat unluckily in the second. So they should be able to travel.

The main strength of Argentina is in one player – that superb fly-half Hugo Porta, who recently scored all his country's points against New Zealand (twenty one in all!). Porta is a genius and prayers will undoubtedly be said by Argentinian Rugby men not only for his delayed retirement but also for his continued good health. However, it is not a 'one-man' team: there is a good scrum-half to partner him in Holmgren, a good full-back in

Miguens and good three-quarters, with the two Lanzas on the wings and useful centres in Cuesta Silva and Turnes.

The pack should also give problems to opponents with the likely no. 8 being Petersen flanked by Ure and Allen. The locks may be Milano and Branca with a front-row of Morel, Cubelli and Cash. It will be mobile and strong and will acquit itself well.

A problem with Argentina in matches abroad has been a tendency to tackle too high, which may have been caused by hard grounds in their own country. Referees will not tolerate this and other occasional lapses in control of temper, which have been seen in the past, should be eliminated if they are to progress without problems.

Fiji

Headquarters: Fiji Rugby Union, P O Box 1234, Suva, Fiji
Secretary: S. Tuinaceva

Fijian Rugby has acquired a reputation for open play and this remains justified, but consistency is probably lacking in their game and they will not be amongst the teams expected to survive beyond the qualifying rounds. In fact, they will do well to win a single match. Recent form, especially on their travels abroad, has not been impressive: a lack of height and weight amongst the forwards has been a major handicap, which has been only partly overcome from time to time by improvisation in the form of using a limited supply of the ball quickly and with skill.

The backs are probably the best part of the Fiji side with Turuva a good full-back and other good mid-field men in Niuqila, Laulau and Cama (when he behaves properly). The wings are good and they will probably select from three – Damu (who can also play at full-back when required), Tuvula and Nabati. The scrum-half, who is another useful player, will very probably be Nawalu.

The problems come amongst the forwards where line-out ball will be at a premium and the lightweight front-row may have serious problems. Rakoro and Hughes with improvisation might win some ball at lock and Rakai, supported by Volavola and Namoro, can usually protect his own ball quite well as the hooker, whilst the back-row, which is likely to consist of Finau, Gale and Teleni (the probable captain), can be expected to show good handling skills. During the tour of Wales and Ireland in 1985 not enough use was made of the promising Tawake, who is tall and agile.

Two tours were made in 1985; one to Australia and the other to Wales and Ireland. Four Tests

Hugo Porta (Argentina's fly-half and captain), who is thought likely to be one of the most important players in the World Cup of 1987 with his flair and goal-kicking.

were played in all and only the one against Ireland in Dublin, when the Fijians were most unlucky to lose by a single point, showed them to advantage. Australia, twice, and Wales had overwhelming victories and the former complained bitterly that the visitors were extremely physically dangerous with their tactics.

In fact, discipline may well be as big a problem as their inability to obtain enough good ball, and with referees being instructed to take tough action against all offenders they will have to improve this part of their game. Scenes such as those against Newport in 1985 cannot be tolerated.

Italy

Headquarters: Federazione Italiana Rugby, Viale Tiziano 70, 00100, Roma, Italy
Secretary: Signor Sandro di Santo

The Italians have been playing Rugby for a long time, but so far they have made only a very modest impression on the world scene, although in a recent match against Queensland they won (15-13). That and a victory over a young Romanian team in

December 1985 (19-3) have been encouraging points offset by a thorough thrashing by France 'A' (away) this season (19-0). The set-back and defeat suffered at Twickenham on a fine April afternoon in 1985 (21-9) showed that Italy probably does not travel well in Rugby terms and this augurs badly for World Cup prospects. After all, the Twickenham defeat was against a side containing no current England caps (it was a 'B' team) and only four of those opposing players have since gained England honours. France 'A' was in effect a good National second fifteen.

The impression given by the Italian team beaten at Twickenham was one of a lack of concentration allied to an ignorance of the laws which led them to be offside too frequently. The scrum was also on the light side and the backs, especially the full-back Ghizzoni, tended to take their eyes off the ball when faced with opposing tacklers. With better concentration the half-backs, Bettarello and Ghini, looked as if they could become good players, whilst they had two speedy wings in Azzali and Venturi. The best of the forwards on that occasion were in the back-row – Artuso, Innocenti and Zanon.

It could well be that the selectors will experiment in the early stages of the coming season to try out locks with height and weight: it is vitally important to obtain better possession.

So far discipline has been only fair with some players displaying volatile temperaments and this will not please some strict referees. This aspect of play will need attention, but probably they will not be the worst offenders. It would be unreal to expect them to reach even the last eight, but they will not be the worst team at the tournament. If there are to be any shocks the Italians might provide them.

Pool 4

France

Headquarters: 7 Cité d'Antin, Paris (9è) 75009, France
Le Secrétaire Général: J.-L. Boujon

France will start the tournament as one of the favoured teams if form in 1987 follows normal patterns. The fact that they will be rated below New Zealand and Australia as potential winners is because they will be playing away from home. In terms of ability no-one will fail to take their challenge very seriously indeed, particularly as the last time they had even a moderate team was in 1982! Since that time they have been the team to beat in Europe and that has been some problem for most opponents. A lack of discipline has meant that, during this most recent period, only in 1981 did they win the Championship outright, a share having been achieved in 1983 and 1986.

So, the French must be one of the favourites and there is nothing in their recent form to suggest that they will go far wrong. They have a superb pack in terms of actual scrummaging with a great front-row in Marocco, Dubroca (the captain) and Garuet, whilst their rucking and mauling and general good work with the loose ball comes from an excellent back-row of Champ, Joinel and Erbani. Only in the line-outs do they find ball less easy to win, but they still manage a fair share through good tactics. Condom's play in most respects is exemplary.

Behind the scrum they have two world-class scrum-halves in Berbizier and Gallion, whilst either Lescarboura (if passed fit) or Laporte will ensure good ball supply from outside-half. The centres, Sella and Charvet, are wonderful runners and great in defence, whilst the wings are more than adequate if they continue to select Lafond (a converted full-back) and Bonneval. Full-back is Serge Blanco, one of the best in the business.

So, are we talking about the eventual winners? Are there any weaknesses? Alas, there are! Disci-

pline is not always as good as it should be and needless penalties are often conceded, particularly away from home. The team may in twelve months' time have passed its peak if changes are not by then forced on them; seven – two backs and five of the pack – will by then have paid farewell to the twenties and they will need to be replaced sooner rather than later. Without doubt, the French selectors already have replacements in mind, but unless these players are given the chance to acquire experience now they may find themselves pitched into big games without any knowledge of the differences involved.

The French should be very good prospects, if they in fact do justice to their reputations.

Scotland

Headquarters: Murrayfield, Edinburgh EH12 5PJ, Scotland
Secretary: I. A. L. Hogg, CA

Along with France, the Scots would seem to be Europe's best hope for success in the World Cup and it is a pity that two such teams should be drawn in the same pool since the losers of the first match will be fighting for survival from then on. After the Grand Slam success of 1984, Scotland lost six successive matches; but a narrow victory over France at Murrayfield in January 1986 was followed by some memorable Rugby from the men in dark blue and some of their support play, particularly by their back-row, was quite breathtaking as England would readily testify.

Only four of the current team will be over thirty at the time of the World Cup and of those men the two most vital elements are the country's greatest-ever half-backs, John Rutherford and Roy Laidlaw. The former may be considered almost irreplaceable and many prayers will be said by Scottish followers between now and the event for the good health and fitness of him – in fact, of both! Behind them can be seen five superbly talented players from the full-back, Gavin Hastings, through the two wings, Duncan and Baird, to the centres Scott Hastings (the other half of the brotherly pair) and David Johnston. In reserve there are such fine performers as Peter Dods, Ivan Tukalo and Keith Robertson, if the latter continues to play. Scotland's 'B' team has won five of its last six matches, so in a country reputed to lack talent in numbers there are remarkably strong reserves.

The pack has been criticized as being on the light side, but mobility has been a more than adequate substitute, whilst in the scrummaging itself the forwards have always been able to hold their own. Here there are two men who will be over thirty at the time of the World Cup, namely, Alex Brewster at loosehead-prop and Colin Deans, his country's greatest-ever hooker and now the captain. Deans has been playing as well as ever and he remains very quick around the field so he should manage another twelve months, whilst Brewster, who will have to fight off the challenge of David Sole, has been a very brave convert to the front-row. The locks have the estimable Campbell and Iain Paxton, a convert from no. 8 who jumps well in the line-outs but who is light by normal standards. The back-row is just superb and will make many friends amongst the unbiased fans. Finlay Calder has had a very good first season at International level in succession to his twin brother, Jim, whilst John Beattie has returned at no. 8 as a revitalized player. Finally, there is 'The White Shark', John Jeffrey of Kelso, who preyed upon opposition mistakes with relish. From Scotland's point of view it is good to know that there are challengers for most positions; the future would therefore seem to be healthy.

However, having painted a very rosy picture of Scotland's prospects it should be mentioned that the Test record abroad is not good. Only one match has been won (in Australia in 1982) since Scotland started touring seriously in 1960, against six losses. An unofficial series in Argentina in 1972 was drawn one match each. Somehow this problem must be overcome, but the two coaches, Derrick Grant and Ian McGeechan, have toured abroad and know something about the task facing their men.

Zimbabwe

Headquarters: Zimbabwe Rugby Union, PO Box 53, Harare, Zimbabwe
President: D. L. L. Morgan

Zimbabwe will be the rank outsiders in this competition and at this moment it is not too clear who will be their representatives in the Antipodes. Before their independence they were a Currie Cup 'A' team in the South African scene without ever seeming likely to trouble the more successful provinces such as Transvaal and Western Province.

During the pre-independence days, Rhodesia did entertain British Lions teams and other touring sides such as Ireland, but they did not appear likely to worry such opposition even in those days when they probably had stronger teams and were regularly meeting tough opponents. Now they must make do with matches against teams which just do not provide good enough preparation for such a tough task as the World Cup. A recent visit to the Iberian peninsular with poor performances against Portugal and Spain cannot have provided much reassurance.

It would be very bad for the competition if an inexperienced team like Zimbabwe should be overwhelmed and it is hoped that they will find something extra from somewhere.

Romania

Headquarters: Federata Romana de Rugbi, Strada Vasile Conta 16, Bucharest CP 70139, Romania
Secretary: Professor O. Marca

In 1984 Romania soundly beat the visiting Scottish team, which had just won the Five Nations Grand Slam. It is true that the Scots were six people short of full strength and wilted in some fierce heat, but it nevertheless showed the Romanians in a very good light. Earlier in the same season they had overwhelmed a poor Welsh team, also in Bucharest (24-6). With a very fine pack and tremendous locks in Dumitru and L. Constantin with a lot of fine support from S. Constantin at no. 8 they looked formidable indeed. They also had another fine line-out man, Caragea, unavailable at the time. The front-row of Bucan, Munteanu and Pascu was also more than useful.

To back up this array of strength there was the clever tactical play of the captain, Paraschiv, at scrum-half and the kicking skill of Alexandru outside him. It was ten-man Rugby, but it was also highly effective.

Romania should have been on the rampage, but late in 1984 there was a rude shock in store in Bucharest when France came and conquered comfortably with Lescarboura scoring all eighteen points; the home country managed only three in reply. A trip to England produced three defeats including one at Twickenham in a boring match, which at least did not see Romania disgraced. But the decline seems to have set in and this recent season has seen the selectors experiment with the result that a very young team lost badly in Italy (19-3) and, when some of the experienced old-hands had been restored, Scotland returned to Bucharest much better prepared than in 1984 and won comfortably (33-18).

So Romania have twelve months to build a side for the big event knowing that they must overcome either Scotland or France or both to advance to the last eight in the competition. Will they give their older players that responsibility or will they try to build a new side and hope that it will click? It is a difficult problem for them, but teams opposing them must give away no penalties as they have in their new outside-half, Ignat, a very good place-kicker. He, at least, might enjoy the tournament if others transgress.

INTERNATIONALS

Five Nations Championship

The title of 'Champions' was in doubt until the final series of matches on 15th March 1986, and eventually the honour was shared between France and Scotland. Last season's Champions, Ireland, were whitewashed and the final table reads like this:

	P	W	L	F	A	Pts
France	4	3	1	98	52	6
Scotland	4	3	1	76	54	6
Wales	4	2	2	74	71	4
England	4	2	2	62	100	2
Ireland	4	0	4	50	82	0

The scoring statistics suggest correctly that France had the most talented team, but indiscipline, especially when Scotland were attacking, cost them the match at Murrayfield, and their subsequent marvellous displays against Ireland, Wales (in Cardiff) and England could not bring them the title. However, they probably had the best front-row in the tournament, and their backs when on the move were a joy to watch with Sella the outstanding figure in the whole competition; he scored a try in every match.

Scotland, by dint of hard work and an excellent back-row, shared the title and after the previous season's problems no-one would begrudge them their partial success. Perhaps they were lucky to beat France when Gavin Hastings kicked six penalty-goals, but were they all not fairly easy kicks in the French '22'? The match in Cardiff provided a most unlucky defeat as the Scots looked the better team, but England paid for that defeat by going down to a record margin at Murrayfield and the score did not flatter the rampaging home team. If Scotland were lucky at all it was in the final match in Dublin, when the Irish played really well and deserved better from the fates.

Wales by breaking even did no better than their form deserved. Excellent backs were inhibited by a lack of good possession and they had Thorburn to thank for the fact that Scotland were beaten. If only some competent forwards could be discovered then the talents of Jonathan Davies, Robert Jones

Back row (left to right) *S. R. Hilditch (touch judge), D. I. H. Burnett (referee), J.-P. Garuet, P. Marocco, J. Gratton, D. Erbani, J.-L. Joinel, F. Haget, J. Condom, O. A. Doyle (touch judge). Front row (left to right) J.-B. Lafond, P. Sella, G. Laporte, P. Berbizier, D. Dubroca (captain), S. Blanco, P. Estève, P. Chadebech.*

and John Devereux could be given full rein, but at the moment they must live off scraps.

England with a big but largely cumbersome pack did well in their home matches, when they had plenty of possession. Poor initial tactics at Murrayfield played into the hands of the home team and eventually the side was run off its feet. In Paris, early chances to score were spurned and this cannot be done against the French at any time.

The Irish only played well in their home matches, the Welsh game being thrown away due to a lack of concentration in the second half. Against Scotland the team as a whole played really well and defeat was not deserved. In the away matches, the forwards were just not good enough even though the match at Twickenham was close and could have been won with a slice of luck. Ireland had excellent backs with Mullin outstanding; more good possession might have brought different results.

In general, it was a most enjoyable Championship, and the arrival of several new faces – notably Champ and Charvet (France), the two Hastings brothers, Duncan, Sole and Finlay Calder (Scotland) and Robert Jones and Devereux (Wales) – was most encouraging. For England, Dean Richards may also make a name for himself. Jeffrey of Scotland with only three caps before the competition started was another brilliant player, and of the 'old-stagers' it was nice to see consistently good displays from Laporte and Blanco (France), Rutherford, Laidlaw and Deans (Scotland) and Pickering (Wales). Rugby at this level is still good fun and long may it remain so.

First Matches
Saturday, 18th January 1986, at Murrayfield

Scotland	18	France	17

Penalty-goals: G. Hastings (6) *Tries:* Berbizier, Sella (1 each)
Half-time: 12-7 *Dropped-goal:* Laporte
Penalty-goals: Laporte (2)

Scotland: A. G. Hastings *(Cambridge University)*; M. D. F. Duncan *(West of Scotland)*, D. I. Johnston *(Watsonians)*, S. Hastings *(Watsonians)*, G. R. T. Baird *(Kelso)*; J. Y. Rutherford *(Selkirk)*, R. J. Laidlaw *(Jed-Forest)*; D. M. B. Sole *(Bath)*, C. T. Deans *(Hawick) (captain)*, I. G. Milne *(Harlequins)*, J. Jeffrey *(Kelso)*, A. J. Campbell *(Hawick)*, J. R. E. Campbell-Lamerton *(London Scottish)*, F. Calder *(Stewart's-Melville FP)*, J. R. Beattie *(Glasgow Academicals)*. *New caps:* A. G. Hastings, Duncan, S. Hastings, Sole, Campbell-Lamerton, F. Calder

France: S. Blanco *(Biarritz)*; J.-B. Lafond *(Racing Club de France)*, P. Sella *(Agen)*, P. Chadebech *(Brive)*, P. Estève *(Narbonne)*; G. Laporte *(Graulhet)*, P. Berbizier *(Agen)*; P. Marocco *(Montferrand)*, D. Dubroca *(Agen) (captain)*, J.-P. Garuet *(Lourdes)*, J. Gratton *(Agen)*, F. Haget *(Biarritz)*, J. Condom *(Boucau)*, J.-L. Joinel *(Brive)*, D. Erbani *(Agen)*. *New cap:* Marocco

Referee: D. I. H. Burnett *(Ireland)*

France scored both tries in this match and yet their defeat was well merited since their old fault of indiscipline was well in evidence and this gave Gavin Hastings the chance to score a record eighteen points for Scotland on his debut. All bar one of the kicks was from a relatively easy position – he also missed twice from good situations – so it can be assumed fairly that Scotland might in certain instances have scored tries but for defensive misdemeanors. In the forward battle the home team at least held its own although there were six new caps, whilst there was a question mark against each

Back row (left to right) S. G. Johnston (replacement), D. S. Wyllie (replacement), G. J. Callander (replacement), F. Calder, J. R. Beattie, I. A. M. Paxton, J. Jeffrey, J. Y. Rutherford, A. K. Brewster, D. B. White (replacement), N. A. Rowan (replacement),

P. W. Dods (replacement). Front row (left to right) K. W. Robertson, D. I. Johnston, A. G. Hastings, A. J. Campbell, C. T. Deans (captain), I. G. Milne, R. J. Laidlaw, S. Hastings, G. R. T. Baird.

Gavin Hastings scores one of his six penalties for Scotland against France at Murrayfield.

of the French tries; the first was an audacious line-out ploy from an over-powered kick-off by Gavin Hastings, but was the line-out correctly taken by the right person from the right position? The second try after half-time came from a fine move, but there was a suspicious final pass by Blanco. So those who thought that the Scots were lucky might well have been too kind to a poor French performance.

Gavin Hastings in scoring six penalty-goals for Scotland set up a record for his country on his debut; his points tally was eighteen. Gavin and his brother, Scott, were the first brothers to make their International debuts for Scotland in the same match since George and Willie Neilson did so against Wales in 1891; both brothers were with Merchistonians. In 1875, the brothers Ninian and Alex Finlay of Edinburgh Academicals made their debuts against England. Jeremy Campbell-Lamerton joins the list of those players whose fathers have also played International Rugby. Scotland and France have now played each other on fifty six occasions with twenty seven wins each and two matches having been drawn.

First Matches
Saturday, 18th January 1986, at Twickenham

England	21	Wales	18
Dropped-goal: Andrew		*Try:* Bowen	
Penalty-goals: Andrew (6)		*Dropped-goal:* J. Davies	
Half-time: 12-9		*Penalty-goals:* Thorburn (3)	
		Conversion: Thorburn	

England: G. H. Davies *(Wasps)*; S. T. Smith *(Wasps)*, S. J. Halliday *(Bath)*, J. L. B. Salmon *(Harlequins)*, R. Underwood *(Leicester and RAF)*; C. R. Andrew *(Nottingham)*, N. D. Melville *(Wasps) (captain)*; P. A. G. Rendall *(Wasps)*, S. E. Brain *(Coventry)*, G. S. Pearce *(Northampton)*, J. P. Hall *(Bath)*, W. A. Dooley *(Preston Grasshoppers)*, M. J. Colclough *(Swansea)*, P. J. Winterbottom *(Headingley)*, G. L. Robbins *(Coventry)*. *New caps:* Halliday and Robbins

Wales: P. H. Thorburn *(Neath)*; P. I. Lewis *(Llanelli)*, J. Devereux *(South Glamorgan Institute and Bridgend)*, B. Bowen *(South Wales Police)*, A. M. Hadley *(Cardiff)*; J. Davies *(Neath)*, R. Jones *(Swansea)*; J. Whitefoot *(Cardiff)*, W. J. James *(Aberavon)*, I. H. Eidman *(Cardiff)*, M. Brown *(Pontypool)*, S. J. Perkins *(Pontypool)*, D. R. Waters *(Newport)*, D. F. Pickering *(Llanelli) (captain)*, P. T. Davies *(Llanelli)*. *New caps:* Devereux, Jones, Waters

Referee: R. J. Fordham *(Australia)*

Wales scored the only try – a very good effort launched by Pickering from a line-out and touched down by Bowen – in the second half, but on the whole England just about deserved to win this tense struggle, because their pack controlled matters better than their opponents. Andrew's goal-kicking was the other decisive factor and his winning dropped-goal in injury time was scored with his 'weaker' left foot after more good work by the pack and Huw Davies.

England's win was only their tenth over Wales in forty years, during which time they have lost twenty four times and six matches have been drawn. This is the most one-sided series in the Five Nations Championship during that period.

Second Matches
Saturday, 1st February 1986, at National Stadium, Cardiff

Wales	22	Scotland	15
Try: Hadley		*Tries:* Duncan, Jeffrey,	
Dropped-goal: J. Davies		G. Hastings (1 each)	
Penalty-goals: Thorburn (5)		*Penalty-goal:* G. Hastings	
		Half-time: 9-12	

Wales: P. H. Thorburn; P. I. Lewis, J. A. Devereux, B. Bowen, A. M. Hadley; J. Davies, R. J. Jones; J. Whitefoot, W. J. James, I. H. Eidman, M. Brown, S. J. Perkins, D. R. Waters, D. F. Pickering *(captain)*, P. T. Davies. *No new caps*

Scotland: A. G. Hastings *(now London Scottish)*; M. D. F. Duncan, D. I. Johnston, S. Hastings, G. R. T. Baird; J. Y. Rutherford, R. J. Laidlaw; D. M. B. Sole, C. T. Deans *(captain)*, I. G. Milne, J. Jeffrey, A. J. Campbell, I. A. M. Paxton *(Selkirk)*, F. Calder, J. R. Beattie. *No new caps*

Referee: R. C. Francis *(Wairarapa-Bush, New Zealand)*

Scotland, better in almost every phase of forward play and the scorers of three tries to one by the home team, lost this match thanks largely to brave Welsh defensive work under some severe pressure and the superb kicking of Thorburn, who scored five penalty-goals, one being from well over sixty metres and another from half-way. Jonathan Davies dropped an excellent goal in a fine display and Hadley scored a fine second-half try after Thorburn had entered the line to create an overlap. Jones at scrum-half – with some very bad ball – was another Welsh hero.

However, Scotland scored three first-half tries through Duncan (after a blind-side run by Rutherford), the immense Jeffrey (after a fine inside pass from Baird) and Gavin Hastings (after a fine move which involved the Scottish back-row and Rutherford). All were wide out and Gavin Hastings failed to convert any of them apart from missing two penalties, only one of which was fairly simple. In a lengthy period during the second half Scotland laid siege to the Welsh line and some thought that Sole had actually scored but there were also three penalty awards near the line against Wales; could not one have been a penalty-try? In the end Scotland were out of luck, but contributed very well to a fine game, which was well handled by Mr Francis even if he did not always apply the strict letter of the Laws, which would have made for a dull affair.

In forty matches since 1947 Wales have won on twenty seven occasions with Scotland winning the other thirteen, only three of them at Cardiff. This was the first time during that period that Scotland have scored more tries and lost. Thorburn's fourth penalty-goal was estimated as having been from about sixty seven metres!

Second Matches

Saturday, 1st February 1986, at Parc-des-Princes, Paris

France	29	Ireland	6

Tries: Berbizier, Marocco, Sella (1 each)
Dropped-goal: Lafond
Penalty-goals: Laporte (3), Blanco (1)
Conversion: Laporte

Penalty-goals: Kiernan (3)
Half-time: 9-6

France: S. Blanco; J.-B. Lafond, P. Sella, P. Chadebech, P. Estève; G. Laporte, P. Berbizier; P. Marocco, D. Dubroca *(captain)*, J.-P. Garuet, E. Champ *(Toulon)*, F. Haget, J. Condom, D. Erbani, J.-L. Joinel. *No new caps*
Ireland: H. P. MacNeill *(London Irish)*; T. M. Ringland *(Ballymena)*, B. J. Mullin *(Dublin University)*, M. J. Kiernan *(Dolphin)*, M. C. Finn *(Cork Constitution)*; P. M. Dean *(St Mary's College)*, M. T. Bradley *(Cork Constitution)*; P. A. Orr *(Old Wesley)*, C. F. Fitzgerald *(St Mary's College) (captain)*, J. J. McCoy *(Bangor)*, D. Morrow *(Bangor)*, D. G. Lenihan *(Cork Constitution)*, W. A. Anderson *(Dungannon)*, R. K. Kearney *(Wanderers)*, B. J. Spillane *(Bohemians)*. *New cap:* Morrow
Referee: R. Fordham *(Australia)*

France, after their set-back at Murrayfield, were far too good for an Irish team with a revised back-row from last season. Superb tries by Berbizier, Marocco and Sella after half-time produced a rout and there was some French play at its best, which is mostly irresistible. On this form who could bet against the French, who dominated all the forward exchanges and also showed their usual skills at handling with dexterity?

Ireland were simply outclassed and would need a big improvement to avoid the 'wooden-spoon' after last season's Championship success.

The countries have met forty one times since 1947 with France having won on twenty four occasions, Ireland on twelve and five matches having been drawn.

Back row (left to right) *R. Quittenton (touch judge), M. Jones (replacement), F. A. Howard (referee), P. I. Lewis, J. Whitefoot, S. J. Perkins, W. P. Moriarty, D. R. Waters, P. T. Davies, I. H. Eidman, J. A. Devereux, M. H. Titley (replacement), M. Dacey (replacement), M. Douglas (replacement), L. Delaney (replacement), L. Prideaux (touch judge). Front row (left to right) R. N. Jones, P. H. Thorburn, D. F. Pickering (captain), W. J. James, A. M. Hadley, J. Davies, B. Bowen, M. Richards (replacement).*

Third Matches

Saturday, 15th February 1986, at Lansdowne Road, Dublin

Ireland	12	Wales	19
Try: Ringland		*Tries:* Lewis, P. Davies (1 each)	
Penalty-goals: Kiernan (2)		*Penalty-goals:* Thorburn (3)	
Conversion: Kiernan		*Conversion:* Thorburn	
		Half-time: 12-4	

Ireland: H. P. MacNeill; T. M. Ringland, M. J. Kiernan, B. J. Mullin, M. C. Finn; P. M. Dean, M. T. Bradley; A. P. Kennedy *(London Irish)*, C. F. Fitzgerald *(captain)*, D. C. Fitzgerald *(Lansdowne)*, R. K. Kearney, J. Holland *(Wanderers)*, D. G. Lenihan, N. J. Carr *(Ards)*, B. J. Spillane. *New cap:* A. P. Kennedy

Wales: P. H. Thorburn; P. I. Lewis, J. A. Devereux, B. Bowen, A. M. Hadley; J. Davies, R. J. Jones; J. Whitefoot, W. J. James, I. H. Eidman, P. Moriarty *(Swansea)*, S. J. Perkins, D. R. Waters, D. F. Pickering *(captain)*, P. T. Davies. *New cap:* P. Moriarty

Referee: F. A. Howard *(England)*

After a first-half drubbing, Wales recovered well to score fifteen second-half points without reply and keep very much alive their Championship hopes. In the first period Ireland were superior and their forwards gave the Welsh a tough time, which continued well into the second half, but eventually the tide turned and a penalty by Thorburn (not at his kicking best before this), a try by P. Davies after good work by Jonathan Davies and Lewis and two more Thorburn penalties (he also converted the try) completed the recovery. In the first half Kiernan kicked penalties either side of an excellent Lewis try well schemed by Devereux, but then followed a fine run by MacNeill who

Phil Davies (Wales) is tackled by Michael Bradley (Ireland) whilst Phil Lewis (Wales) and Michael Kiernan (Ireland) support.

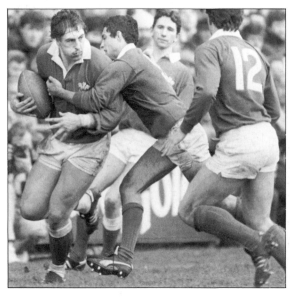

timed his pass well for Ringland to score a good Irish try, which Kiernan converted.

Ireland somehow let their advantage slip and despite their win Wales will have asked questions about their pack. However, a win in Dublin is never easily achieved, which was the main Welsh bonus. Again, this was a well refereed match. Well done Mr Howard!

In thirty nine matches since 1946 Wales have beaten Ireland twenty four times, with three matches having been drawn and Ireland having won on eleven occasions.

Third Matches

Saturday, 15th February 1986, at Murrayfield

Scotland	33	England	6
Tries: Duncan, Rutherford,		*Penalty-goals:* Andrew (2)	
S. Hastings (1 each)		*Half-time:* 12-6	
Penalty-goals: G. Hastings (5)			
Conversions: G. Hastings (3)			

Scotland: A. G. Hastings; M. D. F. Duncan, D. I. Johnston, S. Hastings, G. R. T. Baird; J. Y. Rutherford, R. J. Laidlaw; A. K. Brewster *(Stewart's-Melville FP)*, C. T. Deans *(captain)*, I. G. Milne, J. Jeffrey, A. J. Campbell, I. A. M. Paxton, F. Calder, J. R. Beattie. *No new caps*

England: G. H. Davies; S. T. Smith, S. J. Halliday, J. L. B. Salmon; M. E. Harrison *(Wakefield)*; C. R. Andrew, N. D. Melville *(captain)*; P. A. G. Rendall, S. E. Brain, G. S. Pearce, J. P. Hall, W. A. Dooley, M. J. Colclough, P. J. Winterbottom, G. L. Robbins. *No new caps. Replacements:* N. C. Redman *(Bath)* second-half for Hall, S. T. Barnes *(Bath)* 75 minutes for Davies

Referee: R. C. Francis *(New Zealand)*

Scotland thrashed England by a record margin for the series between the two countries with a devastating onslaught in the second half after their forwards had subdued the heavier Englishmen during the first period, when four penalty goals from four attempts by Gavin Hastings outscored two efforts (out of six) by Andrew.

After the break the more athletic and mobile Scots took control and the final score did not flatter them, although it was not until the last quarter had almost started that they added to their score. Then the floodgates opened and brilliant tries came from Duncan (from a ruck set up by Rutherford and pass by Gavin Hastings), Rutherford (after English passing broke down and Calder and Laidlaw sent in the scorer) and Scott Hastings (after Baird had broken from defence and set up his forwards to send away Jeffrey, Rutherford and then the scorer himself). It was brilliant to watch – if you were Scottish or a neutral. Gavin Hastings converted all three superbly and also kicked another penalty-goal – eight successes from eight kicks and a record twenty one points. Another success in the match was the referee who again used common sense and allowed the game to flow. Well done Mr Francis!

Since 1946 England have beaten Scotland on twenty two occasions, Scotland have won thirteen times and six matches have been drawn. This was Scotland's eleventh win at Murrayfield during that period with three matches there drawn; England have won seven times there.

The score of 33-6 was a record winning margin for the fixture. Scotland's final points tally was also the highest recorded in the series between the countries, whilst the margin of twenty seven points also equalled the previous heaviest margin of defeat suffered by England, which was only in June 1985 in New Zealand in the Second International there (15-42).

Gavin Hastings' twenty one points are a Scottish scoring record in International Rugby. Rutherford and Laidlaw were appearing together for the twenty eighth time – a record for an International half-back pairing. Brewster, having gained three caps between 1977 and 1980 as a flanker, won another as a prop.

Fourth Matches
Saturday, 1st March 1986, at Twickenham

England	25	Ireland	20

Tries: Richards (2), Davies (1), penalty-try
Penalty-goal: Andrew
Conversions: Andrew (3)

Tries: Ringland, Mullin, McCall (1 each)
Penalty-goals: Kiernan (2)
Conversion: Kiernan
Half-time: 9-10

Back row *B. J. Spillane, A. P. Kennedy, D. C. Fitzgerald, B. W. McCall, D. G. Lenihan, R. K. Kearney, H. P. MacNeill, N. J.*

England: G. H. Davies; M. E. Harrison, K. G. Simms *(Liverpool)*, F. J. Clough *(Orrell and Cambridge University)*, R. Underwood; C. R. Andrew, N. D. Melville *(captain)*; G. J. Chilcott *(Bath)*, S. E. Brain, G. S. Pearce, P. J. Winterbottom, W. A. Dooley, M. J. Colclough, G. W. Rees *(Nottingham)*, D. Richards *(Leicester)*. *Replacement:* J. A. Palmer *(Bath)* for Simms, 31 minutes. *New caps:* Clough and Richards

Ireland: H. P. MacNeill; T. M. Ringland, M. J. Kiernan, B. J. Mullin, K. D. Crossan *(Instonians)*; R. P. Keyes *(Cork Constitution)*, M. T. Bradley; A. P. Kennedy, C. F. Fitzgerald *(captain)*, D. C. Fitzgerald, D. Morrow, B. W. McCall, D. G. Lenihan, N. J. Carr, B. J. Spillane. *New cap:* Keyes

Referee: C. Norling *(Wales)*

England's pack, after its mauling at Murrayfield, showed three changes and was too strong for a gallant Irish side which led at half-time. Two 'push-over' tries in the second half provided a memorable debut for Richards, who would have had another before half-time, but an Irish infringement saw a penalty-try awarded instead. England's other try came from a determined dash by Huw Davies after a weak Irish clearance. Irish tries came from Ringland, Mullin (put nicely away by Keyes after a good drive by Lenihan) and McCall, who charged down an attempted clearance by Melville near the end.

On a ground that was only passed fit for play late on the previous day, both teams produced good entertainment and England went on to Paris (two weeks later) with a chance of being Champions. Ireland this season had to settle for last place.

Of the forty matches played between the two countries since 1946 England have won eighteen, Ireland seventeen, and five have been drawn.

Carr, M. T. Bradley. Front row *B. J. Mullin, R. P. Keyes, T. M. Ringland, C. F. Fitzgerald (capt.), M. J. Kiernan, K. D. Crossan.*

Jean-Baptiste Lafond (France) scores the first of his two tries at Cardiff against Wales despite the attentions of Robert Jones and Bleddyn Bowen (in background).

Fourth Matches
Saturday, 1st March 1986, at National Stadium, Cardiff

Wales	15	France	23

Penalty-goals: Thorburn (5)
Half-time: 9-11

Tries: Lafond (2), Sella and Blanco (1 each)
Dropped-goal: Laporte
Conversions: Laporte (2)

Wales: P. H. Thorburn; M. Titley *(Swansea)*, J. A. Devereux, B. Bowen, A. M. Hadley; J. Davies, R. N. Jones; J. Whitefoot, W. J. James, I. H. Eidman, W. P. Moriarty, S. J. Perkins, D. R. Waters, D. F. Pickering *(captain)*, P. T. Davies. *No new caps*

France: S. Blanco; J.-B. Lafond, P. Sella, D. Charvet *(Toulouse)*, E. Bonneval *(Toulouse)*; G. Laporte, P. Berbizier; P. Marocco, D. Dubroca *(captain)*, J.-P. Garuet, D. Erbani, F. Haget, J. Condom, E. Champ, J.-L. Joinel. *New cap:* Charvet

Referee: J. B. Anderson *(Scotland)*

This was another victory for athleticism over sluggish opposition as a swift French side ran in four tries to none by the home team, who only once – when the game was virtually lost – threatened the French line; then Hadley was forced into touch near the corner post.

Before that France had scored two brilliant tries after fine combined work through Sella and Blanco; the other two, by Lafond, owed more to poor defensive work and good opportunism by the scorer. But from the early stages of the match the French pack had looked faster and more skilful, whilst the general work of the Welsh forwards was poor. With the kind of swift service enjoyed, the French backs were able to run freely and the scoring shows how well they did it on a cold but dry day on a firm but very playable ground. The Welsh backs with poor possession tried hard, but usually failed to beat the cover. Thorburn was their best player over the whole game.

This was France's nineteenth victory over Wales since 1946. Wales have won eighteen matches and three have been drawn.

Thorburn's fifty two points for Wales in the Championship are a record for the country. France scored their highest number of points against Wales in an International match. The last try scored against France in the Five Nations Championship was by Jim Calder (Scotland) on 17th March 1984 in the Grand Slam match.

Fifth Matches
Saturday, 15th March 1986, at Parc des Princes, Paris

France	29	England	10

Tries: Laporte, Blanco, Sella (1 each); penalty-try
Penalty-goals: Laporte (3)
Conversions: Laporte (2)

Try: Dooley
Penalty-goals: Barnes (2)
Half-time: 10-0

France: S. Blanco; J.-B. Lafond, P. Sella, D. Charvet, E. Bonneval; G. Laporte, P. Berbizier; P. Marocco, D. Dubroca *(captain)*, J.-P. Garuet, E. Champ, F. Haget, J. Condom, J.-L. Joinel, D. Erbani. *No new caps*

England: G. H. Davies; M. E. Harrison, K. G. Simms, F. J. Clough, R. Underwood; C. R. Andrew, N. D. Melville *(captain)*; G. J. Chilcott, S. E. Brain, G. S. Pearce, P. J. Winterbottom, W. A. Dooley, M. J. Colclough *(2nd captain)*, G. W. Rees, D. Richards. *Replacements:* R. J. Hill *(Bath)* for Melville, 20 minutes; S. Barnes for Davies, 32 minutes. *No new caps*

Referee: D. Bevan *(Wales)*

France were easy winners over an England team disrupted by injuries. England failed to take chances early in the match which might have given them a slim chance of providing a shock result. With just over thirty minutes gone, Melville and Davies had been replaced and France led by ten points, Andrew having missed four penalty chances for England. In the second half, France strolled to victory and scored three tries to add to the one by Laporte before the change-over. The second-half scorers were Blanco, a penalty-try awarded for a deliberate knock-on by Barnes near the England line, and Sella, after a glorious move started by Berbizier and continued by Laporte, Charvet and the scorer himself. England managed a try through Dooley after a line-out, but the visitors, as expected, were well beaten and France had earned at least a share of the Championship.

In forty matches between the two countries since 1946, France have won twenty times, there have been six draws and England have won fourteen times.

England were the only country to use any replacements during the current Championship – five in all, which is a record. They were the first country since 1946 to concede a century of points in the Championship and France (on 98) narrowly missed achieving that distinction in terms of points scored.

Sella (France) became only the fourth player to score a try in all four Championship matches. Others to perform the feat were H. C. Catcheside (England), A. C. Wallace (Scotland) and P. Estève (France). W. Dooley's try for England was the first against the French for two seasons.

P. Berbizier (Agen and France) passes from a scrum against England supported by Erbani and pursued by Hill (England).

Back row (left to right) *R. J. Hill (replacement), S. Barnes (replacement), J. A. Palmer (replacement), P. J. Winterbottom, D. Richards, W. A. Dooley, M. J. Colclough, G. S. Pearce, S. E. Brain, F. J. Clough, G. J. Chilcott, P. Cook (replacement),* *A. Simpson (replacement), P. A. G. Rendall (replacement). Front row (left to right) K. G. Simms, C. R. Andrew, M. E. Harrison, N. D. Melville (captain), R. Underwood, G. H. Davies, G. W. Rees.*

Fifth Matches

Saturday, 15th March 1986, at Lansdowne Road, Dublin

Ireland	9	Scotland	10

Try: Ringland
Penalty-goal: Kiernan
Conversion: Kiernan
Half-time: 9-0

Try: Laidlaw
Penalty-goals: G. Hastings
(2)

Ireland: H. P. MacNeill; T. M. Ringland, B. J. Mullin, M. J. Kiernan, K. D. Crossan; A. J. P. Ward (*Greystones*), M. T. Bradley; P. A. Orr, C. F. Fitzgerald (*captain*), D. C. Fitzgerald, R. D. Morrow, D. G. Lenihan, B. W. McCall, N. J. Carr, W. A. Anderson. *No new caps*

Scotland: A. G. Hastings; K. W. Robertson (*Melrose*), D. I. Johnston, S. Hastings, G. R. T. Baird; J. Y. Rutherford, R. J. Laidlaw; A. K. Brewster, C. T. Deans (*captain*), I. G. Milne, J. Jeffrey, A. J. Campbell, I. A. M. Paxton, F. Calder, J. R. Beattie. *No new caps*

Referee: F. Palmade (*France*)

Scotland won their share of the Championship the hard way. In a thrilling match against an Irish team showing much more commitment than in recent matches, they were rather lucky to win. A strong wind favoured Ireland in the first half, but Scotland failed narrowly to score two tries in the first twenty minutes through Baird and Paxton before Ireland, with Ward and Mullin outstanding, had an inspired spell and scored twice through a Kiernan penalty and a try by Ringland, which had been schemed by Ward and the hard running Mullin. Scotland did not make the best of their second-half wind advantage, but after two penalty-goals by Gavin Hastings – one from half-way – there was a marvellous individual try by Laidlaw, who dummied his way over from a scrum near the Irish '22'. The home team then applied pressure in the last fifteen minutes but Scottish luck plus some fine tackling, particularly by Rutherford, kept them out; a fairly easy penalty attempt by Kiernan went wide and Rutherford also missed with a dropped-goal attempt. Despite the low scoring, this was a very good match to watch and it was also played in a very good spirit even though exchanges were tough. The referee, Mr Palmade, was handling his last representative match and gave his usual efficient performance.

In thirty nine matches between the countries since 1946, Ireland have won on twenty four occasions, there has been one draw and Scotland have won on fourteen occasions.

P. A. Orr (Ireland), by making his fiftieth appearance for his country, equalled the world record for caps by a prop forward, which he holds jointly with A. B. Carmichael (Scotland). K. W. Robertson (Scotland) became the most capped player from Melrose by appearing for a thirty third occasion for his country.

G. Hastings by scoring fifty two points in the Championship set up a new record for Scotland. His missed conversion prevented him from equalling the Championship record of P. Lescarboura in 1984. R. Laidlaw (Scotland) scored his fifth try for his country – four of them against Ireland.

Trevor Ringland (Ireland) has Brendan Mullin and Michael Kiernan in support as he is tackled by Roger Baird (Scotland) and confronts Gavin Hastings. John Rutherford is in close pursuit.

Other Internationals

Bledisloe Cup
Saturday, 29th June 1985, at Eden Park, Auckland

New Zealand	10	Australia	9

Try: Green | *Try:* Black
Penalty-goals: Crowley (2) | *Penalty-goal:* Lynagh
Half-time: 6-3 | *Conversion:* Lynagh

New Zealand: K. Crowley; C. Green, S. Pokere, W. Taylor, J. Kirwan; W. Smith, D. Kirk; G. Knight, A. Dalton (*captain*), J. Ashworth, M. Shaw, M. Pierce, G. Whetton, J. Hobbs, M. Mexted. *Replacement:* A. Whetton for Shaw

Australia: R. Gould; P. Grigg, J. Black, T. Lane, M. Burke; M. Lynagh, N. Farr-Jones; E. Rodriguez, T. Lawton, A. McIntyre, S. Poidevin, S. Cutler, S. Williams (*captain*), D. Codey, S. Tuynman

Referee: D. I. H. Burnett (*Ireland*)

This dour and grim meeting was enlivened by a fine try mid-way through the second half after the Wallabies had snatched the lead earlier in the same period through a fine effort by Burke. Numerous players handled the ball from a tapped penalty (called by Dalton instead of a goal kick) before Green ran in the final pass from Hobbs. This was the best part of a match in which no chances were taken. Dalton was an outstanding captain for the All-Blacks and even saved his side from really bad late problems by taking a strike against the head.

'B' International
Sunday, 20th October 1985, at Sainte Foy la Grande

France 'B'	30	Wales 'B'	13

Tries: Delpoux (2), | *Try:* M. Jones
Peytavin, Bianchi (1 each) | *Dropped-goal:* John
Penalty-goals: Bianchi (2) | *Penalty-goal:* John
Conversions: Bianchi (4) | *Half-time:* 3-9

France 'B': J. Bianchi (*Toulon*); J.-M. Rancoule (*Toulouse*), D. Charvet (*Toulouse*), P. Chadebech (*Brive*), R. Peytavin (*Bayonne*); J.-M. Lescuré (*Narbonne*), G. Ramon (*Narbonne*) (*captain*); P. Marocco (*Montferrand*), C. Rizon (*Montferrand*), P. Laval (*Brive*), J.-P. Pelloux (*Nice*), P. Serrière (*RC Paris*), B. Delbreil (*Agen*), M. Delpoux (*Narbonne*), M. Cecillon (*Bourgoin*)

Wales 'B': P. Rees (*Cardiff*); I. Evans (*Llanelli*), D. Jacob (*Neath*), E. Jones (*South Wales Police*), A. Emyr (*Swansea*); G. John (*Bridgend*), R. Jones (*Swansea*); B. Williams (*Neath*), M. Richards (*Neath*) (*captain*), L. Delaney (*Llanelli*), D. Waters (*Newport*), K. Moseley (*Pontypool*), A. Hopkins (*Llanelli*), P. Moriarty (*Swansea*), M. Jones (*Neath*)

Referee: M. Megson (*Scotland*)

The score slightly flattered France, who only pulled away to their large score late in the game. Of those who played Charvet, Chadebech and Marocco played for France in Five Nations matches with R. Jones, Waters and P. Moriarty appearing for Wales. All played with distinction.

'B' International
Saturday, 7th December 1985, at Old Anniesland, Glasgow

Scotland 'B'	9	Italy 'B'	0

Try: Campbell-Lamerton | *Half-time:* 9-0
Penalty-goal: Cramb |
Conversion: Cramb |

Scotland 'B': S. Hastings (*Watsonians*); M. D. F. Duncan (*West of Scotland*), S. W. McAslan (*Heriot's FP*), S. Scott (*Stewart's-Melville FP*), A. V. Tait (*Kelso*); R. Cramb (*Harlequins*), S. G. Johnston (*Watsonians*); D. M. B. Sole (*Bath*), K. S. Milne (*Heriot's FP*), T. G. Waite (*Kelso*), H. M. Parker (*Kilmarnock*), J. R. E. Campbell-Lamerton (*London Scottish*), P. J. Hogarth (*Hawick*), C. B. S. Richardson (*Edinburgh Academicals*), A. J. Macklin (*London Scottish*)

Italy 'B': A. Bertoncini (*Placenza*); E. Venturi (*Rovigo*), S. Nardo (*Pardova*), C. Spalletta (*l'Aquila*), D. Marrama (*l'Aquila*); O. Albini (*Milano*), P. Spinazze (*Sandona*); M. D'Onofrio (*l'Aquila*), C. Pratichetti (*Milano*), M. Quaglio (*Rovigo*), P. Pedroni (*Milano*), B. D'Onofrio (*l'Aquila*), L. Pelliccione (*l'Aquila*), R. Corvo (*Roma*), R. Dolfato (*Treviso*). *Replacement:* M. Trevisol (*Treviso*) for Pelliccione, first half

Referee: M. Lamoulie (*France*)

International Trial, Scotland
Saturday, 4th January 1986, at Murrayfield

Blues	10	Reds	41

Try: Duncan | *Tries:* G. Hastings,
Penalty-goals: Dods (2) | S. Hastings, Calder, Leslie,
Half-time: 3-13 | Flannigan (1 each)
 | *Penalty-goals:* G. Hastings
 | (4), S. Hastings (1)
 | *Conversions:* G. Hastings (3)

Blues: P. W. Dods (*Gala*); M. D. F. Duncan (*West of Scotland*), K. W. Robertson (*Melrose*), D. I. Johnston (*Watsonians*), I. Tukalo (*Selkirk*); J. Y. Rutherford (*Selkirk*), R. J. Laidlaw (*Jed-Forest*); A. K. Brewster (*Stewart's-Melville FP*), C. T. Deans (*Hawick*) (*captain*), I. G. Milne (*Harlequins*), H. M. Parker (*Kilmarnock*), A. J. Tomes (*Hawick*), J. H. Calder (*Stewart's-Melville FP*), I. A. M. Paxton (*Selkirk*), J. Jeffrey (*Kelso*). *Replacement:* D. G. Leslie (*Dundee HSFP*) for Paxton (Leslie also played part of game for Reds)

Reds: A. G. Hastings (*Cambridge University*); S. W. McAslan (*Heriot's FP*), S. H. Scott (*Stewart's-Melville FP*), S. Hastings (*Watsonians*), G. R. T. Baird (*Kelso*); D. S. Wyllie (*Stewart's-Melville FP*), S. G. Johnston (*Watsonians*); D. M. B. Sole (*Bath*), G. J. Callander (*Kelso*) (*captain*), N. A. Rowan (*Boroughmuir*), A. J. Campbell (*Hawick*), J. R. E. Campbell-Lamerton (*London Scottish*), D. B. White (*Gala*), J. R. Beattie (*Glasgow Academicals*), F. Calder (*Stewart's-Melville FP*). *Replacement:* C. Flannigan (*Melrose*) for A. G. Hastings

Referee: B. Anderson (*Corstorphine*)

International Trial, Ireland
Saturday, 4th January 1986, at Lansdowne Road, Dublin

Ireland XV	21	Combined Provinces	12

Tries: Lenihan, Orr (1 each) *Try:* Anderson
Penalty-goals: Kiernan (3) *Penalty-goals:* Keyes (2)
Conversions: Kiernan (2) *Conversion:* Keyes
Half-time: 12-9

Ireland: H. P. MacNeill (*London Irish*); T. M. Ringland (*Ballymena*), M. J. Kiernan (*Dolphin*), B. J. Mullin (*Dublin University*), P. P. Haycock (*Terenure College*); P. M. Dean (*St Mary's College*), M. T. Bradley (*Cork Constitution*); P. A. Orr (*Old Wesley*), C. F. Fitzgerald (*St Mary's College*) (*captain*), J. J. McCoy (*Bangor*), P. M. Matthews (*Ards*), D. G. Lenihan (*Cork Constitution*), W. A. Anderson (*Dungannon*), R. K. Kearney (*Wanderers*), B. J. Spillane (*Bohemians*)

Combined Provinces: P. I. Rainey (*Ballymena*); J. F. Sexton (*Dublin University*), M. C. Finn (*Cork Constitution*), J. A. Hewitt (*NIFC*), R. L. Anderson (*London Irish*); R. P. Keyes (*Cork Constitution*), R. C. Brady (*Ballymena*); A. P. Kennedy (*London Irish*), H. T. Harbison (*Bective Rangers*), D. C. Fitzgerald (*Lansdowne*), D. P. Fanning (*St Mary's College*) (*captain*), B. W. McCall (*London Irish*), J. J. Holland (*Wanderers*), W. R. Duncan (*Malone*), R. D. Morrow (*Bangor*)

Referee: D. I. H. Burnett (*Irish Panel*)

FIRA Championship
Saturday, 15th February 1986, at Annecy

France 'A'	18	Italy	0

Tries: Rodriguez, Lorieux, Lagisquet (1 each) *Half-time:* 12-0
Conversions: Sallefranque (3)

France 'A': Dupuy (*Lombez-Samatan*); Jehl (*Toulon*), Codorniou (*Narbonne*), Bonneval (*Toulouse*), Lagisquet (*Bayonne*); Sallefranque (*Dax*), G. Camberabero (*La Voulte*); Cremaschi (*Tarbes*), Herrero (*Toulon*), Ondarts (*Biarritz*), Verdy (*Montferrand*), Picard (*Montferrand*), Lorieux (*Aix-les-Bains*), Rodriguez (*Mont-de-Marsan*), Orso (*Nice*). *Replacement:* Macabiau for Camberabero, 78 minutes

Italy: Trolani; Mascioletti, Franscescato, Zorzi, Ghizzoni; Bottarello, Fusco; Cucchiella, Morelli, Rossi, Artuzo, Gardin, Annibal, Innocenti, Colella. *Replacement:* Pavin for Artuso, 32 minutes

Referee: J. M. Fleming (*Scotland*)

'B' International
Sunday, 2nd March 1986, at Villefranche-sur-Saône

France 'B'	10	Scotland 'B'	12

Tries: Berot, Cecillon (1 each) *Penalty-goals:* Flannigan (4)
Conversion: Lescuré *Half-time:* 0-6

France 'B': J. Dupuy; P. Berot, A. Carbonnel, E. Blanc, M. Andrieu; J.-M. Lescuré, G. Ramon (*captain*); E. Alabarde, C. Rizon, P. Ondartz, K. Janik, J.-M. Cadieu, P. Pujade, M. Cecillon, M. Delpoux

Scotland 'B': C. Flannigan (*Melrose*); A. M. Thomson (*Kelso*), S. W. McAslan (*Heriot's FP*), S. H. Scott (*Stewart's-Melville FP*), A. V. Tait (*Kelso*); R. L. Cramb (*Harlequins*), S. G. Johnston (*Watsonians*); D. F. Milne (*Heriot's FP*),

J. G. Runciman (*Melrose*), T. G. Waite (*Kelso*), P. J. Hogarth (*Hawick*) (*captain*), H. M. Parker (*Kilmarnock*), J. S. Hamilton (*Heriot's FP*), A. J. Macklin (*London Scottish*), D. J. Turnbull (*Hawick*)

Referee: G. Simmons (*Wales*)

FIRA Championship
Sunday, 23rd March 1986, at Lisbon

Portugal	18	France 'A'	60

Try: Nuno Durao *Tries:* Malosse (5), Devergle
Penalty-goals: Queimado (4) (2), Beraud, Cecillon,
Conversions: Queimado Capelle, Cassagne,
Half-time: 3-32 Delpoux (1 each)
Conversions: Rui (5),
Dupuy (1)

Portugal: Rossano Garcia; Lupi, Belo, Viera de Almeida, Domingos Megre; Nuno Durao, Queimado; Nuno Morais, Luis Nunes, Faustino, A. Fereira, Jose Luis, P. Ferreira, Marques Pinto, Bernardo. *Replacements:* Luis Filipe for Nuno Morais, 19 minutes; Ricardo Durao for Rossano Garcia, 68 minutes

France 'A': Bianchi (*Toulon*); Malosse (*La Voulte*), Cassagne (*Bourgoin*), Codorniou (*Narbonne*), Lupuyau (*Dax*); Rui (*Castres*), Gallion (*Toulon*); Detrez (*Nîmes*), Herrero (*Toulon*), Ondarts (*Biarritz*), Delpoux (*Narbonne*), Devergie (*Nîmes*), Condom (*Boucau*), Cecillon (*Bourgoin*), Capelle (*Nîmes*). *Replacements:* Dupuy (*Lombez Samatan*) for Bianchi, 20 minutes; Beraud (*Dax*) for Delpoux, 40 minutes

Referee: M. Santi (*Italy*)

Romania v. Scotland
Saturday, 29th March 1986, at Bucharest

Romania	18	Scotland	33

Dropped-goal: Ignat *Tries:* Jeffrey, S. Hastings,
Penalty-goals: Ignat (5) Deans (1 each)
Half-time: 12-15 *Penalty-goals:* G. Hastings
(5)
Conversions: G. Hastings (3)

Romania: L. Hodorca; R. Voinov, A. Lungu, V. David, M. Toader; C. Ignat, M. Paraschiv (*captain*); S. Bucan, M. Munteanu, V. Pascu, F. Muriariu, G. Caragea, L. Constantin, V. Giuglea, S. Constantin. *Replacements:* V. Tufa for Munteanu, 72 minutes; N. Copil for Toader, 75 minutes

Scotland: A. G. Hastings (*Cambridge University, London Scottish*); M. D. F. Duncan (*West of Scotland*), D. I. Johnston (*Watsonians*), S. Hastings (*Watsonians*), G. R. T. Baird (*Kelso*); J. Y. Rutherford (*Selkirk*), R. J. Laidlaw (*Jed-Forest*); A. K. Brewster (*Stewart's-Melville FP*), C. T. Deans (*Hawick*) (*captain*), I. G. Milne (*Harlequins*), J. Jeffrey (*Kelso*), A. J. Campbell (*Hawick*), I. A. M. Paxton (*Selkirk*), F. Calder (*Stewart's-Melville FP*), J. R. Beattie (*Glasgow Academicals*)

Referee: R. C. Quittenton (*England*)

Scotland gained revenge for their defeat in the same stadium in May 1984 with a storming second-half display similar to that against England. Tries came from Jeffrey (after a break by Gavin Hastings and fine inside pass from Duncan), Scott Hastings (after Finlay Calder had collected a

Rutherford kick-off and passed) and Deans, whose second try for Scotland came after Voinov had failed to gather a Rutherford kick allowing Baird to collect and slip a scoring pass to his captain. This was the second time during the season that Scotland scored a total of thirty three points, and Gavin Hastings produced an exact repeat of his Murrayfield tally against England; his was another outstanding performance.

For the home team Ignat scored all the points and one of his penalties was a massive effort from inside his own half, but it was Scotland's afternoon in every other respect. It was also the third time in five seasons that Scotland have exceeded a score of thirty on opposition territory; the other occasions were in Cardiff in 1982 (34-18, against Wales) and in Dublin in 1984 (32-9, against Ireland).

England Under-23 v. Spain
Wednesday, 9th April 1986, at Twickenham

England Under-23	**15**	**Spain**	**10**
Penalty-goals: Barnes (5)		*Try:* Sainz	
Half-time: 3-6		*Penalty-goals:* Puertas (2)	

England Under-23: S. D. Hodgkinson (*Nottingham*); J. M. Goodwin (*Moseley*), K. G. Simms (*Liverpool, Cambridge University*), F. J. Clough (*Orrell, Cambridge University*), R. Underwood (*Leicester, RAF*); S. Barnes (*Bath*), S. M. Bates (*Wasps*); M. S. Linnett (*Moseley*), R. Howe (*Blackheath*), A. R. Mullins (*Durham University, Durham City*), T. Edbrook (*Exeter University*), N. C. Redman (*Bath*)

(*captain*), J. R. Howe (*Hartlepool Rovers*), R. A. Robinson (*Loughborough University, Bath*), D. Richards (*Leicester*)

Spain: F. Puertas (*Canoe NC*); R. Sainz (*CD Arquitectura*), G. Rivero (*Olímpico RC, Agen*), J. Azkargorta (*Guecho*), I. Oller (*UE Santboiana*); J. Moreno (*CD Arquitectura*), J. Díaz (*Getxo RT*); J. Alvárez (*El Salvador*), S. Santos (*Liceo Francés*) (*captain*), T. Pardo (*Valencia RC*), A. Malo (*UE Santboiana*), F. Méndez (*CR Cisneros*), F. Chocarro (*ATSS Sebastián*), S. Loughney (*FC Barcelona*), J. A. Egido (*Canoe NC*). Replacement: J. Urida Hidalgo (*Sporting de Gijon*) for Egido, 74 minutes

Referee: G. Simmons (*Welsh RU*)

Spain scored the only try near the end of this rather scrappy game and surprised many by their staunch display. Their tackling prevented an England Under-23 try, with Rivero outstanding in this respect. Had Puertas been on better kicking form there might have been a surprise result against a side containing six current England squad members.

In another match on the tour Spain lost to Devon & Cornwall at Torquay (30-6). Other players on the tour were: A. Trenzano (*BUC*), C. Encabo (*CD Arquitectura*), L. Núñez (*Olímpico RC*), G. Díaz (*Filosofía y Letras*), A. Ruiz (*Filosofía y Letras*), F. Blanco (*CD Arquitectura*). The team was managed by Sr M. Escoda with Srs J. M. Epalza and C. Murillo as coaches. Sr J. Geijo was physiotherapist and there were two other officials, Srs J. F. Santana and L. Freijido.

England Under-23 v. Spain at Twickenham, 9th April 1986: John Howe (England) is confronted by Javier Díaz (Spain's scrum-half).

France v. Romania

Saturday, 12th April 1986, at Lille

France	25	Romania	13

Tries: Bonneval, Charvet, Sella, Erbani, Lagisquet (1 each)
Penalty-goal: Laporte
Conversion: Laporte

Tries: David, Hodorca (1 each)
Penalty-goal: Ignat
Conversion: Ignat
Half-time: 11-9

France: S. Blanco (*Biarritz*); J.-B. Lafond (*Racing Club de France*), P. Sella (Agen), D. Charvet (*Toulouse*), E. Bonneval (*Toulouse*); G. Laporte (*Graulhet*), P. Berbizier (*Agen*); P. Marocco (*Montferrand*), D. Dubroca (*Agen*) (*captain*), J.-P. Garuet (*Lourdes*), E. Champ (*Toulon*), J. Condom (*Boucau*), F. Haget (*Biarritz*), D. Erbani (*Agen*), J.-L. Joinel (*Brive*). Replacements: P. Lagisquet (*Bayonne*) for Lafond, 19 minutes; T. Picard (*Montferrand*) for Champ, 55 minutes. *No new caps*

Romania: L. Hodorca; M. Toader, A. Lungu, V. David, G. Varzaru; G. Ignat, T. Coman; F. Opris, M. Mot, V. Pascu, F. Muriariu (*captain*), L. Constantin, G. Caragea, M. Giucal, S. Constantin. *Replacement:* R. Voinov for Hodorca, 66 minutes

Referee: M. Waldron (*Australia*)

Romania, with five changes from the team beaten in Bucharest by Scotland, put up a gallant effort and even led by 13 points to 11 with three-quarters of the match completed, before the French recovered their form and scored three late tries to gain their expected victory. Romania were well led by the veteran Muriariu and were much better than they had appeared against the Scots two weeks earlier, so much so that their World Cup prospects looked less futile than before. The French displayed in the end their usual *élan* on a cold and unpleasant day. Sella's try was his fifth in five 1986 matches for France, who conceded two tries themselves for the first time this year.

The Rest v. British Lions at Cardiff, 16th April 1986: Back row (left to right) *D. I. H. Burnett (touch judge), R. C. Francis (referee), H. E. Botha, D. M. Gerber (replacements), M. G. Mexted, S. N. Tuynman (replacement), N. C. Farr-Jones, S. A. G. Cutler, E. E. Rodriguez, P. R. van der Merwe (replacement),*

IB Centenary Celebration

Wednesday, 16th April 1986, at National Ground, Cardiff

British Lions	7	Rest of the World	15

Try: Beattie
Penalty-goal: Hastings
Half-time: 7-6

Tries: Farr-Jones, Poidevin (1 each)
Penalty-goal: Lynagh
Conversions: Lynagh (2)

British Lions: A. G. Hastings (*Cambridge University, London Scottish, Scotland*); T. M. Ringland (*Ballymena, Ireland*), B. J. Mullin (*Dublin University, Ireland*), J. A. Devereux (*South Glamorgan Institute, Wales*), R. Underwood (*Leicester, RAF, England*); J. Y. Rutherford (*Selkirk, Scotland*), R. J. Jones (*Swansea, Wales*); J. Whitefoot (*Cardiff, Wales*), C. T. Deans (*Hawick, Scotland*) (*captain*), D. C. Fitzgerald (*Lansdowne, Ireland*), J. Jeffrey (*Kelso, Scotland*), W. A. Dooley (*Preston Grasshoppers, England*), D. G. Lenihan (*Cork Constitution, Ireland*), J. R. Beattie (*Glasgow Academicals, Scotland*), N. J. Carr (*Ards, Ireland*). Replacements: I. A. M. Paxton (*Selkirk, Scotland*) for Dooley, 30 minutes; M. Dacey (*Swansea, Wales*) for Rutherford, 40 minutes

Rest of the World: S. Blanco (*Biarritz, France*); J. J. Kirwan (*Auckland, New Zealand*), A. G. Slack (*Queensland, Australia*) (*captain*), M. P. Lynagh (*Queensland, Australia*), P. Estève (*Narbonne, France*); W. R. Smith (*Canterbury, New Zealand*); N. C. Farr-Jones (*New South Wales, Australia*), E. E. Rodriguez (*New South Wales, Australia*), T. A. Lawton (*Queensland, Australia*), G. A. Knight (*Manawatu, New Zealand*), M. W. Shaw (*Manawatu, New Zealand*), S. A. G. Cutler (*New South Wales, Australia*), S. W. P. Burger (*Western Province, South Africa*), S. P. Poidevin (*New South Wales, Australia*), M. G. Mexted (*Wellington, New Zealand*)

Referee: R. C. Francis (*New Zealand*). Touch judges: C. Norling (*Wales*), C. A. Waldron (*Australia*)

On a very wet evening, attempts at an open game, especially by the visiting team, were mainly thwarted by the conditions, but the Rest did score two good tries; Blanco, with fine initial runs, set up both of them. The first followed a five-metre

T. A. Lawton, S. W. P. Burger, G. A. Knight, P. Estève, A. G. Dalton (replacement), R. Quittenton, C. Norling (touch judges). Front row (left to right) *J. J. Kirwan, M. P. Lynagh, R. I. Templeton (manager), A. G. Slack (captain), B. J. Lochore (coach), M. W. Shaw, W. R. Smith, S. Blanco.*

Five Nations v. Overseas Unions at Twickenham, 19th April 1986: Back row (left to right) *D. C. T. Rowlands (manager), C. T. Deans (replacement), I. G. Milne, D. C. Fitzgerald (replacement), J. Jeffrey, L. Rodriguez, I. A. M. Paxton, J. Condom, J. R. Beattie (replacement), J. Whitefoot, C. Norling (referee), S. E. Brain.* Front row (left to right) *A. G. Hastings (replacement), T. M. Ringland, M. Dacey, R. Underwood, R. J. Hill, D. G. Lenihan (captain), M. J. Kiernan, S. Blanco, P. Sella, J. Fouroux (coach).* Sitting *R. N. Jones, B. J. Mullin.*

scrum and Farr-Jones went over from clean possession. For the second, Estève started the movement, which was continued well by Blanco, whose inside pass was touched down efficiently by Poidevin. For the Lions, Beattie finished off a move that involved several forwards after a period of pressure by the home team.

For the most part, the visitors were too strong in the scrums. They dominated the line-outs once Dooley had departed injured, even though Paxton had a thoroughly good game in other respects, as did Jeffrey. Outside the scrum, Ringland was the best Lions player. Farr-Jones was an excellent scrum-half for the Rest and received good support from Lynagh, Blanco and Slack, whilst Rodriguez, Knight, Cutler, Mexted and Poidevin in the pack (among an excellent combination) were immense.

IB Centenary Celebration
Saturday, 19th April 1986, at Twickenham

Five Nations	13	Overseas Unions	32

Tries: Kiernan, Ringland (1 each)
Penalty-goal: Kiernan
Conversion: Blanco
Half-time: 7-10

Tries: Gerber (2), Kirwan, Du Plessis, Rodriguez, Shaw (1 each)
Penalty-goals: Botha (2)
Conversion: Botha

Five Nations XV: S. Blanco (*Biarritz, France*); T. M. Ringland (*Ballymena, Ireland*), P. Sella (*Agen, France*), M. J. Kiernan (*Dolphin, Ireland*), R. Underwood (*Leicester, RAF, England*); M. Dacey (*Swansea, Wales*), R. J. Hill (*Bath, England*); J. Whitefoot (*Cardiff, Wales*), S. E. Brain (*Coventry, England*), I. G. Milne (*Harlequins, England*), J. Jeffrey (*Kelso, Scotland*), D. G. Lenihan (*Cork Constitution, Ireland*) (*captain*), J. Condom (*Boucau, France*), L. Rodriguez (*Mont de Marsan, France*), I. A. M. Paxton (*Selkirk, Scotland*)

Overseas Unions XV: R. G. Gould (*Queensland, Australia*); J. Kirwan (*Auckland, New Zealand*), D. M. Gerber (*Eastern Province, South Africa*), W. T. Taylor (*Canterbury, New Zealand*), C. J. Du Plessis (*Western Province, South Africa*); H. E. Botha (*Northern Transvaal, South Africa*), D. S. Loveridge (*Taranaki, New Zealand*), E. E. Rodriguez (*New South Wales, Australia*), A. G. Dalton (*Counties, New Zealand*) (*captain*), P. R. Van Der Merwe (*Western Transvaal, South Africa*), S. P. Poidevin (*New South Wales, Australia*), A. M. Haden (*Auckland, New Zealand*), S. A. G. Cutler (*New South Wales, Australia*), M. W. Shaw (*Manawatu, New Zealand*), S. N. Tuynman (*New South Wales, Australia*)

Referee: D. I. H. Burnett (*Ireland*). *Touch judges:* C. Norling (*Wales*), C. A. Waldron (*Australia*)

In perfect conditions both sides gave a fine exhibition of open Rugby. However, the superior weight and forward skills of the men from the southern hemisphere were too much for the Europeans in the second half, when five magnificent tries were scored with the Five Nations replying right on the final whistle through Ringland.

In the opening half, an early home thrust led to Underwood going over, but he was recalled because of an earlier infringement. Soon Kiernan converted a penalty award which was countered by Botha within two minutes. Fine work by Paxton, Jeffrey, Underwood, Blanco and Ringland led to Kiernan just squeezing over after twenty three minutes; but then the visitors showed their mettle with a fine try by Gerber putting the finishing touches to great work by the whole team.

In the second half, Kirwan, through determined running, finished off a move involving Loveridge, Botha and Taylor. Then with similar expertise, the same combination sent in from behind their own line the excellent Du Plessis for another try before two fine forward drives produced tries by Rodriguez and Shaw. In between, the southerners ran a ball from their own half and a superb sprint and inside pass from Kirwan brought Gerber's second try with forward power assisting the final drive.

It was wonderful stuff and the atheleticism of the southern team was awe-inspiring with Gerber outshining the best centre in Europe, Sella, who nevertheless tackled bravely along with Blanco.

TOURS

Scotland Tour of Canada

Any team that tours a minor Rugby-playing country is on the proverbial 'hiding to nothing'. Victories are to be expected and if they are by relatively small margins they amount to disasters. Defeats are positive calamities. Scotland in Canada met all three problems and it is difficult to comment objectively on this tour for that reason. Tours of this nature must take place so that the other countries can better themselves; when local teams cause shocks they are to be applauded rather than the losers being chastised.

Scotland's first two matches, both in British Columbia, were a disaster followed by calamity. First Vancouver Island put up stiff resistance and then the home province made an astonishing recovery to swamp the Scots in an inspired second-half spell of thoroughly good Rugby, for which they deserve congratulations.

It was to the credit of the visitors that they were able to shake themselves and win the remaining three matches by one huge, one massive and one overwhelming margin, and self-respect was partially restored. The opposition was weak by now and the Scots did not allow their opponents 'off the hook'.

Even in the match that was lost, the Scottish forwards were generally far too strong for their opponents and Leslie is to be applauded for playing in all five matches, in which he scored four tries. Other forwards did as expected of them, but good line-out men are still absent from the Scottish game.

The backs had two stars amongst their number in Hastings and Tukalo. The former was outstanding on the tour in the four matches he played at full-back, while Tukalo was the other player apart from his captain to play in every match and his six tries were a just reward for some clever running. Dods scored seventy five points on tour, which was a Scottish touring record, but he took a long time to find his best form and was seen to the most advantage when playing on the right-wing. For the rest, it became clear that prayers should be said for the continued good health of John Rutherford, Keith Robertson, Gordon Hunter and Roger Baird, who all missed the tour.

Date	Opponents	Venue	Result
8th May	Victoria Island	Victoria Island	W 20-10
11th May	British Columbia	Vancouver	L 13-22
14th May	Pacific Coast Grizzlies	Seattle	W 32-6
18th May	Canadian Wolverines	Edmonton	W 62-6
22nd May	Alberta President's XV	Calgary	W 79-0

Match summary: P 5 W 4 L 1 F 206 A 44

1st Match
Wednesday, 8th May 1985, at Victoria Island

Vancouver Island	10	Scotland	20

Try: Cardinal
Penalty-goals: Wyatt (2)
Half-time: 10-10

Tries: I. Milne, Leslie, Tukalo (1 each)
Penalty-goals: Dods (2)
Conversion: Dods

Vancouver Island: M. Allen; P. Monaghan, M. McDowell, G. Prevost, J. Olsen; M. Wyatt, T. White; G. Dukelow, M. Cardinal, P. Kyle, H. de Goede *(captain)*, M. Felix, M. Moss, R. Frame, B. Miles. *Replacement:* K. Straith for McDowell, 66 minutes

Scotland: A. G. Hastings; P. E. Dods, A. V. Tait, K. T. Murray, I. Tukalo; A. B. M. Ker, D. A. Macdonald; N. A. Rowan, K. S. Milne, I. G. Milne, H. M. Parker, T. J. Smith, D. J. Turnbull, S. K. McGaughey, D. G. Leslie *(captain)*

Referee: C. Parrish *(Vancouver)*

Scotland were very nearly embarrassed in this opening match winning only late in the game with tries by Leslie and Tukalo. Earlier, they had been held well by a brave home side, for whom Wyatt was outstanding as were the whole of the pack with Kyle performing bravely against the formidable Iain Milne, as did Dukelow against Rowan. The second phase for Scotland needed a great improvement.

2nd Match
Saturday, 11th May 1985, at Vancouver

British Columbia	22	Scotland	13

Tries: Palmer (2), Cardinal (1)
Penalty-goals: Wyatt (2)
Conversions: Wyatt (2)

Try: Steven
Penalty-goals: Dods (2), Gass (1)
Half-time: 3-3

British Columbia: T. MacTavish; M. Iannone, S. MacTavish, P. Vason, P. Palmer; M. Wyatt, I. Stuart; G. Dukelow, M. Cardinal, P. Kyle, R. Hindson, H. de Goede *(captain)*, J. Donaldson, R. Frame, W. McKinnon

Scotland: P. W. Dods; P. D. Steven, B. Edwards, D. S. Wyllie,

I. Tukalo; C. W. Gass, D. Bryson; A. K. Brewster, R. Cunningham, I. G. Milne, A. J. Campbell, A. J. Tomes, J. Jeffrey, D. G. Leslie *(captain)*, I. A. M. Paxton

Referee: K. Morrison *(Vancouver)*

This was one of the most embarrassing defeats ever suffered by a Scottish team and it was one for which no excuses can be made. After a level-scoring first half, by which time the Scots should have been well ahead, the visitors then went into a seven-point lead only to allow the spirited Canadians back into the game with a vengeance to score three tries, two converted by Wyatt, and a penalty-goal by Wyatt. In reply the Scots could only manage one penalty-goal by Gass.

The Canadians deserve all credit for this fine performance, but clearly some Scottish players were stale and should have taken the summer off. Dods in particular had a poor match and his future International career must have been in doubt after this.

The Canadian tries were excellent during their spell of superiority in the second half. First, Palmer rounded off a ten-man move initiated by Vason; then Wyatt made a break, which ended with Cardinal scoring a second try (also his second in as many matches). With Scotland trying to recover at 13-16 down, Palmer appeared again to score in injury time for Wyatt to convert as he had done with Cardinal's try. The score reflected the fine work by him and every player, particularly de Goede, Hindson and Kyle.

3rd Match
Tuesday, 14th May 1985, at Seattle

Pacific Coast Grizzlies	6	Scotland	32
Penalty-goals: Inns (2)		*Tries:* Tukalo, Campbell,	
Half-time: 6-6		K. Milne, Tomes (1 each)	
		Penalty-goals: Hastings (4)	
		Conversions: Hastings (2)	

Pacific Coast Grizzlies: M. Inns; K. Higgins, D. Shanagher, T. Sammet, B. Williams; B. Meyersieck, J. Nikel; D. Ochs, J. Everett, J. Jellaco, A. Ward, E. Burlingham *(captain)*, P. Deddeh, B. Vizzard, W. Zimmerman. *Replacement:* B. Malinowskiy for Ochs, half-time

Scotland: A. G. Hastings; P. D. Steven, K. T. Murray, D. S. Wyllie, I. Tukalo; A. B. M. Ker, D. Bryson; A. K. Brewster, K. S. Milne, I. G. Milne, T. J. Smith, A. J. Tomes, D. J. Turnbull, D. G. Leslie *(captain)*, J. Jeffrey. *Replacement:* A. J. Campbell for Jeffrey, 29 minutes

Referee: I. Nixon *(Texas)*

This was a better performance by Scotland but even so the team took time to settle; by the second half when all the tries were scored they were well on top.

The success was due in the main to forward

domination, and Iain Milne was in such superb form that his opposite number retired at half-time having been so badly outplayed. Hastings at full-back was the best player behind the scrum, where the others yet again tended to over-elaborate on a narrow pitch, thus allowing time and opportunities for the tacklers to close down potentially dangerous situations. When the pack played to their basic strengths it was a different story as the four tries confirm.

Hastings's contribution was sixteen points – half the total score.

4th Match
Saturday, 18th May 1985, at Edmonton

Canadian Wolverines	6	Scotland	62
Penalty-goals: Hariyama (2)		*Tries:* Hastings (2), Paxton	
Half-time: 0-32		(2), Leslie (2), Rowan,	
		Tukalo, Cunningham,	
		Edwards, Macdonald (1	
		each)	
		Penalty-goals: Dods (2)	
		Conversions: Dods (6)	

Canadian Wolverines: M. Shifler; K. Karwandy, R. O'Hagan, J. Mooney, S. Gray; G. Hariyama, I. St Clair; W. Spoffard, G. Scott, P. Kyle, H. de Goede *(captain)*, D. Prunty, G. McKinnon, B. Dickson, T. Sinclair. *Replacements:* P. Trelawney for Mooney; D. Holland for Dickson

Scotland: A. G. Hastings; P. W. Dods, D. S. Wyllie, B. Edwards, I. Tukalo; C. W. Gass, D. A. Macdonald; A. K. Brewster, R. Cunningham, N. A. Rowan, H. M. Parker, A. J. Tomes, S. K. McGaughey, D. G. Leslie *(captain)*, I. A. M. Paxton

Scotland at last showed some form against a team that might have accurately been described as Canada 'C'. A crowd of 3,500 saw them score five tries before half-time and six more after the break.

In every aspect of the game the Scots were superior and for once the backs combined well, with Hastings the best of many good performers. The forwards were so superior that they contributed six of the tries – two from the front-row!

5th Match
Wednesday, 22nd May 1985, at Calgary

Alberta	0	Scotland	79
Half-time: 0-19		*Tries:* Dods (4), Tukalo (3),	
		Jeffrey (2), Hastings (2),	
		Leslie, Tait (1 each)	
		Penalty-goal: Dods	
		Conversions: Dods (12)	

Alberta: M. Brister; J. Foster, H. Davis, R. Lesage, J. Disturnal; P. Trelawny, M. Hannigan; J. Williams, J. Vivian, D. Fulton, D. Holland, J. Kemp, P. Paxton, J. Goldgrabe, C. Ogilvy *(captain)*

Scotland: A. G. Hastings; P. W. Dods, A. V. Tait, K. T.

Murray, I. Tukalo; C. W. Gass, D. A. Macdonald; A. K. Brewster, K. S. Milne, I. G. Milne, A. J. Campbell, A. J. Tomes, S. K. McGaughey, D. G. Leslie (*captain*), J. Jeffrey

Referee: A. Piggott (Ontario)

This match was so one-sided that objective comment on it would be misleading. Scotland were so superior that they might even have reached a century of points had the referee not blown for time after seventy five minutes! Even so, the score equalled Scotland's previous record margin for a tour match (Thailand were beaten 82-3 in 1977), and Dods, with four tries, one penalty-goal and twelve conversions, set up a record for an individual of forty three points.

The Gala man, normally a full-back, revelled in the opportunities given to him and even managed to overcome the place-kicking stutter which had haunted him since the Grand Slam days of 1984. After four early misses he found his touch and his four tries showed that perhaps he could emulate Bruce Hay in future and play as a wing, thus allowing Hastings a place as the International full-back. Tukalo was another star of this match and must add to his single cap next season. The forwards encountered no opposition and were just not tested.

For the record, Scotland scored only three tries before half-time – by Jeffrey (a push-over), Tukalo and Leslie. Thereafter, tries were scored at will, frequently as a result of poor Alberta kicking-off and Dods in this period alone scored his four tries and converted all ten that were scored.

Scotland Tour of Canada

Backs	Appearances Representative	Scores PG	DG	C	T	Pts
P. W. Dods *(Gala)*	4	7		19	4	75
D. Bryson *(Gala)*	2					
B. Edwards *(Boroughmuir)*	2				1	4
C. W. Gass *(Hawick)*	3	1				3
A. G. Hastings *(Cambridge University, Watsonians)*	4	4		2	4	32
A. B. M. Ker *(Kelso)*	2					
D. A. Macdonald *(Musselburgh)*	3				1	4
K. T. Murray *(Hawick)*	3					
P. D. Steven *(Heriot's FP)*	2				1	4
A. V. Tait *(Kelso)*	2				1	4
I. Tukalo *(Selkirk)*	5				6	24
D. S. Wyllie *(Stewart's-Melville FP)*	3					
Forwards						
D. G. Leslie *(Gala) (captain)*	5				4	16
A. K. Brewster *(Stewart's-Melville FP)*	4					
A. J. Campbell *(Hawick)*	2(1)				1	4
R. Cunningham *(Bath)*	2				1	4
J. Jeffrey *(Kelso)*	3				2	8
S. K. McGaughey *(Hawick)*	3					
I. G. Milne *(Harlequins)*	4				1	4
K. S. Milne *(Heriot's FP)*	3				1	4
H. M. Parker *(Kilmarnock)*	2					
I. A. M. Paxton *(Selkirk)*	2				2	8
N. A. Rowan *(Boroughmuir)*	2				1	4
T. J. Smith *(Gala)*	2					
A. J. Tomes *(Hawick)*	4				1	4
D. J. Turnbull *(Hawick)*	2					
Totals		12		21	32	206

Figures in brackets are for appearances as a replacement

Tour Officials
D. G. Leslie *(Gala)*, captain; G. B. Masson *(North District)*, manager; C. M. Telfer *(Hawick)*, coach; D. Grant *(Hawick)*, assistant coach

Uncapped players
Gass, Hastings, Bryson, Macdonald, Ker and Tait (backs); K. S. Milne, Parker and Turnbull (forwards)

Ireland Tour of Japan

By scoring thirty three tries in five matches, including eight in the first of the International matches, Ireland showed (as France were to do later) that Japan are not yet ready for proper International Rugby matches. All five matches were won easily enough and Kiernan created an Irish record by scoring twenty five points in the Second Test.

Date	Opponents	Venue	Result
19th May	Kanto Select	Marioka	W 42-15
22nd May	Japan Select	Sendai	W 34-10
26th May	JAPAN	Osaka	W 48-13
29th May	Kansai Select	Kansai	W 44-13
2nd June	JAPAN	Tokyo	W 33-15
Match summary:	P 5	W 5	F 201 A 66

Appearances
Backs: M. C. Finn 5 (2 Tests), H. P. MacNeill 4 (2 Tests), M. J. Kiernan 4 (2 Tests), K. D. Crossan 4 (2 Tests), B. J. Mullin 4 (2 Tests), P. M. Dean 3 (2 Tests), M. T. Bradley 3 (2 Tests), R. P. Keyes 2 (1 replacement, 2nd Test), R. C. Brady 2 (1 replacement, 2nd Test), M. C. Finn 2, P. A. Rainey 2

Forwards: P. Kenny 4, 1 replacement (2 Tests), W. A. Anderson 4 (2 Tests), P. M. Matthews 3 (2 Tests), P. A. Orr 3 (2 Tests), C. F. Fitzgerald (captain) 3 (2 Tests), D. G. Lenihan 3 (2 Tests), B. J. Spillane 3 (2 Tests), J. J. McCoy 3 (2 Tests), B. W. McCall 3, P. Collins 3, M. P. Fitzpatrick 2, P. A. Kennedy 2, H. T. Harbison 2, N. J. Carr 2

Scorers
Tries: Ringland 6 (3 in Tests), Matthews 4 (2 in Tests), Mullin 3 (1 in Tests), Kiernan 3 (all in Tests), MacNeill 2 (1 in Tests), Finn 2, Crossan 2, Rainey 2, Collins 2, Bradley 1, Hewitt 1, Orr 1, Fitzgerald 1 (in Tests), McCoy 1, Anderson 1 (in Tests), Spillane 1

Penalty-goals: Kiernan 5 (all in Tests), Keyes 2

Conversions: Kiernan 19 (9 in Tests), Keyes 5

Leading points scorers: Kiernan 65 (45 in Tests), Ringland 24 (12 in Tests)

1st Match
Sunday, 19th May 1985, at Marioka

Kanto Select XV	15	Ireland	42

Tries: Kasai (2)
Penalty-goal: Mukai
Conversions: Mukai (2)
Half-time: 9-22

Tries: Crossan (2), Ringland, Spillane, Collins, Bradley, Orr, Finn (1 each)
Conversions: M. Kiernan (5)

Kanto Select: S. Mukai; T. Wakaayashi, A. Kaneko, S. Ishikawa, T. Higano; K. Iida, K. Sakashita; M. Tsuchida, Y. Kasai, T. Tsuchiya, T. Kikuhi, H. Taione, M. Aizawa, N. Tada, T. Nakano

Ireland: H. P. MacNeill; T. M. Ringland, M. C. Finn, M. J. Kiernan, K. D. Crossan; P. M. Dean, M. T. Bradley; P. A. Orr, C. F. Fitzgerald (captain), M. P. Fitzpatrick, D. G. Lenihan, B. W. McCall, P. Kenny, P. Collins, B. J. Spillane

Referee: W. D. Bevan (Wales)

The Irish tourists with a very strong selection were too strong for the home team and scored eight tries – five before half-time. The local side rallied well against the odds and Kasai scored two good tries, both of which Mukai (a brave full-back) converted; he also kicked a penalty-goal.

2nd Match
Wednesday, 22nd May 1985, at Sendai

Japan Select XV	10	Ireland	34

Tries: Muria, Tsuchida (1 each)
Conversion: Kitsukawa
Half-time: 6-20

Tries: Mullin (2), Matthews (2), MacNeill, McCoy (1 each)
Conversions: Kiernan (5)

Japan Select: D. Murai, T. Wakabayashi, M. Kikukawa, J. Ikeno, I. Sato; H. Kuchiki, K. Kodama; T. Nagayama, T. Nishii, T. Kimura, K. Suzuki, A. Kono, K. Tsuchiya, Y. Kasai, M. Tsuchida

Ireland: P. I. Rainey; H. P. MacNeill, M. J. Kiernan, B. J. Mullin, K. D. Crossan; R. P. Keyes, R. C. Brady; P. Kennedy, H. T. Harbison, J. J. McCoy, W. A. Anderson, B. W. McCall, P. Collins, P. M. Matthews (captain), N. J. Carr. *Replacement:* P. Kenny for Carr, 53 minutes

Referee: M. Howard (New Zealand)

Ireland won easily enough against enthusiastic but less than skilful opposition, and they did take time after the change-round to add substantially to their score. The best Irish performers were Crossan and Mullin, but Matthews, captaining for this game, did much effective spoiling work and also scored two tries.

3rd Match, First International
Sunday, 26th May 1985, at Osaka

Japan	13	Ireland	48

Tries: Konishi, Ishiyama (1 each)
Penalty-goal: Honjo
Conversion: Honjo

Tries: Ringland (3), Matthews (2), MacNeill, Kiernan, Fitzgerald (1 each)
Penalty-goals: Kiernan (2)
Conversions: Kiernan (5)

Japan: S. Mukai; S. Onuki, T. Yoshino, S. Hirao, D. Murai; K. Honjo, Y. Konishi; J. Ishiyama, T. Fujita, K. Horaguchi (captain), M. Koshiyama, A. Oyagi, T. Hayashi, M. Senda, Y. Kawase

Ireland: H. P. MacNeill; T. M. Ringland, B. J. Mullin, M. J. Kiernan, K. D. Crossan; P. M. Dean, M. T. Bradley; P. A. Orr, C. F. Fitzgerald (captain), J. J. McCoy, D. G. Lenihan, W. A. Anderson, P. M. Matthews, P. Kenny, B. J. Spillane

Referee: W. D. Bevan (Wales)

Ireland had their largest win in International Rugby and did so against inadequate opposition, which was very disappointing. Eight tries for the visitors told their tale of total superiority and there was no weak link in the Irish ranks with Ringland and Matthews outstanding. Even so, the Irish coach considered that the line-out play might have been improved, but it would have needed stronger opponents to bring such a change.

4th Match
Wednesday, 29th May 1985, at Kansai

Kansai Select	13	Ireland	44

Try: Y. Furui
Penalty-goals: Y. Yamakita (3)

Tries: Ringland (2), Rainey (2), Finn, Collins, Hewitt (1 each)
Penalty-goals: Keyes (2)
Conversions: Keyes (5)

Kansai Select: N. Kido; S. Shimosaka, M. Tamura, T. Fukui, U. Sugano; Y. Yamakita, N. Hagimoto; K. Munakumo, M. Nakatani, N. Kasamutsu, H. Takahashi, K. Kawaji, H. Matsuda, K. Nakayama, T. Kimura. *Replacement:* Y. Furui for Shimosaka

Ireland: P. I. Rainey; T. M. Ringland, B. J. Mullin, J. Hewitt, M. C. Finn; R. P. Keyes; R. C. Brady; P. A. Kennedy, H. T. Harbison, M. P. Fitzpatrick, B. W. McCall, W. A. Anderson, P. Collins, N. J. Carr, P. Kenny

Referee: N. Mashimo *(Japan)*

This was all too easy for Ireland who dominated every phase of the game with Ringland increasing his try tally for the tour to six. Rainey scored another two and the outside-half, Keyes, contributed sixteen points with his kicking. The replacement wing, Yasihuro Furui, scored the Japanese team's only try, but the visitors in their turn scored seven.

5th Match, Second International
Sunday, 2nd June 1985, at Tokyo

Japan	15	Ireland	33

Tries: Mukai, Onuki (1 each)
Penalty-goal: Kobayashi
Conversions: Kobayashi (2)
Half-time: 12-12

Tries: Kiernan (2), Mullin, Anderson (1 each)
Penalty-goals: Kiernan (3)
Conversions: Kiernan (4)

Japan: S. Mukai; S. Onuki, T. Yoshino, H. Kobayashi, D. Murai; S. Harao, Y. Konishi; I. Shiyama, T. Fujita, K. Horaguchi *(captain)*, T. Hayashi, A. Oyagi, M. Koshiyama, M. Chida, T. Kawse

Ireland: H. P. MacNeill; T. M. Ringland, B. J. Mullin, M. J. Kiernan, K. D. Crossan; P. M. Dean, M. T. Bradley; P. A. Orr, C. F. Fitzgerald *(captain)*, J. J. McCoy, W. A. Anderson, D. G. Lenihan, P. M. Matthews, P. Kenny, B. J. Spillane. *Replacements:* R. C. Brady for Bradley, R. P. Keyes for Dean

Referee: W. D. Bevan *(Wales)*

Japan really made Ireland fight on this occasion, but a splendid personal effort by Kiernan eventually beat them off. The Irish centre scored twenty five points – an Irish record for an International match – from two tries, three penalties and four conversions. Even so, it was all closer than it seemed after an even first half, when both sides scored two converted tries.

In the end, the superior Irish pack and Kiernan repulsed the brave home challenge, but for once Ringland did not appear amongst the scorers and the fact that only four tries were scored by Ireland was a testimony to greatly improved Japanese defence. Two tries against Ireland were more than Scotland, Wales and England had managed in the Five Nations tournament this year!

England Tour of New Zealand

England have now made three tours to New Zealand and have won only one International out of five; that happened in 1973, when the other matches there were all lost. This time England won all but one of the non-Internationals (losing badly to Auckland) but lost both Tests. Even so the first of the two was lost on a try-count of two to nil in England's favour and it was only when New Zealand had re-grouped their unchanged team that a real rout followed. So it would be fair to say that the tour was not a disaster. England, at the moment, have no means of mounting a real challenge to a full-strength and properly 'tuned-up' New Zealand team, which is ominous. The tour party was probably the best available yet inferior to the home opposition when the real test came.

The biggest problems of the tour arose mainly from the back play, especially at full-back, where Martin had a sad tour after two poor home games against Wales and Ireland, at least in terms of errors made. The unfortunate Metcalfe was unable to take his chance and win his first caps. The centre play was at its best quite good and no more whilst the half-backs, Barnes in particular, could be said to have earned credit marks, although Hill showed that he needed to exercise more personal discipline on the field. Melville was sound and, at times, quite inspiring, but again he suffered more than his share of injuries. The wings did all that was asked of them, and Harrison, with five tries, can look back on his efforts with satisfaction. Goodwin was unlucky with injuries and unable to play a full part, whilst Smith was dependable. The backs – except in the second half of the Wellington Test – all tackled bravely and well.

The pack presented problems regarding selection, but this was caused mostly by the fact that in their various ways all the players had satisfactory trips without anyone – Cooke apart – being outstanding. The front-row did well and the combination for the Tests meant that Sheppard was unlucky not to add to his total of caps; Huntsman came in at loosehead and performed bravely. Brain was a courageous hooker, but it was doubtful if the tour selectors chose the best pairing at lock. Was it right to prefer Bainbridge, a more solid scrummager, to Dooley, whose line-out work was always good? The back-row selection meant the end of Hesford's International career, which he took with good grace, while Rees was unlucky perhaps to miss the two big games although all the three back-row men could say that they had good tours. Teague showed persistence in scoring his try at Christchurch, but he was less good at Wellington.

So England had no reason to reproach its players. The problem, which was shown by the Wallabies in their November 1985 match at Twickenham, was that others were better. Improvements in the British game are not impossible; perhaps a League system (which we will shortly experience) will produce the necessary sharpening effect. Perhaps also, coaches should revert to being guides rather than rigid off-field tacticians.

1st Match

Saturday, 18th May 1985, at Whangarei

North Auckland	14	England	27

Tries: Lambourne, Ngakuru, K. Phillips (1 each)
Conversion: Bean
Half-time: 6-9

Tries: Melville, Goodwin, Hesford, Smith (1 each)
Penalty-goals: Barnes (3)
Conversion: Barnes

North Auckland: S. Bean; K. Woodman, P. Cooper, C. Going, T. Ngakura; I. Dunn, C. Hull; M. Smith, F. Henare, W. Le Clerc, B. Budd (*captain*), H. Harvey, N. Ruddell, F. Lambourne, C. Phillips. *Replacement:* K. Phillips for C. Phillips, 56 minutes

England: C. R. Martin; S. Smith, P. W. Dodge (*captain*), J. L. B. Salmon, J. Goodwin; S. Barnes, N. D. Melville;

Date	Opponents	Venue	Result
18th May	North Auckland	Whangarei	W 27-14
22nd May	Poverty Bay	Gisborne	W 45-0
25th May	Auckland	Auckland	L 6-24
28th May	Otago	Dunedin	W 25-16
1st June	NEW ZEALAND	Christchurch	L 13-18
4th June	Southland	Invercargill	W 15-9
8th June	NEW ZEALAND	Wellington	L 15-42

Match summary: P 7 W 4 L 3 F 146 A 123

P. Huntsman, S. E. Brain, G. S. Pearce, J. Orwin, W. A. Dooley, J. P. Hall, D. A. Cooke, R. Hesford
Referee: K. Lawrence (*Bay of Plenty*)

This opening victory against a team that had not been enjoying too much recent success was a reasonable start to the tour, but it showed that in certain areas England needed to improve if there was to be any chance of Test successes. In the pack much good work was done spasmodically by Dooley and the back-row, but behind the scrum there was a lack of fluency although Melville had a good match.

Melville opened the scoring for England, who led at half-time. After the break the visitors improved greatly and were rampant, particularly in the final quarter. Second-half tries came from Goodwin, Hesford and Smith. The North Auckland response was brave but their third try by the replacement Kim Phillips came in injury time. Bean missed six penalty kicks for the home team, so England could have been embarrassed had he been on better form.

2nd Match

Wednesday, 22nd May 1985, at Gisborne

Poverty Bay	0	England	45

Half-time: 0-25

Tries: Hill (2), Harrison (2), Dodge, Metcalfe, Smith (1 each)
Penalty-goals: Davies (3)
Conversions: Davies (4)

Poverty Bay: P. Roberts, M. White, B. Walters, B. Tupara, A. Walters; J. Whittle (*captain*), I. Ngatai; M. Kingi, S. Donnelly, R. Newlands, G. Williams, P. Evans, M. Winterbottom, G. Law, N. Frankish. *Replacement:* M. Parkes for B. Walters, 21 minutes

England: I. R. Metcalfe; M. E. Harrison, P. W. Dodge (*captain*), B. Barley, J. Goodwin; G. H. Davies, R. J. Hill; M. Preedy, A. Simpson, A. Sheppard, S. Bainbridge, W. A. Dooley, D. H. Cooke, G. W. Rees, M. C. Teague. *Replacement:* S. T. Smith for Goodwin, 43 minutes
Referee: K. Henderson (*Southland*)

England were comfortable winners against a Third Division team, but the fact that a clean scoresheet was maintained was a plus mark, providing good practice for all the players. The forwards in general were good although Bainbridge had his problems at the front of the line-out.

The half-time score showed the superiority of the visitors but there was a second-half spell of twenty minutes when all efforts to advance from a twenty eight point lead failed. Also, the luckless Goodwin injured a knee and was carried off although later the injury did not look quite as bad as had been feared.

The fact that five backs scored was a good testimony to their enterprise, and of the uncapped players both Harrison and Metcalfe looked good. There would be harder days ahead, but at least the team had won both matches.

3rd Match

Saturday, 25th May 1985, at Eden Park, Auckland

Auckland	24	England	6

Tries: Haden, G. Whetton, Stanley (1 each)
Penalty-goals: Fox (2)
Conversions: Fox (3)

Try: Smith
Conversion: Barnes
Half-time: 12-0

Auckland: L. Harris; J. Kirwan, J. Stanley, K. Sherlock, T. Wright; G. Fox, D. Kirk; S. McDowell, I. Abercrombie, M. Gray, G. Whetton, A. Haden (*captain*), A. Whetton, M. Brooke-Cowden, G. Rich.
England: I. R. Metcalfe; S. T. Smith, P.W. Dodge (*captain*), B. Barley, M. E. Harrison; S. Barnes, N. D. Melville; M. Preedy, S. E. Brain, G. S. Pearce, S. Bainbridge, W. A. Dooley, J. P. Hall, D. H. Cooke, M. C. Teague
Referee: B. Francis (*Wairarapa Bush*)

As expected, Auckland were too strong for a brave but unlucky English team, particularly where refereeing decisions were concerned. On one occasion, England found themselves with a good attacking position only to be recalled for a scrum – with their own 'put-in'. Even so, Auckland were superior in too many aspects, although the line-out with Dooley doing well was one exception, and they did deserve to win. This demonstrated just how formidable would be the task of facing the All-Blacks in the Tests.

Auckland led by twelve points at half-time after excellent tries by Haden and Gary Whetton, who scored after Kirwan beat off three tacklers before Barnes pulled him down only for the ball to stay available for Fox to send in Whetton. After half-time, Fox, who had converted both first-half tries, extended the lead with a penalty-goal, after which Smith scored well for England with Barnes converting. Smith actually capitalized on two English errors to do his work. Fox scored another penalty-goal and converted Auckland's third try by Stanley.

4th Match

Tuesday, 28th May, at Carisbrook, Dunedin

Otago	16	England	25

Tries: Young, Kenny (1 each)
Penalty-goals: Cooper (2)
Conversion: Cooper

Tries: Davies, Harrison, Hall, Barnes (1 each)
Penalty-goals: Barnes (3)
Half-time: 6-14

Otago: G. Cooper; N. Pilcher, M. Gibson, J. Waldron, R. Milne; J. Haggart, D. Kenny; J. Latta, P. O'Neill, S. Hotton, R. Knight, G. Macpherson, A. Hollander, P. Young, M. Brewer (*captain*)
England: G. H. Davies; M. E. Harrison, B. Barley, J. L. B. Salmon, C. R. Martin; S. Barnes, R. J. Hill; P. Huntsman, A. Simpson, A. Sheppard, J. Orwin, S. Bainbridge, J. P. Hall, G. W. Rees, R. Hesford (*captain*).
Replacement: S. T. Smith for Martin, 35 minutes
Referee: G. Smith (*Hawkes Bay*)

The match was a good one for England even though history has recorded stronger Otago teams. With the scrummage in command and Bainbridge working wonders at the line-out, the visitors had an admirable supply of the ball even when defending, as they did for a long period late in the match. They should have made better use of that possession at times. Behind the scrum Barnes was exempt from criticism and was outstanding in most respects with a late try scored through sheer determination.

Otago led immediately in this game with two penalty-goals by Cooper before Martin, soon to retire injured with an ankle sprain, set up a try for Davies. Two penalty-goals by Barnes, who also ran well to set up a try by Harrison (the other first-half scorer), gave England a good first-half lead.

However, Otago recovered to 10-14 down (a try by Young) and after Hall had scored another good try the home team again narrowed the gap to 10-18 before Barnes resumed control of the match by scoring another penalty-goal, by kicking well in defence against the inevitable Otago counter-attacks and finally by scoring his try.

5th Match, First International

Saturday, 1st June 1985, at Lancaster Park, Christchurch

New Zealand	18	England	13

Penalty-goals: Crowley (6)
Half-time: 12-13

Tries: Harrison, Teague (1 each)
Penalty-goal: Barnes
Conversion: Barnes

New Zealand: K. Crowley; J. Kirwan, S. Pokere, W. Taylor, C. Green; W. Smith, D. Kirk; J. Ashworth, A. Dalton (*captain*), G. Knight, G. Whetton, M. Pierce, M. Shaw, J. Hobbs, M. Mexted. *New caps:* Crowley, Kirk, Pierce
England: G. H. Davies; S. T. Smith, P. W. Dodge (*captain*), J. L. B. Salmon, M. E. Harrison; S. Barnes, N. D. Melville; P. Huntsman, S. E. Brain, G. S. Pearce, S. Bainbridge,

J. Orwin, J. P. Hall, D. H. Cooke, M. C. Teague. *New caps:* Salmon, Harrison, Huntsman

Referee: K. Fitzgerald (*Queensland, Australia*)

By scoring two tries to nil England took many of the honours from this match, but victory eluded them mainly because too many penalties were conceded in kickable positions and only one could be said to have been a rather harsh award. This happened with fifteen minutes remaining and it gave the All-Blacks the lead for the first time. In fairness, England's penalty awards were in all but two instances in relatively defensive situations, whilst the two kickable positions produced one success for Barnes – and a near miss. Crowley was allowed eight kicks at goal and scored from six, which equalled a New Zealand record. This showed that the New Zealanders held a territorial advantage during the game with England's tries being the result of splendid opportunism. Even so, they gave the All-Blacks too many anxious moments for home comfort, which is a great credit to English Rugby.

England led at half-time by courtesy of an early penalty-goal by Barnes, which was soon cancelled out by a similar effort by Crowley. New Zealand then enjoyed much scrappy possession, which was well used by the gallant Kirk at scrum-half. One piece of good handling by him produced a move that broke down in mid-field as a result of over-ambitious passing and Harrison with great skill fielded the error to run in for a try under the posts; Barnes converted. Two penalties by Crowley narrowed the margin to one point before England were awarded a scrum near the home '22' and Teague fed Melville cleverly for the latter to kick well as he was tackled. The awkward bounce confused the defence and Teague was able to touch down for the second try, which was just too wide for Barnes's conversion attempt. Before half-time Crowley again landed a penalty-goal.

The second half saw much New Zealand pressure with no reward until over an hour had elapsed and here the referee rather harshly (it seemed) adjudged Dodge to be offside at a line-out. Crowley put New Zealand in the lead from a fairly easy kick. He then appeared to give Barnes a compensating award, but his effort went wide. So, New Zealand won a rather unconvincing victory. Their pack had slightly the better of the forward battle, but the service to Kirk was frequently untidy and the scrum-half did well to keep his team out of trouble on many occasions. England's backs looked the better unit with Melville, free of any injury, playing well.

6th Match

Tuesday, 4th June 1985, at Invercargill

Southland	9	England	15
Penalty-goals: B. McKenzie (3)		*Penalty-goals:* Davies (5) *Half-time:* 6-6	

Southland: B. McKenzie; A. Monaghan, P. Laidlaw, J. Chittock, W. Molloy; M. Brown, C. Hiini; P. Cosgrove, B. McCall, K. Molloy, G. McKenzie, A. Byrne, P. Henderson, D. Kelly (*captain*), T. Bokser

England: I. R. Metcalfe; J. Goodwin, B. Barley, J. L. B. Salmon, C. R. Martin; G. H. Davies, R. J. Hill; M. Preedy, A. Simpson, A. Sheppard, W. A. Dooley, S. Bainbridge, D. Cooke (*captain*), G. W. Rees, R. Hesford

Referee: C. Dainty (*Wellington*)

A thoroughly disagreeable match was won by the visitors, whose Huw Davies landed five penalties from seven attempts against three successes by Brent McKenzie from four efforts. This would suggest that England had more of the play territorially and just deserved to win.

The busiest man on the field was the referee, who did well, on the whole, in the sour atmosphere for which both teams were responsible. England teams are not normally noted for bad behaviour, but on this occasion two players fell from grace – Preedy and Hill – with the former evading censure and the latter escaping with no more than a stern warning after his alleged raking of Henderson.

The England management did well to avoid post-match recriminations. Matches like this are best left as pure statistics with other details forgotten.

7th Match, Second International

Saturday, 8th June 1985, at Wellington

New Zealand	42	England	15
Tries: Green (2), Kirwan, Hobbs, Mexted, Shaw (1 each) *Dropped-goal:* Smith *Penalty-goals:* Crowley (3) *Conversions:* Crowley (3)		*Tries:* Hall, Harrison (1 each) *Dropped-goal:* Barnes *Conversions:* Barnes (2) *Half-time:* 13-9	

New Zealand: K. J. Crowley; J. J. Kirwan, S. T. Pokere, W. T. Taylor, C. N. Green; W. R. Smith, D. E. Kirk; J. Ashworth, A. G. Dalton (*captain*), G. A. Knight, G. W. Whetton, M. J. Pierce, M. W. Shaw, M. J. B. Hobbs, M. G. Mexted. *No new caps*

England: G. H. Davies; S. T. Smith, P. W. Dodge (*captain*), J. L. B. Salmon, M. E. Harrison; S. Barnes, N. D. Melville; R. P. Huntsman, S. E. Brain, G. S. Pearce, J. Orwin, S. Bainbridge, J. P. Hall, D. H. Cooke, M. C. Teague. *Replacements:* R. J. Hill for Melville, 40 minutes; W. A. Dooley for Orwin, 65 minutes. *No new caps*

Referee: K. Fitzgerald (*Queensland, Australia*)

In this second and final match of the series, New Zealand played to the form expected of them in more ways than one, but they ended the match as well deserved winners. The game as a whole was no credit to Rugby, and it is to be hoped that by the time the World Cup is staged someone will have persuaded all the teams that take part to desist from the kind of violence that has taken root in too many International fixtures. Were the scenes of this match to be multiplied a few times, the big event of 1987 would turn into a major disaster. Even referees with more natural authority than Mr Fitzgerald will find it difficult to cope. The big problem has been excessive use of the boot against men on the ground; New Zealand do this when they think opponents are killing the ball unnecessarily and the opponents in their turn deny that they indulge in such tactics. But whichever side one takes, the fact is that this was a thoroughly unpleasant match, for which New Zealand can take much of the blame since they suffered fewer serious injuries. This detracts from a fine win.

England suffered a record defeat, but they started well enough with a good try by Hall. However, by half-time New Zealand led (13-9) and after the break the pressure was applied vigorously although with less violence than had been seen in the earlier stages. They ended by scoring six tries, three of which came from scrums; this demonstrated that such a set-piece is still a dangerous situation contrary to many coaching ideas in the British Isles. England's only high spot of the second half was another interception and try by Harrison after he had again collected a bad pass from Pokere.

New Zealand, when they concentrated on Rugby, were a good and powerful outfit with excellent back play well started by Kirk and continued by Smith. Crowley at full-back continued his very good start in International Rugby. The

England Tour of New Zealand

	Appearances			Scores				
	Representative	International	Total	PG	DG	C	T	Pts
Backs								
P. W. Dodge (*Leicester*) (*captain*)	3	2	5				1	4
B. Barley (*Wakefield*)	4		4					
S. Barnes (*Bristol*)	3	2	5	6(1)	(1)	2(3)	1	26(12)
G. H. Davies (*Wasps*)	3	2	5	8		4	1	36
M. E. Harrison (*Wakefield*)	3	2	5				3(2)	12 (8)
R. J. Hill (*Bath*)	3	(1)	3(1)				2	8
C. R. Martin (*Bath*)	3		3					
N. D. Melville (*Wasps*)	2	2	4				1	4
I. R. Metcalfe (*Moseley*)	3		3				1	4
J. Goodwin (*Moseley*)	3		3				1	4
J. L. B. Salmon (*Harlequins*)	3	2	5					
S. T. Smith (*Wasps*)	2(2)	2	4(2)				3	12
Forwards								
S. Bainbridge (*Fylde*)	4	2	6					
S. E. Brain (*Coventry*)	2	2	4					
D. H. Cooke (*Harlequins*)	4	2	6					
W. A. Dooley (*Preston Grasshoppers*)	4	(1)	4(1)					
J. P. Hall (*Bath*)	3	2	5				1(1)	4(4)
R. Hesford (*Bristol*)	3		3				1	4
P. Huntsman (*Headingley*)	2	2	4					
J. Orwin (*RAF, Gloucester*)	2	2	4					
G. S. Pearce (*Northampton*)	2	2	4					
M. Preedy (*Gloucester*)	3		3					
G. W. Rees (*Nottingham*)	3		3					
A. Sheppard (*Bristol*)	3		3					
A. Simpson (*Sale*)	3		3					
M. C. Teague (*Gloucester*)	2	2	4				1	(4)
Totals				15	1	9	20	146

Figures in brackets are for appearances as a replacement

Test match scores are shown in brackets

Tour Officials
P. W. Dodge, captain; W. G. D. Morgan, manager; M. J. Green and W. B. Ashton, coaches

pack owed much again to the brilliant Mexted. England had few stars on a day when they had too many walking wounded, but Barnes was, on the whole, sound and the pack, with the front-row playing very bravely (especially Brain), did not disgrace itself. But in the end it was the home team that showed just how far behind England lag in terms of Rugby expertise.

France Tour of Argentina

The visiting French team after some early easy preliminaries found the Argentina national team a different proposition and the First Test in Buenos Aires was lost. However, the team managed to 'lift' itself for the Second Test, which was won not without a struggle and narrowly. The French found the expected brilliant opposition from Hugo Porta, possibly the best fly-half in the world, and they will vouch for the fact that the South Americans are realistic contenders for the World Cup in 1987.

Date	Opponents	Venue	Result
June 1985	San Isidro Club	Buenos Aires	W 41-18
	Mendoza	Mendoza	W 64-6
	Buenos Aires	Buenos Aires	W 50-15
	Tucuman	Tucuman	W 24-7
	ARGENTINA	Buenos Aires	L 16-24
	Santa Fe	Santa Fe	W 82-7
	ARGENTINA	Buenos Aires	W 23-15
Match summary:	P 7 W 6 L 1 F 300 A 92		

First Test
Saturday, 22nd June 1985, at Buenos Aires

Argentina 24   **France** 16

Tries: Ure, Turnes (1 each)
Penalty-goals: Porta (3)
Dropped-goal: Porta
Conversions: Porta (2)

Tries: Blanco, Lafond (1 each)
Penalty-goals: Lescarboura (2)
Conversion: Lescarboura

Argentina: B. Miguens; J. Lanza, Cuesta Silva, Turnes, Michinni; Porta *(captain)*, J. Miguens; Morel, Cubelli, Cash, Branca, Milano, Allen, Ure, Petersen. *Replacements:* Madero for J. Lanza; P. Lanza for Michinni

France: Blanco; Lafond, Sella, Codorniou, Bonneval; Lescarboura, Berbizier; Dospital, Dintrans *(captain)*, Garuet, Lorieux, Condom, Gratton, Joinel, Champ

Referee: B. Francis *(New Zealand)*

Second Test
Saturday, 29th June 1985, at Buenos Aires

Argentina 15   **France** 23

Try: Cuesta Silva
Penalty-goals: Porta (3)
Conversion: Porta
Half-time: 6-16

Tries: Codorniou, Erbani, Berbizier, Blanco (1 each)
Penalty-goal: Lescarboura
Conversions: Lescarboura (2)

Argentina: B. Miguens; Scolni, Cuesta Silva, Turnes, P. Lanza; Porta *(captain)*, J. Miguens; Morel, Cubelli, Cash, Branca, Milano, Allen, Ure, Petersen

France: Blanco; Lafond, Codorniou, Sella, Pardo; Lescarboura, Berbizier; Chabowski, Dintrans *(captain)*, Dubroca, Picard, Condom, Gratton, Champ, Erbani. *Replacement:* Lorieux for Picard

Referee: B. Francis *(New Zealand)*

United States Tour of Japan

Date	Opponents	Result
June-July 1985	Kyushu	W 20-10
	Japanese Universities	W 29-11
	Kansai	W 29-3
	Japan 'B'	W 28-16
	Kanto	W 34-9
	JAPAN	W 16-15
Match summary:	P 6 W 6 F 156 A 64	

Cardinal Newman Club Tour of Europe

The Newman Club (Buenos Aires) brought thirty nine players on a short tour to England, France and Italy and they experienced mixed results. Among their players were two recent Pumas, Marcello Carrique (centre or full-back) and Eduardo Torello (scrum-half). The latter broke an arm in the first match and his replacement, Espinosa, was not in the same class so that the

Results (1st XV)

Opponents	Venue	Result
Combined London Old Boys	Old Rutlishians, Merton	W 25-3
Gosforth XV	Gosforth	L 0-3
Yorkshire Under-21	Selby	L 15-38
Oxford University	Iffley Road, Oxford	L 7-31
Cambridge University LX Club	Cambridge	W 12-8
Paris University Club	Paris	W 9-7
Selezione Alto Lazio	Rome	W 16-6
Rolly-Go (Roma Rugby Club)	Rome	W 12-4

Match summary (England): P5 W2 L3 F59 A83
All matches: P8 W5 L3 F96 A100

backs did not move as freely as they might have done. The party usually fielded two fifteens at the same time and it was well managed by Sr C. Uranga with another former Puma back, Eduardo Poggi, as their charming and efficient coach. Carrique apart, the best players on the tour were the centre (Llerena), wing (Sundblad), the prop (Brandi) and the two Urangas, who also played in the pack. The teams they met perhaps did not publicize the tour as much as they might have done – only the match against the Combined London Old Boys, which also produced the best performance, being well 'written-up' in advance, whilst some playing conditions were unfamiliar.

Fiji Tour of Wales and Ireland

This was altogether a better tour than that of 1982 to England and Scotland, when all eight matches were lost – mostly by large margins. On this occasion, five of the ten matches were won and only three defeats could be described as bad, which were against Cardiff, Ulster and Wales in the final match, when the visitors gained no worthwhile possession and were routed.

In contrast the Irish match was lost most unluckily and on other occasions the tourists did well even when good ball was in short supply. With inventiveness and improvisation, the backs, of whom Laulau, Niuqila and Nawalu (the scrum-half) were outstanding, managed to turn apparently bad situations into try-scoring moves and when in full flight the side was exciting to watch.

On the debit side there were occasions when the discipline could have been better, and after a serious 'punch-up' late on against Ulster worse

was to follow when Savai was sent off against Newport and suspended for six weeks. Later in the same match there was a serious brawl and other players were lucky not to follow Savai off the field (these could have included at least one from the home side).

However, although the forwards were big and appeared to be physically impressive, they were not good enough for International Rugby, and it can be said that the team left once again leaving a memory of popular and enterprising players.

Date	Opponents	Venue	Result
9th Oct.	Cross Keys	Cross Keys	W 26-12
12th Oct.	Cardiff	Cardiff	L 15-31
16th Oct.	Swansea	Swansea	W 23-14
19th Oct.	IRELAND	Dublin	L 15-16
23rd Oct.	Ulster	Belfast	L 9-23
26th Oct.	Connacht	Galway	W 7-6
30th Oct.	Newport	Newport	W 7-6
2nd Nov.	London Welsh	Richmond	W 22-9
5th Nov.	Llanelli	Llanelli	L 28-31
9th Nov.	WALES	Cardiff	L 3-40

Match summary: P10 W5 L5 F155 A188

1st Match
Wednesday, 9th October 1985, at Pandy Park, Cross Keys

Cross Keys	12	Fijians	26

Try: penalty-try
Dropped-goal: Crane
Penalty-goal: Crane
Conversion: Crane
Half-time: 6-6

Tries: Gale, Bola, Tawake (1 each)
Penalty-goals: Tukania (2), Damu (2)
Conversion: Damu

Cross Keys: I. Evans; K. Holder, D. O'Driscoll, S. Flynn, K. Swain; R. Crane, G. Williams; P. Leader, G. Flynn, R. Donovan, N. Jones, A. Ellison, S. James (*captain*), P. Stokes, S. Rendall

Fijians: E. Turuva; J. Damu, P. Rauluni, A. Niuqila, S. Laulau; T. Tukania, D. Bola; T. Tubananitu, B. Vukiwai, P. Volavola, I. Savai, A. Hughes, I. Finau, P. Gale, E. Teleni (*captain*). *Replacement:* A. Tawake for I. Finau

Referee: G. Simmonds (*Taffs Well*)

This was an uninformative performance by the tourists who eventually won by a comfortable margin. In the first half, many passes were dropped, but later the backs moved fluently. The most impressive visitor was the centre, Niuqila. The home team played bravely and well earned their late penalty-try.

2nd Match
Saturday, 12th October 1985, at the National Stadium, Cardiff

Cardiff	31	Fijians	15

Tries: Hadley (2), Holmes, Rees (1 each)
Penalty-goals: Davies (3)
Conversions: Davies (3)

Tries: Nawalu, Niuqila (1 each)
Penalty-goal: Damu
Conversions: Damu (2)
Half-time: 16-15

Cardiff: P. Rees; G. Cordle, D. Evans, A. Donovan, A. Hadley, G. Davies, T. Holmes; J. Whitefoot, A. Phillips (captain), I. Eidman, R. Lakin, H. Stone, R. Norster, G. Roberts, J. Scott. *Replacement:* T. Crothers for Roberts, 40 minutes

Fijians: E. Turuva; J. Damu, P. Rauluni, A. Niuqila, S. Tuvula; T. Tukania, P. Nawalu; S. Natiuku, E. Rakai, R. Namoro, I. Finau, K. Rakoroi, A. Hughes, P. Gale, E. Teleni (captain). *Replacements:* I. Tawake for Hughes, 27 minutes; J. Kubu for Turuva, 75 minutes

Referee: W. Jones (*Gwaen-cae-Gurwen*)

Once the Fijians had lost Hughes with an ankle injury, any real chance of reasonable possession went with him and Cardiff were comfortable winners, even though the handling of the backs, Holmes and Davies apart, was undistinguished. A score of only four tries did not flatter the home team, but the visitors played bravely whenever they had the ball.

3rd Match
Wednesday, 16th October 1985, at St Helens, Swansea

Swansea	14	Fijians	23

Tries: Dacey, Richards (1 each)
Penalty-goals: Hopkins (2)
Half-time: 10-14

Tries: Nabati (2), Niuqila, Rakoroi (1 each)
Penalty-goal: Nawalu
Conversions: Kubu (2)

Swansea: M. Thomas; M. Titley, D. Richards, K. Hopkins, I. Jeffreys; M. Dacey, H. Davies; K. Colclough, H. Gibson, S. Evans, M. Davies (captain), M. Colclough, J. Williams, R. Moriarty, T. Cheeseman. *Replacement:* K. Williams for H. Davies, 40 minutes

Fijians: J. Kubu; M. Nabati, S. Laulau, T. Cama, S. Tuvula; A. Niuqila, P. Nawalu; S. Natiuku, E. Rakai, P. Volavola, I. Finau (captain), I. Savai, K. Rakoroi, A. Waqailiti, P. Gale

Referee: D. O. Hughes (*Newbridge*)

A weakened Swansea team had its moments, but serious errors gave away not only ground but also scores and the visitors took the opportunities given to them. Even so their pack gave a greatly improved display, although it was early to determine whether there was any hope for success in the big games.

4th Match, First International
Saturday, 19th October 1985, at Lansdowne Road, Dublin

Ireland	16	Fiji	15

Try: Bradley
Penalty-goals: Kiernan (4)
Half-time: 6-6

Tries: Laulau, Tuvula (1 each)
Penalty-goal: Damu
Conversions: Damu (2)

Ireland: H. P. MacNeill (*London Irish*); M. J. Kiernan (*Dolphin*), B. J. Mullin (*Dublin University*), J. A. Hewitt (*North of Ireland FC*), K. D. Crossan (*Instonians*); P. M. Dean (*St Mary's College*), M. T. Bradley (*Cork Constitution*), P. A. Orr (*Old Wesley*), C. F. Fitzgerald (*St Mary's College*) (captain), J. J. McCoy (*Bangor*), P. M. Matthews (*Ards*), W. A. Anderson (*Dungannon*), D. G. Lenihan (*Cork Constitution*), W. J. Sexton (*Garryowen*), B. J. Spillane (*Bohemians*)

Fiji: E. Turuva (*Nadi*); J. Damu (*St John Marist*), T. Cama (*Nabua*), S. Laulau (*Nawaka*), S. Tuvula (*Western Marine*); A. Niuqila (*Nakelo*), P. Nawalu (*St John Marist*); S. Natiuku (*Rewa*), E. Rakai (*Gaunavou*), R. Namoro (*Lutu*), I. Finau (*St Mary's*), K. Rakoroi (*Army/Navy*), A. Hughes (*St John Marist*), P. Gale (*Nadi*), E. Teleni (*Army/Navy*)

Referee: W. D. Bevan (*Wales*)

In a fine match, Fiji were desperately unlucky to lose – and not only because Turuva should have scored a try in the dying seconds. Some thought that he had done so fairly, but the referee spotted a knock-on as he was gathering the ball and the chance was lost. Had he kicked and then touched down over the line, Ireland could have done nothing about it and a fine kick and chase of seventy yards out of defence would have been justly rewarded.

Ireland were never as enterprising as they had been in their Championship-winning days of the previous season, even though they won plenty of possession. The backs were too elaborate and Dean frequently chose the wrong option. Even so, Kiernan twice scored penalties in the first half and Irish pressure looked like producing a try from Spillane, who might have done better to pass. The ball was lost and cleared ninety yards away, where Kiernan kicked dead only for Laulau to score a fine individual try from the drop-out. It was level-pegging at the break.

In the very first minute of the second period Fiji went ahead with a marvellous try by Turuva, who intercepted a pass intended for Kiernan; from his own '22' he raced the full length of the field and scored under the posts. Damu converted this as he had done with the first, but a penalty from Kiernan and try by Bradley, forced over by his own pack, took Ireland ahead only for Fiji to regain the lead briefly through a penalty-goal by Damu. Kiernan scored his fourth penalty-goal and then Damu missed two for Fiji (one was very close indeed) before there was the incident with the luckless Turuva.

So it was a moral victory for the Fijians and the Irish will have learned that there is no room for complacency in Rugby.

5th Match
Wednesday, 23rd October 1985, at Ravenhill, Belfast

Ulster	23	Fijians	9

Tries: Morrow, Matthews, Rainey (1 each)
Penalty-try: Rainey
Penalty-goal: Rainey
Conversions: Rainey (2)

Try: Tuvula
Penalty-goal: Kubu
Conversion: Kubu
Half-time: 13-3

Ulster: P. Rainey (*Ballymena*); J. R. McMaster (*Bangor*), D. A. Irwin (*Instonians*) (*captain*), J. Hewitt (*NIFC*), K. D. Crossan (Instonians); I. D. Brown (*Malone*), R. C. Brady (*Ballymena*); A. P. Kennedy (*London Irish*), J. P. McDonald (*Malone*), J. J. McCoy (*Bangor*), P. M. Matthews (*Ards*), B. W. McCall (*London Irish*), W. A. Anderson (*Dungannon*), W. R. Duncan (*Malone*), D. R. Morrow (*Bangor*). *Replacement:* P. O'Donnell (*London Irish*) for Brown, 38 minutes

Fijians: J. Kubu; M. Nabati, P. Rauluni, T. Cama, S. Tuvula; A. Niuqila, P. Nawalu; S. Natiuku, B. Vukiwai, R. Namoro, I. Finau, K. Rakoroi, A.P.T. Hughes, P. Gale, E. Teleni (*captain*). *Replacement:* I. Tawake for Tuvula

Referee: K. McCartney (*Scottish RU*)

Ulster won their fourteenth consecutive match at representative level against a very disappointing Fijian team, which was outplayed at every phase of the game. By scoring four tries to one (a penalty-try awarded to Rainey included) they emphasized their all-round superiority in every way possible. Hughes at lock was Fiji's best player.

6th Match
Saturday, 26th October 1985, at Galway

Connacht	6	Fijians	7

Penalty-goals: O'Toole (2)
Half-time: 6-0

Try: Nabati
Penalty-goal: Kubu

Connacht: H. O'Toole (*Corinthians*); P. O'Flynn (*Corinthians*), R. Hernon (*UCC*), M. Seely (*Old Belvedere*), C. Hitchcock (*Galwegians*); H. Condon (*London Irish*), C. McCarthy (*UCG*); T. Clancy (*Lansdowne*), C. F. Fitzgerald (*St Mary's College*) (*captain*), M. McClancy (*Old Belvedere*), D. Greaney (*Corinthians*), M. Tarpey (*St Mary's College*), M. Moylett (*Shannon*), J. O'Driscoll (*London Irish*), N. Mannion (*Corinthians*). *Replacements:* J. Daly (*Lansdowne*) for Hitchcock; B. Deegan (*Wanderers*) for Fitzgerald

Fijians: J. Kubu; M. Nabati, S. Laulau, T. Cama, J. Damu; T. Tukania, D. Bola; P. Volavola, E. Rakai, R. Namoro, P. Gale, I. Savai, A. P. T. Hughes, A. Waqailiti, E. Teleni (*captain*). *Replacement:* I. Tawake for R. Namoro

Referee: D. W. Matthews (*RFU*)

Connacht led at half-time by O'Toole's two penalties and there were hopes of a victory over a

touring team, but after the break the visitors came more into the game and not only scored the only try but also earned their hard-won victory.

7th Match
Wednesday, 30th October 1985, at Rodney Parade, Newport

Newport	6	Fijians	7

Dropped-goal: James
Penalty-goal: Callard
Half-time: 3-0

Try: Namoro
Dropped-goal: Kubu

Newport: J. Callard; S. Pill, D. Pitt, P. Daniel, S. McWilliams; K. James, T. Coombs; J. Rawlins, M. J. Watkins (*captain*), R. Morgan, R. Collins, J. Widdicombe, D. Waters, R. Powell, W. Rendall. *Replacements:* A. Perry for Rendall, 24 minutes; C. Jonathan for Coombs, 73 minutes

Fijians: J. Kubu; M. Nabati, S. Laulau, T. Cama, J. Damu; A. Niuqila, P. Nawalu; P. Volavola, E. Rakai, R. Namoro, I. Finau, I. Savai, A. P. T. Hughes, P. Gale, E. Teleni (*captain*)

Referee: R. Jones (*Swansea*)

An opportunist try by Namoro seven minutes from time settled this match, in which Newport were awarded nineteen penalties against two to the visitors, who had Savai sent off in the forty-ninth minute for allegedly butting Daniel. It seemed from the TV recording that the offence was no more than a wild charge into a ruck, but Savai was nevertheless given a six-week suspension, which meant missing the rest of the tour. A brawl a few minutes later between the two sets of forwards would have justified such action (particularly against Volavola) had the referee seen the events in question. Newport had plenty of possession apart from penalty awards and dissipated too many chances, whereas the Fijians fed on crumbs but nevertheless did well with them.

8th Match
Saturday, 2nd November 1985, at Old Deer Park, Richmond

London Welsh	9	Fijians	22

Penalty-goals: Price (3)
Half-time: 3-10

Tries: Niuqila (2), Teleni (1)
Penalty-goals: Kubu (2)
Conversions: Kubu (2)

London Welsh: A. Martin; J. Hughes, R. Ackerman, G. Leleu, C. Rees (*captain*); C. Price, M. Douglas; T. Jones, B. Light, B. Bradley, G. Llewelyn, J. Collins, S. Page, M. Watkins, M. Bowring. *Replacement:* G. Thomas for Douglas, 44 minutes

Fijians: J. Kubu; M. Nabati, S. Laulau, T. Cama, S. Tuvula; A. Niuqila, P. Nawalu; P. Volavola, E. Rakai, R. Namoro, K. Rakoroi, I. Tawake, A. Waqailiti, P. Gale, E. Teleni (*captain*). *Replacements:* S. Natiuku for Gale, 48 minutes; B. Vukiwai for Rakai, 74 minutes

Referee: K. Rowlands (*WRU*)

Without looking too convincing the Fijians were comfortable winners over the London Welsh, who scored first but generally lacked penetration and distinguished themselves bravely in defence rather than as attackers. The Fijian tries were all good examples of opportunism, but many chances were squandered through final passes being knocked on. Mr Rowlands had no problems in controlling a very clean match.

9th Match

Tuesday, 5th November 1985, at Stradey Park, Llanelli

Llanelli	31	Fijians	28

Tries: May, Buchanan, A. Hopkins (1 each, plus 1 penalty)
Dropped-goal: Pearce
Penalty-goals: Pearce (2)
Conversions: Pearce (3)

Tries: Tuvula (2), Damu, Laulau (1 each)
Penalty-goals: Damu (2)
Conversions: Damu (3)
Half-time: 10-28

Llanelli: K. Thomas; P. Hopkins, P. Morgan, N. Davies, C. Davies; G. Pearce, J. Griffiths; A. Buchanan, D. Fox, L. Delaney, A. Hopkins, P. May (*captain*), R. Thomas, M. Perego, M. Lynch
Fijians: E. Turuva; J. Damu, S. Laulau, P. Rauluni, S. Tuvula; A. Niuqila, P. Nawalu; P. Volavola, B. Vukiwai, S. Natiuku, I. Tawake, I. Finau, K. Rakoroi, A. Waqailiti, E. Teleni (*captain*). *Replacement:* P. Gale for Finau, 41 minutes
Referee: I. Peard (*Castleton*)

After falling behind by twenty five points to four brilliant Fijian tries in the first half-hour, Llanelli fought back to their third successive win over a touring side, which was achieved with a try by A. Hopkins ten minutes from no-side. May led his men with great courage and Pearce's kicking (fifteen points) was another decisive factor in the final result.

10th Match, Second International

Saturday, 9th November 1985, at National Stadium, Cardiff

Wales	40	Fiji	3

Tries: P. Davies (2), Holmes, Hadley, Pickering, Titley, James (1 each)
Penalty-goals: Thorburn (2)
Conversions: Thorburn (3)

Penalty-goal: Damu
Half-time: 18-10

Fiji Tour of Wales and Ireland

	Appearances			Scores				
	Representative	International	Total	PG	DG	C	T	Pts
E. Teleni (*captain*) (no. 8)	7	2	9				1	4
S. Natiuku (prop)	4(1)	1	5(1)					
T. Tubananitu (prop)	1		1					
R. Namoro (prop)	5	2	7				1	4
P. Volavola (prop)	6	1	7					
E. Rakai (hooker)	5	2	7					
B. Vukiwai (hooker)	3(1)		3(1)					
P. Gale (flanker/no. 8)	7(1)	2	9(1)				1	4
I. Finau (flanker)	6	2	8					
A. Waqailiti (flanker)	4	4						
I. Tawake (flanker/lock)	2(4)		2(4)				1	4
K. Rakoroi (lock)	5	2	7				1	4
I. Savai (lock)	4		4					
A. P. T. Hughes (lock)	5	2	7					
P. Nawalu (scrum-half)	6	2	8	1			1	7
D. Bola (scrum-half)	2		2				1	4
A. Niuqila (centre/fly-half)	7	2	9				4	16
J. Kubu (full-back)	5(1)	(1)	5(2)	4	1	5		25
T. Cama (centre)	5	2	7					
P. Rauluni (centre)	4		4					
S. Laulau (wing/centre)	6	2	8				1(1)	4(4)
J. Damu (wing)	5	2	7	5(2)		6(2)	1	31(10)
M. Nabati (wing)	5	1	6				3	12
S. Tuvula (wing)	5	2	7				3(1)	12(4)
E. Turuva (full-back)	3	1	4					
T. Tukania (fly-half)	3		3	2				6
Totals				14	1	13	21	155

Figures in brackets are for appearances as a replacement

Test match scores are shown in brackets

Tour Officials
J. Taka, manager; J. Sovau, coach; G. Simkin, coaching adviser

Wales: P. H. Thorburn (*Neath*); M. H. Titley (*Swansea*), R. A. Ackerman (*Cardiff*), B. Bowen (*South Wales Police*), A. M. Hadley (*Cardiff*); J. Davies (*Neath*), T. D. Holmes (*Cardiff*) (captain); J. Whitefoot (*Cardiff*), W. J. James (*Aberavon*), I. H. Eidman (*Cardiff*), M. Davies (*Swansea*), S. J. Perkins (*Pontypool*), R. L. Norster (*Cardiff*), D. F. Pickering (*Llanelli*), P. T. Davies (*Llanelli*). *Replacement:* R. Giles (*Aberavon*) for Holmes, 70 minutes

Fiji: J. Damu (*St John Marist*); M. Nabati (*Kaduvu*), S. Laulau (*Nawaka*), T. Cama (*Nabua*), S. Tuvula (*Western Marine*); A. Niuqila (*Nakelo*), P. Nawalu (*St John Marist*); P. Volavola (*Nawaka*), E. Rakai (*Gaunavou*), R. Namoro (*Lutu*), I. Finau (*St Mary's*), K. Rakoroi (*Army/Navy*), A. P. T. Hughes (*St John Marist*), P. Gale (*Nadi*), E. Teleni (*Army/Navy*) (captain). *Replacement:* J. Kubu (*Waimanu*) for Tuvula, 8 minutes

Referee: S. R. Hilditch (*Irish RFU*)

There was no fairy-tale ending to the Fijian tour with Wales, awarding full caps for the game dominating at forward, both in scrum and line-out and giving massive possession to a set of backs who played poorly, which meant that the margin of victory was not greater. With few scraps of possession the tourists had to improvise when they did have the ball and for once they did not do well in that direction. There was a late penalty-goal by Damu, who started at full-back but soon moved to the wing to replace Tuvula.

Wales, whose sixth try by Titley was the best of the bleak afternoon, were well served by the whole pack, but the selectors will have pondered for a long time about their wasteful backs.

New Zealand Tour of Argentina

Although winning the Test Series by one win and a draw, in which they outscored the Pumas by four tries to nil and should have won, the All-Blacks would be the first to agree that Argentina has arrived as a major Rugby force. There were few easy matches and the World Cup will be all the better for a new challenge.

With players who were not available or retired plus disruptive injuries, the New Zealanders had their problems, but with such fine players as Mexted, Hobbs (the captain) and Shaw amongst their forwards, and excellent backs in Kirwan, Taylor, Fox, Smith, Kirk and Loveridge, they were usually better than the opposition.

Date	Opponents	Venue	Result	
13th Oct.	Atletico San Isidro	Buenos Aires	W	22-9
16th Oct.	Rosario	Rosario	W	28-9
19th Oct.	Buenos Aires XV	Buenos Aires	W	31-13
23rd Oct.	Cordoba	Cordoba	W	72-9
26th Oct.	ARGENTINA	Buenos Aires	W	33-20
30th Oct.	Mar del Plata XV	Mar del Plata	W	56-6
2nd Nov.	ARGENTINA	Buenos Aires	D	21-21

Match summary: P 7 W 6 D 1 F 263 A 87

First International
Saturday, 26th October 1985, at Buenos Aires

Argentina	20	New Zealand	33
Tries: Cuesta Silva, Lanza (1 each)		*Tries:* Kirwan (2), Hobbs, Crowley (1 each)	
Penalty-goals: Porta (3)		*Penalty-goals:* Crowley (4)	
Dropped-goal: Porta		*Dropped-goal:* Fox	
		Conversion: Crowley	

Argentina: Miguens; J. Lanza, Cuesta Silva, Turnes, P. Lanza; Porta (captain), Holmgren; Ure, Allen, Petersen, Milano, Branca, Cash, Cubelli, Morel. *Replacements:* Madero for Miguens; Carosio for Allen
New Zealand: Crowley; Kirwan, Taylor, Simpson, Green; W. Smith, Loveridge; Mexted, Hobbs (captain), Shaw, G. Whetton, Haden, McDowell, Reid, McGrattan

Three late tries (by Crowley, Kirwan, his second, and Hobbs) maintained an unbeaten record for the All-Blacks in 1985, but it was a tough struggle and the Pumas gave a good account of themselves.

Second International
Saturday, 2nd November 1985, at Buenos Aires

Argentina	21	New Zealand	21
Dropped-goals: Porta (3)		*Tries:* Kirwan (2), Mexted, Green (1 each)	
Penalty-goals: Porta (4)		*Penalty-goal:* Crowley	
Half-time: 12-21		*Conversion:* Crowley	

Argentina: B. Miguens; J. Lanza, Cuesta Silva, Turnes, P. Lanza; Porta (captain), Holmgren; Ure, Allen, Petersen, Milano, Branca, Cash, Cubelli, Morel. *Replacements:* Madero for Miguens; Carosio for Allen
New Zealand: Crowley; Kirwan, Taylor, Simpson, Green; W. Smith, Loveridge; Mexted, Hobbs (captain), Shaw, G. Whetton, Haden, McDowell, Reid, McGrattan

Although New Zealand scored four tries to nil they had to struggle near the end to draw as the Pumas spent the last few minutes encamped on the visitors' line. Earlier, Porta with three dropped-goals and four penalties had scored all the Argentinian points whereas Crowley was off form with his kicking, missing three penalty attempts and three conversions.

Japan Tour of France

This was a very sobering lesson not only for the under-sized Japanese but also for the World Cup organizers, who must now hope for a miraculous improvement from France's visitors since a series of heavy routs will embarrass everyone. All six matches were easily lost with the Japanese scoring only forty points and conceding two hundred and seventy six. A lack of physique amongst the forwards is a big disadvantage and it is one that has been a problem ever since Japan started to play internationally; there is no solution. The only problems the French faced were a series of bad injuries.

Date	Opponents	Venue	Result
10th Oct.	French XV	Strasbourg	L 17-44
13th Oct.	Bourgogne	Chalon-sur-Saône	L 8-48
16th Oct.	Litoral	Toulon	L 11-37
20th Oct.	FRANCE	Dax	L 0-50
23rd Oct.	French Barbarians	Cognac	L 4-45
27th Oct.	FRANCE	Nantes	L 0-52

Match summary: P 6 L 6 F 40 A 276

First International
Sunday, 20th October 1985, at Dax

France	50	Japan	0

Tries: Lafond (4), Fabre, Cassagne, Codorniou, Rodriguez, Detrez, Dubroca (1 each)
Conversions: Camberabero (5)
France: S. Blanco; M. Fabre, P. Sella, D. Codorniou, J.-P. Lafond; D. Camberabero, P. Berbizier; P. E. Detrez, P. Dintrans *(captain)*, D. Dubroca, J. Gratton, J. Condom, J.-C. Orso, E. Champ, L. Rodriguez. *Replacements:* C. Delage for Blanco; G. Cassagne for Sella

Japan: Murai; Onuki, Taumoefolau, Matsunaga, Yoshino; Kutsuki, Komishi; Ishiyama, Fujita, Horaguchi *(captain)*, Kassai, Oyagi, Hayashi, Chida, Kawase
Referee: J. Fleming *(Scotland)*

This was an absurdly one-sided match and the French won as they pleased, but at the same time they saw Blanco and Sella injured, which was something they would have liked to avoid. Lafond with four tries had an excellent match as a wing, but the competition was so weak that comparisons with other Internationals would be pointless.

Second International
Sunday, 27th October 1985, at Nantes

France	52	Japan	0
	Half-time: 26-0		

Tries: Camberabero (2), Lafond (2), Charvet (2), Dintrans (2), Fabre, Bonneval (1 each)
Conversions: Camberabero (6)
France: J. Bianchi; M. Fabre, D. Charvet, E. Bonneval, J.-B. Lafond; D. Camberabero, P. Berbizier; E. Champ, L. Rodriguez, J. Gratton, J.-C. Orso, J. Picard, D. Dubroca, P. Dintrans *(captain)*, P. Marocco

Japan: Murai; Onuki, Taumoefolau, Matsunaga, Yoshino; Honjo, Kunishi; Chida, Tauchida, Kasai, Oyagi, Hayashi, Horaguchi *(captain)*, Fujita, Ishiyama. *Replacements:* Kobayashi for Taumoefolau; Mukai for Kobayashi
Referee: C. Norling *(Wales)*

Japan were again completely outclassed and conceded ten tries; this is ominous for the World Cup in 1987, since the credibility of the competition will not be enhanced by such weak countries taking part.

Australia 18 Group Tour

Another superb Australian Schools side came, saw and conquered and in most matches it was again a case of how many they would score. With this in mind one must congratulate those opponents who gave them a good run for their money and the best opposition came from Scotland, Campion School, Ireland (in a very close match) and Ulster. England were gallant in defence, but the physical superiority of the young Australians eventually proved overwhelming.

It was usually a great pleasure to watch these superbly fit young visitors for whom Stuart was a

Date	Opponents	Venue	Result	
7th Dec.	ITALY		W	7-3
11th Dec.	BELGIUM		W	17-6
14th Dec.	SCOTLAND	Murrayfield	W	24-13
17th Dec.	S of Scotland Schools	Hawick	W	57-0
20th Dec.	Campion School	Basildon	W	13-0
23rd Dec.	E Counties Schools	Cambridge	W	52-0
28th Dec.	Leinster	Dublin	Frosted off	
1st Jan.	IRELAND	Belfast	W	13-9
4th Jan.	Ulster Schools	Belfast	W	6-0
8th Jan.	Munster School	Limerick	W	25-0
11th Jan.	Midland Schools	Moseley	W	54-0
15th Jan.	S & S-W Schools	Yeovil	W	15-0
19th Jan.	N of England Schools	New Brighton	W	18-3
22nd Jan.	London Schools	Richmond	W	30-0
26th Jan.	NETHERLANDS	Hilversum	W	66-0
29th Jan.	ENGLAND	Twickenham	W	29-6

Match summary (Britain): P 12 W 12 F 307 A 25
All matches: P 15 W 15 F 426 A 40

fine captain and scrum-half. Fly-half Kahl, the centre Fulivai, the wing O'Connell and the forwards Malloy, Dix and Wilson were all outstanding members of a fine side. Several will be Wallabies before any of us are much older.

All twelve matches in Britain were won – three hundred and seven points being scored against only twenty five conceded on the tour. In only four matches did opponents score against them. They also won the three matches on the Continent. So, not only was their defence almost impregnable, but they were also very enterprising in attack. In short, they were a joy to watch even in unfamiliar conditions!

Striking teachers prevented the team from playing any matches in Wales. Only Belgium and Scotland crossed the Australians' line!

New Zealand Combined Services

Forty years after a famous tour by Charles Saxton's 'Kiwis', the New Zealand Combined Services made an eight-match tour of England and Wales and won each game.

No opponents could really match them and only one try was conceded – against the RAF in the first match. Outstanding players were W. Shelford, the captain, Hohapatu, the scrum-half, D. Shelford at centre, Cookson on the left-wing and the flanker, Henderson.

Opponents	Venue	Result	
RAF	Brize Norton	W	26-9
Army	Aldershot	W	37-6
British Police	Cardiff	W	60-0
Salisbury & Services XV	Old Sarum	W	39-6
Royal Navy	Portsmouth	W	36-6
Combined Services	Devonport	W	41-0
Public Schools Wanderers	Wasps RFC	W	19-3
Middlesex Clubs	Centaurs RFC	W	22-6

Match summary: P 8 W 8 F 280 A 36

Tour Party
Lt Col. S. D. Jameson *(Army)*, manager; Lt Cdr R. W. Petts *(Navy)*, assistant manager; Flt Lt P. W. Wallis *(Air Force)*, coach; Sgt P. L. Sparrow *(Police)*, masseur/physiotherapist; S. McLean *(Police)*, full-back; W. Matene *(Police)*, D. Ngatai *(Army)*, D. Shelford *(Navy)*, S. Menehira *(Army)*, R. Kapa *(Police)*, C. Cookson *(Navy)*, three-quarters; A. Rangihuna *(Police)*, E. Brown *(Army)*, J. Hohapatu *(Navy)*, E. Elgar *(Army)*, half-backs; W. Shelford *(Navy)* *(captain)*, M. Henderson *(Army)*, C. Natapu *(Air Force)*, M. Brown *(Air Force)*, M. Rosenbrook *(Police)*, D. Boland *(Air Force)*, K. Mitchell *(Police)*, A. Kennedy *(Police)*, B. Harvey *(Police)*, S. Hinds *(Police)*, T. Ryan *(Police)*, R. Tarawhiti *(Police)* *(hooker)*, T. Katting *(Air Force)* *(hooker)*, forwards

Queensland Tour of England, Ireland and Wales

In a short tour, the strongest state side from Australia had mixed fortunes, but four of the six matches were won. Playing generally in wet and windy conditions the tourists with a large number of players from the recent Grand Slam team did not really do themselves justice, particularly in their defeats by Middlesex and Leinster. The best performance came against Kent in the opening match and the team also played well against Munster, whilst the removal of Ulster's long unbeaten record was a fine achievement.

In matches in Europe, Queensland beat Holland (54-4) and lost to Italy (13-15).

Tour Party Officials

Joe French, president; J. Breen, manager; R. Templeton, coach; C. O'Brien, physiotherapist; Dr C. Osborne, honorary medical officer; A. Gough, strapper-baggageman

Players

Backs: R. Gould *(captain)*, G. Martin, B. Moon, P. Grigg, R. Hanley, A. Slack, M. Cook, P. Mills, A. Herbert, M. Lynagh, T. Lane, P. Slattery, B. Smith

Forwards: A. McIntyre *(vice-captain)*, M. Crank, S. Phillpotts, R. Lawton, T. Lawton, M. McBain, D. Frawley, T. Coker, S. Nightingale, W. Campbell, J. Gardner, J. Miller, J. Heinke, G. Hassall

Date	Opponents	Venue	Result
5th Jan.	Kent	Blackheath	W 32-9
8th Jan.	Middlesex	Sudbury (Wasps)	L 4-14
11th Jan.	Leinster	Dublin	L 12-15
14th Jan.	Ulster	Belfast	W 6-4
18th Jan.	Munster	Cork	W 24-15
21st Jan.	Llanelli	Llanelli	W 13-12
	(Carwyn James Memorial Match)		
Match summary:	P 6 W 4 L 2 F 91 A 69		

Scorers

Tries: Moon (3), Smith (2), Miller, Heinke, Grigg, Herbert, Lynagh (1 each)
Dropped-goal: Lynagh
Penalty-goals: Lynagh (6), Gould (4), Smith (2)
Conversions: Smith (3), Gould (2), Lynagh (1)
Leading points scorers: Lynagh (27), Smith (20), Gould (16), Moon (12)

Scotland Tour of Spain and France

Immediately after the latest season had ended Scotland sent a strong touring team to Europe and there were mixed results.

Date	Opponents	Venue	Result
1st May	SPAIN	Barcelona	W 39-17
4th May	Côte Basque	Bayonne	L 19-40
7th May	Regional Selection	Tarbes	D 16-16
10th May	French Barbarians	Agen	L 19-32
14th May	Tarn Selection	Graulhet	W 26-7
Match summary:	P 5 W 2 D 1 L 2 F 119 A 119		

Five matches were played in all, starting with victory over Spain in Barcelona by a very comfortable margin in a fine open match. Seven tries were scored and three conceded, but the next game against Côte Basque in Bayonne saw a complete reversal of that situation as the talented home team themselves scored seven tries to three.

A Regional Selection in Tarbes drew with the tourists (thirty two points being shared) and then in Agen a strong French Barbarians team beat the Scots in a splendid open match, which marked the retirement of that fine French prop, Dospital. Victory at Graulhet against a Tarn Selection ended the tour on almost the right note. The margin of success was large, but the game was poorly handled and ill-tempered at times.

The full party was as follows:

Backs: P. W. Dods (*Gala*), C. F. Flannigan (*Melrose*), M. D. F. Duncan (*West of Scotland*), I. Tukalo (*Selkirk*), A. V. Tait (*Kelso*), D. I. Johnston (*Watsonians*), K. T. Murray (*Hawick*), S. Scott (*Stewart's-Melville FP*), R. Cramb (*Harlequins*), D. S. Wyllie (*Stewart's-Melville FP*), S. G. Johnston (*Watsonians*), J. Scott (*Stewart's-Melville FP*)

Forwards: G. J. Callander (*Kelso*) (*captain*), G. Runciman (*Melrose*), A. K. Brewster (*Stewart's-Melville FP*), N. A. Rowan (*Boroughmuir*), G. Waite (*Kelso*), A. D. G. MacKenzie (*Selkirk*), A. J. Tomes (*Hawick*), A. J. Campbell (*Hawick*), I. A. M. Paxton (*Selkirk*), R. E. Paxton (*Kelso*), J. Jeffrey (*Kelso*), D. B. White (*Gala*), D. J. Turnbull (*Hawick*), J. R. Beattie (*Glasgow Academicals*)

Coaches: D. Grant and I. R. McGeechan

England 'B' in Italy

In May 1986 England 'B' led by Bath's John Palmer made a short tour of Italy with the following results:

Date	Opponents	Venue	Result
7th May	ITALY 'B'	Catania	W 27-14
10th May	ITALY	Olympic Stadium, Rome	D 15-15
Match summary:	P 2 W 1 D 1 F 42 A 29		

It was a very strong combination and a number of players enhanced their chances of being selected for the World Cup squad of forty, which was to be chosen during the summer.

ENGLAND

One of the most discouraging tasks nowadays is that of the English International selectors since, with the largest number of players at their disposal, they are only judged to have been successful when England are Champions of the Five Nations – and that has not happened since 1980. Since that wonderful Grand Slam season there have been moderately successful campaigns in 1981 and 1982, followed by three dreadful years. This recent effort has been equivocal to say the least, with the team gaining narrow victories over Wales and Ireland at Twickenham to set against quite horrific routs in Edinburgh and Paris.

But it was never expected to happen that way. The first half of the season suggested that 1986 would see some good results. England were not involved with any touring team, but with the best players in a number of cases being absent from the Thorn EMI County Championship it was fortuitous

David (Ireland's scrum-half, Bradley) halts Goliath (England's lock, Maurice Colclough) in the England v. Ireland match at Twickenham, 1st March 1986.

that the Inter-Divisional Championship had been resumed and this produced some fine play, giving every encouragement to the optimists.

The Thorn EMI Championship is in fact the first major event of the season, allowing for the fact that its final two rounds take place several months after the preliminaries. Also, some areas have stronger participation by club players than others, so the four semi-finalists are not necessarily the four best counties. This season Lancashire qualified on points difference over Yorkshire and Durham, all three played strong sides. Warwickshire in the Midlands were virtually Coventry under a different name and played to their main strength, a massive pack, and duly reached the semi-finals with few problems. Kent were the surprise in the London area, where they overtook Middlesex on points difference, whilst in the South & South-West Gloucestershire, with players mostly from junior clubs, were still too strong for Somerset, Devon and Cornwall. The Warwickshire pack proved to be just strong enough to overcome Lancashire in one semi-final and Kent were winners of the other over the weakened Gloucestershire side. In the final, the Warwickshire pack dominated in a display of nine-man Rugby to take the title; Graham Robbins scored three tries all from scrummage drives.

Robbins was also the outstanding player of the Divisional Championship (which was also generously sponsored by Thorn EMI) and as a result it was the Midlands team that emerged as Champions, having beaten the North, the South & South-West and London Division to achieve it. London finished second with two wins and the North beat the South & South-West on the final day, which was a big initial disappointment for the selectors, who were looking to players from that area for key positions in their first team. So far the new system was working, or was it?

It was not difficult to select a sound-looking England team for the first match against Wales at Twickenham. Only seven members of the side routed in New Zealand in the 1985 tour were back, Dooley having been a replacement then, and new caps were there in Halliday and Robbins. It looked a good blend and the forwards did well enough against Wales to encourage hopes of a fine campaign; Dooley and Colclough were monopolistic in the line-outs and behind the scrum Andrew punished many Welsh indiscretions; no tries were scored but it was a good-looking win.

Murrayfield should have been the next stage in a victorious season, but things went badly wrong. First, the side appeared not to be match fit after a bad cold spell, but since players frequently miss matches the Saturday before an International this is a weak excuse. As it was, the plan for Murrayfield was the same as for the Twickenham success, but it floundered immediately when the English pack failed to dominate the Scots at the first scrum; the lighter home team held firm and continued to do so throughout the match. At the line-outs it was soon clear that the Scots with four-man lines were prepared to vary their tactics as Wales had not done and this source of supply was correspondingly diminished. The rucks and mauls were won decisively by the more athletic and fitter Scots, whilst the kicking skills of Rob Andrew, so vital in the win against Wales, deserted him. The final score did not flatter the winners and they sent the selectors back to draft a new team.

This they did quite cleverly, but it was hard to see why Salmon and Halliday, who had seen little of the ball at Murrayfield owing to Andrew's poor form there, should have dropped. The inclusion of Richards and Rees in the back-row was right and Chilcott was probably a correct choice to replace Rendall. The match against Ireland was narrowly won, but the method lacked charm since it relied on forward power, which came off on this occasion. However, Richards had an outstanding match and his two tries should have been three. The pack had scrummaged well and took a good share of the line-outs, but there was little to show whether the backs were adequate.

The match in Paris was the final one of the campaign and in theory England had a chance of winning at least a share of the spoils for the season, but there were few who took this seriously and they were proved right. The side did play bravely and were the only team to cross the French line during the Championship, but, as at Murrayfield, the final score was not flattering to the winners. The pack did well at the line-outs, but it was outscrummaged and the French were not only more athletic, but they also made better use of the ball from broken play.

It is easy enough to suggest remedies, but would they work? One possibility is that all future Inter-Divisional competitions should be supplemented by an International trial match as was the case before. In this way, such players as Dean Richards, who was on the bench for the Midlands throughout the recent Divisional matches because Robbins was no. 8 for the region, would have been given a second chance to impress the selectors. Other positions could have been improved by having alternative candidates brought under the scrutiny of the selectors. This was a missing element, and it could have made the difference between a mediocre and good campaign. The selectors are making a sound start for World Cup year by choosing forty players for special squad training, but it is hoped that this will not lead to the removal of all intuition and initiative from players restricted by a rigid system. Forward domination and a pack-orientated game have only limited chances of success and it was significant that England's main club competition, the John Player Cup, was won – as was the case with the Thorn EMI County Championship – by Bath, a team which had strong forwards and relied too much on their scrummaging to the detriment of talented backs.

Leagues are about to become a reality in England at the expense of the present Merit Tables, which will be the basis for such leagues. By the start of the 1987-88 season these will commence with three merit tables still decided on percentages on a national basis. To support these there will be two more leagues, North and South, and they will be further supported by four divisional leagues, which will themselves be supported by regional 'feeder' leagues. It is an exciting prospect and should benefit the game if played in the right spirit.

Of course, there were Merit Table competitions this season and Merit Table A was won by Gloucester, a very competent team that won yet again because they were able to create and generate forward power. Backs again did not have too much running to do. Something should be done to change this state of affairs.

Whatever one may think about the coaching in England and the performances of teams at International levels, it cannot be denied that the sport in pure organizational terms has been very well administered. Any visit to Twickenham is a most enjoyable occasion. The man who has been responsible for this for thirteen years is Air Commodore R. H. G. Weighill, who is retiring this summer to become Secretary of the International Board. His efficiency and unfailing courtesy have been appreciated by everyone and he has been a wonderfully good ambassador for both the Rugby Football Union and the game as a whole.

John Smith Table A

	P	W	L	F	A	%
Gloucester	9	8	1	170	120	88.89
Nottingham	7	5	2	146	82	71.43
Wasps	7	5	2	123	104	71.43
Leicester	10	7	3	213	133	70.00
Bath	6	3	3	142	73	50.00
Harlequins	4	2	2	74	52	50.00
Bristol	7	3	4	117	120	42.86
London Scottish	7	3	4	81	139	42.86
Sale	5	2	3	63	97	40.00
Gosforth	5	2	3	52	109	40.00
Moseley	9	2	7	102	156	22.22
Headingley	8	0	8	77	175	0.00

Champions: Gloucester
Relegated: Gosforth and Headingley

John Smith Table B

	P	W	D	L	F	A	%
Orrell	8	6	0	2	144	87	75.00
Coventry	7	5	0	2	133	71	71.43
Saracens	6	4	0	2	83	62	66.67
Rosslyn Park	7	4	0	3	82	100	57.14
Waterloo	9	5	0	4	161	83	55.55
London Irish	9	5	0	4	126	95	55.55
Liverpool	9	4	0	5	133	127	44.44
Blackheath	8	3	1	4	93	136	43.75
Northampton	7	3	0	4	89	96	42.86
London Welsh	6	2	1	3	95	82	41.67
Richmond	10	4	0	6	128	184	40.00
Bedford	9	2	0	7	81	206	22.22

Promoted to Table A: Orrell (Champions) and Coventry

National Merit Table C

	P	W	L	F	A	%
Metropolitan Police	7	6	1	138	71	85.71
Wakefield	6	4	2	124	74	66.67
Vale of Lune	6	4	2	77	54	66.67
Morley	6	4	2	80	78	66.67
West Hartlepool	7	4	3	138	56	57.14
Plymouth Albion	7	4	3	144	96	57.14
Sheffield	7	4	3	87	88	57.14
Roundhay	9	5	4	130	86	55.55
Fylde	8	4	4	95	131	50.00
Birmingham	7	3	4	46	115	42.86
Exeter	8	1	7	59	173	12.50
Nuneaton	10	1	9	86	182	10.00

South-West Merit Table

	P	W	L	%
Gloucester	8	7	1	87.50
Bath	7	6	1	85.71
Plymouth Albion	7	5	2	71.43
Bristol	8	5	3	62.50
Camborne	6	1	5	16.67
Cheltenham	6	1	5	16.67
Exeter	10	1	9	10.00

Cornwall Merit Table

	P	W	D	L	F	A	%
Camborne	20	20	0	0	527	123	100.00
Redruth	20	15	0	5	323	198	75.00
Truro	20	12	1	7	293	214	62.50
St Ives	20	11	1	8	271	232	57.50
Newquay Hornets	20	10	1	9	272	208	52.50
Launceston	20	9	1	10	220	174	47.50
Penryn	20	8	0	12	252	251	40.00
Hayle	20	8	0	12	170	273	40.00
Penzance & Newlyn	20	6	2	12	171	359	35.00
Falmouth	20	4	1	15	140	391	22.50
St Austell	20	3	1	16	125	341	17.50

Devon Merit Table

Table A	P	W	D	L	F	A	%
Sidmouth	16	13	1	2	259	82	84.38
Okehampton	15	12	0	3	310	83	80.00
Tiverton	12	8	0	4	207	130	66.67
Crediton	15	9	1	5	185	137	63.33
Exmouth	16	9	1	6	107	217	59.38
Devon & Cornwall Police	7	3	0	4	82	78	42.86
Bideford	15	5	0	10	200	231	33.33
Paignton	15	5	0	10	157	287	33.33
Newton Abbot	14	2	1	11	81	259	17.86
Teignmouth	15	1	2	12	101	285	13.33

Bass Merit Table

	P	W	D	L	Pts	%
Taunton	12	11	0	1	22	91.67
Lydney	14	11	1	2	23	82.14
Clifton	15	12	0	3	24	80.00
Brixham	13	8	2	3	18	69.23
St Ives	12	7	0	5	14	58.33
Torquay	11	6	0	5	12	55.55
Stroud	15	7	1	7	15	50.00
Redruth	13	6	0	7	12	46.15
Exeter University	10	4	0	6	8	40.00
Devonport Services	12	4	1	7	9	37.50
Weston-super-Mare	15	5	0	10	11	36.67
Bridgwater	15	4	2	9	10	33.33
Tiverton	11	3	0	8	6	27.27
Avon Police	15	0	0	15	0	0.00

London Division Merit Table

	P	W	D	L	F	A	%
Wasps	7	5	0	2	181	140	71.43
Rosslyn Park	7	5	0	2	141	116	71.43
London Scottish	5	3	1	1	88	90	70.00
Harlequins	7	4	0	3	119	80	57.14
London Irish	9	5	0	4	154	112	55.55
Saracens	6	3	0	3	78	112	50.00
Blackheath	7	2	2	3	94	130	42.85
London Welsh	9	2	2	5	135	141	33.33
Richmond	9	3	0	6	122	145	33.33
Metropolitan Police	8	2	1	5	127	173	31.25

Foster Beard Middlesex County Clubs Merit Table

	P	W	D	L	Pts	%
Ealing	9	8	0	1	16	88.88
Hendon	8	7	0	1	14	87.50
Ruislip	9	7	0	1	14	87.50
Twickenham	11	8	0	3	16	72.72
Hampstead	6	2	2	2	6	49.99
Grasshoppers	8	3	1	4	7	43.75
Harrow	6	2	1	3	5	41.66
Finchley	8	2	1	5	5	31.25
Mill Hill	7	2	0	5	4	28.57
Uxbridge	10	2	1	7	5	25.00
Centaurs	8	2	0	6	4	25.00
Osterley	7	0	0	7	0	0.00

Hendon and Ruislip were level on percentage and points. Hendon beat Ruislip on points average. Uxbridge and Centaurs were level on percentage. Uxbridge beat Centaurs on actual match points gained

Bisley Office Equipment Southern Merit Table

	P	W	D	L	F	A	%
Salisbury	10	9	0	1	212	72	90.00
High Wycombe	9	7	1	1	191	71	83.33
Maidenhead	8	6	0	2	183	61	75.00
Abbey	8	5	0	3	115	78	62.50
Guildford & Godalming	7	4	0	3	108	51	57.14
Bournemouth	8	4	1	3	125	117	56.25
Henley	11	6	0	5	167	106	54.55
Havant	8	3	1	4	70	90	43.75
Newbury	9	3	1	5	113	178	38.89
Reading	8	3	0	5	91	95	37.50
Trojans	10	1	0	9	63	264	10.00
Staines	10	0	0	10	44	299	0.00

Mercia Merit Table

	P	W	D	L	F	A	%
Stourbridge	8	8	0	0	131	35	100.00
Lichfield	8	5	0	3	149	100	62.50
Derby	9	5	1	3	112	99	61.11
Solihull	5	3	0	2	54	53	60.00
Wolves	9	5	0	4	79	82	55.55
Stoke	11	6	0	5	142	140	54.54
Walsall	10	5	0	5	135	83	50.00
Stafford	9	4	0	5	125	109	44.44
Newbold	6	2	0	4	36	92	33.33
Dudley KW	10	3	0	7	30	104	30.00
Hinckley	8	2	0	6	67	103	25.00
Burton	7	1	1	5	39	128	21.43

Girobank League, Leading Positions

	P	W	D	L	F	A	%
North-West Division 1							
Widnes	9	8	0	1	161	94	16
West Park	8	7	0	1	169	48	14
Wigton	9	7	0	2	174	59	14

	P	W	D	L	F	A	%
East Area Division 1							
Sandbach	9	8	1	0	140	54	17
Macclesfield	8	6	1	1	138	39	13
Old Aldwinians	9	6	1	2	128	81	13
North Area Division 1							
Moresby	9	7	0	2	137	50	14
Workington	8	5	2	1	152	76	12
Vickers	9	6	0	3	96	73	12
West Area Division 1							
Warrington	9	8	1	0	182	60	17
Merseyside Police	10	7	1	2	200	121	15
Ormskirk	10	6	1	3	142	56	13

Heart of England Merit Table

	P	W	D	L	F	A	%
Barkers' Butts	9	8	0	1	217	71	88.89
Vipers	7	6	0	1	138	64	85.71
Banbury	6	5	0	1	138	44	83.33
Stamford	5	4	0	1	101	37	80.00
Towcestrians	9	6	0	3	153	78	66.67
Wigston	9	5	0	4	121	98	55.55
Oadby-Wyggestonians	7	3	0	4	61	126	42.86
Old Northamptonians	7	2	0	5	59	125	28.57
Long Buckby	8	2	0	6	83	130	25.00
Bletchley	5	1	0	4	35	99	20.00
Bedford Athletic	9	1	1	7	72	185	16.67
Ampthill	7	0	1	6	42	163	7.14

Wyvern Merit Table

	P	W	D	L	F	A	%
Malvern	7	6	1	0	135	45	92.86
Selly Oak	7	4	2	1	109	56	71.43
Bournville	6	3	1	2	88	51	58.33
Droitwich	7	4	0	3	63	36	57.14
Warley	7	3	1	3	40	86	50.00
Woodrush	6	2	1	3	49	35	41.67
Redditch	7	1	0	6	54	124	14.29
Pershore	7	1	0	6	45	150	14.29

Northern Merit Table

	P	W	D	L	F	A	%
Waterloo	9	8	0	1	253	60	88.89
Gosforth	11	9	0	2	180	115	81.82
West Hartlepool	10	8	0	2	155	76	80.00
Orrell	9	7	0	2	203	80	77.78
Sale	11	8	0	3	296	113	72.73
Wakefield	9	5	0	4	128	104	55.36
Liverpool	11	6	0	5	146	203	54.55
Durham	11	5	1	5	172	140	50.00
Morley	8	3	0	5	87	150	37.50
Vale of Lune	9	3	0	6	115	166	33.33
Fylde	9	3	0	6	103	214	33.33
Roundhay	12	3	1	8	113	192	29.17
Headingley	10	2	0	8	96	174	20.00
Middlesbrough	10	2	0	8	53	210	20.00
Sheffield	11	2	0	9	117	200	18.18

John Player Special Cup

First Round

28th September 1985

Aspatria	19	Westoe	24
Berry Hill	36	Bournemouth	6
Bletchley	20	Maidenhead	9
Cheshunt	23	Askeans	23
(Cheshunt win on tries)			
Evesham	9	Bedford	13
Gloucester	87	Exeter University	3
Havant	17	Guildford	7
Maidstone	6	Lewes	21
Matlock	13	Barkers Butts	11
Mid-Whitgiftians	4	Southend	12
Morley	19	Wakefield	27
Nuneaton	19	Lichfield	23
Redcliffians	6	Coney Hill	17
Richmond	21	London Irish	14
Saracens	27	North Walsham	6
Sheffield	13	Vale of Lune	16
St Ives	18	Henley	22
Stourbridge	9	Broughton Park	13
Tynedale	22	Lymm	0
Peterborough	10	Loughborough University	24

Result of the Round

Nuneaton	19	Lichfield	23

Even at this early stage there was much of interest, with London Irish unfortunate to draw Richmond and go out. Lichfield did well to win at Nuneaton and Gloucester, entering at this point, routed Exeter University. It showed that there is something special (no pun intended) about cup knock-out competitions.

Second Round

26th October 1985

Bedford	10	Broughton Park	37
Lichfield	39	Matlock	7
Loughborough University	17	Berry Hill	10
Wakefield	42	Tynedale	6
Westoe	15	Vale of Lune	21
Bletchley	6	Havant	9
Coney Hill	6	Saracens	15
Lewes	10	Gloucester	24
Richmond	30	Cheshunt	6
Southend	19	Henley	3

Result of the Round

Bedford	10	Broughton Park	37

Poor Bedford's awful season continued with a big home defeat at the hands of Broughton Park, but the other 'big guns' survived along with Lichfield and two student teams – Loughborough University and West London Institute. Now further opportunities for fame beckoned.

Third Round

25th January 1986

Camborne	15	Havant	4
Coventry	14	Leicester	21
Gloucester	7	Bristol	4
Harlequins	9	Headingley	6
Lichfield	26	West London Institute	0
London Scottish	16	Sale	6
London Welsh	10	Plymouth	6

Wasps RFC, John Player Special Cup runners-up, at Twickenham, 26th April 1986. Back row (left to right) L. Prideaux, R. Quittenton (touch judges), P. Minihan (replacement), K. Titcombe (replacement), A. Isichei (replacement), M. Rigby, M. A. Rose, J. Bonner, M. C. F. Pinnegar, D. Pegler, J. A. Probyn, A. Simmons, G. Holmes, J. Ellison (replacement), J. Samuel (replacement), P. Balcombe (replacement), official, F. A. Howard (referee), official. Front row (left to right) N. C. Stringer (kneeling), M. D. Bailey, R. Pellow, M. Taylor (coach), R. M. Cardus (captain), G. L. Rees, S. T. Smith, S. M. Bates.

Nottingham	25	Southend	12
Orrell	16	Bath	16
(Bath go through)			
Rosslyn Park	19	Wakefield	23
Saracens	11	Waterloo	8
Wasps	23	Loughborough University	3
West Hartlepool	3	Moseley	33

26th January 1986

| Richmond | 7 | Blackheath | 12 |

1st February 1986

Broughton Park	12	Vale of Lune	6
Gosforth	6	Northampton	6
(Northampton advance)			

Result of the Round

| Rosslyn Park | 19 | Wakefield | 23 |

All team's exempted until now played and one, Rosslyn Park, were shocked at home by unfancied Wakefield. Another Yorkshire club failed narrowly at Stoop against Harlequins, even though they played for more than an hour without the prop, Machell, who was sent off. London's two remaining Exiles survived, both with somewhat lucky wins – Scottish against Sale and, more so, Welsh against Plymouth Albion. Even luckier were the holders, Bath, who went forward by dint of being the visitors in a drawn game at Orrell. The two student teams went out with Lichfield, the conquerors of West London Institute, paying yet another visit to the Fourth Round.

Fourth Round

22nd February 1986

Lichfield	6	Harlequins	23
London Welsh	12	Camborne	9
Moseley	4	Bath	22

8th March 1986

Northampton	6	London Scottish	11
Saracens	6	Gloucester	13
Wakefield	7	Nottingham	26

9th March 1986

| Broughton Park | 6 | Leicester | 40 |

22nd March 1986

| Blackheath | 12 | Wasps | 24 |

Result of the Round

| Moseley | 4 | Bath | 22 |

The round took four weeks to complete, thanks to the weather! Three matches were completed on the scheduled day and the quarter-finals draw was postponed. Bath's win at Moseley was probably the best performance in a round without surprise results. London Welsh (finalists last season) were very lucky to survive at home against Camborne.

Quarter-finals

8th March 1986

| London Welsh | 10 | Bath | 18 |

22nd March 1986

| Harlequins | 8 | Leicester | 15 |
| London Scottish | 12 | Gloucester | 8 |

28th March 1986

| Nottingham | 13 | Wasps | 13 |
| (Wasps qualify on try-count, 2-1) | | | |

Result of the Round

| London Scottish | 12 | Gloucester | 8 |

Another fragmented round ended on Good Friday with Wasps rallying to draw at Nottingham and advance on the try-count. Earlier, Bath eliminated a gallant London Welsh as did Leicester's power against the brave Harlequins. 'Scottish' surprised

Bath RFC, John Player Special Cup winners, at Twickenham, 26th April 1986. Back row (left to right) R. Quittenton (touch judge), Bath official, L. Prideaux (touch judge), replacement, Bath official, G. Dawe, replacement, R. A. Spurrell, N. C. Redman, D. Egerton (replacement), J. Morrison, J. P. Hall, C. R. Martin, M. R. Lee, G. J. Chilcott, three officials, F. A. Howard (referee). Front row (left to right) physiotherapist, replacement (kneeling), replacement, A. Swift, S. J. Halliday, J. A. Palmer (captain), D. M. Trick, S. Barnes, R. J. Hill, replacement, physiotherapist (kneeling).

Gloucester, whose cause was not helped by the 52nd minute dismissal of their lock, Brain, for punching at a maul.

Semi-finals

5th April 1986

Leicester	6	Bath	10
Wasps	11	London Scottish	3

Losing semi-final teams

Leicester: W. Hare; B. Evans, P. Dodge, S. Burnhill, K. Williams; L. Cusworth (*captain*), N. Youngs; S. Redfern, C. Tressler, W. Richardson, J. Wells, J. Davidson, M. Foulkes-Arnold, R. Tebbutt, D. Richards. *Replacement:* S. Kenney for N. Youngs, 18 minutes

Referee: R. Quittenton (*London*)

London Scottish: G. Hastings; L. Batten, L. Renwick, S. Irvine, T. Patterson-Brown; N. Chesworth, A. Cushing; N. Weir, I. Kirk, T. Borthwick, S. Austen, J. Campbell-Lamerton, D. Tosh, I. Morrison, J. Macklin (*captain*)

Referee: L. Prideaux (*North Midlands*)

The two matches were played on the same day and only two weeks behind schedule, with Bath reaching their third successive final and removing Leicester's unbeaten home record in the competition. Hare (Leicester) and Barnes (Bath) each kicked two penalty-goals, but a try for the more powerful visitors just before half-time was decisive. At Sudbury Wasps, despite missing many kicks at goal, deservedly reached their first final through tries by Simon Smith and Rigby with a late penalty following from Stringer shortly after Irvine had kicked one for London Scottish.

Final

Saturday, 26th April 1986, at Twickenham

Bath	25	Wasps	17

Tries: Swift, Spurrell, Hill, Simpson (1 each)
Penalty-goal: Trick
Conversions: Trick (3)
Half-time: 7-13

Tries: Stringer, Pellow Balcombe (1 each)
Penalty-goal: Stringer
Conversion: Stringer

Bath: C. R. Martin; D. M. Trick, J. A. Palmer (*captain*), S. J. Halliday, A. Swift; S. Barnes, R. J. Hill; G. J. Chilcott, G. Dawe, M. R. Lee, R. A. Spurrell, J. Morrison, N. C. Redman, J. P. Hall, P. D. Simpson

Wasps: N. C. Stringer; S. T. Smith, R. M. Cardus (*captain*), R. Pellow, M. D. Bailey; G. L. Rees, S. M. Bates; G. Holmes, A. Simmons, J. A. Probyn, D. Pegler, J. Bonner, M. C. F. Pinnegar, M. Rigby, M. A. Rose. *Replacement:* P. Balcombe for Bates, 34 minutes

Referee: F. A. Howard (*Liverpool Society*)

Bath's success at Twickenham was to be expected and at the end of a fine, if at times ill-tempered, match it could fairly be said that it was deserved.

'We're just good friends!' Is that what Dawe of Bath is saying to Simmons (Wasps) as his colleagues try restraint in the John Player Special Cup final at Twickenham?

But Wasps, badly depleted by injuries, put up a tremendous show on a beautiful spring afternoon and they earned great praise for making it such an enjoyable match. Much of the enterprise came from them and they earned every point they scored.

After early Bath pressure, Wasps broke out and a fine move across the line started by Rigby and Rees led to Bailey trying to go in at the corner; when checked, he passed inside and Stringer went over, failing to convert. Within three minutes, an absolutely brilliant try was produced by the Wasps, who turned a Bath attack into a swift counter starting with a break by Rees, Cardus and Pellow from their own '22'; Stringer passed to Bailey, whose own inside transfer found Cardus and Pellow, who went over for Stringer to convert. The latter then converted a penalty after Bath had fallen offside, although Hall was also warned for a foul on Bailey. Bath fought back before half-time to produce a good try by Swift in the corner and a penalty-goal by Trick.

The second half belonged to the Bath pack, who worked tries for Spurrell and Simpson from short-range scrums and another from Hill, who also ran over after picking up from another five-metre scrum. Trick converted all three well, but Wasps had the last word when Balcombe, a replacement, scored a fine try after being sent away by Smith.

At times, this was a bad-tempered affair and referee Howard had to issue a final warning to both teams after an hour; soon afterwards, a Bath player threw a punch, which luckily for him was not seen by the referee. Generally, however, the entertainment was excellent, with Wasps' enterprising backs being unable in the end to acquire enough ball, so dominant were the Bath forwards against a much-changed and struggling Wasps pack.

This was Bath's third successive victory in the event and ten of their players appeared in all three games – Martin, Trick, Palmer, Hill, Chilcott, Lee, Redman, Spurrell, Hall and Simpson. They have won the competition on those three occasions only and the other three-time winners are Leicester. Gloucester, Coventry and Gosforth have won twice, there has been one shared title between Gloucester and Moseley, and single-time winners are Bedford and Bristol.

Cup Winners, 1972-85

1972	Gloucester	17	Moseley	6
1973	Coventry	27	Bristol	15
1974	Coventry	26	London Scottish	6
1975	Bedford	28	Rosslyn Park	12
1976	Gosforth	23	Rosslyn Park	14
1977	Gosforth	27	Waterloo	11
1978	Gloucester	6	Leicester	3
1979	Leicester	15	Moseley	12
1980	Leicester	21	London Irish	9
1981	Leicester	22	Gosforth	15
1982	Gloucester (Trophy shared)	12	Moseley	12
1983	Bristol	28	Leicester	22
1984	Bath	10	Bristol	9
1985	Bath	24	London Welsh	15

County Cups

Cheshire
Sale beat Birkenhead Park (no score given)

Cumbria
Wigton beat Netherhall (no score given)

Devon
Plymouth Albion	15	Exeter	6

Durham
West Hartlepool	33	Gateshead Fell	6

Lancashire
Vale of Lune beat Preston Grasshoppers (after replay, no score given)

Leicestershire
Syston beat Wigston (no score given)

North Midlands
Stourbridge beat Dixonians (no score given)

Northumberland
Gosforth	9	Tynedale	7

Somerset
Taunton	21	Combe Down	13

Warwickshire
Solihull beat Leamingtonians (no score given)

Yorkshire
Wakefield beat Morley (no score given)

Berkshire Giddy & Giddy Cup
Reading	18	Newbury	0

Buckinghamshire
Marlow	15	High Wycombe	11

Bedfordshire
Leighton Buzzard	10	Luton	3

Cornwall
St Ives	4	Camborne	0

East Midlands
Leighton Buzzard	16	Peterborough	6

Essex
Eton Manor	11	Harlow	0

Essex (William Younger Floodlit Cup)
Harlow	16	Basildon	6

Eastern Counties
Sudbury	31	Saffron Walden	3

Hampshire
Havant	10	United Services, Portsmouth	0

Hertfordshire President's MSB Cup
Hertford	12	Letchworth	6

Hertfordshire Floodlit Cup
Cheshunt	4	Hertford	0

Dorset & Wiltshire Cup
Swindon	12	Bournemouth	6

Kent
Blackheath	13	Askeans	6

Lincolnshire
Lincoln	9	Boston	6

Middlesex
Saracens	19	Wasps	3

Middlesex Agar Cup
Old Gaytonians	18	Grasshoppers	9

Oxfordshire
Oxford	9	Henley	7

Suffolk
Sudbury	13	Ipswich	3

Staffordshire
Lichfield	26	Leek	0

Surrey
London Irish	34	Reigatians	12

Sussex
Worthing	9	East Grinstead	4

Notts, Lincs & Derbys
Paviors	37	Lincoln	3

Thorn EMI County Championship

South-Western Division

Division 1

9th November 1985

Somerset	19	Devon	7
Gloucestershire	13	Cornwall	9

16th November 1985

Cornwall	21	Devon	3
Gloucestershire	23	Somerset	10

23rd November 1985

Cornwall	22	Somerset	3
Devon	6	Gloucestershire	25

	P	W	L	F	A	Pts
Gloucestershire	3	3	0	61	25	6
Cornwall	3	2	1	52	19	4
Somerset	3	1	2	32	52	2
Devon	3	0	3	16	65	0

Gloucestershire qualify for national semi-finals. Devon are relegated to Division 2.

Division 2

9th November 1985

Berkshire	12	Buckinghamshire	10
Oxfordshire	24	Dorset & Wiltshire	28

16th November 1985

Dorset & Wiltshire	9	Buckinghamshire	0
Oxfordshire	3	Berkshire	13

23rd November 1985

Berkshire	9	Dorset & Wiltshire	6
Buckinghamshire	6	Oxfordshire	22

	P	W	L	F	A	Pts
Berkshire	3	3	0	34	19	6
Dorset & Wiltshire	3	2	1	43	33	4
Oxfordshire	3	1	2	49	47	2
Buckinghamshire	3	0	3	16	43	0

Berkshire are promoted to Division 1.

London Division

Group A

16th October 1985

Kent	3	Middlesex	17
Surrey	20	Hertfordshire	9

30th October 1985

Middlesex	10	Surrey	16
Hertfordshire	21	Kent	32

13th November 1985

Kent	23	Surrey	6
Hertfordshire	10	Middlesex	13

	P	W	L	F	A	Pts
Kent	3	2	1	58	44	4
Middlesex	3	2	1	40	29	4
Surrey	3	2	1	42	42	4
Hertfordshire	3	0	3	40	65	0

Hertfordshire are relegated to Group B. Kent qualify for national semi-finals.

Group B

16th October 1985

Sussex	9	Hampshire	6

23rd October 1985

Hampshire	9	Eastern Counties	12

30th October 1985

Eastern Counties	20	Sussex	7

9th November 1985

Hampshire	13	Sussex	6

16th November 1985

Sussex	9	Eastern Counties	9

23rd November 1985

Eastern Counties	7	Hampshire	7

	P	W	D	L	F	A	Pts
Eastern Counties	4	2	2	0	48	32	6
Hampshire	4	1	1	2	28	27	3
Sussex	4	1	1	2	31	48	3

Eastern Counties are promoted to Group A.

Midland Division

Group 1

9th October 1985

Staffordshire	15	Leicestershire	34

15th October 1985

Leicestershire	25	Warwickshire	13

23rd October 1985

Warwickshire	37	Staffordshire	16

	P	W	L	F	A	Pts
Leicestershire	2	2	0	59	28	4
Warwickshire	2	1	1	50	41	2
Staffordshire	2	0	2	31	71	0

Group 2

8th October 1985

Notts, Lincs & Derbys	0	North Midlands	6

15th October 1985

East Midlands	6	Notts, Lincs & Derbys	10

23rd October 1985

North Midlands	24	East Midlands	12

	P	W	L	F	A	Pts
North Midlands	2	2	0	30	12	4
Notts, Lincs & Derbys	2	1	1	10	12	2
East Midlands	2	0	2	18	34	0

Semi-finals

6th November 1985

Leicestershire (at Westleigh)	26	Notts, Lincs & Derbys	9
North Midlands (at Moseley)	4	Warwickshire	46

Final

20th November 1985

Leicestershire (at Leicester)	3	Warwickshire	26

Warwickshire qualify for national semi-finals.

Northern Division

16th October 1985

Cumbria	15	Cheshire	22
Lancashire	24	Yorkshire	26
Northumberland	3	Durham	12

30th October 1985

Cheshire	6	Lancashire	44
Yorkshire	31	Northumberland	6
Durham	27	Cumbria	9

9th November 1985

Cumbria	7	Lancashire	14
Cheshire	17	Northumberland	14
Durham	19	Yorkshire	11

16th November 1985

Yorkshire	24	Cumbria	10
Durham	26	Cheshire	0
Northumberland	3	Lancashire	38

23rd November 1985

Yorkshire	34	Cheshire	12
Northumberland	10	Cumbria	4
Lancashire	25	Durham	9

	P	W	L	F	A	Pts
Lancashire	5	4	1	145	51	8
Yorkshire	5	4	1	126	71	8
Durham	5	4	1	93	48	8
Cumbria	5	1	4	45	87	2
Northumberland	5	1	4	36	102	2
Cheshire	5	1	4	47	133	2

Lancashire qualify for national semi-finals on points difference.

Semi-final

Saturday, 8th March 1986, at Blackheath

Kent	**16**	**Gloucestershire**	**3**

Try: Cokell
Dropped-goal: Colyer
Penalty-goals: Field (3)

Penalty-goal: Russell
Half-time: 13-3

Kent (Blackheath unless otherwise stated): G. Walters; J. Field (*Askeans*), L. Cokell, R. Bodenham (*captain*), D. Osbourne (*Rosslyn Park*); N. Colyer, C. Read (*Plymouth Albion*); P. Essenhigh, R. Howe, K. Rutter, D. Vaughan, D. Hursey, P. McRae (*Askeans*), M. Skinner (*Harlequins*), R. Cheval (*Askeans*).

Gloucestershire: P. Cue (*Bath*); A. Morley (*Bristol*), S. Hogg (*Bristol*), L. Jones (*Matson*), T. Bick (*Berry Hill*); B. Russell (*Gordon League*), W. Hall (*Coney Hill*); G. Sargeant (*Gloucester*) (*captain*), S. Everall (*Cheltenham*), R. Picket (*Berry Hill*), T. Buck (*Berry Hill*), P. Miles (*Bristol*), M. Scuse (*Bristol*), I. Seymour (*Berry Hill*), J. Price (*Coney Hill*). Replacement: T. Davies (*Stroud*) for Hall, 33 minutes

Referee: F. Howard (*Liverpool*)

Kent, Thorn EMI County Championship finalists, at Twickenham, 12th April 1986. Back row (left to right) *three officials, D. J. Hudson (touch judge), L. Prideaux (referee), I. Bullerwell (touch judge), replacement, L. Cokell, S. E. Thresher, P. J. McRae, D. G. Hursey, R. E. Cheval, M. G. Skinner, P. Essenhigh, replacement, K. T. F. Rutter, officials and replacements.* Front row (left to right) *J. H. Field, C. T. Read, N. W. Collyer, R. R. D. Bodenham (captain), R. K. Howe, D. Vaughan, D. Osbourne.*

Semi-final

Saturday, 8th March 1986, at Nuneaton

| Warwickshire | 19 | Lancashire | 15 |

Tries: Johnson, Robbins
P. Thomas (1 each)
Penalty-goal: S. Thomas
Conversions: S. Thomas (2)

Tries: Heslop (2)
Penalty-goal: O'Brien
Conversions: O'Brien (2)
Half-time: 4-11

Warwickshire (Coventry unless otherwise stated): Steve Hall (*Barkers' Butts*); C. Leake (*Nuneaton*), B. Massey, C. Millerchip, Stuart Hall; T. Buttimore (*Leicester*), S. Thomas; L. Johnson, A. Farrington, S. Wilkes, R. Travers, A. Gulliver, B. Kidner, P. Thomas, G. Robbins (*captain*). *Replacement:* B. Masser (*Nuneaton*) for Farrington, 74 minutes

Lancashire (Orrell unless otherwise stated): K. O'Brien (*Broughton Park*); J. Carleton, G. Ainscough, S. Langford, N. Heslop (*Waterloo*); P. Williams, G. Williams; K. Fletcher, N. Hitchin, D. Southern, P. Moss, J. Syddall (*Waterloo*) (*captain*), W. Dooley (*Preston Grasshoppers*), S. Gallagher (*Waterloo*), M. Kenrick (*Sale*)

Referee: R. C. Quittenton (*London*)

One moderate match and one excellent encounter characterized these semi-finals. Despite intense second-half pressure, Kent increased their well-earned half-time lead at Blackheath against a Gloucestershire team minus the stars of both Gloucester and Bristol with one or two honourable exceptions.

At Nuneaton, the home team fought back after being behind by 15 points to 4, thanks to outstanding captaincy by Robbins and a fine rally after Lancashire had dominated much of the match. Kent had reached the final for the first time since 1927, but the Midlanders have a more recent history of continued success.

Final

Saturday, 12th April 1986, at Twickenham

| Kent | 6 | Warwickshire | 16 |

Dropped-goal: Colyer
Penalty-goal: Field
Half-time: 6-6

Tries: Robbins (3)
Conversions: S. Thomas (2)

Kent (Blackheath unless stated): S. E. Thresher (*Harlequins*); J. H. Field (*Askeans*), L. Cokell, R. R. D. Bodenham (*captain*), D. Osbourne (*Rosslyn Park*); N. W. Colyer, C. T. Read (*Plymouth Albion*); P. Essenhigh, R. K. Howe, K. T. F. Rutter, D. Vaughan, D. G. Hursey, P. J. McRae (*Askeans*), M. G. Skinner (*Harlequins*), R. E. Cheval (*Askeans*)

Warwickshire (Coventry unless stated): Steve Hall (*Barkers' Butts*); C. Leake (*Nuneaton*), C. J. Millerchip, R. Massey, Stuart Hall; T. Buttimore (*Leicester*), S. Thomas; L. Johnson, A. Farrington, S. Wilkes, P. Thomas, A. Gulliver, B. Kidner, R. Travers, G. Robbins (*captain*)

Referee: L. Prideaux (*North Midlands*)

An entertaining first half saw the teams change round level on points, with Kent having played with much enterprise to take a six-point lead before the first of three push-over tries by Robbins brought parity for the Midlanders. If anything, Kent deserved to lead at the interval as their backs looked far more convincing.

But after the break Warwickshire's pack took complete control and there was little Kent could do about it. Each mistake was severely punished by some shrewd kicking from Steve Thomas, who kept them 'pegged' back in defence, and two more push-over tries from Robbins resulted. Thomas converted the first as he had done before half-time.

It was a sign of the times that Robbins, the hero of the game, was the only International player on view, and the tournament as a whole seemed to

Warwickshire, at Twickenham, 12th April 1986. Back row (left to right) three officials, I. Bullerwell (touch judge), L. Prideaux (referee), replacement, S. Wilkes, P. Thomas, B. Kidner, A. Gulliver, C. Millerchip, R. Travers, remainder officials. Front row (left to right) L. Johnson, Steve Hall, S. Thomas, Warwickshire president, G. Robbins, R. Massey, A. Farrington. Kneeling (left to right) replacement, replacement, T. Buttimore, Stuart Hall, C. Leake, replacement, replacement.

have lost some prestige due to the 'club v. county' problems which beset players. Even so, Kent had done well to reach this stage, having first disposed of the challenge of Middlesex (on points difference when the actual match between them had been lost by Kent); in the semi-finals, they beat the challenge of an unfamiliar Gloucestershire team. Warwickshire had comfortably won their own regional division, but in the semi-final they were very hard pressed by Lancashire, who had themselves found qualification (on points difference in the end) no easy matter in the North against the challenges of Yorkshire and Durham.

It is a fervent hope that this worthy competition will soon return to its former importance. In the West Country, the playing of county matches in mid-week may ease some of the problems, but Rugby is, after all, an amateur sport and there are times when it would seem that there are too many calls on the players.

This was Warwickshire's ninth success in the competition. Kent have won it on three occasions and were in the final on the last occasion in 1927, when they had the last of their victories.

English County Champions, 1889-1985

1889	Yorkshire	1947	Lancashire beat Gloucestershire (14-3) at Gloucester, after an 8-all draw at Blundell-sands	1962	Warwickshire beat Hampshire (11-6) at Twickenham
1890	Yorkshire				
1891	Lancashire			1963	Warwickshire beat Yorkshire (13-10) at Coventry
1892	Yorkshire				
1893	Yorkshire				
1894	Yorkshire	1948	Lancashire beat Eastern Counties (5-0) at Cambridge	1964	Warwickshire beat Lancashire (8-6) at Coventry
1895	Yorkshire				
1896	Yorkshire				
1897	Kent	1949	Lancashire beat Gloucestershire (9-3) at Blundellsands	1965	Warwickshire beat Durham (15-9) at Hartlepool
1898	Northumberland				
1899	Devon				
1900	Durham	1950	Cheshire beat East Midlands (5-0) at Birkenhead Park	1966	Middlesex beat Lancashire (6-0) at Blundellsands
1901	Devon				
1902	Durham				
1903	Durham	1951	East Midlands beat Middlesex (10-0) at Northampton	1967	Surrey and Durham, after drawing twice, (14-14) at Twickenham and (0-0) at Hartlepool, became joint Champions
1904	Kent				
1905	Durham				
1906	Devon	1952	Middlesex beat Lancashire (9-6) at Twickenham		
1907	Devon and Durham				
1908	Cornwall				
1909	Durham	1953	Yorkshire beat East Midlands (11-3) at Bradford	1968	Middlesex beat Warwickshire (9-6) at Twickenham
1910	Gloucestershire				
1911	Devon				
1912	Devon	1954	Middlesex beat Lancashire (24-6) at Blundellsands	1969	Lancashire beat Cornwall (11-9) at Redruth
1913	Gloucestershire				
1914	Midlands				
1920	Gloucestershire	1955	Lancashire beat Middlesex (14-8) at Twickenham	1970	Staffordshire beat Gloucestershire (11-9) at Burton-on-Trent
1921	Gloucestershire				
1922	Gloucestershire				
1923	Somerset	1956	Middlesex beat Devon (13-9) at Twickenham	1971	Surrey beat Gloucestershire (14-3) at Gloucester
1924	Cumberland				
1925	Leicestershire	1957	Devon beat Yorkshire (12-3) at Plymouth	1972	Gloucestershire beat Warwickshire (11-6) at Coventry
1926	Yorkshire				
1927	Kent	1958	Warwickshire beat Cornwall (16-8) at Coventry		
1928	Yorkshire			1973	Lancashire beat Gloucestershire
1929	Middlesex	1959	Warwickshire beat Gloucestershire (14-9) at Bristol		
1930	Gloucestershire				
1931	Gloucestershire				
1932	Gloucestershire	1960	Warwickshire beat Surrey (9-6) at Coventry		
1933	Hampshire				
1934	East Midlands				
1935	Lancashire	1961	Cheshire beat Devon (5-3) at Birkenhead Park, after a no-points draw at Plymouth		
1936	Hampshire				
1937	Gloucestershire				
1938	Lancashire				
1939	Warwickshire				

	(17-12) at Bristol
1974	Gloucestershire beat Lancashire (22-12) at Blundellsands
1975	Gloucestershire beat Eastern Counties (13-9) at Gloucester
1976	Gloucester beat Middlesex (24-9) at Richmond
1977	Lancashire beat Middlesex (17-6) at Blundellsands
1978	North Midlands beat Gloucestershire (10-7) at Moseley
1979	Middlesex beat Northumberland (19-6) at Twickenham
1980	Lancashire beat Gloucestershire (21-15) at Vale of Lune
1981	Northumberland beat Gloucestershire (15-6) at Gloucester
1982	Lancashire beat North Midlands (7-3) at Moseley
1983	Gloucestershire beat Yorkshire (19-7) at Bristol
1984	Gloucestershire beat Somerset (36-18) at Twickenham
1985	Middlesex beat Notts, Lincs & Derbys (12-9) at Twickenham

The title has gone to Gloucestershire 15 times, Lancashire 12, Yorkshire 10, Warwickshire 9, Middlesex 8, Devon 7 (once jointly), Durham 7 (twice jointly), Kent 3, Hampshire, East Midlands, Cheshire and Northumberland twice each, Surrey twice (once jointly), Cornwall, Midlands, Somerset, Cumberland, Leicestershire, Staffordshire and North Midlands once each.

Thorn EMI Divisional Championship

7th December 1985

London	22	South & South-West	3
(at Stoop Memorial Ground)			
Midlands	28	North	15
(at Nottingham)			

14th December 1985

North	3	London	7
(at Otley)			
South & South-West	9	Midlands	19
(at Gloucester)			

21st December 1985

Midlands	12	London	3
(at Northampton)			
South & South-West	17	North	28
(at Bristol)			

	P	W	L	F	A	Pts
Midlands	3	3	0	59	27	6
London	3	2	1	32	18	4
North	3	1	2	46	52	2
South & South-West	3	0	3	29	69	0

The Thorn EMI Divisional Championship might not have gone the way the selectors had hoped, as Midlands won from London with the well-fancied North and South & South-West trailing badly. Some selection problems were created by all this. The most impressive player in the tournament was the Midlands no. 8, Graham Robbins of Coventry, who had yet to be capped. Others who did well were Huw Davies at full-back for London and Rob Andrew, partnered by the injury-prone Melville, for the North. But, on the strength of these matches alone, it would have been dangerous for the selectors to make judgments; a full-scale trial might have been a good idea.

Teams

London

Backs: G. H. Davies (*Wasps*), SSW, N, M; S. T. Smith (*Wasps*), SSW, N, M; R. Lozowski (*Wasps*), SSW, N, M; J. Salmon (*Harlequins*), SSW, N, M; M. Bailey (*Cambridge University*), SSW, N, M; S. Smith (*Richmond*), SSW, M; S. Bates (*Wasps*), SSW, N, M; N. Colyer (*Blackheath*), N

Forwards: P. Rendall (*Wasps*), SSW, N, M; A. Simmons (*Wasps*), SSW, N, M; J. Probyn (*Wasps*), SSW, N, M; K. Moss (*Wasps*), SSW, N, M; C. Pinnegar (*Wasps*), SSW, N, M; M. Colclough (*Swansea*), SSW, N, M; D. Cooke (*Harlequins*), SSW, N, M (*all as captain*); P. Jackson (*Harlequins*), SSW, N, M

Scorers: v.SSW (*tries*: Davies (2), S. T. Smith; *penalty-goals*: Davies (2); *conversions*: Davies (2)); v. N (*try*: Salmon; *penalty-goal*: Davies); v. M (*penalty-goal*: Davies)

South & South-West

Backs: C. Martin (*Bath*), L, M, N; D. Trick (*Bath*), L; J. Palmer (*Bath*), L, M, N; S. Halliday (*Bath*), L, M; J. Carr (*Bristol*), L; M. Hamlin (*Gloucester*), L; R. Hill (*Bath*), L, M, N; R. Knibbs (*Bristol*), M, N; S. Barnes (*Bath*), M, N; B. Trevaskis (*Bath*), M, N; C. Howard (*Bristol*), N

Forwards: G. Chilcott (*Bath*), L; P. Stiff (*Bristol*), L (r); K. White (*Gloucester*), L; A. Dun (*Bristol*), L; J. Orwin (*Gloucester*), L, M, N; N. Redman (*Bath*), L, M, N; R. Spurrell (*Bath*), L, M, N (*all as captain*); M. Teague (*Cardiff*), L; M. Preedy (*Gloucester*), M, N; K. Bogira (*Bristol*), M, N; R. Pascall (*Gloucester*), L, M, N; J. Hall (*Bath*), M, N; D. Egerton (*Bath*), M, N

Scorers: v. L (*penalty-goal:* Palmer); v. M (*try:* Halliday; *penalty-goal:* Barnes; *conversion:* Barnes); v. N (*tries:* Egerton, Howard, Redman; *conversion:* Barnes; *penalty-goal:* Barnes)

Midlands

Backs: S. Hodgkinson (*Nottingham*), N, SSW, L; S. Holdstock (*Nottingham*), N, SSW, L; P. Dodge (*Leicester*), N, SSW, L; G. Hartley (*Nottingham*), L, SSW, L; J. Goodwin (*Moseley*), N, SSW, L; L. Cusworth (*Leicester*), N, SSW, L; S. Thomas (*Coventry*), N, SSW, L

Forwards: L. Johnson (*Coventry*), N, SSW, L; S. Brain (*Coventry*), N, SSW, L; G. Pearce (*Northampton*), N, SSW, L; N. Mantell (*Nottingham*), N, SSW, L (*all as captain*); V. Cannon (*Northampton*), N, SSW, L; P. Cook (*Nottingham*), N, SSW, L; G. Robbins (*Coventry*), N, SSW, L; G. Rees (*Nottingham*), N, SSW, L

Scorers: v. N (*tries*: Goodwin, Robbins (3); *penalty-goals*: Hodgkinson (2); *conversions*: Hodgkinson (3)); v. SSW (*tries*: Hodgkinson, penalty; *conversions*: Hodgkinson; *penalty-goals*: Hodgkinson (2), Dodge); v. L (*penalty-goals*: Hodgkinson (4))

North

Backs: S. Langford (*Orrell*), M, L, SSW; M. Harrison (*Wakefield*), M, L, SSW; K. Simms (*Cambridge University*), M, L, SSW; J. Buckton (*Saracens*), M, L (*captain*), SSW (*captain*); R. Underwood (*Leicester*), M, L, SSW; R. Andrew (*Nottingham*) M, L, SSW; G. Jenion (*Sale*), M (r); S. Kirkup (*Durham City*), M; N. Melville (*Wasps*), L, SSW

Forwards: P. Huntsman (*Headingley*), M, SSW; A. Simpson (*Sale*), L; J. Curry (*Gosforth*), M; W. Dooley (*Preston Grasshoppers*), M, L, SSW; J. Howe (*Hartlepool Rovers*), M; P. Winterbottom (*Headingley*), M, L, SSW; P. Buckton (*Orrell*), M (*captain*), L; P. Johnston (*West Hartlepool*), M, L, SSW; G. Cook (*West Hartlepool*), L, SSW (r); N. Hitchen (*Orrell*), L, SSW; D. Southern (*Orrell*), L, SSW; J. Syddall (*Waterloo*), L, SSW; S. Hodgson (*Vale of Lune*), SSW

Scorers: v. M (*try*: Jenion; *penalty-goals*: Andrew (2), Langford; *conversion:* Langford); v. L (*penalty-goal:* Andrew); v. SSW (*tries*: Harrison, Simms, Underwood, Hodgson, Andrew; *conversions*: Andrew (4))

Right Oxford v. Cambridge at Twickenham, 10th December 1985: The Cambridge University scrum-half, Jonathan Turner, prepares to pass the ball to his backs, aided by Withyman, Stileman and O'Leary.

Oxford and Cambridge

Second Fifteens
Thursday, 5th December 1985, at Iffley Road, Oxford

Oxford University Greyhounds	9	Cambridge University LX Club	9
Try: Hender		*Dropped-goal*: Vyvyan	
Penalty-goal: Cochrane		*Penalty-goals*: Withers (2)	
Conversion: Cochrane		*Half-time*: 6-6	

Oxford University Greyhounds: P. McLarnon; I. McDonald, K. White, H. Cochrane, L. Phillips (a full blue, 1984); C. Evans (a full blue, 1984), C. Horner; N. Peacock, N. Prichard, M. Welby, D. Davies, A. Welsh (a full blue, 1984), I. Dunham, M. Hender, G. Spackman. *Replacement*: G. Dollar for Horner, 56 minutes

Cambridge University LX Club: P. Beard; D. Pierce, M. Hawkins, S. Withers, J. Wylie; S. Vyvyan, A. Wilmhurst; I. McCausland, B. Gilchrist, N. Hunt, D. Browne, M. Eberlin, P. Hobbs, M. George, G. Armstrong

Referee: M. Gorwyn (*Army*)

In very wet conditions, the Greyhounds scored the only try, converted by Cochrane, early in the game; but the LX Club drew level by half-time with Withers's penalty-goals. In injury time, Vyvyan dropped a goal for the visitors only to see the lead lost when Cochrane landed a penalty moments later.

The University Match
Tuesday, 10th December 1985, at Twickenham

Oxford	7	Cambridge	6
Try: C. MacDonald		*Penalty-goals:* Hastings (2)	
Penalty-goal: Kennedy		*Half-time:* 7-0	

Oxford University: A. P. Kennedy (*Wallace HS, Lisburn, Keble*); S. J. R. Vessey (*Magdalen College School, Merton*), J. M. Risman (*Wellington College, St Edmund Hall*), R. A. Rydon (*Sherborne, Pembroke*), S. B. Pearson (*Uppingham, Trinity*); A. M. Johnson (*Radley, St Catherine's*), S. N. J. Roberts (*Manchester GS, Exeter*); J. M. Dingemans (*Radley, Mansfield*), R. I. Glynn (*Leeds GS, St Edmund Hall*), T. G. Willis (*Wellington College, St Edmund Hall*), T. G. R. Marvin (*Radley, St Catherine's*), N. W. Macdonald (*Cape Town University, University*) (*captain*), C. Crane (*West Monmouth GS, St Edmund Hall*), S. J. M. Griffin (*Christ's College, Brecon, University*), C. P. MacDonald (*Stellenbosch University, University*)

Cambridge University: A. G. Hastings (*George Watson's College, Magdalene*) (*captain*); A. T. Harriman (*Radley, Magdalene*), F. J. Clough (*St John Rigby, Magdalene*), K. G. Simms (*West Park, Emmanuel*), K. T. Wyles (*Wymondham College, Churchill*); M. D. Bailey (*Ipswich, Corpus Christi*), J. M. P. C. Turner (*Sherborne, Downing*); N. J. Herrod (*King Henry VIII, Coventry, Clare Hall*), P. H. Combe (*Marlborough, Magdalene*), T. J. L. Borthwick (*Tonbridge, Magdalene*), S. R. Kelly (*Richard Huish College, Corpus Christi*), W. M. C. Stileman (*Wellington College, Selwyn*), S. T. O'Leary (*Plymouth College, Fitzwilliam*), P. A. Green (*Kent College, Trinity Hall*), T. Withyman (*Spalding GS, Emmanuel*). *Replacement*: D. J. Pierce (*Newcastle RGS, St John's*) for Harriman, 26 minutes

Referee: R. C. Quittenton (*London and Sussex*)

The Annual University Match at Twickenham recovered much of its credibility with this thrilling game, eventually won by Oxford by a single point after some final stages that were unbelievably exciting. Skills were in short supply with defences being so efficient, but total commitment by both sides was there to be witnessed in profusion. The courageous Dark Blues just prevented a sixth successive defeat.

Oxford won, even though they were outplayed in the main phases of the forward battle, because every player tackled with total bravery and this unsettled the Cambridge backs, who were already handicapped by having to play the reluctant Bailey out of position. The only try of the match, scored by the winners, came some seven minutes before half-time, when a scrum won by Cambridge was wheeled and Turner lost possession to Roberts and Griffin; the Oxford forwards then passed like skilled backs for Coll MacDonald to go over in the corner. Kennedy, who had scored from an earlier penalty award, failed to convert; but the lead was enough for an Oxford side that withstood intense second-half pressure from the Light Blues, who were only able to counter with two penalties from Hastings. The match was desperately close and Vessey on the Oxford right made at least three vital tackles.

A thoroughly sporting match was a credit to the game and it was well handled by the referee, who only once had to wave a sternly rebuking finger, at O'Leary's temporary loss of temper. That apart, it was marvellous entertainment and it is hoped that in future years college tutors will admit a few good Rugby players so that this match can continue to justify its pride of place in the Rugby calendar.

The game abounded with heroes – the whole Oxford side, well led by Macdonald, earning praise for its collective courage. For Cambridge, O'Leary, Withyman and Combe were outstanding forwards and the backs, with limited opportunities, still looked a very talented combination.

Oxford v. Cambridge
104 matches played   Oxford 44 wins   Cambridge 47 wins   13 draws

Matches were played at The Oval, 1873-74 to 1879-80; at Blackheath, 1880-81 to 1886-87; at Queen's Club, 1887-88 to 1920-21; then at Twickenham. From 1874-75 no match could be won unless a goal was scored.

1871-72	Oxford 1G, 1T to 0 (at Oxford)
1872-73	Cambridge 1G, 2T to 0 (at Cambridge)
1873-74	Drawn 1T to 1T
1874-75	Drawn Oxford 2T to 0
1875-76	Oxford 1T to 0
1876-77	Cambridge 1G, 2T to 0
1877-78	Oxford 2T to 0
1878-79	Drawn, no score
1879-80	Cambridge 1G, 1DG to 1DG
1880-81	Drawn 1T to 1T
1881-82	Oxford 2G, 1T to 1G
1882-83	Oxford 1T to 0
1883-84	Oxford 3G, 4T to 1G
1884-85	Oxford 3G, 1T to 1T
1885-86	Cambridge 2T to 0
1886-87	Cambridge 3T to 0
1887-88	Cambridge 1DG, 2T to 0
1888-89	Cambridge 1G, 2T to 0
1889-90	Oxford 1G, 1T to 0
1890-91	Drawn 1G to 1G
1891-92	Cambridge 2T to 0
1892-93	Drawn, no score
1893-94	Oxford 1T to 0
1894-95	Drawn 1G to 1G
1895-96	Cambridge 1G to 0
1896-97	Oxford 1G, 1DG to 1G, 1T
1897-98	Oxford 2T to 0
1898-99	Cambridge 1G, 2T to 0
1899-1900	Cambridge 2G, 4T to 0
1900-01	Oxford 2G to 1G, 1T
1901-02	Oxford 1G, 1T to 0
1902-03	Drawn 1G, 1T to 1G, 1T
1903-04	Oxford 3G, 1T, to 2G, 1T
1904-05	Cambridge 3G to 2G

Modern scoring values adopted

1905-06	Cambridge 3G (15) to 2G, 1T (13)
1906-07	Oxford 4T (12) to 1G, 1T (8)
1907-08	Oxford 1G, 4T (17) to 0
1908-09	Drawn 1G (5) to 1G (5)
1909-10	Oxford 4G, 5T (35) to 1T (3)
1910-11	Oxford 4G, 1T (23) to 3G, 1T (18)
1911-12	Oxford 2G, 3T (19) to 0
1912-13	Cambridge 2G (10) to 1T (3)
1913-14	Cambridge 1DG, 3T (13) to 1T (3)
1914-15 to 1918-19. No matches during war
1919-20	Cambridge 1DG, 1PG (7) to 1G (5)

1920-21	Oxford 1G, 4T (17) to 1G, 3T (14)
1921-22	Oxford 1G, 2T (11) to 1G (5)
1922-23	Cambridge 3G, 2T (21) to 1G, 1T (8)
1923-24	Oxford 3G, 2T (21) to 1G, 1PG, 2T (14)
1924-25	Oxford 1G, 2T (11) to 2T (6)
1925-26	Cambridge 3G, 6T (33) to 1T (3)
1926-27	Cambridge 3G, 5T (30) to 1G (5)
1927-28	Cambridge 2G, 2PG, 2T (22) to 1G, 3T (14)
1928-29	Cambridge 1G, 3T (14) to 1DG, 1PG, 1T (10)
1929-30	Oxford 1G, 1DG (9) to 0
1930-31	Drawn Oxford 1PG (3), Cambridge 1T (3)
1931-32	Oxford 1DG, 2T (10) to 1T (3)
1932-33	Oxford 1G, 1T (8) to 1T (3)
1933-34	Oxford 1G (5) to 1T(3)
1934-35	Cambridge 2G, 1DG, 1PG, 4T (29) to 1DG (4)
1935-36	Drawn, no score
1936-37	Cambridge 2T (6) to 1G (5)
1937-38	Oxford 1G, 4T (17) to 1DG (4)
1938-39	Cambridge 1G, 1PG (8) to 2PG (6)
1939-40	Oxford 1G, 1DG, 2T (15) to 1T (3) (at Cambridge)
	Cambridge 3G, 3T (14) to 2G, 1T (13) (at Oxford)
1940-41	Cambridge 1G, 2T (11) to 1G, 1DG (9) (at Oxford)
	Cambridge 2G, 1T (13) to 0 (at Cambridge)
1941-42	Cambridge 1PG, 2T (9) to 1PG, 1T (6) (at Cambridge)
	Cambridge 1G, 2PG, 2T (17) to 1G, 1T (8) (at Oxford)
1942-43	Cambridge 1G, 1DG (9) to 0 (at Oxford)
	Cambridge 2G, 2T (16) to 1T (3) (at Cambridge)
1943-44	Cambridge 2G, 1T (13) to 1DG (4) (at Cambridge)
	Oxford 2T (6) to 1G (5) (at Oxford)
1944-45	Drawn 1T to 1T (at Oxford)
	Cambridge 2G, 2T (16) to 1DG (4) (at Cambridge)
1945-46	Cambridge 1G, 2T (11) to 1G 1PG (8)
1946-47	Oxford 1G, 1DG, 2T (15) to 1G (5)
1947-48	Cambridge 2PG (6) to 0

Dropped-goal reduced to 3 points

1948-49	Oxford 1G, 1DG, 2T (14) to 1G, 1PG (8)
1949-50	Oxford 1T (3) to 0
1950-51	Oxford 1G, 1PG (8) to 0
1951-52	Oxford 2G 1T (13) to 0
1952-53	Cambridge 1PG, 1T (6) to 1G (5)
1953-54	Drawn Oxford 1PG, 1T (6), Cambridge 2PG (6)
1954-55	Cambridge 1PG (3) to 0
1955-56	Oxford 1PG, 2T (9) to 1G (5)
1956-57	Cambridge 1G, 1DG, 1PG, 1T (14) to 2PG, 1T (9)
1957-58	Oxford 1T (3) to 0
1958-59	Cambridge 1G, 1PG, 3T (17) to 1PG, 1T (6)
1959-60	Oxford 3PG (9) to 1PG (3)
1960-61	Cambridge 2G, 1T (13) to 0
1961-62	Cambridge 1DG, 2T (9) to 1DG (3)
1962-63	Cambridge 1G, 1DG, 1PG, 1T (14) to 0
1963-64	Cambridge 2G, 1PG, 2T (19) to 1G, 1DG, 1PG (11)
1964-65	Oxford 2G, 1PG, 2T (19) to 1PG, 1G from a mark (6)
1965-66	Drawn 1G each
1966-67	Oxford 1G, 1T (8) to 1DG, 1T (6)
1967-68	Cambridge 1T, 1PG (6) to 0
1968-69	Cambridge 1T, 1PG, 1DG (9) to 2T (6)
1969-70	Oxford 3PG (9) to 2PG (6)
1970-71	Oxford 1G, 1DG, 2T (14) to 1PG (3)

Try increased to 4 points

1971-72	Oxford 3PG, 3T (21) to 1PG (3)
1972-73	Cambridge 1G, 1T, 1DG, 1PG (16) to 2PG (6)
1973-74	Cambridge 2T, 1DG, 1PG (14) to 1G, 2PG (12)
1974-75	Cambridge 1G, 1T, 2PG (16) to 5PG (15)
1975-76	Cambridge 2G, 1T, 5PG, 1DG (34) to 3PG, 1DG (12)
1976-77	Cambridge 1G, 3PG (15) to 0
1977-78	Oxford 1T, 4PG (16) to 1T, 2PG (10)
1978-79	Cambridge 2G, 1T, 3PG (25) to 1T, 1PG (7)
1979-80	Oxford 1DG, 2PG (9) to 1PG (3)
1980-81	Cambridge 1T, 3PG (13) to 3PG (9)
1981-82	Cambridge 3PG (9) to 2PG (6)
1982-83	Cambridge 3PG, 1DG, 2T (20) to 2T, 1PG, 1Con (13)
1983-84	Cambridge 2T, 4PG (20) to 3PG (9)
1984-85	Cambridge 4G, 2T (32) to 2PG (6)
1985-86	Oxford 1T, 1PG (7) to 2PG (6)

Oxford Blues, 1945-86

Famous personalities before 1945 are included in the list. The dates are those of the year in which the match was actually played. An (r) after the year, i.e. 1985(r), denotes an appearance as a replacement.

Abbott, J. S., 1954-5
Adcock, J. R. L., 1961
Aitken, G. G., 1922-4
Allaway, R. C. P., 1953-4-5
Allison, M. G., 1955
Ashby, C. J., 1973
Asquith, P. R., 1974

Badenoch, D. F., 1971
Baggaley, J. C., 1953-4
Baird, J. S., 1966-7
Baker, D. G. S., 1951-2
Baker, P., 1980(r)
Baker, R. T., 1968
Bannerman, J. MacD., 1927-8
Barker, A. C., 1966-7
Barnes, S., 1981-2-3
Barr, D. C. A., 1980
Barry, D. M., 1968-9-70
Bass, R. C., 1961
Baxter, T. J., 1958-9
Beamish, S. H., 1971
Beare, A., 1982
Bedford, T. P., 1965-6-7
Behn, A. R., 1968-9
Bell, D. L., 1970
Bentley, P. J., 1960
Bettington, R. H. B., 1920-2
Bevan, J. H., 1946
Bibby, A. J., 1980-1
Binham, P. A., 1971
Birrell, H. B., 1953
Boobyer, B., 1949-50-1
Booth, J. L., 1956
Boss, F. H., ten 1958-9-60
Botting, I. J., 1949-50
Boyce, A. W., 1952-3
Boyle, D. S., 1967-8-9
Brace, D. O., 1955-6
Bray, C. N., 1979
Brett, P. V., 1978
Brewer, R. J., 1965
Brewer, T. J., 1951
Bridge, D. J. W., 1946-7-8
Britton, R. B., 1963-4
Brooks, A. W., 1980-1-2
Broughton, R. C., 1965
Bryan, T. A., 1975-6-7
Bryer, L. W., 1953
Bucknall, A. L., 1965-6
Budge, K. J., 1977-8-9
Bullard, G. L., 1950-1
Burnett, P. J., 1960
Burse, R., 1974
Butcher, W. M., 1954
Butler, F. E. R., 1959-60

Cannell, L. B., 1948-9-50
Carroll, B. M., 1970-1
Carroll, P. R., 1968-9-70
Cass, T., 1961
Cawkwell, G. L., 1946-7
Clark, R. B., 1978-9
Clarke, E. J. D., 1973
Clements, B. S., 1975
Coker, J. B. H., 1965
Cole, B. W., 1945

Coleman, D. J., 1982-3
Coles, S. C., 1954-6-7
Collingwood, J. A., 1961-2
Cooke, J. L., 1968-9
Cooke, W. R., 1976
Cooper, A. H., 1951
Cooper, R. M., 1946
Coutts, I. D. F., 1951
Craig, F. J. R., 1963-4-5
Crane, C., 1985
Cranmer, P., 1933-4
Creese, N. A. H., 1951
Croker, J. R., 1966-7
Crowe, P. J., 1981-2-3
Cuff, T. W., 1945
Cunningham, G., 1907-8-9
Currie, J. D., 1954-5-6-7
Curry, J. A. H., 1961
Curtis, A. B., 1949

Davey, P., 1967
Davey, R. A. E., 1972
Davies, D. E., 1951
Davies, D. M., 1958-9-60
Davies, R., 1969
Davies, R. A., 1974-5
Davies, R. H., 1955-6-7
Davies, S. J. T., 1972-3
Davies, W. G., 1977
Davis, T. M., 1978-9-80
Dawkins, P. M., 1959-60-1
Dew, C. J., 1978
Diamond, A. J., 1957
Dickson, W. M., 1912
Dingemans, J. M., 1985
Dixon, P. J., 1967-8-9-70
Donnelly, M. P., 1946
Donovan, T. J., 1971
Dorman, J. M. A., 1964
Douglas, A. I., 1970-1
Drysdale, D., 1925
Dunbar, I. T., 1970-1-3

Edmonds, J. N., 1978
Ellis, A. W., 1975
Emms, D. A., 1949-50
Enevoldson, T. P., 1976-7-8-9-80
Evans, C. D., 1984
Evans, D. P., 1959
Ewart, C. B., 1982

Faktor, S. J., 1977
Fallon, T. J., 1953-5
Fellows-Smith, J. P., 1953-4
Fergusson, E. A. J., 1952-3
Filby, L. L., 1960
Finch, C. J., 1978
Findlay, A. C., 1983
Fisher, S. J., 1976
Franklin, H. W. F., 1923

Gabitass, J. R., 1965-6
Galbraith, J. H., 1947
Gargan, M. F., 1980-2-3
Gent, G. N., 1949
Gill, R. D., 1947-8
Gilthorpe, C. G., 1946-7

Glover, J., 1959-60
Glover, T. R., 1973-4
Glynn, R. I., 1985
Gordon, P. F. C., 1970
Gould, E. J. H., 1963-4-5-6
Green, R., 1948-9-50
Greenhaigh, J. E., 1984
Griffin, S. J. M., 1985
Griffith, C. J. L., 1950-1-2
Griffiths, D. A., 1969-70
Griffiths, R. L., 1969
Gush, E. P., 1963

Habergham, W. D. R., 1980-2
Hadman, W. G., 1964-5-6
Halliday, S. J., 1979-80-1
Harcourt, A. B., 1945-6
Hawkesworth, C. J., 1970-1-2
Heal, M. G., 1971
Hearn, R. D., 1964
Hefer, W. J., 1949-50
Henderson, J. H., 1952
Herrod, N. J., 1981-2-3
Higham, J. R. S., 1959
Hiller, R. B., 1965
Hines, G. W., 1961-2
Hoare, A. H. M., 1956-7
Hobart, A. H., 1981
Hockley, M., 1975
Hofmeyer, K. de J., 1927
Hofmeyr, M. B., 1948-9-50
Hofmeyr, S. J., 1928-9-30
Hofmeyr, S. M., 1979
Holroyd, C. A., 1966
Hood, R. K., 1976
Hoolahan, R. M. C., 1976-7-8
Hopkins, K. M., 1977
Horne, E. C., 1975-6-7
Houston, K. J., 1964
Howard, P. D., 1929-30
Hoyer-Millar, G. C., 1952
Hughes, R. A., 1978
Hugo-Hamman, C. T., 1981-2
Hutchinson, J. M., 1972-3

Ilett, N. L., 1947

James, S., 1970-1
James, S. J. B., 1966
Jenkin, J. M., 1952
Jenkins, A., 1971
Jenkins, P., 1980
Jenkins, V. G. J., 1930-1-2
Jesson, D., 1957-8-9
Johnson, A. M., 1985
Johnson, P. M., 1968-70
Johnstone, P. G., 1952-3-4
Jones, D. K., 1963
Jones, D. R. R., 1972
Jones, I. C., 1962-3-4
Jones, R. O. P., 1969-70-1
Jones, T. W., 1978-9
Jones, V. W., 1954
Joyce, A. L., 1984

Kay, D. C., 1972-3
Kendall-Carpenter, J. MacG. K., 1948-9-50
Kennedy, A. P., 1985
Kent, C. P., 1972-3-4-5
Kent, P. C., 1970

King, B. B., 1963
King, P. E., 1975
Kinnimonth, P. W., 1947-8
Kyrke-Smith, P. St L., 1973-4-5(r)

Laidlaw, C. R., 1968-9
Lamb, R. H., 1962-3-4
Langley, P. J., 1949
Lawrence, W. S., 1954-6
Lawton, T., 1921-2-3
Lee, J. W., 1973-4
Lee, R. J., 1972
Lennox-Cook, J. M., 1945
Leslie, R. E., 1954
Lewin, A. J. A., 1962-3
Lewis, D. J., 1950
Lewis, S. M., 1973
Light, B., 1977
Littlechild, E. J. F., 1972
Lloyd, E. A., 1964-5-6
Lombard, L. T., 1956-7-8
Love, R. D., 1972
Luddington, R. S., 1980-2

McClure, R. N., 1973
Macdonald, C. P., 1985
Macdonald, D. A., 1975-6
Macdonald, D. S. M., 1974-5-6
Macdonald, N. W., 1984-5
McFarland, P. R. E., 1967
McGlashan, J., 1945
Mackenzie, D. W., 1974
MacLachlan, L. P., 1953
MacNeill, H. P., 1982-3-4
McPartlin, J. J., 1960-1-2
Macpherson, G. P. S., 1922-3-4
Macpherson, N. M. S., 1928
McQuaid, A. S. J., 1983
Maddock, W. P., 1972
Mallalieu, J. P. W., 1927
Mallett, N. V., 1979
Marvin, T. G. R., 1984-5
Mead, B. D., 1972-3
Meadows, H. J., 1948
Millerchip, C. J. E., 1981-2
Mills, D. J., 1983-4
Mitchell, M. D., 1977
Moir, M. J. P., 1977
Montgomery, J. R., 1958
Moorcroft, E. K., 1966
Moore, H. R., 1956
Moore, P. B. C., 1945-6
Morgan, A. K., 1963-4
Morgan, D. J., 1979
Morgan, R. de R., 1983
Morrison, W. E. A., 1979-80
Mulvey, R. S., 1968
Murray, G. C., 1959

Neville, T. B., 1971-2
Newman, A. P., 1973
Newman, S. C., 1946-7
Newton-Thompson, J. O., 1945-6

Obolensky, A., 1935-7
O'Brien, T. S., 1983-4
O'Connor, A., 1958
Osborne, E. C., 1969
Owen-Smith, H. G. O., 1932-3

Painter, P. A., 1967

Palmer, M. S., 1960
Payne, C. M., 1960
Pearce, J. K., 1945
Pearson, S. B., 1983-4-5
Peck, A. Q., 1981
Phillips, L. R. L., 1984
Phillips, M. S., 1956-7-8-9
Phillips, R. H., 1966-7-8
Plant, W. I., 1958
Plumbridge, R. A., 1954-5-6
Pollard, D., 1952
Poulton, R. W. (later Poulton-Palmer), 1909-10-11
Prescott, R. E., 1932
Prodger, J. A., 1955

Quinnen, P. N., 1974-5
Quist-Arcton, E. A. K., 1978-9

Rahmatallah, F. J., 1976
Ramsay, A. W., 1952-3
Ramsden, J. E., 1945
Raphael, J. E., 1901-2-3-4
Read, R. F., 1965
Reed, D. K., 1984
Reeler, I. L., 1955-6
Rees, P. S., 1974-5-8
Richards, S. B., 1962
Rigby, J. P., 1955-6
Rimmer, L. I., 1958
Risman, J. M., 1984-5
Rittson-Thomas, G. C., 1949-50
Robbins, P. G. D., 1954-5-6-7
Roberts, M. G., 1968
Roberts, N. T., 1979-80-1
Roberts, S. N. J., 1985
Robinson, D. A. B., 1952-3

Robinson, R. G., 1976-7
Rosier, J. R. H., 1983
Ross, W. S., 1980
Rotherham, A., 1882-3-4
Rudd, E. L., 1963-4
Rydon, R. A., 1985

Sachs, D. M., 1962
Sampson, D. H., 1945
Sampson, H. F., 1910-11
Saunders, C. J., 1951
Sawtell, P. R., 1972
Scott, J. S. M., 1957-8
Searle, J. P., 1981-2
Sexton, C. M., 1976
Seymour, T. M., 1971-3
Sharp, R. A. W., 1959-60-1
Shaw, C., 1974-5
Sheil, A. G. R., 1958
Silk, N., 1961-2-3
Simmie, M. S., 1965-6
Simonet, P. M., 1984
Skipper, D. J., 1952
Slater, N. T., 1960
Small, H. D., 1949-50
Smith, I. S., 1923
Smith, M. J. K., 1954-5
Speed, R. R., 1967-8-9
Spence, K. M., 1951-2
Spencer, B. L., 1960
Stafford, P. M. W., 1961-2
Stagg, P. K., 1961-2
Starmer-Smith, N. C., 1965-6
Steel, J. J., 1953
Stevens, D. T., 1959
Stewart, A., 1947-8
Steyn, S. S. L., 1911-12

Stobie, A. M., 1945
Stobie, W. D. K., 1947
Stoneman, B. M., 1962
Stoop, A. D., 1902-3-4
Strand-Jones, J., 1899-1900-1
Summerskill, W. H. J., 1945
Sutton, M. A., 1945-6
Swan, M. W., 1957
Swarbrick, D. W., 1946-7-8

Tahany, M. P., 1945
Taylor, J. A., 1974
Thomas, A. C., 1979
Thomson, B. E., 1951-2
Thomson, J. B., 1983
Thorburn, C. W., 1964
Thorniley-Walker, M. J., 1967
Tongue, P. K., 1975
Torry, P. J., 1968-9
Travers, B. H., 1946-7

Van Ryneveld, A, J., 1946-7-8
Van Ryneveld, C. B., 1947-8-9
Vassall, H., 1879-80-1
Vassall, H. H., 1906-7-8
Vessey, S. J. R., 1984-5
Vintcent, A. N., 1948-9

Wakelin, W. S., 1964
Waldron, O. C., 1965-7
Walford, M. M., 1935-6-7
Walker, J. C., 1955
Walker, M., 1950-1
Wallace, A. C., 1922-3-4-5
Ward, J. M., 1972
Ware, M. A., 1961-2
Waterman, J. S., 1974

Wates, C. S., 1961
Watkinson, A. F., 1977-8
Watson, P. W., 1954-5
Watt, K. A., 1976
Watts, L. D., 1957-8
Webster, J. G. M., 1980-1
Webster, J. P., 1982-3
Welsh, A. R., 1984
Weston, B. A. G., 1957
White, G. L., 1976-7
Whyte, A. G. D., 1963
Whyte, D. J., 1963
Wilcock, R. M., 1962
Wilcock, S. H., 1957-8-9
Willcox, J. G., 1959-60-1-2
Williams, C. D., 1945
Williams, J. R., 1969
Willis, D. C., 1975-6-7
Willis, T. G., 1985
Wilson, C. T. M., 1948
Wilson, G. A., 1946-8
Wilson, J., 1967-8
Wilson, N. G. C., 1967
Wilson, R. W., 1956
Wilson, S., 1963-4
Wimperis, E. J., 1951
Winn, C. E., 1950
Winn, R. R., 1953
Witney, N. K. J., 1970-1
Wood, D. E., 1952-3
Woodhead, P. G., 1974
Woodrow, D. R., 1978-9-80
Wyatt, D. M., 1981
Wydell, H. A., 1951
Wynter, E. C. C., 1947

Young, J. R. C., 1957-8

Cambridge Blues, 1945-86

Aarvold, C. D., 1925-6-7-8
Ackford, P. J., 1979
Allan, C. J., 1962
Allan, J. L. F., 1956
Allchurch, T. C., 1980-1
Allen, D. B., 1975
Andrew, C. R., 1982-3-4
Anthony, A. J., 1967
Archer, G. M. D., 1950-1
Arthur, T. G., 1962
Asquith, J. P. K., 1953
Attfield, S. J. W., 1982-4

Bailey, M. D., 1982-3-4-5
Bailey, R. C., 1982-3
Balding, I. A., 1961
Barker, R. E., 1966
Barrow, E., 1950
Barter, A. F., 1954-5-6
Bartlett, R. M., 1951
Batten, J. M., 1971-2-3-4
Bearne, K. R. F., 1957-8-9
Beazley, T. A. G., 1971
Bedell-Sivright, D. R., 1899-1900-1-2
Bedell-Sivright, J. V., 1900-1-2
Beer, I. D. S., 1952-3-4
Bennett, N. J., 1981
Beringer, F. R., 1951-2
Beringer, G. G., 1975-6
Berman, J. V., 1966

Berry, S. P., 1971
Bevan, G. A. J., 1951
Biddell, C. W., 1980-1
Biggar, M. A., 1971
Bird, D. R. J., 1958-9
Boggon, R. P., 1956
Bole, E., 1945-6-7
Borthwick, T. J. L., 1985
Boulding, P. V., 1975-6
Bowen, R. W., 1968
Boyd-Moss, R. J., 1980-1-2
Brash, J. C., 1959-60-1
Breakey, N. J. F., 1974-5(r)-7
Briggs, P. D., 1962
Brookstein, R., 1969
Brooman, R. J., 1977-8
Brown, S. L., 1975-6
Bruce-Lockhart, J. H., 1910
Bruce-Lockhart, L., 1945-6
Bruce-Lockhart, R. B., 1937-8
Bryce, R. D. H., 1965
Bush, J. D., 1983
Bussey, W. M., 1960-1-2
Butler, E. T., 1976-7-8

Campbell, H. H., 1946
Campbell, J. W., 1973-4
Cangley, B. G. M., 1946
Carter, C. P., 1965
Chalmers, P. S., 1979
Clarke, B. D. F., 1978

Clarke, S. J. S., 1962-3
Clayton, J. R., 1971
Clements, J. W., 1953-4-5
Clough, F. J., 1984-5
Coley, M., 1964
Collier, R. B., 1960-1
Combe, P., 1984-5
Conway, G. S., 1919-20-1
Cooke, S. J., 1981
Corry, T. M., 1966
Cosh, N. J., 1966
Covell, G. A. B., 1949
Cove-Smith, R., 1919-20-1
Crothers, G., 1977(r)
Crow, W. A. M., 1961-2
Cullen, J. C., 1980-1-2

Dalgleish, K. J., 1951-2-3
Daniell, J., 1898-9-1900
David, P. W., 1983
Davies, G., 1948-9-50
Davies, G. H., 1980-1
Davies, H. J., 1958
Davies, J. C., 1949
Davies, J. S., 1977
Davies, P. M., 1952-3-4
Davies, T. G. R., 1968-9-70
Davies, W. G., 1946-7
De Nobriga, A. P., 1948
Devitt, Sir T. G., 1923-4-5
Dick, R. C. S., 1933

Dickins, J. P., 1972-3
Doherty, H. D., 1950
Dorward, A. F., 1947-8-9
Dovey, B. A., 1960
Downey, W. J., 1954-5-6-7
Doyle, M. G., 1965
Drake, T. R., 1965
Drake-Lee, M. J., 1961-2-3
Drummond, N. W., 1971
Duncan, C., 1966
Dutson, C. S., 1963

Edlmann, S. R. R., 1974-5
Edmonds, G. A., 1976
Edwards, E. F., 1971
Edwards, R. J., 1971-2
Ellis, P. R., 1975
Ellison, J. F., 1983-4
Evans, M. R. M., 1955
Evans, W. R., 1955
Ewbank, C. F., 1983

Fairgrieve, J., 1945
Fleming, R. S., 1964
Folwell, A. J. S., 1967-8
Ford, J. N., 1977-8-9
Fosh, M. K., 1977-8
Fox, S., 1945
Frankcom, G. P., 1961-3-4
French, N. J., 1973
French, R. B., 1969

Fyfe, K. C., 1932-3-4-5

Gatford, H. J. H., 1946
Geoghegan, K. F., 1977
Gethin, D., 1965-6
Gibbs, J. D., 1965
Gibson, C. M. H., 1963-4-5
Gill, S. M., 1980-1
Gilliland, W. D., 1979
Glanvill, S. F., 1977-9-80
Gloag, I. S., 1949-50-2
Gloag, L. G., 1948
Godson, A., 1959-60
Grant, A. R., 1975-6
Grant, J. J. H., 1978
Green, M. J., 1965-6-7
Green, P. A., 1984-5
Greenwood, J. E., 1910-11-12-13-19
Greenwood, J. R. H., 1962-3
Greig, I. A., 1977-8
Griffiths, H. B., 1953
Gwilliam, J. A., 1947-8

Hamilton-Wickes, R. H., 1920-1-2-3
Hamp-Ferguson, A. J. C., 1964-5
Hampel, A. K. R., 1982
Hannaford, C., 1967
Harding, R. M., 1973-4
Harding, Rowe, 1924-5-6-7
Harding, V. S. J., 1958-9-60
Harper, A. G. R., 1983
Harriman, A. T., 1985
Harrison, R. B., 1951
Hartley, J. J., 1974
Hartley, M. J., 1957
Harvey, J. R. W., 1963-4
Hastings, A. G., 1984-5
Heath, N. R. M., 1977-8
Heginbotham, R. C., 1984
Henderson, A. P., 1945-6-7
Herbert, A. J., 1954-5-6
Herrod, N. J., 1985
Heslip, M. R., 1967
Hetherington, J. G. G., 1955
Hewett, B. J., 1963
Higham, C. F. W., 1961-2
Hignell, A. J., 1974-5-6-7
Hinton, N. P., 1969-70
Hockey, J. R., 1957
Hodgson, J. T., 1955
Hodgson, M. E., 1973
Holmes, W. B., 1947-8
Horner, P. J., 1982
Horrocks-Taylor, J. P., 1956-7
Howard, J. M., 1971-2
Hughes, K., 1968-9
Hunter, J. M., 1946

Inglis, F. C., 1959
Jagger, D., 1954
James, A. M., 1948-9
James, J. H. H., 1962-3-4
Jenkins, J. D., 1964
Jenkins, J. M., 1949-51
Jenkins, W. G., 1948
Jessop, A. W., 1972
Johnston, J. N., 1981
Jolliffe, R. L. K., 1965
Jones, B. M., 1949
Jones, C. W., 1933-4-5
Jones, D. G. H., 1951-2
Jones, W. W. A., 1968-9-70-2

Jorden, A. M., 1968-9

Keith-Roach, P. D'A., 1969-70-1
Kelly, S. R., 1985
Kershaw, M. E., 1955
Killick, S. E., 1978
Kimberley, H. M., 1945-6-7-8
King, R. H., 1950
Kingston, C. J., 1980-1-2
Kirby, T. K. M., 1945
Kitchin, P. A., 1965

Laycock, A. M., 1979
Leadbetter, V. H., 1951-2
Leonard, R. J. N., 1957
Lewis, A. D., 1975-6
Lewis, A. R., 1959
Lewis, G. G., 1976
Lewis, G. Windsor, 1956-7-8
Lewis, Windsor H., 1926-7
Lillington, P. M., 1981-2
Linnecar, R. J. D., 1970
Lintott, T. M. R., 1974
Lister, R. C., 1969
Lloyd-Davies, R. H., 1947
Lord, M., 1960
Loveday, B. R., 1956-7
Lowden, G. S., 1945
Lowe, C. N., 1911-12-13
Lyon, D. W., 1967-8

McClung, T., 1954
MacEwen, R. K. G., 1953-4
McGahey, A. M. J., 1979-80-1
MacGregor, G., 1889-90
McKenzie, M. R., 1968
Macklin, A. J., 1979-80-2
Macleod, K. G., 1905-6-7-8
Macleod, L. M., 1903-4
McMorris, L., 1963
MacMyn, D. J., 1921-2-3-4
McRoberts, T. S., 1946-7-8
MacSweeney, D. A., 1957-8-9
Makin, R. L., 1959
Malik, N. A., 1975
Mann, F. T., 1910
Marques, R. W. D., 1954-5-6-7
Marr, T. C. K., 1945
Marsden, E. W., 1950
Marshall, T. R., 1950
Martin, A. W., 1983-4
Martin, N. O., 1965-6-7
Martin, S. A., 1961-2-3
Massey, D. G., 1952
Massey, M. J. O., 1951-2-3
Metcalfe, I. R., 1978-9
Michaelson, R. C. B., 1960-1-2
Miliffe, M. J., 1964
Millard, D. E. S., 1956
Mills, D. C., 1958
Mills, H. H., 1947-8
Mills, P. R., 1958-9
Mitchell, F., 1893-4-5
Monahan, J. D., 1967-8
Monro, A. H., 1973
Moon, R. H. Q. B., 1984
Moore, P. J. de A., 1947-8
Morgan, H. P., 1952-3
Moriarty, S. P., 1980
Morrison, B. J., 1965
Morrison, I. R., 1983-4
Moyes, J. L., 1974-5
Mulligan, A. A., 1955-6-7
Murray, R. A., 1982

Nixon, P. J. L., 1976

O'Brien, T., 1981-2
O'Callaghan, C., 1978
O'Callaghan, M. W., 1974-5-6-7
O'Leary, S. T., 1984-5
Onyett, P. S., 1966-7
Oswald, G. B. R., 1945
Owen, A. V., 1945
Owen, J. E., 1961

Page, J. J., 1968-9-70
Page, R. S., 1972-3
Parker, G. W., 1932-3-4-5
Parr, M. F., 1978
Paterson-Brown, T., 1983
Patterson, W. M., 1956
Pearson, T. C., 1952-3
Peck, I. G., 1979
Pender, A. R., 1963
Perry, D. G., 1958
Perry, S. V., 1946-7
Phillips, G. P., 1971-2
Phillips, R. J., 1964
Pierce, D. J., 1985(r)
Pratt, S. R. G., 1973-4
Price, P. R., 1967
Prosser-Harries, A., 1957

Rae, A. J., 1901
Raffle, N. C. G., 1954-5
Raine, J. B., 1947
Rainforth, J. J., 1958-9
Raybould, W. H., 1966
Redmond, G. F., 1969-70-1
Rees, A. M., 1933-4
Rees, B. I., 1963-4-5-6
Rees, G., 1972-3
Reeve, P. B., 1950-1
Richards, T. B., 1955
Robbie, J. C., 1977-8
Roberts, J., 1952-3-4
Roberts, S. N., 1983
Robertson, I. D., 1967
Robinson, P. J., 1962
Rodgers, A. K., 1968-9-70
Rose, W. M. H., 1979-80-1
Rosser, D. W. A., 1962-3-4
Rosser, M. F., 1972-3
Rotherham, Arthur, 1890-1
Ryan, C. J., 1966
Ryan, P. H., 1952-3

Saville, C. D., 1967-8-9-70
Schwarz, R. O., 1893
Scotland, K. J. F., 1958-9-60
Scott, A. W., 1945-8
Scott, R. R. F., 1957
Shackleton, I. R., 1968-9-70
Shaw, P. A. V., 1977
Shepherd, J. K., 1950
Shipsides, J., 1970
Silk, D. R. W., 1953-4
Sim, R. G., 1966-7
Simms, K. G., 1983-4-5
Skinner, R. C. O., 1970-1
Slater, K. J. P., 1964
Smith, A. R., 1954-5-6-7
Smith, J. M., 1972
Smith, J. V., 1948-9-50
Smith, M. A., 1966-7
Smith, P. K., 1970
Smith, S. R., 1958-9
Smith, S. T., 1982-3

Spencer, J. S., 1967-8-9
Spray, K. A. N., 1946-7
Stead, R. J., 1977
Steele, H. K., 1970
Steele-Bodger, M. R., 1945-6
Stevenson, H., 1977(r)-9
Stewart, A. A., 1975-7
Stileman, W. M. C., 1985
Stothard, N. A., 1979

Tarsh, D. N., 1955
Taylor, D. G., 1982
Thomas, B., 1960-1-2
Thomas, D. R., 1972-3-4
Thomas, J., 1945
Thomas, N. B., 1966
Thomas, R. C. C., 1949
Thompson, M. J. M., 1950
Thompson, R. V., 1948-9
Thornton, J. F., 1976-8-9
Timmons, F. J., 1983
Tredwell, J. R., 1968
Tucker, W. E., 1922-3-4-5
Turner, J. A., 1956
Turner, J. M. P. C., 1985
Turner, M. F., 1946
Tyler, R. H., 1978-9-80

Umbers, R. H., 1954
Vaughan, G. P., 1949
Vaux, J. G., 1957
Vivian, J. M., 1976

Waddell, G. H., 1958-60-1
Wade, M. R., 1959-9-60-1
Wainwright, J. F., 1956
Wainwright, M. A., 1980
Wakefield, W. W., 1921-2
Walker, D. R., 1980-1
Walker, R., 1963
Warfield, P. J., 1974
Warlow, S., 1972-3
Watt, J. R., 1970
Webb, G. K. M., 1964-5
Webster, A. P., 1971
Wells, T. U., 1951
Wetson, M. T., 1958-9-60
Wheeler, P. J. F., 1951-2-3
White, W. N., 1947
Wiggins, C. M., 1964
Wilkinson, R. M., 1971-2-3
Williams, C. C. U., 1950
Williams, C. R., 1971-2-3
Williams, D. B., 1973
Williams, E. J. H., 1946
Williams, J. M., 1949
Williams, N. E., 1950
Williamson, I. S., 1972
Williamson, P. R., 1984
Willis, H., 1949-50-1
Wintle, T. C., 1960-1
Withyman, T. A., 1985
Wood, G. E., 1974-5-6
Wood, G. E. C., 1919
Woodall, B. J. C., 1951
Woodroffe, O. P., 1952
Woods, S. M. J., 1888-9-90
Wooler, W., 1933-4-5
Wordsworth, A. J., 1973-5
Wrench, D. F. B., 1960
Wyles, K. T., 1985

Young, P. D., 1949
Young, S. K., 1974

Universities Athletic Union

Challenge round scores

Brunel	10	Sheffield	6
UWCM	7	Birmingham	18
Loughborough	63	Bristol	10
Durham	57	UMIST	3
Manchester	26	Bath	6
Swansea	81	Kent	4
Exeter	28	Salford	0
Nottingham	19	Newcastle	3

Quarter-finals

Manchester	6	Swansea	12
Exeter	6	Nottingham	7
Brunel	8	Birmingham	15
Loughborough	12	Durham	4

Semi-finals

Loughborough (at Rugby)	17	Birmingham	0
Nottingham (at Stroud)	9	Swansea	3

2nd XV Championship final

Loughborough	20	UC Cardiff	0

First Fifteens Final
Wednesday, 12th March 1986, at Twickenham

Loughborough	14	Nottingham	0

Tries: James, Rowe (1 each) *Half-time:* 4-0
Dropped-goal: Hancock
Penalty-goal: D. Hughes

Loughborough: I. Harris; J. Rowe, C. Allen, D. Hughes, C. James; A. Sutton, M. Hancock; M. Freer, D. Cheesewright, G. Hughes, J. Wilby, M. Upex, A. MacDonald, A. Robinson (*captain*), A. Swain.
Nottingham: A. Hamilton; M. Clark, L. Eales (*captain*), S. Purdy, T. Chalk; M. Simmonds, J. Jenkins; J. Ward, M. Lambert, A. Challis, R. Bridson, S. Howe, D. Nicholls, A. Berry, G. Koral. *Replacement:* B. Evans for Eales, 22 minutes.
Referee: R. Quittenton (*London*)

The Loughborough domination of this event continued, and only gallant resistance by Nottingham prevented a rout. In fact, they lost their captain, Eales, as a brave attempt was made to avoid the first try against them. From then on, enthusiastic play by the underdogs prevented further disasters until near the end, when Hamilton had to release the ball after a kick-ahead by Sutton and the ensuing move produced Rowe's try.

It is no fault of Loughborough's that they monopolize the tournament. It would seem that enough good talent is just not reaching the universities, Durham and the winners excepted, because various extremist lobbies are doing their best to keep players out of team sports. So those who do manage something from very little, such as Nottingham, are worthy of great praise. It is now suggested that the polytechnics and colleges play better Rugby than the universities, and this may well be true.

Loughborough have now won on twenty one occasions with Durham, Liverpool and Swansea having seven successes each, Bristol five, Manchester four, Cardiff three, Bangor and UWIST two each, Aberystwyth, Birmingham, Leeds and Newcastle one each.

The Miller Buckley University Triple Crown Championship

Results

England	14	Wales	21
Wales	42	Scotland	20
Ireland	20	Wales	7
England	10	Ireland	8
Ireland	40	Scotland	6
Scotland	13	England	38

	P	W	L	F	A	Pts
Ireland	3	2	1	63	28	4
England	3	2	1	62	41	4
Wales	3	2	1	70	54	4
Scotland	3	0	3	39	120	0

(Ireland win through scoring most tries)

British Polytechnics Sports Association

Quarter-finals

Newcastle	8	Leicester	17
Kingston	24	Thames	8
South Bank	9	Plymouth	4
Coventry	4	Leeds	16

Semi-finals

Leicester	0	Kingston	17

South Bank (after extra time)	10	Leeds	29

2nd XV final

Bristol	3	Coventry	7

3rd XV final

Kingston	23	Trent	9

First Fifteens Final
Wednesday, 12th March 1986, at London Irish Ground

Kingston	12	Leeds	15

Try: penalty-try   *Try:* Everett
Dropped-goal: Kuhn   *Penalty-goals:* Reeman (3)
Penalty-goal: Wallace   *Conversion:* Reeman
Conversion: Wallace   *Half-time:* 9-9

Kingston: M. Wallace; A.Gratwicke, S. Johnston, S. Tipping, V. Rolandi; R. Kuhn, S.Whitworth; M. Wallwork, J. Meadowcroft, M. Jones, P. Rycroft, A. Rankes, P. Ashworth, S. Hayter (*captain*), M. Downes

Leeds: J. Mallender; R. Widdop, I. Melia (*captain*), A. Manicom, D. Roberts; T. Reeman, J. Everett; T. Smith, A. Buchanan, S. Ellis, E. Saunders, B. Brown, H. Barrett, N. Ashton, D. Cooper

Referee: G. Crawford (*London*)

Leeds caused a surprise by beating Kingston in the final of the 'Polys' tournament and on the whole deserved their success, which brought them the Rugby World Cup. In a gripping encounter, their First XV made a fine start and, had Barrett accepted an opportunity to score an early try, the match might have been over by half-time as Reeman, with some fine kicking, had given them nine points in the first quarter of the game. As it was, Kingston fought back and by scoring a penalty-try before half-time they were actually in the lead. Soon after the break, however, Everett with great determination went over from a scrum, and Reeman converted. The late thrust by Kingston, with a penalty-goal by Wallace, was not enough to change the result. Leeds, mostly PE students, were fitter and better organized.

In a series of matches that were very well organized, the heroes of the main match were the two scrum-halves of each team, Reeman (Leeds), Barrett (Leeds), Rycroft (Kingston) and Downes (Kingston). But it is invidious to pick out names in an excellent match in which no-one was lacking in effort or commitment.

The tournament was first played in the season of 1969-70 and Wales have won on five occasions, followed by Kingston (three times), Glamorgan (twice), Leeds (twice), Liverpool (twice), Middlesex (once), Lanchester (once), Bristol (once).

Hospitals Challenge Cup

First Round

King's College	6	St Bartholomew's	13
St George's	0	The London	17

Second Round

UCH & Middlesex	3	Guy's	12
St Bartholomew's	3	St Mary's	33
St Thomas's	15	Royal Free	0
The London	15	Charing Cross & Westminster	10

Semi-finals

The London	9	St Thomas's	4
St Mary's	36	Guy's	0

(both at Richmond Athletic Ground)

Final
Wednesday, 12th March 1986, at Richmond Athletic Ground

The London	10	St Mary's	6

Try: Rossiter   *Penalty-goals:* Booth (2)
Dropped-goal: Roome   *Half-time:* 7-6
Penalty-goal: Maclean

The London: N. Benson; I. Hamilton, C. Long, B. Barker, N. Rossiter; A. Maclean, C.Roome; J. Brosch, C. Mann, P. Taylor, A. Parnham, A. Justice, P. Barnes, T. Briggs, S. Slack.
Replacement: C. Johns for Benson, 65 minutes

St Mary's: J. Booth; R. Robinson, D. Wilcox, M. Dixon, R. Harvey; A. Field, C. Whitworth; R. Bailey, M. Kenny, A. Budgen, C. Hayward, C. Guest, R. Holland, I. Bain, P. Toozs-Hobson

Referee: R. Glass (*London*)

All pre-match forecasts, which made St Mary's the overwhelming favourites as a result of earlier easy wins, were confounded as The London bravely resisted the grinding efforts of their opponents' bigger and heavier pack and eventually won for the first time since 1968. A first-half try by Rossiter, supplemented by a dropped-goal by Roome, countered two penalties by Booth, and the only score of the second period was a coolly-taken penalty by Maclean for the winners. St Mary's sacrificed much hard-earned advantage by conceding too many such awards, which Roome and Maclean cleverly used to work the touch-line and keep them out.

The cup has been won thirty times by Guy's, twenty five times by St Mary's, seventeen times by St Thomas's, eleven times by The London, nine times by St Bartholomew's, three times by Westminster and St George's and once by Middlesex.

Inter-Services Championship

Stewart Wrightson Trophy
Saturday, 8th March 1986, at Twickenham

Royal Navy   13   **The Army**   3

Try: Woodcock   *Penalty-goal:* Bentley
Dropped-goal: Price   *Half-time:* 3-3
Penalty-goals: Durkin, Kellett
(1 each)

Royal Navy: Lt C. Alcock (*captain*); LPT R. Penfold, WEM (R) D. Oakley, MEAAP A. Kellett, AB M. Speakman; MEM (I) G. Price, Lt M. Durkin; CPO PT R. Ewins, LS (S) SM R. Joy, Sgt J. Martin, Lt H. Howarth, L AEM (M) B. Woodcock, LPT I. Russell, Lt S. Hughes, AEM (M) G. Wood

The Army: Capt. C. Bentley; Dvr S.Walklin, Lt H. Kelly, Lt N. Beazley, Cpl E. Takins; WO2 J. Morgan, L/Cpl M. Sanderson; Cpl N. Kessell, S/Sgt J. Byrne (*captain*), Cpl D. Mathias, Lt R. Bush, Cpl R. Baker, Sgt Inst. S. Peacock, Sgt C. Christopher, Sgt M. Lewis

Referee: G. C. Cromwell (*Gloucester*)

In a dour game, The Army's stronger pack failed to bring victory against a brave Senior Service side led with some inspiration by Alcock from full-back. By scoring the only try, the seamen deserved their success, which provided the chance for a first Championship win since 1981.

Windsor Life Challenge Cup
Saturday, 22nd March 1986, at Twickenham

Royal Navy   9   **Royal Air Force**   20

Dropped-goal: Price   *Tries:* Underwood (2),
Penalty-goals: Price (2)   Parsonage (1)
Half-time: 6-3   *Penalty-goals:* Worrall (2)
     Conversion: Lazenby

Royal Navy: Lt C. Alcock (*captain*); LPT R. Penfold, POWEM (O) J. Pocklington, WEM (R) D. Oakley, AB M. Speakman; MEM (L) G. Price, AB J. Kingston; CPOPT R. Ewins, LS(S)SM R. Joy, Lt B. Howarth, LAEM(M) B. Woodcock, LPT I. Russell, Cpl M. Hewitt, AEM(M) G. Wood, Lt S. Hughes

Royal Air Force: Cpl S. Lazenby; Flt Lt M. Aspinall, Jnr Tech. S. Roke, F/O I. Goslin (*captain*), F/O R. Underwood; Sgt P. A'Herne, Cpl S. Worrall; Cpl M. Whitcombe, SAC K. Davies, SAC A. Billett, Cpl B. Richardson, Cpl R. Burn, Cpl D. Parsonage, F/O I. Stevens, Jnr Tech. D. Gigg. *Replacement:* SAC N. Raikes for A'Herne, 50 minutes

Referee: Dr J. Coulson (*Northumberland*)

After penalties were exchanged and the Royal Navy led (9-6) with twelve minutes remaining, the Air Force put in a splendid counter-offensive and scored fourteen points through two tries by Underwood, the England wing, and Parsonage. Underwood had seen little of the ball until then and in fact scored once in the opposite corner to his own flank. The airmen in the end thoroughly deserved their victory, which left them as favourites to retain the Inter-Services title.

Windsor Life Trophy
Saturday, 5th April 1986, at Twickenham

The Army   13   **Royal Air Force**   16

Tries: Walklin, Peacock   *Tries:* Roke, Lazenby
(1 each)   (1 each)
Penalty-goal: Morgan   *Penalty-goals:* Lazenby (2)
Conversion: Morgan   *Conversion:* Lazenby
     Half-time: 7-6

The Army: Lt M. Greenhalgh; Dvr S. Walklin, Lt H. Kelly, Lt N. Beazley, Cpl E. Atkins; W/O J. Morgan, Capt. F. Drury; Cpl N. Kessell, S/Sgt J. Byrne (*captain*), Capt. C. Harvey, Lt R. Bush, Capt. B. McCall, L/Cpl K. Hopson, C/Sgt G. Williams, Sgt Inst. S. Peacock

Royal Air Force: Cpl S. Lazenby; Flt Lt M. Aspinall, Jnr Tech. S. Roke, F/O I. Goslin (*captain*), F/O R. Underwood; SAC N. Raikes, Cpl S.Worrall; Cpl M. Whitcombe, SAC K. Davies, SAC A. Billett, Cpl D. Parsonage, Cpl B. Richardson, Cpl R. Burn, Jnr Tech. D. Gigg, F/O I. Stevens. *Replacements:* Flt Sgt J. Peters for Billett; Cpl S. Mowbray for Burn

Referee: A. Turner (*Lancashire Society*)

The result eventually turned on kicking successes, with Lazenby outscoring Morgan by one penalty-goal. But it was exciting for all that, and the Air Force just about deserved their second successive title after coming from behind to win. In fact they trailed (12-13) with injury time beckoning, when Underwood cleverly collected a kick ahead by Goslin and passed inside for Lazenby to go over and bring his own tally to twelve points. Earlier, Walklin had beaten Underwood on the turn to score for the men in khaki, whose other try was a fine effort by Peacock. Roke's effort for the airmen was also commendable in poor playing conditions.

	P	W	L	F	A	Pts
Royal Air Force	2	2	0	36	22	4
Royal Navy	2	1	1	22	23	2
The Army	2	0	2	16	29	0

The Army have now won the tournament on twenty five occasions, the Royal Navy fifteen times and the Royal Air Force eleven times. The Army and the Royal Air Force have twice shared the title and there have been eight triple ties since the Championship started in 1920.

In matches between the services, The Army have beaten the Royal Navy thirty six times against thirty defeats with three games drawn. The Royal Navy have recorded thirty five wins over the Royal Air Force against twenty two defeats and four drawn matches. The Army have defeated the Royal Air Force on thirty five occasions, the airmen have won nineteen encounters and there have been seven draws.

The Army last won the tournament in 1983 and the Royal Navy's last success was in 1981.

The Barbarians

Despite counter attractions, which make it difficult for Geoff Windsor-Lewis to produce top-class teams at the drop of his hat, as might have been the case in better days, the 'Baa-Baas' continue to entertain and remain a great attraction. On the whole, the latest season was successful, with five matches out of seven being won and only one of the defeats being a rout – in the final match against Swansea.

In other matches, there were good performances against Leicester and the East Midlands, and Cardiff were beaten for the first time since 1980. The match against Penarth was the final one of the series, which saw the Barbarians win fifty nine of the seventy four matches, with eleven wins for Penarth and four draws. It is sad that this game is now consigned to history, but it is a sign of the times and of the numerous commitments which mean that Geoff Windsor-Lewis must now perform miracles to keep the public happy. For example, in the East Midlands match, he had the services of seven Scots, none of whom were available for the Easter tour owing to the fact that Scotland were playing in Bucharest.

Even so, it would be a sad day if the club could no longer appear, as it is an institution in its own right, and one that reminds us of former values where the game, and even life itself, are concerned.

Mark Douglas, the London Welsh scrum-half, fires out the ball although tackled by the Barbarian Philip Matthews at Twickenham on 14th September 1985.

Date	Opponents	Venue	Result
16th Sept.	London Welsh	Twickenham	W 27-24
22nd Oct.	Newport	Rodney Parade, Newport	L 29-38
28th Dec.	Leicester	Leicester	W 19-16
5th Mar.	East Midlands	Northampton	W 35-6
28th Mar.	Penarth	Penarth	W 39-15
29th Mar.	Cardiff	Cardiff RFC	W 24-19
31st Mar.	Swansea	Swansea	L 13-48

Match summary: P 7 W 5 L 2 F 186 A 166

Players

Backs: P. Dods (*Gala*), LW; S.Smith (*Wasps*), LW, N; M. Kiernan (*Lansdowne*), LW; K. Simms (*Cambridge University, Liverpool*), LW, C, S; R. Underwood (*Leicester*), LW; M. Dacey (*Swansea*), LW; N. Melville (*Wasps*), LW; H. Davies (*Wasps*), N; I. Evans (*Llanelli*), N, L; R.Cardus (*Wasps*), N (r); B. Bowen (*South Wales Police*), N; M. Harrison (*Wakefield*), N, C; R. Andrew (*Nottingham*), N; R. Moon (*Nottingham*), N, EM (r); H. MacNeill (*London Irish*), L; M. Titley (*Swansea*), L, P; S. Halliday (*Bath*), L; A. Emyr (*Swansea*), L, P; S. Barnes (*Bath*), L, P; R. Hill (*Bath*), L, S; R. Jones (*Swansea*), L (r), C; K. Townley (*Llanelli*), L (r); G. Hastings (*Cambridge University, London Scottish*), EM; M. Duncan (*West of Scotland*), EM; J. Palmer (*Bath*), EM, P; J. Devereux (*South Glamorgan Institute*), EM, C, S (r); M. Bailey (*Wasps*), EM; D.Wyllie (*Stewart's-Melville FP*), EM; S. Johnston (*Watsonians*), EM; F. Clough (*Orrell*), P, S; G. Davies (*Cardiff*), P; M. Douglas (*London Welsh*), P; P. Thorburn (*Neath*), C, S; K. Crossan (*Instonians*), C; J. Davies (*Neath*), C; P. Lewis (*Llanelli*), S; A. Hadley (*Cardiff*), S; G. Pearce (*Llanelli*), S

Forwards: I. Stephens (*Bridgend*), LW; C. Deans (*Hawick*), LW, EM; M. Hobley (*Wasps*), LW; W. Anderson (*Dungannon*), LW, EM; R. Norster (*Cardiff*), LW, S; P. Matthews (*Ards*), LW; G. Rees (*Nottingham*), LW, C; J. Jeffrey (*Kelso*), LW; T. Jones (*London Welsh*), N; A. Simpson (*Sale*), N; D. Fitzgerald (*Lansdowne*), N; R. Kearney (*Wanderers*), N; J. Orwin (*Gloucester*), N; W. Dooley (*Preston Grasshoppers*), N, L; P. Buckton (*Orrell*), N; M. Teague (*Cardiff*), N; J. Whitefoot (*Cardiff*), L; A. Phillips (*Cardiff*), L; G. Pearce (*Northampton*), L, C; M. Colclough (*Swansea*), L; D. Pickering (*Llanelli*), L; D. Leslie (*Dundee HSFP*), L; P. Winterbottom (*Headingley*), L, C; P. Orr (*Old Wesley*), EM; L. Delaney (*Llanelli*), EM, P, S; N. Redman (*Bath*), EM; D. White (*Gala*), EM; G. Roberts (*Cardiff*), EM; I. Paxton (*Selkirk*), EM; R. Lee (*Bath*), P; W. Burns (*Lansdowne*), P, C (r), S; P. May (*Llanelli*), P, C, S; D. Waters (*Newport*), P; A. Keay (*Saracens*), P, S; S. McGaughey (*Hawick*), P, S; O. Williams (*Glamorgan Wanderers*), P; G. Robbins (*Coventry*), P (r), C, S; P. Rendall (*Wasps*), C; C. F. Fitzgerald (*St Mary's College*), C; J. Campbell-Lamerton (*London Scottish*), C; P. Winterbottom (*Headingley*), C; I. Eidman (*Cardiff*), S

Middlesex Seven-a-Side Tournament

Sixth round

Nottingham	32	Worthing	6
Rosslyn Park II	10	Blackheath	8
Rosslyn Park	28	Richmond	6
Kelso	24	Richmond II	4
Loughborough Students	24	Sale	12
Saracens	10	London Welsh	0
Harlequins	22	Wasps II	0
Wasps	24	Hendon	3

Quarter-finals

Nottingham	20	Rosslyn Park II	10
Rosslyn Park	20	Kelso	10
Saracens	16	Loughborough Students	10
Harlequins	18	Wasps	10

Semi-finals

Nottingham	24	Rosslyn Park	4
Harlequins	16	Saracens	4

Final

Harlequins	**18**	**Nottingham**	**10**

Harlequins: S. Hunter, A. Thompson, R. Lawrence, A. Woodhouse, A. Dent, J. Olver, M. Skinner

Nottingham: C. Oti, G. Hartley, S. Hodgkinson, R. Moon, S. Hughes, B. Moore, P. Thornley

Referee: A. Trigg (*London*)

By winning the Middlesex Sevens for the first time since 1978 Harlequins drew level with Richmond as the club that has won on the most occasions, nine times each. It was a well deserved reward for probably the best Seven in the competition and supplemented the success in their own Sevens in September 1985.

Harlequins' road to the final involved successive victories over the Wasps seconds and, in the quarter-finals, over their first Seven, which saw the holders depart in a fairly close encounter; in the semi-finals, Saracens were comfortably dismissed. The other finalists were Nottingham, who reached that stage with wins over Worthing, Rosslyn Park seconds and Rosslyn Park first Seven in the semi-finals.

Nottingham opened and closed the scoring in the final, but were well outplayed in the period between those scores. Dent in the first period, followed by Woodhouse and the powerful wing, Hunter, took 'Quins well clear as all three tries were converted by Lawrence, and that was virtually that! Nottingham's final scorers were Hartley and Moon with Hodgkinson converting the second.

Of the visiting teams, Kelso were weakened by a Scottish tour of Spain and France and they went out to Rosslyn Park first Seven in the quarter-finals. Sale, the other guests, went out in the sixth round to Loughborough Students, who were Saracens' victims in the next stage. Apart from Worthing, the other junior team, Hendon, also tried hard, but they were sixth round losers to Wasps' first Seven.

All the Harlequins players were stars of the tournament in their own right, with Hunter's powerful running being too much for each opponent in turn. Nottingham's stars were Oti and Moon, and another player to shine was the Rosslyn Park wing, Offiah.

One point of criticism must be made and it is not directed at the organizers. Why do clubs enter teams for this important Sevens tournament, or for any such event, with players wearing numbers that bear little or no resemblance to those printed in the official programme? Can they not send their men onto the field numbered from one to seven? Perhaps next year the organizers should insist on teams following the programme numbers or face penalties, such as the concession of an immediate twelve points to their opponents each time they offend.

Richmond have won this event nine times (one by Richmond II), Harlequins nine times, London Welsh eight times, London Scottish six times, St Mary's Hospital and Loughborough Colleges five, Rosslyn Park four, Wasps three, Blackheath and St Luke's College (now Exeter University) twice, Barbarians, Sale, Metropolitan Police, Cardiff, Cambridge University, Notts (now Nottingham), Heriot's FP and Stewart's-Melville FP once each.

Middlesex Sevens action between Harlequins (the eventual winners) and Wasps II.

Tournament Winners, 1926-85

1926	Harlequins	1946	St Mary's Hospital
1927	Harlequins	1947	Rosslyn Park
1928	Harlequins	1948	Wasps
1929	Harlequins	1949	Heriot's FP
1930	London Welsh	1950	Rosslyn Park
1931	London Welsh	1951	Richmond II
1932	Blackheath	1952	Wasps
1933	Harlequins	1953	Richmond
1934	Barbarians	1954	Rosslyn Park
1935	Harlequins	1955	Richmond
1936	Sale	1956	London Welsh
1937	London Scottish	1957	St Luke's College
1938	Metropolitan Police	1958	Blackheath
1939	Cardiff	1959	Loughborough Colleges
1940	St Mary's Hospital	1960	London Scottish
1941	Cambridge University	1961	London Scottish
1942	St Mary's Hospital	1962	London Scottish
1943	St Mary's Hospital	1963	London Scottish
1944	St Mary's Hospital	1964	Loughborough Colleges
1945	Notts	1965	London Scottish
1966	Loughborough Colleges	1976	Loughborough Colleges
1967	Harlequins	1977	Richmond
1968	London Welsh	1978	Harlequins
1969	St Luke's College	1979	Richmond
1970	Loughborough Colleges	1980	Richmond
1971	London Welsh	1981	Rosslyn Park
1972	London Welsh	1982	Stewart's-Melville FP
1973	London Welsh	1983	Richmond
1974	Richmond	1984	London Welsh
1975	Richmond	1985	Wasps

Other Sevens Tournaments

Harlequins

Harlequins	20	Kelso	18

London Welsh Centenary

Public Schools Wanderers	38	Leicester	6

Rosslyn Park Sturges Sevens

Rosslyn Park	34	Cambridge University	4

Oxfordshire

Richmond	20	London Welsh	6

Schools

Schools Internationals

18-Group

Scotland (at Murrayfield)	6	France	13
France (at St Raphael)	18	England	19
England (at Nottingham)	13	Ireland	6
Wales (at Neath)	15	Scotland	4
Scotland (at Braidholm, Edinburgh)	10	England	7
England (at Otley)	18	Wales	7
Ireland (at Galway)	17	Wales	3
Ireland (at Dublin)	16	Japan	6

16-Group

Italian Regional XV (at Bergamo)	7	England	25
Italy (at Varese)	14	England	20

Youths

France	40	Wales	12
Wales	14	England	4
Scotland	43	Sweden	4
England	6	France	35
Italy	4	Scotland	22

Under-21

Italy	6	Scotland	22

As always, there were several outstanding schools, with unbeaten records in Inter-School matches being maintained by Ardingly, Bishop's Stortford, Campion (who gave the visiting Australians a hard match), Harrow (whose Rees became a first-team player for Wasps and a Middlesex regular in the Thorn EMI Championship), Kent College (Canterbury) and Oratory. Others also maintained fine records: Arnold, Cheltenham GS, Forest, King Edward VI (Birmingham), Nottingham High School, St Bees, Taunton and West Buckland all suffered only one defeat. Harrow's perfect record was the first in their history, earning them an award from *Rugby World & Post*.

The England Youth team before joining battle with the French Juniors at the Old Deer Park, Richmond. France won 35-6.

English Clubs

Bath

Address: Recreation Ground, Bath, Somerset. Tel: (0225) 25192. The Horse Show Ground, Bath, Somerset. Tel: (0225) 310548
Founded: 1865
Secretary: C. A. Howard, 24 The Green, Hinton Charterhouse, Bath BA3 6BT. Tel: (022122) 2406 (h), (0225) 62827 (w)
Fixtures secretary: J. W. P. Roberts, Grove House, Ashley, Box, Wilts. Tel: (0225) 742251
Captain 1985-86: J. A. Palmer
Most capped players: J. P. Hall, 15 for England; R. A. Gerrard, 14 for England
Colours: Blue, white and black/black/blue, white and black
Directions to ground: From A4 (London Road) proceed into centre of city and turn left after Post Office into Pulteney Street passing Library. Cross over Avon Bridge and the Recreation Ground is on the right
Clubhouse: Bars, tearoom, changing-rooms
Teams run: 3
1st XV 1985-86: P 43 W 33 D 3 L 7 F 1055 A 504

For Bath this was another very good season with the John Player Special Cup won for the third successive year. In the John Smith Merit Table A only six fixtures were completed with three wins being achieved. The team's overall record was superb. Eight players appeared in the Five Nations Championship this season: Halliday, Palmer, Barnes, Hill, Chilcott, Hall and Redman for England, and Sole for Scotland.

Bedford

Address: Goldington Road, Bedford. Tel: (0234) 59160/54619
Founded: 1886
Secretary: A. D. Mills, 7 Sandy Road, Bedford. Tel: (0234) 47796 (h)
Fixtures secretary: J. R. Saunders, College Farm, Oakley, Beds. Tel: (02302) 2328 (h)
Captain 1985-86: I. G. Peck
Most capped player: D. P. Rogers, 34 for England, 2 for British Lions
Colours: Oxford and Cambridge blue wide hoops
Directions to ground: From town centre proceed east following A428 sign to St Neots. Ground is on left soon after start of Goldington Road
Clubhouse: Bars, tearooms, changing-rooms
Teams run: 3
1st XV 1985-86: P 39 W 14 D 2 L 23 F 431 A 859

Bedford, with their centenary season approaching, had a dreadful time, winning only two (of nine) John Smith Merit Table B matches to finish last. In the John Player Special Cup (won in 1975) elimination came in ignominious fashion in the second round at home to Broughton Park. The overall record was also mediocre.

Birkenhead Park

Address: Upper Park, Park Road North, Birkenhead, Merseyside. Tel: 051-652 4646
Founded: 1871
Secretary: G. Marrs, 501 Tower Building, Water Street, Liverpool 3. Tel: 051-652 1536 (h), 051-236 3191 (w)

Fixtures secretary: M. H. Pearson, The Hollies, Viner Road South, Birkenhead. Tel: 051-653 9372 (h), 051-236 9891 (w)
Captain 1985-86: C. Plummer
Most capped player: J. R. Paterson, 21 for Scotland
Colours: Red, navy and white hoops
Clubhouse: Changing-rooms, bars
1st XV 1985-86: P 44 W 26 D 2 L 16 F 786 A 525

Park had a useful season playing outside the main merit tables winning twenty six of their forty four matches.

Birmingham

Address: Forshaw Heath Lane, Earlswood, Solihull, West Midlands B94 5LH. Tel: (0564) 822955
Founded: 1911
Secretary: S. MacAleavey, 18 Leander Gardens, Kings Heath, Birmingham B14 6EZ. Tel: 021-443 2154 (h), 021-550 9201 (w)
Fixtures secretary: A. Morden, 134 Old Station Road, Hampton-in-Arden, Solihull B92 0HE. Tel: (06755) 2462 (h), 021-643 2736 (w)
Captain 1985-86: D. Read
Colours: Red/white/red, black and white
Clubhouse: Usual facilities
1st XV 1985-86: P 34 W 15 D 2 L 17 F 417 A 592

Birmingham finished tenth (out of twelve) in Merit Table C and just failed to break even over the whole season in terms of results.

Blackheath

Address: Rectory Field, Blackheath, London SE3. Tel: 01-858 1578/3677
Founded: 1858
Secretary: D. J. Piper, 12 Manor Way, Blackheath, London SE3
Fixtures secretary (1st XV): D. Blacklocks, Home Farm, Smeeth, Ashford, Kent. Tel: 030-381 3104 (h), (0679) 20593 (w)
Captain 1985-86: R. Bodenham
Coach 1985-86: H. McHardy
Most capped players: C. N. Lowe, 25 caps for England; N. S. Bruce, 31 caps for Scotland
Colours: Red and black hoops/black/black and red
Directions to ground: From central London proceed towards South Circular road, then follow A207 towards Dartford. Ground is near park on right. British Rail to Blackheath
Clubhouse: Bar, changing-rooms
1st XV 1985-86: P 32 W 15 D 2 L 15 F 475 A 522

Blackheath provided half the Kent team, which reached the Thorn EMI County Championship final. 'The Club' also reached the last sixteen of the John Player Special Cup, but finished in the lower reaches of John Smith Merit Table B, and the London Merit Table. They were the winners of the Kent Cup (XV-a-side).

Bradford & Bingley

Address: Wagon Lane, Bingley, West Yorkshire. Tel: (0274 56) 0468
Founded: 1982, on merger of Bradford and Bingley clubs
Secretary: W. P. Dennis, 2 Hesp Hills, Beckfoot Lane, Bingley, West Yorkshire. Tel: (0274 56) 7500 (h), (0274 72) 2118 (w)

Fixtures secretary: P. W. Crowther, 1 Manor Close, Bramhope, Leeds LS16 9HQ. Tel: (0532) 842926 (h), (0943) 464680 (w)
Captain 1985-86: R. Hood
Most capped player: E. Myers (Bradford), 18 for England
Colours: Red, amber and black hoops/dark blue/black with red and amber tops
Clubhouse: Usual facilities
1st XV 1985-86: P 34 W 9 D 1 L 24 F 221 A 547

The combined club had a poor season and had to suffer some heavy defeats. With national merit tables coming along there will be a need for improvement or they will find themselves playing amongst lesser sides.

Bristol

Address: Memorial Ground, Filton Avenue, Horfield, Bristol BS7 0AG. Tel: (0272) 48360
Founded: 1888
Secretary: T. A. B. Mahoney, 2 Raymend Walk, Bristol BS3 5AP. Tel: (0272) 664782
Fixtures secretary: B. W. Redwood, 205 Stoke Lane, Westbury, Bristol BS9 3RX. Tel: (0272) 684382 (h), (0272) 44273 (w)
Captain 1985-86: P. Polledri
Most capped players: J. V. Pullin, 42 for England, 7 for British Lions; J. S. Tucker, 27 for England; J. D. Currie, 25 for England
Colours: Blue and white/blue/blue and white
Directions to ground: Take A38 towards Cheltenham. Ground is on Filton road
Clubhouse: Bars, tearoom
Teams run: 3
1st XV 1985-86: P 42 W 26 D 0 L 16 F 902 A 502

Bristol had a mediocre season with only two John Smith Merit Table A matches (out of six) being won and in the John Player Special Cup a tough encounter in the third round at Gloucester was narrowly lost. Alan Morley continued to play for the club and was as effective as ever.

Broughton Park

Address: Chelsfield Grove, Chorlton, Manchester 21. Tel: 061-881 2481
Founded: 1882
Secretary: R. W. Greenall, 260 Barlow Moor Road, Chorlton, Manchester M21 2HA. Tel: 061-861 0457 (h), 061-766 6098 (w)
Fixtures secretary: P. W. Barratt, The Corner House, Brooklane, Alderley Edge, Cheshire SK9 7RU
Captain 1985-86: J. Wilde
Most capped player: A. Neary, 43 for England, 1 for British Lions
Colours: Black and white hoops/black
Clubhouse: Usual facilities
1st XV 1985-86: P 43 W 26 D 1 L 16 F 633 A 487

Broughton Park did not figure in any national merit table, but they had an excellent record in club matches winning nearly two-thirds of them. With national merit tables being organized on a wider basis in 1987 they should figure prominently.

Cambridge University

Address: Grange Road, Cambridge. Tel: (0223) 54131
Founded: 1872
Fixtures secretary: Dr D. H. Marrian, 244 Hills Road, Cambridge. Tel: (0223) 242719
Captain: A. G. Hastings (1985), F. J. Clough (1986)
Coach 1985-86: A. K. Rodgers
Most capped players: C. M. H. Gibson, 69 for Ireland, 12 for British Lions; T. G. R. Davies, 46 for Wales, 5 for British Lions; A. R. Smith, 33 for Scotland, 3 for British Lions
Colours: Light blue and white hoops/white/light blue and white
Clubhouse: Club room with bar, changing-rooms
Teams run: 3
1st XV 1985-86: P 21 W 10 D 0 L 11 F 374 A 353

Cambridge University were runners-up in the Rosslyn Park Sevens and, as the University Match was lost, it might be said that Cambridge University had a less satisfactory season than usual, but they remained an attractive team to watch and if certain players, who are rumoured to be taking up residence, actually do arrive prospects under F. J. Clough should be good. The most capped International player in the world, C. M. H. Gibson, was in residence from 1963 to 1966; he was capped for Ireland in his freshman year.

Coventry

Address: Coundon Road, Coventry. Tel: (0203) 591274
Founded: 1874
Secretary: P. A. J. Sharp, 17 Asthill Grove, Coventry. Tel: (0203) 502468 (h), (0203) 57411 (w)
Fixtures secretary: J. Barton, 5 The Riddings, Coventry. Tel: (0203) 73148 (h), (0203) 58381 (w)
Most capped players: D. J. Duckham, 36 for England, 3 for British Lions; F. E. Cotton 31 for England, 7 for British Lions; P. E. Judd, 22 for England
Colours: Navy and white hoops/navy
Clubhouse: Excellent facilities for players and spectators with bars, changing-rooms, plus other social attractions
1st XV 1985-86: P 41 W 29 D 0 L 12 F 867 A 521

Coventry finished second in the John Smith Merit Table B and are promoted. In the John Player Special Cup they were beaten in the third round by Leicester at Coundon Road. Steve Brain continued effectively as England's hooker and Graham Robbins played twice in the all-white. Most of the highly successful Warwickshire team, including the whole pack, were Coventry players. Coventry won the first ever John Player Special Cup in 1974, having won the RFU knock-out competition the previous season.

Fylde

Address: The Woodlands Memorial Ground, Blackpool Road, Ansdell, Lytham St Annes, Lancashire. Tel: (0253) 734733
Founded: 1919
Secretary: P. Makin, Links Way, Greenway, St Annes-on-Sea, Lancs. Tel: (0253) 722713 (h), (0772) 59625 (w)
Fixtures secretary: H. M. Whittle, Windrush, Lilac Avenue, Ballam Road, Lytham St Annes, Lancs. Tel: (0253) 735157 (h), (0772) 22626 (w)
Captain 1985-86: A. Macfarlane
Most capped player: W. B. Beaumont, 34 for England (19 as captain), 7 for British Lions (4 as captain)
Colours: Claret, gold and white
Directions to ground: On A584 Lytham to Blackpool road
Clubhouse: Usual, excellent, facilities for playing and social activities
1st XV 1985-86: P 43 W 20 D 0 L 23 F 642 A 767

Fylde played in Merit Table C and finished in ninth place with a break-even record. The overall record for the season was modest.

Gloucester

Address: Kingsholm, Kingsholm Road, Gloucester GL1 3AX.
Tel: (0452) 28385 (clubhouse), (0452) 20901 (office)
Founded: 1873
Secretary: T. R. Tandy, 48 Cotteswold Road, Gloucester. Tel:
(0452) 23049
Fixtures secretary: P. J. Ford, Rivermead, Sandhurst Lane,
Gloucester. Tel: (0452) 424101
Captain 1985-86: J. Orwin
Most capped player: A. T. (Tom) Voyce, 27 for England
Colours: Cherry and white stripes/white/cherry and white
Directions to ground: From city centre take Worcester Street
and go straight into Kingsholm Road
Clubhouse: Bars, changing-rooms, tearooms
Teams run: 3
1st XV 1985-86: P 44 W 32 D 0 L 12 F 1006 A 477
   Victory in the John Smith Merit Table A was the high spot
and the overall record was good. Success in the John Player
Special Cup eluded the team again in a stormy match at Richmond
against London Scottish when Brain of Gloucester was sent off.
There was also an absence of International honours, which
made no sense in the light of the team's consistency.

Gosforth

Address: New Ground, Great North Road, Gosforth,
Newcastle-upon-Tyne NE3 2DT. Tel: (0632) 856915
Founded: 1877
Secretary: B. J. Colledge, 12 Waterbury Road, Brunton Park,
Gosforth, Newcastle-upon-Tyne NE3 5AJ. Tel: (0632) 363680
Fixtures secretary (1st XV): J. M. Smith, 3 Oaklands Avenue,
Gosforth, Newcastle-upon-Tyne 3. Tel: (0912) 853377 (h), (0912)
655193 (w)
Captain 1985-86: S. Gustard
Most capped players: R. J. McLoughlin, 40 for Ireland, 3 for
British Lions; R. M. Uttley, 23 for England, 4 for British Lions
Colours: Green and white hoops/white/green and white hoops
Directions to ground: On A1 Great North Road leaving New-
castle for Scotland
Clubhouse: Usual good facilities for playing and social activities
1st XV 1985-86: P 36 W 27 D 1 L 8 F 553 A 338
   Gosforth finished tenth in John Smith Merit Table A but
were relegated (and Moseley survived) on a technicality. Twice
previous winners of the John Player Cup (in 1976 and 1977),
Gosforth this season had an unlucky exit in the third round after
a draw at home against Northampton. They won the Northumberland Cup. In most respects it was a good season in terms
of overall results and the team should bounce back.

Halifax

Address: Ovenden Park, Halifax. Tel: (0422) 65926
Founded: 1873
Secretary: I. P. Booth, 33 Trenance Gardens, Greetland, Halifax,
West Yorkshire HX4 8NN. Tel: (0422) 72399
Fixtures secretary: S. J. Battersby, 3 Townend Road, Holmfirth,
West Yorks. Tel: (0484) 685162
Captain 1985-86: A. Davidson
Most capped players: J. P. Horrocks-Taylor, 9 for England, 1
for British Lions; G. T. Thomson, 9 for England
Colours: Dark blue, light blue and white narrow hoops
Clubhouse: Changing-rooms, bars
1st XV 1985-86: P 36 W 14 D 2 L 20 F 417 A 493
   Outside any national merit table Halifax had a moderate
season which was not relieved by John Player Cup success.

Harlequins

Address: Stoop Memorial Ground, Craneford Way, Twicken-
ham, Middlesex. Tel: 01-892 3080. They also play at RFU
Ground, Twickenham
Founded: 1866
Secretary: C. M. Herridge, 11 Langley Avenue, Surbiton, Surrey
KT6 9QN. Tel: 01-390 0201 (h), (0895) 440641 (w)
Fixtures secretary: R. F. Read, Brookside, Lodge Lane, Salfords,
Redhill, Surrey RH1 5DH. Tel: (02934) 3711 (h), 01-661 5107
(w)
Captain 1985-86: D. H. Cooke
Most capped players: I. G. Milne, 33 for Scotland; W. W.
Wakefield, 31 for England
Colours: Light blue, magenta, chocolate, French grey, black
and light green/white shorts
Directions to ground: From Richmond take A316 to Twickenham
and turn right at third roundabout. Ground is quarter of mile
ahead. By BR (Southern) to Twickenham, turn right, cross
road and go straight for ten minutes (approximately), crossing
main A316
Clubhouse: Large upstairs bar and clubroom, downstairs
dressing-rooms
1st XV 1985-86: P 34 W 20 D 0 L 14 F 603 A 462
   Harlequins had a good season but it could have been better.
In the John Player Special Cup the team reached the last eight
and in the John Smith Merit Table A the team finished sixth,
but played only four matches.

Harrogate

Address: Claro Road, Harrogate. Tel: (0423) 66966/64933
Founded: 1871
Secretary: F. Carter, 6 Blackthorn Lane, Burnbridge, Harrogate.
Tel: (0423) 870654 (h), (0532) 445831 (w)
Fixtures secretary: C. T. Wood, 17 Beech Road, Harrogate.
Tel: (0423) 872572
Captain 1985-86: P. J. Squires
Most capped player: P. J. Squires, 29 for England, 1 for British
Lions
Colours: Red, amber and black
Clubhouse: Usual facilities
1st XV 1985-86: P 38 W 20 D 0 L 18 F 540 A 631
   An even season ended with Harrogate winning twenty of
thirty eight matches. The club was not in any national merit
table but, with the new structure starting in 1987, they hope to
be prominent.

Hartlepool Rovers

Address: The Friarage, West View Road, Hartlepool, Cleveland.
Tel: (0429) 67741
Founded: 1879
Secretary: K. Lister, 12 The Grove, Hartlepool, Cleveland
TS26 9NE. Tel: (0429) 67246 (h), (0429) 68151 (w)
Fixtures secretary: W. J. Dale, 21 Knapton Avenue, Billingham,
Cleveland. Tel: (0642) 556314
Captain 1985-86: C. Winspear
Most capped player: G. S. Conway, 18 for England
Colours: White/black/red
Clubhouse: Usual facilities
1st XV 1985-86: P 38 W 29 D 0 L 9 F 624 A 350
   Hartlepool Rovers had a good season with twenty nine wins
in thirty eight matches, but they were not concerned in any
national merit table, although this will change when the 1987-88
season starts and they should be well to the fore.

Headingley

Address: Bridge Road, Kirkstall, Leeds 5. Tel: (0532) 755029
Founded: 1878
Secretary: M. Beaumont, Stoneycroft, 44 Larkfield Avenue, Leeds LS19 6EN. Tel: (0532) 506574 (h), (0637) 61212 (w)
Fixtures secretary: P. A. W. Stephens, c/o Salesplan Ltd, 48 York Place, Leeds LS1 2RU. Tel: (0532) 436334
Captain 1985-86: T. Sinclair
Most capped players: I. R. McGeechan, 32 for Scotland, 8 for British Lions; P. J. Winterbottom, 19 for England, 4 for British Lions
Colours: Green, black and white/blue
Clubhouse: Good facilities for playing and social activities
1st XV 1985-86: P 39 W 19 D 0 L 20 F 565 A 500

Headingley had a poor season in John Smith Merit Table A, losing all eight matches and thus suffering relegation. In the John Player Special Cup the team lost narrowly in the third round away to Harlequins after having a forward dismissed early in the game. The overall record was just short of an even return, so things can improve. Peter Winterbottom regained his England place after a season's absence through injury.

Huddersfield

Address: Tandem, Waterloo, Huddersfield. Tel: (0484) 23864
Founded: 1909
Secretary: J. Newsome, 230 Huddersfield Road, Liversedge, West Yorkshire W15 7QQ. Tel: (0924) 403372
Fixtures secretary: B. Starbuck, 7 Whitegates Grove, Fenay Bridge, Huddersfield, West Yorks. Tel: (0484) 603750 (h), (0484) 682266 (w)
Captain 1985-86: P. Urwin
Most capped player: N. M. Hall, 17 for England
Colours: White, claret and gold
Clubhouse: Usual facilities
1st XV 1985-86: P 31 W 8 D 1 L 22 F 332 A 561

Huddersfield were a much improved side this season due to the forward power provided by the Kiwi contingent of players. The team is now looking to improve the performance of its backs to match that of its forwards and thus achieve better match results.

Hull & East Riding

Address: The Circle, Anlaby Road, Kingston-upon-Hull, North Humberside. Tel: (0482) 507098/507918
Founded: 1901
Secretary: C. K. Rockingham, 30 St Margarets Avenue, Cottingham, North Humberside HU16 5NF. Tel: (0482) 867131 (h), (0482) 825301 (w)
Fixtures secretary: S. Elliott, 73 Kingtree Avenue, Cottingham, North Humberside HU16 4DR. Tel: (0482) 443466 (h), (0482) 222316 (w)
Captain 1985-86: I. Furlong
Most capped player: R. D. Sangwin, 2 for England (1964)
Colours: Cherry and white hoops/navy
Clubhouse: Usual facilities for players and spectators
1st XV 1985-86: P 36 W 22 D 2 L 12 F 678 A 423

Apart from the excellent playing record the club had a very good fly-half in S. Girking, who not only played for the country 'B' side but also scored 353 points for the club – 23 tries, 48 conversions, 49 penalty-goals and 6 dropped-goals. The First XV reached the semi-finals of the county cup losing away to Morley (10-9). Hull & East Riding provided three players for the full Yorkshire team – Paul Sellar, the hooker, Tony Rice (the club captain) and D. Goodall. S. Hadi and R. Kernan played for Yorkshire Colts.

Kendal

Address: Mint Bridge, Shap Road, Kendal, Cumbria. Tel: (0539) 24239
Founded: 1880, newly constituted in 1909
Secretary: P. W. Sharp, 3 Beechmount, Redhills Road, Arnside, via Carnforth, Lancs. Tel: (0524) 791963 (h), (0539) 20277 (w)
Fixtures secretary: R. Short, Cockin Farm, Whinfell, near Kendal, Cumbria. Tel: (053 984) 251 (h), (0539) 22636 (w)
Captain 1985-86: G. Barton
Most capped player: S. A. Martindale, 1 for England
Colours: Black and amber
Directions to ground: Follow A6 out of Kendal towards Shap
Clubhouse: Usual facilities
1st XV 1985-86: P 33 W 16 D 0 L 17 F 486 A 418

Kendal concentrated on the qualifying division of the Northern Merit Table and finished halfway in a modest season. As a result, they missed playing in the Cumbria Cup, which they might well have won.

Leicester

Address: The Clubhouse, Aylestone Road, Leicester LE2 7LF. Tel: (0533) 540276
Founded: 1880
Secretary: J. A. Allen, 60 Dorchester Road, Leicester. Tel: (0533) 858407 (h), (0533) 554321 (w)
Fixtures secretary: J. H. Berry, Bunnystone Cottage, Bunnison Lane, Colston Bassett, Notts. Tel: (09497) 428 (w)
Captain 1985-86: I. Smith
Most capped players: P. J. Wheeler, 41 for England, 7 for British Lions; P. W. Dodge, 32 for England, 2 for British Lions
Colours: Scarlet, green and white jerseys
Directions to ground: From city centre take A50 (Welford Road) then fork right on to A426 (Aylestone Road). Ground is close by on left
Clubhouse: First-class social and playing facilities with bars for members, changing-rooms
1st XV 1985-86: P 36 W 26 D 0 L 10 F 834 A 486

Leicester maintained a good position in John Smith Merit Table A and reached the semi-finals of the John Player Special Cup, losing at home to Bath. Dean Richards made a very successful debut for England.

Liverpool

Address: St Michael's, Church Road, Liverpool L17 7BD. Tel: 051-727 6330
Founded: 1857
Secretary: J. Boyce, 34 Mersey Road, Liverpool 17. Tel: 051-427 2124 (h), 051-709 1608 (w)
Fixtures secretary: W. E. Rickarby, 6 Daventry Road, Aigburth, Liverpool 17. Tel: 051-727 3142 (h), 051-236 3778/5107 (w)
Captain 1985-86: J. Hescot
Most capped player: M. A. C. Slemen, 31 for England, 1 for British Isles
Colours: Red, blue and black horizontal stripes/white
1st XV 1985-86 (John Smith Merit Table B): P 9 W 4 D 0 L 5 F 133 A 127

After a very poor start in John Smith Merit Table B Liverpool with some late wins fought back and finished in seventh place.

London Irish

Address: The Avenue, Sunbury-on-Thames, Middlesex. Tel: (09327) 83034
Founded: 1898
Secretary: K. Kehoe, S. Reid's, 91 Fleet Street, London EC4 1DH. Tel: 01-353 3904
Fixtures secretary: R. G. McLennan, 20 Haselbury Road, London N18. Tel: 01-801 3374 (h), 01-440 9411 (w)
Captain 1985-86: P. O'Donnell
Most capped players: K. W. Kennedy, 45 for Ireland, 4 for British Lions; M. G. Molloy, 27 for Ireland; H. P. MacNeill, 21 for Ireland, 3 for British Lions
Colours: Green/white/green and white
Directions to ground: Take A316 towards M3; leave at first junction, turn left towards Sunbury and right before Kempton Park Racecourse into the Avenue. Ground is on right
Clubhouse: Upstairs bar and tearoom, downstairs dressing-rooms. New function room extension completed. These excellent facilities are now used for the finals of the Polytechnic Cups
1st XV 1985-86: P 33 W 20 D 2 L 11 F 665 A 496

This was a mediocre season with a modest John Smith Merit Table B position achieved; it was the same in the London Merit Table. In the John Player Cup there was first round elimination to Richmond. The Surrey Cup was won. The final, overall record was good enough to show potential for the future.

London Scottish

Address: Richmond Athletic Ground, Richmond, Surrey. Tel: 01-940 0397
Founded: 1878
Secretary: V. J. W. M. Lawrence, 22A Queen's Ride, Barnes, London SW13 0HX. Tel: 01-878 1456 (h), 01-289 1611 (w)
Fixtures secretary: S. R. G. Pratt, 34 Hillside Road, Ashtead, Surrey KT21 1RX. Tel: (03722) 73420
Captain 1985-86: A. J. Macklin
Coach 1985-86: A. F. McHarg
Most capped players: A. F. McHarg, 44 for Scotland; N. S. Bruce, 31 for Scotland; I. H. P. Laughland, 31 for Scotland
Colours: Dark blue with red lion badge/white/red
Directions to ground: Richmond Station (LT and BR Southern Region) turn right, then left at main roundabout. Ground is on the right on A316, Lower Mortlake Road
Clubhouse: Large bar, tearoom, changing-rooms
1st XV 1985-86: P 26 W 18 D 1 L 7 F 419 A 363

London Scottish reached the semi-finals of the John Player Special Cup losing to Wasps. In John Smith Merit Table A they finished in seventh place with three wins and four defeats.

London Welsh

Address: Old Deer Park, Kew Road, Richmond, Surrey TW9 2AZ. Tel: 01-940 2520
Founded: 1885
Secretary: Roland Hobbs, 73 Downs Road, Epsom, Surrey. Tel: (03727) 22252
Fixtures secretary (1st XV): D. Edgar Thomas, 241 Kent House Road, Beckenham, Kent. Tel: 01-778 4062
Captain 1985-86: Clive Rees
Coach 1985-86: John Vaughan
Most capped player: J. P. R. Williams, 55 for Wales, 8 for British Lions
Colours: Red with white shorts
Directions to ground: From Richmond Station (LT and BR Southern Region) ten minutes walk on Kew Road towards Kew Gardens. By road take road to Kew from main Great Chertsey Road (ground on left) or from Kew Bridge take road to Richmond (on right)
Clubhouse: Changing-rooms for home and visiting teams, two bars and tearoom
1st XV 1985-86: P 35 W 10 D 3 L 22 F 529 A 698

The London Welsh centenary season was very poor mainly due to injuries to, and departures of, key players. Mark Douglas and Russell (for virtually the whole season) were big sufferers as was fly-half, Colyn Price. Clive Rees, after a distinguished career, retired at the end of the season. The club reached the last eight of the John Player Special Cup, in which they will not compete in 1986-87 owing to a poor position in the London Merit Table. Several special events were staged to mark the club's centenary season, including a Sevens tournament won by Public Schools Wanderers.

Manchester

Address: Grove Lane, Cheadle Hulme, Cheshire. Tel: 061-485 1115
Founded: 1860
Secretary: G. T. Dodds, 8 Dennison Road, Cheadle Hulme, Cheadle, Cheshire SK8 6LW. Tel: 061-485 2104 (h)
Fixtures secretary: C. Williams, 45 Marina Drive, Marple, Cheshire. Tel: 061-445 8352
Captain 1985-86: G. Stewart
Most capped player: G. S. Conway, 18 for England
Colours: Red and white hoops/white/red
Clubhouse: Bars, changing-rooms
1st XV 1985-86: P 34 W 9 D 0 L 25 F 266 A 656

Manchester had a very poor season winning only nine matches out of thirty four.

Metropolitan Police

Address: Police Sports Club, Imber Court, Embercourt Road, East Molesey, Surrey. Tel: 01-398 1267
Founded: 1923
Secretary: K. Will, 60 Ivanhoe Drive, Kenton, Middlesex. Tel: 01-907 0094 (h), 01-577 4257 (w)
Fixtures secretary: George Crawford, 9 Elmwood Drive, Ewell, Epsom, Surrey. Tel: 01-393 5009 (h), 01-720 8011 (w)
Captain 1985-86: G. Porter
Most capped player: A. M. Rees, 13 for Wales
Colours: Navy blue/dark blue/dark blue
Clubhouse: About to become the finest in England
1st XV 1985-86: P 39 W 18 D 1 L 20 F 586 A 656

By winning Merit Table C Metropolitan Police did very well, although their overall record looked less impressive with their strong fixture list. Their results included a first-ever win against Harlequins. Richmond ended their John Player Special Cup ambitions in a preliminary round.

Middlesbrough

Address: Acklam Park, Green Lane, Middlesbrough, Cleveland. Tel: (0642) 88567
Founded: 1872
Secretary: D. Brydon, 20 Westwood Avenue, Linthorpe, Middlesbrough, Cleveland JS5 5PY. Tel: (0642) 819954 (h), (0642) 245432 ext. 3756 (w)
Fixtures secretary: G. D. Baxter, 3 Hambledon Road, Middlesbrough. Tel: (0642) 822107

Captain 1985-86: A. Robinson
Most capped player: A. G. B. Old, 16 for England
Colours: Maroon/white/maroon
Clubhouse: Full facilities
1st XV 1985-86: P 37 W 17 D 1 L 19 F 490 A 571

Middlesbrough had a mediocre season and will need to improve when the national merit tables commence.

Morley

Address: Scatcherd Lane, Morley, Leeds. Tel: (0532) 533487
Founded: 1878
Secretary: T. Long, Birch House, 41 Westfield Road, Horbury, West Yorks WF4 6YS. Tel: (0924) 272972 (h)
Fixtures secretary: T. Richmond, 101 Carlinghow Hill, Batley, West Yorks. Tel: (0924) 472705
Captain 1985-86: K. Plant
Most capped player: G. H. Marsden, 3 for England
Colours: Maroon jerseys
Clubhouse: Usual facilities
1st XV 1985-86: P 34 W 19 D 0 L 15 F 510 A 538

Morley did well to finish in fourth place in Merit Table C with four wins in six matches and the overall record was good with nineteen wins in thirty four matches. The club went out in the first round of the John Player Special Cup at home to Wakefield, but did well in the Yorkshire Cup.

Moseley

Address: The Reddings, Reddings Road, Moseley, Birmingham B13 8IW. Tel: 021-449 2149
Founded: 1873
Secretary: B. J. Malin, 59 Spiceland Road, Northfield, Birmingham B31 1NL. Tel: 021-476 6890 (h), 021-475 4220 (w)
Fixtures secretary: S. N. H. Cooper, 30 Conifer Court, Moor Green Lane, Moseley, Birmingham B13 8NB. Tel: 021-449 8940
Captain 1985-86: G. N. J. Cox
Most capped player: N. E. Horton, 20 for England
Colours: Black and red hooped jerseys
1st XV 1985-86: P 45 W 29 D 0 L 16 F 834 A 502

In a season of 'might-have-beens' one small mercy emerged in that relegation from John Smith Merit Table A was avoided. There was also a second place in the Midlands Merit Table to record, but John Player Special Cup progress was halted in the fourth round by Bath at the Reddings. The final playing record was good with twenty nine matches being won.

New Brighton

Address: Reeds Lane, Leasowe Road, Moreton, Wirral L46 3RH. Tel: 051-677 1873
Founded: 1875
Secretary: K. Roberts, 19 Heron Road, Meols, Merseyside L47 9RU. Tel: 051-632 5722 (h), 051-709 6882 (w)
Fixtures secretary: Major J. Ledsham, MBE, 'Ashley', Leighton Road, Neston, South Wirral L64 3SE. Tel: 051-336 4310 (h), (0244) 37922 (w)
Captain 1985-86: S. Miles
Most capped player: A. W. Maxwell, 7 for England
Colours: Dark blue, light blue, white hoops/white
Clubhouse: Bars, changing-rooms, usual facilities
1st XV 1985-86: P 33 W 6 D 0 L 27 F 250 A 656

New Brighton had a wretched season winning only six times in thirty three matches.

Northampton

Address: Franklin Gardens, Northampton. Tel: (0604) 51543
Founded: 1880
Secretary: G. R. Allen, 37 Winston Close, Nether Heyford, Northampton. Tel: (0327) 40135 (h), (0604) 34833 ext. 5261 (w)
Fixtures secretary: F. J. Hobbs, 101 Mendip Road, Duston, Northampton. Tel: (0604) 53854
Captain 1985-86: D. K. Woodrow
Most capped players: C. R. Jacobs, 29 for England; J. Butterfield, 28 for England, 4 for British Lions; G. O. Pearce, 27 for England
Colours: Black, green and gold jerseys
Clubhouse: Full facilities for players and members alike
1st XV 1985-86: P 38 W 16 D 1 L 21 F 623 A 656

John Player Special Cup progress took Northampton to the fourth round and a defeat at home by London Scottish. In Merit Table B ninth place out of twelve was achieved and the overall record was modest. Gary Pearce needed three more England caps to break the club record.

Northern

Address: McCracken Park, Great North Road, Newcastle-upon-Tyne 3. Tel: (0632) 363369
Founded: 1876
Secretary: E. Wilkins, 27 Kingsley Avenue, Melton Park, Gosforth, Newcastle-upon-Tyne. Tel: (0632) 365557 (h), (0632) 611063 (w)
Fixtures secretary: I. Nicholson, 5 West Road, Ponteland, Northumberland. Tel: (0661) 6272 (h), (0661) 23863 (w)
Captain 1985-86: G. Longstaffe
Most capped player: J. D. Currie, 25 for England
Colours: White/navy blue/red
Directions to ground: On A1 road to Scotland
Clubhouse: Usual facilities
1st XV 1985-86: P 39 W 14 D 3 L 22 F 554 A 591

Northern had a modest season winning only fourteen matches out of thirty nine.

Nottingham

Address: Ireland Avenue, Beeston, Nottingham. Tel: (0602) 254238
Founded: 1877
Secretary: J. L. Drapkin, 'Crailing', Wellin Lane, Edwalton, Nottingham NG12 4AH. Tel: (0602) 231662 (h), (0602) 506111 ext. 2138 (w)
Fixtures secretary: J. H. Addison, Wycliffe Mills, High Church Street, New Basford, Nottingham. Tel: (0602) 785466
Captain 1985-86: N. D. Mantell
Coach 1985-86: A. Davies
Most capped player: V. H. Cartwright, 14 for England
Colours: Green and white/green
Clubhouse: Excellent facilities for players, members and spectators
1st XV 1985-86: P 32 W 27 D 1 L 4 F 927 A 292

Nottingham had a fine season without winning anything. They reached the last eight of the John Player Special Cup before being eliminated at home against Wasps on a 2-1 try-count. In the John Smith Merit Table A the club finished a very good second to Gloucester. Rob Andrew and Gary Rees both appeared for England and the team also reached the final of the Middlesex Sevens.

Nuneaton

Address: Cleaver Ground, Attleborough Road, Nuneaton. Tel: (0203) 383206
Founded: 1879
Secretary: A. McElvanney, 17 Shetland Drive, Nuneaton, Warks CV10 7LA. Tel: (0203) 346949 (h), 021-235 4842 (w)
Fixtures secretary: D. J. Sharp, 11 Greenside Close, Nuneaton, Warks. Tel: (0203) 340542
Captain 1985-86: G. Mumford
Most capped player: W. A. Holmes, 16 for England
Colours: Black, red and white hoops/black
Clubhouse: Bars, changing-rooms, social facilities
1st XV 1985-86: P 37 W 11 D 1 L 25 F 592 A 713
   In a poor season Nuneaton finished last in Merit Table C and only eleven matches out of thirty seven were won overall. In the John Player Special Cup there was a narrow first-round defeat at home to Lichfield.

Orrell

Address: Edge Hall Road, Orrell, Wigan, Greater Manchester WN5 8TL. Tel: (0695) 623193
Founded: 1927
Secretary: J. Arrowsmith, 1 Fisher Drive, Orrell, Wigan, Greater Manchester WN5 8QX. Tel: (0942) 216879 (h), 051-928 0881 ext. 46 (w)
Fixtures secretary: J. B. Cooper, Sunnylands Farm, 100 Higgins Lane, Burscough, Ormskirk. Tel: (0704) 893239 (h), 051-236 9231 ext. 6 (w)
Captain 1985-86: D. Southern
Most capped player: J. Carleton, 25 for England, 6 for British Isles
Colours: Amber and black hoops/black/black
Clubhouse: Usual full facilities for players, members and visitors
1st XV 1985-86: P 45 W 33 D 2 L 10 F 984 A 470
   Orrell won John Smith Merit Table B and enjoyed a very good season overall suffering only ten defeats. In the John Player Cup there was an unlucky third-round exit to holders and eventual winners, Bath, who were the away team in a drawn match. F. J. Clough played for England.

Otley

Address: Cross Green, Otley, West Yorkshire. Tel: (0943) 461180
Founded: 1865, present club in 1907
Secretary: G. Hinchliffe, 22 Cyprus Drive, Thackley, Bradford, West Yorks BD10 0AJ. Tel: (0274) 615543 (h), (0274) 724282 (w)
Fixtures secretary: W. H. Lambert, Crabbapple Cottage, Ghyll Royd, Guiseley, Leeds. Tel: (0943) 74493 (h), (0532) 441244 (w)
Captain 1985-86: R. Stead
Most capped player: A. H. Bateson, 4 for England
Colours: Black and white hoops/black/black
Clubhouse: Usual facilities
1st XV 1985-86: P 36 W 19 D 1 L 16 F 630 A 456
   Otley, scene of the famous North of England 1979 victory over the All-Blacks, had a fair season winning more than half their fixtures.

Oxford University

Address: University Rugby Ground, Iffley Road, Oxford. Tel: (0865) 242017
Founded: 1869
Secretary: J. J. McPartlin, St Edward's School, Woodstock Road, Oxford. Tel: (0865) 55863 (h), (0865) 59529 (school)
Fixtures secretary: J. H. C. Anelay, 1 St Giles, Oxford. Tel: (0865) 53136 (h), (0865) 242468 (w)
Captain: N. W. Macdonald (1985), S. J. M. Griffin (1986)
Coach 1985-86: L Davies
Most capped players: J. M. Bannerman, 37 for Scotland; P. K. Stagg, 28 for Scotland; J. D. Currie, M. S. Phillips, 25 each for England; H. P. MacNeill, 25 for Ireland, 3 for British Lions
Colours: All dark blue
Directions to ground: From centre of Oxford travel to The Plain then take A4158 (Iffley Road) towards Wallingford. Ground is half-mile on right
Clubhouse: Two dressing-rooms, bar
Teams run: 3
1st XV 1985-86: P 20 W 8 D 0 L 12 F 301 A 411
   Oxford University were the winners of the Bowring Bowl and emerged brave victors in the annual match against Cambridge. With most of the team returning plus the addition of the All-Black scrum-half, D. E. Kirk, who will be in residence, prospects look better than for many seasons.

Preston Grasshoppers

Address: Lightfoot Green, Fulwood, Preston. Tel: (0772) 863546/863027
Founded: 1869
Secretary: L. Anson, Oak Tree, 110 Whittingham Lane, Broughton, Preston PR3 5DD. Tel: (0772) 862050 (w)
Fixtures secretary: J. M. Powell, 88 Lansdown Hill, Fulwood, Preston. Tel: (0772) 862050 (w)
Captain 1985-86: B. Horton
Most capped player: W. A. Dooley, 10 for England
Colours: Navy blue and white/navy blue/navy blue
Clubhouse: Usual facilities
1st XV 1985-86: P 40 W 21 D 2 L 17 F 622 A 516
   Preston Grasshoppers had a good season, particularly in the county cup. The overall record was also good, even though the season ended with a bad defeat at Liverpool. Wade Dooley took his England caps total to double figures.

Richmond

Address: Richmond Athletic Ground, Richmond, Surrey. Tel: 01-930 0397
Founded: 1861
Secretary: P. N. Quinnen, 67 Upper Grotto Road, Strawberry Hill, Twickenham, Middlesex. Tel: 01-892 9336 (h), 01-382 6336 (w)
Fixtures secretary: Dr T. E. Roberts, 7 Homestead Road, Basingstoke, Hants. Tel: (0256) 64999
Captain 1985-86: M. Slagter
Coach 1985-86: D. Rollitt
Most capped player: C. W. Ralston, 22 for England
Colours: Old gold, red and black/black/old gold, red and black
Directions to ground: Richmond Station (LT and BR Southern Region) turn right, then left at main roundabout. Ground is on right on A316 to Twickenham
Clubhouse: Large bar, tearoom, changing-rooms
1st XV 1985-86: P 34 W 14 D 1 L 19 F 588 A 581
   Despite winning the Oxfordshire Sevens, Richmond had a mediocre season and finished eleventh (out of twelve) in John Smith Merit Table B with four wins from ten matches. In the John Player Special Cup the team were eliminated in the third round by Blackheath.

Rosslyn Park

Address: Priory Lane, Upper Richmond Road, Roehampton, London SW15. Tel: 01-876 1879
Founded: 1879
Secretary: D. Henderson, 1 Cedars Road, Barnes, London SW13. Tel: 01-876 2646 (h), 01-992 3222 (w)
Fixtures secretary: C. Morgan, 96 Thames Street, Sunbury-on-Thames, Middlesex. Tel: (09327) 85012
Captain 1985-86: S. Henderson
Most capped player: A. G. Ripley, 24 for England
Colours: Red and white hoops/black/red, white and black
Directions to ground: From Barnes Station (BR Southern Region) turn right; ground is only a few minutes' walk. Ground is on left from Putney on Upper Richmond Road
Clubhouse: General bar with full licence and tea; Members' Bar and committee room; changing-rooms. Rosslyn Park has a floodlit pitch
1st XV 1985-86: P 33 W 22 D 0 L 11 F 659 A 487

Until the New Year Rosslyn Park were London's best team, but a shock third-round defeat in the John Player Special Cup meant a slump, although the final record was still excellent. In John Smith Merit Table B the team finished in fourth place and they were top of the London Merit Table. They won their own Sevens tournament.

Roundhay

Address: Chandos Park, Chandos Avenue, Lidget Lane, Leeds LS8 1QX. Tel: (0532) 661815
Founded: 1924
Secretary: D. B. Stead, 470 Spen Lane, West Park, Leeds LS16 6JD. Tel: (0532) 672146 (h), (0532) 456089 (w)
Fixtures secretary: T. Kay, 12 Lakeview Court, West Avenue, Leeds LS8 2JS. Tel: (0532) 562558 (h), (0274) 582266 (w)
Captain 1985-86: P. Gray
Most capped player: D. T. Wilkins, 13 for England
Colours: Emerald, scarlet, white/white
Clubhouse: Usual facilities
1st XV 1985-86: P 41 W 23 D 2 L 16 F 664 A 379

Roundhay finished eighth in Merit Table C and had a generally good season, winning just over half their fixtures.

Rugby

Address: Webb Ellis Road, Rugby, Warks. Tel: (0788) 4907
Founded: 1873
Secretary: J. W. Llewellyn, 11 Rokeby Street, Rugby CV21 3RH. Tel: (0788) 72287 (h), (0788) 77111 ext. 681 (w)
Fixtures secretary: R. Pebody, 107 Bawnmore Road, Rugby, Warks. Tel: (0788) 815011
Captain 1985-86: G. Steele-Bodger
Most capped player: G. S. Conway, 18 for England
Colours: White/navy/red and white
Directions to ground: Off Bilton Road
Clubhouse: Usual facilities
1st XV 1985-86: P 38 W 11 D 0 L 27 F 394 A 678

Rugby had an extremely poor season, winning only eleven matches out of thirty eight played.

St Ives

Address: Alexandra Road, St Ives, Cornwall
Founded: 1887
Secretary: M. Gee, Hellesvean Close, St Ives, Cornwall. Tel: (0736) 797168 (h), (0736) 794166 (w)

Directions to ground: Leaving St Ives towards Penzance and Land's End the ground is at top of hill on Alexandra Road (a right turn)
Clubhouse: Bar, changing-rooms
1st XV 1985-86: P 47 W 30 D 1 L 16 F 713 A 530

St Ives won the Cornwall Cup and finished with a good overall record by winning thirty matches out of forty seven played. They had to play a secondary role in Cornwall to the rampant Camborne team.

Sale

Address: Heywood Road, Brooklands, Sale, Cheshire. Tel: 061-973 6348
Founded: 1861
Secretary: D. Smith, 2 Riddings Road, Hale, Altrincham, Cheshire. Tel: 061-941 1717 (h), 061-736 5843 ext. 264 (w)
Fixtures secretary: L. J. Davies, 8 Beeston Road, Sale, Cheshire
Captain 1985-86: A. Bond
Coach 1985-86: S. J. Smith
Most capped players: F. E. Cotton, 31 for England, 7 for British Lions; E. Evans, 30 for England; S. J. Smith, 28 for England
Colours: Blue and white hoops/blue/blue
Directions to ground: Take A57 road from Manchester towards M6. In Sale turn left towards Brooklands Station along Heywood Road. Ground is on right
Clubhouse: Large clubhouse with excellent facilities including changing-rooms, bar, refreshments
1st XV 1985-86: P 35 W 26 D 0 L 9 F 759 A 383

Although many fixtures were cancelled owing to bad weather Sale had another good season, winning twenty six matches out of thirty five. In John Smith Merit Table A the team finished in ninth place with two wins in five outings. In the John Player Special Cup elimination was at the hands of London Scottish (away) in the third round.

Saracens

Address: Bramley Sports Ground, Chase Side, London N14. Tel: 01-449 3770
Founded: 1876
Secretary: B. D. W. Richards, 36 Stone Hall Road, London N21. Tel: 01-360 4061
Fixtures secretary: D. H. J. Grammer, 18 Branscombe Gardens, London N21. Tel: 01-886 7392
Captain 1985-86: Alex Keay
Coach 1985-86: Tony Russ
Most capped player: V. S. Harding, 6 for England
Colours: Black with red badge/black/red
Directions to ground: Southgate (LT) is the nearest station. By road take A111 towards Potters Bar
Clubhouse: Large licensed bar, changing-rooms
Teams run: 7
1st XV 1985-86: P 39 W 28 D 1 L 10 F 846 A 467

Saracens enjoyed an excellent season reaching the fourth round of the John Player Special Cup and finishing third in John Smith Merit Table B, having led for a long time . In the London Merit Table the club had a mid-way position, whilst the second team, the Crusaders, won the Middlesex Cup.

Sheffield

Address: Abbeydale Park, Totley Rise, Sheffield. Tel: (0742) 362040 (club steward), (0742) 360992 (club groundsman)
Founded: 1902

Secretary: P. J. Tear, 463 Abbey Lane, Sheffield S7 2QZ. Tel: (0742) 368008 (h), (0742) 77901 (w)
Fixtures secretary: H. A. Cotton, 9 Endcliffe Crescent, Sheffield S10 3EB. Tel: (0742) 686144 (h), (0742) 755266 (w)
Captain 1985-86: D. Parsonage
Most capped player: A. G. B. Old, 16 for England
Colours: Blue and white bands/red
Clubhouse: Usual facilities
1st XV 1985-86: P 34 W 20 D 1 L 13 F 546 A 417

Sheffield finished seventh in Merit Table C with four wins from seven games and of the thirty four matches played overall twenty were won with one drawn – a reasonable performance.

Vale of Lune

Address: Powderhouse Lane, Lancaster. Tel: (0524) 64029
Founded: 1900
Secretary: I. K. Clays, 9 Hatlex Lane, Hest Bank, near Lancaster. Tel: (0524) 822264
Fixtures secretary: F. W. Swarbrick, Oxendale Farm, Wyresdale Road, Lancaster. Tel: (0524) 37601 (h), (0524) 64055 (w)
Captain 1985-86: J. Ashworth
Colours: Cherry and white hoops/navy/red
Clubhouse: Bars, changing-rooms
1st XV 1985-86: P 40 W 24 D 2 L 14 F 726 A 488

Vale of Lune won the Lancashire County Cup and finished third in Merit Table C. There was also a good run in the John Player Special Cup which ended in the third round with defeat at Broughton Park. The full record was good with twenty four wins in forty matches.

Wakefield

Address: College Grove, Wakefield, West Yorkshire. Tel: (0924) 2038/63431
Founded: 1901
Secretary: R. D. Foster, 27 Carr Lane, Sandal, Wakefield, West Yorkshire WF2 6HI. Tel: (0924) 250116 (h), (0924) 371501 (w)
Captain 1985-86: M. Dearman
Most capped player: B. Barley, 4 for England
Colours: Black and gold
Clubhouse: Bar, refreshments, changing-rooms
1st XV 1985-86: P 36 W 25 D 1 L 10 F 689 A 488

Wakefield won the Yorkshire County Cup and finished second in Merit Table C. In every respect it was a good season as the club also reached the fourth round of the John Player Special Cup, disposing of Rosslyn Park (away) in the process.

Wasps

Address: Repton Avenue, Rugby Avenue, Sudbury, Middlesex. Tel: 01-902 4220
Founded: 1867
Secretary: I. A. Montlake, Stonedene House, 92/3 Hartfield Road, Forest Row, Sussex RH18 5LY. Tel: (0342) 822980
Fixtures secretary: Neville Compton, 29 Dukes Wood Avenue, Gerrards Cross, Bucks SL9 7LA. Tel: (0753) 85507
Captain 1985-86: R. Cardus
Coach 1985-86: D. Arnold
Most capped player: R. M. Uttley, 23 for England
Colours: All black
Directions to ground: London Transport to Sudbury Town then ten minute walk to ground after passing straight outside ground then turning left and crossing road before right turn at Rugby

Avenue. By road from London through Wembley turning right at roundabout towards Harrow then right at next roundabout
Clubhouse: Upstairs and downstairs bar, changing-rooms, committee room
1st XV 1985-86: P 33 W 22 D 1 L 10 F 713 A 500

An excellent season ended with Wasps, short of four International players, playing gallantly in the final of the John Player Special Cup before losing to Bath. In John Smith Merit Table A a very creditable third place was achieved. Four Wasps players appeared for England – Davies, Smith, Melville and Rendall – but only Smith was fit for the Twickenham final.

Waterloo

Address: St Anthony's Road, Blundellsands, Liverpool L23 8TW. Tel: 051-924 4552
Founded: 1882
Secretary: K. Alderson, 66 St Michaels Road, Blundellsands, Liverpool L23 7UW. Tel: 051-924 1168 (h), 051-546 5691 (w)
Fixtures secretary: G. Poynton, 13 Heyes Grove, Rainford, St Helens, Lancs. Tel: (074 488) 4128
Captain 1985-86: L. Connor
Most capped player: H. G. Periton, 21 for England
Colours: Green, red and white hoops
Clubhouse: Usual excellent facilities for players and spectators
1st XV 1985-86: P 38 W 28 D 0 L 10 F 977 A 334

Waterloo won the Northern Merit Table, but failed to gain promotion from John Smith Merit Table B, finishing only fifth. The overall record was good. The team went out of the John Player Special Cup in the third round at Saracens.

West Hartlepool

Address: Brierton Lane, Hartlepool, Cleveland. Tel: (0429) 72640
Founded: 1881
Secretary: F. M. Gibbon, Regent House, York Road, Hartlepool, Cleveland. Tel: (0740) 30410 (h), (0429) 34455 (w)
Fixtures secretary: L. W. B. Smith, 30 Newquay Close, Cliffords Green, Hartlepool, Cleveland. Tel: (0429) 31000
Captain 1985-86: J. Groves
Most capped player: C. D. Aarvold, 16 for England, 4 for British Lions
Colours: Green, red and white hoops/white/green and red
Clubhouse: Usual facilities for players and spectators
1st XV 1985-86: P 44 W 33 D 0 L 11 F 92 A 503

West Hartlepool finished fifth in Merit Table C and also won the Durham Cup. The John Player venture was a disaster, but the overall record was very good.

Wilmslow

Address: Memorial Ground, Pownall Park, Wilmslow, Cheshire. Tel: (0625) 22274/24148
Founded: 1886, new club in 1923
Secretary: J. B. Fisher, 26 Lees Road, Bramhall, Cheshire. Tel: 061-439 2972 (h), 061-236 2065 (w)
Fixtures secretary: G. Mitchell, Greenbank Farm, Brookhouse Lane, Smallwood, near Sandbach, Cheshire. Tel: (047 75) 329
Captain 1985-86: C. Barltrop
Colours: Sky blue, maroon and white/white/maroon
Clubhouse: Usual facilities
1st XV 1985-86: P 28 W 7 D 1 L 20 F 292 A 451

Wilmslow had a very poor season, winning only seven matches of twenty eight played.

SCOTLAND

Review of the Season

by Bill McLaren

The Hawick forward Colin Deans, now just one cap behind Ken Kennedy's world record of forty five caps as a hooker, will remember the 1985-86 season with particular fondness for not only did he reach several personal peaks but there were a number of heartening features for the Scottish game as a whole.

Deans was captain of the South of Scotland side that won a four-game 'grand slam' District Championship for the fourth season in a row. He then assumed the mantle of national captain in succession to David Leslie who returned to his original club side, Dundee High School FP, and helped them to gain promotion to Division 3 of the National Leagues and to win the Midlands Cup. Deans not only survived a remarkable national trial in which the senior side he led was comprehensively outplayed (41-10), but he then led Scotland to an unexpected share of the Championship with France after some thoroughly exciting fifteen-man play. In April he received the Division 1 Championship Trophy as Hawick captain following their 26-3 win over John Rutherford's Selkirk at Philiphaugh before proceeding to Cardiff where he had the honour of leading the British Lions against the Overseas XV as part of the Centenary celebrations of the International Board. It was an impressive run of generally successful captaincies, although there was one big disappointment at the season's end when Melrose beat a Hawick side containing nine reserves at the Greenyards (18-9). Hawick were thus denied a share of the Border League title, which went instead to Kelso for the first time since 1937.

Scotland's performances in the Championship reflected credit upon the national selectors, Robin Charters (convener), Ian MacGregor, Jim Telfer, Bob Munro, Derrick Grant, Ian McGeechan, and upon the new coaching duo, Derrick Grant and Ian McGeechan. In the wake of six successive International defeats, the selectors reacted to that trial upset in a positive manner, appointing six new caps for the opening match at home against France – Gavin Hastings (Cambridge University and Watsonians), Matt Duncan (West of Scotland), Scott Hastings (Watsonians), David Sole (Bath), Jeremy Campbell-Lamerton (London Scottish) and Finlay Calder (Stewart's-Melville FP). Although Scotland's display in that match hardly hinted at the thrilling style that was to follow against Wales and England, the Scottish scrummage proved stronger than expected, with Sole emerging as a prop of great potential and sharing in the very impressive defensive work in which Duncan's marking of Patrick Estève and the finality of Scott Hastings's tackling were outstanding features. The Scots reacted spiritedly to the shock concession of a Pierre Berbizier try within twenty two seconds of kick-off and capitalized on French indiscipline (they were penalized twenty one times to Scotland's twelve) for Gavin Hastings to equal the world record of six penalty-goals in one International and clinch a narrow victory (18-17). The French Federation president, Albert Ferrasse, commented at the post-match function on the fact that France had scored two tries to none and had still lost.

Scotland's visit to Cardiff differed from their French experience in two ways. This time, instead of having John Rutherford embracing a tight punting format, the Scots were positive and adventurous in scoring three brilliant tries to one. However, Wales successfully kicked *their* goals and won a magnificent contest (22-15). One of the five penalty-goals by Welsh full-back Paul Thorburn was a monumental effort from eight metres inside his own half to give Wales a 19-15 lead. Scotland's first-half display had all the elements of a fifteen-man pattern for their three tries – one by Matt Duncan on receipt of his first pass in ninety one minutes of major International football, the others by the outstanding John

Jeffrey and by Gavin Hastings. Scotland probably would have gone on to win had two scores by Sole not been disallowed by New Zealand referee, Bob Francis, in a torrid ten-minute spell of seige during which Sole, Laidlaw (also twice), Calder and Beattie were denied.

No-one could have anticipated the dramatic events of England's visit to Murrayfield, which coincided with one of the greatest displays ever given by Scotland. Their 33-6 margin was the biggest ever recorded against England by any country and it included a new record for a Scot in an International – twenty one points for Gavin Hastings from five penalty-goals and three conversions. He attempted eight kicks and landed the lot. There was in this Scottish performance a distinct resemblance to the All-Blacks whose methods had so impressed the Grand Slam coaches Jim Telfer and Derrick Grant when they toured New Zealand with the Lions in 1966. The Scots surprisingly made the line-out a profitable source with a series of five-man formations in which John Beattie excelled. For the second match running Scotland scored three tries – through Matt Duncan (two in his first three Internationals), Rutherford (who thus equalled the legendary Herbert Waddell's record for a Scottish stand-off of seven) and by Scott Hastings, arguably the try of the Championship to rank alongside Philippe Sella's superb score against England. Amid all the euphoria, Grant stayed calm and restrained: 'We've only won another game. We are keeping our feet on the ground'.

Perhaps he had a premonition of the disappointment that was to attend Scotland's final Championship game in Dublin. Ireland, heading for a whitewash, succeeded in closing them down in attack and in themselves putting together some delightful handling, especially in the closing spell when, at 9-10 down, they should have won. One penalty decision in their favour was reversed by French referee, Francis Palmade, on the advice of his countryman touch judge, Guy Maurette, and a second penalty was pushed wide by Michael Kiernan. Scotland's try on the left of a scrummage was by Roy Laidlaw, four of whose five International tries have been against Ireland. When Gavin Hastings failed to convert that try it was his first miss in eleven consecutive International goal-kicks. His two penalty-goals, however, gave him a new record Scottish aggregate for a Championship of fifty two. It was indicative of the character of the match: whereas Ireland succeeded in working the ball to their open side wing five times, Scotland did not manage it once. But Deans gave an inspiring example, especially in his tackling, and Finlay

Alister Campbell (Scotland's lock) feeds Roy Laidlaw (no. 9) with Finlay Calder, John Jeffrey and Colin Deans looking on in support against England at Murrayfield.

Roy Laidlaw, scorer of a brilliant individual try for Scotland, passes the ball out despite the interference of Ireland's Nigel Carr.

Calder put his stamp on the improvement he had shown on every International outing.

Scotland had not had much of a set piece platform in Dublin but they scrummaged very effectively in Bucharest when they beat Romania (33-18) on March 29th. Iain Milne gave Ion Bucan a torrid time and the Scots again scored three tries through Jeffrey, Scott Hastings and Deans. There was widespread sympathy for Roger Baird when his try was chalked off as touch judge Laurie Prideaux signalled foot in touch. It would have been Baird's first try for Scotland in twenty five Internationals. Gavin Hastings registered twenty one points for the second time and so ended his first season in major International Rugby with seventy three points in five games. He is already third in Scotland's all-time scoring list behind Andy Irvine (273 points) and Peter Dods (150).

So Scotland earned high honour with four wins in five Internationals and ten good tries in the basket. They also had a splendid attack-defence record, second only to the remarkable French:

	Tries scored	Tries conceded
France	13	1
Scotland	7	4
Ireland	5	9
Wales	4	8
England	4	11

There were other encouraging aspects of Scotland's International play. Their 'B' side,

Under-21's, Under-19's and Under-18's all had good victories as follows:

Date	Team	Opponents	Venue	Result
7th Dec.	'B'	Italy 'B'	Old Anniesland	W 9-0
25th Feb.	U21	Scottish Universities	Murrayfield	W 22-3
2nd Mar.	'B'	France 'B'	Villefranche	W 12-10
2nd Apr.	U21	Combined Services U21	Murrayfield	W 34-0
5th Apr.	U18	Sweden U18	Murrayfield	W 43-4
12th Apr.	U19	Italy U19	Piacenza	W 22-4
12th Apr.	U21	Italy U21	Piacenza	W 22-6

In their District Championship 'grand slam' the South beat Glasgow (19-16), North & Midlands (29-0), Edinburgh (10-3) and Anglo-Scots (16-13), and have now remained unbeaten in their last twenty four District Championship games. Against Edinburgh their only uncapped player was the Kelso wing, Sandy Thomson, who raised his tries tally in fourteen district games to twelve. There was a milestone for Gala's International full-back, Peter Dods, who became the first to score over 400 points in district matches. His total now is 427 in fifty six games. The South underlined their strength at Murrayfield on March 1st when, in a special match to beat the frost, they overcame a Scottish Districts XV containing eleven International players (21-19).

In winning the Division 1 National League championship for the ninth time in thirteen seasons Hawick did not play to the style that they would have wished. In the absence of Jim Renwick, who went back to junior Rugby and was a key figure in his old club, Hawick Harlequins, winning the Border Junior title, and with their other International centre, Keith Murray, out of action for over two months, Hawick reverted to a tight strategy built around their magnificent pack and kicking halves, Greg Oliver and Colin Gass. They were much indebted to Gass who finished top scorer in the upper Divisions of the Leagues with 121 of Hawick's 241 league points. Ironically, Hawick's only defeat in thirteen league games was at the hands of Kilmarnock by a convincing 24-12, four tries to one margin, not altogether explained by the fact that Hawick were short of their entire first choice back-row and of Deans. It proved to be Kilmarnock's only win and they were relegated along with Preston Lodge FP. It was good for the Scottish game, however, that the sternest challenge to Hawick came from two sides who favoured a fluent, fifteen-man style, Kelso and Stewart's-Melville FP.

Kelso had the best defence record in Division 1 – only ninety four points conceded in twelve games – and Stewart's-Melville FP were the top scorers with 289 points in twelve games. Hawick beat Kelso 13-9 in a bruising contest in which Kelso led 9-0 and, in the crucial match that was regarded as a championship decider, the 'Greens' won over the College at Inverleith by 16-6 with mighty forward power, although the gale hindered Stewart's-Melville from stitching together the sharp inter-passing that had marked their championship campaign. The varying styles of the big three are reflected in the number of tries they scored: Stewart's-Melville FP scored fifty tries in twelve games; Kelso thirty eight in twelve games; and Hawick twenty nine in thirteen games.

Kelso were worthy runners-up in Division 1 and climaxed another heartening campaign by winning the Border League. However, the Scottish tour to Spain and France created the sad depletion of teams, especially Hawick, for the vital play-off games. All the same, Kelso can point to their 12-6 home win over Hawick on an April evening as the match that really brought them the title.

Edinburgh hosted a knock-out fifteen-a-side cup competition for the first time called the River Series Trophy. It was won by Boroughmuir who beat Stewart's-Melville FP in the final (32-18).

Following defeats by Australia, France and Wales the senior Scottish Schools side ended their season on a successful note with a 10-7 win over English Schools at Braidholm.

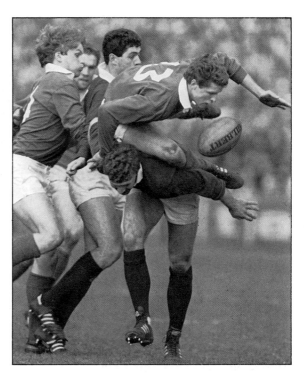

Leap-frog? Brendan Mullin (Ireland) finds his progress halted by Iain Paxton (Scotland) as Trevor Ringland (Ireland) and Gavin Hastings (Scotland) lend support.

Schweppes Scottish National Leagues

Division 1

	P	W	D	L	F	A	Pts
Hawick	13	12	0	1	241	117	24
Kelso	12	10	0	2	266	94	20
Stewart's-Melville FP	12	9	0	3	289	103	18
Watsonians	13	8	0	5	214	145	16
Heriots	13	8	0	5	201	161	16
Gala	12	7	0	5	202	153	14
West of Scotland	12	7	0	5	199	192	14
Boroughmuir	13	7	0	6	143	163	14
Jed-Forest	13	5	0	8	132	218	10
Melrose	13	4	0	9	149	170	8
Edinburgh Academicals	13	4	0	9	115	206	8
Selkirk	13	4	0	9	118	208	8
Preston Lodge FP	13	3	0	10	90	258	6
Kilmarnock	13	1	0	12	123	294	2

Champions: Hawick
Runners-up: Kelso
Relegated: Preston Lodge and Kilmarnock

Division 2

	P	W	D	L	F	A	Pts
Glasgow Academicals	12	12	0	0	214	93	24
Ayr	13	9	0	4	308	118	18
Stirling County	13	9	0	4	178	110	18
Musselburgh	12	8	0	4	154	104	16
Glasgow High Kel	12	7	0	5	158	185	14
Dunfermline	12	6	0	6	148	149	12
Haddington	12	6	0	6	153	160	12
Royal High	13	6	0	7	124	158	12
Howe of Fife	13	5	1	7	201	146	11
Langholm	13	5	1	7	133	134	11
Edinburgh Wanderers	12	5	1	6	128	181	11
Portobello FP	12	5	0	7	120	136	10
Clarkston	12	1	1	10	72	216	3
Jordanhill	11	0	0	11	42	243	0

Champions: Glasgow Academicals
Promoted: Ayr
Relegated: Clarkston and Jordanhill

Division 3

	P	W	D	L	F	A	Pts
Corstorphine	12	12	0	0	273	49	24
Hillhead	13	10	0	3	186	142	20
Highland	13	7	1	5	218	130	15
Perthshire	12	7	0	5	129	118	14
Hutchesons	13	6	0	7	158	148	12
Gordonians	13	6	0	7	107	111	12
Cambuslang	12	6	0	6	131	150	12
Greenock Wanderers	12	6	0	6	137	171	12
Kirkcaldy	13	5	1	7	136	166	11
Aberdeen GSFP	13	5	0	8	126	174	10
Morgan Academy FP	13	5	0	8	151	208	10
Dalziel HSFP	13	4	1	8	138	136	9
Madras College FP	13	4	1	8	132	200	9
Edinburgh University	13	4	0	9	105	224	8

Champions: Corstorphine
Promoted: Hillhead
Relegated: Madras College FP and Edinburgh University

Division 4

	P	W	D	L	F	A	Pts
Currie	13	12	0	1	269	65	24
Dundee HSFP	13	12	0	1	245	93	24
Cartha QP	13	11	0	2	235	94	22
Peebles	12	9	0	3	155	94	18
Grangemouth	13	8	0	5	172	155	16
Dumfries	12	6	0	6	97	186	12
Harris Academy FP	11	5	0	6	101	129	10
Alloa	12	5	0	7	90	131	10
Trinity Academicals	13	4	0	9	107	141	8
Broughton	13	4	0	9	116	202	8
Glenrothes	11	3	1	7	75	119	7
Leith Academicals	12	3	0	9	132	142	6
Lenzie	13	2	1	10	114	186	5
Marr	13	2	0	11	83	254	4

Champions: Currie
Promoted: Dundee HSFP
Relegated: Lenzie and Marr

Division 5

	P	W	D	L	F	A	Pts
East Kilbride	13	12	0	1	301	74	24
Biggar	13	11	0	2	200	101	22
Ardrossan Academicals	12	9	0	3	197	120	18
Hillfoots	12	8	1	3	217	86	17
Moray	11	7	0	4	189	121	14
Lismore	12	7	0	5	171	148	14
Linlithgow	12	5	1	6	130	88	11
Livingston	11	5	0	6	82	171	10
Aberdeen University	12	4	1	7	172	141	9
Drumpellier	13	4	0	9	112	186	8
Penicuik	13	4	0	9	117	259	8
Panmure	11	3	1	7	119	260	7
Hamilton Academicals	12	2	0	10	90	183	4
Allan Glens	13	2	0	11	75	234	4

Champions: East Kilbride
Promoted: Biggar
Relegated: Hamilton Academicals and Allan Glens

Final Positions in Border League

	P	W	L	D
Kelso	12	11	1	0
Hawick	12	10	2	0
Jed-Forest	11	5	5	1
Selkirk	11	4	6	1
Gala	11	4	7	0
Melrose	10	3	7	0
Langholm	9	0	9	0

Division 1 and 2 top points scorers
121 Colin Gass (*Hawick*)
110 Gordon Forbes (*Watsonians*)
101 Duncan Cameron (*Glasgow Academicals*)
91 Peter Dods (*Gala*)
84 Peter Hewitt (*Heriots*)
80 Steve Munro (*Ayr*)

Division 1 and 2 top try scorers
20 Steve Munro (*Ayr*)
10 Chris Spence (*Stewart's-Melville FP*)
8 David Brown (*Ayr*)
8 Ian Rankin (*Howe of Fife*)

7 Phil Manning (*Ayr*)
7 David Michie (*Glasgow High Kel*)
7 John Jeffrey (*Kelso*)
7 Alan Tait (*Kelso*)
7 Matt Duncan (*West of Scotland*)

Top club scores
312 Wigtownshire
308 Ayr
301 East Kilbride
289 Stewart's-Melville FP

Division 6	P	W	D	L	F	A	Pts
Wigtownshire	12	11	1	0	312	62	23
Crieff	13	9	1	3	167	142	19
Dunbar	12	8	0	4	206	91	16
Earlston	13	6	3	4	123	100	15
North Berwick	13	6	2	5	118	134	14
Paisley	13	6	1	6	156	100	13
Montrose	12	5	1	6	127	141	11
Strathclyde Police	13	5	1	7	97	138	11
Old Aloysians	11	4	2	5	98	138	10
Dalkeith	13	4	2	7	114	179	10
Walkerburn	12	5	0	7	81	180	10
Stewartry	13	4	1	8	114	126	9
Cumbernauld	13	4	1	8	78	142	9
Stobswell	13	3	0	10	114	232	6

Champions: Wigtownshire
Promoted: Crieff
Relegated: Cumbernauld and Stobswell

Division 7	P	W	D	L	F	A	Pts
St Boswells	12	11	0	1	235	76	22
Murrayfield	13	10	0	3	267	109	20
Aberdeenshire	13	10	0	3	257	116	20
Clydebank	12	8	1	3	142	93	17
Dundee University	11	7	0	4	178	135	14
Garioch	11	6	1	4	166	95	13
Waid Academy FP	12	6	0	6	181	146	12
Falkirk	12	6	0	6	127	132	12
Cumnock	12	5	0	7	213	126	10
Waysiders	12	5	0	7	215	138	10
Edinburgh Northern	13	5	0	8	109	212	10
Garnock	11	2	0	9	74	139	4
Uddingston	12	2	0	10	64	295	4
Stirling University	12	0	0	12	29	445	0

Champions: St Boswells
Promoted: Murrayfield
Relegated: Garnock, Uddingston and Stirling University
Promoted from district leagues: Birkmyre (West),
Carnoustie HSFP (Midlands) and Duns (East)

Scottish Border Sevens Tournaments

Autumn Winners

Selkirk

Melrose	20	Hawick	16

(after extra time)

Kelso

Public Schools Wanderers	38	Gala	12

Spring Finals

Gala

Hawick	36	Melrose	12

Teams in final and scorers
Hawick: K. Mitchell, K. Murray, J. Hogg, G. Oliver; S.
McGaughey, S. McGuigan, D. Turnbull. (Murray (3), Mitchell
(2), Oliver (1) tries; Hogg 6 conversions)
Melrose: C. Ruthven, K. Robertson, I. Ramsay, D. Shiel; K.
McLeish, G. Runciman, D. Little. (Robertson 2 tries; Ramsay
2 conversions)

Melrose

Kelso	22	Racing Club de France	16

Teams in final and scorers
Kelso: D. Robeson, E. Common, A. Ker, R. Hogarth; E.
Paxton, G. Callander, J. Jeffrey. (Jeffrey (2), Hogarth (1), Ker
(1) tries; Hogarth 3 conversions)
Racing Club de France: P. Guillard, J.-M. Lafond, V. Rousset,
P. Collett; L. Pardo, J.-P.Genet, C. Monbat. (Rousset (2),
Guillard (1) tries; Rousset 2 conversions)

Hawick

Hawick	26	Jed-Forest	12

Teams in final and scorers
Hawick: A. Stanger, K. Murray, J. Hogg, G. Oliver; K.
Campbell, S. McGaughey, D. Turnbull. (Stanger, Campbell,
Murray 1 try each and penalty-try; Hogg 3 conversions)
Jed-Forest: H. Hogg, G. McKechnie, D. Miller, R. Laidlaw; G.
Hume, R. Lindores, B. Law. (Miller 1 try and 1 penalty-try;
McKechnie 2 conversions)

Earlston

Melrose	26	Musselburgh	4

Jed-Forest

Kelso	26	Melrose	10

Teams in final and scorers
Kelso: D. Robeson, E. Common, A. Ker, R. Hogarth; E.
Paxton, M. Minto, S. Edwards. (Robeson (2), Hogarth (1),
Ker (1), Edwards (1) tries; Hogarth 3 conversions)
Melrose: G. Shirra-Gibb, E. Weatherly, I. Ramsay, D. Shiel;
A. Dobie, A. Kerr, N. Anderson. (Shiel 2 tries; Ramsay 2
conversions)

Langholm

Jed-Forest	32	Melrose	8

Teams in final and scorers
Jed-Forest: H. Hogg, G. McKechnie, P. Douglas, R. Laidlaw;
G. Hume, R. Lindores, B. Law. (Laidlaw (2), Hume (2), Hogg
(1), McKechnie (1) tries; McKechnie 4 conversions)
Melrose: A. Redburn, E. Weatherly, I. Ramsay, D. Shiel; N.
Anderson, A. Kerr, A. Dobie. (Redburn, Weatherly 1 try
each)

Summary of Spring Tournaments

For once all six tournaments were won by Border clubs; Kelso and Hawick managed two successes each with Melrose and Jed-Forest taking the other two titles. Jed-Forest pleased everyone by winning at Langholm for the first time since 1920; they have been knocking on the door for some time and deserve reward for their efforts. Kelso at full strength are probably the best Sevens exponents, but many would like to see a resurgence by Gala and some victories for Selkirk and Langholm.

Scottish Inter-District Championship

30th November 1985				
Edinburgh (at Murrayfield)	29	North & Midlands	12	
South (at Murrayfield)	19	Glasgow	16	
7th December 1985				
South (at Jed-Forest)	29	North & Midlands	0	
14th December 1985				
Edinburgh (at Watsonians RFC)	3	South	10	
North & Midlands (at St Andrews)	6	Anglo-Scots	28	
16th December 1985				
Glasgow (at Hillhead)	13	Anglo-Scots	17	
21st December 1985				
Anglo-Scots (at Richmond)	9	Edinburgh	23	
North & Midlands (at Robert Gordon's, Aberdeen)	10	Glasgow	30	

28th December 1985				
Edinburgh (at Murrayfield)	10	Glasgow	7	
Anglo-Scots (at Murrayfield)	13	South	16	

	P	W	L	F	A	Pts
South	4	4	0	74	32	8
Edinburgh	4	3	1	65	38	6
Anglo-Scots	4	2	2	67	58	4
Glasgow	4	1	3	66	56	2
North & Midlands	4	0	4	28	116	0

The five districts scored exactly 300 points in their ten matches and the title went to the South yet again, although they were less than convincing in any of their matches. The best display came from Edinburgh against the well-fancied Anglo-Scots at Richmond.

Cup Results

Royal Bank of Scotland Youth Final			
Grangemouth	4	Stirling County	19
River Series Trophy Final (Edinburgh Seniors)			
Boroughmuir	32	Stewart's-Melville FP	18
Murrayfield Cup Final (Seniors)			
Falkirk	6	Duns	12
Midland Cup Final (Seniors)			
Dundee HSFP (after extra time)	18	Howe of Fife	10
Lanarkshire Cup Final (Seniors)			
Drumpelier	0	Dalziel HSFP	24
Lanarkshire Consolation Cup Final (Seniors)			
Hamilton Academicals	17	Lanark	11
Dunbartonshire Cup Final (Seniors)			
Clydebank	13	Strathendrick	3
Border League (Seniors)			
Kelso 1st, Hawick 2nd (Kelso's first success since 1937)			
Glasgow Cup Final			
Kilmarnock	24	Dalziel HSFP	9

Schools

Dollar Academy had the best record of the Scottish Schools with only one defeat in seventeen matches; but the record of Fettes, with two defeats and two draws in seventeen matches, is as praiseworthy, because they had a tougher fixture list. Another Edinburgh school, Merchiston, maintained its high standards of recent seasons with only three defeats in fifteen matches; they produced Baird and Jeffrey of the current successful Scottish national team. Similarly, Boroughmuir, Heriot's and Glasgow Academy all have much to cheer about. George Watson's had seven wins and four defeats early on and were, as always, difficult to beat, but their final record is not available.

The Scottish Schools representative side had a mixed season, but they did beat England.

Scottish Clubs

Ayr

Address: Millbrae, Alloway, Ayr. Tel: (0292) 41944
Founded: 1897
Captain 1985-86: D. W. Brown
Most capped player: S. Munro, 10 for Scotland
Colours: Pink and black
Clubhouse: Bar, changing-rooms
1st XV 1985-86 (2nd Division):
P 13 W 9 D 0 L 4 F 308 A 118
  Ayr in a very satisfactory season recovered their national First Division status by finishing second in Division Two.

Boroughmuir

Address: Meggetland, Colinton Road, Edinburgh EH14 1AS. Tel: 031-443 7571
Founded: 1919, Boroughmuir FP until 1974
Fixtures secretary: John Thorburn, 15 Moat Terrace, Edinburgh. Tel: 031-444 1600
Captain 1985-86: B. H. Hay
Most capped players: B. H. Hay, 23 for Scotland, 3 for British Lions; K. Ross, 11 for Scotland
Colours: Navy blue/emerald green
Clubhouse: Bar, changing-rooms
1st XV 1985-86 (1st Division):
P 13 W 7 D 0 L 6 F 143 A 163
  Boroughmuir continued to be one of Scotland's top clubs. For a time they challenged for national First Division honours, but some late defeats spoiled their chances. They did, however, become the first winners of the new River Series Trophy for Edinburgh clubs. Norrie Rowan continued to be a steadfast deputy for Iain Milne in the Scotland squad.

Clarkston

Address: Braidholm, Giffnock, Glasgow. Tel: 041-637 5850
Founded: 1937
Secretary: John Revill, 16 Cedarwood Avenue, Newton Mearns, Glasgow G77 5GD. Tel: 041-639 3860 (h), 041-221 9277
Captain 1985-86: K. Fairbairn
Colours: Scarlet, white and green
Clubhouse: Changing-rooms, bar
1st XV 1985-86 (2nd Division):
P 12 W 1 D 1 L 10 F 72 A 216
  Only Jordanhill did worse than Clarkston in the national Second Division and the club will play in the Third Division next season.

Corstorphine

Address: Union Park, Carrick Kowe, Edinburgh. Tel: 031-334 8063
Secretary: G. F. G. Welsh, Glenesk, 7 Ladywell Ave. Edinburgh EH12 7LG. Tel: 031-334 2723 (h), 031-229 9292 ext. 3403 (w)
Colours: Red and blue quartered jerseys/white/blue
1st XV 1985-86 (3rd Division):
P 12 W 12 D 0 L 0 F 273 A 49

Corstorphine, in an exeptional season, are now one step away from playing against clubs that have previously sent their second teams to provide opposition. This is the result of a record of twelve wins out of twelve and promotion from the Third Division of the National League. In conceding only forty nine league points, the club had the best defensive record in the whole competition during the season just ended.

Dunfermline

Address: McKane Park, Dunfermline, Fife
Founded: 1904
Secretary: Graeme Wyles, 5 Ardeer Place, Dunfermline KY11 4YX. Tel: (0383) 726655 (h), 031-556 8555 ext. 2356 (w)
Captain 1985-86: A. Orr
Most capped players: J. T. Greenwood, 20 for Scotland, 4 for British Lions; R. J. C. Glasgow, 10 for Scotland
Colours: Royal blue and white
Clubhouse: Changing-rooms, bar
1st XV 1985-86 (2nd Division):
P 12 W 6 D 0 L 6 F 148 A 149
  Dunfermline had a mixed season and finished sixth in national Division Two, so they never really challenged.

Edinburgh Academicals

Address: Raeburn Place, Edinburgh. Tel: 031-332 1070
Founded: 1857
Secretary: D. W. Pearson, 55 Queen Street, Edinburgh. Tel: 031-557 0825 (h), 031-226 4081 (w)
Captain 1985-86: C. B. S. Richardson
Most capped player: W. I. D. Elliott, 29 for Scotland
Colours: Blue and white striped jerseys
Clubhouse: Bars, changing-rooms
Teams run: 3
1st XV 1985-86 (1st Division):
P 13 W 4 D 0 L 9 F 115 A 208
  Edinburgh Academicals finished eleventh in the Schweppes First Division and their captain, C. B. S. Richardson, played for Scotland 'B', but they have had better seasons.

Edinburgh Wanderers

Address: Murrayfield, Edinburgh EH12 8RH
Founded: 1868
Secretary: D. M. Martin, 53 Strathalmond Road, Edinburgh EH4 8HP. Tel: 031-339 7771 (h), 031-556 2433 ext. 286 (w)
Captain 1985-86: K. R. Gillies
Most capped player: A. R. Smith, 33 for Scotland, 3 for British Lions
Colours: Red and black hoops/black
Directions to ground: As for SRU ground at Murrayfield
Clubhouse: As for Murrayfield
1st XV 1985-86 (2nd Division):
P 12 W 5 D 1 L 6 F 128 A 181
  Edinburgh Wanderers survived comfortably enough in the Schweppes Second Division without appearing to be likely promotion candidates. They live in the shadow of the more famous Edinburgh clubs.

Gala

Address: Netherdale, Galashiels, Borders. Tel: (0896) 3811
Founded: 1875
Secretary: R. McVittie, Viewbank, 33 Balmoral Place, Galashiels
TD1 1JD. Tel: (0896) 4248 (h), (0896) 4751 (w)
Captain 1985-86: D. Bryson
Coach 1985-86: J. Aitken
Most capped players: P. C. Brown, 27 for Scotland; J. Aitken,
24 for Scotland; J. N. M. Frame, 23 for Scotland; J. W. C.
Turner, 20 for Scotland, 4 for British Lions; N. A. MacEwan,
20 for Scotland
Colours: Maroon/white/maroon and white
Directions to ground: From town centre follow signs for
Netherdale
Clubhouse: Bar for members, changing-rooms
Teams run: 3
1st XV 1985-86 (1st Division):
P 12 W 7 D 0 L 5 F 202 A 153
   Gala finished only sixth in the National League First Division
and in the Border League they ended below Kelso and Hawick.
No major Sevens events were won in a transitional season,
when only Dods appeared in the full Scotland squad.

Glasgow Academicals

Address: New Anniesland, Anniesland Road, Glasgow. Tel:
041-959 1101/1323
Founded: 1886
Secretary: T. R. Cole, 1 Blythswood Square, Glasgow G2 4AA.
Tel: 041-334 0325 (h), 041-221 0683 (w)
Captain 1985-86: A. G. Ker
Most capped players: J. B. Nelson, 25 for Scotland; J. R.
Beattie, 21 for Scotland, 1 for British Lions
Colours: Blue and white hoops/blue
Clubhouse: Usual facilities
1st XV 1985-86 (2nd Division):
P 12 W 12 D 0 L 0 F 214 A 93
   Glasgow Accies won all their Schweppes National League
Second Division matches and the title most impressively, and
also had John Beattie restored to the Scotland team with selection
for the British Lions in Cardiff as a bonus. He now needs five
caps to beat the club record of twenty five Scotland caps held by
J. B. Nelson.

Glasgow High/Kelvinside

Address: Old Anniesland, Glasgow. Tel: 041-959 1154
Founded: 1982, by a merger of two clubs
Secretary: D. J. Forbes, 54 West Nile Street, Glasgow G1 2NP.
Tel: 041-632 2240(h), 041-221 0981 (w)
Most capped player: J. W. Y. Kemp, 27 for Scotland; A.
Cameron, 17 for Scotland, 2 for British Lions (with Glasgow
HSFP)
Colours: Chocolate and gold
Clubhouse: Bars, changing-rooms
1st XV 1985-86 (2nd Division):
P 12 W 7 D 0 L 5 F 158 A 185
   Glasgow High/Kelvinside made a strong bid for promotion
from the Second Division of the National League, but eventually
finished fifth.

Gordonians

Address: Seafield, Thorngrove, Aberdeen. Tel: (0224) 37027
Founded: 1903
Secretary: A. M. Matheson, 15 Golden Square, Aberdeen AB9
1JF. Tel: (0224) 33548 (h), (0224) 644333 (w)
Captain 1985-86: J. S. P. Hutchison
Most capped player: I. G. McCrae, 6 for Scotland
Colours: Blue with gold hoops/blue
Clubhouse: Changing-rooms, bars
1st XV 1985-86 (3rd Division):
P 13 W 6 D 0 L 7 F 107 A 111
   Gordonians remain in the Third Division of the National
League having finished sixth in an uneven season.

Haddington

Address: Neilson Park, Haddington, Midlothian. Tel: (062 082)
3702
Founded: 1911
Secretary: A. Pacey, Carlowrie, 160 Barleyknowe Road, Gore-
bridge, Midlothian EH23 4PS. Tel: (0875) 4920235 (h), (0875)
4920156 (w)
Captain 1985-86: G. Hamilton
Colours: Scarlet/navy blue
Clubhouse: Bars, changing-rooms
1st XV 1985-86 2nd Division:
P 12 W 6 D 0 L 6 F 153 A 160
   Haddington did not threaten an early return to the top division,
breaking even on Second Division results.

Hawick

Address: Mansfield Park, Mansfield Road, Hawick, Borders.
Tel: (0450) 4291
Founded: 1873
Secretary: G. M. Adams, 28 Wilton Hill, Hawick TD9 8BA.
Tel: (0450) 73212
Captain 1985-86: C. T. Deans
Coach 1985-86: Derrick Grant
Most capped players: J. M. Renwick, 52 for Scotland, 1 for
British Lions; C. T. Deans, 44 for Scotland; A. J. Tomes, 41 for
Scotland; H. F. McLeod, 40 for Scotland, 6 for British Lions
Colours: Green/white/green and white
Clubhouse: Large stand with bars, changing-rooms
1st XV 1985-86 (1st Division):
P 13 W 12 D 0 L 1 F 241 A 117
   Hawick won the National League First Division for a ninth
time, but they lost the Border League title to Kelso. Sevens
wins were recorded at Galashiels and at their own tournament.
Colin Deans became the club's second most capped player after
J. M. Renwick; he also captained Scotland in all the season's
International matches.

Heriot's FP

Address: Goldenacre, Inverleith Row, Edinburgh. Tel: 031-
552 5925 (pavilion), 031-552 4097 (groundsman)
Founded: 1890
Secretary: A. G. Fisken, 77 Swanston Avenue, Edinburgh EH10
7DA. Tel: 031-445 1939 (h), 031-226 6605 (w)
Fixtures secretary: C. D. Bisset, 23 Bonaly Rise, Edinburgh
EH13 0QB. Tel: 031-441 4987 (h), 031-336 6001 (w)
Captain 1985-86: P. T. O'Neill

Most capped players: A. R. Irvine, 51 for Scotland, 9 for British Lions; I. G. Milne, 33 for Scotland; K. J. F. Scotland, 27 for Scotland, 5 for British Lions
Colours: Blue and white horizontal stripes
Directions to ground: From St Andrews Square proceed north – there are several streets going in that direction – until you reach Inverleith Row. Ground is on right. The walking time is about twenty minutes
Clubhouse: Bar, tearoom, changing-rooms
1st XV 1985-86 (1st Division):
P 13 W 8 D 0 L 5 F 201 A 161

Heriot's challenged for top honours, but had to be content with an honourable fifth place. No current players appeared for Scotland, but the Edinburgh District side and Scotland 'B' called on players from the club. Peter Hewitt scored eighty four points in First Division matches.

Highland

Address: Northern Meeting Park, Inverness, Highland Region. Tel: (0463) 38644
Founded: 1922
Secretary: R. R. Sinclair, 33 Academy Street, Inverness IV1 1JN. Tel: (0463) 234849 (h), (0463) 239494 (w)
Captain 1985-86: R. D. K. Graham
Most capped player: N. A. MacEwan, 20 for Scotland
Colours: Green with red band/black/red and green hoops
Clubhouse: Full facilities, at Canal Park
1st XV 1985-86 (3rd Division):
P 13 W 7 D 1 L 5 F 218 A 130

Highland were third in the Third Division of the National League, but they were well behind Corstorphine and Hillhead, who were both promoted.

Hillhead

Address: Hughenden & Garscadden, Glasgow
Founded: Formerly Hillhead High School FP
Secretary: A. H. M. MacPherson, 65 Bath Street, Glasgow G2 2DT. Tel: 041-775 1545 (h), 041-332 9411 (w)
Most capped players: W. C. W. Murdoch and I. A. A. MacGregor, 9 each for Scotland
Colours: Chocolate, navy and gold
Clubhouse: Bar, changing-rooms
1st XV 1985-86 (3rd Division):
P 13 W 10 D 0 L 3 F 186 A 142

Hillhead, after some lean times, return to better company as a result of being promoted as runners-up to Corstorphine in the National League Third Division.

Howe of Fife

Address: Duffus Park, Cupar, Fife. Tel: (0334) 528190
Founded: 1922
Secretary: J. Manson, Averon Bank, North Union Street, Cupar KY15 4DU, Fife. Tel: (0334) 54466 (h), (0592) 754411 ext. 3437 (w)
Captain 1985-86: C. D. Reekie
Most capped player: D. M. D. Rollo, 40 for Scotland
Colours: Royal blue and white hooped jerseys
Clubhouse: There is a separate clubhouse at 15 Provost's Wynd, Cupar, with full facilities
1st XV 1985-86 (2nd Division):
P 13 W 6 D 0 L 7 F 201 A 146

Howe of Fife remained comfortably in the Second Division of the National League by finishing ninth with eleven points. Ian Rankin scored eight tries.

Jed-Forest

Address: Riverside Park, Jedburgh, Borders. Tel: (0835) 62232/2486
Founded: 1885
Secretary: W. Mabon, 70 Howden Road, Jedburgh TD8 6JS. Tel: (0835) 62388 (h), (0835) 62497 (w)
Captain 1985-86: R. J. Laidlaw
Most capped player: R. J. Laidlaw, 36 for Scotland, 4 for British Lions
Colours: Royal blue/white/royal blue
Clubhouse: Bar, changing-rooms
1st XV 1985-86 (1st Division):
P 13 W 5 D 0 L 8 F 132 A 218

Jed-Forest did well to avoid relegation from the First Division of the National League and had moderate Border League results. In Spring Sevens tournaments three finals were reached and in the last of them victory was achieved at Langholm. R. J. Laidlaw joined the exclusive band of players who have appeared in forty International matches. His national partnership with J. Y. Rutherford (Selkirk) reached thirty, a world half-back record.

Jordanhill

Address: Kilmardinny Playing Fields, Milngavie Road, Bearsden, Glasgow G61 3TB. Tel: 041-942 8980
Founded: 1972, when the College and School FP clubs were amalgamated
Secretary: R. D. Baillie, 1270 Dumbarton Road, Glasgow G14 9PR. Tel: 041-954 9569 (h), 041-445 2241 (w)
Most capped player: J. (Ian) McLauchlan, 43 for Scotland, 8 for British Lions
Clubhouse: Changing-rooms, bar
1st XV 1985-86 (2nd Division):
P 11 W 0 D 0 L 11 F 42 A 243

In an ignominious season Jordanhill lost all eleven Second Division matches and were duly relegated.

Kelso

Address: Poynder Park, Kelso, Roxburghshire. Tel: (0896) 8224300
Founded: 1876
Secretary: T. McNally, Pringlebank, 25 Bowman Street, Kelso. Tel: (0896) 8224363
Fixtures secretary: B. H. Cuthbert, 58 Grovehill, Kelso. Tel: (0896) 8224271
Captain 1985-86: R. E. Paxton
Most capped player: G. R. T. Baird, 25 for Scotland, 4 for British Lions
Colours: Black and white hoops/black/red
Clubhouse: Bar with full licence, changing-rooms
Teams run: 3
1st XV 1985-86 (2nd Division):
P 12 W 10 D 0 L 2 F 266 A 94

Kelso narrowly failed to take the First Division title for the first time, but won the Border League and the Spring Sevens tournaments at Melrose and Jedburgh. Baird and Jeffrey played in all of Scotland's International matches and G. J. Callander led Scotland's touring party to Spain and France in May.

Kilmarnock

Address: Bellsland, Queens Drive, Kilmarnock, Ayrshire. Tel: (0560) 22314
Founded: 1868
Secretary: J. R. Colman, c/o Clubhouse. Tel: (0560) 6356 (h), (0560) 4341 (w)
Captain 1985-86: D. A. J. Fulton
Most capped player: W. Cuthbertson, 20 for Scotland
Colours: White with red hooped jerseys (white Maltese Cross)
Clubhouse: Bars, changing-rooms
1st XV 1985-86 (1st Division):
P 13 W 1 D 0 L 12 F 123 A 294
Only one victory – over Champions Hawick – meant a return to the Second Division for Kilmarnock. Parker, their lock, had a 1st XV place in the Scottish trial at Murrayfield, but finished on the losing side (10-41).

Langholm

Address: Milntown, Langholm, Dumfriesshire. Tel: (0541) 80386
Founded: 1871
Secretary: Kenneth A. Pool, 80 Henry Street, Langholm. Tel: (0541) 80370
Fixtures secretary: A. Reid, 2 Walter Street, Langholm. Tel: (0541) 80434
Captain 1985-86: B. Hislop
Most capped players: C. Elliott, 12 for Scotland. W. C. C. Steele, 23 for Scotland, was first capped as a Langholm player; he also played in two Tests for the British Lions
Colours: Red/white/red
Directions to ground: One mile from town centre on A7 road to Edinburgh, on left by Ewes Water
Clubhouse: Bar, dressing-rooms
Teams run: 3
1st XV 1985-86 (2nd Division):
P 13 W 5 D 1 L 7 F 133 A 134
Langholm again failed to gain promotion from the National League Second Division, finishing in the lower half of the table. They made little impression in either the Border League or the Sevens tournaments. Langholm's best season was in 1958-59, when the National League and Border League were won for the only time in each case. The 1st XV were unbeaten and the club's own Sevens tournament was also won.

Melrose

Address: Greenyards, Melrose, Borders. Tel: (089682) 2559/2993
Founded: 1877
Secretary: Stewart Henderson, The Greenyards, Melrose TD6 9SA. Tel: (089 682) 2069 (h), and at club
Captain 1985-86: J. G. Runciman
Most capped players: K. W. Robertson, 33 for Scotland; F. A. L. Laidlaw, 32 for Scotland, 2 for British Lions; J. W. Telfer, 25 for Scotland, 9 for British Lions
Colours: Yellow and black/white/yellow and black
Clubhouse: Fine facilities, bars, changing-rooms
1st XV 1985-86 (1st Division):
P 13 W 4 D 0 L 9 F 149 A 170
A last gasp victory over Edinburgh Academicals at home rescued Melrose from relegation from the First Division of the National League and victory over Hawick at home in the final

match of the season gave the Border League title to Kelso. Melrose were winners of the Selkirk & Earlston Sevens. Keith Robertson became the club's most capped player for Scotland.

Musselburgh

Address: Stoneyhill and Pinkie, Musselburgh, Midlothian. Tel: 031-665 3435
Founded: 1921
Secretary: D. M. C. Thomson, 15 Stoneyhill Court, Musselburgh EN21 6SD. Tel: 031-685 3545 (h), 031-225 2211 (w)
Colours: Blue and white stripes
Clubhouse: Bar, changing-rooms
1st XV 1985-86 (2nd Division):
P 12 W 8 D 0 L 4 F 154 A 104
Musselburgh challenged strongly for promotion from the Second Division of the National League and finished a creditable fourth. D. A. Macdonald, the scrum-half, went on Scotland's 1985 tour of Canada.

Portobello FP

Address: Cavalry Park, Duddingston Road West, Edinburgh
Founded: 1954, present club
Secretary: Ford Paterson, 11 Nantwich Drive, Edinburgh EH7 6QS. Tel: 031-669 6036 (h), 031-225 5333 (w)
Captain 1985-86: A. T. I. Denham
Colours: Old gold and navy blue hoops
Clubhouse: Usual facilities
1st XV 1985-86 (2nd Division):
P 12 W 5 D 0 L 7 F 120 A 136
Although they finished in twelfth position in the Second Division of the National League, Portobello FP were never in any real danger of descending lower, although they will look for better results next season.

Preston Lodge

Address: Pennypit Park, Prestonpans, East Lothian
Founded: 1929
Secretary: A. S. Dickson, 56 Stoneyhill Drive, Musselburgh, East Lothian EH21 6SQ. Tel: 031-665 4839 (h), 031-553 3516 (w)
Captain 1985-86: S. Love
Colours: Black, maroon and white/white/black, maroon and white
Clubhouse: Bar, changing-rooms
1st XV 1985-86 (1st Division):
P 13 W 3 D 0 L 10 F 90 A 258
Preston Lodge made a most gallant attempt to stay in the First Division and had a chance after beating Melrose in a late season match, but the Borderers then beat Edinburgh Academicals and stayed up.

Royal High

Address: Jock's Lodge, 30 Piersfield Terrace, Edinburgh. Tel: 031-556 2033
Founded: 1867
Secretary: H. H. Penman, 33A Queens Crescent, Edinburgh EH9 2BA. Tel: 031-667 2524
Captain 1985-86: N. A. Stewart

Most capped players: J. P. Fisher, 25 for Scotland; M. C. Morrison, 23 for Scotland
Colours: Black and white hoops/black
Directions to ground: Take London Road going east. Pass by Meadowbank Stadium on left. Jock's Lodge is a further half-mile on right
Clubhouse: Bars, changing-rooms
Teams run: 3
1st XV 1985-86 (2nd Division):
P 13   W 6   D 0   L 7   F 124   A 158
   Royal High finished eighth in the Second Division and never really challenged for promotion. With their best players being persuaded to join leading clubs, prospects cannot improve until they offer good enough standards to keep them.

Selkirk

Address: Philphaugh, Selkirk, Borders. Tel: (0750) 20403
Founded: 1907
Secretary: W. Jackson, 44 Raeburn Meadow, Selkirk. Tel: (0750) 21023 (h), (0750) 21601 (w)
Fixtures secretary: B. Duffy, 63 Back Row, Selkirk. Tel: (0750) 21665
Captain 1985-86: K. Laurie
Coach 1985-86: David Bell
Most capped players: J. Y. Rutherford, 37 for Scotland, 1 for British Lions; I. A. M. Paxton, 25 for Scotland, 4 for British Lions
Colours: Navy blue/white/navy blue
Directions to ground: Leave centre of town on A708 road for St Mary's Lock. Ground is on left
Clubhouse: Bars, changing-rooms, committee rooms
Teams run: 3
1st XV 1985-86 (1st Division):
P 13   W 4   D 0   L 9   F 118   A 208
   Selkirk, despite their star names, only just avoided relegation from the First Division of the National League finishing one place above Preston Lodge. Border League results were little better and no Sevens tournaments were won. Had John Rutherford and Iain Paxton been more regularly available it might have been a different story.

Stewart's-Melville FP

Address: Inverleith & Ferryfield, Ferry Road, Edinburgh EH5 2DW. Tel: 031-522 3004/2112
Founded: 1973, when Daniel Stewart's College and Melville College were amalgamated
Secretary: I. W. Forsyth, 8 Barnton Park Dell, Edinburgh EH4 6HW. Tel: 031-336 6995 (h), 031-655 6000 (w)
Captain 1985-86: J. H. Calder
Most capped players: J. H. Calder, 27 for Scotland, 1 for British Lions; A. J. W. Hinshelwood, 21 for Scotland, 3 for British Lions; D. W. Morgan, 21 for Scotland, 2 for British Lions
Colours: Scarlet with broad black band divided by narrow gold band/white/black
Directions to ground: From St Andrews Square proceed up Broughton Street and Inverleith Row. Turn left at junction onto Ferry Road. Ground is half-mile (approx.) on left
Clubhouse: Bars, tearoom, changing-rooms. Excellent facilities
Teams run: 3
1st XV 1985-86 (1st Division):
P 12   W 9   D 0   L 3   F 289   A 103

Stewart's-Melville had an excellent season in the First Division of the National League finishing third behind Hawick and Kelso after having led for much of the season. Finlay Calder succeeded his brother, Jim, in the Scotland senior team.

Stirling County

Address: Bridgehaugh Park, Stirling. Tel: (0786) 4827
Founded: 1904
Secretary: J. R. Muirhead, 2 Clifford Road, Stirling. Tel: (0786) 2585 (h), (0786) 4144 (w)
Captain 1985-86: E. T. N. Pollock
Most capped player: Dr W. Welsh, 8 for Scotland
Colours: Red, white and black
Clubhouse: Changing-rooms, bar
1st XV 1985-86 (2nd Division):
P 13   W 9   D 0   L 4   F 178   A 110
   Stirling County had a fine season just missing promotion to the First Division of the National League on points difference from Ayr.

Watsonians

Address: Myreside, Edinburgh. Tel: 031-447 1395
Founded: 1875
Secretary: D. D. Carmichael, 1 Royal Terrace, Edinburgh EH7 5AD. Tel: 031-557 4455
Captain 1985-86: G. N. Buchan
Most capped players: D. I. Johnston, 27 for Scotland; J. C. MacCallum, 26 for Scotland
Colours: Maroon and white
Directions to ground: Off Colinton Road on south-west side of city
Clubhouse: Good facilities with changing-rooms and bars
1st XV 1985-86 (1st Division):
P 13   W 8   D 0   L 5   F 214   A 145
   Watsonians were, in effect, Scotland's fourth best team and they had a very good season. Representative honours were in abundance with the Hastings brothers and David Johnston (now the club's most capped player) appearing in all of Scotland's International matches. Duncan Forbes scored 110 league points for the club.

West of Scotland

Address: Burnbrae, Glasgow Road, Milngavie, Glasgow G62 6HX. Tel: 041-956 2891/1960
Founded: 1865
Secretary: J. F. Livingston, 28 Cleveden Gardens, Glasgow G12 0PT. Tel: 041-339 1341 (h), 041-204 0771 (w)
Captain 1985-86: G. M. McGuinness
Most capped players: A. B. Carmichael, 50 for Scotland; G. L. Brown, 30 for Scotland, 8 for British Lions; W. P. Scott, 21 for Scotland
Colours: Red and yellow hoops
Directions to ground: Off A879 (Glasgow Road) in Milngavie
Clubhouse: Bar, changing-rooms and other facilities
1st XV 1985-86 (1st Division):
P 12   W 7   D 0   L 5   F 199   A 192
   West of Scotland did well to finish as high as seventh in the First Division of the National League. Matt Duncan made a very good debut for Scotland with two tries in his four appearances. He also scored seven tries in league matches.

IRELAND

Review of the Season
by Sean Diffley, Irish Independent

The signs for the reigning Five Nations Champions were ominous from the start. In October, the touring Fijians gave the Irish the fright of their lives; Ireland finally won by one point, but it was a hugely lucky escape. Tuvula, the Fiji full-back, went clear of the Irish defence five minutes from the end of the International at Lansdowne Road. A match-winning try seemed certain; but the referee, Derek Bevan (Wales), well up with the play let it be stressed, ruled that Tuvula, in attempting to gather the ball a few yards from the Irish line and well clear of any attention from the Irish defence, knocked the ball forward. Then, a

Ireland skipper, Ciaran Fitzgerald, makes some points to Donal Lenihan (no.5) during the short half-time break against Wales at Lansdowne Road, Dublin.

minute before full-time, the Fijian place-kicker, Damu, from a very feasible distance and angle indeed, kicked the ball narrowly wide. Many of the Lansdowne Road spectators were convinced that Tuvula had knocked the ball back rather than forward and that the Fijians had really gained a moral victory despite losing (16-15). Fiji in fact scored two tries to Ireland's one.

So, the team that had won the Five Nations title the previous season had just escaped from contributing a 'first' to Rugby history by becoming the first of the Five Nations to lose to Fiji.

Before that game with Fiji, the Irish coach Mick Doyle had talked to the visiting Australian captain, Andrew Slack, who advised against taking the Fijians on at their own game and trying to imitate their style of running and passing with gay abandon. Experience had shown that even the classy Australians found it necessary to put the pressure on the flying Fijians in the forwards. But the euphoria of the previous Five Nations Championship, in which the Irish had concentrated on mobility and on keeping the ball as far from the forward mauling as possible, still hovered over Lansdowne Road and the Fijians, allowed to fulfil their own style of play, nearly toppled the Irish.

But, if many felt that Doyle and his fellow selectors were rather unwisely dismissing the necessity of getting their platform organized with their cavalier attitude towards hard-grinding scrum-maging practice, the reality was that Ireland was suffering a dearth of good scrummagers. The signs were there in the Irish trial in early January 1986. The Irish XV beat the Combined Provinces (21-12) but, in the second half of the trial, it was noticeable that the Irish XV forwards were anything but comfortable in the scrums.

On the first day of February 1986 the Irish bubble burst resoundingly at the Parc des Princes. In the very first scrum they were demolished, and for the rest of the match they struggled in desperation.

The French won (29-9) to score their highest total ever against Ireland. There was no doubt that the Irish badly missed their world-class flanker, Philip Matthews, who had injured an elbow playing for Ulster against Queensland and was out of action for the season. There was a bad loss too because of the broken jaw sustained by that lively left-wing Keith Crossan, who could not play until the third match against England at Twickenham.

After the Paris debacle, Ireland brought in two new props. They picked Paul Kennedy (London Irish) instead of Phil Orr and Des Fitzgerald (Lansdowne) instead of Jim McCoy. Also, Willie Anderson was dropped from lock and replaced by Jerry Holland (Wanderers), with talented Nigel Carr, recovered from injury, playing at flank. There was a better organization about the team that played Wales, but, in the end, the Irish fell apart again after faltering at half-time at Lansdowne Road with their 12-4 interval lead, which included a superb try by Trevor Ringland. But the cooler, shrewder Welsh (not a vintage side by any means) controlled the second half as the Irish pack once again failed. Wales eventually won 19-12, and the Irish season was in disarray.

At Twickenham, Ireland brought on twenty four-year-old Ralph Keyes for his first cap instead of the injured Paul Dean at fly-half. Brian McCall (London Irish) was at lock instead of the injured Jerry Holland and Davy Morrow was back at flank instead of another injured player, Ronan Kearney.

It was the match at Twickenham that underlined the unfortunate aspect of the whole season; the fact that the Irish had an excellent back division, starved of opportunities to show their class because of the unsatisfactory forward platform.

Keyes, who might have been excused of nervousness playing his first International at Twickenham, was cool and composed and made a neat half-break to give Brendan Mullin an excellent try at the posts. And there was the almost inevitable try from Trevor Ringland. But the scrums were disastrous. England's no. 8, Dean Richards, scored two tries when the Irish scrum was pushed over their line. There was also a penalty-try after an illegal attempt to foil another push-over, and a try by Huw Davies, the direct result of a series of powerful and embarrassingly strong scrums on the Irish line.

After that the selectors had the wisdom to recall Phil Orr, who never should have been dropped after Paris; they also brought back Willie Anderson and played him at no. 8 instead of Brian Spillane. And, with both Dean and Keyes injured, the veteran Tony Ward was recalled to the team to the clear delight of his fans.

So, Scotland at Lansdowne Road stood between Ireland and the whitewash. And, in fairness, this was a much improved Irish forward display. The return of Orr steadied the scrum and Anderson played a blinder at no. 8. In fact, this was a match that the Irish should have won. Trevor Ringland

Trevor Ringland (Ireland) escapes the despairing tackle of Adrian Hadley (Wales) to score in the corner.

scored his seventh try for Ireland but was guilty of an indiscretion that led to the referee reversing his decision to award Ireland a penalty kick in front of the posts. And then Michael Kiernan, of all people, with yet another chance to win the match, missed a penalty kick from just left of the Scottish posts. The 'little people' who had smiled on the Irish the previous season were certainly looking the other way in 1986.

The irony of that missed opportunity by Kiernan was that the Irish pack, to the undisguised delight of Phil Orr, actually 'walked' the Scottish pack back towards their own line, forcing them to concede what should have been a match-winning penalty-goal. Could this be the same Irish pack that had been so humiliated throughout the season?

It is indeed amazing what a couple of judicious changes can do.

So the Irish will be fervently hoping this season that they can get their act together in the forwards with the World Cup on the horizon. But the signs that a strong pack will be available are not too obvious. The Irish did not initially support the World Cup and required many assurances, particularly with respect to the amateur laws, before accepting an invitation. But as this new season begins the doubts are surfacing in Ireland again. The unofficial tour of South Africa by New Zealand and the seemingly powerless position of the Rugby authorities, have posed many questions in a country of firm believers in the amateur ethos of world Rugby.

Irish Roll of Honour, 1985-86

compiled by Frank Byford

Connacht Branch IRFU

Senior Cup Final
Galwegians   10   Athlone   0
Senior League
Galway Corinthians
Schools Senior Cup
St Josephs, Garbally Park, Ballinasloe

Leinster Branch IRFU

Senior Cup Final
Lansdowne   15   Blackrock College   9
(at Lansdowne Road, Dublin)
Senior League
Lansdowne
Schools Senior Cup
Blackrock College

Munster Branch IRFU

Senior Cup Final (Centenary Cup, 1886-1986)
Shannon   17   Garryowen   6
(at Thomond Park, Limerick)
Senior League
Shannon
Cork Charity Cup
Cork Constitution
Limerick Charity Cup
Shannon
Schools Senior Cup
Crescent College Comprehensive, Limerick

Ulster Branch IRFU

Ulster Senior Cup Final
Bangor   17   Malone   6
(at Ravenhill, Belfast)
Ulster Senior Plate Final
Dungannon   9   Ballynahinch   6
Senior League
Ballymena
Bass Boston Floodlit Cup
Bangor
Schools Senior Cup
Bangor Grammar School

Team of the Year in Ireland
Shannon (P 28   W 27   D 1   F 521   A 156)
Inter-Provincial Champions
Ulster
Dudley Cup – Irish University Championship
University College, Dublin

Dudley Cup – Irish Universities Championship

	P	W	L	F	A	Pts
University College, Dublin	4	4	0	67	16	8
Dublin University	4	3	1	79	32	6
University College, Cork	4	2	2	38	41	4
University College, Galway	3	0	3	9	53	0
Queens University, Belfast	3	0	3	22	73	0

The match between Queens University, Belfast and University College, Galway was not played

Irish Inter-Provincial Championship

h November 1985
t Belfast)

| Ulster | 23 | Munster | 3 |

einster
t Dublin)

| | 6 | Connacht | 9 |

3rd November 1985
onnacht
t Galway)

| | 6 | Ulster | 16 |

Iunster
t Cork)

| | 6 | Leinster | 15 |

7th December 1985

| Leinster | 13 | Ulster | 19 |

(at Dublin)

| Munster | 16 | Connacht | 9 |

(at Cork)

	P	W	L	F	A	Pts
Ulster	3	3	0	58	22	6
Leinster	3	1	2	35	37	2
Connacht	3	1	2	24	38	2
Munster	3	1	2	28	48	2

Leinster Senior League

Final

unday, 29th December 1985, at Donnybrook

| ansdowne | 16 | Terenure College | 6 |

ry: Spring
enalty-goals: Dilger (4)

Penalty-goals: O'Kelly (2)

ansdowne: P. Danaher; J. Daly, R. Moroney, W. Dawson, P. Purcell; G. Dilger, E. Costello; T. Clancy, W. Burns, D. Fitzgerald, M. Ryan (*captain*), V. Ryan, J. Malone, C. Quinn, A. Corcoran. *Replacement:* D. Spring

Terenure College: R. Hopkins, P. Haycock, P. O'Sullivan, D. McGowan, P. Walsh; B. O'Kelly, P. Joyce (*captain*); D. Egan, T. D'Arcy, M. D'Arcy, C. Sampson, L. O'Dea, B. Twomey, L. Kinsella, J. O'Brien

Referee: O. A. Doyle (*Leinster Branch*)

Irish Clubs

Armagh

ddress: Palace Grounds, Ring Road, Armagh. Tel: (0861) 22248
ounded: 1875
ecretary: T. Galbraith, 22 Brentwood Park, Richhill, Co. rmagh. Tel: (0762) 871706

rmagh RFC, April 1986

Fixtures secretary: S. M. Smyth, 2 Rosemount Avenue, Armagh. Tel: (0861) 524242
Captain 1985-86: S. R. Wilson
Coach 1985-86: J. Wilson
Most capped player: Brian McCall, 4 for Ireland
Colours: Red and black hoops/white
Directions to ground: Off Ring Road, Armagh
Clubhouse: 6 changing-rooms, 2 bars, function room
Teams run: 5 plus Under-20s
1st XV 1985-86: P 24   W 11   D 1   L 12   F 292   A 354

Armagh achieved their highest league position since going senior in 1981. They reached the semi-finals of the Senior Plate.

Ballymena

Address: Eaton Park, Ballymena, Co. Antrim. Tel: (0266) 6746
Founded: 1922
Captain 1985-86: F. Allen
Most capped players: W. J. McBride, 63 for Ireland, 17 for British Lions; S. Millar, 37 for Ireland, 9 for British Lions; T. M. Ringland, 21 for Ireland, 1 for British Lions
Colours: Black/white/black and white

Clubhouse: Changing-rooms, bar
1st XV 1985-86: P 24　W 16　D 0　L 8　F 357　A 322
　　Ballymena had a good season and won the Ulster Senior League.

Bangor

Address: Upritchard Park, Bloomfield Road South, Bangor, Co. Down
Founded: 1885
Captain 1985-86: S. Todd
Most capped player: R. A. Milliken, 14 for Ireland
Colours: Old gold, royal blue and black
Clubhouse: Changing-rooms, bar
1st XV 1985-86: P 32　W 25　D 0　L 7　F 574　A 310
　　Bangor, in an excellent season, won the Ulster Senior Cup.

Bective Rangers

Address: Donnybrook, Dublin 4. Tel: 0001-693894
Founded: 1881
Captain 1985-86: T. Kavanagh
Most capped player: J. L. Farrell, 29 for Ireland, 5 for British Lions
Colours: Red, green and white stripes/white
Clubhouse: Changing-rooms, bar
1st XV 1985-86: P 26　W 13　D 1　L 12　F 333　A 328
　　Bective Rangers broke even in a modest season.

Blackrock College

Address: Stadbrook Road, Blackrock, Dublin. Tel: 0001-805697
Founded: 1882
Captain 1985-86: D. Coakley
Most capped players: J. F. Slattery, 61 for Ireland, 4 for British Isles; H. P. MacNeill, 25 for Ireland, 3 for British Lions
Colours: Narrow royal blue and white stripes/navy/navy
Clubhouse: Changing-rooms, bar
1st XV 1985-86: P 27　W 17　D 1　L 9　F 494　A 371
　　Blackrock College had a good season without winning anything at senior level. At schools level the Senior Cup was won.

Bohemians

Address: Thomond Park, Limerick. Tel: (061) 51877
Founded: 1922
Secretary: M. Leydon, Belvoir, 22 Revington Park, North Circular Road, Limerick. Tel: (061) 54853 (h), (061) 44388 (w)
Fixtures secretary: D. Fitzpatrick, Trenton, Avondale Drive, Greystones, Limerick. Tel: (061) 53562 (h)
Captain 1985-86: T. Lenahan
Most capped player: M. A. F. English, 16 for Ireland
Colours: Red and white
Clubhouse: Changing-rooms, bar
1st XV 1985-86: P 27　W 10　D 2　L 15　F 290　A 399
　　Bohemians had a poor season with no competition won.

City of Derry

Address: Branch Road, Londonderry. Tel: (0504) 264528
Founded: 1881
Secretary: Robert Logue, Sportsfield House, Airfield Road, Eglinton. Tel: (0504) 810085

Fixtures secretary: George Tees, 19 Baywater, Londonderr
Tel: (0504) 42836
Captain 1985-86: Ian Crowe
Coach 1985-86: Mike Balmer
Most capped player: Ken Goodall, 19 for Ireland
Colours: Green/white/green and black
Directions to ground: Across New Foyle Bridge, turn left, tu
right at traffic lights into Buncrana Road, club is three quarte
mile further out
Clubhouse: Large modern building comprising 7 changing-room
2 shower-rooms, squash courts and separate changing/show
facilities, main Members' Bar, function room and kitchens
Teams run: 6 plus Colts XV
1st XV 1985-86: P 25　W 13　D 0　L 12　F 315　A 326
　　City of Derry started off the season with a very good recor
winning ten games and losing six but deteriorated in the seco
half following a spate of injuries.

CIYMS

Address: Circular Road, Belfast. Tel: (0232) 768225/760120
Founded: 1922
Captain 1985-86: I. McIlmoyle
Most capped player: A. C. Pedlow, 30 for Ireland, 2 for Briti
Isles
Colours: Black and white hoops/black/blue
Clubhouse: Changing-rooms, bar
1st XV 1985-86: P 23　W 3　D 2　L 18　F 223　A 391
　　CIYMS had a desperate season with only three victories.

Clontarf

Address: Castle Avenue, Clontarf, Dublin. Tel: 0001-336214
Founded: 1876
Captain 1985-86: G. Carr
Most capped player: G. J. Morgan, 19 for Ireland, 1 for Briti
Isles
Colours: Red and blue/white/red and blue
Directions to ground: Turn left off Clontarf Road before Clonta
Baths when proceeding from city centre
Clubhouse: Changing-rooms, bar
　　Clontarf won no trophies during the season.

Collegians

Address: Deramore Park, Belfast. Tel: (0232) 665943
Captain 1985-86: W. Kettyle
Founded: 1890
Most capped player: J. McVicker, 20 for Ireland, 3 for Britis
Isles
Colours: White and maroon, navy stockings with maroon top
Clubhouse: Changing-rooms, bar
1st XV 1985-86: P 25　W 13　D 0　L 12　F 336　A 308
　　Collegians broke even in a modest season.

Corinthians

Address: Corinthian Park, Tuam Road, Galway
Founded: 1932
Captain 1985-86: J. O'Connell
Colours: Blue, black and white
Clubhouse: Changing-rooms, bars
　　Corinthians won the Connacht Senior League.

Cork Constitution

Address: Temple Hill, Cork. Tel: (021) 292563
Founded: 1892
Secretary: Mark O'Sullivan
Fixtures secretary: Ciaran Bourke, Discovery, Douglas Road, Cork. Tel: (021) 363798 (h), (021) 961011 (w)
Captain 1985-86: Paul Derham
Coach 1985-86: Noel Murphy
Most capped player: Tom Kiernan, 54 for Ireland, 5 for British Lions
Colours: Blue, black and white
Directions to ground: Blackrock Road from city centre to Temple Hill south-east of city
Clubhouse: 6 dressing-rooms, function and dance hall, bar and committee room
Teams run: 6 adult, 6 youth (12-18 years)
1st XV 1985-86: P 31 W 18 D 4 L 9 F 445 A 307

Cork Constitution had a successful season, winning the Cork Charity Cup, the Munster Junior (2nd XV) Cup, the Denneay Cup and the Under-18 Cup and League. The senior side included five International players and Donal Lenihan captained the Five Nations team at Twickenham. Five members of the current senior team have captained Munster provincial teams.

Dolphin

Address: Musgrave Park, Cork. Tel: (021) 22069
Founded: 1902
Secretary: M. J. O'Riordan, Greenwood, Temple Hill, Carrigrohane, Co. Cork. Tel: (021) 80257 (h)
Fixtures secretary: J. V. O'Callaghan, 3 Ard na Ri Avenue, Gouladuff Road, Cork. Tel: (021) 965 745 (h), (021) 966333 (w)
Captain 1985-86: Donal Daly
Most capped player: J. S. McCarthy, 28 for Ireland
Colours: Navy blue
Clubhouse: Changing-rooms, bar

Dolphin had no competition successes.

Dublin University

Address: College Park, Trinity College, Dublin 2. Tel: 0001-778423
Founded: 1854
Captain 1985-86: P. Clinch
Most capped player: J. D. Clinch, 30 for Ireland
Colours: White/white/black and red
Directions to ground: In Kimmage district of Dublin, very close to college
Clubhouse: Changing-rooms, bar
1st XV 1985-86: P 23 W 11 D 0 L 12 F 342 A 318

Dublin University finished runners-up in the Dudley Cup; they lost the Colours Match to University College, Dublin.

Dungannon

Address: Stevenson Park, Dungannon, Co. Tyrone. Tel: (08687) 22387
Founded: 1873
Captain 1985-86: F. Patton
Most capped player: S. A. McKinney, 25 for Ireland
Colours: Royal blue and white hoops/white
Clubhouse: Changing-rooms, bar
1st XV 1985-86: P 26 W 8 D 2 L 16 F 249 A 354

Dungannon had a poor season, relieved by success in the Ulster Senior Plate.

Galwegians

Address: Glenina, Galway, Co. Galway. Tel: (091) 62484
Founded: 1922
Captain 1985-86: M. Quaid
Most capped player: P. J. A. O'Sullivan, 15 for Ireland
Colours: Sky blue/white/sky blue and black
Clubhouse: Changing-rooms, bar

Galwegians had a modest season, relieved only by victory in the Connacht Senior Cup.

Garryowen

Address: Dooradoyle, Limerick. Tel: (061) 46094
Founded: 1884
Secretary: G. McKeon, 24 Highfield, Ennis Road, Limerick. Tel: (061) 54398 (h), (061) 61555 (w)
Fixtures secretary: W. S. Purcell, 27 Fortfield, Raheen, Limerick. Tel: (061) 28828 (h), (061) 316411 (w)
Captain 1985-86: D. O'Donovan
Most capped player: B. G. M. Wood, 29 for Ireland, 2 for British Lions
Colours: Light blue jerseys, with white star on breast
Clubhouse: Changing-rooms, bar

In a modest season Garryowen lost the final of the Munster Senior Cup to Shannon.

Greystones

Address: Dr J. J. Hickey Park, Delgany Road, Greystones, Co. Wicklow. Tel: 0001-874640 (steward), 0001-874814 (members)
Founded: 1937
Secretary: Tom Nolan, 96 Beachdale, Kilcoole, Co. Wicklow. Tel: 0001-877219 (h), 0001-862525 (w)
Fixtures secretary: Charley O'Reilly, The Bungalow, Killincarrig, Delgany, Co. Wicklow. Tel: 0001-874527 (h)
Captain 1985-86: Tony Doyle
Coach 1985-86: Terry Diaper
Most capped players: Tony Ward, 17 for Ireland (1 with Greystones), 1 for British Lions; Paul McNaughton, 15 for Ireland (all Greystones)
Colours: Green and white hoops/white/green
Directions to ground: On 84 bus route from Dublin just outside Greystones
Clubhouse: Members lounge, function room, 4 changing-rooms, fully equipped kitchen
Teams run: 7 senior, 4 youth
1st XV 1985-86: P 33 W 23 D 1 L 9 F 569 A 400

The 1st XV had a poor start to the season because of injuries which affected the League campaign. From December the team had an excellent run of results right up to the Cup campaign when the top players did not play well on the day. Youths (U18 and U12) had an exceptionally successful year.

Instonians

Address: Shane Park, Stockmans Lane, Belfast. Tel: (0232) 660629
Founded: 1919
Captain 1985-86: J. McKibbin
Most capped player: D. Hewitt, 18 for Ireland, 6 for British Isles
Colours: Yellow, black and purple
Clubhouse: Changing-rooms, bar

Lansdowne

Address: Lansdowne Road, Dublin 4. Tel: 0001-689300
Founded: 1872
Secretary: Aidan F. Browne, 3 Creggin, Bailey View, Harbour Road, Dalkey, Co. Dublin. Tel: 0001-804917
Fixtures secretary: Aidan F. Browne
Captain 1985-86: Willy Burns
Coaches 1985-86: Paddy Boylan and Donal Caniffe
Most capped player: Moss Keane, 51 for Ireland, 1 for British Lions
Colours: Red, yellow and black
Clubhouse: Bar, gymnasium, 5 dressing-rooms, weights room
Teams run: 8

The club achieved the Cup and League double at senior level. The double has only been achieved three times in the history of Leinster Rugby, once previously by Blackrock and Lansdowne on the other occasion.

Malone

Address: Gibson Park Avenue, Cregagh Road, Belfast BT6 9GL. Tel: (0232) 57819/51312 (office)
Founded: 1892
Captain 1985-86: W. Duncan
Most capped player: W. E. Crawford, 30 for Ireland
Colours: White/blue/red
Clubhouse: Changing-rooms, bar
1st XV 1985-86: P 26 W 16 D 1 L 9 F 364 A 270

In a good season Malone lost the Ulster Senior Cup final to Bangor.

Monkstown

Address: Sydney Parade, Dublin 4. Tel: 0001-691794
Founded: 1883
Captain 1985-86: I. Counihan
Most capped player: J. C. Parke, 20 for Ireland
Colours: Royal blue and gold
Directions to ground: From city centre, left off Merrion Road near hospital
Clubhouse: Changing-rooms, bar

Monkstown had no successes in 1985-86.

North of Ireland Cricket & Football Club

Address: The Pavilion, Shaftesbury Avenue, Ormean Road, Belfast BT7 2ES. Tel: (0232) 21096/23342
Founded: 1859
Secretary: J. Gilbert Paton, 7 Cleaver Park, Belfast BT9. Tel: (0232) 667814 (h)
Fixtures secretary: D. J. Kelly Wilson, 4 Cairnburn Road, Belfast BT4. Tel: (0232) 768267 (h)
Captain 1985-86: Dr Stephen Hall
Coach 1985-86: Ian Bremner
Most capped player: C. M. H. Gibson MBE, 69 for Ireland, 14 for British Lions (current world record)
Colours: Red, black and blue
Teams run: 7
1st XV 1985-86: P 22 W 12 D 0 L 10 F 370 A 246

NIFC had a moderate season, suffering disruptions caused by poor weather conditions.

Old Belvedere

Address: Anglesea Road, Ballsbridge, Dublin 4. Tel: 000 689748
Founded: 1930
Captain 1985-86: M. McClany
Most capped player: A. J. F. O'Reilly, 29 for Ireland, 10 British Lions
Colours: Black and white/black
Directions to ground: Anglesea Road starts where Merri Road takes over from Pembroke Road
Clubhouse: Changing-rooms, bar
1st XV 1985-86: P 25 W 15 D 0 L 10 F 442 A 313

Old Belvedere had a fair season but won no competitions.

Old Wesley

Address: Donnybrook, Dublin 4. Tel: 0001-689149
Founded: 1891
Captain 1985-86: P. Orr
Most capped player: P. Orr, 50 for Ireland, 1 for British Lion
Colours: White and red/white
Clubhouse: Changing-rooms, bar
1st XV 1985-86: P 27 W 16 D 3 L 8 F 432 A 310

Old Wesley won nearly two-thirds of the matches playe Phil Orr became the most capped British prop forward (eq with J. McLauchlan of Scotland).

Palmerston

Address: Milltown Road, Clonskeagh, Dublin 6. Tel: 000 973126
Founded: 1899
Captain 1985-86: K. Tobin
Colours: Black, green and white/black
Clubhouse: Changing-rooms, bar

Palmerston had no successes in 1985-86.

Portadown

Address: Chambers Park, Portadown, Co. Armagh. Tel: (076 335269
Founded: 1879
Secretary: A. Gribben, 10 Knockmena Park, Portadown. T (0762) 332206 (h)
Fixtures secretary: R. Stewart, 10 Margretta Park, Portadow Tel: (0762) 334168 (h)
Captain 1985-86: S. J. Grattan
Coach 1985-86: W. Gribben
Most capped player: C. Murtagh, 1 for Ireland
Colours: Royal blue/white/royal blue with white
Directions to ground: Situated off Bridge Street
Clubhouse: Changing pavilion containing 6 changing-room and gymnasium; clubhouse containing extensive social ameniti and 2 changing-rooms; one pitch fully floodlit
Teams run: 7 senior teams; U20, U18, U16 youth teams; Mi Rugby
1st XV 1985-86: P 31 W 11 D 2 L 18 F 284 A 435

A mid-table position was achieved in the Ulster Senior Leagu Portadown were winners of the Galwegians RFC Sevens a Senior Plate.

Queen's University

Postal address: Students' Union, Queen's University of Belfas Belfast BT7 1NF. Tel:(0232) 224803. Telex: 74487

Ground: Dub Pavilion, Malone Playing Fields, Belfast BT9
ND. Tel: (0232) 611879/611950
Founded: 1869
Secretary: David T. Cromie, 50 Hampton Park, Belfast BT7
JP. Tel: (0232) 640279
Fixtures secretary: Dr John Neill, 37 Priory Park, Belfast BT10
AE. Tel: (0232) 612289
Captain 1985-86: David Armstrong
Coach 1985-86: Bill Buchanan
Most capped player: J. Kyle, 46 for Ireland, 6 for British Lions
Colours: Royal blue/white
Directions to ground: From Queen's University follow Malone
Road for 2 miles to roundabout, then follow Upper Malone Road
or 1 mile
Clubhouse: Changing facilities, bar, snacks, discos
Teams run: 7
1st XV 1985-86: P 30 W 10 D 0 L 20 F 389 A 546
    Queen's University had a poor season not relieved by any cup
successes.

St Mary's College

Address: Templeville Road, Dublin 6. Tel: 0001-900440
Founded: 1900
Captain 1985-86: T. Kennedy
Most capped players: J. J. Moloney, 27 for Ireland; C. F.
Fitzgerald, 25 for Ireland, 4 for British Isles
Colours: Royal blue with white star/white/royal blue
Directions to ground: On right off Templeville Road (Templeogue
district)
Clubhouse: Changing-rooms, bar
1st XV 1985-86: P 27 W 11 D 2 L 14 F 376 A 371
    No tournaments were won by St Mary's College this season.

Shannon

Address: Gortatogher, Parteen, Co. Clare. Tel: (061) 52350
Founded: 1884
Secretary: M. G. Ryan, Curragour, Parteen, Co. Clare. Tel:
(061) 40563
Fixtures secretary: R. Keane, 8 Oakland Drive, Greystones,
Limerick. Tel: (061) 52494 (h), (061) 315599 (w)
Captain 1985-86: G. McMahon
Most capped player: G. A. J. McLoughlin, 18 for Ireland
Colours: Black and blue/black/black and blue
Clubhouse: Usual facilities
1st XV 1985-86: P 28 W 27 D 1 L 0 F 521 A 156
    Shannon were Ireland's most successful club, being unbeaten.
They won the Munster Senior Cup and Senior League.

Sunday's Well

Address: Musgrave Park, Cork. Tel: (021) 965735
Founded: 1923
Secretary: M. Cooper, 1 Lee Road, Cork. Tel: (021) 43595
Fixtures secretary: M. Barry, Browningstown Park, Douglas,
Cork
Captain 1985-86: Olan Trevor
Most capped player: J. C. Walsh, 27 for Ireland
Colours: Red, green and white/white/red, green and white
Clubhouse: Usual facilities
1st XV 1985-86: P 22 W 8 D 3 L 11 F 222 A 305
    In a season badly disrupted by the weather Sunday's Well had
very moderate results.

Terenure College

Address: Lakelands Park, Terenure, Dublin 6. Tel: 0001-907572
Founded: 1941
Captain 1985-86: N. Williamson
Most capped player: M. L. Hipwell, 12 for Ireland
Colours: Purple, black and white
Directions to ground: Proceeding north along Templeogue Road,
on left after convent school
    Terenure College had no successes this season.

University College, Cork

Address: Mardyke, Western Road, Cork. Tel: (021) 45772
Founded: 1872
Secretary: D. Keohane, Tara, 3 Bishopscourt Road, Wilton,
Cork. Tel: (021) 41878
Fixtures secretary: J. Crowley, Western Star, Western Road,
Cork. Tel: (021) 430470
Captain 1985-86: P. Culhane
Most capped player: J. Russell, 19 for Ireland
Colours: Red with black skull and crossbones/white/black, red
and white
Clubhouse: Full facilities
1st XV 1985-86: P 22 W 8 D 0 L 14 F 244 A 367
    University College, Cork won only eight matches out of
twenty two played and finished in third place in the Irish Uni-
versities Championship, for the Dudley Cup.

University College, Dublin

Address: University College, Dublin, Belfield, Dublin 4. Tel:
0001-693616
Founded: 1910
Most capped player: R. J. McLoughlin, 40 for Ireland, 3 for
British Lions
Colours: St Patrick's blue/white/navy with St Patrick's blue
tops
Directions to ground: In University College, Dublin grounds
Clubhouse: Usual facilities
1st XV 1985-86: P 23 W 14 D 1 L 8 F 361 A 261
    University College, Dublin had a fine season and won the
Dudley Cup for the five Irish Universities. The overall record
was also good.

Wanderers

Address: Lansdowne Road, Dublin 2. Tel: 0001-689277
Founded: 1870
Secretary: George Stringer, 39 Bellevue Road, Glenageary,
Co. Dublin. Tel: 0001-854776
Fixtures secretary: Gordon Black, 64 Dangan Park, Dublin 12.
Tel: 0001-554394
Captain 1985-86: I. Burns
Coach 1985-86: Gerry Murphy
Most capped player: J. R. Kavanagh, 35 for Ireland
Colours: Blue, black and white hoops/navy/black with blue and
white tops
Directions to ground: IRFU ground, but there is a second
ground on Merrion Road (on right going south)
Clubhouse: IRFU ground. Merrion Road has a fine clubhouse
with bar, changing-rooms and social facilities. Tel: 0001-
693227/695272
Teams run: 7
1st XV 1985-86: P 28 W 16 D 2 L 10 F 423 A 394
    Wanderers had a fair season without winning any tournaments.
Their cause was not helped by a long injury list.

WALES

Eighties' Slump Continues

The slump that has overtaken Welsh Rugby in the eighties continued this past season, and there were few signs to indicate that there will be an instant improvement, which is very worrying with the World Cup to be faced next year. In spite of the fact that the National team won three of its five matches during the season, these results are misleading; and the club Rugby scene was none too healthy into the bargain.

Bad Season for Discipline

Before the season was very old, the good name of Welsh Rugby had been severely tarnished by a number of unsavoury incidents. First, in September, there was a brawl at Bristol that led to the London referee, George Crawford, walking off the pitch; and the match between the home team and Newport was completed under the attention of another official. The action of Mr Crawford won him no friends with his 'bosses', but it was a pity that he felt bound to act as he did and there was much sympathy for him.

Next, Pontypool and Newbridge had a dispute after the Newbridge forward, Jarman, was taken to hospital following an alleged punching incident. At the end of the season, Newbridge were again in the wars at Pontypool, when they finished with only thirteen men after using both their replacements. Pontypool immediately announced the cancellation of future matches between the clubs, although they were criticized at the time for not first advising Newbridge of their decision (it was announced through the press). It was also felt that they were 'getting their retaliation in first', since no-one could blame Newbridge for the injuries their own players had received; they in their turn were criticized by 'Pooler' players and officials for picking Jarman for the match. They called it 'provocation', although how he could be described as a provocation is hard to understand.

If that was not enough, Newport were involved in three more unfortunate incidents. There was a brawl with the touring Fijians, who had seen one of their own forwards dismissed; soon after that a match against London Welsh at the Old Deer Park saw them lose two forwards, sent off, in a match where 'the Welsh' also had a player dismissed. Near the end of the season, a young prop was also sent off and that player missed being on the replacements bench for the Schweppes final.

The authorities took this indiscipline by players very seriously and swingeing new measures were announced to penalize miscreants, including a threat of indefinite suspensions for the worst offenders. No player would be selected for Wales in any season when he was dismissed.

Immediately, Wales found themselves condemned to face the Five Nations programme without two important forwards – Norster of Cardiff and Richard Moriarty of Swansea – as each had fallen foul of referees. These were two self-inflicted wounds and they did the country's International chances no good, but they did at least go some way to restoring confidence and respect for the good intentions of the Principality.

International Matches

The first major International fixtures of the season took place early in the winter of 1985, when Wales 'B' were soundly thrashed in France and the senior side took on Fiji, who had given Ireland a very close run earlier in their tour. Possibly on the strength of this, Wales decided to award full caps for the occasion, but it was a very hollow victory that was achieved by a team playing none too well against poor opposition. The case for giving caps was based on the fact that in 1983 Romania (a non-IB country) were met in Bucharest and full caps were awarded then, but most people would place the Eastern Europeans in a class well above the Fijians. A further argument is that weaker national teams will be met in the World Cup where caps will be awarded for each match played. There will be accusations that the honour of winning a cap is being devalued, particularly if (as is intended) full awards are made for the games on the South Pacific tour at the close of this season.

However, that Fijian match was the last Terry Holmes played for Wales, and it was ironical that he had to be replaced near the end of the match by

Left *J. Davies (Wales), tackled by C. R. Andrew (England) passes the ball to Bleddyn Bowen, who goes on to touch down.*

Right *'It's my try!' Bowen announces his score but there is no happy ending to the Twickenham match: Wales lose 21-18.*

Ray Giles. Terry's professional debut ended the same way. With the 'own goals' conceded by Norster and Richard Moriarty, the National squad was by now badly weakened particularly amongst the forwards. Stuart Evans, the young prop, joined the unavailable list by breaking an ankle.

The first Five Nations match was at Twickenham against opponents whose record in the fixture over forty years had been disastrous, but on this occasion the Welsh forward weakness was badly exposed. There were three new caps in the young South Glamorgan Institute centre, John Devereux, the Swansea scrum-half, Robert Jones, and the veteran Newport lock, David Waters. England 'cleaned out' the line-outs and were stronger scrummagers, but even so Wales scored the only try through Bowen in a narrow defeat (21-18).

Next it was Cardiff, with Scotland trying for a third successive win there and the home team can count themselves lucky that they did not succeed. Thorburn's magnificent boot (fifteen points) kept Wales in contention and his best effort was a massive penalty from at least sixty metres. But Scotland did score three tries to one, and several Welsh players thought that they had scored a fourth! Again, the scrummaging was not good, but Perkins and Waters did better in the line-outs without dominating. In the mauls and rucks the more athletic Scots were superior and deserved better from the fates.

A poor first-half effort in Dublin left Wales trailing (4-12), but after the change the team did perform well and a good try by Phil Davies, which supplemented a fine earlier effort from Lewis, helped the team to an uneasy but satisfying win. Thorburn, with another eleven points, was again on target when it mattered.

The French came to Cardiff, they saw enough and conquered well. The try-count was four-nil in their favour and again it was Thorburn who kept Wales in striking distance with five more penalty-goals, which left him with a Welsh record of fifty two points for the tournament. But the home team was not helped by some poor tackling, which allowed the French at least two avoidable tries.

So, it would seem on paper that the season was not too bad, there being three victories to set against two defeats, but signs of a new 'Golden Era' in Welsh Rugby were just not there. Promising backs certainly were in evidence both within and without the National team, and Jonathan Davies already looks a great player with John Devereux and Robert Jones highly promising. But new forwards are a priority to ensure that there is an adequate supply of the ball; athleticism is another requirement.

Clubs

Pontypool again dominated the club scene and won both the Western Mail and Whitbread Merit Tables comfortably. They were an efficient outfit

The talented back, Robert Jones (Wales), beats a tackle by Ronan Kearney (Ireland) in Dublin on 15th February. He is a man to watch in the future.

based mainly on forward power, with Graham Price, Perkins and Brown outstanding. Price did, however, blot his copybook by being sent off for the first time in a distinguished career in a late season game at Coventry. Perkins has now retired from International Rugby, but Brown will no doubt hope to attract the selectors' attention again, having been dropped by them after the Scotland game. It must be said that although the wings were given plenty of scoring chances it was not generally true to say that 'Pooler' were an attractive team to watch, and their running feud with Newbridge was something the Welsh game could do without.

Glamorgan Wanderers were the next best team in both Merit Tables and they also managed a total of one thousand points, but their young full-back, Hembury, was their only player to gain recognition and he went on the South Pacific tour.

Cardiff and Newport contested the Schweppes final and both had their days. Swansea and Neath looked good at times but lacked consistency, as did Bridgend. Neath twice beat the all-conquering Pontypool, but went out of the Schweppes Cup at

home to Glamorgan Wanderers. It was good to see Penarth improve, but they are still usually on the proverbial 'hiding to nothing' at most times.

For other clubs the season provided varied fortunes. South Wales Police on their day were a match for anyone and Ebbw Vale had a fine spell after Christmas, but Cross Keys (in their centenary year), Tredegar, Abertillery and Pontypridd usually struggled for success. Maesteg could be reasonably happy with their progress but Aberavon had little cause for satisfaction apart from their cup success at Llanelli, a team that also experienced its ups and downs.

If the pools companies were ever to follow Rugby results they could thrive in modern Wales, where apart from Pontypool, many teams are very inconsistent. A proper new challenger for the Gwent club is badly needed. Perhaps club loyalty is less evident than before and regular moves by players do not help in team planning.

Schools, Youths and Universities

Owing to industrial action by teachers, the schools played no representative matches against the touring Australians. This was a considerable blow and results were very mediocre when a team was

inally selected. A victory over Scotland could be
et against defeat by England.

The youth team lost badly against France, but
ad a very useful win over England some time
ater. Booth, the scrum-half who has played for
Neath, looks a fine prospect.

The Welsh Universities should have won the
Miller-Buckley Triple Crown, but after convincing
wins over England and Scotland they floundered
n Ireland, whose team took the trophy on a try-
count. Domestically, the universities did well with
University College, Swansea performing bravely
n the Schweppes Welsh Challenge Cup, which is
covered later in this section.

The Swansea Polytechnic lost its grip on their
trophy, which was eventually won by Leeds; but it
was an exceptionally bad winter for cancelled fixtures and this must have hampered preparations.

Summary

The World Cup will dominate all talking and
thinking over the next twelve months. Wales have
the backs, but forwards must be found if any impression is to be made in the Antipodes next year.

Whitbread Merit Table

	P	W	D	L	F	A	%
Pontypool	25	23	0	2	626	238	92.00
Glamorgan Wanderers	17	12	0	5	267	228	70.58
Neath	26	18	0	8	543	281	69.23
Newport	27	17	3	7	548	291	68.51
Swansea	23	13	1	9	432	328	58.69
Aberavon	28	15	2	11	410	403	57.14
Maesteg	21	11	0	10	304	326	52.38
Llanelli	23	11	1	11	486	313	50.00
Newbridge	24	10	2	10	342	395	50.00
Bridgend	27	12	0	15	399	419	44.44
Ebbw Vale	23	9	1	12	293	415	41.30
Abertillery	22	7	0	15	248	442	31.81
London Welsh	11	3	1	7	185	221	31.81
Pontypridd	24	7	0	17	272	344	29.16
Cross Keys	24	6	0	18	267	561	25.00
Penarth	19	3	0	16	191	434	15.78

The £150 Club of the Month award was won by Swansea.
They scored 21 tries in four games

Team tries

245	Pontypool	138	Maesteg
218	Llanelli	135	Aberavon
198	South Wales Police	118	Newbridge
187	Neath	111	Cross Keys
175	Bridgend	96	Ebbw Vale
164	Glamorgan Wanderers	92	Pontypridd
162	Swansea	91	Tredegar
144	Newport	86	Penarth
140	Cardiff	70	London Welsh

Western Mail Championship

	P	W	D	L	F	A	%
Pontypool	40	35	0	5	1027	402	87.50
Glamorgan Wanderers	33	24	1	8	648	411	74.24
Cardiff	38	27	1	10	834	513	72.36
Neath	46	29	1	16	902	556	64.13
Newport	40	22	4	14	732	470	60.00
Aberavon	35	20	2	13	535	452	60.00
Swansea	41	24	1	16	860	588	59.75
South Wales Police	38	21	3	14	847	530	59.21
Llanelli	42	23	3	16	982	632	58.33
Tredegar	30	16	1	13	417	462	55.00
Bridgend	43	23	1	19	704	627	54.65
Maesteg	35	17	1	17	543	554	50.00
Newbridge	41	16	5	20	605	656	45.12
Ebbw Vale	38	16	2	20	494	644	44.73
Penarth	32	11	0	21	404	624	34.37
Cross Keys	33	10	0	23	447	751	30.30
Pontypridd	41	12	0	29	362	815	29.26
London Welsh	29	6	3	20	424	612	25.86
Abertillery	35	8	0	27	407	707	22.85

Leading try scorers

39	Glen Webbe (*Bridgend*) (includes 1 for Neath)	18	Clive Barber (*South Wales Police*)
35	Mark Brinkworth (*South Wales Police*)	18	Shaun McWilliams (*Newport*)
28	Nick Ward (*Glamorgan Wanderers*)	18	Owain Williams (*Glamorgan Wanderers*)
27	Goff Davies (*Pontypool*)	17	Allan Bateman (*Maesteg*)
25	Bleddyn Taylor (*Pontypool*)	17	Eamonn Holland (*Glamorgan Wanderers*)
24	Carwyn Davies (*Llanelli*)	17	Leighton May (*Cross Keys*)
24	Andrew Hughes (*South Wales Police*)	17	Nigel Whitehouse (*South Wales Police*)
24	Chris Huish (*Pontypool*)	16	Roger Bidgood (*Pontypool*)
22	Paul Moriarty (*Swansea*)	16	Mark Brown (*Pontypool*)
23	Peter Hopkins (*Llanelli*)		
21	Graham Davies (*Neath*)	16	Andy Francis (*Glamorgan Wanderers*)
21	Martin Gravelle (*Llanelli*)	16	Ray Giles (*Aberavon*)
21	Adrian Hadley (*Cardiff*)		
20	Arthyr Emyr (*Swansea*)		

Leading points scorers

420	Gary Pearce (*Llanelli*)	232	Geraint John (*Bridgend*)
338	Gareth Davies (*Cardiff*)	229	Paul Thornburn (*Neath*)
324	Mark Hambury (*Glamorgan Wanderers*)	191	Richard Bevan (*Swansea*) (includes 83 for Aberavon)
321	Roddy Crane (*Cross Keys*) (includes 20 for Pontypridd, 3 for Penarth)	191	Paul Turner (*Newport*)
309	Peter Lewis (*Pontypool*)	159	Gwyn Evans (*Maesteg*)
285	Brian Bolderson (*Tredegar*)	159	Bleddyn Taylor (*Pontypool*)
278	Peter Goodfellow (*Newbridge*)	156	Glen Webbe (*Bridgend*) (includes 4 for Neath)

Schweppes Welsh Challenge Cup

First Round

16th November 1986

Aberavon Quins	7	Treorchy	6
British Steel (Port Talbot)	6	Carmarthen	15
Burry Port	4	Cross Keys	6
Caerleon	9	Oakdale	12
Cardigan	7	Caldicot	6
Cilfynydd	22	Penygroes	0
Dunvant	4	Pontypridd	0
Gilfach Goch	3	South Wales Police	22
Glamorgan Wanderers	8	Carmarthen Athletic	6
Kenfig Hill	16	Whitland	7
Kidwelly	8	Tenby United	6
Llantrisant	13	Ystradgynlais	7
Mountain Ash	18	Blaengarw	9
Mumbles	7	Seven Sisters	15
Narberth	0	Aberavon	14
Neath	26	Old Illtydians	9
Neath Athletic	12	Gowerton	6
Newport	28	Abertillery	8
Pencoed	10	Gorseinon	3
Pill Harriers	9	Ebbw Vale	27
Pontyclun	0	Bridgend	46
Pontypool United	13	Penarth	18
Pyle	21	Ruthin	7
Risca	6	Pontypool	28
South Glamorgan Institute	16	Cardiff	25
Swansea	22	Llanharan	6
Tredegar	3	University College, Swansea	12
Tumble	6	Maesteg	11
Vardre	3	Newbridge	19
Wrexham	10	Llandovery	6
Ystrad Rhondda	3	Rumney	21

26th November 1985

Pontarddulais	12	Llanelli	37

Result of the Round

Tredegar	3	University College, Swansea	12

For once all the senior sides had survived the preliminary rounds, but two were to go out here to lesser mortals – Tredegar at home to University College, Swansea and Pontypridd at Dunvant. Other senior casualties were Abertillery at Newport, but Penarth advanced at Pontypool United to earn a tie at Neath.

Second Round

21st December 1985

Aberavon Quins	9	Aberavon	36
Bridgend	59	Oakdale	9
Cardiff	24	Pencoed	3
Cardigan	0	South Wales Police	40
Ebbw Vale	16	Cross Keys	9
Glamorgan Wanderers	16	Rumney	6
Kenfig Hill	4	Pontypool	5
Kidwelly	6	Swansea	1
Llanelli	48	Llantrisant	0
Neath	17	Penarth	9
Newbridge	3	Neath Athletic	10
Newport	35	Mountain Ash	12
University College, Swansea	0	Dunvant	10
Wrexham	36	Pyle	10

26th December 1985

Carmarthen	0	Seven Sisters	9

14th January 1986

Cilfynydd	6	Maesteg	17

Result of the Round

Newbridge	3	Neath Athletic	10

Struggling Newbridge were the only senior team to be 'giant-killed' – at home to Neath Athletic. Other senior departures were Penarth, gallantly at Neath, and Cross Keys at Ebbw Vale. Swansea had a struggle at Kidwelly, but on the whole the 'big-boys' had few problems.

Third Round

25th January 1986

Aberavon	19	Seven Sisters	3
Bridgend	38	Dunvant	0
Llanelli	27	Pontypool	6
Maesteg	9	South Wales Police	4
Neath	9	Glamorgan Wanderers	12
Neath Athletic	0	Cardiff	22
Newport	29	Wrexham	0
Swansea	21	Ebbw Vale	12

Result of the Round

Neath	9	Glamorgan Wanderers	12

Glamorgan Wanderers, who do not normally make any impact on Cup matters, were the heroes with a gallant win at the Gnoll. Neath also lost their other team, Athletic, to a defeat at home by Cardiff. The outstanding match of the round saw the holders, Llanelli, trounce Pontypool at Stradey Park. The junior teams finally bowed out bravely and form in general, the surprise apart, followed expectations.

Fourth Round

22nd February 1986

Llanelli	10	Aberavon	1

8th March 1986

Cardiff	21	Glamorgan Wanderers	12
Maesteg	9	Bridgend	9
(Bridgend go through as try scorers)			
Newport	10	Swansea	1

Llanelli	10	Aberavon	11

Out went the holders, Llanelli, beaten at home by Aberavon, whose Ray Giles scored the winning try and generally commanded the match. Maesteg lost at home to Bridgend on the strength of the fact that the visitors scored the only try of the match. Newport beat Swansea in a tough encounter and Gareth Davies of Cardiff scored all their points against Glamorgan Wanderers.

Semi-finals

2nd March 1986

Aberavon (at Cardiff)	6	Newport	15
Bridgend (at Swansea)	9	Cardiff	17

The teams were level at half-time in Cardiff, but Newport's powerful pack took charge and tries by Turner and Collins were enough. Turner scored the other points. Cardiff were too strong for Bridgend with outside-half, Gareth Davies, outstanding; he scored eleven points for his side.

Final

Saturday, 26th April 1986, at National Stadium, Cardiff

Cardiff	28	Newport	21

Tries: Hadley (3), O'Brien (1)
Penalty-goals: Davies (2)
Conversions: Davies (3)
Half-time: 19-6

Tries: Pitt, Turner, Collins (1 each)
Penalty-goal: Turner
Conversions: Turner (3)

Cardiff: M. Rayer; G. Cordle, A. Donovan, M. Ring, A. Hadley; G. Davies, N. O'Brien; J. Whitefoot, A Phillips (*captain*), I. Eidman, O. Golding, K. Edwards, R. Norster, G. Roberts, J. Scott

Newport: R. Knight; M. Batten, D. Pitt, P. Daniel, J. White; P. Turner, N. Callard; J. Rawlins, M. Watkins (*captain*), R. Morgan, R. Collins, J. Widdecombe, A. Perry, R. Powell, D. Waters

Referee: K. Rowlands (*Ynysybwl*)

This was not the grim, defensive encounter many had predicted it would be and a fine match was won by Cardiff thanks largely to their first-half opportunism, which brought them a thirteen-point lead. This was increased after the change-over to twenty two points before a brave and late rally by Newport made the final tally look respectable. This was Cardiff's fourth win in six seasons.

In the first half Cardiff were quickly ahead through a try by Hadley, who collected a shrewd punt by Gareth Davies and went over for the latter to convert; he also kicked a penalty before O'Brien ended some intense Cardiff pressure with a determined effort for their second try. In between all this, Pitt had followed up his own punt to punish indecision by Davies and Rayer and go over for a try, which Turner converted; this reduced the deficit temporarily to three points, which were soon lost to that O'Brien try and another piece of opportunism by Hadley.

After the break Cardiff continued to pressurize Newport. The lead was extended through a penalty-goal by Gareth Davies and a try from Hadley (his third) after fine running by several Cardiff players including Ring, who played well after having spent much of the season out through injury. Newport's late rally was started by clever play from Turner, who was able to gather his own punt and run over in the corner. He converted that well, as he also did for a try by Collins, whose determination beat off some indecisive tackling by a relaxed Cardiff defence.

Cardiff were the better side and deserved victory, but Newport's late points rush showed that no-one can relax even when victory would seem to be assured. For that they deserved credit and it made for a good match, which Mr Rowlands handled well.

Welsh Cup Finals

Welsh Brewers Cup

Tonmawr (at Cardiff Arms Park)	9	Cardiff International AC	6

WWRU President's Cup

Bonymaen (at Stradey Park, Llanelli)	12	Tumble	19

Wrexham Lager Trophy

Tondu (at Aberavon Athletic)	20	Ynysybwl	15

Welsh Youth Cup

Cardiff (at National Ground, Cardiff)	3	Llanelli	19

Mid-Wales Emlyn Hooson Cup

Newtown (Newtown win for sixth successive season)	23	Welshpool	15

Welsh Counties Cup

Glamorgan (at The Gnoll, Neath. Breconshire win title for the first time)	12	Breconshire	16

President's Cup

Cardiff Athletic (at Glamorgan Wanderers, Ely, Cardiff)	21	St Peter's	16

Enoch Lewis Cup

Heol-y-Cyw	32	Tondu	3

C. G. Davies Cup

Neath Athletic	4	Bryncoch	17

Silver Ball

Winners: St Peter's

Cup Winners, 1972-85

at National Ground, Cardiff

1972	Neath	15	Llanelli	9
1973	Llanelli	30	Cardiff	7
1974	Llanelli	12	Aberavon	10
1975	Llanelli	15	Aberavon	6
1976	Llanelli	15	Swansea	4
1977	Newport	16	Cardiff	15
1978	Swansea	13	Newport	9
1979	Bridgend	18	Pontypridd	12

1980	Bridgend	15	Swansea	
1981	Cardiff	14	Bridgend	
1982	Cardiff	12	Bridgend	1

(Cardiff won by scoring most tries)

1983	Pontypool	18	Swansea	
1984	Cardiff	24	Neath	1
1985	Llanelli	15	Cardiff	1

Llanelli have five wins, Cardiff four, Bridgend two, Neath Newport, Swansea and Pontypool one each. Cardiff have playe in the most finals (seven), but Llanelli, having played in si have lost only once.

Welsh Clubs

Aberavon

Address: Talbot Athletic Ground, Manor Street, Port Talbot, West Glamorgan. Tel: (0639) 882427/886038
Founded: 1876
Secretary: W. Lewis, 82 Talbot Road, Port Talbot, West Glamorgan SA13 1LA. Tel: (0639) 882427/886038
Fixtures secretary: J. S. Dolan, Oakwood House, Oakwood Avenue, Port Talbot, West Glamorgan. Tel: (0639) 882771
Captain 1985-86: R. Giles
Most capped player: A. J. Martin, 34 for Wales, 1 for British Lions
Colours: Red and black hoops/white/red
Directions to ground: M4 to Port Talbot. Ground is visible on left-hand side of road (from Junction 39)
Clubhouse: Usual facilities for playing side and social events
1st XV 1985-86: P 46 W 29 D 2 L 14 ab 1 F 836 A 539
  Aberavon had a modest season, but the club reached the last eight of the Schweppes Welsh Challenge Cup beating Llanelli, the holders, (away) in the process. Roy Giles made one replacement appearance for Wales and was captain of the Wales 'B' touring side in Italy.

Abertillery

Address: The Park, Oak Street, Abertillery, Gwent. Tel: (0495) 212226
Founded: 1884
Secretary: M. Lewis, Wildacre, Cwm Farm Lane, Abertillery, Gwent NP3 2PA. Tel: (0495) 213227 (h), (0495) 212555 (hq)
Fixtures secretary: A. Rees, 63 Powell Street, Abertillery, Gwent. Tel: (0495) 212627
Captain 1985-86: G. Everett
Most capped players: H. J. Morgan, 27 for Wales, 4 for British Lions; A. E. I. Pask, 26 for Wales, 8 for British Lions
Colours: Green and white or all green
Directions to ground: Junction 27 of M4. Take A467, then A4048 to Newbridge. Through Newbridge to Abertillery, where the park is in a prominent situation just outside the town centre
Clubhouse: Usual facilities for players, members and spectators

1st XV 1985-86: P 42 W 14 D 0 L 28 F 564 A 777
  Abertillery had a very poor season and won only one-third o matches played, losing the rest.

Bridgend

Address: Brewery Field, Tondu Road, Bridgend, Mi Glamorgan. Tel: (0656) 2707, (0656) 59032
Founded: 1878
Secretary: W. A. D. Lawrie, 12 Hillsboro', Bridgend, Mi Glamorgan CF31 4DJ. Tel: (0656) 2911
Fixtures secretary: E. Jones, 21 Austin Avenue, Laleston Bridgend, Mid Glamorgan CF32 0LG. Tel: (0656) 56399
Captain 1985-86: G. P. Williams
Most capped players: J. P. R. Williams, 55 for Wales, 8 fo British Lions; S. P. Fenwick, 30 for Wales, 4 for British Lions
Colours: Blue and white stripes
Directions to ground: M4 to Junction 36; follow signs to tow centre. Located on Tondu Road after going round one-wa system. Left over bridge after cenotaph, on right
Clubhouse: Bars, lounge reception, changing-rooms
1st XV 1985-86: P 52 W 29 D 2 L 20 ab 1 F 984 A 68
  Bridgend had a mixed season overall, but did well to reac the Schweppes Welsh Challenge Cup semi-finals before bowin out to Cardiff, the eventual winners. Glen Webbe was selecte for the Pacific tour and became Wales' first black full Inte national. He scored thirty eight tries for the club during th 1985-86 season.

Cardiff

Address: Cardiff Arms Park, Westgate Street, Cardiff. Te (0222) 23546
Founded: 1876
Secretary: A. J. Priday, Cardiff Arms Park, Westgate Stree Cardiff. Tel: (0222) 23546
Fixtures secretary: Brian Mark, 7 Tygwyn Crescent, Penylar Cardiff. Tel: (0222) 483798
Captain 1985-86: A. Phillips

Most capped players: G. O. Edwards, 53 for Wales, 10 for British Lions; T. G. R. Davies, 46 for Wales, 5 for British Lions; G. I. Morgan, 29 for Wales, 4 for British Lions
Colours: Cambridge blue and black stripes/sky blue
Directions to ground: From BR and bus stations cross road to Westgate Street. Ground is at far end on left (behind National Stadium); or off Junction 32 of M4
Clubhouse: Full facilities for players, members and spectators
1st XV 1985-86: P 44 W 33 D 1 L 10 F 971 A 574

Victory in the final of the Schweppes Welsh Challenge Cup was a fine achievement; it was a fourth win in six seasons. Overall results were good with third place being attained in the Western Mail Championship. Welsh caps were won by Terry Holmes (before he went North), A. M. Hadley, J. Whitefoot and I. Eidman. Robert Norster missed the Five Nations matches but not against Fiji).

Cross Keys

Address: Pandy Park, Cross Keys, Gwent. Tel: (0495) 270289
Founded: 1885
Secretary: D. B. Evans, Glanant, 17 Caerphilly Close, Rhiwderin, Gwent NP1 9RB. Tel: (0633) 893070 (h), (0633) 892722 (w)
Fixtures secretary: A. Rumble, 10 Clyde Street, Risca, Gwent. Tel: (0633) 615068 (h), (0222) 753271 ext. 2537 (w)
Captain 1985-86: S. James
Most capped player: S. Morris, 19 for Wales
Colours: Black and white hoops
Directions to ground: Junction 27 of M4. A467 to Cross Keys. Pandy Park is prominently situated just outside the town centre
Clubhouse: Usual facilities for players, members and visitors
1st XV 1985-86: P 48 W 21 D 0 L 25 ab 2 F 768 A 886

Cross Keys in their centenary year had a miserable time with moderate results and problems with the access to the ground. One happy occasion was a 'Golden Oldies' match the evening before the Wales v. France game at Cardiff for veterans from the two countries; by all accounts a good time was had by all!

Ebbw Vale

Address: Eugene Cross Park, Ebbw Vale, Gwent. Tel: (0495) 302955/302157
Founded: 1880
Secretary: R. Powell, 68 Letchworth Road, Ebbw Vale, Gwent NP3 6LB. Tel: (0495) 304792
Fixtures secretary: C. Lapham, 5 Northfield Close, Caerleon, Gwent. Tel: (0633) 420823 (h), (0633) 420106 (w)
Captain 1985-86: N. Robinson
Most capped player: Denzil Williams, 36 for Wales, 5 for British Lions
Colours: Red, green and white
Directions to ground: Junction 27 of M4. A467 to Cross Keys. A4048 to Newbridge. A4046 to Ebbw Vale. Glamorgan CCC play at Eugene Cross Park which is prominently situated by the side of Ebbw River
Clubhouse: Usual facilities for players, members and visitors
1st XV 1985-86: P 46 W 23 D 2 L 21 F 676 A 707

Ebbw Vale had a moderate season and did nothing of note in any competition.

Glamorgan Wanderers

Address: Memorial Ground, Ely, Cardiff. Tel: (0222) 591039
Founded: 1893
Secretary: G. W. Thomas, 4 St John's Crescent, Whitchurch,

Cardiff CF4 7AF. Tel: (0222) 620853 (h), (0222) 407219 (w)
Fixtures secretary: D. Lloyd, 62 Coryton Rise, Whitchurch, Cardiff. Tel: (0222) 628858 (h), (0222) 397571 (w)
Captain 1985-86: J. Davies
Colours: Cambridge blue, black and white
Directions to ground: West Cardiff rear Ely BR station (on A4119)
Clubhouse: Excellent clubhouse facilities for players, members and spectators
1st XV 1985-86: P 45 W 35 D 1 L 9 F 1002 A 509

Glamorgan Wanderers enjoyed a tremendous season – the best in the club's history. Second place was achieved in both the leading Welsh Merit Tables and the last eight was reached in the Schweppes Welsh Challenge Cup which ended with honourable defeat at neighbours Cardiff. Mark Hembury was selected for Wales' South Pacific tour and was likely to become the club's first capped player. The team was awarded a Whitbread 'Team of the Month' award in *Rugby World & Post* for February 1986. This season also marked the first time that the club have reached 1000 points.

Llanelli

Address: Stradey Park, Llanelli, Dyfed. Tel: (0554) 774060
Founded: 1872
Secretary: Ken Jones, Homestead, 6 Ael-y-Bryn Drive, Llanelli, Dyfed SA15 4LE. Tel: (0554) 755607
Fixtures secretary: J. D. W. Maclean, Ro-Fawr Farm, Dryslwyn, Carmarthen, Dyfed. Tel: (055 84) 505
Captain 1985-86: P. May
Most capped players: J. J. Williams, 30 for Wales, 7 for British Lions; P. Bennett, 29 for Wales, 8 for British Lions; W. D. Thomas, 25 for Wales, 6 for British Lions; N. R. Gale, 25 for Wales
Colours: Scarlet with white collar/navy blue
Directions to ground: M4 to Junction 48; follow signs into town centre. Then follow signposts to Stradey Park
Clubhouse: Excellent general facilities
1st XV 1985-86: P 51 W 31 D 3 L 17 F 1337 A 703

Llanelli had a fair season, but failed to win anything; the Schweppes Welsh Challenge Cup was lost at home when Aberavon came and left with a narrow win. David Pickering captained Wales in the Five Nations Championship and on the Pacific tour. Other caps were won by Phil Lewis and P. T. Davies.

Maesteg

Address: The Old Parish Ground, Llynvi Road, Maesteg, Mid Glamorgan. Tel: (0656) 782283
Founded: 1882
Secretary: Graham Rhys Court, End Bungalow, Priory Terrace, Maesteg, Mid Glamorgan. Tel: (0656) 737004 (h), (0639) 883161 ext. 3222 (w)
Fixtures secretary: G. M. Evans, 26 Shelley Drive, Cefn Glas, Bridgend, Mid Glamorgan. Tel: (0656) 5037 (h), (0443) 402867 (w)
Captain 1985-86: P. Francis
Most capped player: G. Evans, 10 for Wales, 2 for British Lions
Colours: Black and amber
Directions to ground: Junction 39 (M4). A4107 to Maesteg. In Maesteg town go through town to bus depot (on hill top). Ground next door
Clubhouse: Good facilities for players, members and visitors
1st XV 1985-86: P 48 W 29 D 2 L 17 F 915 A 656

In a fair season Maesteg reached the last eight of the Schweppes Welsh Challenge Cup and had a reasonable overall record.

Neath

Address: The Gnoll, Gnoll Park Road, Neath, West Glamorgan. Tel: (0639) 4420
Founded: 1871
Secretary: Allan Benjamin, 24 The Pines, Brynamlwg Parc, Penscynor, Neath, West Glamorgan SA10 8AL. Tel: (0639) 2172 (h), (0639) 850237 (w)
Fixtures secretary: Berwyn Davies, 48 Abernant Road, Aberdare, Mid Glamorgan. Tel: (0685) 876857 (h), (0685) 874629 (w)
Captain 1985-86: Jonathan Davies
Coach 1985-86: Brian Thomas
Most capped players: W. D. Morris, 34 for Wales; J. R. G. Stephens, 32 for Wales, 2 for British Lions
Colours: All black with Maltese Cross or red
Directions to ground: M4 to Junction 41. A474 to Neath (through Briton Ferry). From the A465 road north of Neath the ground is clearly visible
Clubhouse: Facilities for players, members and visitors
1st XV 1985-86: P 54 W 36 D 1 L 17 F 1136 A 619

After a good spell Neath had a slump and were surprisingly eliminated from the Schweppes Welsh Challenge Cup at home by Glamorgan Wanderers. However, the final, overall results were good. Jonathan Davies won numerous 'Player of the Year' awards (including that of *Rugby World & Post*) as he continued to look very good. Paul Thorburn also played in all Wales' matches; he broke all his country's Five Nations records for a season's work.

Newbridge

Address: Welfare Ground, Bridge Street, Newbridge, Gwent. Tel: (0495) 243247
Founded: 1890
Secretary: B. Wellington, 11 Treowen Road, Newbridge, Gwent NP1 4DL. Tel: (0495) 243525 (h), (0633) 65491 (w)
Fixtures secretary: R. Morgan, 30 Homeleigh, Newbridge, Gwent.
Captain 1985-86: J. Stokes
Most capped player: D. Hayward, 15 for Wales, 3 for British Lions
Colours: Sky blue and black or red
Directions to ground: Junction 27 (M4). A467 through Risca. A4048 through Cross Keys into Newbridge; ground is by dual carriageway on Risca side
Clubhouse: Usual facilities for players, members and visitors
1st XV 1985-86: P 48 W 22 D 5 L 21 F 737 A 694

Newbridge did well to break even during a difficult season. It is hoped that their feud with Pontypool will soon end even though from afar it would seem that they were not the guilty party. Games played in bad spirit do Rugby's name no good.

Newport

Address: Rodney Parade, Newport, Gwent. Tel: (0633) 58193/59649
Founded: 1874
Secretary: D. A. G. Ackerman, Greystones, 18 Canberra Crescent, Newport, Gwent. Tel: (0633) 66626 (h), (0633) 271288 ext. 263 (w)
Fixtures secretary: R. Atkins, 644 Chepstow Road, Newport, Gwent. Tel: (0633) 275222 (h), (0633) 273081 (w)
Captain 1985-86: M. Watkins
Most capped players: K. J. Jones, 44 for Wales, 3 for British Lions; B. V. Meredith, 34 for Wales, 8 for British Lions; B. Price, 32 for Wales, 4 for British Lions

Colours: Black and amber
Directions to ground: Junction 27 (M4) into Newport. Near town centre on east side of Usk
Clubhouse: Usual excellent facilities for players, members and visitors
1st XV 1985-86: P 49 W 29 D 4 L 15 ab 1 F 910 A 53

Newport had a season of troughs and peaks with the latter including a fine fight in the final of the Schweppes Welsh Challenge Cup and the good form of Paul Turner, among others. The bad news was a poor disciplinary record which saw the team involved in two very bad brawls – against Bristol and the Fijians; in the former the referee, George Crawford, walked off the field. Three players were also sent off during the season.

Penarth

Address: Athletic Grounds, Lavernock Road, Penarth, South Glamorgan. Tel: (0222) 708402
Founded: 1880
Secretary: Cyril Lewis, 3 Birch Lane, The Paddocks, Penarth, South Glamorgan. Tel: (0222) 700156 (h), (0222) 44531 (w)
Fixtures secretary: K. G. Bush, 12 Timbers Road, Roath, Cardiff. Tel: (0222) 482254
Captain 1985-86: R. McPherson
Most capped player: J. Bassett, 15 for Wales
Colours: Royal blue or blue and white hoops
Directions to ground: Junction 32 (M4). Ground is near Cefn Mably public house
Clubhouse: Facilities for members, players and visitors
1st XV 1985-86: P 41 W 17 D 1 L 22 ab 1 F 566 A 73

Penarth, under the inspiring leadership of R. McPherson, had a greatly improved season. Among the stars who turned out for them was the former Wales lock, Allan Martin. The Barbarians were met for the last time, which was a sad event.

Pontypool

Address: Pontypool Park, Pontypool, Gwent. Tel: (049 55) 349
Founded: 1901
Secretary: R. Jeremiah, 138 Blaendare Road, Pontypool, Gwent NP4 5RT. Tel: (049 55) 4120 (h)
Fixtures secretary: K. Childs, 177 Henllys Way, St Dials, Cwmbran, Gwent. Tel: (0633) 633820
Captain 1985-86: S. J. Perkins
Most capped player: G. Price, 41 for Wales, 12 for British Lions
Colours: Red, white and black hoops/royal blue
Directions to ground: Junction 26 (M4). A4051 to Pontypool. Pontypool Park is near town centre
Clubhouse: Headquarters are at Elm House, Park Road, Pontypool. Tel: (049 55) 2524
1st XV 1985-86: P 51 W 45 D 0 L 6 F 1485 A 492

By any standards this was another very fine season for 'Pooler' although the Cup provided an early exit at the hands of Llanelli. As adequate consolation was victory in both the Western Mail Championship (for the third season in a row) and the Whitbread Merit Table, and the selection for Wales of Perkins and Brown. It is hoped that the dispute with Newbridge will end soon.

Pontypridd

Address: Sardis Road, Pwllgwaun, Pontypridd, Mid Glamorgan CF37 1EU. Tel: (0443) 405006
Founded: 1876

Secretary: Stan Thomas, 11 Llandraw Road, Maesycoed, Pontypridd, Mid Glamorgan CF37 1EU. Tel: (0443) 404450 (h), (0443) 506135 (w)
Fixtures secretary: G. Gittins, 9 Hilltop Crescent, The Common, Pontypridd, Mid Glamorgan CF37 4AD. Tel: (0443) 404959 (h)
Captain 1985-86: J. O'Callaghan
Most capped player: R. J. Robins, 13 for Wales, 4 for British Lions
Colours: Black and white hoops or red
Directions to ground: Junction 32 (M4). A470 through Caerphilly to Pontypridd. Sardis Road runs along the River Taff
Clubhouse: Usual facilities. Tel: (0443) 407170 (dressing-rooms)
1st XV 1985-86: P 47 W 15 D 0 L 32 F 550 A 882
   With only fifteen matches won out of forty seven played, this was a poor season.

South Glamorgan Institute

Address: Cyncoed Road, Cyncoed, Cardiff. Tel: (0222) 55111
Secretary: Leighton Davies, 167 Park Street, Bridgend, Mid Glamorgan CF31 4BB. Tel: (0656) 3715 (h), (0222) 55111 ext. 3378 (w)
Fixtures secretary: Eifion Morgan, Tutor's Flat, South Glamorgan Institute of Higher Education, Cyncoed, Cardiff. Tel: (0222) 754864 (h), (0222) 755755 (w)
Most capped player: There have been many capped players from the Institute, who have won most honours after leaving. The latest is J. A. Devereux with four recent appearances for Wales
Colours: Maroon and amber
Clubhouse: Changing-rooms, refreshments
   South Glamorgan Institute continued to produce stars (John Devereux is the latest) and they are now a top club in their own right. They won the British Colleges Cup.

South Wales Police

Address: Recreation Ground, Waterton Cross, Bridgend, Mid Glamorgan. Tel: (0685) 55555
Founded: 1969
Secretary: David W. Rees, 6 Heol Trelales, Laleston, Bridgend, Mid Glamorgan CF32 0HW. Tel: (0656) 67094 (h), (0656) 55555 ext. 247 (w)
Fixtures secretary: Supt W. R. Morgan, MBE, Hawen, Corntown, near Bridgend, Mid Glamorgan. Tel: (0656) 3665 (h), (0639) 883101 ext. 203 (w)
Captain 1985-86: S. Sutton
Most capped player: B. Bowen, 10 for Wales
Colours: Red/white/royal blue
Directions to ground: Junction 35 (M4). Take A473 to Bridgend. Rugby ground is on left at Waterton Cross
Clubhouse: The Police Club at Bridgend has very good facilities in every aspect
1st XV 1985-86: P 47 W 28 D 3 L 15 ab 1 F 1093 A 592
   South Wales Police had a very good season and the club is now a major force in Welsh Rugby. At times discipline by the players was not good and two were sent off against Rosslyn Park, where the supporters did fine work to repair the damage caused. Bleddyn Bowen became the club's most capped player by playing for Wales in all the season's Internationals. He should have added to his figure of ten after going on tour with Wales to Fiji, Tonga and Western Samoa.

Swansea

Address: St Helens Ground, Swansea, West Glamorgan. Tel: (0792) 466872 (dressing-rooms), (0792) 464918 (club office)
Founded: 1874
Secretary: D. P. Price, c/o Club Office, The Pavilion, Bryn Road, Swansea, West Glamorgan SA2 0AR. Tel: (0792) 464918
Fixtures secretary: Vivian Dvies, c/o The Pavilion (as above)
Captain 1985-86: M. Davies
Most capped players: T. M. Davies, 38 for Wales, 8 for British Lions; R. M. Owen, 35 for Wales; D. I. E. Bebb, 34 for Wales, 8 for British Lions
Colours: All white or red and black
Directions to ground: Junction 41 (M4) at Briton Ferry. Left over bridge, follow A483 into Swansea. Follow signposts for Mumbles. Ground is on right in Mumbles Road
Clubhouse: Excellent with all facilities (social club tel: (0792) 466593)
1st XV 1985-86: P 48 W 29 D 1 L 18 F 990 A 660
   Swansea had a patchy season with, for them, a moderate overall record, but a semi-final place in the Schweppes Welsh Cup was a good performance. Robert Jones, a very promising scrum-half, made his debut for Wales, who also capped both Moriartys. The material and potential are there for success.

Swansea University

Address: University Ground, Sketty Lane, Seansea, West Glamorgan. Tel: (0792) 208317/205678
Secretary: R. G. Elias, Department of Zoology, University College, Singleton Park, Swansea, West Glamorgan SA2 8PP. Tel: (0792) 260688 (h), (0792) 295445 (w), (0792) 205678 ext. 83 (hq)
Fixtures secretary: G. B. Lewis, Department of Geography, University College, Singleton Park, Swansea, West Glamorgan SA2 8PP. Tel: (0792) 402434 (h), (0792) 295235 (w)
Colours: Green and white or red
Directions to ground: Follow signs to Mumbles passing Swansea RFC ground
   Swansea University distinguished themselves by dismissing Tredegar (away) in the Schweppes Welsh Challenge Cup, but once again their raid on the UAU Championship foundered during the knock-out stages.

Tredegar

Address: Tredegar Recreation Ground, Park Hill, Tredegar, Gwent. Tel: (049 525) 2879
Founded: 1899
Secretary: J. L. Williams, 5 Vale View, Tredegar, Gwent. Tel: (049 525) 2037 (h), (0495) 303401 ext. 213 (w)
Fixtures secretary: Ian Lewis, 24 Tredomen Terrace, Ystrad Mynach, Mid Glamorgan. Tel: (0443) 812322 (h)
Captain 1985-86: F. Jacas
Colours: Red, black and white or red
Directions to ground: Junction 27 (M4). A467 through Risca. A4045 through Cross Keys and Newbridge; go through Abertillery to Tredegar Park
1st XV 1985-86: P 41 W 26 D 1 L 14 F 647 A 538
   Apart from the shock of elimination from the Schweppes Cup by University College, Swansea, at home the club had a fair season with wins comfortably outnumbering defeats. Brian Bolderson scored 285 points.

FRANCE

Introduction

In twelve months, France have only lost twice at full International level. Their 'A' team won all its matches so that the FIRA title was retained comfortably, the 'B' team beat Wales but lost to Scotland and the other teams won all matches that mattered apart from a defeat for France's schoolboys at the hands of England. No-one could quibble about all that, but it should have been better at

the very top level and there ought to have been another Grand Slam title.

At club level the standard is probably now the highest in Europe, so why is it that France do not win a Grand Slam every season? The answer is simple – poor field discipline.

International Matches

The summer of 1985 saw France tour Argentina where the Test series was drawn each side winning a game for a total of thirty nine points each. Both were very hard matches and the French did well to recover after the first International was lost in Buenos Aires.

Back home, Japan toured in the autumn and were no match for anyone with the Tests providing a total of more than one hudred points for the French with none conceded. It was not very good practice for the forthcoming Five Nations matches nor was a game involving the 'B' teams of France and Wales, which the French (at home) won comfortably. Marocco was the star of this confrontation and he went on to do great things after the New Year, when four matches out of five at full level were won. So what happened to the other match?

That was the notorious affair at Murrayfield where the newcomer Gavin Hastings scored all Scotland's points from penalties against two tries and some successful kicks by the French; the ultimate winning score for the Scots was 18-17. On paper it sounds as if the better team lost and the media have worked hard to foster that impression, but better teams do not wantonly give away points and this is precisely what was done. A new and exciting looking side with a controversial choice of hooker and captain in that admirable prop, Dubroca, played well up to a point and started with an audacious piece of gamesmanship, bringing a dubious try by Berbizier.

Perhaps the fact that it was awarded persuaded the French that anything would be passed that day, but things soon went sour as stupid infringements

Philippe Sella, the devastating French centre from Agen, break, away against Wales in Cardiff.

were committed in easy scoring positions and the Scots soon took the lead, which was only briefly relinquished once. An excellent second-half try by Sella merely reduced the lead and in the end the French were probably lucky that their lack of discipline had only cost them eighteen points, since at least two more kickable awards were missed by the debutant Scotland full-back. The home team may never have looked like scoring a try, but who can blame them for not bothering to take chances when Santa Claus at the other end was giving them regular scoring opportunities to keep them in front? If a side is irresponsible it deserves to lose and it was hard on Scotland that credit for a good performance was denied them because of a possibly misleading final scoreline.

However, when France lose they are very dangerous in the next match and an Ireland team weakened by injuries to a couple of key players was no match for the French in Paris. Three glorious tries were scored after half-time and the French front-row, which had failed to subdue the Scots, had no such problems with the men in green. Sella, scorer of France's uncontroversial try in Edinburgh, went over for the third of the trio and it was a real gem, one of several during the campaign for Les Tricolors.

Cardiff is not usually an easy place for the French, but with two changes from the Irish game (Charvet and Bonneval replaced Chadebech and Estève) they again played with dash and enterprise against a poor Welsh team, which tackled and handled badly. Even so, it was a fine victory. Four tries to nil (including one from Sella) told their tale.

The same team faced England in the last game in Paris when four tries were scored, including a penalty-try, whilst one was conceded – for the first time in the Five Nations Championship for two years. Again, the front-row excelled, but the rest of the pack also did well, particularly the flankers, with the result that England, bravely though they played, were never in with a chance. Again, Sella (who had thus scored in every match) was on the scoresheet to prove himself the outstanding man of the whole campaign. Others to shine were Blanco (as usual), Laporte, Berbizier and the front-row.

But all that fine play produced only a share of the title with Scotland. A subsequent hard-earned win over Romania at Lille did not necessarily suggest that they were better than the Scots, who had also beaten the Eastern Europeans on their own territory, whilst their 'B' team had also won for a second successive time on French soil.

Indian winter? Guy Laporte (Graulhet and France) returned to the national team at fly-half at the age of thirty three.

So France departed on a world tour probably feeling, with some justification, that they were Europe's best, but, with at least seven of the team destined to be over thirty by 1987, the need for new faces was important. Also, it was interesting to guess how the French line-out ploy (scrum-half throwing in) would work under very tough playing conditions. Would their brilliant, but in two cases ageing, front-row be able to dominate in the southern hemisphere? After all, the strong man, Garuet, is well over thirty, and Dubroca is now almost a veteran, as are Condom, Joinel and Erbani plus the admirable fly-half Laporte, who made such a brave return to International Rugby.

So, again the Internationals promised well for the future, but with how many immediate changes? Also, can the team avoid donating matches to opponents through indiscipline? If they can they will be unbeatable, but recent history is against them.

The French Championship

The French Championship runs a long and harrowing course for some teams, which means that in the end the very best – and only those teams – reach the ultimate stages of the competition. The First Division is divided into two groups (A and B) and there is promotion and relegation between them. There are also lower divisions with the usual 'ups' and 'downs', so any team can, if successful and ambitious enough, reach the top level and play amongst the best.

The big surprise in the 'barrages' was the victory of Graulhet (the team of Laporte) over Valence, and Grenoble also beat the form book by disposing of the higher rated Aurillac. Those matches were on neutral grounds, but the last sixteen were played on each other team's ground in turn and there were some sensational aggregate scores.

Nearly all the teams had to come from deficits to go through with Montferrand only surviving on penalty-goals scored against Nice after the match had ended level. Graulhet again did well to go through narrowly against Narbonne, whilst Perpignan (against Racing Club de France) and Biarritz (the team of Blanco) scraped through against Narbonne.

The quarter-finals were all on neutral grounds and were all close matches bar one, in which Toulouse beat Biarritz (16-3). All of the other matches were very close and they saw Toulon (against Perpignan), Graulhet (against Montferrand, after extra time) and Agen (over Béziers) go through.

The semi-finals in Group A were in the end comfortable victories for Agen and Toulouse, although they both had their anxious moments. Eventually, after being behind at half-time (6-9), Agen ran away from Toulon (38-18), but Toulouse fumbled their way to success against Graulhet, who had done very well to reach this stage. The score was 21-12.

In Group B the finalists were Angoulême, whose locks included Maurice Colclough, and who won comfortably against Albi; but Voiron had to go to a lengthy period of extra time before advancing past Saint-Gaudens.

Amongst the famous clubs that failed to make the play-offs and thus faced the threat of relegation from Group A were Mont-de-Marsan, Boucau, Dax, Tulle, Tyrosse, La Voulte, Castres, Bourgoin and Bègles. It is a tough tournament!

Quarter-finals, Group A

Toulon (at Valence)	15	Perpignan	10
Agen (at Toulouse)	16	Béziers	12
Graulhet (after extra time, at Aurillac)	15	Montferrand	12
Toulouse (at Agen)	16	Biarritz	3

Semi-finals, Group B

Angoulême (at Merignac)	15	Albi	6
Voiron (after extra time, at Avignon)	9	Saint-Gaudens	3

Semi-finals, Group A

Toulouse (at Tarbes)	21	Graulhet	12
Agen (at Toulouse)	38	Toulon	18

Final, Group B
at Vichy

Angoulême	22	Voiron	17

Tries: Chasson, Dufau (1 each)
Dropped-goals: Larrieu (2)
Penalty-goals: Larrieu (2)
Conversion: Larrieu

Tries: Chevallier, Montagny, Font (1 each)
Penalty-goal: Darme
Conversion: Darme
Half-time: 15-9

Angoulême: Chaumeil; Chasson, Graulout, Dufau, Joussin; Larrieu, Vilquin; Vergez, Ducluzeau, Artero, Vialeix, Martin, Colclough (*England*), Giraud, Holmes

Voiron: Darme; Nemoz, Cretier, Galland, Font; Perez, Besson; Colussi, Poulet, Curzit, Gafforoni, Piarulli, Montagny, Chevallier, Rebout

Referee: M. Bertrand (*Languedoc*)

Final, Group A
Saturday, 24th May 1986, at Parc des Princes, Paris

Stade Toulousain	16	Agen	6

Try: Bonneval
Penalty-goals: Gabernet (1), Lopez (3)

Penalty-goals: Berot (2)
Half-time: 6-3

Stade Toulousain: S. Gabernet (*captain*); J.-M. Rancoule, E. Bonneval, D. Charvet, G. Noves; P. Rougé-Thomas, M. Lopez; G. Portolan, S. Laïrle, C. Portolan, T. Maset, J.-M. Giraud, J. M. Cadieu, K. Janik, A. Cigagna. *Replacements:* Santamans (19) and Lecompte (20) for G. Portolan and Cigagna, 64 minutes

Agen: P. Berot; E. Gleyze, P. Sella, P. Mothe, B. Lacombe; C. DeIarge, P. Berbizier; J.-L. Tolot, J.-L. Dupont, D. Dubroca (*captain*), J. Gratton, P. Pujade, B. Mazzer, B. Delbreil, D. Erbani. *Replacement:* Boué for Dubroca, 24 minutes (Berbizier took over as captain)

Referee: André Peytavin (*Ile de France*)

A dour and hard-fought match almost experienced tragedy in the twenty fourth minute when the Agen (and France) captain, Dubroca, was injured in a clash with Maset. Dubroca lost consciousness and appeared to have swallowed his tongue, but swift medical action saved his life and his final sufferings were none too serious.

However, the incident seemed to overshadow much of the rest of the game, which was being led at the time by a penalty-goal for Toulouse from Gabernet. Almost immediately Berot, with a penalty award, brought the scores level, but five minutes from the break Lopez regained the lead for Toulouse, the holders, with a short-range penalty award.

Soon after the restart Lopez converted another penalty, to which Berot replied with his second a few minutes later and the score remained that way until twelve minutes from time, during which period an award to Agen in a good position was ruined by some crazy folly from Erbani, which caused Mr Peytavin to reverse his original decision. Lopez then kicked another penalty and, in injury time, Bonneval seized on an error by Mothe to score the game's only try and bring victory for Toulouse; Bonneval ran in determined fashion to beat Sella's brave attempt at a tackle.

It seemed that too much was at stake in this match and defences were largely on top with the brilliant Sella for Agen having virtually no opportunities to show his abilities. In contrast, both Bonneval and Charvet contrived to look dangerous whenever they were in possession and the holders' scrum-half, Lopez, was the man of the match as he outshone the regular French scrum-half, Berbizier.

In a curtain-raising match Racing Club de France won the Cadets Championship by beating Narbonne in the final (19-4); the winners were the better team, but in the latter stages of the match there were some ugly brawls, which the referee should have penalized severely, but did not.

French Championship Winners, 1892-1985

1892	Racing Club de France	1901	Stade Français
1893	Stade Français	1902	Racing Club de France
1894	Stade Français	1903	Stade Français
1895	Stade Français	1904	Bordeaux UC
1896	Olympique de Paris	1905	Bordeaux UC
1897	Stade Français	1906	Bordeaux UC
1898	Stade Français	1907	Bordeaux UC
1899	Bordeaux UC	1908	Stade Français
1900	Racing Club de France	1909	Bordeaux UC

1910	FC Lyon	1952	Lourdes
1911	Bordeaux UC	1953	Lourdes
1912	Stade Toulousain	1954	Grenoble
1913	Bayonne	1955	Perpignan
1914	Perpignan	1956	Lourdes
1920	Tarbes	1957	Lourdes
1921	Perpignan	1958	Lourdes
1922	Stade Toulousain	1959	Racing Club de France
1923	Stade Toulousain	1960	Lourdes
1924	Stade Toulousain	1961	Béziers
1925	Perpignan	1962	Agen
1926	Stade Toulousain	1963	Mont-de-Marsan
1927	Stade Toulousain	1964	Pau
1928	Pau	1965	Agen
1929	Quillan	1966	Agen
1930	Agen	1967	Montauban
1931	Toulon	1968	Lourdes
1932	Lyon Olympique U	1969	Bègles
1933	Lyon Olympique U	1970	La Voulte
1934	Bayonne	1971	Béziers
1935	Biarritz	1972	Béziers
1936	Narbonne	1973	Tarbes
1937	Vienne	1974	Béziers
1938	Perpignan	1975	Béziers
1939	Biarritz	1976	Agen
1940-42	No competition	1977	Béziers
1943	Bayonne	1978	Béziers
1944	Perpignan	1979	Narbonne
1945	Agen	1980	Béziers
1946	Pau	1981	Béziers
1947	Stade Toulousain	1982	Agen
1948	Lourdes	1983	Béziers
1949	Castres	1984	Béziers
1950	Castres	1985	Toulouse
1951	Carmaux		

During the First World War the Championship was replaced by 'La Coupe de L'Espérance'.

Lourdes won the 1968 final on a superior try-count against Toulon. The match was drawn (9-9).

The French Cup

Last eight

Béziers	21	Toulouse	3
(at Carcassonne)			
Aurillac	32	Narbonne	12
(at Albi)			
Grenoble	23	Tarbes	3
(at Nîmes)			

Hyères beat Bergerac at Foix, no score given

Semi-finals

Aurillac	26	Hyères	15
(at Castlenaudary)			
Béziers	20	Grenoble	15
(at Valence)			

Final

| Béziers | 40 | Aurillac | 9 |
| (at Castres) | | | |

AUSTRALIA

After the euphoria of the Grand Slam tour of Britain late in 1984, anything short of a miracle would have been an anticlimax. There were no miracles and the 1985 season was one of transition, with the National team trying to come to terms with the departure from the game of Mark Ella, who had played a key role in scheming those four victories in the British Isles. Who would succeed him and could there be a successful replacement?

The heir-apparent was Michael Lynagh, but the home International programme was scarcely one that would give a reliable indication of the potential of a recast team. Two touring teams came, and both left with very poor results to show for all their efforts. Neither side tested Australia to the full.

First came Canada for a tour of nine matches including two Tests, but they were just not up to International standards and their tour results were very poor. The visitors won four of their games against Queensland Country (13-6), Northern Territories (30-12), South Australia (24-16) and Brisbane (24-16). Outside the Tests they lost badly to Western Australia (6-16), which was a first ever win for that state over a touring side; other defeats were at the hands of New South Wales (6-31), and New South Wales Country (23-31), both matches showing that their defence was simply not good enough. It proved defective again in the Internationals, which were both lost – in Sydney (3-59) and Brisbane (15-43). The points tally on the tour was 144 to 230 against, but at least in the last Test they showed some fighting spirit.

Fiji followed and they barely offered stiffer resistance playing ten matches and also winning four, of which only New South Wales Country could be described as serious opposition. There was a creditable draw with Sydney (28-28), but outside the Internationals there were losses to Brisbane, New South Wales and Australian Capital Territory. The Tests themselves produced crashing defeats in Brisbane (52-28) and Sydney (32-9). In fact, all Fiji really achieved was notoriety for alleged 'over-robust' play, and they were seriously criticized for it.

So far, therefore, it had not been a distinguished season, but there were high hopes for the only 'real' International match of the campaign – the Bledisloe Cup in Auckland. All the players had been on the tour of the British Isles with Lynagh replacing Mark Ella; Black and Lane were the centres with Burke on the wing for Campese, whilst the forwards were the Grand Slam octet. A dour and unenterprising encounter saw New Zealand retain the cup by a single point (10-9) with each side scoring a try, that of the Wallabies coming from James Black after half-time, when for a brief period Australia held the lead.

As usual after the end of the season, there were tours to the northern hemisphere. These involved the Australian Schools side, which won all its matches in Europe and should produce new stars for the Wallabies very soon, and Queensland, who took a very strong team to England, Ireland, Wales and Europe, but won only four matches and lost three, including one against Italy, who won 'on penalties'. The latter tour was probably the most effective as a testing ground for promising young players, since the established players such as Gould, Grigg, Moon, Lynagh, McIntyre and Lawton must have learned nothing they did not already know.

The real interest now centres on the 1987 World Cup and Australia must have secret hopes of success. In the new season, France will pay a visit and this will give a more reliable guide as to prospects than the Bledisloe Cup, since the All-Blacks may have their two best fifteens suspended and will not, in such circumstances, provide a proper trial. The

B. Moon (Australia) scores a try against the French Barbarians in the semi-finals of the Hong Kong International Sevens.

Wallabies will need to find yet another new captain, as Steve Williams has now retired after a distinguished Rugby career to concentrate on stock-broking. In some ways it is a pity that Australia cancelled a projected tour by Romania, since they would have given some useful opposition, but the powers at the top did not like the idea of another loss-making tour to follow those by Canada and Fiji in 1985.

Already this season the Wallabies have been seen in action in two major Sevens tournaments – in Sydney and Hong Kong. The former was thought to be a likely source of success, but the Australians lost in the final to an abrasive and very fit New Zealand team, who also won in Hong Kong, when the Wallabies went out in the semi-finals to the French Barbarians.

So, it should be an interesting season, but the potential controversy that surrounds the unofficial New Zealand tour of South Africa and the possibility that Australian players could soon become involved in a professional circus cannot be ignored. It is perhaps unlikely that this will be considered by the players until after the World Cup, for which the Wallabies are one of the favourites, but it is an open secret that many players would be tempted if the right offer were to be made. Dr Vanderfield, the Australian Rugby Union chairman, has threatened dire penalties for any deviations from strict amateur discipline, even though Australia was the first nation to stretch the rules regarding tour payments for players; but can they afford to impose rigid penalties if things do go wrong? We wait and see.

New South Wales International Sevens

Pool A
Australia	18	Netherlands	0
Spain	24	England	6
Spain	12	Netherlands	6
Australia	24	England	6
England	20	Netherlands	16
Australia	18	Spain	10

Pool B
New Zealand	22	Tonga	0
Wales	18	USA	0
Tonga	18	USA	4
Wales	18	New Zealand	12
Wales	18	Tonga	12
New Zealand	28	USA	0

Pool C
Western Samoa	24	Romania	6
Argentina	27	Japan	0
Romania	12	Japan	6
Argentina	18	Western Samoa	0
Argentina	21	Romania	4
Western Samoa	10	Japan	6

Pool D
Fiji	32	Canada	0
France	16	South Korea	16
South Korea	10	Canada	10
Fiji	14	France	12
France	28	Canada	0
Fiji	18	South Korea	6

Quarter-finals
Australia	14	Western Samoa	4
Wales	12	France	8
Argentina	12	Spain	6
New Zealand	16	Fiji	0

Semi-finals
Australia	18	Wales	6
New Zealand	24	Argentina	4

Final
Sunday, 23rd March 1986, at Sydney

New Zealand	32	Australia	0

New Zealand: M. Clamp, C. Green, F. Botica, D. Kirk (*captain*); W. Shelford, M. Brooke-Cowden, Z. Brooke

Australia: I. Williams, G. Ella, M. Lynagh, P. Cox; R. Gould (*captain*), S. Poidevin, P. Lucas. *Replacements:* B. Moon for Ella; S. Tuynman for Gould

Referee: R. Fordham (*New South Wales*)

The only sad thing from the Australian point of view was the thrashing administered to their highly-favoured Seven in the final by an All-Black team whose try scorers in the game were Brooke (2), Botica (2), Kirk and Clamp, with Botica converting four.

Until fatigue and injuries hit them, Wales were a star team with Jonathan Davies (Neath) outstanding – he scored seven tries. But Australia beat them in the semi-finals. In the final, the hosts themselves suffered from injuries, of which one was inflicted on Ella by Shelford, who was in every other respect outstanding.

England had a disastrous campaign with a weakened team; defeats were suffered against Spain, complete novices at this kind of activity, and Australia, which was expected. Only brave play by Hill (Bath) against Holland prevented a whitewash. The success of Spain and Western Samoa was, however, good for the future of the game in those improving countries.

NEW ZEALAND

There was a time when the course of New Zealand Rugby could be predicted accurately for years to come. In the past, events proceeded in a completely orderly sequence; but everything changes in time and the only thing that is certain about the next twelve months is that the future can no longer be forecast with accuracy, and certainly not with any feelings of confidence.

The first big event of the season was the tour by England, and the visitors put up some brave resistance. The first two matches of the tour (against North Auckland and Poverty Bay) were won comfortably enough, but defeat at Auckland showed that it would be a struggle for the men in white in the Internationals. Otago at Dunedin provided a stiff trial immediately before the Christchurch Test, but in that match at least the All-Blacks were rather lucky to win, thanks to Crowley's accurate boot; England scored the only two tries of the game. The tourists then disposed of Southland in a close encounter, but the Second Test provided very few anxious moments for the home country, which inflicted a record margin of defeat on the Englishmen (42-15). Wellington will not be a very happy memory for England.

Thoughts now turned to a tour of South Africa, those thoughts fully occupying the attentions of the Rugby authorities, who were in favour of the tour, and the government, who were against. But first there was the little matter of the Bledisloe Cup challenge and a visit from the Wallabies, who returned home beaten by the narrowest of margins in a very dour match.

So, it was off to South Africa – or was it? Those against the tour obtained an injunction in the High Court, which meant at the very least a short postponement of the team's departure for South Africa. The New Zealand RFU had no alternative but to bow to the decision. Talks of a tour taking place with a team of individuals travelling to South Africa remained just that – talk. The whole event seemed to have petered out, and that seemed to be the end of all tours to the Republic.

Meanwhile, negotiations for a substitute and shorter tour of Argentina were started and successfully concluded, and that was to complete the International action of 1985.

But first the traditional Ranfurly Shield with its unique form of contest held the attention of New Zealanders; and the question everyone was asking was whether Canterbury could do it for a twenty sixth time. Their earlier easy win against North Auckland at Lancaster Park was their twenty fifth successful defence and this equalled a record set up by Auckland from 1960 to 1963. September 14th had been set as a date for a challenge by Auckland, when it was thought that the visitors would be weakened by having many key men away touring South Africa, but the cancellation of that tour meant that all their players would, in fact, be available for the game.

Each side fielded seven All-Blacks, those of Canterbury being Craig Green, Robbie Deans, Victor Simpson, Warwick Taylor, Wayne Smith, Jock Hobbs and Albert Anderson. Auckland's Internationals were John Kirwan, Grant Fox, David Kirk, Andy Haden, Gary Whetton and Steve McDowell. Another, Steve Pokere, was held in reserve.

The first half saw Auckland play with the help of a stiff breeze and by half-time they held an incredible lead of 24-0. Tries by Joe Stanley, Terry Wright, John Kirwan and the massive prop, John Drake, were supplemented by two penalties and a conversion by Grant Fox. It had been a nightmare first half for the defenders, none being less happy than full-back Deans.

But Canterbury did fight back. Bruce Deans crossed for Canterbury, but a fine move restored Auckland's twenty four-point lead as McDowell went over in his turn. A try by Green was then converted by Robbie Deans, who also kicked a penalty-goal. Wayne Smith and Anderson scored tries and Deans converted the second so it was now 23-28. Smith tried a long kick, which Green was just unable to gather over the line so that Fox and Kirwan were able to scramble the ball clear, and Auckland had won the Ranfurly Shield. No fewer than 52,000 people saw this epic.

So, the All-Blacks departed for Argentina and a tour of seven matches, which started with four easy wins; only a Buenos Aires XV, a very useful side, gave any semblance of trouble, but by the time the First International was played the visitors knew how to score. In that match, the New Zealanders were quickly leading by nine points, but the Pumas fought back and themselves took a single-point lead. But at half-time it was the turn of the All-Blacks to lead by one point. After an hour there had been six more points each and New Zealand led 21-20, but then the All-Blacks scored three late and unconverted tries to win 33-20. One came from Jock Hobbs, who had taken over the captaincy of the tourists from the unavailable Andy Dalton.

A win by a wide margin over Cordoba preceded the Second International, which like the first was played in Buenos Aires. It was a real thriller and ended in forty two points being exactly shared. Porta of Argentina, that wonderful fly-half, scored all his side's points with four penalty-goals and three dropped goals against four tries from New Zealand scored by Kirwan (2), Mexted and Green. The difference between the sides was the kicking, with the unfortunate Crowley only managing to land two efforts against the virtuosity of Hugo Porta. But four wins and a draw out of five International matches in the last twelve months put New Zealand at the top of the League.

Normally, the summer months in the southern hemisphere are a time for quiet and cricket, but this has not happened. First, there has been disagreement about the new shirt designs for future All-Black teams and, not surprisingly, Andy Haden has been one of the people involved in trying to promote a new type of shirt and logo. As this is being written, it is not clear how that controversy will be resolved. Further debate has arisen because the New Zealand RFU chairman, Ces Blazey, is about to retire after seven years in office and his successor is soon to be named from a suggested list of three – Bob Thomas, Bob Stuart (the All-Black captain in Europe, 1953-54) and Ivan Vodanovitch. Thomas and Vodanovitch are former successful coaches; all are men of the highest integrity, and the man selected will undoubtedly adorn the office with distinction.

Well into 1986, New Zealand's International activities have so far started with appearances in two International Sevens tournaments with two successes. First, the celebration event in Sydney was won easily enough in the final against the home country, and then the Hong Kong Sevens were also won with new stars emerging such as Zinzan Brooke and Brooke-Cowden; other successes have been Kirk at scrum-half and the flanker, Wayne Shelford, who during the northern hemisphere winter months had led a most successful New Zealand Services team in Europe. Several players, notably Kirwan and the evergreen Andy Haden, took part in the IB Centenary matches in

Jock Hobbs, the New Zealand flanker and captain during the 1985 matches in Argentina.

Britain with distinction, but while they were there the 'baloon went up'.

The 'baloon' was the recent unofficial tour by thirty one New Zealanders with the title of 'Cavaliers' in South Africa. So, the problem has not gone away, just as instructions to the organizers to cancel the tour and to the tourists to return home were predictably ignored. Since the New Zealanders selected almost everyone who would normally expect to be included in an All-Blacks party with the exception of Kirwan and Kirk, it can be appreciated that much embarrassment has been caused by the affair.

What happens now to the participating players is anyone's guess, but with international commitments to be met this year against France and Australia it will provide some dreadful headaches for the selectors if the 'rebels' are disciplined. What price will the bookmakers place on New Zealand's World Cup prospects if lengthy suspensions are imposed on the players in question? Or, for that matter, what price will the same bookmakers place on any serious disciplinary measures actually being taken at all?

What all this means is that the admirable Mr Blazey will have a knotty problem to pass on to his successor, one which no-one would like to be responsible for solving. As we stated at the beginning of this account, the future of New Zealand Rugby is no longer either ordered or predictable. How many of the country's leading players will be professionals this time next year? Will New Zealand Rugby be by then a wholly professional sport? Who knows?

Hong Kong International Sevens

Preliminary results

Australia	38	Malaysia	6
Irish Wolfhounds	36	Thailand	0
Scottish Co-Optimists	26	Papua New Guinea	0
French Barbarians	26	Kwang Hua-Taipei	0
New Zealand	34	Indonesia	0
Tonga	30	Sri Lanka	6
Western Samoa	32	Brunei	4
Kenya	32	Malaysia	0
Bahrain	4	Thailand	4
Canada	14	Papua New Guinea	0
Fiji	40	Singapore	0
Kwang Hua-Taipei	10	Solomon Islands	6
Hong Kong	40	Indonesia	0
Korea	24	Sri Lanka	0
Japan	34	Brunei	0
American Eagles	36	Singapore	0
Australia	30	Kenya	10
Irish Wolfhounds	32	Bahrain	6
Scottish Co-Optimists	14	Canada	8
French Barbarians	28	Solomon Islands	0
New Zealand	42	Hong Kong	0
Tonga	18	Korea	6
Western Samoa	30	Japan	10
Fiji	26	American Eagles	0

Quarter-finals

Australia	26	Irish Wolfhounds	6
French Barbarians	22	Scottish Co-Optimists	10
New Zealand	26	Tonga	0
Fiji	8	Western Samoa	4

Semi-finals

French Barbarians	20	Australia	14
New Zealand	28	Fiji	6

Bowl final

Papua New Guinea	22	Sri Lanka	10

Plate final

American Eagles	24	Canada	18

Final

Sunday, 6th April 1986, at Hong Kong

New Zealand	**32**	**French Barbarians**	**12**

New Zealand: Botica, Brooke-Cowden, Brooke, Clamp, Kirk, Shelford, Smith

French Barbarians: Rodriquez, Cabannes, Janeczek, Fournials, Cecillon, Peuchlestrad, Bonal. *Replacement:* Rutherford (*Scottish Co-Optimists*)

New Zealand did a notable double by adding Cathay Pacific Hong Kong International Sevens to the Sydney Tournament they won in March, and they did so with six of the team that had won in Australia. In the final, they beat a talented but injury-hit French Barbarians. Their star player was their forward, Zinzan Brooke, although the 'Man of the Tournament' award went to Tommy Smith of the American Eagles, who won the Plate.

The talented Australians went no further than the semi-finals where they lost to the French Barbarians, who had beaten the Scottish Co-Optimists in the last eight. New Zealand's victims in the knock-out rounds were Tonga and Fiji respectively. The other quarter-finalists were the Tongans and the Irish Wolfhounds, whose Welsh star, Jonathan Davies, was injured on the first day and retired from the tournament.

The crowd on the second day numbered 25,000 and again the tournament was organized in a masterly fashion.

The winning New Zealand Seven at the 1986 Hong Kong Sevens. Shelford (kneeling, first from the left) later joined the 'Cavaliers' in South Africa.

SOUTH AFRICA

Politics now play such an important part in South African Rugby – both inside the Republic and internationally – that it might be easier to concentrate on this aspect and forget that the game is actually played there. The 1985 season was one of continuing melodrama, and the 1986 campaign looked as though it might follow a similar path.

The main event in 1985 should have been a tour by the New Zealand All-Blacks, but this never materialized owing to events that are described elsewhere in this book, so in the end domestic events largely dominated the scene. The principal domestic competition is the Currie Cup and this was won in Durban (for a fourth successive year) by Western Province, who defeated Northern Transvaal, led by fly-half Naas Botha, in the final (22-15). Botha, a failure in an attempt to play in American Football, was the best player for his team and with three dropped-goals and two penalties scored all the points, but Western Province were superior and were well led by Rob Louw. They scored both the game's tries (by Hennie Bekker and Niel Burger) and their other points came from Calla Schultz, the full-back, who sent over a dropped-goal, three penalties and a conversion to make a personal contribution of fourteen points.

In spite of international disapproval, there are regular tours to the Republic by lesser touring teams, but such a description would not do justice to the strength, on paper, of Crawshay's Welsh team, which made a (for them) pre-season tour and came away with results, which suggested that despite boycotts and other factors, the standard of Rugby in the southern hemisphere is superior to that in the north. Crawshay's included such well-known Internationals as Elgan Rees, Mark Titley, Alan Donovan, Ray Giles, Graham Price, Ian Stephens, Alan Phillips, Terry Shaw, Allan Martin, Phil Davies and David Pickering, but after initial victories over Winelands at Vredendal in the Cape (19-13) and over a Western Province League Fifteen at Newlands (37-23), four losses were sustained – against Eastern Province at Port Elizabeth (16-31), Natal President's XV in Durban (18-40), Northern Transvaal at Pretoria (9-34) and Free State 'B' at Bloemfontein (17-40). The scores show that the visitors, who were captained by the former

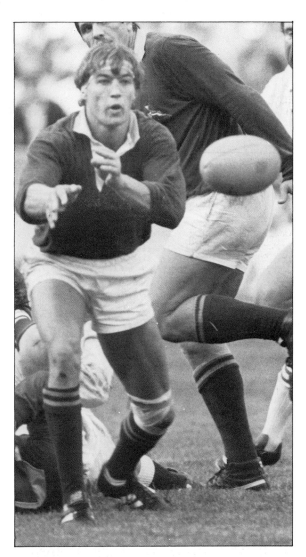

Rob Louw (South Africa), a great no.8, who now plays as a professional.

Cambridge blue, Chris Williams, were outclassed and several of the matches were not played in the best of spirits. A final scoring tally of 116 points scored to 181 conceded tells its own tale and the team, although it had its star names, suffered among other things for having too many people who were not match fit.

The season ended in Cape Town with an International Sevens Tournament, which was won by

Danie Gerber (South Africa) – the best centre in the world? His recognized International appearances are restricted by politics.

Pretoria University ('Tukkies') in the final on 31st March (14-6). Naas Botha started the match for the losers, but was injured and left the field before half-time. Stellenbosch University ('Maties') were the favourites to take the honours but they were destroyed by 'Tukkies' in a semi-final (40-6), their worst defeat in one hundred years of Rugby.

This season's Currie Cup was played in two groups as in 1985, with the first two in each going forward to the semi-finals; group winners meet opposite group runners-up at that stage. The teams involved were Western Province (long-term holders), Northern Transvaal, Free State, Transvaal, Eastern Province, Northern Free State, Vaal Triangle, Western Transvaal, Eastern Transvaal, Griqualand West, Natal and South West Africa. There was a good deal of controversy with accusations of 'under-the-counter payments' being made freely. Numerous players, particularly in the Transvaal, have changed clubs and, as a result, Northern Transvaal entered the Currie Cup with several important forwards missing. A club in the Transvaal was also alleged to have enticed thirteen players to its ranks amidst allegations of corrupt practices. Natal as a province has also suffered badly from transfers. So some inter-club relations are becoming strained!

A move to clean up on dirty play has also been announced, but its likely effectiveness will be open to question. A 'sin-bin' system is generally considered to be a joke as it can encourage unscrupulous players to 'take out' opponents by foul play in the full knowledge that a temporary suspension from the game will have no adverse effect on the offending side.

Another thorny point is the question of non-white players in the sport. In recent seasons there has been a realistic attempt to integrate the sport, and three players, Williams, Tobias and Cupido, have earned Springbok colours on merit with no 'window-dressing' involved. Others would follow, but there is the problem that the present unrest will discourage the potential members of the South African Rugby Federation from joining, owing to the dangers inherent in not being seen to support the political aspirations of the majority of the population.

Thus it is inevitable that politics are involved. The tour by the New Zealand 'Cavaliers' denotes a victory to some people of Rugby over politics and politicians. However, this is a debatable point. It is clear that, just as those who caused the cancellation of the projected tour of 1985 took the New Zealand RFU by surprise, so this recent tour

Northern Transvaal, who beat Eastern Province in the final (17-16).

During the summer months there were rumours and counter-rumours about the formation of a professional circus, and players leaving to play Rugby League in Britain. The latter sport did claim Rob Louw and another Springbok in Ray Mordt, but Danie Gerber, who was also thought likely to make the change, did not do so and in fact was one of the South Africans who distinguished themselves in the IB Centenary matches in April 1986 at Twickenham and Cardiff.

The club Champions this year are the Free State University team known as the Shimlas, who beat caught many people off guard, and perhaps a projected Western Samoan tour was a 'smoke screen' to conceal real intentions.

Certainly, many arrived at the IB Centenary Congress in England without realizing that anything sinister was afoot; these people included both Ces Blazey of New Zealand and the veteran South African maestro, Danie Craven. Whilst the congress was still in progress rumours started about the tour and these were soon confirmed as being factually correct. Efforts to have the tour cancelled were unlikely to succeed, as the main organizers were the Transvaal RU; in South Africa, there is strong provincial autonomy and Danie Craven was virtually powerless to do anything about it, as was Ces Blazey.

Now the IB, having had its authority flouted, must decide the action, which could or should be taken against South Africa, in the full knowledge that any drastic action, whether it be expulsion or suspension, would merely advance the date of professionalism in the sport. Indeed, it might be a 'nine-day wonder' as far as the Republic is concerned. Professional players are not going to give up the game merely because they are banned from playing as amateurs and it is almost certain that a professional game would spread eventually to all the major countries. Then what would happen?

So, for the moment at least, South Africa holds many of the cards – and enough cash also! It will be interesting to see the outcome, but meanwhile, since it was a very strong touring party, the relative strengths of the two leading nations are now assessable; there is also the possibility that it will become clear before the World Cup that the best team is absent from it.

Unofficial New Zealand Tour of South Africa 1986

An astonished Rugby public learned during the course of the IB Centenary celebrations that an unofficial New Zealand team called the 'Cavaliers' would tour South Africa during April and May 1986. Almost all the leading players from New Zealand were taking part, with only Kirk, the scrum-half, and the wing, Kirwan, being absent.

All efforts to have the tour halted were unsuccessful and it went ahead as secretly planned with South Africa winning the series (3-1) against a team that was virtually a full-strength All-Black selection. The New Zealanders, whilst being made welcome, will not remember the tour with much pleasure, since they suffered numerous injuries.

Date	Opponents	Venue	Result
23rd Apr.	Junior Springboks	Johannesburg	W 22-21
26th Apr.	Northern Transvaal	Pretoria	W 10-9
30th Apr.	Orange Free State	Bloemfontein	W 31-9
3rd May	Transvaal	Johannesburg	L 19-24
6th May	Western Province	Cape Town	W 25-16
10th May	SOUTH AFRICA	Cape Town	L 15-21
13th May	Natal	Durban	W 37-24
17th May	SOUTH AFRICA	Durban	W 19-18
20th May	South African Barbarians	Johannesburg	W 42-13
24th May	SOUTH AFRICA	Pretoria	L 18-33
27th May	Western Transvaal	Potchefstroom	W 26-18
31st May	SOUTH AFRICA	Johannesburg	L 10-24

Amongst their casualties was Andy Dalton, the captain, who was ruled out of events after the second match as a result of a broken jaw.

The 'Tests' were hard-fought affairs, but the Springboks, apart from losing rather unluckily in the second of the series, were generally superior and the fine kicking of Naas Botha at fly-half was a match-winning factor on its own. In the Final Test the New Zealanders complained bitterly about the refereeing of Ken Rowlands, the Welshman, who sent off Gary Knight and South Africa's Smal for a five-minute cooling-off period; but Hika Reid, the Cavaliers' hooker, was lucky he was still on the field at the end of the match after showing almost violent dissent at some decisions.

After South Africa's fine display in this series it would be difficult to describe the 1987 World Cup as really including all the best sides.

Tour Party

Backs: R. Deans *(Canterbury)*, K. Crowley *(Taranaki)*, M. Clamp *(Wellington)*, C. Green *(Canterbury)*, M. Purcell *(United States)*, B. Robins *(Taranaki)*, V. Simpson *(Canterbury)*, S. Pokere *(Auckland)*, W. Osborne *(Wanganui)*, W. Taylor *(Canterbury)*, W. Smith *(Canterbury)*, G. Fox *(Auckland)*, A. Donald *(Wanganui)*, D. Loveridge *(Taranaki)*

Forwards: A. Dalton *(Counties) (captain)*, H. Reid *(Bay of Plenty)*, J. Mills *(Canterbury) (replacement for Dalton)*, G. Knight *(Manawatu)*, J. Ashworth *(Canterbury)*, S. McDowell *(Auckland)*, S. Crichton *(Wellington)*, G. Whetton *(Auckland)*, A. Haden *(Auckland)*, A. Anderson *(Canterbury)*, M. Pierce *(Wellington)*, J. Hobbs *(Canterbury)*, F. Shelford *(Bay of Plenty)*, M. Shaw *(Manawatu)*, A. Whetton *(Auckland)*, M. Mexted *(Wellington)*, W. Shelford *(North Harbour)*

Manager: C. Meads; *coach:* I. Kirkpatrick

Test Scorers

South Africa: Botha (1 try, 2 dropped-goals, 15 penalty-goals, 7 conversions) 69 points; Reinach (2 tries) 8 points; C. Du Plessis, Schmidt, Gerber and Wright (1 try each); M. Du Plessis (1 dropped-goal)

New Zealand: Fox (1 dropped-goal, 9 penalty-goals, 3 conversions) 36 points; Deans (2 penalty-goals) 6 points; Taylor, Mexted, Crowley, Donald (1 try each); 1 penalty-try

RECORDS

Major Tours Summary

British Isles to Australia and New Zealand

Year	Captain	P	W	D	L	F	A	Notes
1888	R. L. Seddon A. E. Stoddart	35	27	6	2	292	98	Stoddart took over as captain after Seddon was drowned in Australia. No Tests played.
1899	Rev. M. Mullineux	21	18	0	3	333	90	Australia only. Won three Tests out of four.
1904	D. R. Bedell-Sivright	19	16	1	2	287	84	Unbeaten in Australia, winning all three Tests, but lost only Test in New Zealand.
1908	A. F. Harding	26	16	1	9	323	201	Anglo-Welsh. Lost two and drew one Test – all in New Zealand.
1930	F. D. Prentice	28	20	0	8	624	318	Lost four Tests out of five – three defeats in New Zealand.
1950	Dr K. D. Mullen	29	22	1	6	570	214	Lost three Tests and drew one in New Zealand, but won two in Australia out of two.
1959	A. R. Dawson	31	25	0	6	756	336	Beat Australia twice in Tests but lost three and won one in New Zealand.
1966	M. J. Campbell-Lamerton	33	22	3	8	502	329	Won both Tests in Australia and lost all four in New Zealand.
1971	S. J. Dawes	26	23	1	2	570	231	Won Test series in New Zealand with two wins, a draw and one defeat.
1977	P. Bennett	26	21	0	5	607	320	New Zealand and Fiji only. Lost Test series (1-3) and only match in Fiji.
1983	C. F. Fitzgerald	18	12	0	6	478	276	New Zealand only. Lost all four Tests.

British Isles to South Africa

Year	Captain	P	W	D	L	F	A	Notes
1891	W. E. Maclagan	19	19	0	0	224	1	Won all three Tests.
1896	J. Hammond	21	19	1	1	310	45	Won three Tests out of four.
1903	M. C. Morrison	22	11	3	8	231	138	Drew two and lost final Test.
1910	Dr T. Smyth	24	13	3	8	290	236	Won one Test out of three.
1924	Dr R. Cove-Smith	21	9	3	9	175	155	Drew one Test and lost other three.
1938	S. Walker	23	17	0	6	407	272	Won one and lost two of the Tests.
1955	R. H. Thompson	24	18	1	5	418	271	Shared the four-Test series.
1962	A. R. Smith	24	15	4	5	351	208	Drew one and lost three tests in series.
1968	T. J. Kiernan	20	15	1	4	377	181	Same Test record as 1962.
1974	W. J. McBride	22	21	1	0	729	207	Won all but the final Test (drawn) of four.
1980	W. B. Beaumont	18	15	0	3	401	244	Lost three and drew one of the Tests.

Scotland, Ireland and Wales to New Zealand and Australia

Year	Captain	P	W	D	L	F	A	Notes
1967	T. J. Kiernan	6	4	0	2	119	80	Ireland to Australia. Won only Test.
1969	B. Price	9	5	0	4	112	103	Wales, also to Fiji. Lost Tests to New Zealand (0-2), beat Australia (once) and Fiji.

Year	Captain	P	W	D	L	F	A	Notes
1970	F. A. L. Laidlaw	6	3	0	3	109	94	Scotland to Australia. Lost only Test.
1975	J. McLauchlan	7	4	0	3	157	104	Scotland to New Zealand. Lost only Test.
1976	T. O. Grace	8	5	0	3	96	68	Ireland to Australia and Fiji. Lost Test in New Zealand.
1978	T. J. Cobner	9	5	0	4	227	106	Wales to Australia. Lost Tests (0-2).
1979	J. F. Slattery	8	7	0	1	184	75	Ireland to Australia. Won Tests (2-0).
1981	A. R. Irvine	8	5	0	3	189	125	Scotland to New Zealand. Lost Tests (0-2).
1982	A. R. Irvine	9	6	0	3	220	113	Scotland to Australia. Shared Tests (1-1).

England to Australia and New Zealand

Year	Captain	P	W	D	L	F	A	Notes
1963	M. P. Weston	6	1	0	5	54	91	Lost to New Zealand (2) and Australia (once).
1973	J. V. Pullin	5	2	0	3	60	72	New Zealand and Fiji. Won the Test in New Zealand and beat Fiji.
1975	A. Neary	8	4	0	4	217	110	Australia only. Lost Test series (0-2).
1985	P. W. Dodge	7	4	0	3	146	123	New Zealand only. Lost Tests (0-2).

Four Home Nations to South Africa

Year	Captain	P	W	D	L	F	A	Notes
1960	G. H. Waddell	3	2	0	1	61	45	Scotland. Lost Test.
1961	A. R. Dawson	4	3	0	1	59	36	Ireland. Lost Test.
1964	D. C. T. Rowlands	4	2	0	2	43	58	Wales. Lost Test.
1972	J. V. Pullin	7	6	1	0	166	58	England. Won Test.
1981	J. F. Slattery	7	3	0	4	207	90	Ireland. Lost Tests (0-2).
1984	J. P. Scott	7	4	1	2	156	145	England. Lost Tests (0-2).

France to New Zealand and Australia

Year	Captain	P	W	D	L	F	A	Notes
1961	F. Moncla	15	8	0	7	180	179	Lost every Test in New Zealand (0-3), but won only Test in Australia.
1968	C. Carrère	14	9	0	5	195	142	Lost series in New Zealand (0-3) and Australia (0-1).
1972	W. Spanghero	9	8	1	0	254	122	Australia only. Won one Test and drew the other.
1979	J.-P. Rives	9	6	0	3	168	116	New Zealand and Fiji. Shared New Zealand Tests (1-1).
1981	J.-P. Rives	9	6	0	3	189	112	Australia. Lost both Tests.
1984	P. Dintrans	8	6	0	2	224	138	New Zealand. Lost both Tests.

France to South Africa

Year	Captain	P	W	D	L	F	A	Notes
1958	M. Celaya	10	5	2	3	137	124	Won one Test and drew other.
1964	M. Crauste	6	5	0	1	117	55	Won only Test.
1967	C. Darrouy	13	8	1	4	209	161	Lost Test series (1-1-2).
1971	C. Carrère	9	7	1	1	228	92	Lost one Test and drew other.
1975	R. Astre/J. Fouroux	11	6	1	4	282	190	Lost both Tests.
1980	J.-P. Rives	4	3	0	1	90	95	Lost only Test.

Australia to British Isles and France

Year	Captain	P	W	D	L	F	A	Notes
1908-09	Dr H. M. Moran	31	25	1	5	438	149	England and Wales. Beat England; lost to Wales.
1927-28	A. C. Wallace	31	24	2	5	432	207	New South Wales 'Waratahs'. Beat Ireland, Wales and France; lost to Scotland and England.
1947-48	W. M. McLean	35	29	0	6	500	243	Lost to Wales and France, but beat other three nations.
1957-58	R. A. L. Davidson	34	16	3	15	285	244	Lost to all Five Nations.
1966-67	J. E. Thornett	34	17	3	14	348	322	Beat Wales and England, but lost to other three nations.
1968	P. G. Johnson	5	2	0	3	38	40	Ireland and Scotland. Lost to both nations.
1971	G. V. Davis	8	4	0	4	110	101	France only. Shared Tests (1-1).
1973	P. D. Sullivan	8	2	1	5	85	131	England and Wales. Lost to both nations.
1975-76	J. N. B. Hipwell	26	19	1	6	496	349	British Isles and United States. Only beat Ireland and United States; lost to other three countries.
1976	G. A. Shaw	10	4	0	6	114	163	France and Italy. Lost twice to France.
1981-82	A. A. Shaw	23	16	1	6	431	219	British Isles only. Only beat Ireland of four home nations.
1983	M. G. Ella	11	6	2	3	190	157	France and Italy. Beat Italy but drew one and lost one to France.
1984	A. G. Slack	18	13	1	4	400	232	British Isles only. Beat all four home nations.

Australia to South Africa

Year	Captain	P	W	D	L	F	A	Notes
1933	A. W. Ross	23	12	1	10	299	195	Lost Test series (2-3).
1953	H. J. Solomon	27	16	1	10	450	413	Lost Test series (1-3).
1961	K. Catchpole	6	3	1	2	90	80	Short tour. Lost Test series (0-2).
1963	J. E. Thornett	24	15	1	8	303	233	Drew Test series (2-2).
1969	G. V. Davis	26	15	0	11	465	353	Lost all four Tests.

New Zealand to British Isles and France

Year	Captain	P	W	D	L	F	A	Notes
1888-89	J. A. Warbrick	74	49	5	20	394	188	The Maoris. Beat Ireland, but lost to England and Wales.
1905-06	D. Gallaher	33	32	0	1	868	47	Beat all nations except Wales.
1924-25	C. G. Porter	30	30	0	0	721	112	Did not play Scotland but beat other four nations. G. Nepia played in every match.
1926-27	W. P. Barclay	31	22	2	7	459	194	The Maoris. Won only Test, against France.
1935-36	J. E. Manchester	28	24	1	3	431	180	British Isles only. Lost to Wales, England and Swansea; beat Scotland and Ireland.
1953-54	R. C. Stuart	31	25	2	4	446	129	Lost to Cardiff, Wales, French Selection and France; beat the other nations.
1963-64	W. J. Whineray	34	32	1	1	568	153	Lost only to Newport and drew with Scotland; won other four Tests.
1967	B. J. Lochore	15	14	1	0	294	129	Did not play in Ireland, but won all other matches except against East Wales (drawn).
1972-73	I. A. Kirkpatrick	30	23	2	5	568	254	Lost to France, drew with Ireland but beat Wales, Scotland and England.
1974	A. R. Leslie	8	7	1	0	127	50	Ireland, Wales and England. Beat Ireland and Wales XV; drew with Barbarians.

Year	Captain	P	W	D	L	F	A	Notes
1977	G. N. K. Mourie	9	8	0	1	216	86	France and Italy. Shared two-match Test series with France (1-1).
1978	G. N. K. Mourie	18	17	0	1	364	147	British Isles only. Beat all four home nations; lost only to Munster.
1979	G. N. K. Mourie	11	10	0	1	192	95	England, Scotland and Italy. Beat England and Scotland; lost to North of England.
1980	G. N. K. Mourie	7	7	0	0	197	41	Wales and North America. Beat Wales.
1981	G. N. K. Mourie	10	8	1	1	170	108	France and Romania. Beat France twice and Romania once.
1983	S. S. Wilson	8	5	1	2	162	116	Scotland and England. Lost to England and Midlands and drew with Scotland.

New Zealand to South Africa

Year	Captain	P	W	D	L	F	A	Notes
1928	M. J. Brownlie	22	16	1	5	339	144	Shared Test series (2-2).
1949	F. R. Allen	24	14	3	7	230	146	Lost all four Tests.
1960	W. J. Whineray	26	20	2	4	441	164	Won one and drew one in four-match Test series.
1970	B. J. Lochore	24	21	0	3	687	228	Lost Test series (1-3).
1976	A. R. Leslie	24	18	0	6	610	291	Lost Test series (1-3).

South Africa to British Isles and France

Year	Captain	P	W	D	L	F	A	Notes
1906-07	P. J. Roos	28	25	1	2	553	79	Lost to Scotland but beat Ireland and Wales drawing with England.
1912-13	W. A. Millar	27	24	0	3	441	101	Beat all Five Nations.
1931-32	B. L. Osler	26	23	2	1	407	124	France excluded. Beat all four home nations.
1951-52	B. J. Kenyon	31	30	0	1	562	167	Beat all Five Nations. Lost only to London Counties.
1960-61	A. S. Malan	34	31	2	1	567	132	Lost to Barbarians, drew with France and won other Tests.
1965	A. S. Malan	5	0	1	4	37	53	Ireland and Scotland only. Lost four matches including both Tests.
1968	D. J. de Villiers	6	5	0	1	84	43	France only. Won both Tests.
1969-70	D. J. de Villiers	24	15	4	5	323	157	British Isles only. Lost to Scotland and England; drew with Wales and Ireland.
1974	J. F. K. Marais	9	8	0	1	170	74	France only. Won both Tests.

South Africa to Australia and New Zealand

Year	Captain	P	W	D	L	F	A	Notes
1921	T. B. Pienaar	23	19	2	2	327	119	No Tests in Australia. Drew series in New Zealand (1-1-1).
1937	P. J. Nel	26	24	0	2	753	169	Won series in Australia (2-0) and New Zealand (2-1).
1956	S. S. Viviers	29	22	1	6	520	203	Won series in Australia (2-0); lost in New Zealand (1-3).
1965	D. J. de Villiers	30	22	0	8	669	375	Lost series in Australia (0-2) and in New Zealand (1-3).
1971	J. F. K. Marais	13	13	0	0	396	102	Australia only. Won Tests (3-0).
1981	W. Claassen	17	14	1	2	535	190	New Zealand and United States. Lost series in New Zealand (1-2). Beat United States once.

Results of International Matches
1871 to 30th April 1986

The years given for Five Nations matches refer to the period after 1st January, i.e. 1964 refers to the season 1963-64. Years for matches against touring teams record the year the match was actually played. British Isles matches are given from 1910, the first year the four home nations co-operated fully to send a touring party to South Africa. Matches involving IB countries against Romania and Argentina are recognized as full Internationals for all matches played since 1st January 1981.

Points-scoring was not introduced until 1886 when Scotland, Wales and Ireland formed an International Board. Points-values varied between countries until England joined the Board in 1890 when values were standardized. The goal from mark was abolished when free-kicks were introduced (1977-78).

Northern hemisphere seasons	Try	Penalty-goal	Dropped-goal	Goal from mark	Conversion
1890-91	1	2	3	3	2
1891-92 to 1892-93	2	3	4	4	3
1893-94 to 1904-05	3	3	4	4	2
1905-06 to 1947-48	3	3	4	3	2
1948-49 to 1970-71	3	3	3	3	2
1971-72 to present	4	3	3	3	2

England v. Ireland
98 matches played   England 55 wins   Ireland 35 wins   8 draws

1875 England 1G, 1DG, 1T to 0 (at The Oval, London)
1876 England 1G, 1T to 0 (at Dublin)
1877 England 2G, 2T to 0 (at The Oval)
1878 England 2G, 1T to 0 (at Dublin)
1879 England 2G, 1DG, 2T to 0 (at The Oval)
1880 England 1G, 1T to 1T (at Dublin)
1881 England 2G, 2T to 0 (at Manchester)
1882 Drawn, 2T each (at Dublin)
1883 England 1G, 3T to 1T (at Manchester)
1884 England 1G to 0 (at Dublin)
1885 England 2T to 1T (at Manchester)
1886 England 1T to 0 (at Dublin)
1887 Ireland 2G to 0 (at Dublin)
1888 No match
1889 No match
1890 England 3T to 0 (at Blackheath, London)
1891 England 2G, 3T (9) to 0 (at Dublin)
1892 England 1G, 1T (7) to 0 (at Manchester)
1893 England 2T (4) to 0 (at Dublin)
1894 Ireland 1DG, 1T (7) to 1G (5) (at Blackheath)
1895 England 2T (6) to 1T (3) (at Dublin)
1896 Ireland 2G (10) to 1DG (4) (at Leeds)
1897 Ireland 1GM, 3T (13) to 2PG 1T (9) (at Dublin)
1898 Ireland 1PG, 2T (9) to 1PG, 1T (6) (at Richmond, London)
1899 Ireland 1PG, 1T (6) to 0 (at Dublin)
1900 England 1G, 1DG, 2T (15) to 1DG (4) (at Richmond)
1901 Ireland 2G (10) to 1PG, 1T (6) (at Dublin)
1902 England 2T (6) to 1T (3) (at Leicester)
1903 Ireland 1PG, 1T (6) to 0 (at Dublin)
1904 England 2G, 3T (19) to 0 (at Blackheath)
1905 Ireland 1G, 4T (17) to 1T (3) (at Cork)
1906 Ireland 2G, 2T (16) to 2T (6) (at Leicester)
1907 Ireland 1G, 1GM, 3T (17) to 1PG, 2T (9) (at Dublin)

1908 England 2G, 1T (13) to 1PG (3) (at Richmond)
1909 England 1G, 2T (11) to 1G (5) (at Dublin)
1910 Drawn, no score (at Twickenham)
1911 Ireland 1T (3) to 0 (at Dublin)
1912 England 5T (15) to 0 (at Twickenham)
1913 England 1PG, 4T (15) to 1DG (4) (at Dublin)
1914 England 1G, 4T (17) to 1G, 1DG, 1T (12) (at Twickenham)
1920 England 1G, 3T (14) to 1G, 1PG, 1T (11) (at Dublin)
1921 England 1G, 1DG, 2T (15) to 0 (at Twickenham)
1922 England 4T (12) to 1T (3) (at Dublin)
1923 England 2G, 1DG, 3T (23) to 1G (5) (at Leicester)
1924 England 1G, 3T (14) to 1T (3) (at Belfast)
1925 Drawn, 2T (6) each (at Twickenham)
1926 Ireland 2G, 1PG, 2T (19) to 3G (15) (at Dublin)
1927 England 1G, 1T (8) to 1PG, 1T (6) (at Twickenham)
1928 England 1DG, 1T (7) to 2T (6) (at Dublin)
1929 Ireland 2T (6) to 1G (5) (at Twickenham)
1930 Ireland 1DG (4) to 1T (3) (at Dublin)
1931 Ireland 1PG, 1T (6) to 1G (5) (at Twickenham)
1932 England 1G, 2PG (11) to 1G, 1PG (8) (at Dublin)
1933 England 1G, 4T (17) to 1PG, 1T (6) (at Twickenham)
1934 England 2G, 1T (13) to 1T (3) (at Dublin)
1935 England 1G, 3PG (14) to 1T (3) (at Twickenham)
1936 Ireland 2T (6) to 1T (3) (at Dublin)
1937 England 1PG, 2T (9) to 1G, 1T (8) (at Twickenham)
1938 England 6G, 1PG, 1T (36) to 1G, 3T (14) (at Dublin)

1939 Ireland 1G (5) to 0 (at Twickenham)
1947 Ireland 2G, 1PG, 3T (22) to 0 (at Dublin)
1948 Ireland 1G, 2T (11) to 2G (10) (at Twickenham)
1949 Ireland 1G, 2PG, 1T (14) to 1G (5) (at Dublin)
1950 England 1T (3) to 0 (at Twickenham)
1951 Ireland 1PG (3) to 0 (at Dublin)
1952 England 1T (3) to 0 (at Twickenham)
1953 Drawn, 2PG, 1T (9) each (at Dublin)
1954 England 1G, 1PG, 2T (14) to 1PG (3) (at Twickenham)
1955 Drawn, Ireland 1PG, 1T (6), England 2T (6) (at Dublin)
1956 England 1G, 3PG, 2T (20) to 0 (at Twickenham)
1957 England 1PG, 1T (6) to 0 (at Dublin)
1958 England 1PG, 1T (6) to 0 (at Twickenham)
1959 England 1PG (3) to 0 (at Dublin)
1960 England 1G, 1DG (8) to 1G (5) (at Twickenham)
1961 Ireland 1G, 2PG (11) to 1G, 1T (8) (at Dublin)
1962 England 2G, 1PG, 1T (16) to 0 (at Twickenham)
1963 Drawn, no score (at Dublin)
1964 Ireland 3G, 1T (18) to 1G (5) (at Twickenham)
1965 Ireland 1G (5) to 0 (at Dublin)
1966 Drawn, 1PG, 1T (6) each (at Twickenham)
1967 England 1G, 1PG (8) to 1PG (3) (at Dublin)
1968 Drawn, England 2PG, 1DG (9), Ireland 3PG (9) (at Twickenham)
1969 Ireland 1G, 2PG, 1DG, 1T (17) to 4PG, 1T (15) (at Dublin)
1970 England 2DG, 1T (9) to 1PG (3) (at Twickenham)
1971 England 3PG (9) to 2T (6) (at Dublin)
1972 Ireland 1G, 1DG, 1PG, 1T (16) to 1G, 2PG (12) (at Twickenham)
1973 Ireland 2G, 1PG, 1DG (18) to 1G, 1PG

(9) (at Dublin)
1974 Ireland 2G, 1PG, 1DG, 2T (26) to 1G 5PG (21) (at Twickenham)
1975 Ireland 2G (12) to 1G, 1DG (9) (at Dublin)
1976 Ireland 2PG, 1DG, 1T (13) to 4PG (12) (at Twickenham)
1977 England 1T (4) to 0 (at Dublin)
1978 England 2G, 1PG (15) to 2PG, 1DG

(9) (at Twickenham)
1979 Ireland 1G, 1PG, 1DG (12) to 1PG, 1T (7) (at Dublin)
1980 England 3G, 2PG (24) to 3PG (9) (at Twickenham)
1981 England 1G, 1T (10) to 2DG (6) (at Dublin)
1982 Ireland 1G, 2PG, 1T (16) to 1G, 3PG (15) (at Twickenham)

1983 Ireland 1G, 5PG, 1T (25) to 5PG (15) (at Dublin)
1984 England 1DG, 3PG (12) to 3PG (9) (at Twickenham)
1985 Ireland 1DG, 2PG, 1T (13) to 2PG, 1T (10) (at Dublin)
1986 England 3G, 1PG, 1T (25) to 1G, 2PG, 2T (20) (at Twickenham)

England v. Scotland
102 matches played   England 48 wins   Scotland 38 wins   16 draws

1871 Scotland 1G, 1T to 1T (at Raeburn Place, Edinburgh)
1872 England 1G, 1DG, 2T to 1DG (at The Oval, London)
1873 Drawn, no score (at Glasgow)
1874 England 1DG to 1T (at The Oval)
1875 Drawn, no score (at Raeburn Place)
1876 England 1G, 1T to 0 (at The Oval)
1877 Scotland 1DG to 0 (at Raeburn Place)
1878 Drawn, no score (at The Oval)
1879 Drawn, Scotland 1DG, England 1G (at Raeburn Place)
1880 England 2G, 3T to 1G (at Manchester)
1881 Drawn, Scotland 1G, 1T, England 1DG, 1T (at Raeburn Place)
1882 Scotland 2T to 0 (at Manchester)
1883 England 2T to 1T (at Raeburn Place)
1884 England 1G to 1T (at Blackheath, London)
1885 No match
1886 Drawn, no score (at Raeburn Place)
1887 Drawn, 1T each (at Manchester)
1888 No match
1889 No match
1890 England 1G, 1T to 0 (at Raeburn Place)
1891 Scotland 2G, 1DG (9) to 1G (3) (at Richmond, London)
1892 England 1G (5) to 0 (at Raeburn Place)
1893 Scotland 2DG (8) to 0 (at Leeds)
1894 Scotland 2T (6) to 0 (at Raeburn Place)
1895 Scotland 1PG, 1T (6) to 1PG (3) (at Richmond)
1896 Scotland 1G, 2T (11) to 0 (at Glasgow)
1897 England 1G, 1DG, 1T (12) to 1T (3) (at Manchester)
1898 Drawn, 1T (3) each (at Powderhall, Edinburgh)
1899 Scotland 1G (5) to 0 (at Blackheath)
1900 Drawn, no score (at Inverleith, Edinburgh)
1901 Scotland 3G, 1T (18) to 1T (3)(at Blackheath)
1902 England 2T (6) to IT (3) (at Inverleith)
1903 Scotland 1DG, 2T (10) to 2T (6) (at Richmond)
1904 Scotland 2T (6) to 1T (3) (at Inverleith)
1905 Scotland 1G, 1T (8) to 0 (at Richmond)
1906 England 3T (9) to 1T (3) (at Inverleith)
1907 Scotland 1G, 1T (8) to 1T (3) (at Blackheath)
1908 Scotland 1G, 2DG, 1T (16) to 2G (10) (at Inverleith)
1909 Scotland 3G, 1T (18) to 1G, 1T (8) (at Richmond)
1910 England 1G, 3T (14) to 1G (5) (at Inverleith)
1911 England 2G, 1T (13) to 1G, 1T (8) (at Twickenham)
1912 Scotland 1G, 1T (8) to 1T (3) (at Inverleith)
1913 England 1T (3) to 0 (at Twickenham)
1914 England 2G, 2T (16) to 1G, 1DG, 2T (15) (at Inverleith)
1920 England 2G, 1T (13) to 1DG (4) (at Twickenham)
1921 England 3G, 1T (18) to 0 (at Inverleith)
1922 England 1G, 2T (11) to 1G (5) (at Twickenham)
1923 England 1G, 1T (8) to 2T (6) (at Inverleith)
1924 England 3G, 1DG, (19) to 0 (at Twickenham)
1925 Scotland 2G, 1DG (14) to 1G, 1PG, 1T (11) (at Murrayfield)
1926 Scotland 2G, 1DG, 1T (17) to 3T (9) (at Twickenham)
1927 Scotland 1G, 1DG, 4T (21) to 2G, 1PG (13) (at Murrayfield)
1928 England 2T (6) to 0 (at Twickenham)
1929 Scotland 4T (12) to 2T (6) (at Murrayfield)
1930 Drawn, no score (at Twickenham)
1931 Scotland 5G, 1T (28) to 2G, 1PG, 2T (19) (at Murrayfield)
1932 England 2G, 2T (16) to 1T (3) (at Twickenham)
1933 Scotland 1T (3) to 0 (at Murrayfield)
1934 England 2T (6) to 1T (3) (at Twickenham)
1935 Scotland 2G (10) to 1DG, 1T (7) (at Murrayfield)
1936 England 3T (9) to 1G, 1PG (8) (at Twickenham)
1937 England 2T (6) to 1PG (3) (at Murrayfield)
1938 Scotland 2PG, 5T (21) to 1DG, 3PG, 1T (16) (at Twickenham)
1939 England 3PG (9) to 2T (6) (at Murrayfield)
1947 England 4G, 1DG (24) to 1G (5) (at Twickenham)
1948 Scotland 2T (6) to 1PG (3) (at Murrayfield)
1949 England 2G, 3T (19) to 1PG (3) (at Twickenham)
1950 Scotland 2G, 1T (13) to 1G, 1PG, 1T (11) (at Murrayfield)
1951 England 1G (5) to 1T (3) (at Twickenham)
1952 England 2G, 1DG, 2T (19) to 1T (3) (at Murrayfield)
1953 England 4G, 2T (26) to 1G, 1T (8) (at Twickenham)
1954 England 2G, 1T (13) to 1T (3) (at Murrayfield)
1955 England 1PG, 2T (9) to 1PG, 1T (6) (at Twickenham)
1956 England 1G, 2PG (11) to 1PG, 1T (6) (at Murrayfield)
1957 England 2G, 1PG, 1T (16) to 1PG (3) (at Twickenham)
1958 Drawn, 1PG (3) each (at Murrayfield)
1959 Drawn, 1PG (3) each (at Twickenham)
1960 England 3G, 1DG, 1PG (21) to 3PG, 1T (12) (at Murrayfield)
1961 England 1PG, 1T (6) to 0 (at Twickenham)
1962 Drawn, 1PG (3) each (at Murrayfield)
1963 England 2G (10) to 1G, 1DG (8) (at Twickenham)
1964 Scotland 3G (15) to 1PG, 1T (6) (at Murrayfield)
1965 Drawn, England 1T (3), Scotland 1DG (3) (at Twickenham)
1966 Scotland 1PG, 1T (6) to 1DG (3) (at Murrayfield)
1967 England 3G, 2PG, 1DG, 1T (27) to 1G, 2PG, 1T (14) (at Twickenham)
1968 England 1G, 1PG (8) to 1PG, 1DG (6) (at Murrayfield)
1969 England 1G, 1T (8) to 1PG (3) (at Twickenham)
1970 Scotland 1G, 2PG, 1T (14) to 1G (5) (at Murrayfield)
1971 Scotland 2G, 1DG, 1T (16) to 3PG, 2T (15) (at Twickenham)
1971 Scotland 4G, 1PG, 1T (26) to 1PG, 1DG (6) (at Murrayfield) (Special Centenary match – non-championship)
1972 Scotland 4PG, 1DG, 2T (23) to 3PG (9) (at Murrayfield)
1973 England 2G, 2T (20) to 1G, 1PG, 1T (13) (at Twickenham)
1974 Scotland 1G, 2PG, 1T (16) to 1DG, 1PG, 2T (14) (at Murrayfield)
1975 England 1PG, 1T (7) to 2PG (6) (at Twickenham)
1976 Scotland 2G, 2PG, 1T (22) to 1G, 2PG (12) (at Murrayfield)
1977 England 2G, 2PG, 2T (26) to 2PG (6) (at Twickenham)
1978 England 2G, 1PG (15) to 0 (at Murrayfield)
1979 Drawn, 1PG, 1T (7) each (at Twickenham)
1980 England 2G, 2PG, 3T (30) to 2G, 2PG (18) (at Murrayfield)
1981 England 1G, 3PG, 2T (23) to 1G, 1PG, 2T (17) (at Twickenham)
1982 Drawn, Scotland 2PG, 1DG (9), England 3PG (9) (at Murrayfield)
1983 Scotland 1G, 3PG, 1DG, 1T (22) to 3PG, 1DG (12) (at Twickenham)
1984 Scotland 2G, 2PG (18) to 2PG (6) (at Murrayfield)
1985 England 2PG, 1T (10) to 1PG, 1T (7) (at Twickenham)
1986 Scotland 3G, 5PG (33) to 2PG (6) (at Murrayfield)

England v. Wales

91 matches played   England 36 wins   Wales 43 wins   12 draws

1881 England 7G, 1DG, 6T to 0 (at Blackheath, London)
1882 No match
1883 England 2G, 4T to 0 (at Swansea)
1884 England 1G, 2T to 1G (at Leeds)
1885 England 1G, 4T to 1G, 1T (at Swansea)
1886 England 1GM, 2T to 1G (at Blackheath)
1887 Drawn, no score (at Llanelli)
1888 No match
1889 No match
1890 Wales 1T to 0 (at Dewsbury)
1891 England 2G, 1T (7) to 1G (3) (at Newport)
1892 England 3G, 1T (17) to 0 (at Blackheath)
1893 Wales 1G, 1PG, 2T (12) to 1G, 3T (11) (at Cardiff)
1894 England 4G, 1GM (24) to 1T (3) (at Birkenhead)
1895 England 1G, 3T (14) to 2T (6) (at Swansea)
1896 England 2G, 5T (25) to 0 (at Blackheath)
1897 Wales 1G, 2T (11) to 0 (at Newport)
1898 England 1G, 3T (14) to 1DG, 1T (7) (at Blackheath)
1899 Wales 4G, 2T (26) to 1T (3) (at Swansea)
1900 Wales 2G, 1PG (13) to 1T (3) (at Gloucester)
1901 Wales 2G, 1T (13) to 0 (at Cardiff)
1902 Wales 1PG, 2T (9) to 1G, 1T (8) (at Blackheath)
1903 Wales 3G, 2T (21) to 1G (5) (at Swansea)
1904 Drawn, England 1G, 1PG, 2T (14), Wales 2G, 1GM (14) (at Leicester)
1905 Wales 2G, 5T (25) to 0 (at Cardiff)
1906 Wales 2G, 2T (16) to 1T (3) (at Richmond, London)
1907 Wales 2G, 4T (22) to 0 (at Swansea)
1908 Wales 3G, 1DG, 1PG, 2T (28) to 3G, 1T (18) (at Bristol)
1909 Wales 1G, 1T (8) to 0 (at Cardiff)
1910 England 1G, 1PG, 1T (11) to 2T (6) (at Twickenham)
1911 Wales 1PG, 4T (15) to 1G, 2T (11) (at Swansea)
1912 England 1G, 1T (8) to 0 (at Twickenham)
1913 England 1G, 1DG, 1T (12) to 0 (at Cardiff)
1914 England 2G (10) to 1G, 1DG (9) (at Twickenham)

1920 Wales 1G, 2DG, 1PG, 1T (19) to 1G (5) (at Swansea)
1921 England 1G, 1DG, 3T (18) to 1T (3) (at Twickenham)
1922 Wales 2G, 6T (28) to 2T (6) (at Cardiff)
1923 England 1DG, 1T (7) to 1T (3) (at Twickenham)
1924 England 1G, 4T (17) to 3T (9) (at Swansea)
1925 England 1PG, 3T (12) to 2T (6) (at Twickenham)
1926 Drawn, 1T (3) each (at Cardiff)
1927 England 1G, 1PG, 1GM (11) to 1PG, 2T (9) (at Twickenham)
1928 England 2G (10) to 1G, 1T (8) (at Swansea)
1929 England 1G, 1T (8) to 1T (3) (at Twickenham)
1930 England 1G, 1PG, 1T (11) to 1T (3) (at Cardiff)
1931 Drawn, England 1G, 2PG (11), Wales 1G, 1GM, 1T (11), (at Twickenham)
1932 Wales 1G, 1DG, 1PG (12) to 1G (5) (at Swansea)
1933 Wales 1DG, 1T (7) to 1T (3) (at Twickenham)
1934 England 3T (9) to 0 (at Cardiff)
1935 Drawn, England 1PG (3), Wales 1T (3) (at Twickenham)
1936 Drawn, no score (at Swansea)
1937 England 1DG (4) to 1T (3) (at Twickenham)
1938 Wales 1G, 2PG, 1T (14) to 1G, 1T (8) (at Cardiff)
1939 England 1T (3) to 0 (at Twickenham)
1947 England 1G, 1DG (9) to 2T (6) (at Cardiff)
1948 Drawn, England 1PG (3), Wales 1T (3) (at Twickenham)
1949 Wales 3T (9) to 1DG (3) (at Cardiff)
1950 Wales 1G, 1PG, 1T (11) to 1G (5) (at Twickenham)
1951 Wales 4G, 1T (23) to 1G (5) (at Swansea)
1952 Wales 1G, 1T (8) to 2T (6) (at Twickenham)
1953 England 1G, 1PG (8) to 1PG (3) (at Cardiff)
1954 England 3T (9) to 1PG, 1T (6) (at Twickenham)
1955 Wales 1PG (3) to 0 (at Cardiff)
1956 Wales 1G, 1T (8) to 1PG (3) (at Twickenham)
1957 England 1PG (3) to 0 (at Cardiff)

1958 Drawn, England 1T (3), Wales 1PG (3) (at Twickenham)
1959 Wales 1G (5) to 0 (at Cardiff)
1960 England 1G, 2PG, 1T (14) to 2PG (6) (at Twickenham)
1961 Wales 2T (6) to 1T (3) (at Cardiff)
1962 Drawn, no score (at Twickenham)
1963 England 2G, 1DG (13) to 1PG, 1T (6) (at Cardiff)
1964 Drawn, 2T (6) each (at Twickenham)
1965 Wales 1G, 1DG, 2T (14) to 1PG (3) (at Cardiff)
1966 Wales 1G, 2PG (11) to 1PG, 1T (6) (at Twickenham)
1967 Wales 5G, 2PG, 1DG (34) to 4PG, 3T (21) (at Cardiff)
1968 Drawn, England 1G, 1PG, 1T (11), Wales 1G, 1DG, 1T (11) (at Twickenham)
1969 Wales 3G, 2PG, 1DG, 2T (30) to 3PG (9) (at Cardiff)
1970 Wales 1G, 1DG, 3T (17) to 2G, 1PG (13) (at Twickenham)
1971 Wales 2G, 2DG, 1PG, 1T (22) to 1PG, 1T (6) (at Cardiff)
1972 Wales 1G, 2PG (12) to 1PG (3) (at Twickenham)
1973 Wales 1G, 1PG, 4T (25) to 2PG, 1DG (9) (at Cardiff)
1974 England 1G, 2PG, 1T (16) to 1G, 2PG (12) (at Twickenham)
1975 Wales 1G, 2PG, 2T (20) to 1T (4) (at Cardiff)
1976 Wales 3G, 1PG (21) to 3PG (9) (at Twickenham)
1977 Wales 2PG, 2T (14) to 3PG (9) (at Cardiff)
1978 Wales 3PG (9) to 2PG (6) (at Twickenham)
1979 Wales 2G, 1DG, 3T (27) to 1PG (3) (at Cardiff)
1980 England 3PG (9) to 2T (8) (at Twickenham)
1981 Wales 1G, 4PG, 1DG (21) to 5PG, 1T (19) (at Cardiff)
1982 England 3PG, 2T (17) to 1DG, 1T (7) (at Twickenham)
1983 Drawn, 1DG, 2PG, 1T each (at Cardiff)
1984 Wales 1G, 2DG, 4PG (24) to 5PG (15) (at Twickenham)
1985 Wales 2G, 1DG, 3PG (24) to 1G, 1DG, 2PG (15) (at Cardiff)
1986 England 1DG, 6PG (21) to 1G, 1DG, 3PG (18) (at Twickenham)

England v. France

61 matches played   England 32 wins   France 22 wins   7 draws

1906 England 4G, 5T (35) to 1G, 1T (8) (at Paris)
1907 England 5G, 1DG, 4T (41) to 2G, 1PG (13) (at Richmond, London)
1908 England 2G, 3T (19) to 0 (at Paris)
1909 England 2G, 4T (22) to 0 (at Leicester)
1910 England 1G, 2T (11) to 1T (3) (at Paris)
1911 England 5G, 2PG, 2T (37) to 0 (at Twickenham)

1912 England 1G, 1DG, 3T (18) to 1G, 1T (8) (at Paris)
1913 England 1G, 5T (20) to 0 (at Twickenham)
1914 England 6G, 3T (39) to 2G, 1T (13) (at Paris)
1920 England 1G, 1PG (8) to 1T (3) (at Twickenham)
1921 England 2G (10) to 2PG (6) (at Paris)

1922 Drawn, England 1G, 2PG (11), France 1G, 2T (11), (at Twickenham)
1923 England 1G, 1DG, 1T (12) to 1PG (3) (at Paris)
1924 England 2G, 3T (19) to 1DG, 1T (7) (at Twickenham)
1925 England 2G, 1GM (13) to 1G, 2T (11) (at Paris)
1926 England 1G, 2T (11) to 0 (at

Twickenham)
1927 France 1T (3) to 0 (at Paris)
1928 England 3G, 1T (18) to 1G, 1T (8) (at Twickenham)
1929 England 2G, 2T (16) to 2T (6) (at Paris)
1930 England 1G, 2T (11) to 1G (5) (at Twickenham)
1931 France 2DG, 2T (14) to 2G, 1T (13) (at Paris)
1947 England 2T (6) to 1PG (3) (at Twickenham)
1948 France 1G, 1DG, 2T (15) to 0 (at Paris)
1949 England 1G, 1DG (8) to 1DG (3) (at Twickenham)
1950 France 2T (6) to 1T (3) (at Paris)
1951 France 1G, 1DG, 1T (11) to 1T (3) (at Twickenham)
1952 England 2PG (6) to 1T (3) (at Paris)
1953 England 1G, 2T (11) to 0 (at Twickenham)
1954 France 1G, 1DG, 1T (11) to 1T (3) (at Paris)
1955 France 2G, 2DG (16) to 2PG, 1T (9) (at Twickenham)
1956 France 1G, 2PG, 1T (14) to 2PG, 1T (9) (at Paris)
1957 England 3T (9) to 1G (5) (at Twickenham)
1958 England 1G, 1PG, 2T (14) to 0 (at Paris)
1959 Drawn, 1PG (3) each (at Twickenham)
1960 Drawn, France 1PG (3), England 1T (3) (at Paris)
1961 Drawn, 1G (5) each (at Twickenham)
1962 France 2G, 1T (13) to 0 (at Paris)
1963 England 2PG (6) to 1G (5) (at Twickenham)
1964 England 1PG, 1T (6) to 1T (3) (at Paris)
1965 England 2PG, 1T (9) to 1PG, 1T (6) (at Twickenham)
1966 France 2G, 1T (13) to 0 (at Paris)
1967 France 2G, 1DG, 1PG (16) to 3PG, 1DG (12) (at Twickenham)
1968 France 1G, 2DG, 1PG (14) to 1DG, 2PG (9) (at Paris)
1969 England 2G, 3PG, 1T (22) to 1G, 1DG (8) (at Twickenham)
1970 France 4G, 2DG, 1PG, 2T (35) to 2G, 1PG (13) (at Paris)
1971 Drawn, England 1G, 3PG (14), France 1G, 1PG, 1DG, 1T (14) (at Twickenham)
1972 France 5G, 1PG, 1T (37) to 1G, 2PG (12) (at Paris)
1973 England 2PG, 2T (14) to 1G (6) (at Twickenham)
1974 Drawn, 1G, 1PG, 1DG (12) each (at Paris)
1975 France 4G, 1PG (27) to 4PG, 2T (20) (at Twickenham)
1976 France 3G, 3T (30) to 1G, 1PG (9) (at Paris)
1977 France 1T (4) to 1PG (3) (at Twickenham)
1978 France 2G, 1PG (15) to 2 DG (6) (at Paris)
1979 England 1PG, 1T (7) to 1G (6) (at Twickenham)
1980 England 1PG, 2DG, 2T (17) to 1G, 1PG, 1T (13) (at Paris)
1981 France 1G, 2DG, 1T (16) to 4PG (12) (at Twickenham)
1982 England 2G, 5PG (27) to 1G, 2PG, 1DG (15) (at Paris)
1983 France 2G, 1PG, 1T (19) to 4PG, 1DG (15) (at Twickenham)
1984 France 3G, 1DG, 1PG, 2T (32) to 2G, 2PG (18) (at Paris)
1985 Drawn, England 1DG, 2PG (9), France 3DG (9) (at Twickenham)
1986 France 2G, 3PG, 2T (29) to 2PG, 1T (10) (at Paris)

England v. Australia

11 matches played England 4 wins Australia 7 wins

1909 Australia 3T (9) to 1T (3) (at Blackheath)
1948 Australia 1G, 2T (11) to 0 (at Twickenham)
1958 England 1PG, 2T (9) to 1DG, 1PG (6) (at Twickenham)
1963 Australia 3G, 1T (18) to 3T (9) (at Sydney)
1967 Australia 1G, 3DG, 2PG, 1T (23) to 1G, 2PG (11) (at Twickenham)
1973 England 1G, 2PG, 2T (20) to 1PG (3) (at Twickenham)
1975 **1** Australia 2PG, 2DG, 1T (16) to 1G, 1PG (9) (at Sydney)
2 Australia 2G, 2PG, 3T (30) to 2G, 3PG (21) (at Brisbane)
Australia won series 2-0
1976 England 1G, 3PG, 2T (23) to 2PG (6) (at Twickenham)
1982 England 1G, 3PG (15) to 1PG, 2T (11) (at Twickenham)
1984 Australia 2G, 1PG, 1T (19) to 1PG (3) (at Twickenham)

England v. New Zealand

15 matches played England 3 wins New Zealand 12 wins

1905 New Zealand 5T (15) to 0 (at Crystal Palace, London)
1925 New Zealand 1G, 1PG, 3T (17) to 1G, 1PG, 1T (11) (at Twickenham)
1936 England 1DG, 3T (13) to 0 (at Twickenham)
1954 New Zealand 1G (5) to 0 (at Twickenham)
1963 **1** New Zealand 3G, 1DG, 1PG (21) to 1G, 2PG (11) (at Auckland)
2 New Zealand 1GM, 2T (9) to 1PG, 1T (6) (at Christchurch)
New Zealand won series 2-0
1964 New Zealand 1G, 2PG, 1T (14) to 0 (at Twickenham)
1967 New Zealand 4G, 1T (23) to 1G, 1PG, 1T (11) (at Twickenham)
1973 New Zealand 1G, 1DG (9) to 0 (at Twickenham)
1973 England 2G, 1T (16) to 1G, 1T (10) (at Auckland)
1978 New Zealand 1G, 2PG, 1T (16) to 1PG, 1DG (6) (at Twickenham)
1979 New Zealand 2PG, 1T (10) to 3PG (9) (at Twickenham)
1983 England 1G, 3PG (15) to 1G, 1PG (9) (at Twickenham)
1985 **1** New Zealand 6PG (18) to 1G, 1PG, 1T (13) (at Christchurch)
2 New Zealand 3G, 1DG, 3PG, 3T (42) to 2G, 1DG (15) (at Wellington)
New Zealand won series 2-0

England v. South Africa

9 matches played England 2 wins South Africa 6 wins 1 drawn

1906 Drawn, 1T (3) each (at Crystal Palace, London)
1913 South Africa 2PG, 1T (9) to 1T (3) (at Twickenham)
1932 South Africa 1DG, 1T (7) to 0 (at Twickenham)
1952 South Africa 1G, 1PG (8) to 1T (3) (at Twickenham)
1961 South Africa 1G (5) to 0 (at Twickenham)
1969 England 1G, 1PG, 1T (11) to 1G, 1PG (8) (at Twickenham)
1972 England 1G, 4PG (18) to 3PG (9) (at Twickenham)
1984 **1** South Africa 3G, 5PG (33) to 1DG, 4PG (15) (at Port Elizabeth)
2 South Africa 4G, 1PG, 2T (35) to 3PG (9) (at Johannesburg)
South Africa won series 2-0

England v. Argentina

1981 **1** Drawn, Argentina 1G, 2DG, 1PG, 1T (19), England 2G, 1PG, 1T (19) (at Buenos Aires)
2 England 1G, 2PG (12) to 1G (6) (at Buenos Aires)
England won series 1-0, with 1 draw

England v. Romania

1985 England 2DG, 4PG, 1T (22) to 5PG (15) (at Twickenham)

Ireland v. Scotland
96 matches played   Ireland 44 wins   Scotland 48 wins   4 draws

1877	Scotland 4G, 2DG, 2T to 0 (at Belfast)	
1878	No match	
1879	Scotland 1G, 1DG, 1T to 0 (at Belfast)	
1880	Scotland 1G, 2DG, 2T to 0 (at Glasgow)	
1881	Ireland 1DG to 1T (at Belfast)	
1882	Scotland 2T to 0 (at Glasgow)	
1883	Scotland 1G, 1T to 0 (at Belfast)	
1884	Scotland 2G, 2T to 1T (at Raeburn Place, Edinburgh)	
1885	Scotland 1G, 2T to 0 (at Raeburn Place)	
1886	Scotland 3G, 1DG, 2T to 0 (at Raeburn Place)	
1887	Scotland 1G, 1GM, 2T to 0 (at Belfast)	
1888	Scotland 1G to 0 (at Raeburn Place)	
1889	Scotland 1DG to 0 (at Belfast)	
1890	Scotland 1DG, 1T to 0 (at Raeburn Place)	
1891	Scotland 3G, 1DG, 2T (14) to 0 (at Belfast)	
1892	Scotland 1T (2) to 0 (at Raeburn Place)	
1893	Drawn, no score (at Belfast)	
1894	Ireland 1G (5) to 0 (at Dublin)	
1895	Scotland 2T (6) to 0 (at Raeburn Place)	
1896	Drawn, no score (at Dublin)	
1897	Scotland 1G, 1PG (8) to 1T (3) (at Powderhall, Edinburgh)	
1898	Scotland 1G, 1T (8) to 0 (at Belfast)	
1899	Ireland 3T (9) to 1PG (3) (at Inverleith, Edinburgh)	
1900	Drawn, no score (at Dublin)	
1901	Scotland 3T (9) to 1G (5) (at Inverleith)	
1902	Ireland 1G (5) to 0 (at Belfast)	
1903	Scotland 1T (3) to 0 (at Inverleith)	
1904	Scotland 2G, 3T (19) to 1T (3) (at Dublin)	
1905	Ireland 1G, 2T (11) to 1G (5) (at Inverleith)	
1906	Scotland 2G, 1GM (13) to 2T (6) (at Dublin)	
1907	Scotland 3G (15) to 1PG (3) (at Inverleith)	
1908	Ireland 2G, 2T (16) to 1G, 1PG, 1T (11) (at Dublin)	
1909	Scotland 3T (9) to 1PG (3) (at Inverleith)	
1910	Scotland 1G, 3T (14) to 0 (at Belfast)	
1911	Ireland 2G, 2T (16) to 1DG, 2T (10) (at Inverleith)	
1912	Ireland 1DG, 1PG, 1T (10) to 1G, 1T (8) (at Dublin)	
1913	Scotland 4G, 3T (29) to 2G, 1DG (14) (at Inverleith)	

1914	Ireland 2T (6) to 0 (at Dublin)	
1920	Scotland 2G, 1PG, 2T (19) to 0 (at Inverleith)	
1921	Ireland 3T (9) to 1G, 1T (8) (at Dublin)	
1922	Scotland 2T (6) to 1T (3) (at Inverleith)	
1923	Scotland 2G, 1T (13) to 1T (3) (at Dublin)	
1924	Scotland 2G, 1T (13) to 1G, 1T (8) (at Inverleith)	
1925	Scotland 2G, 1DG (14) to 1G, 1PG (8) (at Dublin)	
1926	Ireland 1T (3) to 0 (at Murrayfield)	
1927	Ireland 2T (6) to 0 (at Dublin)	
1928	Ireland 2G, 1T (13) to 1G (5) (at Murrayfield)	
1929	Scotland 2G, 2T (16) to 1DG, 1T (7) (at Dublin)	
1930	Ireland 1G, 3T (14) to 1G, 2T (11) (at Murrayfield)	
1931	Ireland 1G, 1T (8) to 1G (5) (at Dublin)	
1932	Ireland 4G (20) to 1G, 1T (8) (at Murrayfield)	
1933	Scotland 2DG (8) to 2T (6) (at Dublin)	
1934	Scotland 2G, 1PG, 1T (16) to 3T (9) (at Murrayfield)	
1935	Ireland 4T (12) to 1G (5) (at Dublin)	
1936	Ireland 1DG, 2T (10) to 1DG (4) (at Murrayfield)	
1937	Ireland 1G, 2T (11) to 1DG (4) (at Dublin)	
1938	Scotland 2G, 1DG, 1PG, 2T (23) to 1G, 3T (14) (at Murrayfield)	
1939	Ireland 1PG, 1GM, 2T (12) to 1T (3) (at Dublin)	
1947	Ireland 1T (3) to 0 (at Murrayfield)	
1948	Ireland 2T (6) to 0 (at Dublin)	
1949	Ireland 2G, 1PG (13) to 1PG (3) (at Murrayfield)	
1950	Ireland 3G, 2PG (21) to 0 (at Dublin)	
1951	Ireland 1DG, 1T (6) to 1G (5) (at Murrayfield)	
1952	Ireland 1PG, 3T (12) to 1G, 1PG (8) (at Dublin)	
1953	Ireland 4G, 2T (26) to 1G, 1PG (8) (at Murrayfield)	
1954	Ireland 2T (6) to 0 (at Belfast)	
1955	Scotland 2PG, 1DG, 1T (12) to 1PG (3) (at Murrayfield)	
1956	Ireland 1G, 3T (14) to 2G (10) (at Dublin)	
1957	Ireland 1G (5) to 1PG (3) (at Murrayfield)	
1958	Ireland 2PG, 2T (12) to 2T (6) (at Dublin)	

1959	Ireland 1G, 1PG (8) to 1PG (3) (at Murrayfield)	
1960	Scotland 1DG, 1T (6) to 1G (5) (at Dublin)	
1961	Scotland 2G, 1PG, 1T (16) to 1G, 1T (8) (at Murrayfield)	
1962	Scotland 1G, 1DG, 2PG, 2T (20) to 1PG, 1T (6) (at Dublin)	
1963	Scotland 1PG (3) to 0 (at Murrayfield)	
1964	Scotland 2PG (6) to 1PG (3) (at Dublin)	
1965	Ireland 2G, 1DG, 1T (16) to 1DG, 1PG (6) (at Murrayfield)	
1966	Scotland 1G, 2T (11) to 1PG (3) (at Dublin)	
1967	Ireland 1G (5) to 1PG (3) (at Murrayfield)	
1968	Ireland 1G, 1PG, 2T (14) to 2PG (6) (at Dublin)	
1969	Ireland 2G, 2T (16) to 0 (at Murrayfield)	
1970	Ireland 2G, 2T (16) to 1G, 1DG, 1T (11) (at Dublin)	
1971	Ireland 1G, 2PG, 2T (17) to 1G (5) (at Murrayfield)	
1972	No match	
1973	Scotland 2PG, 3DG, 1T (19) to 2PG, 2T (14) (at Murrayfield)	
1974	Ireland 1G, 1PG (9) to 2PG (6) (at Dublin)	
1975	Scotland 2PG, 2DG, 2T (20) to 1G, 1PG, 1T (13) (at Murrayfield)	
1976	Scotland 4PG, 1DG (15) to 2PG (6) (at Dublin)	
1977	Scotland 2PG, 1DG, 3T (21) to 1G, 3PG, 1DG (18) (at Murrayfield)	
1978	Ireland 1G, 2PG (12) to 3PG (9) (at Dublin)	
1979	Drawn, 1PG, 2T (11) each (at Murrayfield)	
1980	Ireland 1G, 3PG, 1DG, 1T (22) to 2G, 1PG (15) (at Dublin)	
1981	Scotland 1PG, 1DG, 1T (10) to 1G, 1PG (9) (at Murrayfield)	
1982	Ireland 6PG, 1DG (21) to 1G, 2PG (12) (at Dublin)	
1983	Ireland 1G, 3PG (15) to 2PG, 1DG, 1T (13) (at Murrayfield)	
1984	Scotland 3G, 2PG, 2T (32) to 1G, 1PG (9) (at Dublin) (Scotland's score includes one penalty-try)	
1985	Ireland 2G, 1DG, 1PG (18) to 4PG, 1DG (15) (at Murrayfield)	
1986	Scotland 2PG, 1T (10) to 1G, 1PG (9) (at Dublin)	

Ireland v. Wales
88 matches played   Ireland 29 wins   Wales 54 wins   5 draws

1882	Wales 2G, 2T to 0 (at Dublin)	
1883	No match	
1884	Wales 1DG, 2T to 0 (at Cardiff)	
1885	No match	
1886	No match	
1887	Wales 1DG, 1T to 3T (at Birkenhead)	
1888	Ireland 1G, 1DG, 1T to 0 (at Dublin)	
1889	Ireland 2T to 0 (at Swansea)	
1890	Drawn, 1G each (at Dublin)	
1891	Wales 1G, 1DG (6) to 1DG, 1T (4) (at Llanelli)	

1892	Ireland 1G, 2T (8) to 0 (at Dublin)	
1893	Wales 1T (2) to 0 (at Llanelli)	
1894	Ireland 1PG (3) to 0 (at Belfast)	
1895	Wales 1G (5) to 1T (3) (at Cardiff)	
1896	Ireland 1G, 1T (8) to 1DG (4) (at Dublin)	
1897	No match	
1898	Wales 1G, 1PG, 1T (11) to 1PG (3) (at Limerick)	

1899	Ireland 1T (3) to 0 (at Cardiff)	
1900	Wales 1T (3) to 0 (at Belfast)	
1901	Wales 2G (10) to 3T (9) (at Swansea)	
1902	Wales 1G, 1DG, 2T (15) to 0 (at Dublin)	
1903	Wales 6T (18) to 0 (at Cardiff)	
1904	Ireland 1G, 3T (14) to 4T (12) (at Belfast)	
1905	Wales 2G (10) to 1T (3) (at Swansea)	
1906	Ireland 1G, 2T (11) to 2T (6) (at	

Belfast)

1907 Wales 2G, 1DG, 1PG, 4T (29) to 0 (at Cardiff)
1908 Wales 1G, 2T (11) to 1G (5) (at Belfast)
1909 Wales 3G, 1T (18) to 1G (5) (at Swansea)
1910 Wales 1DG, 5T (19) to 1T (3) (at Dublin)
1911 Wales 2G, 1PG, 1T (16) to 0 (at Cardiff)
1912 Ireland 1G, 1DG, 1T (12) to 1G (5) (at Belfast)
1913 Wales 2G, 1PG, 1T (16) to 2G, 1PG (13) (at Swansea)
1914 Wales 1G, 2T (11) to 1T (3) (at Belfast)
1920 Wales 3G, 1DG, 3T (28) to 1DG (4) (at Cardiff)
1921 Wales 1PG, 1T (6) to 0 (at Belfast)
1922 Wales 1G, 2T (11) to 1G (5) (at Swansea)
1923 Ireland 1G (5) to 1DG (4) (at Dublin)
1924 Ireland 2G, 1T (13) to 1DG, 2T (10) (at Cardiff)
1925 Ireland 2G, 1PG, 2T (19) to 1T (3) (at Belfast)
1926 Wales 1G, 2T (11) to 1G, 1PG (8) (at Swansea)
1927 Ireland 2G, 1PG, 2T (19) to 1G, 1DG (9) (at Dublin)
1928 Ireland 2G, 1T (13) to 2G (10) (at Cardiff)
1929 Drawn, 1G (5) each (at Belfast)
1930 Wales 1PG, 3T (12) to 1DG, 1PG (7) (at Swansea)
1931 Wales 1G, 1DG, 2T (15) to 1T (3) (at Belfast)
1932 Ireland 4T (12) to 1DG, 2T (10) (at Cardiff)
1933 Ireland 1DG, 1PG, 1T (10) to 1G (5)

(at Belfast)

1934 Wales 2G, 1T (13) to 0 (at Swansea)
1935 Ireland 2PG, 1T (9) to 1PG (3) (at Belfast)
1936 Wales 1PG (3) to 0 (at Cardiff)
1937 Ireland 1G (5) to 1PG (3) (at Belfast)
1938 Wales 1G, 1PG, 1T (11) to 1G (5) (at Swansea)
1939 Wales 1DG, 1T (7) to 0 (at Belfast)
1947 Wales 1PG, 1T (6) to 0 (at Swansea)
1948 Ireland 2T (6) to 1T (3) (at Belfast)
1949 Ireland 1G (5) to 0 (at Swansea)
1950 Wales 2T (6) to 1PG (3) (at Belfast)
1951 Drawn, Wales 1PG (3) to Ireland 1T (3) (at Cardiff)
1952 Wales 1G, 1PG, 2T (14) to 1PG (3) (at Dublin)
1953 Wales 1G (5) to 1T (3) (at Swansea)
1954 Wales 1DG, 3PG (12) to 2PG, 1T (9) (at Dublin)
1955 Wales 3G, 1PG, 1T (21) to 1PG (3) (at Cardiff)
1956 Ireland 1G, 1DG, 1PG (11) to 1PG (3) (at Dublin)
1957 Wales 2PG (6) to 1G (5) (at Cardiff)
1958 Wales 3T (9) to 1PG, 1T (6) (at Dublin)
1959 Wales 1G, 1T (8) to 1PG, 1T (6) (at Cardiff)
1960 Wales 2G (10) to 2PG, 1T (9) (at Dublin)
1961 Wales 2PG, 1T (9) to 0 (at Cardiff)
1962 Drawn, Ireland 1DG (3), Wales 1PG (3) (at Dublin)
1963 Ireland 1G, 1DG, 2PG (14) to 1DG, 1T (6) (at Cardiff)
1964 Wales 3G (15) to 2PG (6) (at Dublin)
1965 Wales 1G, 1DG, 1PG, 1T (14) to 1G, 1PG (8) (at Cardiff)
1966 Ireland 1DG, 1PG, 1T (9) to 1PG, 1T (6) (at Dublin)

1967 Ireland 1T (3) to 0 (at Cardiff)
1968 Ireland 1PG, 1DG, 1T (9) to 1PG, 1DG (6) (at Dublin)
1969 Wales 3G, 1DG, 1PG, 1T (24) to 1G, 2PG (11) (at Cardiff)
1970 Ireland 1G, 1DG, 1PG, 1T (14) to 0 (at Dublin)
1971 Wales 1G, 2PG, 1DG, 3T (23) to 3PG (9) (at Cardiff)
1972 No match
1973 Wales 1G, 2PG, 1T (16) to 1G, 2PG (12) (at Cardiff)
1974 Drawn, Ireland 3PG (9), Wales 1G, 1PG (9) (at Dublin)
1975 Wales 3G, 2PG, 2T (32) to 1T (4) (at Cardiff)
1976 Wales 3G, 4PG, 1T (34) to 3PG (9) (at Dublin)
1977 Wales 2G, 2PG, 1DG, 1T (25) to 3PG (9) (at Cardiff)
1978 Wales 4PG, 2T (20) to 3PG, 1DG, 1T (16) (at Dublin)
1979 Wales 2G, 4PG (24) to 2G, 3PG (21) (at Cardiff)
1980 Ireland 3G, 1PG (21) to 1PG, 1T (7) (at Dublin)
1981 Wales 2PG, 1DG (9) to 2T (8) (at Cardiff)
1982 Ireland 1G, 2PG, 2T (20) to 1G, 1PG, 1DG (12) (at Dublin)
1983 Wales 1G, 3PG, 2T (23) to 3PG (9) (at Cardiff)
1984 Wales 1G, 4PG (18) to 3PG (9) (at Dublin)
1985 Ireland 2G, 3PG (21) to 1G, 1DG (9) (at Cardiff)
1986 Wales 1G, 3PG, 1T (19) to 1G, 2PG (12) (at Dublin)

Ireland v. France

59 matches played   Ireland 25 wins   France 29 wins   5 draws

1909 Ireland 2G, 1PG, 2T (19) to 1G, 1T (8) (at Dublin)
1910 Ireland 1G, 1T (8) to 1T (3) (at Paris)
1911 Ireland 3G, 1DG, 2T (25) to 1G (5) (at Cork)
1912 Ireland 1G, 2T (11) to 2T (6) (at Paris)
1913 Ireland 3G, 3T (24) to 0 (at Cork)
1914 Ireland 1G, 1T (8) to 2T (6) (at Paris)
1920 France 5T (15) to 1DG, 1T (7) (at Dublin)
1921 France 4G (20) to 2G (10) (at Paris)
1922 Ireland 1G, 1PG (8) to 1T (3) (at Dublin)
1923 France 1G, 3T (14) to 1G, 1T (8) (at Paris)
1924 Ireland 2T (6) to 0 (at Dublin)
1925 Ireland 1PG, 2T (9) to 1T (3) (at Paris)
1926 Ireland 1G, 1PG, 1T (11) to 0 (at Belfast)
1927 Ireland 1G, 1PG (8) to 1T (3) (at Paris)
1929 Ireland 2T (6) to 0 (at Paris)
1930 France 1G (5) to 0 (at Belfast)
1931 France 1T (3) to 0 (at Paris)
1947 France 4T (12) to 1G, 1PG (8) (at Dublin)
1948 Ireland 2G, 1T (13) to 2T (6) (at Paris)
1949 France 2G, 2PG (16) to 3PG (9) (at Dublin)
1950 Drawn, France 1DG (3), Ireland 1PG

(3) (at Paris)

1951 Ireland 1PG, 2T (9) to 1G, 1T (8) (at Dublin)
1952 Ireland 1G, 1PG, 1T (11) to 1G, 1PG (8) (at Paris)
1953 Ireland 2G, 2T (16) to 1DG (3) (at Belfast)
1954 France 1G, 1T (8) to 0 (at Paris)
1955 France 1G (5) to 1PG (3) (at Dublin)
1956 France 1G, 2DG, 1T (14) to 1G, 1PG (8) (at Paris)
1957 Ireland 1G, 1PG, 1T (11) to 2PG (6) (at Dublin)
1958 France 1G, 1DG, 1PG (11) to 2PG (6) (at Paris)
1959 Ireland 1DG, 1PG, 1T (9) to 1G (5) (at Dublin)
1960 France 1G, 3DG, 3T (23) to 2T (6) (at Paris)
1961 France 2DG, 2PG, 1T (15) to 1PG (3) (at Dublin)
1962 France 1G, 2T (11) to 0 (at Paris)
1963 France 3G, 2DG, 1T (24) to 1G (5) (at Dublin)
1964 France 3G, 1DG, 3T (27) to 1DG, 1T (6) (at Paris)
1965 Drawn, 1T (3) each (at Dublin)
1966 France 1G, 1PG, 1T (11) to 1DG, 1PG (6) (at Paris)

1967 France 1G, 2DG (11) to 1PG, 1T (6) (at Dublin)
1968 France 2G, 1PG, 1DG (16) to 2PG (6) (at Paris)
1969 Ireland 1G, 1DG, 3PG (17) to 2PG, 1T (9) (at Dublin)
1970 France 1G, 1DG (8) to 0 (at Paris)
1971 Drawn, Ireland 1T (9), France 2PG, 1DG (9) (at Dublin)
1972 Ireland 2PG, 2T (14) to 1G, 1PG (9) (at Paris)
1972 Ireland 3G, 2PG (24) to 1G, 2T (14) (at Dublin)
Non-championship match
1973 Ireland 2PG (6) to 1T (4) (at Dublin)
1974 France 1G, 1PG (9) to 2PG (6) (at Paris)
1975 Ireland 2G, 1PG, 2DG, 1T (25) to 1PG, 1DG (6) (at Dublin)
1976 France 2G, 2PG, 2T (26) to 1PG (3) (at Paris)
1977 France 1G, 3PG (15) to 2PG (6) (at Dublin)
1978 France 2PG, 1T (10) to 3PG (9) (at Paris)
1979 Drawn, Ireland 3PG (9), France 1G, 1PG (9) (at Dublin)
1980 France 1G, 2PG, 1DG, 1T (19) to 1G, 3PG, 1DG (18) (at Paris)

| 1981 | France 3PG, 2DG, 1T (19) to 3PG, 1T (13) (at Dublin) | 1983 | Ireland 1G, 4PG, 1T (22) to 1G, 2PG, 1T (16) (at Dublin) | 1985 | Drawn, Ireland 5PG (15), France 2G, 1PG (15) (at Dublin) |
| 1982 | France 1G, 4PG, 1T (22) to 3PG (9) (at Paris) | 1984 | France 1G, 4PG, 1DG, 1T (25) to 4PG (12) (at Paris) | 1986 | France 1G, 1DG, 4PG, 2T (29) to 3PG (9) (at Paris) |

Ireland v. Australia
10 matches played   Ireland 6 wins   Australia 4 wins

1947	Australia 2G, 2T (16) to 1PG (3) (at Dublin)		Sydney)		Sydney)
1958	Ireland 1PG, 2T (9) to 2T (6) (at Dublin)	1968	Ireland 2G (10) to 1T (3) (at Dublin)		Ireland won series 2-0
1967	Ireland 2DG, 1PG, 2T (15) to 1G, 1DG (8) (at Dublin)	1976	Australia 1G, 2PG, 2T (20) to 2PG, 1T (10) (at Dublin)	1981	Australia 3PG, 1DG, 1T (16) to 4PG (12) (at Dublin)
1967	Ireland 1G, 1DG, 1T (11) to 1G (5) (at	1979	**1** Ireland 2G, 4PG, 1DG (27) to 1G, 2PG (12) (at Brisbane)	1984	Australia 3DG, 1PG, 1T (16) to 3PG (9) (at Dublin)
			2 Ireland 1PG, 2DG (9) to 1PG (3) (at		

Ireland v. New Zealand
9 matches played   New Zealand 8 wins   1 draw

1905	New Zealand 3G (15) to 0 (at Dublin)		to 1PG (3) (at Dublin)		(at Dublin)
1924	New Zealand 1PG, 1T (6) to 0 (at Dublin)	1963	New Zealand 1PG, 1T (6) to 1G (5) (at Dublin)	1976	New Zealand 1PG, 2T (11) to 1PG (3) (at Wellington)
1935	New Zealand 1G, 2PG, 2T (17) to 2PG, 1T (9) (at Dublin)	1973	Drawn, Ireland 2PG, 1T (10), New Zealand 1G, 1T (10) (at Dublin)	1978	New Zealand 2DG, 1T (10) to 2PG (6) (at Dublin)
1954	New Zealand 1G, 1DG, 1PG, 1T (14)	1974	New Zealand 1G, 3PG (15) to 2PG (6)		

Ireland v. South Africa
10 matches played   Ireland 1 win   South Africa 8 wins   1 draw

1906	South Africa 1PG, 4T (15) to 1PG, 3T (12) (at Belfast)		(5) (at Dublin)	1970	Drawn, 1G, 1PG (8) each (at Dublin)
1912	South Africa 4G, 6T (38) to 0 (at Dublin)	1960	South Africa 1G, 1T (8) to 1PG (3) (at Dublin)	1981	**1** South Africa 1G, 3PG, 2T (23) to 2G, 1PG (15) (at Cape Town)
1931	South Africa 1G, 1T (8) to 1PG (3) (at Dublin)	1961	South Africa 3G, 1PG, 2T (24) to 1G, 1PG (8) (at Cape Town)		**2** South Africa 1PG, 3DG (12) to 2PG, 1T (10) (at Durban)
1951	South Africa 1G, 1DG, 3T (17) to 1G	1965	Ireland 2PG, 1T (9) to 1PG, 1T (6) (at Dublin)		South Africa won series 2-0

Scotland v. Wales
90 matches played   Scotland 37 wins   Wales 51 wins   2 draws

1883	Scotland 3G to 1G (at Raeburn Place, Edinburgh)	1904	Wales 3G, 1PG, 1T (21) to 1T (3) (at Swansea)	1928	Wales 2G, 1T (13) to 0 (at Murrayfield)
1884	Scotland 1DG, 1T to 0 (at Newport)	1905	Wales 2T (6) to 1T (3) (at Inverleith)	1929	Wales 1G, 3T (14) to 1DG, 1PG (7) (at Swansea)
1885	Drtawn, no score (at Glasgow)	1906	Wales 3T (9) to 1PG (3) (at Cardiff)	1930	Scotland 1G, 1DG, 1T (12) to 1G, 1DG (9) (at Murrayfield)
1886	Scotland 2G, 1T to 0 (at Cardiff)	1907	Scotland 2T (6) to 1PG (3) (at Inverleith)	1931	Wales 2G, 1T (13) to 1G, 1T (8) (at Cardiff)
1887	Scotland 4G, 8T to 0 (at Raeburn Place)	1908	Wales 2T (6) to 1G (5) (at Swansea)	1932	Wales 1PG, 1T (6) to 0 (at Murrayfield)
1888	Wales 1T to 0 (at Newport)	1909	Wales 1G (5) to 1PG (3) (at Inverleith)	1933	Scotland 1G, 1PG, 1T (11) to 1T (3) (at Swansea)
1889	Scotland 2T to 0 (at Raeburn Place)	1910	Wales 1G, 3T (14) to 0 (at Cardiff)	1934	Wales 2G, 1T (13) to 1PG, 1T (6) (at Murrayfield)
1890	Scotland 1G, 2T to 1T (at Cardiff)	1911	Wales 2G, 1DG, 6T (32) to 1DG, 2T (10) (at Inverleith)	1935	Wales 1DG, 2T (10) to 2T (6) (at Cardiff)
1891	Scotland 1G, 2DG, 6T (15) to 0 (at Raeburn Place)	1912	Wales 2G, 2DG, 1T (21) to 2T (6) (at Swansea)	1936	Wales 2G, 1T (13) to 1T (3) (at Murrayfield)
1892	Scotland 1G, 1T (7) to 1T (2) (at Swansea)	1913	Wales 1G, 1T (8) to 0 (at Inverleith)	1937	Scotland 2G, 1T (13) to 2T (6) (at Swansea)
1893	Wales 1PG, 3T (9) to 0 (at Raeburn Place)	1914	Wales 2G, 2DG, 1PG, 1T (24) to 1G (5) (at Cardiff)	1938	Scotland 1G, 1PG (8) to 2T (6) (at Murrayfield)
1894	Wales 1DG, 1T (7) to 0 (at Newport)	1920	Scotland 2PG, 1T (9) to 1G (5) (at Inverleith)	1939	Wales 1G, 1PG, 1T (11) to 1PG (3) (at Cardiff)
1895	Scotland 1G (5) to 1GM (4) (at Raeburn Place)	1921	Scotland 1G, 1PG, 2T (14) to 2DG (8) (at Swansea)	1947	Wales 2G, 1PG, 3T (22) to 1G, 1PG (8) (at Murrayfield)
1896	Wales 2T (6) to 0 (at Cardiff)	1922	Drawn, Scotland 1PG, 2T (9), Wales 1G, 1DG (9) (at Inverleith)	1948	Wales 1G, 1PG, 2T (14) to 0 (at Cardiff)
1897	No match	1923	Scotland 1G, 2T (11) to 1G, 1PG (8) (at Cardiff)	1949	Scotland 2T (6) to 1G (5) (at Murrayfield)
1898	No match	1924	Scotland 4G, 1PG, 4T (35) to 2G (10) (at Inverleith)	1950	Wales 1DG, 1PG, 2T (12) to 0 (at Swansea)
1899	Scotland 1GM, 2DG, 3T (21) to 2G (10) (at Inverleith, Edinburgh)	1925	Scotland 1G, 1DG, 5T (24) to 1G, 1PG, 2T (14) (at Swansea)		
1900	Wales 4T (12) to 1T (3) (at Swansea)	1926	Scotland 1G, 1PG (8) to 1G (5) (at Murrayfield)		
1901	Scotland 3G, 1T (18) to 1G, 1T (8) (at Inverleith)	1927	Scotland 1G (5) to 0 (at Cardiff)		
1902	Wales 1G, 3T (14) to 1G (5) (at Cardiff)				
1903	Scotland 1PG, 1T (6) to 0 (at Inverleith)				

1951 Scotland 2G, 1DG, 1PG, 1T (19) to 0 (at Murrayfield)
1952 Wales 1G, 2PG (11) to 0 (at Cardiff)
1953 Wales 1PG, 3T (12) to 0 (at Murrayfield)
1954 Wales 1PG, 4T (15) to 1T (3) (at Swansea)
1955 Scotland 1G, 1DG, 1PG, 1T (14) to 1G, 1T (8) (at Murrayfield)
1956 Wales 3T (9) to 1PG (3) (at Cardiff)
1957 Scotland 1DG, 1PG, 1T (9) to 1PG, 1T (6) (at Murrayfield)
1958 Wales 1G, 1T (8) to 1PG (3) (at Cardiff)
1959 Scotland 1PG, 1T (6) to 1G (5) (at Murrayfield)
1960 Wales 1G, 1PG (8) to 0 (at Cardiff)
1961 Scotland 1T (3) to 0 (at Murrayfield)
1962 Scotland 1G, 1T (8) to 1DG (3) (at Cardiff)
1963 Wales 1DG, 1PG (6) to 0 (at Murrayfield)
1964 Wales 1G, 1PG, 1T (11) to 1T (3) (at

Cardiff)
1965 Wales 1G, 2PG, 1T (14) to 2DG, 2PG (12) (at Murrayfield)
1966 Wales 1G, 1T (8) to 1PG (3) (at Cardiff)
1967 Scotland 1G, 1DG, 1T (11) to 1G (5) (at Murrayfield)
1968 Wales 1G (5) to 0 (at Cardiff)
1969 Wales 1G, 2PG, 2T (17) to 1PG (3) (at Murrayfield)
1970 Wales 3G, 1T (18) to 1DG, 1PG, 1T (9) (at Cardiff)
1971 Wales 2G, 1PG, 2T (19) to 4PG, 2T (18) (at Murrayfield)
1972 Wales 3G, 3PG, 2T (35) to 1G, 2PG (12) (at Cardiff)
1973 Scotland 1G, 1T (10) to 3PG (9) (at Murrayfield)
1974 Wales 1G (6) to 0 (at Cardiff)
1975 Scotland 3PG, 1DG (12) to 2PG, 1T (10) (at Murrayfield)
1976 Wales 2G, 3PG, 1DG, 1T (28) to 1G (6) (at Cardiff)

1977 Wales 2G, 2PG (18) to 1G, 1DG (9) (at Murrayfield)
1978 Wales 1PG, 1DG, 4T (22) to 2PG, 2T (14) (at Cardiff)
1979 Wales 1G, 3PG, 1T (19) to 3PG, 1T (13) (at Murrayfield)
1980 Wales 1G, 1PG, 2T (17) to 1G (6) (at Cardiff)
1981 Scotland 2G, 1PG (15) to 2PG (6) (at Murrayfield) (Scotland's score includes one penalty-try)
1982 Scotland 4G, 2DG, 1T (34) to 1G, 4PG (18) (at Cardiff)
1983 Wales 1G, 3PG, 1T (19) to 1G, 3PG (15) (at Murrayfield)
1984 Scotland 2G, 1PG (15) to 1G, 1PG (9) (at Cardiff)
1985 Wales 1G, 1DG, 4PG, 1T (25) to 2G, 2DG, 1PG (21) (at Murrayfield)
1986 Wales 1DG, 5PG, 1T (22) to 1PG, 3T (15) (at Cardiff)

Scotland v. France

56 matches played   Scotland 27 wins   France 27 wins   2 draws

1910 Scotland 3G, 4T (27) to 0 (at Inverleith, Edinburgh)
1911 France 2G, 2T (16) to 1G, 1DG, 2T (15) (at Paris)
1912 Scotland 5G, 1PG, 1T (31) to 1T (3) (at Inverleith)
1913 Scotland 3G, 2T (21) to 1T (3) (at Paris)
1914 No match
1920 Scotland 1G (5) to 0 (at Paris)
1921 France 1T (3) to 0 (at Inverleith)
1922 Drawn, 1T (3) each (at Paris)
1923 Scotland 2G, 2T (16) to 1GM (3) (at Inverleith)
1924 France 4T (12) to 1DG, 1PG, 1T (10) (at Paris)
1925 Scotland 2G, 5T (25) to 1DG (4) (at Inverleith)
1926 Scotland 1G, 1PG, 4T (20) to 1PG, 1T (6) (at Paris)
1927 Scotland 4G, 1PG (23) to 2T (6) (at Murrayfield)
1928 Scotland 5T (15) to 2T (6) (at Paris)
1929 Scotland 1PG, 1T (6) to 1T (3) (at Murrayfield)
1930 France 1DG, 1T (7) to 1T (3) (at Paris)
1931 Scotland 2PG (6) to 1DG (4) (at Murrayfield)
1947 France 1G, 1T (8) to 1PG (3) (at Paris)
1948 Scotland 2PG, 1T (9) to 1G, 1PG (8) (at Murrayfield)
1949 Scotland 1G, 1T (8) to 0 (at Paris)
1950 Scotland 1G, 1T (8) to 1G (5) (at Murrayfield)

1951 France 1G, 2PG, 1T (14) to 2PG, 2T (12) (at Paris)
1952 France 2G, 1PG (13) to 1G, 2PG (11) (at Murrayfield)
1953 France 1G, 1DG, 1PG (11) to 1G (5) (at Paris)
1954 France 1T (3) to 0 (at Murrayfield)
1955 France 1PG, 4T (15) to 0 (at Paris)
1956 Scotland 2PG, 2T (12) to 0 (at Murrayfield)
1957 Scotland 1DG, 1PG (6) to 0 (at Paris)
1958 Scotland 1G, 1PG, 1T (11) to 2PG, 1T (9) (at Murrayfield)
1959 France 2DG, 1T (9) to 0 (at Paris)
1960 France 2G, 1T (13) to 1G, 1PG, 1T (11) (at Murrayfield)
1961 France 1G, 1DG, 1PG (11) to 0 (at Paris)
1962 France 1G, 2PG (11) to 1PG (3) (at Murrayfield)
1963 Scotland 1G, 1DG, 1PG (11) to 1DG, 1PG (6) (at Paris)
1964 Scotland 2G (10) to 0 (at Murrayfield)
1965 France 2G, 2T (16) to 1G, 1T (8) (at Paris)
1966 Drawn, Scotland 1T (3), France 1PG (3) (at Murrayfield)
1967 Scotland 2PG, 1DG (9) to 1G, 1T (8) (at Paris)
1968 France 1G, 1T (8) to 1PG, 1T (6) (at Murrayfield)
1969 Scotland 1PG, 1T (6) to 1PG (3) (at Paris)
1970 France 1G, 1DG, 1T (11) to 2PG, 1T

(9) (at Murrayfield)
1971 France 2G, 1PG (13) to 1G, 1PG (8) (at Paris)
1972 Scotland 1G, 1PG, 1DG, 2T (20) to 1G, 1PG (9) (at Murrayfield)
1973 France 3PG, 1DG, 1T (16) to 2PG, 1DG, 1T (13) (at Paris)
1974 Scotland 1G, 3PG, 1T (19) to 1PG, 1DG (6) (at Murrayfield)
1975 France 1PG, 1DG, 1T (10) to 3PG (9) (at Paris)
1976 France 3PG, 1T (13) to 1PG, 1DG (6) (at Murrayfield)
1977 France 2G, 1PG, 2T (23) to 1PG (3) (at Paris)
1978 France 1G, 3PG, 1T (19) to 1G, 1PG, 1DG, 1T (16) (at Murrayfield)
1979 France 2PG, 1DG, 3T (21) to 1G, 1PG, 2T (17) (at Paris)
1980 Scotland 2G, 2PG, 1T (22) to 1PG, 1DG, 2T (14) (at Murrayfield)
1981 France 1G, 2PG, 1T (16) to 1G, 1PG (9) (at Paris)
1982 Scotland 3PG, 1DG, 1T (16) to 1PG, 1T (7) (at Murrayfield)
1983 France 1G, 1T, 3PG (19) to 1G, 2DG, 1PG (15) (at Paris)
1984 Scotland 1G, 5PG (21) to 1DG, 1PG (12) (at Murrayfield)
1985 France 1PG, 2T (11) to 1PG (3) (at Paris)
1986 Scotland 6PG (18) to 1DG, 2PG, 2T (17) (at Murrayfield)

Scotland v. Australia

10 matches played   Scotland 6 wins   Australia 4 wins

1947 Australia 2G, 2T (16) to 1DG, 1PG (7) (at Murrayfield)
1958 Scotland 2PG, 2T (12) to 1G, 1T (8) (at Murrayfield)
1966 Scotland 1G, 1PG, 1T (11) to 1G (5) (at Murrayfield)
1968 Scotland 2PG, 1T (9) to 1PG (3) (at

Murrayfield)
1970 Australia 1G, 1PG, 5T (23) to 1PG (3) (at Sydney)
1975 Scotland 1G, 1T (10) to 1PG (3) (at Murrayfield)
1981 Scotland 1G, 5PG, 1DG (24) to 1PG, 3T (15) (at Murrayfield)

1982 **1** Scotland 1G, 1PG, 1DG (12) to 1PG, 1T (7) (at Brisbane)
2 Australia 3G, 5PG (33) to 3PG (9) (at Sydney)
Series drawn 1-1
1984 Australia 3G, 5PG, 1T (37) to 4PG (12) (at Murrayfield)

Scotland v. New Zealand
12 matches played   New Zealand 10 wins   2 draws

1905 New Zealand 4T (12) to 1DG, 1T (7) (at Inverleith, Edinburgh)
1935 New Zealand 3G, 1T (18) to 1G, 1T (8) (at Murrayfield)
1954 New Zealand 1PG (3) to 0 (at Murrayfield)
1964 Drawn, no score (at Murrayfield)
1967 New Zealand 1G, 2PG, 1T (14) to 1DG (3) (at Murrayfield)

1972 New Zealand 1G, 2T (14) to 1DG, 2PG (9) (at Murrayfield)
1975 New Zealand 4G (24) to 0 (at Auckland)
1978 New Zealand 2G, 2PG (18) to 1G, 1DG (9) (at Murrayfield)
1979 New Zealand 2G, 2T (20) to 2PG (6) (at Murrayfield)
1981 **1** New Zealand 1PG, 2T (11) to 1T (4)

(at Dunedin)
2 New Zealand 6G, 1T (40) to 1G, 2PG, 1DG (15) (at Auckland)
New Zealand won series 2-0
1983 Drawn, Scotland 5PG, 2DG, 1T (25), New Zealand 2G, 3PG, 1T (25) (at Murrayfield)

Scotland v. South Africa
8 matches played   Scotland 3 wins   South Africa 5 wins

1906 Scotland 2T (6) to 0 (at Glasgow)
1912 South Africa 2G, 2T (16) to 0 (at Inverleith)
1932 South Africa 2T (6) to 1T (3) (at Murrayfield)
1951 South Africa 7G, 1DG, 2T (44) to 0 (at Murrayfield)
1960 South Africa 3G, 1T (18) to 2G (10) (at

Port Elizabeth)
1961 South Africa 2PG, 2T (12) to 1G (5) (at Murrayfield)
1965 Scotland 1G, 1DG (8) to 1G (5) (at Murrayfield)
1969 Scotland 1PG, 1T (6) to 1PG (3) (at Murrayfield)

Scotland v. Romania

1981 Scotland 4PG (12) to 2PG (6) (at Murrayfield)
1982 Romania 2G, 1DG, 3PG, 1T (28) to 1G, 1DG, 3PG, 1T (22) (at Bucharest)
1986 Scotland 3G, 5PG (33) to 1DG, 5PG (18) (at Bucharest)

Wales v. France
59 matches played   Wales 36 wins   France 20 wins   3 draws

1908 Wales 3G, 1PG, 6T (36) to 1DG (4) (at Cardiff)
1909 Wales 7G, 4T (47) to 1G (5) (at Paris)
1910 Wales 8G, 1PG, 2T (49) to 1G, 2PG, 1T (14) (at Swansea)
1911 Wales 3G (15) to 0 (at Paris)
1912 Wales 1G, 3T (14) to 1G, 1T (8) (at Newport)
1913 Wales 1G, 2T (11) to 1G, 1T (8) (at Paris)
1914 Wales 5G, 2T (31) to 0 (at Swansea)
1920 Wales 2T (6) to 1G (5) (at Paris)
1921 Wales 2PG, 2T (12) to 1DG (4) (at Cardiff)
1922 Wales 1G, 2T (11) to 1T (3) (at Paris)
1923 Wales 2G, 1PG, 1T (16) to 1G, 1T (8) (at Swansea)
1924 Wales 1DG, 2T (10) to 2T (6) (at Paris)
1925 Wales 1G, 2T (11) to 1G (5) (at Cardiff)
1926 Wales 1DG, 1T (7) to 1G (5) (at Paris)
1927 Wales 2G, 5T (25) to 1DG, 1T (7) (at Swansea)
1928 France 1G, 1T (8) to 1T (3) (at Paris)
1929 Wales 1G, 1T (8) to 1T (3) (at Cardiff)
1930 Wales 2DG, 1T (11) to 0 (at Paris)
1931 Wales 5G, 1DG, 2T (35) to 1T (3) (at Swansea)
1947 Wales 1PG (3) to 0 (at Paris)
1948 France 1G, 2T (11) to 1PG (3) (at Swansea)
1949 France 1G (5) to 1T (3) (at Paris)
1950 Wales 3G, 1PG, 1T (21) to 0 (at

Cardiff)
1951 France 1G, 1PG (8) to 1T (3) (at Paris)
1952 Wales 1DG, 2PG (9) to 1G (5) (at Swansea)
1953 Wales 2T (6) to 1PG (3) (at Paris)
1954 Wales 2G, 3PG (19) to 2G, 1PG (13) (at Cardiff)
1955 Wales 2G, 2PG (16) to 1G, 1DG, 1PG (11) (at Paris)
1956 Wales 1G (5) to 1T (3) (at Cardiff)
1957 Wales 2G, 1PG, 2T (19) to 2G, 1T (13) (at Paris)
1958 France 2G, 2DG (16) to 1PG, 1T (6) (at Cardiff)
1959 France 1G, 1PG, 1T (11) to 1PG (3) (at Paris)
1960 France 2G, 2T (16) to 1G, 1PG (8) (at Cardiff)
1961 France 1G, 1T (8) to 2T (6) (at Paris)
1962 Wales 1PG (3) to 0 (at Cardiff)
1963 France 1G (5) to 1PG (3) (at Paris)
1964 Drawn, 1G, 2PG (11) each (at Cardiff)
1965 France 2G, 1PG, 1DG, 2T (22) to 2G, 1T (13) (at Paris)
1966 Wales 2PG, 1T (9) to 1G, 1T (8) (at Cardiff)
1967 France 1G, 2DG, 1PG, 2T (20) to 1G, 2PG, 1DG (14) (at Paris)
1968 France 1G, 1PG, 1DG, 1T (14) to 2PG, 1T (9) (at Cardiff)
1969 Drawn, France 1G, 1PG (8), Wales 1G, 1T (8) (at Paris)
1970 Wales 1G, 2PG (11) to 2T (6) (at

Cardiff)
1971 Wales 1PG, 2T (9) to 1G (5) (at Paris)
1972 Wales 4PG, 2T (20) to 2PG (6) (at Cardiff)
1973 France 3PG, 1DG (12) to 1DG (3) (at Paris)
1974 Drawn, 3PG, 1DG, 1T (16) each (at Cardiff)
1975 Wales 1G, 1PG, 4T (25) to 2PG, 1T (10) (at Paris)
1976 Wales 5PG, 1T (19) to 1G, 1PG, 1T (13) (at Cardiff)
1977 France 1G, 2PG, 1T (16) to 3PG (9) (at Paris)
1978 Wales 1G, 2DG, 1T (16) to 1DG, 1T (7) (at Cardiff)
1979 France 2PG, 2T (14) to 3PG, 1T (13) (at Paris)
1980 Wales 1G, 3T (18) to 1G, 1DG (9) (at Cardiff)
1981 France 5PG, 1T (19) to 1G, 3PG (15) (at Paris)
1982 Wales 6PG, 1T (22) to 1G, 2PG (12) (at Cardiff)
1983 France 1DG, 3PG, 1T (16) to 1G, 1PG (9) (at Paris)
1984 France 1G, 4PG, 1DG (21) to 1G, 2PG, 1T (16) (at Cardiff)
1985 France 2PG, 2T (14) to 1PG (3) (at Paris)
1986 France 2G, 1DG, 2T (23) to 5PG (15) (at Cardiff)

Wales v. Australia
11 matches played   Wales 7 wins   Australia 4 wins

1908 Wales 1PG, 2T (9) to 2T (6) (at Cardiff)
1947 Wales 2PG (6) to 0 (at Cardiff)
1958 Wales 1DG, 1PG, 1T (9) to 1T (3) (at Cardiff)
1966 Australia 1G, 1DG, 1PG, 1T (14) to 1G, 1PG, 1T (11) (at Cardiff)

1969 Wales 2G, 2PG, 1T (19) to 2G, 2PG (16) (at Sydney)
1973 Wales 4PG, 3T (24) to 0 (at Cardiff)
1975 Wales 3G, 1PG, 1DG, 1T (28) to 1PG (3) (at Cardiff)
1978 **1** Australia 1G, 4PG (18) to 2T (8) (at Brisbane)

2 Australia 3PG, 2DG, 1T (19) to 2PG, 1DG, 2T (17) (at Sydney)
Australia won series 2-0
1981 Wales 1G, 3PG, 1DG (18) to 1G, 1PG, 1T (13) (at Cardiff)
1984 Australia 3G, 2PG, 1T (28) to 1G, 1PG (9) (at Cardiff)

Wales v. New Zealand
11 matches played   Wales 3 wins   New Zealand 8 wins

1905 Wales 1T (3) to 0 (at Cardiff)
1924 New Zealand 2G, 1PG, 2T (19) to 0 (at Swansea)
1935 Wales 2G, 1T (13) to 1G, 1DG, 1T (12) (at Cardiff)
1953 Wales 2G, 1PG (13) to 1G, 1PG (8) (at Cardiff)
1963 New Zealand 1DG, 1PG (6) to 0 (at

Cardiff)
1967 New Zealand 2G, 1PG (13) to 1DG, 1PG (6) (at Cardiff)
1969 **1** New Zealand 2G, 1PG, 2T (19) to 0 (at Christchurch)
      2 New Zealand 3G, 1DG, 5PG (33) to 2PG, 2T (12) (at Auckland)
      New Zealand won series 2-0

1972 New Zealand 5PG, 1T (19) to 4PG, 1T (16) (at Cardiff)
1978 New Zealand 3PG, 1T (13) to 4PG (12) (at Cardiff)
1980 New Zealand 2G, 1PG, 2T (23) to 1PG (3) (at Cardiff)

Wales v. South Africa
7 matches played   South Africa 6 wins   1 draw

1906 South Africa 1G, 2T (11) to 0 (at Swansea)
1912 South Africa 1PG (3) to 0 (at Cardiff)
1931 South Africa 1G, 1T (8) to 1T (3) (at Swansea)
1951 South Africa 1DG, 1T (6) to 1T (3) (at

Cardiff)
1960 South Africa 1PG (3) to 0 (at Cardiff)
1964 South Africa 3G, 1DG, 2PG (24) to 1PG (3) (at Durban)
1970 Drawn, 1PG, 1T (6) each (at Cardiff)

Wales v. Romania

1983 Romania 1G, 2PG, 3T (24) to 2PG (6) (at Bucharest)

British Isles v. Australia
7 matches played   British Isles 6 wins   Australia 1 win

1930 Australia 2T (6) to 1G (5) (at Sydney)
1950 **1** British Isles 2G, 2PG, 1DG (19) (at Brisbane)
      2 British Isles 3G, 1PG, 2T (24) to 1T (3) (at Sydney)
      British Isles won series 2-0

1959 **1** British Isles 1G, 2PG, 1DG, 1T (17) to 2PG (6) (at Brisbane)
      2 British Isles 3G, 1PG, 2T (24) to 1PG (3) (at Sydney)
      British Isles won series 2-0
1966 **1** British Isles 1G, 1PG, 1T (11) to 1G,

1PG (8) (at Sydney)
      2 British Isles 5G, 1PG, 1DG (31) to 0 (at Brisbane)
      British Isles won series 2-0

British Isles v. New Zealand
28 matches played   British Isles 5 wins   New Zealand 21 wins   2 draws

1930 **1** British Isles 2T (6) to 1T (3) (at Dunedin)
      2 New Zealand 2G, 1GM (13) to 2G (10) (at Christchurch)
      3 New Zealand 1G, 1DG, 2T (15) to 2G (10) (at Auckland)
      4 New Zealand 2G, 4T (22) to 1G, 1PG (8) (at Wellington)
      New Zealand won series 3-1
1950 **1** Drawn, 2T, 1PG (9) each (at Dunedin)
      2 New Zealand 1G, 1T (8) to 0 (at Christchurch)
      3 New Zealand 1PG, 1T (6) to 1PG (3) (at Wellington)
      4 New Zealand 1G, 1DG, 1T (11) to 1G, 1PG (8) (at Auckland)
      New Zealand won series 3-0, with 1 draw
1959 **1** New Zealand 6PG (18) to 1G, 1PG, 3T (17) (at Dunedin)
      2 New Zealand 1G, 2T (11) to 1G, 1PG

(8) (at Wellington)
      3 New Zealand 2G, 1PG, 1DG, 2T (22) to 1G, 1PG (8) (at Christchurch)
      4 British Isles 3T (9) to 2PG (6) (at Auckland)
      New Zealand won series 3-1
1966 **1** New Zealand 1G, 2PG, 1DG, 2T (20) to 1PG (3) (at Dunedin)
      2 New Zealand 2G, 1PG, 1T (16) to 3PG, 1DG (12) (at Wellington)
      3 New Zealand 2G, 2PG, 1T (19) to 2T (6) (at Christchurch)
      4 New Zealand 3G, 1PG, 1DG, 1T (24) to 1G, 1PG, 1T (11) (at Auckland)
      New Zealand won series 4-0
1971 **1** British Isles 2PG, 1T to 1PG (3) (at Dunedin)
      2 New Zealand 2G, 1PG, 3T (22) to 1PG, 1DG, 2T (12) (at Christchurch)
      3 British Isles 2G, 1DG (13) to 1T (3) (at Wellington)
      4 Drawn, British Isles 1G, 2PG, 1DG

(14), New Zealand 1G, 2PG, 1T (14) (at Auckland)
      British Isles won series 2-1, with 1 draw
1977 **1** New Zealand 2G, 1T (16) to 4PG (12) (at Wellington)
      2 British Isles 3PG, 1T (13) to 3PG (9) (at Christchurch)
      3 New Zealand 1G, 2PG, 1DG, 1T (19) to 1PG, 1T (7) (at Dunedin)
      4 New Zealand 2PG, 1T (10) to 1G, 1PG (9) (at Auckland)
      New Zealand won series 3-1
1983 **1** New Zealand 3PG, 1DG, 1T (16) to 3PG, 1DG (12) (at Christchurch)
      2 New Zealand 1G, 1PG (9) to 0 (at Wellington)
      3 New Zealand 1G, 3PG (15) to 2T (8) (at Dunedin)
      4 New Zealand 4G, 2PG, 2T (38) to 2PG (6) (at Auckland)
      New Zealand won series 4-0

British Isles v. South Africa
30 matches played   British Isles 8 wins   South Africa 18 wins   4 draws

1910 **1** South Africa 1G, 4T (14) to 1DG, 2T (10) (at Johannesburg)
      2 British Isles 1G, 1T (8) to 1T (3) (at Port Elizabeth)
      3 South Africa 3G, 1PG, 1T (21) to 1G (5) (at Cape Town)
      South Africa won series 2-1

1924 **1** South Africa 1DG, 1T (7) to 1T (3) (at Durban)
      2 South Africa 1G, 1PG, 3T (17) to 0 (at Johannesburg)
      3 Drawn, 1T (3) each (at Port Elizabeth)
      4 South Africa 1DG, 4T (16) to 1PG,

2T (9) (at Cape Town)
      South Africa won series 3-0, with 1 draw
1938 **1** South Africa 4G, 2PG (26) to 4PG (12) (at Johannesburg)
      2 South Africa 2G, 2PG, 1T (19) to 1T (3) (at Port Elizabeth)

3 British Isles 1G, 1PG, 1DG, 3T (21) to 2G, 1PG, 1T (16) (at Cape Town)
South Africa won series 2-1

1955 1 British Isles 4G, 1T (23) to 2G, 2PG, 2T (22) (at Johannesburg)
2 South Africa 2G, 5T (25) to 1PG, 2T (9) (at Cape Town)
3 British Isles 1PG, 1DG, 1T (9) to 2PG (6) (at Pretoria)
4 South Africa 2G, 1DG, 3T (22) to 1G, 1T (8) (at Port Elizabeth)
Series drawn 2-2

1962 1 Drawn, 1T (3) each (at Johannesburg)
2 South Africa 1PG (3) to 0 (at Durban)
3 South Africa 1G, 1PG (8) to 1DG (3)

(at Cape Town)
4 South Africa 5G, 2PG, 1T (34) to 1G, 1PG, 2T (14) (at Bloemfontein)
South Africa won series 3-0, with 1 draw

1968 1 South Africa 2G, 4PG, 1T (25) to 1G, 5PG (20) (at Pretoria)
2 Drawn, 2PG (6) each (at Port Elizabeth)
3 South Africa 1G, 2PG (11) to 2PG (6) (at Cape Town)
4 South Africa 2G, 1DG, 2T (19) to 2PG (6) (at Johannesburg)
South Africa won series 3-0, with 1 draw

1974 1 British Isles 3PG, 1DG (12) to 1DG (3) (at Cape Town)

2 British Isles 1G, 1PG, 1DG, 4T (28) to 2PG, 1DG (9) (at Pretoria)
3 British Isles 1G, 2PG, 2DG, 2T (26) to 3PG (9) (at Port Elizabeth)
4 Drawn, British Isles 1G, 1PG, 1T (13), South Africa 3PG, 1T (13) (at Johannesburg)
British Isles won series 3-0, with 1 draw

1980 1 South Africa 3G, 2T (26) to 5PG, 1DG, 1T (22) (at Cape Town)
2 South Africa 2G, 2PG, 2T (26) to 1G, 3PG, 1T (19) (at Bloemfontein)
3 South Africa 1G, 1PG, 1DG (12) to 2PG, 1T (10) (at Port Elizabeth)
4 British Isles 1G, 1PG, 2T (17) to 3PG, 1T (13) (at Pretoria)
South Africa won series 3-1

France v. Australia
15 matches played   France 9 wins   Australia 4 wins   2 draws

1948 France 2G, 1T (13) to 2PG (6) (at Paris)
1958 France 2G, 2DG, 1T (19) to 0 (at Paris)
1961 France 2DG, 3T (15) to 1G, 1PG (8) (at Sydney)
1967 France 1G, 1DG, 4PG (20) to 1G, 1DG, 1PG, 1T (14) (at Paris)
1968 Australia 1G, 1DG, 1PG (11) to 2G (10) (at Sydney)
1971 1 Australia 1G, 1PG, 1T (13) to 1PG, 2T (11) (at Toulouse)
2 France 1G, 4PG (18) to 3PG (9) (at

Paris)
Series drawn 1-1
1972 1 Drawn, Australia 2PG, 2T (14), France 1G, 2T (14) (at Sydney)
2 France 2G, 1T (16) to 5PG (15) (at Brisbane)
France won series 1-0, with 1 draw
1976 1 France 3G (18) to 4PG, 1DG (15) (at Bordeaux)
2 France 2G, 1PG, 1DG, 4T (34) to 2PG (6) (at Paris)
France won series 2-0

1981 1 Australia 1G, 1PG, 2T (17) to 1G, 2PG, 1DG (15) (at Bisbane)
2 Australia 2G, 4PG (24) to 2DG, 2T (14) (at Sydney)
Australia won series 2-0
1983 1 Drawn, France 3PG, 2DG (15), Australia 1G, 1PG, 2DG (15) (at Clermont-Ferrand)
2 France 1G, 3PG (15) to 1PG, 1DG (6) (at Paris)
France won series 1-0, with 1 draw

France v. New Zealand
20 matches played   France 4 wins   New Zealand 16 wins

1906 New Zealand 4G, 6T (38) to 1G, 1T (8) (at Paris)
1925 New Zealand 3G, 5T (30) to 2T (6) (at Toulouse)
1954 France 1T (3) to 0 (at Paris)
1961 1 New Zealand 2G, 1DG (13) to 2DG (6) (at Auckland)
2 New Zealand 1G (5) to 1T (3) (at Wellington)
3 New Zealand 4G, 3PG, 1T (32) to 1T (3) (at Christchurch)
New Zealand won series 3-0
1964 New Zealand 1DG, 1PG, 2T (12) to 1PG (3) (at Paris)
1967 New Zealand 3G, 1PG, 1T (21) to 3PG, 1DG, 1T (15) (at Paris)

1968 1 New Zealand 3PG, 1T (12) to 1DG, 2PG (9) (at Christchurch)
2 New Zealand 3PG (9) to 1PG (3) (at Wellington)
3 New Zealand 2G, 1DG, 2PG (19) to 1DG, 3T (12) (at Auckland)
New Zealand won series 3-0
1973 France 1G, 1PG, 1T (13) to 2PG (6) (at Paris)
1977 1 France 1G, 1DG, 3PG (18) to 1DG, 2PG, 1T (13) (at Toulouse)
2 New Zealand 1G, 1DG, 2PG (15) to 1PG (3) (at Paris)
Series drawn 1-1
1979 1 New Zealand 1G, 3PG, 2T (23) to 1G, 1DG (9) (at Christchurch)

2 France 1G, 1PG, 1DG, 3T (24) to 1G, 3PG, 1T (19) (at Auckland)
Series drawn 1-1
1981 1 New Zealand 2PG, 1DG, 1T (13) to 2PG, 1DG (9) (at Toulouse)
2 New Zealand 2G, 2PG (18) to 2PG (6) (at Paris) (New Zealand's score includes one penalty-try)
New Zealand won series 2-0
1984 1 New Zealand 2PG, 1T (10) to 1G, 1DG (9) (at Christchurch)
2 New Zealand 2G, 5PG, 1T (31) to 2PG, 3T (18) (at Auckland)
New Zealand won series 2-0

France v. South Africa
19 matches played   France 3 wins   South Africa 12 wins   4 draws

1913 South Africa 4G, 1PG, 5T (38) to 1G (5) (at Bordeaux)
1952 South Africa 2G, 1PG, 4T (25) to 1DG (3) (at Paris)
1958 1 Drawn, South Africa 1T (3), France 1DG (3) (at Cape Town)
2 France 2DG, 1PG (9) to 1G (5) (at Johannesburg)
France won series 1-0, with 1 draw
1961 Drawn, no score (at Paris)
1964 France 1G, 1PG (8) to 1PG, 1T (6) (at Springs, South Africa)
1967 1 South Africa 4G, 1PG, 1T (26) to 1T (3) (at Durban)
2 South Africa 2G, 1PG, 1T (16) to

1PG (3) (at Bloemfontein)
3 France 2G, 2DG, 1PG (19) to 1G, 2PG, 1T (14) (at Johannesburg)
4 Drawn, South Africa 1DG, 1PG (6), France 1PG, 1T (6) (at Cape Town)
South Africa won series 2-1, with 1 draw
1968 1 South Africa 4PG (12) to 3T (9) (at Bordeaux)
2 South Africa 2G, 1PG, 1T (16) to 1G, 2DG (11) (at Paris)
South Africa won series 2-0
1971 1 South Africa 2G, 1DG, 3PG (22) to 2PG, 1T (9) (at Bloemfontein)
2 Drawn, 1G, 1DG (8) each (at

Durban)
South Africa won series 1-0, with 1 draw
1974 1 South Africa 3PG, 1T (13) to 1T (4) (at Toulouse)
2 South Africa 2PG, 1T (10) to 2T (8) (at Paris)
South Africa won series 2-0
1975 1 South Africa 3G, 4PG, 2T (38) to 3G, 1PG, 1T (25) (at Bloemfontein)
2 South Africa 2G, 7PG (33) to 1G, 3PG, 1DG (18) (at Pretoria)
South Africa won series 2-0
1980 South Africa 4G, 3PG, 1T (37) to 1G, 3PG (15) (at Pretoria)

France v. Romania
30 matches played   France 22 wins   Romania 8 wins

1981   France 18 to 9 (at Narbonne)
1982   Romania 13 to 9 (at Bucharest)
1983   France 26 to 15 (at Toulouse)

1984   France 18 to 3 (at Bucharest)
1986   France 25 to 13 (at Lille)

Australia v. New Zealand
79 matches played   Australia 19 wins   New Zealand 56 wins   4 draws

1903   New Zealand 1G, 1PG, 2GM, 2T (22) to 1PG (3) (at Sydney)
1905   New Zealand 1G, 3T (14) to 1T (3) (at Dunedin)
1907   **1** New Zealand 4G, 2T (26) to 1PG, 1GM (6) (at Sydney)
2 New Zealand 1G, 3T (14) to 1G (5) (at Brisbane)
3 Drawn, 1G (5) each (at Sydney)
New Zealand won series 2-0, with 1 draw
1910   **1** New Zealand 2T (6) to 0 (at Sydney)
2 Australia 1G, 2T (11) to 0 (at Sydney)
3 New Zealand 2G, 6T (28) to 2G, 1PG (13) (at Sydney)
New Zealand won series 2-1
1913   **1** New Zealand 3G, 5T (30) to 1G (5) (at Wellington)
2 New Zealand 3G, 1DG, 2T (25) to 2G, 1T (13) (at Dunedin)
3 Australia 2G, 2T (16) to 1G (5) (at Christchurch)
New Zealand won series 2-1
1914   **1** New Zealand 1G (5) to 0 (at Sydney)
2 New Zealand 1G, 4T (17) to 0 (at Brisbane)
3 New Zealand 2G, 4T (22) to 1DG, 1T (7) (at Sydney)
New Zealand won series 3-0
1929   **1** Australia 2PG, 1T (9) to 1G, 1PG (8) (at Sydney)
2 Australia 1G, 2PG, 2T (17) to 1PG, 2T (9) (at Brisbane)
3 Australia 3PG, 2T (15) to 2G, 1T (13) (at Sydney)
Australia won series 3-0
1931   New Zealand 1G, 4PG, 1T (20) to 2G, 1T (13) (at Auckland)
1932   **1** Australia 2G, 2PG, 2T (22) to 2G, 1DG, 1T (17) (at Sydney)
2 New Zealand 1G, 1DG, 1PG, 3T (21) to 1T (3) (at Brisbane)
3 New Zealand 3G, 2T (21) to 2G, 1T (13) (at Sydney)
New Zealand won series 2-1
1934   **1** Australia 2G, 3PG, 2T (25) to 1G, 2T (11) (at Sydney)
2 Drawn, 1T (3) each (at Sydney)
Australia won series 1-1, with 1 draw
1936   **1** New Zealand 1G, 2T (11) to 1PG, 1T (6) (at Wellington)
2 New Zealand 4G, 1PG, 5T (38) to 2G, 1PG (13) (at Dunedin)
New Zealand won series 2-0
1938   **1** New Zealand 3G, 2PG, 1T (24) to 3PG (9) (at Sydney)
2 New Zealand 2G, 1DG, 2T (20) to 1G, 1PG, 2T (14) (at Brisbane)
3 New Zealand 1G, 2PG, 1T (14) to 1PG, 1T (6) (at Sydney)
New Zealand won series 3-0
1946   **1** New Zealand 5G, 2T (31) to 1G, 1T

(8) (at Dunedin)
2 New Zealand 1G, 3PG (14) to 2G (10) (at Auckland)
New Zealand won series 2-0
1947   **1** New Zealand 2G, 1T (13) to 1G (5) (at Brisbane) (New Zealand's score includes one penalty-try)
2 New Zealand 3G, 4PG (27) to 1G, 3PG (14) (at Sydney)
New Zealand won series 2-0
1949   **1** Australia 1G, 2T (11) to 1PG, 1T (6) (at Wellington)
2 Australia 2G, 1PG, 1T (16) to 1DG, 1PG, 1T (9) (at Auckland)
Australia won series 2-0
1951   **1** New Zealand 1G, 1PG (8) to 0 (at Sydney)
2 New Zealand 1G, 1DG, 3T (17) to 1G, 1PG, 1T (11) (at Sydney)
3 New Zealand 2G, 2T (16) to 2PG (6) (at Brisbane)
New Zealand won series 3-0
1952   **1** Australia 1G, 1DG, 2T (14) to 1PG, 2T (9) (at Christchurch)
2 New Zealand 1DG, 2PG, 2T (15) to 1G, 1PG (8) (at Wellington)
Series drawn 1-1
1955   **1** New Zealand 2G, 1PG, 1T (16) to 1G, 1PG (8) (at Wellington)
2 New Zealand 1G, 1DG (8) to 0 (at Dunedin)
3 Australia 1G, 1T (8) to 1T (3) (at Auckland)
New Zealand won series 2-1
1957   **1** New Zealand 2G, 3PG, 2T (25) to 1G, 2PG (11) (at Sydney)
2 New Zealand 2G, 1DG, 1GM. 2T (22) to 2PG, 1T (9) (at Brisbane)
New Zealand won series 2-0
1958   New Zealand 2G, 5T (25) to 1T (3) (at Wellington)
2 Australia 1PG, 1T (6) to 1T (3) (at Christchurch)
3 New Zealand 1G, 4PG (17) to 1G, 1PG (8) (at Auckland)
New Zealand won series 2-1
1962   **1** New Zealand 1G, 1DG, 1PG, 3T (20) to 2PG (6) (at Brisbane)
2 New Zealand 1G, 2PG, 1T (14) to 1G (5) (at Sydney)
New Zealand won series 2-0
1962   **1** Drawn, New Zealand 2PG, 1T (9), Australia 3PG (9) (at Wellington)
2 New Zealand 1PG (3) to 0 (at Dunedin)
3 New Zealand 2G, 1DG, 1T (16) to 1G, 1PG (8) (at Auckland)
New Zealand won series 2-0, with 1 draw
1964   New Zealand 1G, 1DG, 2PG (14) to 2PG, 1T (9) (at Dunedin)

2 New Zealand 3G, 1T (18) to 1T (3) (at Christchurch)
3 Australia 1G, 1DG, 3PG, 1T (20) to 1G (5) (at Wellington)
New Zealand won series 2-1
1967   New Zealand 4G, 1DG, 2PG (29) to 1PG, 2T (9) (at Wellington)
1968   **1** New Zealand 3G, 1PG, 3T (27) to 1G, 2PG (11) (at Sydney)
2 New Zealand 2G, 2PG, 1T (19) to 5PG, 1T (18) (at Brisbane) (New Zealand's score includes one penalty-try) New Zealand won series 2-0
1972   **1** New Zealand 3G, 1DG, 2T (29) to 2PG (6) (at Wellington)
2 New Zealand 2G, 2PG, 3T (30) to 1G, 1DG, 2T (17) (at Christchurch)
3 New Zealand 4G, 2PG, 2T (38) to 1PG (3) (at Auckland)
New Zealand won series 3-0
1974   **1** New Zealand 1PG, 2T (11) to 1G (6) (at Sydney)
2 Drawn, 1G, 2PG, 1T (16) each (at Brisbane)
3 New Zealand 2G, 1T (16) to 2PG (6) (at Sydney)
New Zealand won series 2-0, with 1 draw
1978   **1** New Zealand 3PG, 1T (13) to 1G, 2PG (12) (at Wellington)
2 New Zealand 2G, 1PG, 1DG, 1T (22) to 1PG, 1DG (6) (at Christchurch)
3 Australia 2G, 1PG, 1DG, 3T (30) to 1G, 2PG, 1T (16) (at Auckland)
New Zealand won series 2-1
1979   Australia 3PG, 1DG (12) to 1PG, 1DG (6) (at Sydney)
1980   **1** Australia 1G, 1DG, 1T (13) to 3PG (9) (at Sydney)
2 New Zealand 1G, 2PG (12) to 1G, 1PG (9) (at Brisbane)
3 Australia 2G, 1PG, 1DG, 2T (26) to 2PG, 1T (10) (at Sydney)
Australia won series 2-1
1982   **1** New Zealand 2G, 1PG, 2T (23) to 1G, 2PG, 1T (16) (at Christchurch)
2 Australia 1G, 3PG, 1T (19) to 1G, 2PG, 1T (16) (at Wellington)
3 New Zealand 2G, 5PG, 2DG (33) to 1G, 3PG, 1DG (18) (at Auckland)
New Zealand won series 2-1
1983   New Zealand 1G, 4PG (18) to 2T (8) (at Sydney)
1984   **1** Australia 1G, 1DG, 1PG, 1T (16) to 1DG, 2PG (9) (at Sydney)
2 New Zealand 2G, 5T (19) to 1G, 3PG (15) (at Brisbane)
3 New Zealand 1G, 5PG, 1T (25) to 1G, 6PG (24) (at Sydney)
New Zealand won series 2-1
1985   New Zealand 2PG, 1T (10) to 1G, 1PG (9) (at Auckland)

Australia v. South Africa

28 matches played   Australia 7 wins   South Africa 21 wins

1933 **1** South Africa 1G, 1PG, 3T (17) to 1PG (3) (at Cape Town)
2 Australia 3G, 1PG, 1T (21) to 1PG, 1T (6) (at Durban)
3 South Africa 1G, 1DG, 1T (12) to 1T (3) (at Johannesburg)
4 South Africa 1G, 1PG, 1T (11) to 0 (at Port Elizabeth)
5 Australia 1G, 1DG, 2T (15) to 1DG (4) (at Bloemfontein)
South Africa won series 3-2

1937 **1** South Africa 1PG, 2T (9) to 1G (5) (at Sydney)
2 South Africa 4G, 2T (26) to 1G, 2PG, 2T (17) (at Sydney)
South Africa won series 2-0

1953 **1** South Africa 2G, 2PG, 3T (25) to 1PG (3) (at Johannesburg)
2 Australia 3G, 1T (18) to 1G, 3T (14) (at Cape Town)
3 South Africa 3G, 1T (18) to 1G, 1PG (8) (at Durban)
4 South Africa 2G, 2DG, 2PG (22) to 2PG, 1T (9) (at Port Elizabeth)
South Africa won series 3-1

1956 **1** South Africa 1PG, 2T (9) to 0 (at Sydney)
2 South Africa 1DG, 2T (9) to 0 (at Brisbane)
South Africa won series 2-0

1961 **1** South Africa 2G, 6T (28) to 1PG (3) (at Johannesburg)
2 South Africa 1G, 1DG, 3PG, 2T (23) to 1G, 2PG (11) (at Port Elizabeth)
South Africa won series 2-0

1963 **1** South Africa 1G, 2PG, 1T (14) to 1T (3) (at Pretoria)
2 Australia 1DG, 1PG, 1T (9) to 1G (5) (at Cape Town)
3 Australia 1G, 1DG, 1PG (11) to 3PG (9) (at Johannesburg)
4 South Africa 2G, 3PG, 1T (22) to 1DG, 1PG (6) (at Port Elizabeth)
Series drawn 2-2

1965 **1** Australia 4PG, 2T (18) to 1G, 1PG, 1T (11) (at Sydney)
2 Australia 4PG (12) to 1G, 1T (8) (at Brisbane)
Australia won series 2-0

1969 **1** South Africa 3G, 3PG, 2T (30) to 1G, 2PG (11) (at Johannesburg)
2 South Africa 2G, 1PG, 1T (16) to 3PG (9) (at Durban)
3 South Africa 1G, 1PG, 1T (11) to 1PG (3) (at Cape Town)
4 South Africa 2G, 2PG, 1T (19) to 1G, 1PG (8) (at Bloemfontein)
South Africa won series 4-0

1971 **1** South Africa 2G, 1DG, 1PG, 1T (19) to 1G, 2PG (11) (at Sydney)
2 South Africa 1G, 1PG, 2T (14) to 1DG (6) (at Brisbane)
3 South Africa 3G, 1PG (18) to 1PG, 1T (6) (at Sydney)
South Africa won series 3-0

Australia v. Argentina

1983 **1** Argentina 2G, 1DG, 1PG (18) to 1PG (3) (at Brisbane)
2 Australia 3G, 1PG, 2T (29) to 1DG, 2PG, 1T (13) (at Sydney)
Series drawn 1-1

New Zealand v. South Africa

37 matches played   New Zealand 15 wins   South Africa 20 wins   2 draws

1921 **1** New Zealand 2G, 1T (13) to 1G (5) (at Dunedin)
2 South Africa 1G, 1DG (9) to 1G (5) (at Auckland)
3 Drawn, no score (at Wellington)
Series drawn 1-1, with 1 draw

1928 **1** South Africa 2DG, 2PG, 1T (17) to 0 (at Durban)
2 New Zealand 1DG, 1PG (7) to 1PG, 1GM (6) (at Johannesburg)
3 South Africa 1G, 2T (11) to 2T (6) (at Port Elizabeth)
4 New Zealand 1DG, 2PG, 1T (13) to 1G (5) (at Cape Town)
Series drawn 2-2

1937 **1** New Zealand 1DG, 2PG, 1T (13) to 1DG, 1T (7) (at Wellington)
2 South Africa 2G, 1PG (13) to 2T (6) (at Christchurch)
3 South Africa 1G, 4T (17) to 2PG (6) (at Auckland)
South Africa won series 2-1

1949 **1** South Africa 5PG (15) to 1G, 1DG, 1PG (11) (at Cape Town)
2 South Africa 1DG, 1PG, 2T (12) to 1DG, 1PG (6) (at Johannesburg)
3 South Africa 3PG (9) to 1T (3) (at Durban)

4 South Africa 1G, 1DG, 1PG (11) to 1G, 1T (8) (at Port Elizabeth)
South Africa won series 4-0

1956 **1** New Zealand 2G (10) to 1PG, 1T (6) (at Dunedin)
2 South Africa 1G, 1T (8) to 1T (3) (at Wellington)
3 New Zealand 1G, 2PG, 2T (17) to 2G (10) (at Christchurch)
4 New Zealand 1G, 2PG (11) to 1G (5) (at Auckland)
New Zealand won series 3-1

1960 **1** South Africa 2G, 1PG (13) to 0 (at Johannesburg)
2 New Zealand 1G, 1DG, 1PG (11) to 1T (3) (at Cape Town)
3 Drawn, 1G, 2PG (11) each (at Bloemfontein)
4 South Africa 1G, 1PG (8) to 1PG (3) (at Port Elizabeth)
South Africa won series 2-1, with 1 draw

1965 **1** New Zealand 2T (6) to 1DG (3) (at Wellington)
2 New Zealand 2G, 1T (13) to 0 (at Dunedin)
3 South Africa 2G, 1PG, 2T (19) to 2G, 1PG, 1T (16) (at Christchurch)

4 New Zealand 1G, 1DG, 4T (20) to 1PG (3) (at Auckland)
New Zealand won series 3-1

1970 **1** South Africa 1G, 2PG, 1DG, 1T (17) to 1PG, 1T (6) (at Pretoria)
2 New Zealand 1PG, 2T (9) to 1G, 1PG (8) (at Cape Town)
3 South Africa 2G, 2PG, 1T (14) to 1PG (3) (at Port Elizabeth)
4 South Africa 1G, 4PG, 1T (20) to 1G, 4PG (17) (at Johannesburg)
South Africa won series 3-1

1976 **1** South Africa 1G, 1PG, 1DG, 1T (16) to 1PG, 1T (7) (at Durban)
2 New Zealand 1G, 2PG, 1DG (15) to 3PG (9) (at Bloemfontein)
3 South Africa 1G, 2PG, 1DG (15) to 2PG, 1T (10) (at Cape Town)
4 South Africa 1G, 2PG, 1DG (15) to 1PG, 1DG, 2T (14) (at Johannesburg)
South Africa won series 3-1

1981 **1** New Zealand 1G, 2T (14) to 1G, 1DG (9) (at Christchurch)
2 South Africa 1G, 5PG, 1DG (24) to 4PG (12) (at Wellington)
3 New Zealand 1G, 4PG, 1DG, 1T (25) to 2G, 2PG, 1T (22) (at Auckland)
New Zealand won series 2-1

New Zealand v. Argentina

1985 **1** New Zealand 1G, 1DG, 4PG, 3T (33) to 1DG, 3PG, 2T (20) (at Buenos Aires)
2 Drawn, Argentina 3DG, 4PG, (21), Romania 1G, 1PG, 4T (21) (at Buenos Aires)
New Zealand won series 1-0, with 1 draw

New Zealand v. Romania

1981 New Zealand 1DG, 1PG, 2T (14) to 1DG, 1PG (6) (at Bucharest)

International Records

England

Team Records

Greatest scores
36 v. Ireland at Dublin, 1938 (36-14)
30 v. Scotland at Murrayfield, 1980 (30-18)
25 v. Wales at Blackheath, London, 1896 (25-0)
41 v. France at Richmond, 1907 (41-13)
23 v. Australia at Twickenham, 1976 (23-6)
16 v. New Zealand at Auckland, 1973 (16-10)
18 v. South Africa at Johannesburg, 1972 (18-9)

Greatest winning margins
22 v. Ireland at Dublin, 1938 (36-14)
20 v. Scotland at Twickenham, 1977 (26-6)
25 v. Wales at Blackheath, 1896 (25-0)
37 v. France at Twickenham, 1911 (37-0)
17 v. Australia at Twickenham, 1973 (20-3); at Twickenham, 1976 (23-6)
13 v. New Zealand at Twickenham, 1936 (13-0)
9 v. South Africa at Johannesburg, 1972 (18-9)

Greatest scores by opposing team
26 v. Ireland at Twickenham, 1974 (21-26)
33 v. Scotland at Murrayfield, 1986 (6-33)
34 v. Wales at Cardiff, 1967 (21-34)
37 v. France at Colombes, 1972 (12-37)
30 v. Australia at Brisbane, 1975 (21-30)
42 v. New Zealand at Wellington, 1985 (15-42)
35 v. South Africa at Johannesburg, 1984 (9-35)

Greatest losing points margins
22 v. Ireland at Dublin, 1947 (0-22)
27 v. Scotland at Murrayfield, 1986 (6-33)
25 v. Wales at Cardiff, 1905 (0-25)
25 v. France at Colombes, 1972 (12-37)
16 v. Australia at Twickenham, 1984 (3-19)
27 v. New Zealand at Wellington, 1985 (15-42)
26 v. South Africa at Johannesburg, 1984 (9-35)

Most points in Five Nations Championship season
82, 1913-14

Most tries in Five Nations Championship season
20, 1913-14

Most tries in Internationals
9 v. France at Parc des Princes, Paris, 1906 (35-8); v. France at Richmond, 1907 (41-13); v. France at Colombes, 1914 (39-13). (In 1881 England scored 13 tries v. Wales at Blackheath before uniform scoring had been settled)

Most tries against England in Internationals
8 by Wales at Cardiff, 1922 (6-28)

Players' Records

Most capped player
A. Neary 43 caps, 1971-80
By position
Full-back: W.H. Hare 25 caps, 1974-84
Wing: M.A.C. Slemen 31 caps, 1976-84

(David Duckham, England's most capped back, played 14 times at centre, 22 times on the wing, and a total of 36 caps)
Centre: P.W. Dodge 30 caps, 1978-85
Fly-half: W.J.A. Davies 22 caps, 1913-23 (M.P. Weston won 5 of his 29 caps as a fly-half, and 24 in the centre)
Scrum-half: S.J. Smith 28 caps, 1973-83
Prop: F.E. Cotton 31 caps, 1971-81
Hooker: J.V. Pullin 42 caps, 1966-76
Lock: W.B. Beaumont 34 caps, 1975-82
Flanker: A. Neary 43 caps, 1971-80
No. 8: J.P. Scott 31 caps, 1978-84. (Scott also won 3 caps as a lock)

Captain in most Internationals
21, W.B. Beaumont, 1978-82

Longest International career
13 seasons, J. Heaton, 1935-47

Most points in an International
22, D. Lambert v. France at Twickenham, 1911

Most points in Internationals
240, W.H. Hare, 25 matches

Most tries in an International
5, D. Lambert v. France at Richmond, 1907 (on his debut)

Most tries in Internationals
18, C.N. Lowe, 25 matches, 1913-23

Most conversions in an International
6, J.E. Greenwood v. France at Paris, 1914; G.W. Parker v. Ireland at Dublin, 1938 (L. Stokes kicked 6 v. Wales at Blackheath, 1881, before uniform scoring had been settled)

Most points in Five Nations Championship season
44, W.H. Hare, 4 matches, 1983-84

Most tries in Five Nations Championship season
8, C.N. Lowe, 4 matches, 1913-14

Most conversions in Five Nations Championship season
7, G.S. Conway, 4 matches, 1923-24

Most penalty-goals in Five Nations Championship season
14, W.H. Hare, 4 matches, 1982-83

Most points in a tour match[*]
36, W.N. Bennett v. Western Australia, Perth, 1975

Most points on an overseas tour[*]
48, W.N. Bennett, 4 matches, Australia, 1975

Most tries in a tour match[*]
4, A.J. Morley v. Western Australia, Perth, 1975; P.S. Preece v. New South Wales, Sydney, 1975

[*]IB countries only. England have played Argentina (twice) and Romania (once)

Ireland

Team Records

Greatest scores
26 v. England at Twickenham, 1974 (26-21)

26 v. Scotland at Murrayfield, 1953 (26-8)
21 v. Wales at Cardiff, 1979 (21-24); at Dublin, 1980 (21-7); at Cardiff, 1985 (21-9)
25 v. France at Cork, 1911 (25-5); at Dublin, 1975 (25-6)
27 v. Australia at Brisbane, 1979 (27-12)
10 v. New Zealand at Dublin, 1973 (10-10)
15 v. South Africa at Cape Town, 1981 (15-23)

Greatest winning margins
22 v. England at Dublin, 1947 (22-0)
21 v. Scotland at Dublin, 1950 (21-0)
16 v. Wales at Belfast, 1925 (19-3)
24 v. France at Cork, 1913 (24-0)
15 v. Australia at Brisbane, 1979 (27-12)
Never won v. New Zealand
3 v. South Africa at Dublin, 1965 (9-6)

Greatest scores by opposing team
36 v. England at Dublin, 1938 (14-36)
32 v. Scotland at Dublin, 1984 (9-32)
34 v. Wales at Dublin, 1976 (9-34)
29 v. France at Paris, 1986 (9-29)
20 v. Australia at Dublin, 1976 (10-20)
17 v. New Zealand at Dublin, 1935 (9-17)
38 v. South Africa at Dublin, (0-38)

Greatest losing points margins
22 v. England at Dublin, 1938 (14-36)
23 v. Scotland at Dublin, 1984 (9-32)
29 v. Wales at Cardiff, 1976 (0-29)
23 v. France at Paris, 1976 (3-26)
13 v. Australia at Dublin, 1947 (3-16)
15 v. New Zealand at Dublin, 1905 (0-15)
38 v. South Africa at Dublin, 1912 (0-38)

Most points in Five Nations Championship season
71, 1982-83

Most tries in Five Nations Championship season
12, 1927-28, 1952-53

Most tries in Internationals
6 v. France at Cork, 1913 (24-0); v. Scotland at Murrayfield, 1953 (26-8)

Most tries against Ireland in Internationals
10 v. South Africa at Dublin, 1912 (0-38)

Players' Records

Most capped player
C.M.H. Gibson 69 caps, 1964-79
By position
Full-back: T.J. Kiernan 54 caps, 1960-73
Wing: A.T.A. Duggan 25 caps, 1964-72; T.O. Grace 25 caps, 1972-78
Centre: C.M.H. Gibson 40 caps, 1964-79 (Gibson also won 25 caps at fly-half and 4 as a wing. G.V. Stephenson won 37 caps as a centre and 5 on the wing. N.J. Henderson won 35 caps as a centre and 5 as a full-back)
Fly-half: J.W. Kyle 40 caps, 1947-58
Scrum-half: M. Sugden 28 caps, 1925-31. (J.J. Moloney won 23 caps at scrum-half and 4 as a wing)
Prop: P.A. Orr 48 caps, 1976-85
Hooker: K.W. Kennedy 45 caps, 1965-75
Lock: W.J. McBride 63 caps, 1962-75
Flanker: J.F. Slattery 61 caps, 1970-84
No. 8: W.P. Duggan 39 caps, 1975-84 (Duggan also won 2 caps as a flanker)

Captain in most Internationals
24, T.J. Kiernan, 1963-73

Longest International career
16 seasons, A.J.F. O'Reilly, 1955-70; C.M.H. Gibson, 1964-79. (Gibson's last match was in an Australian season)

Most points in an International
21, S.O. Campbell v. Scotland at Dublin, 1982; S.O. Campbell v. England at Dublin, 1983

Most points in Internationals
217, S.O. Campbell, 22 matches, 1976-84

Most tries in an International
3, J.P. Quinn v. France at Cork, 1913; E.O'D. Davy v. Scotland at Murrayfield, 1930; S.Byrne v. Scotland at Murrayfield, 1953

Most tries in Internationals
14, G.V. Stephenson, 41 matches, 1920-30

Most conversions in an International
4, P.F. Murray v. Scotland at Murrayfield, 1932; R.J. Gregg v. Scotland at Murrayfield, 1953

Most points in Five Nations Championship season
52, S.O. Campbell, 4 matches, 1982-3

Most tries in Five Nations Championship season
5, J.E. Arigho, 3 matches, 1927-8

Most conversions in Five Nations Championship season
7, R.A. Lloyd, 4 matches, 1912-13

Most penalty-goals in Five Nations Championship season
14, S.O. Campbell, 5 matches, Australia 1979

Most points in a tour match*
19, A.J.P. Ward v. Australian Capital Territory at Canberra, 1979; S.O. Campbell v. Australia at Brisbane, 1979

Most points on an overseas tour*
60, S.O. Campbell, 5 matches, Australia, 1979

Most tries in a tour match*
3, A.T.A. Duggan v. Victoria at Melbourne, 1965; J.F. Slattery v. S.A. President's XV at East London, 1981; M.J. Kiernan v. Gold Cup XV at Oudtshoorn, South Africa, 1981

*IB countries only

Scotland

Team Records
Greatest scores
33 v. England at Murrayfield, 1986 (33-6)
32 v. Ireland at Dublin, 1984 (32-9)
35 v. Wales at Inverleith, 1924 (35-10)
31 v. France at Inverleith, 1912 (31-30)
24 v. Australia at Murrayfield, 1981 (24-15)
25 v. New Zealand at Murrayfield, 1983 (25-25)
33 v. Romania at Bucharest, 1986 (33-18)
10 v. South Africa at Port Elizabeth, 1960 (10-18)

Greatest winning margins
27 v. England at Murrayfield, 1986 (33-6)
23 v. Ireland at Dublin, 1984 (32-9)
25 v. Wales at Inverleith, 1924 (35-10)
28 v. France at Inverleith, 1912 (31-3)

9 v. Australia at Murrayfield, 1981 (24-15)
Never won v. New Zealand
15 v. Romania at Bucharest, 1986 (33-18)
6 v. South Africa at Hampden Park, Glasgow, 1906 (6-0)

Greatest scores by opposing team
30 v. England at Murrayfield, 1980 (18-30)
26 v. Ireland at Murrayfield, 1953 (8-26)
33 v. Wales at Cardiff, 1972 (12-35)
23 v. France at Parc des Princes, Paris, 1977 (3-23)
37 v. Australia at Murrayfield, 1984 (12-37)
40 v. New Zealand at Auckland, 1981 (15-40)
28 v. Romania at Bucharest, 1984 (22-28)
44 v. South Africa at Murrayfield, 1951 (0-44)

Greatest losing points margins
20 v. England at Twickenham, 1977 (6-26)
21 v. Ireland at Dublin, 1950 (0-21)
23 v. Wales at Cardiff, 1972 (12-35)
20 v. France at Parc des Princes, Paris, 1977 (3-23)
25 v. Australia at Murrayfield, 1984 (12-37)
25 v. New Zealand at Auckland, 1981 (15-40)
6 v. Romania at Bucharest, 1986 (22-28)
44 v. South Africa at Murrayfield, 1951 (0-44)

Most points in Five Nations Championship season
86, 1983-84

Most tries in Five Nations Championship season
17, 1924-25

Most tries in Internationals
8 v. Wales at Inverleith, 1924 (35-10). (12 tries scored v. Wales at Raeburn Place, 1887, before uniform scoring was settled)

Most tries against Scotland in Internationals
9 by South Africa at Murrayfield, 1951 (0-44)

Players' Records
Most capped player
J.M. Renwick 52 caps, 1972-84
By position
Full-back: A.R. Irvine 47 caps, 1972-82 (Irvine was also chosen 4 times as a wing)
Wing: A.R. Smith 33 caps, 1955-62
Centre: J.M. Renwick 52 caps, 1972-84 (Renwick played once as a replacement on the wing)
Fly-half: J.Y. Rutherford 37 caps, 1979-85 (I.R. McGeechan, 32 caps, won 12 as a fly-half and 20 at centre)
Scrum-half: R.J. Laidlaw 36 caps, 1980-85
Prop: A.B. Carmichael 50 caps, 1967-78
Hooker: C.T. Deans 44 caps, 1978-85
Lock: A.F. McHarg 42 caps, 1968-79 (McHarg also won 2 caps at no. 8)
Flanker: W.I.D. Elliot 29 caps, 1947-54
No.8: J.W. Telfer 22 caps, 1964-70. (Telfer also won 3 caps as flanker. D.G. Leslie, 32 caps, has won 27 as flanker and 5 as no.8)

Captain in most Internationals
19, J. McLauchlan, 1973-79

Longest International career
14 seasons, W.C.W. Murdoch, 1935-48

Most points in an International
21, A.G. Hastings v. England at Murrayfield, 1986; A.G. Hastings v. Romania at Bucharest, 1986

Most points in Internationals
273, A.R. Irvine, 51 matches, 1972-82 (This includes one penalty-try)

Most tries in an International
4, W.A. Stewart v. Ireland at Inverleith, 1913; I.S. Smith v. France at Inverleith, 1925; I.S. Smith v. Wales at Swansea, 1925. (G.C. Lindsay scored 5 tries v. Wales at Raeburn Place, 1887, before uniform scoring was settled. I.S. Smith scored 6 tries in succession in 1925, 3 v. France at the end of the match and 3 v. Wales at the beginning of the next)

Most tries in Internationals
24, I.S. Smith, 32 matches, 1924-33

Most conversions in an International
5, F.H. Turner v. France at Inverleith, 1912; J.W. Allan v. England at Murrayfield, 1931

Most points in Five Nations Championship season
52, A.G. Hastings, 4 matches, 1985-86

Most tries in Five Nations Championship season
8, I.S. Smith, 4 matches, 1924-25

Most conversions in Five Nations Championship season
8, P.W. Dods, 4 matches, 1983-84

Most penalty-goals in Five Nations Championship season
14, A.G. Hastings, 4 matches, 1985-86

Most points in a tour match*
24, D.W. Morgan v. Wellington at Wellington, 1975; A.R. Irvine v. King Country at Taumarunui, New Zealand, 1981; A.R. Irvine v. Wairarapa-Bush at Masterton, New Zealand, 1981

Most points on an overseas tour
56, W. Lauder, 5 matches, Australia, 1970; A.R. Irivine, 4 matches, New Zealand, 1981

Most tries in a tour match*
3, A.R. Smith v. Eastern Transvaal at Springs, South Africa, 1960

*IB countries only

Wales

Team Records
Greatest scores
34 v. England at Cardiff, 1967 (34-21)
34 v. Ireland at Dublin, 1976 (34-9)
35 v. Scotland at Cardiff, 1972 (35-12)
49 v. France at Swansea, 1910 (49-14)
28 v. Australia at Cardiff, 1975 (28-3)
16 v. New Zealand at Cardiff, 1972 (16-19)
6 v. South Africa at Cardiff, 1970 (6-6)

Greatest winning margins
25 v. England at Cardiff, 1905 (25-0)
29 v. Ireland at Cardiff, 1907 (29-0)
23 v. Scotland at Cardiff, 1972 (35-12)
42 v. France at Colombes, 1909 (47-5)
25 v. Australia at Cardiff, 1975 (28-3)
5 v. New Zealand at Cardiff, 1953 (13-8)
Never won v. South Africa

Greatest scores by opposing team
25 v. England at Blackheath, 1896 (0-25)
21 v. Ireland at Cardiff, 1979 (24-21); at Dublin, 1980 (7-21); at Cardiff, 1985 (9-21)
35 v. Scotland at Inverleith, 1924 (10-35)
23 v. France at Cardiff, 1986 (15-23)

'8 v. Australia at Cardiff, 1984 (9-28)
33 v. New Zealand at Auckland, 1969 (12-33)
24 v. South Africa at Durban, 1964 (3-24)

Greatest losing points margins
25 v. England at Blackheath, 1896 (0-25)
16 v. Ireland at Belfast, 1925 (3-19)
25 v. Scotland at Inverleith, 1924 (10-35)
11 v. France at Paris, 1985 (3-14)
19 v. Australia at Cardiff, 1984 (9-28)
21 v. New Zealand at Auckland, 1969 (12-33)
21 v. South Africa at Durban, 1964 (3-24)

Most points in Five Nations Championship season
102, 1975-76

Most tries in Five Nations Championship season
21, 1909-1910

Most tries in Internationals
11 v. France at Colombes, 1909 (47-5)

Most tries against Wales in Internationals
8 v. Scotland at Inverleith, 1924 (10-35)
(England scored 13 tries v. Wales in 1881,
and Scotland 12 in 1887, before uniform
scoring was settled)

Players' Records

Most capped player
J.P.R. Williams 55 caps, 1969-81

By position
Full-back: J.P.R. Williams 54 caps, 1969-81
(Williams also won one cap as a flanker)
Wing: K.J. Jones 44 caps, 1947-57. (T.G.R.
Davies won 35 caps as a wing and 11 as a
centre)
Centre: S.P. Fenwick 30 caps, 1975-81
Fly-half: C.I. Morgan 29 caps, 1951-58. (P.
Bennet, 29 caps, won one at full-back, as a
replacement, one on the wing and two at
centre, once as a replacement)
Scrum-half: G.O. Edwards 53 caps, 1967-78
Prop: G. Price 41 caps, 1975-83
Hooker: B.V. Meredith 34 caps, 1954-62
Lock: A.J. Martin 34 caps, 1973-81
Flanker: W.D. Morris 32 caps 1967-74
(Morris also won 2 caps, his first, at no.8)
No.8: T.M. Davies 38 caps, 1969-76

Captain in most Internationals
18, A.J. Gould, 1889-97

Longest International career
14 seasons, W.J. Trew, 1900-13; T.H. Vile,
1908-21; H. Tanner, 1936-49

Most points in an International
19, J. Bancroft v. France at Swansea, 1910;
K.S. Jarrett v. England at Cardiff, 1967; P.
Bennett v. Ireland at Dublin, 1976

Most points in Internationals
166, P. Bennett, 29 matches, 1969-78

Most tries in an International
4, W. Llewellyn v. England at Swansea, 1899
(on his debut); R.A. Gibbs v. France at
Cardiff, 1908; M.C.R. Richards v. England
at Cardiff, 1969

Most tries in Internationals
20, G.O. Edwards, 53 matches, 1967-78;
T.G.R. Davies, 46 matches, 1966-78

Most conversions in an International
8, J. Bancroft v. France at Swansea, 1910

Most points in Five Nations Championship season
52, P.H. Thorburn, 4 matches, 1985-86

Most tries in Five Nations Championship season
6, R.A. Gibbs, 1907-08; M.C.R. Richards,
1968-9

Most conversions in Five Nations Championship season
11, J. Bancroft, 4 matches, 1908-9

Most penalty-goals in Five Nations Championship season
16, P.H. Thorburn, 4 matches, 1985-86

Most points in a tour match*
15, K.S. Jarrett v. Otago 1969 at Dunedin

Most points on an overseas tour*
55, S.P. Fenwick, 7 matches, Australia, 1978

Most tries in a tour match*
3, M.C.R. Richards v. Otago 1969 at Dunedin

*IB countries only. Wales awarded caps for
two matches as follows: 1983, v. Romania at
Bucharest (L 3-23); 1985, v. Fiji at Cardiff
(W 40-3)

British Isles

Team Records

Greatest scores
31 v. Australia at Brisbane, 1966 (31-0)
17 v. New Zealand at Dunedin, 1959 (17-18)
28 v. South Africa at Pretoria, 1974 (28-9)

Greatest winning margins
31 v. Australia at Brisbane, 1966 (31-0)
10 v. New Zealand at Wellington, 1971 (13-3)
19 v. South Africa at Pretoria, 1974 (28-9)

Greatest scores by opposing team
8 v. Australia at Sydney, 1966 (11-8)
38 v. New Zealand at Auckland, 1983 (6-38)
34 v. South Africa at Bloemfontein, 1962
(14-34)

Greatest losing points margins
1 v. Australia at Sydney, 1930 (5-6)
32 v. New Zealand at Auckland, 1983 (6-38)
20 v. South Africa at Bloemfontein, 1962
(14-34)

Most tries in Internationals
5 v. Australia at Sydney, 1950 (24-3); v. South
Africa at Johannesburg, 1955 (23-22);
v. Australia at Sydney, 1959 (24-3);
v. Australia at Brisbane, 1966 (31-0);
v. South Africa at Pretoria, 1974 (28-9)

Most tries against British Isles in Internationals
7, by South Africa at Cape Town, 1955 (9-25)

Most points on an overseas tour (all matches)
842 in Australia, New Zealand and Canada,
33 matches, 1959 (includes 582 points in
25 matches in New Zealand)

Most tries on an overseas tour (all matches)
165 in Australia, New Zealand and Canada,
33 matches, 1959 (includes 113 tries in 25
matches in New Zealand)

Players' Records

Most capped player
W.J. McBride 17 caps, 1962-74

By position
Full-back: J.P.R. Williams 8 caps, 1971-74
(A.R. Irvine, in 9 Tests, played 7 times
as wing)
Wing: A.J.F. O'Reilly 9 caps, 1955-59
(O'Reilly also played once as a centre)

Centre: C.M.H. Gibson 8 caps, 1966-71
(Gibson in 12 Tests also played 4 times as a
fly-half. I.R. McGeechan in 8 Tests played 7
times as a centre and once on the wing as a
replacement)
Fly-half: P. Bennett 8 caps, 1974-77
Scrum-half: R.E.G. Jeeps 13 caps, 1955-62
Prop: G. Price 12 caps, 1977-83
Hooker: B.V. Meredith 8 caps, 1955-62
Lock: W.J. McBride 17 caps, 1962-74
Flanker: N.A.A. Murphy 8 caps, 1959-66
No. 8: T.M. Davies 8 caps, 1971-74. (Both
A.E.I. Pask and J.W. Telfer played 4 Tests
at no. 8 and 4 Tests as a flanker)

Captain in most Internationals
6, A.R. Dawson, 1959

Most points in an International
18, A.J.P. Ward v. South Africa at Cape
Town, 1980

Most points in Internationals
44, P. Bennett, 8 matches, 1974-77

Most points in International series
35, T.J. Kiernan, 4 matches, South Africa,
1968

Most tries in an International
2, C.D. Aarvold v. New Zealand at
Christchurch, 1930; J.E. Nelson v.
Australia at Sydney, 1950; M.J. Price v.
Australia at Sydney, 1959; M.J. Price v.
New Zealand at Dunedin, 1959; D.K. Jones
v. Australia at Brisbane, 1966; T.G.R.
Davies v. New Zealand at Christchurch,
1971; J.J. Williams v. South Africa at
Pretoria, 1974; J.J. Williams v. South Africa
at Port Elizabeth, 1974

Most tries in Internationals
6, A.J.F. O'Reilly, 10 matches, 1955-59

Most conversions in an International
5, S. Wilson v. Australia at Brisbane, 1966

Most tries in an International series
4, J.J. Williams, 4 matches, South Africa,
1974

Most tries on an overseas tour
22 (including one penalty-try), A.J.F.
O'Reilly, 23 matches, Australia/New
Zealand/Canada, 1959 (17 tries in 17
matches in New Zealand)

Most points in a tour match
37, A.G.B. Old v. South Western Districts at
Mossel Bay, South Africa, 1974

Most points on an overseas tour
188, B. John, 17 matches, Australia/New
Zealand, 1971 (180 points in 16 matches in
New Zealand)

Most tries in a tour match
6, D.J. Duckham, v. West Coast-Buller at
Greymouth, New Zealand, 1971; J.J.
Williams v. South Western Districts at
Mossel Bay, 1974. (A.R. Irvine scored 5
tries from full-back v. King Country-
Wanganui at Taumarunui, New Zealand,
1977)

France

Team Records

Greatest scores
37 v. England at Colombes, 1972 (37-12)
27 v. Ireland at Colombes, 1964 (27-6)

23 v. Scotland at Parc des Princes, Paris, 1977 (23-3)
23 v. Wales at Cardiff, 1986 (23-15)
34 v. Australia at Parc des Princes, 1976 (34-6)
24 v. New Zealand at Auckland, 1979 (24-19)
25 v. South Africa at Bloemfontein, 1975 (25-38)

Greatest winning margins
25 v. England at Colombes, 1972 (37-12)
23 v. Ireland at Parc des Princes, 1976 (26-3)
20 v. Scotland at Parc des Princes, 1977 (23-3)
11 v. Wales at Parc des Princes, 1985 (14-3)
28 v. Australia at Parc des Princes, 1976 (34-6)
 7 v. New Zealand at Parc des Princes, 1973 (13-6)
 5 v. South Africa at Johannesburg, 1967 (19-14)

Greatest scores by opposing team
41 v. England at Richmond, 1907 (13-41)
25 v. Ireland at Cork, 1911 (5-25); at Dublin, 1975 (6-25)
31 v. Scotland at Inverleith, Edinburgh 1912, (3-31)
49 v. Wales at Swansea, 1910 (14-49). (South Africa beat 'France' 55-6 at Parc des Princes on 3rd January 1907. However, it is not considered an official International match)
24 v. Australia at Sydney, 1981 (14-24)
38 v. New Zealand at Parc des Princes, 1906 (8-38); 38 v. South Africa at Bordeaux, 1913 (5-38); 38 v. South Africa at Bloemfontein, 1975 (25-38)

Greatest losing points margins
37 v. England at Twickenham, 1911 (0-37) .
24 v. Ireland at Cork, 1913 (0-24)
28 v. Scotland at Inverleith, 1912 (3-31)
42 v. Wales at Colombes, 1909 (5-47). (The 6-55 defeat by South Africa in Paris, 1907, is considered to be unofficial)
10 v. Australia at Sydney, 1981 (14-24)
30 v. New Zealand at Parc des Princes, 1906 (8-38)
33 v. South Africa at Bordeaux, 1913 (5-38)

Most points in Five Nations Championship season
98, 1985-86

Most tries in Five Nations Championship season
13, 1975-76

Most tries in Internationals
6 v. Ireland at Colombes, 1964 (27-6);
 v. England at Colombes, 1970, (35-13);
 v. England at Colombes, 1972 (37-12);
 v. England at Parc des Princes, 1976 (30-9);
 v. Australia at Parc des Princes, 1976 (34-6)

Most tries against France in Internationals
11 v. Wales at Colombes, 1909 (5-47)
 (South Africa's 13 tries in Paris, 1907, are not considered official)

Most points on tour (all matches)*
282 in South Africa, 11 matches, 1975

Players' Records
Most capped player
R. Bertranne 52 caps, 1971-81
By position
Full-back: M. Vannier 30 caps, 1953-61
Wing: J. Dupuy 28 caps, 1956-64; C. Darrouy, 1957-67
Centre: R. Bertranne 39 caps, 1971-81
 (Bertranne also won 13 caps as a wing)

Fly-half: P. Albaladejo 23 caps, 1954-64
 (Albaladejo also won one cap, his first, as a full-back)
Scrum-half: G. Dufau 33 caps, 1948-57
Prop: R. Paparemborde 46 caps, 1975-83
Hooker: P. Dintrans 34 caps, 1979-85
Lock: E. Cester 30 caps, 1966-74. (B. Dauga won 29 caps as lock and 21 at no. 8. M. Celaya won 18 caps as lock, 15 at no. 8 and 2 as a flanker)
Flanker: J.-P. Rives 47 caps, 1975-84
No. 8: G. Basquet 26 caps, 1947-52. (W. Spanghero won 21 caps at no. 8, 16 at lock and 5 as a flanker. J.-L. Joinel, 45 caps, won 18 as flanker and 27 at no. 8)

Captain in most Internationals
32, J.-P. Rives, 1979-84

Longest International career
13 seasons, A. Boniface, 1954-66

Most points in an International
18, J.-P. Lescarboura v. Romania at Bucharest, 1984

Most points in Internationals
164, J.-P. Lescarboura, 1982-85 (20 matches)

Most tries in an International
3, M. Crauste v. England at Colombes, 1962; C. Darrouy v. Ireland at Dublin, 1963

Most tries in Internationals
14, C. Darrouy, 28 matches, 1957-67

Most conversions in an International
5, P. Villepreux v. England at Paris, 1972

Most points in Five Nations Championship season
54, J.-P. Lescarboura, 4 matches, 1983-84

Most tries in Five Nations Championship season
5, P. Estève, 4 matches, 1982-83. (Estève scored in each Championship match. This has only been achieved twice before (by A.C. Wallace of Scotland in 1925, and by H.C. Catcheside of England in 1924) and once since (by P. Sella of France in 1986))

Most conversions in Five Nations Championship season
7, P. Villepreux, 4 matches, 1971-72

Most penalty-goals in Five Nations Championship season
10, J.-P. Lescarboura, 4 matches, 1983-84

Most points in a tour match
19, J.L. Dehez v. South Western Districts (South Africa) 1967 at George. (P. Estève scored 32 points against East Japan in 1984)

Most points on an overseas tour
71, J.-P. Romeu, 7 matches, South Africa, 1975

Most tries in a tour match*
4, R. Bertranne v. Western Transvaal at Potchesftroom, 1971; M. Bruel v. Australian Capital Territory at Canberra, 1981. (P. Estève scored 8 tries against East Japan in 1984)

*IB countries only

Australia

All records are against recognized International teams.

Team Records
Greatest scores
30 v. England at Brisbane, 1975 (30-21)
20 v. Ireland at Dublin, 1976 (20-10)
37 v. Scotland at Murrayfield, 1984 (37-12)
28 v. Wales at Cardiff, 1984 (28-9)
24 v. France at Sydney, 1981 (24-14)
30 v. New Zealand at Auckland, 1978 (30-16)
21 v. South Africa at Durban, 1933 (21-6)
 8 v. British Isles at Sydney, 1966 (8-11)
(Australia scored 50 against Japan (not an IB country) at Brisbane 1975)

Greatest winning margins
16 v. England at Twickenham, 1984 (19-3)
13 v. Ireland at Dublin, 1947 (16-3)
25 v. Scotland at Murrayfield, 1984 (37-12)
19 v. Wales at Cardiff, 1984 (28-9)
10 v. France at Sydney, 1981 (24-14)
16 v. New Zealand at Sydney, 1980 (26-10)
15 v. South Africa at Durban, 1933 (21-6)
 1 v. British Isles at Sydney, 1930 (6-5)
(Australia beat US (not an IB country) by 46 points (49-3) at Sydney, 1983)

Greatest scores by opposing team
23 v. England at Twickenham, 1976 (6-23)
27 v. Ireland at Brisbane, 1979 (12-27)
24 v. Scotland at Murrayfield, 1981 (15-24)
28 v. Wales at Cardiff, 1975 (3-28)
34 v. France at Parc des Princes, Paris, 1976 (6-34)
38 v. New Zealand at Dunedin, 1936 (13-38); v. New Zealand at Auckland, 1972 (3-38)
30 v. South Africa at Johannesburg, 1969 (11-30)
31 v. British Isles at Brisbane, 1966 (0-31)

Greatest losing points margins
17 v. England at Twickenham, 1973 (3-20); v. England at Twickenham, 1976 (6-23)
15 v. Ireland at Brisbane, 1979 (12-27)
 9 v. Scotland at Murrayfield, 1981 (15-24)
25 v. Wales at Cardiff, 1975 (3-28)
28 v. France at Parc des Princes, 1976 (6-34)
35 v. New Zealand at Auckland, 1972 (3-38)
25 v. South Africa at Johannesburg, 1961 (3-28)
31 v. British Isles at Brisbane, 1966 (0-31)

Most tries in Internationals
6 v. Scotland at Sydney, 1970 (23-3)
 (Australia scored 9 against US (not an IB country) at Sydney in 1983)

Most tries against Australia in Internationals
8 by South Africa at Johannesburg, 1961 (3-28)

Most points on an overseas tour (all matches)
500 in British Isles/France, 35 matches, 1947-48

Most tries on an overseas tour (all matches)
115 in British Isles/France, 35 matches, 1947-48

Players' Records
Most capped players
P.G. Johnson 39 caps, 1959-71; G.V. Davis 39 caps, 1963-72
By position
Full-back: R.G. Gould 21 caps, 1980-85
Wing: B.J. Moon 25 caps, 1978-84
Centre: G.A. Shaw 21 caps, 1969-79
 (M.J. Hawker, 24 caps, has won 20 as a centre and 1 as a wing in recognized Internationals. In other matches, he has played as a centre 4 times and once as a

fly-half. A.G. Slack, 27 caps, has only played 21 matches at centre in recognized Internationals)
Fly-half: P.F. Hawthorne 21 caps, 1962-67 (P.E. McLean has won 8 caps at full-back, 1 at centre, and 13 at fly-half. M.G. Ella has won 25 caps as a fly-half, but only 20 against IB countries)
Scrum-half: J.N.B. Hipwell 34 caps, 1968-82
Prop: R.B. Prosser 24 caps, 1967-72
Hooker: P.G. Johnson 39 caps, 1959-71
Lock: G. Fay 20 caps, 1971-79. (A.R. Miller won 12 caps as a prop, 19 at lock. S.A. Williams has won 23 caps as a lock, but only 18 against IB countries)
Flanker: G.V. Davis 39 caps, 1963-72
No. 8: M.E. Loane 20 caps, 1974-82

Captain in most Internationals
16, J.E. Thornett, 1962-67; G.V. Davis, 1969-72

Longest International career
16 seasons, G.M. Cooke, 1932-47/8 (Cooke's career ended during a tour to Europe); A.R. Miller, 1952-67

Most points in an International
21, P.E. McLean v. Scotland at Sydney, 1982; M.P. Lynagh v. Scotland at Murrayfield, 1984

Most points in Internationals
162, P.E. McLean, 22 matches, 1974-82 (against IB countries only)

Most tries in an International
4, G.Cornelsen v. New Zealand at Auckland, 1978. (D.I. Campese scored 4 against US (not an IB country) at Sydney in 1983)

Most tries in Internationals
9, B.J. Moon, 25 matches, 1978-84 (against IB countries only)

Most conversions in an International
3, R.R. Biilmann v. South Africa at Durban, 1933; P.F. Ryan v. England at Sydney, 1963; P.E. McLean v. Scotland at Sydney, 1982; R.G. Gould v. Wales at Cardiff, 1984; M.P. Lynagh v. Scotland at Murrayfield, 1984. (P.E. McLean kicked 6 against Japan (not an IB country) at Brisbane in 1975)

Most points in an International series
42, M.P. Lynagh, 4 matches, British Isles, 1984

Most tries in International series on tour
4, G. Cornelsen, 3 matches, New Zealand, 1978; M.G. Ella, 4 matches, British Isles, 1984. (Ella scored in every match of the series)

Most points in a tour match
23, J.C. Hindmarsh v. Glamorgan at Neath, 1975

Most points on an overseas tour
23, C.J. Russell, British Isles, 1908-09

Most tries in a tour match
6, J.S. Boyce v. Wairarapa at Masterton, New Zealand, 1962

New Zealand

Team Records
Greatest scores
42 v. England at Twickenham, 1967 (42-15)

17 v. Ireland at Dublin, 1935 (17-9)
40 v. Scotland at Auckland, 1981 (40-15)
33 v. Wales at Auckland, 1969 (33-12)
38 v. France at Parc des Princes, 1906 (38-8)
38 v. Australia at Auckland, 1972 (38-3)
25 v. South Africa at Auckland, 1981 (25-22)
38 v. British Isles at Auckland, 1983 (38-6)
(New Zealand scored 51 against America in 1913 at Berkeley)

Greatest winning margins
27 v. England at Wellington, 1985 (42-15)
15 v. Ireland at Dublin, 1905 (15-0)
25 v. Scotland at Auckland, 1981 (40-15)
21 v. Wales at Auckland, 1969 (33-12)
30 v. France at Parc des Princes, 1906 (38-8)
35 v. Australia at Auckland, 1972 (38-3)
17 v. South Africa at Auckland, 1965 (20-3)
32 v. British Isles at Auckland, 1983 (38-6)

Greatest scores by opposing team
16 v. England at Auckland, 1973 (10-16)
10 v. Ireland at Dublin, 1973 (10-10)
25 v. Scotland at Murrayfield, 1983 (25-25)
16 v. Wales at Cardiff, 1972 (19-16)
24 v. France at Auckland, 1979 (19-24)
30 v. Australia at Auckland, 1978 (16-30)
24 v. South Africa at Wellington, 1981 (12-24)
17 v. British Isles at Dunedin, 1959 (18-17)

Greatest losing points margins
13 v. England at Twickenham, 1936 (0-13)
No defeat by Ireland
No defeat by Scotland
 5 v. Wales at Cardiff, 1953 (8-13)
 7 v. France at Parc des Princes, 1973 (6-13)
16 v. Australia at Sydney, 1980 (10-26)
17 v. South Africa at Durban, 1928 (0-17)
10 v. British Isles at Wellington, 1971 (3-13)

Most tries in Internationals
10 v. France at Parc des Princes, 1906 (38-8)

Most tries against New Zealand in Internationals
5 by South Africa at Auckland, 1937 (6-17); by Australia at Auckland, 1978 (16-30)

Most points on an overseas tour (all matches)
868 in British Isles/France, 33 matches, 1905-06

Most tries on an overseas tour (all matches)
215 in British Isles/France, 33 matches, 1905-06

Players' Records
Most capped player
C.E.Meads 55 caps, 1957-71
By position
Full-back: D.B. Clarke 31 caps, 1956-64
Wing: B.G. Williams 36 caps, 1970-78 (Williams also won 2 caps at centre)
Centre (includes 2nd five-eighth): B.J. Robertson 34 caps, 1972-81
1st five-eighth: O.D. Bruce 14 caps, 1976-78
Scrum-half: S.M. Going 29 caps, 1967-77
Prop: W.J. Whineray 32 caps, 1957-65
Hooker: A.G. Dalton 35 caps, 1977-84
Lock: C.E. Meads 48 caps, 1957-71. (Meads also won 5 caps as a flanker, 2 as a no. 8)
Flanker: K.R. Tremain 36 caps, 1959-68 (Tremain also won 2 caps as a no. 8) I.A. Kirkpatrick 36 caps, 1967-77 (Kirkpatrick also won 3 caps as a no. 8)
No. 8: M.G. Mexted 34 caps, 1979-84

Captain in most Internationals
30, W.J. Whineray, 1958-65

Longest International career
15 seasons, E.E. Hughes, 1907-21; C.E. Meads, 1957-71

Most points in an International
26, A.R. Hewson v. Australia at Auckland, 1982

Most points in Internationals
207, D.B. Clarke, 31 matches, 1956-64

Most tries in an International
4, D. McGregor v. England at Crystal Palace, 1905

Most tries in Internationals
19, S.S. Wilson, 34 matches, 1977-83

Most conversions in an International
6, A.R. Hewson v. Scotland at Auckland, 1981

Most points in an International series
46, A.R. Hewson, 4 matches v. British Isles, 1983

Most tries in an International series
5, K.S. Svenson, 4 matches, British Isles/France, 1924-25. (Svenson scored in every match of the International series)

Most tries on an overseas tour
42, J. Hunter, 23 matches, British Isles/France, 1905-06

Most points in a tour match
43, R.M. Deans, v. South Australia at Adelaide, 1984

Most points on an overseas tour
230, W.J. Wallace, 25 matches, British Isles/France, 1905-06

Most points in International series on tour
32, W.F. McCormick, 4 matches, British Isles/France, 1967; R.M. Deans, 3 matches, Australia, 1984

Most tries in a tour match
8, T.R. Heeps v. Northern New South Wales at Quirindi, 1962

South Africa

Unless otherwise stated, records refer only to matches involving IB countries and the British Isles.

Team Records
Greatest scores
35 v. England at Johannesburg, 1984 (35-9)
38 v. Ireland at Dublin, 1912 (38-0)
44 v. Scotland at Murrayfield 1951 (44-0)
24 v. Wales at Durban, 1964 (24-3)
38 v. France at Bordeaux, 1913 (38-5); at Bloemfontein, 1975 (38-25)
30 v. Australia at Johannesburg, 1969 (30-11)
24 v. New Zealand at Wellington, 1981 (24-12)
34 v. British Isles at Bloemfontein, 1962 (34-14)
(South Africa beat France 55-6 at Parc des Princes, Paris in 1907, but it is not considered an official International match. In 1982, at Pretoria, South Africa won 50-18 v. South America (not an IB country))

Greatest scores by opposing team
18 v. England at Johannesburg, 1972 (9-18)
15 v. Ireland at Cape Town, 1981 (23-15)
10 v. Scotland at Port Elizabeth, 1960 (18-10)
 6 v. Wales at Cardiff, 1970 (6-6)

25 v. France at Bloemfontein, 1975 (38-25)
21 v. Australia at Durban, 1933 (6-21)
25 v. New Zealand at Auckland, 1981 (22-25)
28 v. British Isles at Pretoria, 1974 (9-28)

Greatest losing points margins
9 v. England at Johannesburg, 1972 (9-18)
3 v. Ireland at Dublin, 1965 (6-9)
6 v. Scotland at Glasgow, 1906 (0-6)
Never defeated by Wales
5 v. France at Johannesburg, 1967 (14-19)
15 v. Australia at Durban, 1933 (6-21)
17 v. New Zealand at Auckland, 1965 (3-20)
19 v. British Isles at Pretoria, 1974 (9-28)

Most tries in Internationals
10 v. Ireland at Dublin, 1912 (38-0)
(South Africa scored 13 tries in an
'unofficial' match v. France in Paris, 1907)

*Most tries against South Africa in
Internationals*
5 by British Isles at Johannesburg, 1955
(22-23); by New Zealand at Auckland, 1965
(3-20); by British Isles at Pretoria, 1974,
(9-28)

Most points on an overseas tour (all matches)
753 in Australia/New Zealand, 26 matches,
1937

Most tries on an overseas tour (all matches)
161 in Australia/New Zealand, 26 matches,
1937

Players' Records

Most capped player
F.C.H. du Preez 38 caps, 1960-71; J.H.Ellis 38
caps, 1965-76
By position
Full-back: L.G. Wilson 27 caps, 1960-65
Wing: J.P.Engelbrecht 33 caps, 1960-69
Centre: J.L. Gainsford 33 caps, 1960-67
Fly-half: P.J. Visagie 25 caps, 1967-71
Scrum-half: D.J. de Villiers 25 caps, 1962-70
Prop: J.F.K. Marais 35 caps, 1963-74
Hooker: G.F. Malan 18 caps, 1958-65
Lock: F.C.H. du Preez 31 caps, 1960-71
(Du Preez also won 7 caps as a flanker)
Flanker: J.H. Ellis 38 caps, 1965-76
No. 8: D.J. Hopwood 22 caps, 1960-65. (T.P.
Bedford won 19 caps at no. 8, and 6 as a
flanker)

Captain in most Internationals
22, D.J. de Villiers, 1965-70

Longest International career
13 seasons, J.M. Powell, 1891-1903;
B.H. Heatlie, 1891- 1903

Most points in an International
22, G.R. Bosch v. France at Pretoria 1975
(D. Mare scored 22 points in an 'unofficial'
match v. France in Paris, 1907)

Most points in Internationals
130, P.J. Visagie, 25 matches, 1967-71
(H.E. Botha, 17 matches, scored 173
points, but only 102 in 10 matches against
IB countries or British Isles)

Most points in International series
43, P.J. Visagie, 4 matches v. Australia, 1969

Most tries in an International
3, E.E. McHardy v. Ireland at Dublin, 1912;
J.A. Stegmann v. Ireland at Dublin, 1912;
K.T. van Vollenhoven v. British Isles at
Cape Town, 1955; H.J. van Zyl v. Australia
at Johannesburg, 1961; R.H. Mordt v. New
Zealand at Auckland, 1981; D.M. Gerber

v. England at Johannesburg, 1984
(Gerber, against South America at
Pretoria, 1982, and Mordt, against US at
Glenville, 1981, have each scored 3 tries in
an International against non IB countries
when caps were awarded)

Most tries in Internationals
8, J.L. Gainsford, 33 matches, 1960-67; J.P.
Engelbrecht, 33 matches, 1960-69
(Although D.M. Gerber has scored 14 tries,
only 6 were in matches against IB countries)

Most conversions in an International
7, A. Geffin v. Scotland at Murrayfield, 1951

Most points in an International series
35, H.E. Botha, 3 matches, New Zealand,
1981

Most tries in an International series
6, E.E.McHardy, 5 matches, British Isles/
France, 1912-13

Most tries on an overseas tour
22, J.A. Loubser, 20 matches, British
Isles/France, 1906-07

Most points in a tour match
31, H.E. Botha v. Nelson Bays at Nelson,
1981. (W.J. de W. Ras scored 35 points
against British Schools Old Boys in a match
at Montevideo, 1980, but this was not in an
IB country)

Most points on an overseas tour
190, G.H. Brand, 20 matches, Australia/
New Zealand, 1937

Most tries in a tour match
6, R.G. Dryburgh v. Queensland at Brisbane,
1956

World

From 1890-91, when points-scoring was
standardized by IB countries to 30th April
1986. Both team and individual records are for
recognized International matches, matches
involving British Isles, and for special celebration matches for which caps were awarded.

Team Records

Greatest score
49, Wales v. France at Swansea, 1910 (49-14)

Greatest winning margin
44, South Africa v. Scotland at Murrayfield,
1951 (44-0)

Most tries in an International
11, Wales v. France at Colombes, Paris (47-5)

Most tries in an International series
16, South Africa v. British Isles, 4 matches, in
South Africa, 1955; New Zealand v.
Australia, 3 matches, in New Zealand, 1972

Most tries on an overseas tour (all matches)
215, New Zealand v. British Isles/France, 33
matches, 1905-06

Most points on an overseas tour (all matches)
868, New Zealand v. British Isles/France, 33
matches, 1905-06

Most points in an International series
97, New Zealand v. Australia, 3 matches, in
New Zealand, 1972

Greatest win on a major tour (all matches)
117-6 New Zealand v. South Australia at
Adelaide, 1974

*Most tries in Five Nations Championship
season*
21, Wales, 1909-10
*Most points in Five Nations Championship
season*
102, Wales, 1975-76

Players' Records

(including matches for British Isles in
brackets)
Most capped player
C.M.H. Gibson *(Ireland)* 81 (12) caps, 1964-
79. (Gibson played 40 matches for Ireland
as a centre and 8 for the Lions, 48 at centre
in total. As a fly-half he played 25 matches
for Ireland and 4 for the Lions, 29 in total.
He also played four matches for Ireland on
the wing. His 69 caps for Ireland, out of 81
in total, are the record for an individual
country)
By position
Full-back: J.P.R. Williams *(Wales)* 62 (8)
caps, 1969-81. (Williams also played once
for Wales as a flanker)
Wing: K.J. Jones *(Wales)* 47 (3) caps, 1947-57
(T.G.R. Davies *(Wales)*, 51 (5), won 39
caps as a wing and 12 as a centre, one of
them for the Lions)
Centre (or 2nd five-eighth): J.M. Renwick 52
(Scotland) 1972-84. (Renwick also won 53
caps for Scotland and the Lions but played
once as a replacement wing. R. Bertranne
(France) has played most matches, 52, for
an individual country as a three-quarter. He
played 39 times in the centre and 13 on the
wing)
Fly-half (or 1st five-eighth): J.W. Kyle
(Ireland) 52 (6) caps, 1947-58
Scrum-half: G.O. Edwards *(Wales)* 63 (10)
caps (1967-78)
Prop: G. Price *(Wales)* 53 (12) caps, 1975-83
Hooker: K.W. Kennedy *(Ireland)* 49 (4) caps,
1965-75; J.V. Pullin *(England)* 49 (7) caps,
1966-76
Lock: W.J.McBride *(Ireland)* 80 (17) caps,
1962-75
Flanker: J.F. Slattery *(Ireland)* 65 (4) caps,
1970-84
No. 8: T.M. Davies *(Wales)* 46 (8) caps, 1969-
76. (B. Dauga *(France)* won 21 caps at no. 8
and 29 at lock)

Captain in most Internationals
32, J.-P. Rives *(France)*, 1979-84

Most points in an International
26, A.R. Hewson *(New Zealand)* v. Australia
at Auckland, 1982

Most points in Internationals
301, A.R. Irvine *(Scotland)*, 60 (9) matches,
1972-82. (The total is made up of 273 points
for Scotland and 28 for British Isles; it
includes one penalty-try)

Most tries in an International
5, D. Lambert *(England)* v. France at
Richmond, 1907

Most tries in Internationals
24, I.S. Smith *(Scotland)*, 32 matches, 1924-33

Most penalty-goals in an International
6, D.B. Clarke *(New Zealand)* v. British Isles
at Dunedin, 1959; G.R. Bosch *(South
Africa)* v. France at Pretoria, 1975; G.
Evans *(Wales)* v. France at Cardiff, 1982;
S.O. Campbell *(Ireland)* v. Scotland at

Dublin, 1982; C.R. Andrew (*England*) v. Wales, 1986; A.G. Hastings (*Scotland*) v. France, 1986

Most conversions in an International
8, J. Bancroft (*Wales*) v. France at Swansea, 1910

Most dropped-goals in an International
3, P. Albaladejo (*France*) v. Ireland at Colombes, Paris, 1960; P.F. Hawthorne (*Australia*) v. England at Twickenham, 1967; H.E. Botha (*South Africa*) v. Ireland at Durban, 1981; J.-P. Lescarboura (*France*) v. England at Twickenham, 1985

Most points in Five Nations Championship season
54, J.-P. Lescarboura (*France*), 4 matches, 1983-84

Most tries in Five Nations Championship season
8, C.N. Lowe (*England*), 4 matches, 1913-14; I.S. Smith (*Scotland*) 4 matches, 1924-25

Most conversions in Five Nations Championship season
11, J. Bancroft (*Wales*), 4 matches, 1908-09

Most penalty-goals in Five Nations Championship season
16, P.H. Thorburn (*Wales*), 4 matches, 1985-86

Most dropped-goals in Five Nations Championship season
5, G. Camberabero (*France*), 3 matches, 1966-67. (J.-P. Lescarboura (*France*) dropped a goal in each Championship match 1983-84, which is unique)

Most tries on an overseas tour
42, J. Hunter (*New Zealand*), 23 matches in British Isles/France, 1905-06

Most points in a tour match
43, R.M. Deans (*New Zealand*) v. South Australia at Adelaide, 1984

Most points on an overseas tour
230, W.J. Wallace (*New Zealand*), 25 matches in British Isles/France, 1905-06

Most tries in a tour match
8, T.R. Heeps (*New Zealand*) v. Northern New South Wales at Quirindi, 1962. (P. Estève scored 8 for France against East Japan in 1984, but this was not a full International tour)

Winners of the Grand Slam

Wales: 1908, 1909, 1911, 1950, 1952, 1971, 1976, 1978 (8 times)
England: 1913, 1914, 1921, 1923, 1924, 1928, 1957, 1980 (8 times)
France: 1968, 1977, 1981 (3 times)
Scotland: 1925, 1984 (twice)
Ireland: 1948 (once)

Winners of the Triple Crown

Wales: 1893, 1900, 1902, 1905, 1908, 1909, 1911, 1950, 1952, 1965, 1969, 1971, 1976, 1977, 1978, 1979 (16 times)
England: 1883, 1884, 1892, 1913, 1914, 1921, 1923, 1924, 1928, 1934, 1937, 1954, 1957, 1960, 1980, (15 times)
Scotland: 1891, 1895, 1901, 1903, 1907, 1925, 1933, 1938, 1984 (9 times)
Ireland: 1894, 1899, 1948, 1949, 1982, 1985 (6 times)

International Champions

1883	England	1912	England and Ireland	1948	Ireland	1973	All Five Nations tied
1884	England	1913	England	1949	Ireland	1974	Ireland
1886	England and Scotland	1914	England	1950	Wales	1975	Wales
1887	Scotland	1920	England, Scotland and Wales	1951	Ireland	1976	Wales
1890	England and Scotland	1921	England	1952	Wales	1977	France
1891	Scotland	1922	Wales	1953	England	1978	Wales
1892	England	1923	England	1954	England, France and Wales	1979	Wales
1893	Wales	1924	England	1955	France and Wales	1980	England
1894	Ireland	1925	Scotland	1956	Wales	1981	France
1895	Scotland	1926	Scotland and Ireland	1957	England	1982	Ireland
1896	Ireland	1927	Scotland and Ireland	1958	England	1983	France and Ireland
1899	Ireland	1928	England	1959	France	1984	Scotland
1900	Wales	1929	Scotland	1960	France and England	1985	Ireland
1901	Scotland	1930	England	1961	France	1986	France and Scotland
1902	Wales	1931	Wales	1962	France		
1903	Scotland	1932	England, Wales and Ireland	1963	England		
1904	Scotland	1933	Scotland	1964	Scotland and Wales		
1905	Wales	1934	England	1965	Wales		
1906	Ireland and Wales	1935	Ireland	1966	Wales		
1907	Scotland	1936	Wales	1967	France		
1908	Wales	1937	England	1968	France		
1909	Wales	1938	Scotland	1969	Wales		
1910	England	1939	England, Wales and Ireland	1970	France and Wales		
1911	Wales	1947	Wales and England	1971	Wales		

Matches were not completed, for various reasons, in 1885, 1888, 1889, 1897, 1898 and 1972.

Wales have won the title outright 21 times, England 18 times, Scotland 12, Ireland 10 and France 7.

International Referees

The list records matches from 1946-47 to 30th April 1986 between the International Board countries and British Isles, and special celebration matches for which caps were awarded. Referees who have officiated at five or more International matches have the totals shown in brackets after their details.

Ackermann, C.J. (*South Africa*) 1953 *SA v. A (2)*; 1955 *SA v. BI*; 1958 *SA v. F*

Anderson, J.B. (*Scotland*) 1981 *W v. E, I v. A*; 1983 *I v. E, A v. NZ*; 1984 *E v. W*; 1986 *W v. F (6)*

Austin, A.W.C. (*Scotland*) 1952 *W v. F*; 1953 *I v. E*; 1954 *I v. W*

Austry, R. (*France*) 1972 *E v. I*

Baise, M. (*South Africa*) 1967 *SA v. F (2)*; 1968 *SA v. BI (2)*; 1969 *SA v. A*; 1974 *SA v. BI (2) (7)*

Baise, S. (*South Africa*) 1969 *SA v. A*

Bevan, W.D. (*Wales*) 1986 *F v. E*

Bezuidenhout, G.P. (*South Africa*) 1976 *SA v. NZ (3)*

Bonnet, J.-P. (*France*) 1979 *W v. E*; 1980 *S v. E, SA v. BI (2)*; 1981 *I v. E*; 1982 *W v. S (6)*

Boundy, L.M. (*England*) 1955 *S v. I*; 1956 *W v. S*; 1957 *F v. S, I v. F, S v. I*; 1958 *S v. F*; 1959 *S v. I*; 1961 *S v. SA (8)*

Brook, P.G. (*England*) 1963 *F v. W*; 1964 *W v. S*; 1965 *W v. I, I v. SA*; 1966 *F v. I (5)*

Brown, D.A. (*England*) 1960 *I v. W*

Burmeister, R.D. (*South Africa*) 1949 *SA v. NZ (2)*; 1953 *SA v. A*; 1955 *SA v. BI (2)*; 1960 *SA v. NZ (2)*; 1961 *SA v. A (8)*

Burnett, D.I.H. (*Ireland*) 1977 *W v. E*; 1979 *F v. W*; 1980 *E v. W*; 1981 *S v. W, E v. S*; 1982 *W v. F*; 1983 *E v. F*; 1984 *S v. E, A v. NZ*; 1985 *E v. F, NZ v. A*; 1986 *S v. F (12)*

Burnett, R.T. (*Australia*) 1974 *A v. NZ*; 1975 *A v. E*; 1978 *A v. W*

Burrell, G. (*Scotland*) 1958 *E v. I*; 1959 *W v. I*

Burrell, R.P. (*Scotland*) 1966 *I v. W*; 1967 *I v. F, F v. NZ*; 1969 *I v. E, F v. W (5)*

Byres, R.G. (*Australia*) 1978 *A v. W*; 1979 *A v. I (2), A v. NZ*; 1980 *A v. NZ*; 1981 *NZ v. S*; 1982 *A v. S (2)*; 1983 *NZ v. BI (2)*; 1984 *I v. W, W v. F (12)*

Calitz, M. (*South Africa*) 1961 *SA v. I*

Calmet, R. (*France*) 1970 *E v. W*

Carlson, K.R.V. (*South Africa*) 1962 *SA v. BI*

Chevner, G. (*France*) 1980 *I v. S*

Clark, K.H. (*Ireland*) 1973 *E v. F*; 1974 *S v. F*; 1976 *F v. E*

Collett, C.K. (*Australia*) 1981 *NZ v. S*

Cooney, W.M. (*Australia*) 1972 *A v. F*; 1975 *A v. E*

Cooper, Dr P.F. (*England*) 1952 *I v. W*; 1953 *S v. W, W v. I, W v. NZ*; 1954 *I v. NZ, W v. S*; 1956 *F v. I, W v. F*; 1957 *F v. W (9)*

Crowe, K.J. (*Australia*) 1965 *A v. SA*; 1966 *A v. BI*; 1968 *A v. NZ*

Cuny, Dr A. (*France*) 1976 *W v. S*

D'Arcy, D.P. (*Ireland*) 1967 *E v. F, E v. S, F v. W*; 1968 *E v. W, S v. E, F v. SA*; 1969 *E v. F, W v. E*; 1970 *W v. S*; 1971 *W v. I*; 1973 *F v. NZ, F v. W*; 1975 *E v. S, W v. A (14)*

De Bruyn, C.J. (*South Africa*) 1969 *SA v. A*; 1974 *SA v. BI (2)*

Dickie, A.I. (*Scotland*) 1954 *F v. I, E v. I, W v. F*; 1955 *I v. E, W v. I*; 1956 *E v. I, I v. W*; 1957 *W v. E, I v. E*; 1958 *W v. A, W v. F (11)*

Domercq, G. (*France*) 1972 *S v. NZ*; 1973 *W v. E*; 1976 *E v. W*; 1977 *S v. W*; 1978 *I v. W (5)*

Doocey, T.F. (*New Zealand*) 1976 *NZ v. I*; 1983 *E v. S, F v. W*

Dowling, M.J. (*Ireland*) 1947 *S v. W*; 1950 *W v. S, S v. E, W v. F*; 1951 *W v. E, S v. W, F v. W, E v. S, SA v. W*; 1952 *W v. S, F v. SA, S v. E*; 1953 *W v. E, E v. S*; 1954 *E v. W*; 1955 *S v. W*; 1956 *S v. F, S v. E (18)*

Doyle, O.E. (*Ireland*) 1984 *W v. S, W v. A*

Duffy, B. (*New Zealand*) 1977 *NZ v. BI*

Durand, C. (*France*) 1969 *E v. S*; 1970 *I v. S*; 1971 *E v. S*

Elliott, H.B. (*England*) 1955 *F v. S*; 1956 *I v. S*

Engelbrecht, Dr G.K. (*South Africa*) 1964 *SA v. W*

Evans, W.J. (*Wales*) 1958 *I v. A, F v. E*

Farquhar, A.B. (*New Zealand*) 1961 *NZ v. F (3)*; 1962 *NZ v. A (2)*; 1964 *NZ v. A (6)*

Ferguson, C.F. (*Australia*) 1963 *A v. E*; 1965 *A v. SA*; 1968 *A v. F*; 1969 *A v. W*; 1971 *A v. SA (2) (6)*

Finlay, A.K. (*Australia*) 1962 *A v. NZ*

Fitzgerald, K.V.J. (*Australia*) 1985 *I v. F, W v. I*

Fleming, J.M. (*Scotland*) 1985 *I v. E*

Fleury, A.L. (*New Zealand*) 1959 *NZ v. BI*

Fong, A.S. (*New Zealand*) 1946 *NZ v. A*; 1950 *NZ v. BI*

Fordham, R. (*Australia*) 1986 *E v. W, F v. I (2)*

Forsyth, R.A. (*New Zealand*) 1958 *NZ v. A*

Francis, R.C. (*New Zealand*) 1984 *E v. A, I v. A*; 1986 *W v. S, S v. E*

Fright, W.H. (*New Zealand*) 1956 *NZ v. SA (2)*

Frood, J. (*New Zealand*) 1952 *NZ v. A*

Garling, A.F. (*Australia*) 1981 *A v. NZ (2)*

Gillies, C.R. (*New Zealand*) 1958 *NZ v. A (2)*; 1959 *NZ v. BI (2)*

Gilliland, R.W. (*Ireland*) 1965 *S v. W, E v. F, F v. W*; 1966 *E v. W*; 1967 *F v. A (5)*

Gillmore, W.N. (*England*) 1958 *I v. S*

Glasgow, O.B. (*Ireland*) 1953 *F v. S, F v. W*; 1954 *S v. E*; 1955 *W v. E, F v. W (5)*

Gourlay, I.W. (*South Africa*) 1976 *SA v. NZ*

Gouws, Dr J. (*South Africa*) 1977 *SA v. Wld*

Grierson, T.F.E. (*Scotland*) 1970 *I v. SA*; 1972 *F v. E*; 1973 *W v. I*; 1975 *E v. F*

Griffiths, A.A. (*New Zealand*) 1952 *NZ v. A*

Harrison, G.L. (*New Zealand*) 1981 *A v. F*; 1983 *F v. A (2)*

Haydon, N.V. (*Australia*) 1957 *A v. NZ*

Hilditch, S.R. (*Ireland*) 1984 *S v. A*

Hill, E.D. (*New Zealand*) 1949 *NZ v. A*

Hofmeyr, E.W. (*South Africa*) 1949 *SA v. NZ (2)*; 1961 *SA v. A*; 1963 *SA v. A*

Hosie, A.M. (*Scotland*) 1973 *I v. E*; 1974 *F v. I*; 1975 *W v. E*; 1976 *E v. I, F v. A*; 1977 *F v. W, I v. F*; 1979 *W v. I, I v. E*; 1980 *W v. F, F v. I*; 1981 *E v. F*; 1982 *E v. I, NZ v. A (2)*; 1983 *I v. F, E v. NZ*; 1984 *F v. E (18)*

Hourquet, R. (*France*) 1983 *S v. NZ*; 1984 *E v. I, SA v. E (2)*; 1985 *S v. W (5)*

Howard, F.A. (*England*) 1984 *I v. S*; 1986 *I v. W (2)*

Hughes, D.M. (*Wales*) 1966 *S v. F, I v. S*; 1967 *I v. E, S v. I*

Hughes, P.E. (*England*) 1978 *I v. S*

Jamison, G.A. (*Ireland*) 1972 *W v. S*

Johnson, R.F. (*England*) 1970 *F v. I, E v. W (r)*; 1971 *W v. I*; 1972 *I v. F, W v. NZ*; 1973 *I v. F*; 1974 *W v. S, I v. NZ, F v. SA*; 1975 *S v. I, S v. A (11)*

Jones, T. (*Wales*) 1947 *E v. F*; 1948 *E v. I, F v. E*; 1949 *E v. F*; 1950 *S v. F*; 1951 *I v. E (6)*

Jones, W. (*Wales*) 1984 *S v. F, NZ v. F (2)*

Jones, W.K.M. (*Wales*) 1968 *I v. A*; 1970 *F v. E*; 1971 *S v. I*

Joseph, M. (*Wales*) 1966 *S v. A*; 1967 *I v. A*; 1968 *I v. S, E v. I*; 1969 *S v. I, S v. SA*; 1970 *S v. E*; 1971 *I v. E, S v. E (C)*; 1972 *S v. F, S v. E*; 1973 *I v. NZ, S v. P (C)*; 1974 *E v. I*; 1976 *E v. A, F v. A*; 1977 *E v. S, S v. I, F v. S (19)*

Joynson, D.C. (*Wales*) 1955 *E v. S*

Keenan, H. (*England*) 1963 *I v. NZ*

Kelleher, J.C. (*Wales*) 1973 *E v. S*; 1974 *F v. E*; 1977 *E v. F*

Kelleher, K.D. (*Ireland*) 1960 *W v. S*; 1961 *W v. E, E v. S*; 1962 *S v. E, W v. F*; 1963 *W v. E*; 1964 *E v. W*; 1965 *F v. S, W v. E*; 1966 *S v. E, W v. A*; 1967 *E v. A, F v. S, S v. W, S v. NZ*; 1968 *S v. F*; 1969 *S v. W, E v. SA*; 1970 *W v. F*; 1971 *F v. S (21)*

King, M.H.R. (*England*) 1961 *S v. I*

Laidlaw, H.B. (*Scotland*) 1963 *I v. E*; 1964 *W v. F*; 1965 *I v. E*; 1968 *F v. E, W v. F (5)*

Lamb, G.C. (*England*) 1968 *F v. I, W v. S, F v. SA*; 1969 *F v. S, I v. F*; 1970 *S v. F, W v. SA, v. W*; 1971 *I v. F, F v. A (10)*

Lambert, N.H. (*Ireland*) 1947 *S v. A*; 1948 *E v. A, S v. E*; 1949 *W v. E, S v. W, E v. S, F v. W*; 1950 *E v. W, F v. E*; 1951 *W v. SA*; 1952 *E v. W (11)*

Lewis, A.R. (*Wales*) 1970 *E v. I*; 1971 *E v. F*; 1972 *F v. I*; 1973 *S v. I, E v. A (5)*

Lewis, E.M. (*Wales*) 1971 *F v. A*

Lewis, M.S. (*Wales*) 1975 *F v. S*; 1976 *I v. S*

Llewellyn, V.S. (*Wales*) 1951 *E v. F*

Lloyd, D.M. (*Wales*) 1975 *I v. F*; 1976 *S v. E*

Louw, L.L. (*South Africa*) 1953 *SA v. A*

Luff, A.C. (*England*) 1963 *W v. I*; 1964 *I v. S, v. W*

McAuley, C.J. (*New Zealand*) 1962 *NZ v. A*

McDavitt, P.A. (*New Zealand*) 1972 *NZ v. A*; 1975 *NZ v. S*; 1977 *NZ v. BI*

McMahon, D.C.J. (*Scotland*) 1961 *W v. I*; 1963 *E v. F*; 1964 *E v. NZ*; 1967 *E v. NZ, W v. E*; 1969 *W v. I (6)*

McMullen, R.F. (*New Zealand*) 1973 *NZ v. A*

Malan, Dr W.C. (*South Africa*) 1970 *SA v. NZ*; 1971 *SA v. F (2)*

Marie, B. (*France*) 1965 *F v. W (r)*; 1966 *E v. I*

Matheson, A.M. (*New Zealand*) 1946 *NZ v. A*

Millar, D.H. (*New Zealand*) 1965 *NZ v. SA*; 1968 *NZ v. F*; 1977 *NZ v. BI (2)*; 1978 *NZ v. A (3) (7)*

Mitchell, R. (*Ireland*) 1955 *E v. F*; 1956 *E v. W*; 1957 *E v. S*

Moolman, Dr J. (*South Africa*) 1972 *SA v. E*

Moore, T.W. (*Australia*) 1947 *A v. NZ*; 1950 *A v. BI*; 1951 *A v. NZ*; 1956 *A v. SA*

Murdoch, W.C.W. (*Scotland*) 1951 *W v. I, I v. SA*; 1952 *E v. SA, F v. E*

Murphy, J.P. (*New Zealand*) 1959 *NZ v. BI*; 1963 *NZ v. E*; 1964 *NZ v. A (2)*; 1965 *NZ v. SA (3)*; 1966 *NZ v. BI (3)*; 1968 *NZ v. F*; 1969 *NZ v. W (2) (13)*

Myburgh, P.A. (*South Africa*) 1962 *SA v. BI*; 1963 *SA v. A (3)*

Norling, C. (*Wales*) 1978 *I v. NZ*; 1979 *E v. S*; 1980 *F v. E*; 1981 *I v. F, NZ v. SA (2), F v. NZ*; 1982 *I v. S*; 1984 *F v. I*; 1985 *E v. S*; 1986 *E v. I (11)*

O'Callaghan, B.J. (*Australia*) 1959 *A v. BI*

Palmade, F. (*France*) 1973 *F v. S (r), S v. W*; 1974 *I v. S*; 1975 *I v. E*; 1977 *I v. E*; 1978 *E v. I*; 1979 *S v. W*; 1980 *SA v. BI (2)*; 1981 *W v. I, SA v. I (2)*; 1982 *E v. W*; 1983 *NZ v. BI (2)*; 1985 *W v. E*; 1986 *I v. S (17)*

Parfitt, V.J. (*Wales*) 1953 *E v. F*; 1954 *I v. S*

Parkes, Dr N.M. (*England*) 1958 *W v. S, F v. A, I v. W, F v. I*; 1959 *F v. W*; 1960 *W v. F*; 1961 *F v. W*; 1962 *W v. S, I v. S (9)*

Parkinson, F.G.M. (*New Zealand*) 1955 *NZ v. A*; 1956 *NZ v. SA (2)*

Pattinson, K.A. (*England*) 1973 *F v. S, W v. A*; 1974 *I v. W*; 1975 *F v. W*; 1976 *S v. F (5)*

Pearce, T.N. (*England*) 1948 *F v. I, S v. W*; 1949 *I v. F, W v. I*; 1950 *F v. I, I v. S*; 1951 *v. S, I v. F, S v. I*; 1952 *F v. I (10)*

Price, F.G. (*Wales*) 1963 *I v. F*

Prideaux, L. (*England*) 1980 *W v. S, I v. W*; 1981 *S v. I, NZ v. SA*; 1985 *F v. S (5)*

Priest, T.E. (*England*) 1953 *I v. F*

Pring, J.P.G. (*New Zealand*) 1966 *NZ v. BI*; 1967 *NZ v. A*; 1968 *NZ v. F*; 1971 *NZ v. BI (4)*; 1972 *NZ v. A (8)*

Quittenton, R.C. (*England*) 1978 *W v. NZ;*
1979 *I v. F, F v. S, S v. NZ;* 1981 *S v. W;* 1982
NZ v. A; 1983 *S v. W;* 1984 *A v. NZ (2)*

Rea, M.D.M. (*Ireland*) 1982 *F v. E*
Reilly, J.R. (*Australia*) 1972 *A v. F*
Richards, A. (*Wales*) 1981 *A v. F;* 1982 *E v. A;*
1983 *F v. S*
Robbertse, P. (*South Africa*) 1967 *SA v. F;*
1969 *SA v. A;* 1970 *SA v. NZ (2)*
Robson, C.F. (*New Zealand*) 1963 *NZ v. E*
Rowlands, K. (*Wales*) 1981 *F v. S;* 1982 *S v. E*

St Guilhem, J. (*France*) 1974 *S v. E;* 1975
W v. I
Sanson, N.R. (*Scotland*) 1974 *W v. F, F v. SA;*
1975 *I v. P (C), SA v. F (2);* 1976 *I v. A, I v.
W;* 1977 *W v. I;* 1978 *F v. E, E v. W, E v. NZ;*
1979 *E v. NZ (12)*
Schoeman, J.P.J. (*South Africa*) 1968 *SA v. BI*
Short, J.A. (*Scotland*) 1982 *I v. W*
Slabber, M.J. (*South Africa*) 1955 *SA v. BI;*
1960 *SA v. NZ*
Strasheim, Dr E.A. (*South Africa*) 1958 *SA v.
F;* 1960 *SA v. S, SA v. NZ;* 1962 *SA v. BI
(2);* 1964 *SA v. F;* 1967 *SA v. F;* 1968 *SA v.
BI (8)*
Strydom, S. (*South Africa*) 1985 *S v. I, F v.
W*
Sullivan, G. (*New Zealand*) 1950 *NZ v. BI*

Taylor, A.R. (*New Zealand*) 1965 *NZ v. SA
(r);* 1972 *NZ v. A*
Taylor, J.A.S. (*Scotland*) 1957 *W v. I;* 1960 *E
v. W, F v. E, W v. SA;* 1962 *E v. W, F v. I, I v.
W (7)*
Thomas, C. (*Wales*) 1979 *S v. I;* 1980 *E v. I*
Thomas, C.G.P. (*Wales*) 1977 *F v. NZ;* 1978 *S
v. F, F v. I*
Tierney, A.T. (*Australia*) 1957 *A v. NZ;* 1959
A v. BI
Tindill, E.W.T. (*New Zealand*) 1950 *NZ v. BI
(2);* 1955 *NZ v. A*
Titcomb, M.H. (*England*) 1966 *W v. S;* 1967
W v. I, W v. NZ; 1968 *I v. W, S v. A;* 1971 *S v.
W, E v. P (C);* 1972 *W v. F (8)*
Tolhurst, H.A. (*Australia*) 1951 *A v. NZ (2)*
Tomalin, L.C. (*Australia*) 1947 *A v. NZ;* 1950
A v. BI
Treharne, G.J. (*Wales*) 1960 *I v. SA;* 1961 *E v.
SA, I v. E, I v. F;* 1963 *S v. I (5)*
Trigg, J.A.F. (*England*) 1982 *S v. F;* 1983
W v. I

Vanderfield, Dr I.R. (*Australia*) 1956 *A v. SA;*
1961 *A v. F;* 1962 *A v. NZ;* 1966 *A v. BI;*
1967 *A v. I;* 1968 *A v. NZ;* 1970 *A v. S;* 1971
A v. SA; 1974 *A v. NZ (2) (10)*

Walsh, L. (*New Zealand*) 1949 *NZ v. A*
Walters, D.G. (*Wales*) 1959 *F v. S, I v. E, E v.
S, I v. F;* 1960 *S v. F, E v. I, I v. S, F v. I;* 1961
F v. SA, E v. I; 1962 *E v. I, F v. E;* 1963 *E v.
S;* 1964 *E v. I, F v. E, F v. I;* 1965 *I v. F, S v. I,
E v. S, S v. SA;* 1966 *F v. E (21)*
Welsby, A. (*England*) 1976 *F v. I;* 1978 *W v. F;*
1981 *F v. W;* 1982 *E v. I*
West, J.R. (*Ireland*) 1974 *E v. W;* 1975 *S v. W;*
1976 *W v. F;* 1977 *F v. NZ;* 1978 *W v. S, S v.
E, S v. NZ;* 1979 *E v. F, NZ v. F (2);* 1980 *S
v. F, SA v. F, W v. NZ;* 1981 *F v. NZ, W v. A;*
1983 *W v. E (16)*
Whittaker, J.B.G. (*England*) 1947 *I v. F,
W v. I*

Williams, R.C. (*Ireland*) 1957 *S v. W, E v. F;*
1958 *E v. W, E v. A, S v. A, S v. E;* 1959 *W v.
E, S v. W, E v. F;* 1960 *S v. E;* 1961 *F v. S, S v.
W;* 1962 *S v. F;* 1963 *F v. S, S v. W, W v. NZ;*
1964 *S v. F, S v. NZ, F v. NZ, S v. E (20)*
Wolstenholme, B.H. (*New Zealand*) 1955
NZ v. A
Woolley, A. (*South Africa*) 1970 *SA v. NZ*

Yché, J.-C. (*France*) 1983 *S v. I*
Young, J. (*Scotland*) 1971 *S v. W;* 1972 *E v. W;*
1973 *E v. NZ*

Other Internationals

The following referees officiated at other
major Internationals for which an IB country
awarded caps.

Anderson, J.B. (*Scotland*) 1982 *R v. F*

Bean, A.S. (*England*) 1945 *W v. F;* 1946
F v. W
Beattie, R.A. (*Scotland*) 1945 *B v. F*
Bevan, W.D. (*Wales*) 1985 *E v. R, I v. Fi, J v. I
(2)*
Bonnet, J.-P. (*France*) 1981 *Arg v. E (2)*
Boundy, L.M. (*England*) 1957 *R v. F*
Brook, P.G. (*England*) 1966 *It v. F, R v. F*
Brown, D.A. (*England*) 1960 *It v. F*
Burnett, D.I.H. (*Ireland*) 1982 *F v. Arg*
Burnett, R.T. (*Australia*) 1973 *A v. Tg;* 1975
A v. J
Byres, R.G. (*Australia*) 1976 *A v. Fi*

Camardon, J. (*Argentina*) 1960 *Arg v. F*
Cooney, W.M. (*Australia*) 1975 *A v. J;* 1976
A v. Fi
Cooper, Dr P.F. (*England*) 1953 *F v. It;* 1954 *It
v. F;* 1956 *It v. F*
Costello, J. (*Fiji*) 1972 *Fi v. A*
Crowe, K.J. (*Australia*) 1976 *A v. Fi*
Curnow, J. (*Canada*) 1976 *US v. F*

D'Arcy, D.P. (*Ireland*) 1967 *F v. R;* 1973 *F v.
R;* 1975 *F v. Arg*
Doyle, O.E. (*Ireland*) 1984 *R v. S*

Elliott, H.B. (*England*) 1955 *F v. It*

Finlay, A.K. (*Australia*) 1961 *A v. Fi*
Fitzgerald, K.V.F. (*Australia*) 1985 *Arg v. NZ
(2)*
Fleming, J. (*Scotland*) 1985 *F v. J (1)*
Francis, R.C. (*New Zealand*) 1985 *Arg v. F (2)*
Fornes, E. (*Argentina*) 1954 *Arg v. F (2)*
Furness, D.C. (*Australia*) 1952 *A v. Fi (2);*
1954 *A v. Fi*

Gilliland, R.W. (*Ireland*) 1964 *It v. F;* 1965 *F v.
R*
Gillmore, W.N. (*England*) 1956 *F v. Cz;* 1958
It v. F
Grierson, T.F.E. (*Scotland*) 1971 *F v. R*
Griffiths, A.A. (*New Zealand*) 1946 *M v. A*

Harrison, G.L. (*New Zealand*) 1980 *Fi v. A;*
1983 *A v. US;* 1984 *Fi v. A*

Hilditch, S.R. (*Ireland*) 1985 *W v. Fi*
Hosie, A.M. (*Scotland*) 1981 *R v. NZ*
Hourquet, R. (*France*) 1984 *SA v. S Am (2)*
Hughes, D.M. (*Wales*) 1965 *F v. It*
Hughes, P.E. (*England*) 1977 *F v. R*

Johnson, R.F. (*England*) 1969 *F v. R*
Joseph, M. (*Wales*) 1968 *R v. F;* 1973 *F v. J;*
1975 *F v. Arg*

Keenan, H.B. (*England*) 1962 *It v. F*
Kelleher, J.C. (*Wales*) 1976 *R v. F*
Kelleher, K.D. (*Ireland*) 1963 *F v. R;* 1964
R v. F
Knox, J. (*Argentina*) 1949 *Arg v. F*

Lacroix, M. (*Belgium*) 1962 *R v. F*
Lamb, G.C. (*England*) 1970 *R v. F*
Lathwell, H.G. (*England*) 1946 *I v. F*
Lewis, A.R. (*Wales*) 1974 *Arg v. F (2)*

Marie, B. (*France*) 1960 *Arg v. F (2)*
Moore, T.W. (*Australia*) 1954 *A v. Fi*
Morgan, E.R. (*Wales*) 1976 *F v. It*
Morrison, D. (*USA*) 1981 *US v. SA*
Muller, F. (*South Africa*) 1982 *SA v. S Am*

Noon, O. (*Argentina*) 1949 *Arg v. F*
Norling, C. (*Wales*) 1983 *A v. Arg (2);* 1986
F v. J (2)

O'Leary, J. (*Australia*) 1958 *A v. M*

Parkes, N.M. (*England*) 1959 *F v. It*
Pattinson, K.A. (*England*) 1974 *R v. F*
Pontin, A.C. (*USA*) 1976 *US v. A*
Pozzi, S. (*Italy*) 1957 *F v. R;* 1960 *R v. F*
Prideaux, L. (*England*) 1980 *S Am v. SA (2)*
Priest, T.E. (*England*) 1952 *It v. F*

Quittenton, R.C. (*England*) 1977 *Arg v. F (2);*
1983 *F v. R;* 1986 *R v. S (3)*

Rea, M.D.M. (*Ireland*) 1978 *R v. F;* 1981
S v. R
Richards, A. (*Wales*) 1980 *R v. F*
Rowlands, K. (*Wales*) 1980 *SA v. S Am (2)*

Sanson, N.R. (*Scotland*) 1975 *F v. R*
Short, J.A. (*Scotland*) 1979 *F v. R*
Strydom, S. (*South Africa*) 1979 *Arg v. A (2);*
1982 *SA v. S Am*

Tagnini, S. (*Italy*) 1968 *Cz v. F*
Taylor, J.A.S. (*Scotland*) 1961 *F v. It*
Tierney, A.T. (*Australia*) 1958 *A v. M*
Tomalin, L.C. (*Australia*) 1949 *A v. M (2)*
Trigg, J.A.F. (*England*) 1981 *F v. R*

Vanderfield, I.R. (*Australia*) 1958 *A v. M;*
1961 *A v. Fi (2);* 1973 *A v. Tg*

Waldron, C.A. (*Australia*) 1986 *F v. R*
Waldron, H. (*England*) 1957 *F v. It*
Walters, D.G. (*Wales*) 1963 *F v. R;* 1964
F v. Fi
Warden, G. (*England*) 1946 *F v. NZA*
West, J.R. (*Ireland*) 1982 *F v. Arg;* 1984 *R v.
F*
Williams, R.C. (*Ireland*) 1961 *F v. R*
Wyllie, W.D. (*Australia*) 1949 *A v. M*

Yché, J.-C. (*France*) 1983 *R v. W, It v. A*
Young, J. (*Scotland*) 1972 *R v. F*

International Caps

1946 to 30th April 1986

A	Australia	G	Germany
Arg	Argentina	I	Ireland
AW	Anglo-Welsh	It	Italy
B	British Forces Teams	J	Japan
BI	British Isles	M	Maoris
Cz	Czechoslovakia	NSW	New South Wales
E	England	NZA	New Zealand Army
F	France	NZ	New Zealand
Fi	Fiji	R	Romania

S	Scotland
SA	South Africa
S Am	South America
(ST)	Short Tour
(T)	Tour
Tg	Tonga
US	United States
W	Wales
Wld	World Invitation XV

(C) Centenary match, 1971 (non-championship)
P President's XV
(r) replacement

Note: (2[1r]) denotes two matches played, one as replacement, for certain tours.

The year in which each match is played is shown on the attached lists except in the case of Five Nations matches which show the concluding year in the appropriate season, e.g. 1963-64 is shown as 1964. This is logical since, with very few exceptions, the matches are played after New Year's Day. Where a series is played the matches are given numbers, e.g. A 2 means the second International in a series played by, say, Wales in Australia against the home country. Matches played against Romania and Argentina since 1st January 1981 by the nations listed are given full International status.

England

Adey, G.J. (*Leicester*) 1976 *I, F*

Adkins, S.J. (*Coventry*) 1950 *I, F, S;* 1953 *W, I, F, S*

Agar, A.E. (*Harlequins*) 1952 *SA, W, S, I, F;* 1953 *W, I*

Allison, D.F. (*Coventry*) 1956 *W, I, S, F;* 1957 *W;* 1958 *W, S*

Andrew, C.R. (*Cambridge U, Nottingham*) 1985 *R, F, S, I, W;* 1986 *W, S, I, F*

Arthur, T.G. (*Wasps*) 1966 *W, I*

Ashby, R.C. (*Wasps*) 1966 *I, F;* 1967 *A*

Ashcroft, A. (*Waterloo*) 1956 *W, I, S, F;* 1957 *W, I, F, S;* 1958 *W, A, I, F, S;* 1959 *I, F, S*

Bailey, M.D. (*Cambridge U, Wasps*) 1984 *SA 1, 2*

Bainbridge, S. (*Gosforth*) 1982 *F, W;* 1983 *F, W, S, I, NZ;* 1984 *S, I, F, W;* 1985 *NZ 1, 2*

Baker, D.G.S. (*OMTs*) 1955 *W, I, F, S*

Bance, J.F. (*Bedford*) 1954 *S*

Barley, B. (*Wakefield*) 1984 *I, F, W, A*

Barnes, S. (*Bristol*) 1984 *A;* 1985 *R (r), NZ 1, 2;* 1986 *S (r), F (r)*

Bartlett, J.T. (*Waterloo*) 1951 *W*

Bartlett, R.M. (*Harlequins*) 1957 *W, I, F, S;* 1958 *I, F, S*

Barton, J. (*Coventry*) 1967 *I, F, W;* 1972 *F*

Baume, J.L. (*Northern*) 1950 *S*

Bazley, R.C. (*Waterloo*) 1952 *I, F;* 1953 *W, I, F, S;* 1955 *W, I, F, S*

Beaumont, W.B. (*Fylde*) 1975 *I, A 1 (r), 2;* 1976 *A, W, S, I, F;* 1977 *S, I, F, W;* 1978 *F, W, S, I, NZ;* 1979 *S, I, F, W, NZ;* 1980 *I, F, W, S;* 1981 *W, S, I, F, Arg 1, 2;* 1982 *A, S*

Beer, I.D.S. (*Harlequins*) 1955 *F, S*

Beese, M.C. (*Liverpool*) 1972 *W, I, F*

Bell, P.J. (*Blackheath*) 1968 *W, I, F, S*

Bendon, G.J. (*Wasps*) 1959 *W, I, F, S*

Bennett, N.O. (*St Mary's Hospital, Waterloo*) 1947 *W, S, F;* 1948 *A, W, I, S*

Bennett, W.N. (*Bedford, London Welsh*) 1975 *S, A 1;* 1976 *S (r);* 1979 *S, I, F, W*

Berridge, M.J. (*Northampton*) 1949 *W, I*

Blakeway, P.J. (*Gloucester*) 1980 *I, F, W, S;* 1981 *W, S, I, F;* 1982 *I, F, W;* 1984 *I, F, W, SA 1;* 1985 *R, F, S, I*

Bond, A.M. (*Sale*) 1978 *NZ;* 1979 *S, I, NZ;* 1980 *I;* 1982 *I*

Boobbyer, B. (*Oxford U, Rosslyn Park*) 1950 *W, I, F, S;* 1951 *W, F;* 1952 *S, I, F*

Botting, I.J. (*Oxford U*) 1950 *W, I*

Boyle, S.B. (*Gloucester*) 1983 *W, S, I*

Brain, S.E. (*Coventry*) 1984 *SA 2, A (r);* 1985 *R, F, S, I, W, NZ 1, 2;* 1986 *W, S, I, F*

Braithwaite-Exley, B. (*Headingley*) 1949 *W*

Brinn, A. (*Gloucester*) 1972 *W, I, S*

Brooke, T.J. (*Richmond*) 1968 *F, S*

Brophy, T.J. (*Liverpool*) 1964 *I, F, S;* 1965 *I, W;* 1966 *W, I, F*

Bucknall, A.L. (*Richmond*) 1969 *SA;* 1970 *I, W, S, F;* 1971 *W, I, F, S (2[1C])*

Bulpitt, M.P. (*Blackheath*) 1970 *S*

Burton, M.A. (*Gloucester*) 1972 *W, I, F, S, SA;* 1974 *F, W;* 1975 *S, A 1, 2;* 1976 *A, W, S, I, F;* 1978 *F, W*

Butcher, C.J.S. (*Harlequins*) 1984 *SA 1, 2, A*

Butler, P.E. (*Gloucester*) 1975 *A 1;* 1976 *F*

Butterfield, J. (*Northampton*) 1953 *F, S;* 1954 *W, NZ, I, S, F;* 1955 *W, I, F, S;* 1956 *W, I, S, F;* 1957 *W, I, F, S;* 1958 *W, A, I, F, S;* 1959 *W, I, F, S*

Cain, J.I. (*Waterloo*) 1950 *W*

Cannell, L.B. (*Oxford U, St Mary's Hospital*) 1948 *F;* 1949 *W, I, F, S;* 1950 *W, I, F, S;* 1952 *SA, W;* 1953 *W, I, F;* 1956 *I, S, F;* 1957 *W, I*

Caplan, D.W.N. (*Headingley*) 1978 *S, I*

Cardus, R.M. (*Roundhay*) 1979 *F, W*

Carleton, J. (*Orrell*) 1979 *NZ;* 1980 *I, F, W, S;* 1981 *W, S, I, F, Arg 1, 2;* 1982 *A, S, I, F, W;* 1983 *F, W, S, I, NZ;* 1984 *S, I, F, W, A*

Challis, R. (*Bristol*) 1957 *I, F, S*

Chilcott, G.J. (*Bath*) 1984 *A;* 1986 *I, F*

Clarke, S.J.S. (*Cambridge U, Blackheath*) 1963 *W, I, F, S, NZ 1, 2, A;* 1964 *NZ, W, I;* 1965 *I, F, S*

Clements, J.W. (*O Cranleighans*) 1959 *I, F, S*

Clough, F.J. (*Cambridge U, Orrell*) 1986 *I, F*

Colclough, M.J. (*Angoulême, Wasps, Swansea*) 1978 *S, I;* 1979 *NZ;* 1980 *F, W, S;* 1981 *W, S, I, F;* 1982 *A, S, I, F, W;* 1983 *F, NZ;* 1984 *S, I, F, W;* 1986 *W, S, I, F*

Collins, P.J. (*Camborne*) 1952 *S, I, F*

Cook, P.W. (*Richmond*) 1965 *I, F*

Cooke, D.A. (*Harlequins*) 1976 *W, S, I, F*

Cooke, D.H. (*Harlequins*) 1981 *W, S, I, F;* 1984 *I;* 1985 *R, F, S, I, W, NZ 1, 2*

Cooper, M.J. (*Moseley*) 1973 *F, S, NZ (r);* 1975 *F, W;* 1976 *A, W;* 1977 *S, I, F, W*

Corless, B.J. (*Coventry, Moseley*) 1976 *A, I (r);* 1977 *S, I, F, W;* 1978 *F, W, S, I*

Cotton, F.E. (*Loughborough Colls, Coventry, Sale*) 1971 *S (2[1C]), P;* 1973 *W, I, F, S, NZ, A;* 1974 *S, I;* 1975 *I, F, W;* 1976 *A, W, S, I, F;* 1977 *S, I, F, W;* 1978 *S, I;* 1979 *NZ;* 1980 *I, F, W, S;* 1981 *W*

Coulman, M.J. (*Moseley*) 1967 *A, I, F, S, W;* 1968 *W, I, F, S*

Cowling, R.J. (*Leicester*) 1977 *S, I, F, W;* 1978 *F, NZ;* 1979 *S, I*

Cowman, A.R. (*Loughborough Colls, Coventry*) 1971 *S (2[1C]), P;* 1973 *W, I*

Creed, R.N. (*Coventry*) 1971 *P*

Currie, J.D. (*Bristol*) 1956 *W, I, S, F;* 1957 *W, I, S, F;* 1958 *W, A, I, F, S;* 1959 *W, I, F, S;* 1960 *W, I, F, S;* 1961 *SA;* 1962 *W, I, F*

Cusworth, L. (*Leicester*) 1979 *NZ;* 1982 *F, W;* 1983 *F, W, NZ;* 1984 *S, I, F, W*

Dalton, T.J. (*Coventry*) 1969 *S (r)*

Danby, T. (*Harlequins*) 1949 *W*

Davies, G.H. (*Cambridge U, Coventry*) 1981 *S, I, F, Arg 1, 2;* 1982 *A, S, I;* 1983 *F, W, S;* 1984 *S, SA 1, 2;* 1985 *R (r), NZ 1, 2;* 1986 *W, S, I, F*

Davies, W.P.C. (*Harlequins*) 1953 *S;* 1954 *NZ, I;* 1955 *W, I, F, S;* 1956 *W;* 1957 *F, S;* 1958 *W*

Davis, A.M. (*Harlequins*) 1963 *W, I, S, NZ 1, 2;* 1964 *NZ, W, I, F, S;* 1966 *W;* 1967 *A;* 1969 *SA;* 1970 *I, W, S*

Dee, J.M. (*Hartlepool R*) 1962 *S;* 1963 *NZ 1*

Dixon, P.J. (*Harlequins, Gosforth*) 1971 *P; 1972 S, I, W, F;* 1973 *I, F, S;* 1974 *S, I, F, W;* 1975 *I;* 1976 *W, F;* 1977 *S, I, F, W;* 1978 *F, S, I, NZ*

Doble, S.A. (*Moseley*) 1972 *SA;* 1973 *NZ, W*

Dodge, P.W. (*Leicester*) 1978 *W, S, I, NZ;* 1979 *S, I, F, W;* 1980 *W, S;* 1981 *W, S, I, F, Arg 1, 2;* 1982 *A, S, F, W;* 1983 *F, W, S, I, NZ;* 1985 *R, F, S, I, W, NZ 1, 2*

Donnelly, M.P. (*Oxford U*) 1947 *I*

Dooley, W.A. (*Preston Grasshoppers*) 1985 *R, F, S, I, W, NZ 2 (r);* 1986 *W, S, I, F*

Dovey, B.A. (*Rosslyn Park*) 1963 W, I

Drake-Lee, N.J. (*Cambridge U, Leicester*) 1963 W, I, F, S; 1964 NZ, W, I; 1965 W

Duckham, D.J. (*Coventry*) 1969 I, F, S, W, SA; 1970 I, W, S, F; 1971 W, I, F, S (2[1C]), P; 1972 W, I, F, S; 1973 NZ, W, I, F, S, NZ, A; 1974 S, I, F, W; 1975 I, F, W; 1976 A, W, S

Dun, A.F. (*Wasps*) 1984 W

Estcourt, N.S.D. (*Blackheath*) 1955 S

Evans, E. (*Sale*) 1948 A; 1950 W; 1951 I, F, S; 1952 SA, W, S, I, F; 1953 I, F, S; 1954 W, NZ, I, F; 1956 W, I, S, F; 1957 W, I, F, S; 1958 W, A, I, F, S

Evans, G.W. (*Coventry*) 1972 S; 1973 W (r), F, S, NZ; 1974 S, I, F, W

Fairbrother, K.E. (*Coventry*) 1969 I, F, S, W, SA; 1970 I, W, S, F; 1971 W, I, F

Fidler, J.H. (*Gloucester*) 1981 Arg 1, 2; 1984 SA 1, 2

Fielding, K.J. (*Moseley, Loughborough Colls*) 1969 I, F, S, SA; 1970 I, F; 1972 W, I, F, S

Finlan, J.F. (*Moseley*) 1967 I, F, S, W, NZ; 1968 W, I; 1969 I, F, S, W; 1970 F; 1973 NZ

Ford, P.J. (*Gloucester*) 1964 W, I, F, S

Frankcom, G.P. (*Cambridge U, Bedford*) 1965 W, I, F, S

French, R.J. (*St Helens*) 1961 W, I, F, S

Gavins, M.N. (*Leicester*) 1961 W

Gay, D.J. (*Bath*) 1968 W, I, F, S

George, J.T. (*Falmouth*) 1947 S, F; 1949 I

Gibbs, G.A. (*Bristol*) 1947 F; 1948 I

Gibbs, N. (*Harlequins*) 1954 S, F

Gittings, W.J. (*Coventry*) 1967 NZ

Glover, P.B. (*Bath*) 1967 A; 1971 F, P

Godwin, H.O. (*Coventry*) 1959 F, S; 1963 S, NZ 1, 2, A; 1964 NZ, I, F, S; 1967 NZ

Gray, A. (*Otley*) 1947 W, I, S

Greenwood, J.R.H. (*Waterloo*) 1966 I, F, S; 1967 A; 1969 I

Gregory, J.A. (*Blackheath*) 1949 W

Guest, R.H. (*Waterloo*) 1939 W, I, S; 1947 W, I, S, F; 1948 A, W, I, S; 1949 F, S

Hale, P.M. (*Moseley*) 1969 SA; 1970 I, W

Hall, J.P. (*Bath*) 1984 S (r), I, F, SA 1, 2, A; 1985 R, F, S, I, W, NZ 1, 2; 1986 W, S

Hall, N.M. (*Richmond*) 1947 W, I, S, F; 1949 W, I; 1952 SA, W, S, I, F; 1953 W, I, F, S; 1955 W, I

Halliday, S.J. (*Bath*) 1986 W, S

Hancock, A.W. (*Northampton*) 1965 F, S; 1966 F

Hancock, J.H. (*Newport*) 1955 W, I

Hannaford, R.C. (*Bristol*) 1971 W, I, F

Harding, R.M. (*Bristol*) 1985 R, F, S

Harding, V.S.J. (*Saracens*) 1961 F, S; 1962 W, I, F, S

Hardy, E.M.P. (*Blackheath*) 1951 I, F, S

Hare, W.H. (*Nottingham, Leicester*) 1974 W; 1978 F, NZ; 1979 NZ; 1980 I, F, W, S; 1981 W, S, Arg 1, 2; 1982 F, W; 1983 F, W, S, I, NZ; 1984 S, I, F, W, SA 1, 2

Harrison, M.E. (*Wakefield*) 1985 NZ 1, 2; 1986 S, I, F

Hastings, G.W.D. (*Gloucester*) 1955 W, I, F, S; 1957 W, I, F, S; 1958 W, A, I, F, S

Hazell, D.St G. (*Leicester*) 1955 W, I, F, S

Hearn, R.D. (*Bedford*) 1966 F, S; 1967 I, F, S, W

Heaton, J. (*Waterloo*) 1935 W, I, S; 1939 W, I, S; 1947 I, S, F

Henderson, A.P. (*Edinburgh Wands*) 1947 W, I, S, F; 1948 I, S, F; 1949 W, I

Herbert, A.J. (*Wasps*) 1958 F, S; 1959 W, I, F, S

Hesford, R. (*Bristol*) 1981 S (r); 1982 A, S, F (r); 1983 F (r); 1985 R, F, S, I, W

Hetherington, J.G.G. (*Northampton*) 1958 A, I; 1959 W, I, F, S

Hewitt, E.N. (*Coventry*) 1951 W, I, F

Higgins, R. (*Liverpool*) 1954 W, NZ, I, S; 1955 W, I, F, S; 1957 W, I, F, S; 1959 W

Hignell, A.J. (*Cambridge U, Bristol*) 1975 A 2; 1976 A, W, S, I; 1977 S, I, F, W; 1978 W; 1979 S, I, F, W

Hill, R.J. (*Bath*) 1984 SA 1, 2; 1985 I (r), NZ 2 (r); 1986 F (r)

Hiller, R. (*Harlequins*) 1968 W, I, F, S; 1969 I, F, S, W, SA; 1970 I, W, S; 1971 I, F, S (2[1C]), P; 1972 W, I

Hodgson, S.A.M. (*Durham City*) 1960 W, I, F, S; 1961 SA, W, I, F, S; 1964 W

Hofmeyr, M.B. (*Oxford U*) 1950 W, F, S

Holmes, C.B. (*Manchester*) 1947 S; 1948 I, F

Holmes, W.A. (*Nuneaton*) 1950 W, I, F, S; 1951 W, I, F, S; 1952 SA, S, I, F; 1953 W, I, F, S

Holmes, W.B. (*Cambridge U*) 1949 W, I, F, S

Hook, W.G. (*Gloucester*) 1951 S; 1952 SA, W

Horrocks-Taylor, J.P. (*Cambridge U, Leicester, Middlesbrough*) 1958 W, A; 1961 S; 1962 S; 1963 NZ 1, 2, A; 1964 NZ, W

Horsfall, E.L. (*Harlequins*) 1949 W

Horton, A.L. (*Blackheath*) 1965 W, I, F, S; 1966 F, S; 1967 NZ

Horton, J.P. (*Bath*) 1978 W, S, I, NZ; 1980 I, F, W, S; 1981 W; 1983 S, I; 1984 SA 1, 2

Horton, N.E. (*Moseley, Toulouse*) 1969 I, F, S, W; 1971 I, F, S,; 1974 S; 1975 W; 1977 S, I, F, W; 1978 F, W; 1979 S, I, F, W; 1980 I

Hosen, R.W. (*Bristol, Northampton*) 1963 NZ 1, 2, A; 1964 F, S; 1967 A, I, F, S, W

Hosking, G.R.d'A. (*Devonport Services*) 1949 W, I, F, S; 1950 W

Huntsman, P. (*Headingley*) 1985 NZ 1, 2

Hurst, A.C.B. (*Wasps*) 1962 S

Hyde, J.P. (*Northampton*) 1950 F, S

Jackson, B.S. (*Broughton Park*) 1970 S (r), F

Jackson, P.B. (*Coventry*) 1956 W, I, F; 1957 W, I, F, S; 1958 W, A, F, S; 1959 W, I, F, S; 1961 S; 1963 W, I, F, S

Jacobs, C.R. (*Northampton*) 1956 W, I, F, S; 1957 W, I, F, S; 1958 W, A, I, F, S; 1960 W, I, F, S; 1961 SA, W, I, F, S; 1963 NZ 1, 2, A; 1964 W, I, F, S

Janion, J.P.A.G. (*Bedford*) 1971 W, I, F, S (2[1C]), P; 1972 W, S, SA; 1973 A; 1975 A 1, 2

Jeavons, N.C. (*Moseley*) 1981 S, I, F, Arg 1, 2; 1982 A, S, I, F, W; 1983 F, W, S, I

Jeeps, R.E.G. (*Northampton*) 1956 W; 1957 W, I, F, S; 1958 W, A, I, F, S; 1959 I; 1960 W, I, F, S; 1961 SA, W, I, F, S; 1962 W, I, F, S

Jennins, C.R. (*Waterloo*) 1967 A, I, F

Jones, H.A. (*Barnstaple*) 1950 W, I, F

Jorden, A.M. (*Cambridge U, Blackheath, Bedford*) 1970 F; 1973 I, F, S; 1974 F; 1975 W, S

Judd, P.E. (*Coventry*) 1962 W, I, F, S; 1963 S, NZ 1, 2, A; 1964 NZ; 1965 I, F, S; 1966 W, I, F, S; 1967 A, I, F, S, W, NZ

Keeling, J.H. (*Guy's Hospital*) 1948 A, W

Keen, B.W. (*Newcastle U*) 1968 W, I, F, S

Kelly, G.A. (*Bedford*) 1947 W, I, S; 1948 W

Kendall-Carpenter, J.MacG.K. (*Oxford U. Bath*) 1949 I, F, S; 1950 W, I, F, S; 1951 I, F, S; 1952 SA, W, S, I, F; 1953 W, I, F, S; 1954 W, NZ, I, F

Kennedy, R.D. (*Camborne S of M*) 1949 I, F, S

Kent, C.P. (*Rosslyn Park*) 1977 S, I, F, W; 1978 F (r)

Keyworth, M. (*Swansea*) 1976 A, W, S, I

King, I. (*Harrogate*) 1954 W, NZ, I

Kingston, P. (*Gloucester*) 1975 A 1, 2; 1979 I, F, W

Knight, P.M. (*Bristol*) 1972 F, S, SA

Labuschagne, N.A. (*Harlequins, Guy's Hospital*) 1953 W; 1955 W, I, F, S

Lampkowski, M.S. (*Headingley*) 1976 A, W, S, I

Larter, P.J. (*Northampton, RAF*) 1967 A, NZ; 1968 W, I, F, S; 1969 I, F, S, W, SA; 1970 I, W, F, S; 1971 W, I, F, S (2[1C]), P; 1972 SA; 1973 NZ, W

Leadbetter, M.M. (*Broughton Park*) 1970 F

Leadbetter, V.H. (*Edinburgh Wands*) 1954 S, F

Lewis, A.O. (*Bath*) 1952 SA, W, S, I, F; 1953 W, I, F, S; 1954 F

Lloyd, R.H. (*Harlequins*) 1967 NZ; 1968 W, I, F, S

Lozowski, R.A.P. (*Wasps*) 1984 A

Luya, H.F. (*Waterloo, Headingley*) 1948 W, I, S, F; 1949 W

McFadyean, C. W. (*Moseley*) 1966 I, S, F; 1967 I, F, S, W, A, NZ; 1968 I, W

Madge, R.J.P. (*Exeter*) 1948 A, W, I, S

Manley, D.C. (*Exeter*) 1963 W, I, F, S

Mantell, N.D. (*Rosslyn Park*) 1975 A 1

Marques, R.W.D. (*Harlequins*) 1956 W, I, S, F; 1957 W, I, F, S; 1958 W, A, I, F, S; 1959 W, I, F, S; 1960 W, I, F, S; 1961 SA, W

Marriott, V.R. (*Harlequins*) 1963 NZ 1, 2, A; 1964 NZ

Martin, C.R. (*Bath*) 1985 F, S, I, W

Martin, N.O. (*Harlequins*) 1972 F (r)

Matthews, J.R.C. (*Harlequins*) 1949 F, S; 1950 I, F, S; 1952 SA, W, S, I, F

Maxwell, A.W. (*New Brighton, Headingley*) 1975 A 1; 1976 A, W, S, I, F; 1978 F

Melville, N.D. (*Wasps*) 1984 A; 1985 I, W, NZ 1, 2; 1986 W, S, I, F

Mills, S.G.F. (*Gloucester*) 1981 Arg 1, 2; 1983 W; 1984 SA, I, A

Moore, P.B.C. (*Blackheath*) 1951 W

Mordell, R.J. (*Rosslyn Park*) 1978 W

Morgan, W.G.D. (*Medicals, Newcastle*) 1960 W, I, F, S; 1961 SA, W, I, F, S

Morley, A.J. (*Bristol*) 1972 SA; 1973 NZ, W, I; 1975 A, 1, 2

Mycock, J. (*Sale*) 1947 W, I, S, F; 1948 A

Neale, B.A. (*Rosslyn Park*) 1951 I, F, S

Neary, A. (*Broughton Park*) 1971 W, I, F, S (2[1C]), P; 1972 W, I, F, S, SA; 1973 NZ, W, I, F, S, NZ, A; 1974 S, I, F, W; 1975 I, F, W, S, A I; 1976 A, W, S, I, F; 1977 I; 1978 F (r); 1979 S, I, F, W, NZ; 1980 I, F, W, S

Nelmes, B.G. (*Cardiff*) 1975 A 1, 2; 1978 W, S, I, NZ

Newman, S.C. (*Oxford U*), 1947 F; 1948 A, W

Newton-Thompson, J.O. (*Oxford U*) 1947 S, F

Ninnes, B.F. (*Coventry*) 1971 *W*
Novak, M.J. (*Harlequins*) 1970 *W, S, F*

Oakley, L.F.L. (*Bedford*) 1951 *W*
Old, A.G.B. (*Middlesbrough, Leicester, Sheffield*) 1972 *W, I, F, S, SA;* 1973 *NZ, A;* 1974 *S, I, F, W;* 1975 *I, A 2;* 1976 *S, I;* 1978 *F*
Orwin, J. (*Gloucester, RAF*) 1985 *R, F, S, I, W, NZ 1, 2*
Owen, J.E. (*Coventry*) 1963 *W, I, F, S, A;* 1964 *NZ;* 1965 *W, I, F, S;* 1966 *I, F, S;* 1967 *NZ*

Page, J.J. (*Bedford, Northampton*) 1971 *W, I, F, S;* 1975 *S*
Pallant, J.N. (*Notts*) 1967 *I, F, S*
Palmer, J.A. (*Bath*) 1984 *SA 1, 2;* 1986 *I (r)*
Pargetter, T.A. (*Coventry*) 1962 *S;* 1963 *F, NZ 1*
Parsons, M.J. (*Northampton*) 1968 *W, I, F, S*
Patterson, W.M. (*Sale*) 1961 *SA, S*
Payne, C.M. (*Harlequins*) 1964 *I, F, S;* 1965 *I, F, S;* 1966 *W, I, F, S*
Pearce, G.S. (*Northampton*) 1979 *S, I, F, W;* 1981 *Arg 1, 2;* 1982 *A, S;* 1983 *F, W, S, I, NZ;* 1984 *S, SA 2, A;* 1985 *R, F, S, I, W, NZ 1, 2;* 1986 *W, S, I, F*
Peart, T.G.A.H. (*Hartlepool R*) 1964 *F, S*
Perry, D.G. (*Bedford*) 1963 *F, S, NZ 1, 2, A;* 1964 *NZ, W, I;* 1965 *W, I, F, S;* 1966 *W, I, F*
Perry, S.V. (*Cambridge U, Waterloo*) 1947 *W, I;* 1948 *A, W, I, S, F*
Phillips, M.S. (*Oxford U, Fylde*) 1958 *A, I, F, S;* 1959 *W, I, F, S;* 1960 *W, I, F, S;* 1961 *W;* 1963 *W, I, F, S, NZ 1, 2, A;* 1964 *NZ, W, I, F, S*
Pickering, R.D.A. (*Bradford*) 1967 *I, F, S, W;* 1968 *F, S*
Plummer, K.C. (*Bristol*) 1969 *W;* 1976 *S, I, F*
Powell, D.L. (*Northampton*) 1966 *W, I;* 1969 *I, F, S, W;* 1971 *W, I, F, S (2/1C])*
Preece, I. (*Coventry*) 1948 *I, S, F;* 1949 *F, S;* 1950 *W, I, F, S;* 1951 *W, I, F*
Preece, P.S. (*Coventry*) 1972 *SA;* 1973 *NZ, W, I, F, S, NZ;* 1975 *I, F, W, A 2;* 1976 *W (r)*
Preedy, M. (*Gloucester*) 1984 *SA 1*
Preston, N.J. (*Richmond*) 1979 *NZ;* 1980 *I, F*
Price, J. (*Coventry*) 1961 *I*
Price, T.W. (*Cheltenham*) 1948 *S, F;* 1949 *W, I, F, S*
Prout, D.H. (*Northampton*) 1968 *W, I*
Pullin, J.V. (*Bristol*) 1966 *W;* 1968 *W, I, F, S;* 1969 *I, F, S, W, SA;* 1970 *I, W, S, F;* 1971 *W, I, F, S (2/1C]), P;* 1972 *W, I, F, SA;* 1973 *NZ, W, I, F, S, NZ, A;* 1974 *S, I, F, W;* 1975 *I, W (r), S, A 1, 2;* 1976 *F*
Purdy, S.J. (*Rugby*) 1962 *S*

Quinn, J.P. (*New Brighton*) 1954 *W, NZ, I, S, F*

Rafter, M. (*Bristol*) 1977 *S, F, W;* 1978 *F, W, S, I, NZ;* 1979 *S, I, F, W, NZ;* 1980 *W (r);* 1981 *W, Arg 1, 2*
Ralston, C.W. (*Richmond*) 1971 *S (C), P;* 1972 *W, I, F, S, SA;* 1973 *NZ, W, I, F, S, NZ, A;* 1974 *S, I, F, W;* 1975 *I, F, W, S*
Ranson, J.M. (*Rosslyn Park*) 1963 *NZ 1, 2, A;* 1964 *W, I, F, S*
Redfern, S. (*Leicester*) 1984 *I (r)*
Redman, N.C. (*Bath*) 1984 *A;* 1986 *S (r)*
Redmond, G.F. (*Cambridge U*) 1970 *F*
Redwood, B.W. (*Bristol*) 1968 *W, I*

Rees, G.W. (*Nottingham*) 1984 *SA 2 (r), A;* 1986 *I, F*
Regan, M. (*Liverpool*) 1953 *W, I, F, S;* 1954 *W, NZ, I, S, F;* 1956 *I, S, F*
Rendall, P.A.G. (*Wasps*) 1984 *W, SA 2;* 1986 *W, S*
Richards, D. (*Leicester*) 1986 *I, F*
Richards, S.B. (*Richmond*) 1965 *W, I, F, S;* 1967 *A, I, F, S, W*
Rimmer, G. (*Waterloo*) 1949 *W, I;* 1950 *W;* 1951 *W, I, F;* 1952 *SA, W;* 1954 *W, NZ, I, S*
Rimmer, L.I. (*Bath*) 1961 *SA, W, I, F, S*
Ripley, A.G. (*Rosslyn Park*) 1972 *W, I, F, S, SA;* 1973 *NZ, W, I, F, S, NZ, A;* 1974 *S, I, F, W;* 1975 *I, F, S, A 1, 2;* 1976 *A, W, S*
Risman, A.B.W. (*Loughborough Colls*) 1959 *W, I, F, S;* 1961 *SA, W, I, F*
Rittson-Thomas, G.C. (*Oxford U*) 1951 *W, I, F*
Robbins, G.L. (*Coventry*) 1986 *W, S*
Robbins, P.G.D. (*Moseley*) 1956 *W, I, S, F;* 1957 *W, I, F, S;* 1958 *W, A, I, S;* 1960 *W, I, F, S;* 1961 *SA, W;* 1962 *S*
Roberts, J. (*Sale*) 1960 *W, I, F, S;* 1961 *SA, W, I, F, S;* 1962 *W, I, F, S;* 1963 *W, I, F, S;* 1964 *NZ*
Roberts, V.G. (*Harlequins*) 1947 *F;* 1949 *W, I, F, S;* 1950 *I, F, S;* 1951 *W, I, F, S;* 1956 *W, I, S, F*
Robinson, E.F. (*Coventry*) 1954 *S;* 1961 *I, F, S*
Rogers, D.P. (*Bedford*) 1961 *I, F, S;* 1962 *W, I, F;* 1963 *W, I, F, S, NZ 1, 2, A;* 1964 *NZ, W, I, F, S;* 1965 *W, I, F, S;* 1966 *W, I, F, S;* 1967 *A, S, W, NZ;* 1969 *I, F, S, W*
Rollitt, D.M. (*Bristol*) 1967 *I, F, S, W;* 1969 *I, F, S, W;* 1975 *S, A 1, 2*
Rose, W.M.H. (*Cambridge U, Coventry*) 1981 *I, F;* 1982 *A, S, I*
Rossborough, P.A. (*Coventry*) 1971 *W;* 1973 *NZ, A;* 1974 *S, I;* 1975 *I, F*
Rosser, D.W.A. (*Wasps*) 1965 *W, I, F, S;* 1966 *W*
Roughley, D. (*Liverpool*) 1973 *A;* 1974 *S, I*
Rowell, R.E. (*Leicester*) 1964 *W;* 1965 *W*
Rudd, E.L. (*Liverpool*) 1965 *W, I, S;* 1966 *W, I, S*
Rutherford, D. (*Gloucester*) 1960 *W, I, F, S;* 1961 *SA;* 1965 *W, I, F, S;* 1966 *W, I, F, S;* 1967 *NZ*
Ryan, P.H. (*Richmond*) 1955 *W, I*

Salmon, J.L.B. (*Harlequins*) 1985 *NZ 1,2;* 1986 *W, S*
Sanders, D.L. (*Harlequins*) 1954 *W, NZ, I, S, F;* 1956 *W, I, S, F*
Sangwin, R.D. (*Hull & E Riding*) 1964 *NZ, W*
Sargent, G.A.F. (*Gloucester*) 1981 *I (r)*
Savage, K.F. (*Northampton*) 1966 *W, I, F, S;* 1967 *A, I, F, S, W, NZ;* 1968 *W, F, S*
Scott, E.K. (*St Mary's Hospital, Redruth*) 1947 *W;* 1948 *A, W, I, S*
Scott, H. (*Manchester*) 1955 *F*
Scott, J.P. (*Rosslyn Park, Cardiff*) 1978 *F, W, S, I, NZ;* 1979 *S (r), I, W, F, NZ;* 1980 *I, F, W, S;* 1981 *W, S, I, F, Arg 1, 2;* 1982 *I, F, W;* 1983 *F, W, S, I, NZ;* 1984 *S, I, F, W, SA 1, 2*
Scott, J.S.M. (*Oxford U*) 1958 *F*
Shackleton, I.R. (*Cambridge U*) 1969 *SA;* 1970 *I, W, S*
Sharp, R.A.W. (*Oxford U, Wasps, Redruth*) 1960 *W, I, F, S;* 1961 *I, F;* 1962 *W, I, F;* 1963 *W, I, F, S;* 1967 *A*
Sheppard, A. (*Bristol*) 1981 *W (r);* 1985 *W*
Sherriff, G.A. (*Saracens*) 1966 *S;* 1967 *A, NZ*

Shuttleworth, D.W. (*Headingley*) 1951 *S;* 1953 *S*
Silk, N. (*Harlequins*) 1965 *W, I, F, S*
Simms, K.G. (*Cambridge U, Liverpool*) 1985 *R, F, S, I, W;* 1986 *I, F*
Simpson, C.P. (*Harlequins*) 1965 *W*
Simpson, P.D. (*Bath*) 1983 *NZ;* 1984 *S*
Slemen, M.A.C. (*Liverpool*) 1976 *I, F;* 1977 *S, I, F, W;* 1978 *F, W, S, I, NZ;* 1979 *S, I, F, W, NZ;* 1980 *I, F, W, S;* 1981 *W, S, I, F;* 1982 *A, S, I, F, W;* 1983 *NZ;* 1984 *S*
Small, H.D. (*Oxford U*) 1950 *W, I, F, S*
Smart, C.E. (*Newport*) 1979 *F, W, NZ;* 1981 *S, I, F, Arg 1, 2;* 1982 *A, S, I, F, W;* 1983 *F, W, S, I*
Smith, J.V. (*Cambridge U, Rosslyn Park*) 1950 *W, I, F, S*
Smith, K. (*Roundhay*) 1974 *F, W;* 1975 *W, S*
Smith, M.J.K. (*Oxford U*) 1956 *W*
Smith, S.J. (*Sale*) 1973 *I, F, S, A;* 1974 *I, F;* 1975 *W (r);* 1976 *F;* 1977 *F (r);* 1979 *NZ;* 1980 *I, F, W, S;* 1981 *W, S, I, F, Arg 1, 2;* 1982 *A, S, I, F, W;* 1983 *F, W, S*
Smith, S.R. (*Richmond*) 1959 *W, F, S;* 1964 *F, S*
Smith, S.T. (*Wasps*) 1985 *R, F, S, I, W, NZ 1, 2;* 1986 *W, S*
Smith, T.A. (*Northampton*) 1951 *W*
Spencer, J. (*Harlequins*) 1966 *W*
Spencer, J.S. (*Cambridge U, Headingley*) 1969 *I, F, S, W, SA;* 1970 *I, W, S, F;* 1971 *W, I, S'(2/1C]), P*
Squires, P.J. (*Harrogate*) 1973 *F, S, NZ, A;* 1974 *S, I, F, W;* 1975 *I, F, W, S, A 1, 2;* 1976 *A, W;* 1977 *S, I, F, W;* 1978 *F, W, S, I, NZ;* 1979 *S, I, F, W*
Starmer-Smith, N.C. (*Harlequins*) 1969 *SA;* 1970 *I, W, S, F;* 1971 *S (C), P*
Steeds, J.H. (*Saracens*) 1949 *F, S;* 1950 *I, F, S*
Steele-Bodger, M.R. (*Cambridge U*) 1947 *W, I, S, F;* 1948 *A, W, I, S, F*
Stevens, C.B. (*Penzance-Newlyn, Harlequins*) 1969 *SA;* 1970 *I, W, S;* 1971 *P;* 1972 *W, I, F, S, SA;* 1973 *NZ, W, I, F, S, NZ, A;* 1974 *S, I, F, W;* 1975 *I, F, W, S*
Stirling, R.V. (*Leicester, RAF, Wasps*) 1951 *W, I, F, S;* 1952 *SA, W, S, I, F;* 1953 *W, I, F, S;* 1954 *W, NZ, I, S, F*
Stringer, N.C. (*Wasps*) 1982 *A (r);* 1983 *NZ (r);* 1984 *SA 1 (r), A;* 1985 *R*
Swarbrick, D.W. (*Oxford U*) 1947 *W, I, F;* 1948 *A, W;* 1949 *I*
Swift, A.H. (*Swansea*) 1981 *Arg 1, 2;* 1983 *F, W, S;* 1984 *SA 2*
Syddall, J.P. (*Waterloo*) 1982 *I;* 1984 *A*
Sykes, F.D. (*Northampton*) 1955 *F, S;* 1963 *NZ 2, A*
Sykes, P.W. (*Wasps*) 1948 *F;* 1952 *S, I, F;* 1953 *W, I, F*
Syrett, R.E. (*Wasps*) 1958 *W, A, I, F;* 1960 *W, I, F, S;* 1962 *W, I, F*

Taylor, P.J. (*Northampton*) 1955 *W, I;* 1962 *W, I, F, S*
Taylor, R.B. (*Northampton*) 1966 *W;* 1967 *I, F, S, W, NZ;* 1969 *F, S, W, SA;* 1970 *I, W, S, F;* 1971 *S (2/1C])*
Teague, M.C. (*Gloucester*) 1985 *F (r)*
Thompson, P.H. (*Headingley, Waterloo*) 1956 *W, I, S, F;* 1957 *W, I, F, S;* 1958 *W, A, I, F, S;* 1959 *W, I, F, S*
Thorne, J.D. (*Bristol*) 1963 *W, I, F*
Tindall, V.R. (*Liverpool U*) 1951 *W, I, F, S*
Towell, A.C. (*Bedford*) 1948 *F;* 1951 *S*

Travers, B.H. (*Harlequins*) 1947 *W, I*; 1948 *A, W*; 1949 *F, S*
Treadwell, W.T. (*Wasps*) 1966 *I, F, S*
Trick, D.M. (*Bath*) 1983 *I*; 1984 *SA 1*
Turner, M.F. (*Blackheath*) 1948 *S, F*

Underwood, A.M. (*Exeter*) 1962 *W, I, F, S*; 1964 *I*
Underwood, R. (*Leicester, RAF*) 1984 *I, F, W, A*; 1985 *R, F, S, I, W*; 1986 *W, I, F*
Uren, R. (*Waterloo*) 1948 *I, S, F*; 1950 *I*
Uttley, R.M. (*Gosforth*) 1973 *I, F, S, NZ, A*; 1974 *I, F, W*; 1975 *F, W, S, A 1, 2*; 1977 *S, I, F, W*; 1978 *NZ*; 1979 *S*; 1980 *I, F, W, S*

Vaughan, D.B. (*Headingley*) 1948 *A, W, I, S*; 1949 *I, F, S*; 1950 *W*

Wackett, J.A.S. (*Rosslyn Park*) 1959 *W, I*
Wade, M.R. (*Cambridge U*) 1962 *W, I, F*
Walker, H.W. (*Coventry*) 1947 *W, I, S, F*; 1948 *A, W, I, S, F*
Wardlow, C.S. (*Northampton*) 1969 *SA (r)*; 1971 *W, I, F, S (2[1C])*
Warfield, P.J. (*Rosslyn Park, Durham U, Cambridge U*) 1973 *NZ, W, I*; 1975 *I, F, S*
Watkins, J.A. (*Gloucester*) 1972 *SA*; 1973 *NZ, W, NZ, A*; 1975 *F, W*
Watt, D.E.J. (*Bristol*) 1967 *I, F, S, W*
Webb, R.E. (*Coventry*) 1967 *S, W, NZ*; 1968 *I, F, S*; 1969 *I, F, S, W*; 1972 *I, F*
Webb, St.L.H. (*Bedford*) 1959 *W, I, F, S*
Webster, J.G. (*Moseley*) 1972 *W, I, SA*; 1973 *NZ, W, NZ*; 1974 *S, W*; 1975 *I, F, W*

Weighill, R.H. (*RAF, Harlequins*) 1947 *S, F*; 1948 *S, F*
West, B.R. (*Loughborough Colls, Northampton*) 1968 *W, I, F, S*; 1969 *SA*; 1970 *I, W, S*
Weston, L.E. (*W of Scotland*) 1972 *F, S*
Weston, M.P. (*Richmond, Durham City*) 1960 *W, I, F, S*; 1961 *SA, W, I, F, S*; 1962 *W, I, F*; 1963 *W, I, F, S, NZ 1, 2, A*; 1964 *NZ, W, I, F, S*; 1965 *F, S*; 1966 *S*; 1968 *F, S*
Wheeler, P.J. (*Leicester*) 1975 *F, W*; 1976 *A, W, S, I*; 1977 *S, I, F, W*; 1978 *F, W, S, I, NZ*; 1979 *S, I, F, W, NZ*; 1980 *I, F, W, S*; 1981 *W, S, I, F*; 1982 *A, S, I, F, W*; 1983 *F, S, I, NZ*; 1984 *S, I, F, W*
White, C. (*Gosforth*) 1983 *NZ*; 1984 *S, I, F*
White, D.F. (*Northampton*) 1947 *W, I, S*; 1948 *I, F*; 1951 *S*; 1952 *SA, W, S, I, F*; 1953 *W, I, S*
Wightman, B.J. (*Moseley, Coventry*) 1959 *W*; 1963 *W, I, NZ 2, A*
Wilkins, D.T. (*United Services, RN, Roundhay*) 1951 *W, I, F, S*; 1952 *SA, W, S, I, F*; 1953 *W, I, F, S*
Wilkinson, R.M. (*Bedford*) 1975 *A 2*; 1976 *A, W, S, I, F*
Willcox, J.G. (*Oxford U, Harlequins*) 1961 *I, F, S*; 1962 *W, I, F, S*; 1963 *W, I, F, S*; 1964 *NZ, W, I, F, S*
Williams, C.G. (*Gloucester, RAF*) 1976 *F*
Williams, J.E. (*O Millhillians, Sale*) 1954 *F*; 1955 *W, I, F, S*; 1956 *I, S, F*; 1965 *W*
Williams, J.M. (*Penzance-Newlyn*) 1951 *I, S*
Wilson, D.S. (*Met Police, Harlequins*) 1953 *F*; 1954 *W, I, S, F*; 1955 *F, S*

Wilson, K.J. (*Gloucester*) 1963 *F*
Winn, C.E. (*Rosslyn Park*) 1952 *SA, W, S, I, F*; 1954 *W, S, F*
Winterbottom, P.J. (*Headingley*) 1982 *A, S, I, F, W*; 1983 *F, W, S, I, NZ*; 1984 *S, F, W, SA 1, 2*; 1986 *W, S, I, F*
Wintle, T.C. (*Northampton*) 1966 *S*; 1969 *I, F, S, W*
Woodgate, E.E. (*Paignton*) 1952 *W*
Woodruff, C.G. (*Harlequins*) 1951 *W, I, F, S*
Woodward, C.R. (*Leicester*) 1980 *I (r), F, W, S*; 1981 *W, S, I, F, Arg 1, 2*; 1982 *A, S, I, F, W*; 1983 *I, NZ*; 1984 *S, I, F, W*
Woodward, J.E. (*Wasps*) 1952 *SA, W, S*; 1953 *W, I, F, S*; 1954 *W, NZ, I, S, F*; 1955 *W, I*; 1956 *S*
Wordsworth, A.J. (*Cambridge U*) 1975 *A 1 (r)*
Wrench, D.F.B. (*Harlequins*) 1964 *F, S*
Wright, I.D. (*Northampton*) 1971 *W, I, F, S (r)*
Wright, T.P. (*Blackheath*) 1960 *W, I, F, S*; 1961 *SA, W, I, F, S*; 1962 *W, I, F, S*
Wyatt, D.M. (*Bedford*) 1976 *S (r)*

Yarranton, P.G. (*RAF, Wasps*) 1954 *W, NZ, I*; 1955 *F, S*
Young, J.R.C. (*Oxford U, Harlequins*) 1958 *I*; 1960 *W, I, F, S*; 1961 *SA, W, I, F*
Young, M. (*Gosforth*) 1977 *S, I, F, W*; 1978 *F, W, S, I, NZ*; 1979 *S*
Young, P.D. (*Dublin Wands*) 1954 *W, NZ, I, S, F*; 1955 *W, I, F, S*
Youngs, N.G. (*Leicester*) 1983 *I, NZ*; 1984 *S, I, F, W*

Ireland

Club Abbreviations: *NIFC*, North of Ireland Football Club; *CIYMS*, Church of Ireland Young Men's Society.
Note: Ireland's two matches against France in 1972 were both recognized Internationals and caps were awarded.

Agar, R.D. (*Malone*) 1947 *F, E, S, W*; 1948 *F*; 1949 *S, W*; 1950 *F, E, W*
Agnew, P.J. (*CIYMS*) 1974 *F (r)*; 1976 *A*
Anderson, F.E. (*Queen's U, Belfast, NIFC*) 1953 *F, E, S, W*; 1954 *NZ, F, E, S, W*; 1955 *F, E, S, W*
Anderson, W.A. (*Dungannon*) 1984 *A*; 1985 *S, F, W, E*; 1986 *F, S*
Armstrong, W.K. (*NIFC*) 1960 *SA*; 1961 *E*

Bailey, N. (*Northampton*) 1952 *E*
Becker, V. (*Lansdowne*) 1974 *F, W*
Bell, W.E. (*Belfast Collegians*) 1953 *F, E, S, W*
Berkery, P.J. (*Lansdowne*) 1954 *W*; 1955 *W*; 1956 *S, W*; 1957 *F, E, S, W*; 1958 *A, E, S*
Blake-Knox, S.E.F. (*NIFC*) 1976 *E, S*; 1977 *F (r)*
Blayney, J. (*Wanderers*) 1950 *S*
Bornemann, W.W. (*Wanderers*) 1960 *E, S, W, SA*
Bowen, D.St.J. (*Cork Constitution*) 1977 *W, E, S*
Bradley, M.T. (*Cork Constitution*) 1984 *A*; 1985 *S, F, W, E*; 1986 *F, W, E, S*
Brady, A.M. (*UC Dublin, Malone*) 1966 *S*; 1968 *E, S, W*
Brady, J.A. (*Wanderers*) 1976 *E, S*
Brady, J.R. (*CIYMS*) 1951 *S, W*; 1953 *F, E, S, W*; 1954 *W*; 1956 *W*; 1957 *F, E, S, W*
Brennan, J.I. (*CIYMS*) 1957 *S, W*
Bresnihan, F.P.K. (*UC Dublin, Lansdowne, London Irish*) 1966 *E, W*; 1967 *A1, E, S, W, F*; 1968 *F, E, S, W, A*; 1969 *F, E, S, W*; 1970 *SA, F, E, S, W*; 1971 *F, E, S, W*
Brophy, N.H. (*Blackrock Coll, UC Dublin*) 1957 *F, E*; 1959 *E, S, W, F*; 1960 *F, SA*; 1961 *S, W*; 1962 *E, S, W*; 1963 *E, W*; 1967 *E, S, W, F, A 2*
Brown, E.L. (*Instonians*) 1958 *F*
Brown, W.J. (*Malone*) 1970 *SA, F, S, W*
Browne, A.W. (*Dublin U*) 1951 *SA*
Buckley, J.H. (*Sunday's Well*) 1973 *E, S*
Burges, J.H. (*Rosslyn Park*) 1950 *F, E*
Burns, I.J. (*Wanderers*) 1980 *E (r)*
Butler, L. (*Blackrock Coll*) 1960 *W*
Byrne, E.M.J. (*Blackrock Coll*) 1977 *S, F*; 1978 *F, W, E, NZ*
Byrne, F. (*UC Dublin*) 1962 *F*
Byrne, S.J. (*UC Dublin, Lansdowne*) 1953 *S, W*; 1955 *F*

Callan, C.P. (*Lansdowne*) 1947 *F, E, S, W*; 1948 *F, E, S, W*; 1949 *F, E*
Campbell, C.E. (*Old Wesley*) 1970 *SA*
Campbell, S.O. (*Old Belvedere*) 1976 *A*; 1979 *A 1, 2*; 1980 *E, S, F, W*; 1981 *F, W, E, S, SA 1*; 1982 *W, E, S, F*; 1983 *S, F, W, E*; 1984 *F, W*
Canniffe, D.M. (*Lansdowne*) 1976 *W, E*
Cantrell, J.L. (*UC Dublin, Blackrock Coll*) 1976 *A, F, W, E, S*; 1981 *S, SA 1, 2, E, A*
Carr, N.J. (*Ards*) 1985 *S, F, W, E*; 1986 *W, E, S*
Carroll, R. (*Lansdowne*) 1947 *F*; 1950 *S, W*

Casey, P.J. (*Lansdowne*) 1963 *F, E, S, W, NZ*; 1964 *E, S, W, F*; 1965 *F, E, S*
Chambers, R.R. (*Instonians*) 1951 *F, E, S, W*; 1952 *F, W*
Clegg, R.J. (*Bangor*) 1973 *F*; 1975 *E, S, F, W*
Clifford, T. (*Young Munster*) 1949 *F, E, S, W*; 1950 *F, E, S, W*; 1951 *F, E, SA*; 1952 *F, S, W*
Condon, H.C. (*London Irish*) 1984 *S (r)*
Corcoran, J.C. (*London Irish*) 1947 *A*; 1948 *F*
Costello, P. (*Bective Rangers*) 1960 *F*
Crossan, K.D. (*Instonians*) 1982 *S*; 1984 *F, W, E, S*; 1985 *S, F, W, E*; 1986 *E, S*
Crowe, J. (*UC Dublin*) 1974 *NZ*
Crowe, L. (*Old Belvedere*) 1950 *S, W*
Cullen, T.J. (*UC Dublin*) 1949 *F*
Culliton, M.G. (*Wanderers*) 1959 *E, S, W, F*; 1960 *E, S, W, F, SA*; 1961 *E, S, W, F*; 1962 *S, F*; 1964 *E, S, W, F*
Cunningham, M.J. (*UC Cork*) 1955 *F, E, S, W*; 1956 *F, S, W*
Curtis, A.B. (*Oxford U*) 1950 *F, E, S*

Dargan, M. (*Old Belvedere*) 1952 *S, W*
Davidson, J.C. (*Dungannon*) 1969 *F, E, S, W*; 1973 *NZ*; 1976 *NZ*
Dawson, A.R. (*Wanderers*) 1958 *A, E, S, W, F*; 1959 *E, S, W, F*; 1960 *F, SA*; 1961 *E, S, W, F, SA*; 1962 *S, F, W*; 1963 *F, E, S, W, NZ*; 1964 *E, S, F*
Dean, P.M. (*St Mary's Coll*) 1981 *SA 1, 2, A*; 1982 *W, E, S, F*; 1984 *A*; 1985 *S, F, W, E*; 1986 *F, W*
Deering, S.M. (*Garryowen, St Mary's Coll*) 1974 *W*; 1976 *F, W, E, S*; 1977 *W, E*; 1978 *NZ*
De Lacy, H. (*Harlequins*) 1948 *E, S*

Dennison, J.P. (*Garryowen*) 1973 *F*; 1975 *E, S*

Dick, C.J. (*Ballymena*) 1961 *W, F, SA*; 1962 *W*; 1963 *F, E, S, W*

Dick, J.S. (*Queen's U, Belfast*) 1962 *E*

Doherty, A. (*Old Wesley*) 1974 *P (r)*

Donaldson, J.A. (*Belfast Collegians*) 1958 *A, E, S, W*

Dooley, J.F. (*Galwegians*) 1959 *E, S, W*

Doyle, J.A.P. (*Greystones*) 1984 *E, S*

Doyle, M.G. (*Blackrock Coll, UC Dublin*) 1965 *F, E, S, W, SA*; 1966 *F, E, S, W*; 1967 *A 1, 2, E, S, W, F*; 1968 *F, E, S, W, A*

Doyle, T.J. (*Wanderers*) 1968 *E, S, W*

Duggan, A.T.A. (*Lansdowne*) 1963 *NZ*; 1964 *F*; 1966 *W*; 1967 *A 1, 2, S, W*; 1968 *F, E, S, W*; 1969 *F, E, S, W*; 1970 *SA, F, E, S, W*; 1971 *F, E, S, W*; 1972 *F 2*

Duggan, W.P. (*Blackrock Coll*) 1975 *E, S, F, W*; 1976 *A, F, W, S, NZ*; 1977 *W, E, S, F*; 1978 *S, F, W, E, NZ*; 1979 *S, A 1, 2*; 1980 *E*; 1981 *F, W, E, S, SA 1, 2, A*; 1982 *W, E, S*; 1983 *S, F, W, E*; 1984 *W, E*

Duncan, W.R. (*Malone*) 1984 *W, E*

Dwyer, P.J. (*UC Dublin*) 1962 *W*; 1963 *F, NZ*; 1964 *S, W*

Elliott, W.R.J. (*Bangor*) 1979 *S*

English, M.A.F. (*Lansdowne, Limerick Bohemians*) 1958 *W, F*; 1959 *E, S, F*; 1960 *E, S*; 1961 *S, W, F*; 1962 *F, W*; 1963 *E, S, W, NZ*

Ennis, F.N.G. (*Wanderers*) 1979 *A 1 (r)*

Ensor, A.H. (*Wanderers*) 1973 *W, F*; 1974 *F, W, E, S, P, NZ*; 1975 *E, S, F, W*; 1976 *A, F, W, E, NZ*; 1977 *E*; 1978 *S, F, W, E*

Fagan, C. (*Wanderers*) 1956 *F, E, S*

Feddis, N. (*Lansdowne*) 1956 *E*

Feighery, C.F.P. (*Lansdowne*) 1972 *F 1, 2, E*

Feighery, T.A.O. (*St Mary's Coll*) 1977 *W, E*

Finn, M.C. (*UC Cork, Cork Constitution*) 1979 *F*; 1982 *W, E, S, F*; 1983 *S, F, W, E*; 1984 *E, S, A*; 1986 *F, W*

Finn, R. (*UC Dublin*) 1977 *F*

Fitzgerald, C.F. (*St Mary's Coll*) 1979 *A 1, 2*; 1980 *E, S, F, W*; 1982 *W, E, S, F*; 1983 *F, W, E*; 1984 *F, W, A*; 1985 *S, F, W, E*; 1986 *F, W, E, S*

Fitzgerald, D.C. (*Lansdowne*) 1984 *E, S*; 1986 *W, E, S*

Fitzpatrick, M.P. (*Wanderers*) 1978 *S*; 1980 *S, F, W*; 1981 *F, W, E, S, A*; 1985 *F (r)*

Flynn, M.K. (*Wanderers*) 1959 *F*; 1960 *F*; 1962 *E, S, F, W*; 1964 *E, S, W, F*; 1965 *F, E, S, W, SA*; 1966 *F, E, S*; 1972 *F 1, 2, E*; 1973 *NZ*

Foley, B.O. (*Shannon*) 1976 *F, E*; 1977 *W (r)*; 1980 *F, W*; 1981 *F, E, S, SA 1, 2, A*

Fortune, J.J. (*Clontarf*) 1963 *NZ*; 1964 *E*

Gaston, J.T. (*Dublin U*) 1954 *NZ, F, E, S, W*; 1955 *W*; 1956 *F, E*

Gavin, T.J. (*Moseley, London Irish*) 1949 *F, E*

Gibson, C.M.H. (*Cambridge U, NIFC*) 1964 *E, S, W, F*; 1965 *F, E, S, W, SA*; 1966 *F, E, S, W*; 1967 *A 1, 2, E, S, W, F*; 1968 *E, S, W, A*; 1969 *E, S, W*; 1970 *SA, F, E, S, W*; 1971 *F, E, S, W*; 1972 *F 1, E, F2*; 1973 *NZ, E, S, W, F*; 1974 *F, W, E, S, P*; 1975 *E, S, F, W*; 1976 *A, F, W, E, S, NZ*; 1977 *W, E, S, F*; 1978 *F, W, E, NZ*; 1979 *S, A 1, 2*

Gibson, M.E. (*Lansdowne*) 1979 *F, W, E, S*; 1981 *W (r)*

Gilpin, F.G. (*Queen's U, Belfast*) 1962 *E, S, F*

Glass, D.C. (*Belfast Collegians*) 1958 *F*; 1960 *W*; 1961 *W, SA*

Glennon, J.J. (*Skerries*) 1980 *E, S*

Godfrey, R.P. (*UC Dublin*) 1954 *S, W*

Goodall, K.G. (*City of Derry, Newcastle U*) 1967 *A 1, 2, E, S, W, F*; 1968 *F, E, S, W, A*; 1969 *F, E, S*; 1970 *SA, F, E, S, W*

Grace, T.O. (*UC Dublin, St Mary's Coll*) 1972 *F 1, E*; 1973 *NZ, E, S, W*; 1974 *E, S, P, NZ*; 1975 *E, S, F, W*; 1976 *A, F, W, E, S, NZ*; 1977 *W, E, S, F*; 1978 *S*

Grant, E.L. (*CIYMS*) 1971 *F, E, S, W*

Gregg, R.J. (*Queen's U, Belfast*) 1953 *F, E, S, W*; 1954 *F, E, S*

Griffin, C.S. (*London Irish*) 1951 *F, E*

Griffin, J.L. (*Wanderers*) 1949 *S, W*

Grimshaw, C. (*Queen's U, Belfast*) 1969 *E (r)*

Guerin, B.N. (*Galwegians*) 1956 *S*

Hakin, R.F. (*CIYMS*) 1976 *W, S, NZ*; 1977 *W, E, F*

Harbison, H.T. (*Bective Rangers*) 1984 *W (r), E, S*

Hardy, G.G. (*Bective Rangers*) 1962 *S*

Harper, J. (*Instonians*) 1947 *F, E, S*

Henderson, N.J. (*Queen's U, Belfast, NIFC*) 1949 *S, W*; 1950 *F*; 1951 *F, E, S, W, SA*; 1952 *F, S, W, E*; 1953 *F, E, S, W*; 1954 *NZ, F, E, S, W*; 1955 *F, E, S, W*; 1956 *S, W*; 1957 *F, E, S, W*; 1958 *A, E, S, W, F*; 1959 *E, S, W, F*

Hewitt, D. (*Queen's U, Belfast, Instonians*) 1958 *A, E, S, F*; 1959 *S, W, F*; 1960 *E, S, W, F*; 1961 *E, S, W, F*; 1962 *S, F*; 1965 *W*

Hewitt, J.A. (*NIFC*) 1981 *SA 1 (r), 2 (r)*

Hewitt, W.J. (*Instonians*) 1954 *E*; 1956 *S*; 1959 *W*; 1961 *SA*

Hickie, D.J. (*St Mary's Coll*) 1971 *F, E, S, W*; 1972 *F 1, E*

Higgins, J.A.D. (*Civil Service*) 1947 *S, W, A*; 1948 *F, S, W*

Hillary, M. (*UC Dublin*) 1952 *E*

Hingerty, D. (*UC Dublin*) 1947 *F, E, S, W*

Hipwell, M.L. (*Terenure Coll*) 1962 *E, S*; 1968 *F, A*; 1969 *F (r), S (r)*; 1971 *F, E, S, W*; 1972 *F 2*

Holland, J.J. (*Wanderers*) 1981 *SA 1, 2*; 1986 *W*

Hooks, K.J. (*Queen's U, Belfast*) 1981 *S*

Houston, K.J. (*Oxford U, London Irish*) 1961 *SA*; 1964 *S, W*; 1965 *F, E, SA*

Hunter, L. (*Civil Service*) 1968 *W, A*

Hunter, W.R. (*CIYMS*) 1962 *E, S, W, F*; 1963 *F, E, S*; 1966 *F, E, S*

Hutton, S.A. (*Malone*) 1967 *S, W, F, A 2*

Irwin, D.G. (*Queen's U, Belfast*) 1980 *F, W*; 1981 *F, W, E, S, SA 1, 2, A*; 1982 *W*; 1983 *S, F, W, E*; 1984 *F, W*

Kavanagh, J.R. (*UC Dublin, Wanderers*) 1953 *F, E, S, W*; 1954 *NZ, S, W*; 1955 *F, E*; 1956 *E, S, W*; 1957 *F, E, S, W*; 1958 *A, E, S, W*; 1959 *E, S, W, F*; 1960 *E, S, W, F, SA*; 1961 *E, S, W, F, SA*; 1962 *F*

Kavanagh, P. (*UC Dublin, Wanderers*) 1952 *E*; 1955 *W*

Keane, M.I. (*Lansdowne*) 1974 *F, W, E, S, P, NZ*; 1975 *E, S, F, W*; 1976 *A, F, W, E, NZ*; 1977 *W, E, S, F*; 1978 *S, F, W, E, NZ*; 1979 *F, W, E, S, A 1, 2*; 1980 *E, S, F, W*; 1981 *F, W, E, S*; 1982 *W, E, S*; 1983 *S, F, W, E*; 1984 *F, W, E, S*

Kearney, R.K. (*Wanderers*) 1982 *F*; 1984 *A*; 1986 *F, W*

Keeffe, E. (*Sunday's Well*) 1947 *F, E, S, W, A*; 1948 *F*

Kelly, J.C. (*UC Dublin*) 1962 *F, W*; 1963 *F, E, S, W, NZ*; 1964 *E, S, W, F*

Kelly, S. (*Lansdowne*) 1954 *S, W*; 1955 *S*; 1960 *W, F*

Kennedy, A.G. (*Belfast Collegians*) 1956 *F*

Kennedy, A.P. (*London Irish*) 1986 *W, E*

Kennedy, K.W. (*Queen's U, Belfast, London Irish*) 1965 *F, E, S, W, SA*; 1966 *F, E, W*; 1967 *A 1, E, S, W, F, A 2*; 1968 *F, A*; 1969 *F, E, S, W*; 1970 *SA, F, E, S, W*; 1971 *F, E, S, W*; 1972 *F 1, 2, E*; 1973 *NZ, E, S, W, F*; 1974 *F, W, E, S, P, NZ*; 1975 *F, W*

Kennedy, T.J. (*St Mary's Coll*) 1978 *NZ*; 1979 *F, W, E (r), A 1, 2*; 1980 *S, F, W*; 1981 *SA 1, 2, A*

Keogh, F.S. (*Bective Rangers*) 1964 *W, F*

Keyes, R.P. (*Cork Constitution*) 1986 *E*

Kiely, M.D. (*Lansdowne*) 1962 *W*; 1963 *F, E, S, W*

Kiernan, M.J. (*Dolphin, Lansdowne*) 1982 *(r), E, S, F*; 1983 *S, F, W, E*; 1984 *E, S, A*; 1985 *S, F, W, E*; 1986 *F, W, E, S*

Kiernan, T.J. (*UC Cork, Cork Constitution*) 1960 *E, S, W, F, SA*; 1961 *E, S, W, F, SA*; 1962 *E, W*; 1963 *F, S, W, NZ*; 1964 *E, S*; 1965 *F, E, S, W, SA*; 1966 *F, E, S, W*; 1967 *A 1, 2, E, S, W, F*; 1968 *F, E, S, W, A*; 1969 *F, E, S, W*; 1970 *SA, F, E, S, W*; 1971 *F*; 1972 *F 1, 2, E*; 1973 *NZ, E, S*

Kyle, J.W. (*Queen's U, Belfast, NIFC*) 1947 *F, E, S, W, A*; 1948 *F, E, S, W*; 1949 *F, E, S, W*; 1950 *F, E, S, W*; 1951 *F, E, S, W, SA*; 1952 *F, S, W, E*; 1953 *F, E, S, W*; 1954 *NZ, F*; 1955 *F, E, W*; 1956 *F, E, S, W*; 1957 *F, E, S, W*; 1958 *A, E, S*

Lamont, R.A. (*Instonians*) 1965 *F, E, SA*; 1966 *F, E, S, W*; 1970 *SA, F, E, S, W*

Lane, M.F. (*UC Cork*) 1947 *W*; 1949 *F, E, S, W*; 1950 *F, E, S, W*; 1951 *F, S, W, SA*; 1952 *F, S*; 1953 *F, E*

Lane, P. (*Old Crescent*) 1964 *W*

Lavery, P. (*London Irish*) 1974 *W*; 1976 *W*

Lawler, P.J. (*Clontarf*) 1951 *S, SA*; 1952 *F, S, W, E*; 1953 *F*; 1954 *NZ, E, S*; 1956 *F, E*

Leahy, M.W. (*UC Cork*) 1964 *W*

Lenihan, D.G. (*UC Cork, Cork Constitution*) 1981 *A*; 1982 *W, E, S, F*; 1983 *S, F, W, E*; 1984 *F, W, E, S, A*; 1985 *S, F, W, E*; 1986 *F, W, E, S*

L'Estrange, L.P.F. (*Dublin U*) 1962 *E*

Lydon, C. (*Galwegians*) 1956 *S*

Lynch, J.F. (*St Mary's Coll*) 1971 *F, E, S, W*; 1972 *F 1, 2, E*; 1973 *NZ, E, S, W*; 1974 *F, W, E, S, P, NZ*

Lynch, L. (*Lansdowne*) 1956 *S*

McBride, W.J. (*Ballymena*) 1962 *E, S, F, W*; 1963 *F, E, S, W, NZ*; 1964 *E, S, F*; 1965 *F, E, S, W, SA*; 1966 *F, E, S, W*; 1967 *A 1, 2, E, S, W, F*; 1968 *F, E, S, W, A*; 1969 *F, E, S, W*; 1970 *SA, F, E, S, W*; 1971 *F, E, S, W*; 1972 *F 1, E, F 2*; 1973 *NZ, E, S, W, F*; 1974 *F, W, E, S, P, NZ*; 1975 *E, S, F, W*

McCall, B.W. (*London Irish*) 1985 *F (r)*; 1986 *E, S*

McCallan, B. (*Ballymena*) 1960 *E, S*

McCarten, R.J. (*London Irish*) 1961 *E, W, F*

McCarthy, J.S. (*Dolphin*) 1948 *F, E, S, W*; 1949 *F, E, S, W*; 1950 *W*; 1951 *F, E, S, W, SA*; 1952 *F, S, W, E*; 1953 *F, E, S*; 1954 *NZ, F, E, S, W*; 1955 *F, E*

McCombe, W.McM. (*Dublin U, Bangor*) 1968 *F;* 1975 *E, S, F, W*

McConnell, A.A. (*Collegians*) 1947 *A;* 1948 *F, E, S, W;* 1949 *F, E*

McCourt, D. (*Queen's U, Belfast*) 1947 *A*

McCoy, J.J. (*Dungannon*) 1984 *W, A;* 1985 *S, F, W, E;* 1986 *F*

McCracken, H. (*NIFC*) 1954 *W*

McDermott, S.J. (*London Irish*) 1955 *S, W*

McGann, B.J. (*Lansdowne*) 1969 *F, E, S, W;* 1970 *SA, F, E, S, W;* 1971 *F, E, S, W;* 1972 *F 1, 2;* 1973 *NZ, E, S, W;* 1976 *F, W, E, S, NZ*

McGrath, D.G. (*UC Dublin*) 1984 *S*

McGrath, P.J. (*UC Cork*) 1965 *E, S, W, SA;* 1966 *F, E, S, W;* 1967 *A 1, 2*

McGrath, R.J.M. (*Wanderers*) 1977 *W, E, F (r);* 1981 *SA 1, 2, A;* 1982 *W, E, S, F;* 1983 *S, F, W, E;* 1984 *F, W*

McGrath, T. (*Garryowen*) 1956 *W;* 1958 *F;* 1960 *E, S, W, F;* 1961 *SA*

McGuire, E.P. (*UC Galway*) 1963 *E, S, W, NZ;* 1964 *E, S, W, F*

MacHale, S. (*Lansdowne*) 1965 *F, E, S, W, SA;* 1966 *F, E, S, W;* 1967 *S, W, F*

McIlrath, J.A. (*Ballymena*) 1976 *A, F, NZ;* 1977 *W, E*

McKay, J.W. (*Queen's U, Belfast*) 1947 *F, E, S, W, A;* 1948 *F, E, S, W;* 1949 *F, E, S, W;* 1950 *F, E, S, W;* 1951 *F, E, S, W, SA;* 1952 *F*

McKee, W.D. (*NIFC*) 1947 *A;* 1948 *F, E, S, W;* 1949 *F, E, S, W;* 1950 *F;* 1951 *SA*

McKelvey, J.M. (*Queen's U, Belfast*) 1956 *F, E*

McKibbin, A.R. (*Instonians, London Irish*) 1977 *W, E, S;* 1978 *S, F, W, E, NZ;* 1979 *F, W, E, S;* 1980 *E, S*

McKibbin, C.H. (*Instonians*) 1976 *S (r)*

McKibbin, D. (*Instonians*) 1950 *F, E, S, W;* 1951 *F, E, S, W*

McKinney, S.A. (*Dungannon*) 1972 *F 1, 2, E;* 1973 *W, F;* 1974 *F, E, S, P, NZ;* 1975 *E, S;* 1976 *A, F, W, E, S, NZ;* 1977 *W, E, S;* 1978 *S (r), F, W, E*

McLennan, A.C. (*Wanderers*) 1977 *F;* 1978 *S, F, W, E, NZ;* 1979 *F, W, E, S;* 1980 *E, F;* 1981 *F, W, E, S, SA 1, 2*

McLoughlin, F.M. (*Northern*) 1976 *A*

McLoughlin, G.A.J. (*Shannon*) 1979 *F, W, E, S, A 1, 2;* 1980 *E;* 1981 *SA 1, 2;* 1982 *W, E, S, F;* 1983 *S, F, W, E;* 1984 *F*

McLoughlin, R.J. (*Blackrock Coll*) 1962 *E, S, F;* 1963 *E, S, W, NZ;* 1964 *E, S;* 1965 *F, E, S, W, SA;* 1966 *F, E, S, W;* 1971 *F, E, S, W;* 1972 *F 1, 2, E;* 1973 *NZ, E, S, W, F;* 1974 *F, W, E, S, P, NZ;* 1975 *E, S, F, W*

McMaster, A.W. (*Ballymena*) 1972 *F 1, 2, E;* 1973 *W, F;* 1974 *F, E, S, P;* 1975 *F, W;* 1976 *A, F, W, NZ*

McMorrow, A. (*Garryowen*) 1951 *W*

McNaughton, P.P. (*Greystones*) 1978 *S, F, W, E;* 1979 *F, W, E, S, A 1, 2;* 1980 *E, S, F, W;* 1981 *F*

MacNeill, H.P. (*Dublin U, Oxford U, Blackrock Coll*) 1981 *F, W, E, S, A;* 1982 *W, E, S, F;* 1983 *S, F, W, E;* 1984 *F, W, E, A;* 1985 *S, F, W;* 1986 *F, W, E, S*

MacSweeney, D.A. (*Blackrock Coll*) 1955 *S*

Madden, M.N. (*Sunday's Well*) 1955 *E, S, W*

Maloney, J. (*UC Dublin*) 1950 *S*

Marshall, B.D.E. (*Queen's U, Belfast*) 1963 *E*

Matthews, P.M. (*Ards*) 1984 *A;* 1985 *S, F, W, E*

Mattsson, J. (*Wanderers*) 1948 *E*

Mays, K.M.A. (*UC Dublin*) 1973 *NZ, E, S, W*

Millar, S. (*Ballymena*) 1958 *F;* 1959 *E, S, W, F;* 1960 *E, S, W, F, SA;* 1961 *E, S, W, F, SA;* 1962 *E, S, F;* 1963 *F, E, S, W;* 1964 *F;* 1968 *F, E, S, W, A;* 1969 *F, E, S, W;* 1970 *SA, F, E, S, W*

Millar, W.H.J. (*Queen's U, Belfast*) 1951 *E, S, W;* 1952 *S, W*

Milliken, R.A. (*Bangor*) 1973 *E, S, W, F;* 1974 *F, W, E, S, P, NZ;* 1975 *E, S, F, W*

Moffett, J.W. (*Ballymena*) 1961 *E, S*

Molloy, M.G. (*UC Galway, London Irish*) 1966 *F, E;* 1967 *A 1, 2, E, S, W, F;* 1968 *F, E, S, W, A;* 1969 *F, E, S, W;* 1970 *F, E, S, W;* 1971 *F, E, S, W;* 1973 *F;* 1976 *A*

Moloney, J.J. (*St Mary's Coll*) 1972 *F 1, 2, E;* 1973 *NZ, E, S, W, F;* 1974 *F, W, E, S, P NZ;* 1975 *E, S, F, W;* 1976 *S;* 1978 *S, F, W, E;* 1979 *A 1, 2;* 1980 *S, W*

Moloney, L.A. (*Garryowen*) 1976 *W (r), S;* 1978 *S (r), NZ*

Monteith, J.D.E. (*Queen's U, Belfast*) 1947 *E, S, W*

Moore, T.A.P. (*Highfield*) 1967 *A 2;* 1973 *NZ, E, S, W, F;* 1974 *F, W, E, S, P, NZ*

Moroney, J.C.M. (*Garryowen*) 1968 *W, A;* 1969 *F, E, S, W*

Moroney, R.J.M. (*Lansdowne*) 1984 *F, W;* 1985 *F*

Moroney, T.A. (*UC Dublin*) 1964 *W;* 1967 *A 1, E*

Morrow, R.D. (*Bangor*) 1986 *F, E, S*

Mortell, M. (*Bective Rangers, Dolphin*) 1953 *F, E, S, W;* 1954 *NZ, F, E, S, W*

Mulcahy, W.A. (*UC Dublin, Bective Rangers*) 1958 *A, E, S, W, F;* 1959 *E, S, W, F;* 1960 *E, S, W, SA;* 1961 *E, S, W, SA;* 1962 *E, S, F, W;* 1963 *F, E, S, W, NZ;* 1964 *E, S, W, F;* 1965 *F, E, S, W, SA*

Mullan, B. (*Clontarf*) 1947 *F, E, S, W;* 1948 *F, E, S, W*

Mullen, K.D. (*Old Belvedere*) 1947 *F, E, S, W, A;* 1948 *F, E, S, W;* 1949 *F, E, S, W;* 1950 *F, E, S, W;* 1951 *F, E, S, W, SA;* 1952 *F, S, W*

Mulligan, A.A. (*Wanderers*) 1956 *F, E;* 1957 *F, E, S, W;* 1958 *A, E, S, F;* 1959 *E, S, W, F;* 1960 *E, S, W, F, SA;* 1961 *W, F, SA*

Mullin, B.J. (*Dublin U*) 1984 *A;* 1985 *S, W, E;* 1986 *F, W, E, S*

Murphy, C.J. (*Lansdowne*) 1939 *E, S, W;* 1947 *F, E*

Murphy, J.G.M.W. (*London Irish*) 1951 *SA;* 1952 *S, W;* 1954 *NZ;* 1958 *W*

Murphy, J.J. (*Greystones*) 1981 *SA 1;* 1982 *W (r);* 1984 *S*

Murphy, N.A.A. (*Cork Constitution*) 1958 *A, E, S, W, F;* 1959 *E, S, W, F;* 1960 *E, S, W, F, SA;* 1961 *E, S, W;* 1962 *E;* 1963 *NZ;* 1964 *E, S, W, F;* 1965 *F, E, S, W, SA;* 1966 *F, E, S, W;* 1967 *A 1, E, S, W, F;* 1969 *F, E, S, W*

Murphy-O'Connor, J. (*Bective Rangers*) 1954 *E*

Murray, J.B. (*UC Dublin*) 1963 *F*

Murtagh, C.W. (*Portadown*) 1977 *S*

Neely, M.R. (*Collegians*) 1947 *F, E, S, W*

Nelson, J.E. (*Malone*) 1947 *A;* 1948 *E, S, W;* 1949 *F, E, S, W;* 1950 *F, E, S, W;* 1951 *F, E, W;* 1954 *F*

Nesdale, T.J. (*Garryowen*) 1961 *F*

Norton, G.W. (*Bective Rangers*) 1949 *F, E, S, W;* 1950 *F, E, S, W;* 1951 *F, E, S*

Notley, J.R. (*Wanderers*) 1952 *F, S*

O'Brien, B.A.P. (*Shannon*) 1968 *F, E, S*

O'Brien, D.J. (*London Irish, Cardiff, Old Belvedere*) 1948 *E, S, W;* 1949 *F, E, S, W;* 1950 *F, E, S, W;* 1951 *F, E, S, W, SA;* 1952 *F, S, W, E*

O'Brien, K.A. (*Broughton Park*) 1980 *E;* 1981 *SA 1 (r), 2*

O'Callaghan, M.P. (*Sunday's Well*) 1962 *W;* 1964 *E, F*

O'Callaghan, P. (*Dolphin*) 1967 *A 1, 2, E;* 1968 *F, E, S, W;* 1969 *F, E, S, W;* 1970 *SA, F, E, S, W;* 1976 *F, W, E, S, NZ*

O'Connell, W.J. (*Lansdowne*) 1955 *F*

O'Connor, H.S. (*Dublin U*) 1957 *F, E, S, W*

O'Donnell, R.C. (*St Mary's Coll*) 1979 *A 1, 2;* 1980 *S, F, W*

O'Donoghue, P.J. (*Bective Rangers*) 1955 *F, E, S, W;* 1956 *W;* 1957 *F, E;* 1958 *A, E, S, W*

O'Driscoll, B.J. (*Manchester*) 1971 *F (r), E, S, W*

O'Driscoll, J.B. (*London Irish, Manchester*) 1978 *S;* 1979 *A 1, 2;* 1980 *E, S, F, W;* 1981 *F, W, E, S, SA 1, 2, A;* 1982 *W, E, S, F;* 1983 *S, F, W, E;* 1984 *F, W, E, S*

O'Flanagan, K.P. (*London Irish*) 1947 *A*

O'Flanagan, M. (*Lansdowne*) 1948 *S*

O'Hanlon, B. (*Dolphin*) 1947 *E, S, W;* 1948 *F, E, S, W;* 1949 *F, E, S, W;* 1950 *F*

O'Leary, A. (*Cork Constitution*) 1952 *S, W, E*

O'Meara, J.A. (*UC Cork, Dolphin*) 1951 *F, E, S, W, SA;* 1952 *F, S, W, E;* 1953 *F, E, S, W;* 1954 *NZ, F, E, S;* 1955 *F, E;* 1956 *S, W;* 1958 *W*

O'Neill, W.A. (*UC Dublin*) 1952 *F;* 1953 *F, E, S, W;* 1954 *NZ*

O'Reilly, A.J.F. (*Old Belvedere, Leicester*) 1955 *F, E, S, W;* 1956 *F, E, S, W;* 1957 *F, S, W;* 1958 *A, E, S, W, F;* 1959 *E, S, W, F;* 1960 *E;* 1961 *E, F, SA;* 1963 *F, S, W;* 1970 *E*

Orr, P.A. (*Old Wesley*) 1976 *F, W, E, S, NZ;* 1977 *W, E, S, F;* 1978 *S, F, W, E, NZ;* 1979 *F, W, E, S, A 1, 2;* 1980 *E, S, F, W;* 1981 *F, W, E, S, SA 1, 2, A;* 1982 *W, E, S, F;* 1983 *S, F, W, E;* 1984 *F, W, E, S, A;* 1985 *S, F, W, E;* 1986 *F, S*

O'Sullivan, P.J.A. (*Galwegians*) 1957 *F, E, S, W;* 1959 *E, S, W, F;* 1960 *SA;* 1961 *E, S;* 1962 *F, W;* 1963 *F, NZ*

Parfrey, P. (*UC Cork*) 1974 *NZ*

Patterson, C.S. (*Instonians*) 1978 *NZ;* 1979 *F, W, E, S, A 1, 2;* 1980 *E, S, F, W*

Pedlow, A.C. (*CIYMS*) 1953 *W;* 1954 *NZ, F, E;* 1955 *F, E, S, W;* 1956 *F, E, S, W;* 1957 *F, E, S, W;* 1958 *A, E, S, W, F;* 1959 *E;* 1960 *E, S, W, F, SA;* 1961 *S;* 1962 *W;* 1963 *F*

Phipps, G.C. (*Army*) 1950 *E, W;* 1952 *F, W, E*

Quinlan, S.V.J. (*Blackrock Coll*) 1956 *F, E, W;* 1958 *W*

Quinn, B.T. (*Old Belvedere*) 1947 *F*

Quinn, F.P. (*Old Belvedere*) 1981 *F, W, E*

Quinn, K. (*Old Belvedere*) 1947 *F, A;* 1953 *F, E, S*

Quinn, M.A.M. (*Lansdowne*) 1973 *F;* 1974 *F, W, E, S, P, NZ;* 1977 *S, F;* 1981 *SA 2*

Quirke, J.T.M. (*Blackrock Coll*) 1962 *E, S;* 1968 *S*

Rea, H.H. (*Edinburgh U*) 1967 *A 1;* 1969 *F*

Reid, P.J. (*Garryowen*) 1947 *A;* 1948 *F, E, W*

Reid, T.E. (*Garryowen*) 1953 *E, S, W;* 1954 *F, NZ;* 1955 *E, S;* 1956 *F, E;* 1957 *F, E, S, W*

Reidy, G.F. (*Dolphin, Lansdowne*) 1953 *W;* 1954 *F, E, S, W*

Ringland, T.M. (*Queen's U, Belfast, Ballymena*) 1981 *A*; 1982 *W, E, F*; 1983 *S, F, W, E*; 1984 *F, W, E, S, A*; 1985 *S, F, W, E*; 1986 *F, W, E, S*

Ritchie, J.S. (*London Irish*) 1956 *F, E*

Robbie, J.C. (*Dublin U, Greystones*) 1976 *A, F, NZ*; 1977 *S, F*; 1981 *F, W, E, S*

Roche, R.E. (*UC Galway*) 1955 *E, S*; 1957 *S, W*

Roe, R. (*Lansdowne*) 1952 *E*; 1953 *F, E, S, W*; 1954 *F, E, S, W*; 1955 *F, E, S, W*; 1956 *F, E, S, W*; 1957 *F, E, S, W*

Ross, G.R.P. (*CIYMS*) 1955 *W*

Scott, D. (*Malone*) 1961 *F, SA*; 1962 *S*

Scott, R.D. (*Queen's U, Belfast*) 1967 *E, F*; 1968 *F, E, S*

Sexton, W.J. (*Garryowen*) 1984 *A*

Sherry, B.F. (*Terenure Coll*) 1967 *A 1, 2, E, S*; 1968 *F, E*

Sherry, M.J.A. (*Lansdowne*) 1975 *F, W*

Slattery, J.F. (*UC Dublin, Blackrock Coll*) 1970 *SA, F, E, S, W*; 1971 *F, E, S, W*; 1972 *F 1, 2, E*; 1973 *NZ, E, S, W, F*; 1974 *F, W, E, S, P, NZ*; 1975 *E, S, F, W*; 1976 *A*; 1977 *S, F*; 1978 *S, F, W, E, NZ*; 1979 *F, W, E, S, A*

1, 2; 1980 *E, S, F, W*; 1981 *F, W, E, S, SA 1, 2, A*; 1982 *W, E, S, F*; 1983 *S, F, W, E*; 1984 *F*

Smith, J.H. (*London Irish*) 1951 *F, E, S, W, SA*; 1952 *F, S, W, E*; 1954 *NZ, W, F*

Spillane, B.J. (*Bohemians*) 1985 *S, F, W, E*; 1986 *F, W, E*

Spring, D.E. (*Dublin U*) 1978 *S, NZ*; 1979 *S*; 1980 *S, F, W*; 1981 *W*

Spring, R.M. (*Lansdowne*) 1979 *F, W, E*

Steele, H.W. (*Ballymena*) 1976 *F*; 1977 *F*; 1978 *F, W, E*; 1979 *F, W, E, A 1, 2*

Stevenson, J.B. (*Instonians*) 1958 *A, E, S, W, F*

Strathdee, E. (*Queen's U, Belfast*) 1947 *E, S, W, A*; 1948 *W, F*; 1949 *E, S, W*

Tector, W.R. (*Wanderers*) 1955 *F, E, S*

Thompson, R.H. (*Instonians*) 1951 *SA*; 1952 *F*; 1954 *NZ, F, E, S, W*; 1955 *F, S, W*; 1956 *W*

Tucker, C.C. (*Shannon*) 1979 *F, W*; 1980 *F (r)*

Turley, N. (*Blackrock Coll*) 1962 *E*

Tydings, J. (*Young Munster*) 1968 *A*

Uprichard, R.J.H. (*Harlequins, RAF*) 1950 *S, W*

Waldron, O.C. (*Oxford U, London Irish*) 1966 *S, W*; 1968 *A*

Wall, H. (*Dolphin*) 1965 *S, W*

Walsh, J.C. (*UC Cork, Sunday's Well*) 1960 *S, SA*; 1961 *E, S, F, SA*; 1963 *E, S, W, NZ*; 1964 *E, S, W, F*; 1965 *F, S, W, SA*; 1966 *F, S, W*; 1967 *E, S, W, F, A 2*

Ward, A.J.P. (*Garryowen, St Mary's Coll*) 1978 *S, F, W, E, NZ*; 1979 *F, W, E, S*; 1981 *W, E, S, A*; 1983 *E (r)*; 1984 *E, S*; 1986 *S*

Whelan, P.C. (*Garryowen*) 1975 *E, S*; 1976 *NZ*; 1977 *W, E, S, F*; 1978 *S, F, E, NZ*; 1979 *F, W, E, S*; 1981 *F, W, E*

Wilkinson, R.W. (*Wanderers*) 1947 *A*

Wilson, F. (*CIYMS*) 1977 *W, E, S*

Wood, B.G.M. (*Garryowen*) 1954 *E, S*; 1956 *F, E, S, W*; 1957 *F, E, S, W*; 1958 *A, E, S, W, F*; 1959 *E, S, W, F*; 1960 *E, S, W, F, SA*; 1961 *E, S, W, F, SA*

Young, R.M. (*Collegians*) 1965 *F, E, S, W, SA*; 1966 *F, E, S, W*; 1967 *W, F*; 1968 *W, A*; 1969 *F, E, S, W*; 1970 *SA, F, E, S, W*; 1971 *F, E, S, W*

Scotland

Abercrombie, J.G. (*Edinburgh U*) 1949 *F, W, I*; 1950 *F, W, I, E*

Aitken, J. (*Gala*) 1977 *E, I, F*; 1981 *F, W, E, I, NZ 1, 2, R, A*; 1982 *E, I, F, W*; 1983 *F, W, E, NZ*; 1984 *W, E, I, F, R*

Aitken, R. (*London Scottish*) 1947 *W*

Allan, J.L. (*Melrose*) 1952 *F, W, I*; 1953 *W*

Allan, J.L.F. (*Cambridge U*) 1957 *I, E*

Allan, R.C. (*Hutchesons' GSFP*) 1969 *I*

Allardice, W.D. (*Aberdeen GSFP*) 1948 *A, F, W, I*; 1949 *F, W, I, E*

Anderson, E. (*Stewart's Coll FP*) 1947 *I, E*

Arneil, R.J. (*Edinburgh Acads, Leicester, Northampton*) 1968 *I, E, A*; 1969 *F, W, I, E, SA*; 1970 *F, W, I, E, A*; 1971 *F, W, I, E (2/1C])*; 1972 *F, W, E, NZ*

Baird, G.R.T. (*Kelso*) 1981 *A*; 1982 *E, I, F, W, A 1, 2*; 1983 *I, F, W, E, NZ*; 1984 *W, E, I, F, A*; 1985 *I, W, E*; 1986 *F, W, E, I, R*

Barnes, I.A. (*Hawick*) 1972 *W*; 1974 *F (r)*; 1975 *E (r), NZ*; 1977 *I, F, W*

Bearne, K.R.F. (*Cambridge U, London Scottish*) 1960 *F, W*

Beattie, J.R. (*Glasgow Acads*) 1980 *I, F, W, E*; 1981 *F, W, E, I*; 1983 *F, W, E, NZ*; 1984 *E (r), R, A*; 1985 *I*; 1986 *F, W, E, I*

Bell, D.L. (*Watsonians*) 1975 *I, F, W, E*

Biggar, A.G. (*London Scottish*) 1969 *SA*; 1970 *F, I, E, A*; 1971 *F, W, I, E (2/1C])*; 1972 *F, W*

Biggar, M.A (*London Scottish*) 1975 *I, F, W, E*; 1976 *W, E, I*; 1977 *I, F, W*; 1978 *I, F, W, E, NZ*; 1979 *W, E, I, F, NZ*; 1980 *I, F, W, E*

Birkett, G.A. (*Harlequins, London Scottish*) 1975 *NZ*

Black, A.W. (*Edinburgh U*) 1947 *F, W*; 1948 *E*; 1950 *W, I, E*

Black, W.P. (*Glasgow HSFP*) 1948 *F, W, I, E*; 1951 *E*

Blaikie, C.F. (*Heriot's FP*) 1963 *I, E*; 1966 *E*; 1968 *A*; 1969 *F, W, I, E*

Bos, F.H. ten (*Oxford U, London Scottish*)

1959 *E*; 1960 *F, W, SA*; 1961 *F, SA, W, I, E*; 1962 *F, W, I, E*; 1963 *F, W, I, E*

Boyle, A.C.W. (*London Scottish*) 1963 *F, W, I*

Boyle, A.H.W. (*St Thomas's Hospital, London Scottish*) 1966 *A*; 1967 *F, NZ*; 1968 *F, W, I*

Brash, J.C. (*Cambridge U*) 1961 *E*

Breakey, R.W. (*Gosforth*) 1978 *E*

Brewster, A.K. (*Stewart's-Melville FP*) 1977 *E*; 1980 *I, F*; 1986 *E, I, R*

Brown, A.R. (*Gala*) 1971 *E (2/1C])*; 1972 *F, W, E*

Brown, G.L. (*W of Scotland*) 1969 *SA*; 1970 *F, W (r), I, E, A*; 1971 *F, W, I, E (2/1C])*; 1972 *F, W, E, NZ*; 1973 *E (r), P*; 1974 *F, W, E, I, F*; 1975 *I, F, W, E, A*; 1976 *F, W, E, I*

Brown, P.C. (*W of Scotland, Gala*) 1964 *F, NZ, W, I, E*; 1965 *I, E, SA*; 1966 *A*; 1969 *I, E*; 1970 *W, E*; 1971 *F, W, I, E (2/1C])*; 1972 *F, W, E, NZ*; 1973 *F, W, I, E, P*

Bruce, C.R. (*Glasgow Acads*) 1947 *F, W, I, E*; 1949 *F, W, I, E*

Bruce, N.S. (*Blackheath, Army, London Scottish*) 1958 *F, A, I, E*; 1959 *F, W, I, E*; 1960 *F, W, I, E, SA*; 1961 *F, SA, W, I, E*; 1962 *F, W, I, E*; 1963 *F, W, I, E*; 1964 *F, NZ, W, I, E*

Bruce, R.M. (*Gordonians*) 1947 *A*; 1948 *F, W, I*

Bruce-Lockhart, L. (*London Scottish*) 1948 *E*; 1950 *F, W*; 1953 *I, E*

Bryce, R.D.H. (*W of Scotland*) 1973 *I (r)*

Budge, G.M. (*Edinburgh Wands*) 1950 *F, W, I, E*

Burnet, P.J. (*London Scottish, Edinburgh Acads*) 1960 *SA*

Burnett, J.N. (*Heriot's FP*) 1980 *I, F, W, E*

Burrell, G. (*Gala*) 1950 *F, W, I*; 1951 *SA*

Calder, F. (*Stewart's-Melville FP*) 1986 *F, W, E, I, R*

Calder, J.H. (*Stewart's-Melville FP*) 1981 *F, W, E, I, NZ 1, 2, R, A*; 1982 *E, I, F, W, A*

1, 2; 1983 *I, F, W, E, NZ*; 1984 *W, E, I, F, A*; 1985 *I, F, W*

Callander, G.J. (*Kelso*) 1984 *R*

Cameron, A. (*Glasgow HSFP*) 1948 *W*; 1950 *I, E*; 1951 *F, W, I, E, SA*; 1953 *I, E*; 1955 *F, W, I, E*; 1956 *F, W, I*

Cameron, A.D. (*Hillhead HSFP*) 1951 *F*; 1954 *F*

Cameron, D. (*Glasgow HSFP*) 1953 *I, E*; 1954 *F, NZ, I, E*

Cameron, N.W. (*Glasgow U*) 1952 *E*; 1953 *F, W*

Campbell, A.J. (*Hawick*) 1984 *I, F, R*; 1985 *I, F, W, E*; 1986 *F, W, E, I*

Campbell, H.H. (*Cambridge U, London Scottish*) 1947 *I, E*; 1948 *I, E*

Campbell, N.M. (*London Scottish*) 1956 *F, W*

Campbell-Lamerton, J.R.E. (*London Scottish*) 1986 *F*

Campbell-Lamerton, M.J. (*Halifax, Army, London Scottish*) 1961 *F, SA, W, I*; 1962 *W, I, E*; 1963 *W, I, E*; 1964 *I, E*; 1965 *F, W, I, E, SA*; 1966 *F, W, I, E*

Carmichael, A.B. (*W of Scotland*) 1967 *I, NZ*; 1968 *F, W, I, E, A*; 1969 *F, W, I, E, SA*; 1970 *F, W, I, E, A*; 1971 *F, W, I, E (2/1C])*; 1972 *F, W, E, NZ*; 1973 *F, W, I, E, P*; 1974 *W, E, I, F*; 1975 *I, F, W, E, NZ, A*; 1976 *F, W, E, I*; 1977 *E, I, (r), F, W*; 1978 *I*

Cawkwell, G.L. (*Oxford U*) 1947 *F*

Charters, R.G. (*Hawick*) 1955 *W, I, E*

Chisholm, D.H. (*Melrose*) 1964 *I, E*; 1965 *E, SA*; 1966 *F, I, E, A*; 1967 *F, W, NZ*; 1968 *F, W, I*

Chisholm, R.W.T. (*Melrose*) 1955 *I, E*; 1956 *F, W, I, E*; 1958 *F, W, A, I*; 1960 *SA*

Clark, R.L. (*Edinburgh Wands, Royal Navy*) 1972 *F, W, E, NZ*; 1973 *F, W, I, E, P*

Coltman, S. (*Hawick*) 1948 *I*; 1949 *F, W, I, E*

Connell, G.C. (*Trinity Acads, London Scottish*) 1968 *E, A*; 1969 *F, E*; 1970 *F*

Cordial, I.F. (*Edinburgh Wands*) 1952 *F, W, I, E*

Coughtrie, S. (*Edinburgh Acads*) 1959 F, W, I, E; 1962 W, I, E; 1963 F, W, I, E

Coutts, F.H. (*Melrose, Army*) 1947 W, I, E

Coutts, I.D.F. (*Old Alleynians*) 1951 F; 1952 E

Cowan, R.C. (*Selkirk*) 1961 F; 1962 F, W, I, E

Cowie, W.L.K. (*Edinburgh Wands*) 1953 E

Cranston, A.G. (*Hawick*) 1976 W, E, I; 1977 E, W; 1978 F (r), W, E, NZ; 1981 NZ 1, 2

Cunningham, R.F. (*Gala*) 1978 NZ; 1979 W, E

Currie, L.R. (*Dunfermline*) 1947 A; 1948 F, W, I; 1949 F, W, I, E

Cuthbertson, W. (*Kilmarnock, Harlequins*) 1980 I; 1981 W, E, I, NZ 1, 2, R, A; 1982 E, I, F, W, A 1, 2; 1983 I, F, W, NZ; 1984 W, E, A

Dalgleish, K.J. (*Edinburgh Wands, Cambridge U*) 1951 I, E; 1953 F, W

Davidson, J.A. (*London Scottish, Edinburgh Wands*) 1959 E; 1960 I, E

Davidson, J.N.G. (*Edinburgh U*) 1952 F, W, I, E; 1953 F, W; 1954 F

Dawson, J.C. (*Glasgow Acads*) 1947 A; 1948 F, W; 1949 F, W, I; 1950 F, W, I, E; 1951 F, W, I, E, SA; 1952 F, W, I, E; 1953 E

Deans, C.T. (*Hawick*) 1978 F, W, E, NZ; 1979 W, E, I, F, NZ; 1980 I, F; 1981 F, W, E, NZ 1, 2, R, A; 1982 E, I, F, W, A 1, 2; 1983 I, F, W, E, NZ; 1984 W, E, I, F, A; 1985 I, F, W, E; 1986 F, W, E, I, R

Deans, D.T. (*Hawick*) 1968 E

Deas, D.W. (*Heriot's FP*) 1947 F, W

Dick, L.G. (*Loughborough Colls, Jordanhill, Swansea*) 1972 W (r), E; 1974 W, E, I, F; 1975 I, F, W, E, NZ, A; 1976 F; 1977 E

Dickson, G. (*Gala*) 1978 NZ; 1979 W, E, I, F, NZ; 1980 W; 1981 F; 1982 W (r)

Docherty, J.T. (*Glasgow HSFP*) 1955 F, W; 1956 E; 1958 F, W, A, I, E

Dods, P.W. (*Gala*) 1983 I, F, W, E, NZ; 1984 W, E, I, F, R, A; 1985 I, F, W

Dorward, A.F. (*Cambridge U, Gala*) 1950 F; 1951 SA; 1952 W, I, E; 1953 F, W, E; 1955 F; 1956 I, E; 1957 F, W, I, E

Douglas, J. (*Stewart's Coll FP*) 1961 F, SA, W, I, E; 1962 F, W, I, E; 1963 F, W, I

Drummond, C.W. (*Melrose*) 1947 F, W, I, E; 1948 F, I, E; 1950 F, W, I, E

Duffy, H. (*Jed-Forest*) 1955 F

Duncan, M.D.F. (*W of Scotland*) 1986 F, W, E, R

Dunlop, Q. (*W of Scotland*) 1971 E (2/1C/)

Edwards, D.B. (*Heriot's FP*) 1960 I, E, SA

Elgie, M.K. (*London Scottish*) 1954 NZ, I, E, W; 1955 F, W, I, E

Elliot, C. (*Langholm*) 1958 E; 1959 F; 1960 F; 1963 E; 1964 F, NZ, W, I, E; 1965 F, W, I

Elliot, T. (*Gala*) 1955 W, I, E; 1956 F, W, I, E; 1957 F, W, I, E; 1958 W, A, I

Elliot, T.G. (*Langholm*) 1968 W, A; 1969 F, W; 1970 E

Elliot, W.I.D. (*Edinburgh Acads*) 1947 F, W, A; 1948 F, W, I, E; 1949 F, W, I, E; 1950 F, W, I, E; 1951 F, W, I, E, SA; 1952 F, W, I, E; 1954 NZ, I, E, W

Fergusson, E.A.J. (*Oxford U*) 1954 F, NZ, I, E, W

Finlay, R. (*Watsonians*) 1948 E

Fisher, A.T. (*Waterloo, Watsonians*) 1947 I, E

Fisher, C.D. (*Waterloo*) 1975 NZ, A; 1976 W, E, I

Fisher, J.P. (*Royal HSFP, London Scottish*) 1963 E; 1964 F, NZ, W, I, E; 1965 F, W, I, E, SA; 1966 F, W, I, E, A; 1967 F, W, I, E, NZ; 1968 F, W, I, E

Forsyth, I.W. (*Stewart's Coll FP*) 1972 NZ; 1973 F, W, I, E, P

Fox, J. (*Gala*) 1952 F, W, I, E

Frame, J.N.M. (*Edinburgh U, Gala*) 1967 NZ; 1968 F, W, I, E; 1969 W, I, E, SA; 1970 F, W, I, E, A; 1971 F, W, I, E (2/1C/); 1972 F, W, E; 1973 P

Friebe, J.P. (*Glasgow HSFP*) 1952 E

Fulton, A.K. (*Edinburgh U, Dollar Acads*) 1952 F; 1954 F

Gammell, W.B.B. (*Edinburgh Wands*) 1977 I, F, W; 1978 W, E

Geddes, K.I. (*London Scottish*) 1947 F, W, I, E

Gemmill, R. (*Glasgow HSFP*) 1950 F, W, I, E; 1951 F, W, I

Gilbert-Smith, D.S. (*London Scottish*) 1952 E

Gill, A.D. (*Gala*) 1973 P; 1974 W, E, I, F

Glasgow, R.J.C. (*Dunfermline*) 1962 F, W, E; 1963 I, E; 1964 I, E; 1965 W, I

Glen, W.S. (*Edinburgh Wands*) 1955 W

Gloag, L.G. (*Cambridge U*) 1949 F, W, I, E

Gordon, R. (*Edinburgh Wands*) 1951 W; 1952 F, W, I, E; 1953 W

Gordon, R.J. (*London Scottish*) 1982 A 1, 2

Gossman, B.M. (*W of Scotland*) 1980 W; 1983 F, W

Gossman, J.S. (*W of Scotland*) 1980 E (r)

Grant, D. (*Hawick*) 1965 F, E, SA; 1966 F, W, I, A, E; 1967 F, W, I, E, NZ; 1968 F

Grant, M.L. (*Harlequins*) 1955 F; 1956 F, W; 1957 F

Grant, T.O. (*Hawick*) 1960 I, E, SA; 1964 F, NZ, W

Gray, D. (*W of Scotland*) 1978 E; 1979 I, F, NZ; 1980 I, F, W, E; 1981 F

Gray, T. (*Northampton, Heriot's FP*) 1950 E; 1951 F, E

Greenwood, J.T. (*Dunfermline, Perthshire Acads*) 1952 F; 1955 F, W, I, E; 1956 F, W, I, E; 1957 F, W, E; 1958 F, W, A, I, E; 1959 F, W, I

Hannah, R.S.M. (*W of Scotland*) 1971 I

Hart, J.G.M. (*London Scottish*) 1951 SA

Hart, W. (*Melrose*) 1960 SA

Hastie, A.J. (*Melrose*) 1961 W, I, E; 1964 I, E; 1965 E, SA; 1966 F, W, I, E, A; 1967 F, W, I, NZ; 1968 F, W

Hastie, I.R. (*Kelso*) 1955 F; 1958 F, E; 1959 F, W, I

Hastings, A.G. (*Cambridge U, London Scottish*) 1986 F, W, E, I, R

Hastings, S. (*Watsonians*) 1986 F, W, E, I, R

Hay, B.H. (*Boroughmuir*) 1975 NZ, A; 1976 F; 1978 I, F, W, E, NZ; 1979 W, E, I, F, NZ; 1980 I, F, W, E; 1981 F, W, E, I, NZ 1, 2

Hegarty, C.B. (*Hawick*) 1978 I, F, W, E

Hegarty, J.J. (*Hawick*) 1951 F; 1953 F, W, I, E; 1955 F

Henderson, B.C. (*Edinburgh Wands*) 1963 E; 1964 F, I, E; 1965 F, W, I, E; 1966 F, W, I, E

Henderson, I. C. (*Edinburgh Acads*) 1939 I, E; 1947 F, W, E, A; 1948 I, E

Henderson, J.H. (*Oxford U, Richmond*) 1953 F, W, I, E; 1954 F, NZ, I, E, W

Henriksen, E.H. (*Royal HSFP*) 1953 I

Hepburn, D.P. (*Woodford*) 1947 A; 1948 F, W, I, E; 1949 F, W, I, E

Hinshelwood, A.J.W. (*London Scottish*) 1966 F, W, I, E, A; 1967 F, W, I, E, NZ; 1968 F, W, I, E, A; 1969 F, W, I, SA; 1970 F, W

Hodgson, C.G. (*London Scottish*) 1968 I, E

Hogg, C.G. (*Boroughmuir*) 1978 F (r), W (r)

Hoyer-Millar, G.C. (*Oxford U*) 1953 I

Hunter, I.G. (*Selkirk*) 1984 I (r); 1985 F (r), W, E

Hunter, J.M. (*Cambridge U*) 1947 F

Hunter, M.D. (*Glasgow High*) 1974 F

Hunter, W.J. (*Hawick*) 1964 F, NZ, W; 1967 F, W, I, E

Inglis, H.M. (*Edinburgh Acads*) 1951 F, W, I, E, SA; 1952 W, I

Inglis, J.M. (*Selkirk*) 1952 E

Innes, J.R.S. (*Aberdeen GSFP*) 1939 W, I, E; 1947 A; 1948 F, W, I, E

Irvine, A.R. (*Heriot's FP*) 1972 NZ; 1973 F, W, I, E, P; 1974 W, E, I, F; 1975 I, F, W, E, NZ, A; 1976 F, W, E, I; 1977 E, I, F, W; 1978 I, F, E, NZ; 1979 W, E, I, F, NZ; 1980 I, F, W, E; 1981 F, W, E, I, NZ 1, 2, R, A; 1982 E, I, F, W, A 1, 2

Jackson, T.G.H. (*Army*) 1947 F, W, E, A; 1948 F, W, I, E; 1949 F, W, I, E

Jackson, W.D. (*Hawick*) 1964 I; 1965 E, SA; 1968 A; 1969 F, W, I, E

Jeffrey, J. (*Kelso*) 1984 A; 1985 I, E; 1986 F, W, E, I, R

Johnston, D.I. (*Watsonians*) 1979 NZ; 1980 I, F, W, E; 1981 R, A; 1982 E, I, F, W, A 1, 2; 1983 I, F, W, NZ; 1984 W, E, I, F, R; 1986 F, W, E, I, R

Johnston, J. (*Melrose*) 1951 SA; 1952 F, W, I, E

Keddie, R.R. (*Watsonians*) 1967 NZ

Keith, G.J. (*Wasps*) 1968 F, W

Keller, D.H. (*London Scottish*) 1949 F, W, I, E; 1950 F, W, I

Kemp, J.W.Y. (*Glasgow HSFP*) 1954 W; 1955 F, W, I, E; 1956 F, W, I, E; 1957 F, W, I, E; 1958 F, W, A, I, E; 1959 F, W, I, E; 1960 F, W, I, E, SA

Kennedy, A.E. (*Watsonians*) 1983 NZ; 1984 W, E, A

Kerr, W. (*London Scottish*) 1953 E

King, J.H.F. (*Selkirk*) 1953 F, W, E; 1954 E

Kininmonth, P.W. (*Oxford U, Richmond*) 1949 F, W, E; 1950 F, W, I, E; 1951 F, W, I, E, SA; 1952 F, W, I; 1954 F, NZ, I, E, W

Laidlaw, F.A.L. (*Melrose*) 1965 F, W, I, E, SA; 1966 F, W, I, E, A; 1967 F, W, I, E, NZ; 1968 F, W, I, A; 1969 F, W, I, E, SA; 1970 F, W, I, E, A; 1971 F, W, I

Laidlaw, R.J. (*Jed-Forest*) 1980 I, F, W, E; 1981 F, W, E, I, NZ 1, 2, R, A; 1982 E, I, F, W, A 1, 2; 1983 I, F, W, E, NZ; 1984 W, E, I, F, R, A; 1985 I, F; 1986 F, W, E, I, R

Lambie, I.K. (*Watsonians*) 1978 NZ (r); 1979 W, E, NZ

Lauder, W. (*Neath*) 1969 I, E, SA; 1970 F, W, I, A; 1973 F; 1974 W, E, I, F; 1975 I, F, NZ, A; 1976 F; 1977 E

Laughland, I.H.P. (*London Scottish*) 1959 *F;*
1960 *F, W, I, E;* 1961 *SA, W, I, E;* 1962 *F,*
W, I, E; 1963 *F, W, I;* 1964 *F, NZ, W, I, E;*
1965 *F, W, I, E, SA;* 1966 *F, W, I, E;* 1967 *E*
Lawrie, K.G. (*Gala*) 1980 *F (r), W, E*
Lawson, A.J.M. (*Edinburgh Wands, London*
Scottish) 1972 *F (r), E;* 1973 *F;* 1974 *W, E;*
1976 *E, I;* 1977 *E;* 1978 *NZ;* 1979 *W, E, I, F,*
NZ; 1980 *W (r)*
Lees, J.B. (*Gala*) 1947 *I, A;* 1948 *F, W, E*
Leslie, D.G. (*Dundee HSFP, W of Scotland,*
Gala) 1975 *I, F, W, E, NZ, A;* 1976 *F, W, E,*
I; 1978 *NZ;* 1980 *E;* 1981 *W, E, I, NZ 1, 2,*
R, A; 1982 *E;* 1983 *I, F, W, E;* 1984 *W, E, I,*
F, R; 1985 *F, W, E*
Lumsden, I.J.M. (*Bath, Watsonians*) 1947 *F,*
W, A; 1949 *F, W, I, E*
Lyall, G.G. (*Gala*) 1947 *A;* 1948 *F, W, I, E*

McClung, T. (*Edinburgh Acads*) 1956 *I, E;*
1957 *W, I, E;* 1959 *F, W, I;* 1960 *W*
McCrae, I.G. (*Gordonians*) 1967 *E;* 1968 *I;*
1969 *F (r), W;* 1972 *F, NZ*
McDonald, C. (*Jed-Forest*) 1947 *A*
Macdonald, D.C. (*Edinburgh U*) 1953 *F, W;*
1958 *I, E*
Macdonald, D.S.M. (*Oxford U, London*
Scottish, W of Scotland) 1977 *E, I, F, W;*
1978 *I, W, E*
Macdonald, J.D. (*London Scottish, Army*)
1966 *F, W, I, E;* 1967 *F, W, I, E*
Macdonald, K.R. (*Stewart's Coll FP*) 1956 *F,*
W, I; 1957 *W, I, E*
Macdonald, R. (*Edinburgh U*) 1950 *F, W, I, E*
Macdonald, W.G. (*London Scottish*) 1969 *I*
(r)
MacEwan, N.A. (*Gala, Highland*) 1971 *F, W,*
I, E (2/1C); 1972 *F, W, E, NZ;* 1973 *F, W,*
I, E, P; 1974 *W, E, I, F;* 1975 *W, E*
MacEwen, R.K.G. (*Cambridge U, London*
Scottish) 1954 *F, NZ, I, W;* 1956 *F, W, I, E;*
1957 *F, W, I, E;* 1958 *W*
McGaughey, S.K. (*Hawick*) 1984 *R*
McGeechan, I.R. (*Headingley*) 1972 *NZ;*
1973 *F, W, I, E, P;* 1974 *W, E, I, F;* 1975 *I, F,*
W, E, NZ, A; 1976 *F, W, E, I;* 1977 *E, I, F,*
W; 1978 *I, F, W, NZ;* 1979 *W, E, I, F*
McGlashan, T.P.L. (*Royal HSFP*) 1947 *F, I,*
E; 1954 *F, NZ, I, E, W*
MacGregor, I.A.A. (*Hillhead HSFP,*
Llanelli) 1955 *I, E;* 1956 *F, W, I, E;* 1957 *F,*
W, I
McGuinness, G.M. (*W of Scotland*) 1982 *A 1,*
2; 1983 *I;* 1985 *I, F, W, E*
McHarg, A.F. (*W of Scotland, London*
Scottish) 1968 *I, E, A;* 1969 *F, W, I, E;* 1971
F, W, I, E (2/1C); 1972 *F, E, NZ;* 1973 *F,*
W, I, E, P; 1974 *W, E, I, F;* 1975 *I, F, W, E,*
NZ, A; 1976 *F, W, E, I;* 1977 *E, I, F, W;*
1978 *I, F, W, NZ;* 1979 *W, E*
McKeating, E. (*Heriot's FP*) 1957 *F, W;* 1961
SA, W, I, E
Mackenzie, A.D.G. (*Selkirk*) 1984 *A*
Mackenzie, D.D. (*Edinburgh U*) 1947 *W, I,*
E; 1948 *F, W, I*
Mackie, G.Y. (*Highland*) 1975 *A;* 1976 *F, W;*
1978 *F*
MacLachlan, L.P. (*Oxford U, London*
Scottish) 1954 *NZ, I, E, W*
McLauchlan, J. (*Jordanhill*) 1969 *E, SA;* 1970
F, W; 1971 *F, W, I, E (2/1C);* 1972 *F, W, E,*
NZ; 1973 *F, W, I, E, P;* 1974 *W, E, I, F;* 1975
I, F, W, E, NZ, A; 1976 *F, W, E, I;* 1977 *W;*
1978 *I, F, W, E, NZ;* 1979 *W, E, I, F, NZ*

McLean, D.I. (*Royal HSFP*) 1947 *I, E*
Maclennan, W.D. (*Watsonians*) 1947 *F, I*
McLeod, H.F. (*Hawick*) 1954 *F, NZ, I, E, W;*
1955 *F, W, I, E;* 1956 *F, W, I, E;* 1957 *F, W,*
I, E; 1958 *F, W, A, I, E;* 1959 *F, W, I, E;*
1960 *F, W, I, E, SA;* 1961 *F, SA, W, I, E;*
1962 *F, W, I, E*
McMillan, K.H.D. (*Sale*) 1953 *F, W, I, E*
McPartlin, J.J. (*Harlequins, Oxford U*) 1960
F, W; 1962 *F, W, I, E*
Macphail, J.A.R. (*Edinburgh Acads*) 1949 *E;*
1951 *SA*
Madsen, D.F. (*Gosforth*) 1974 *W, E, I, F;*
1975 *I, F, W, E;* 1976 *F;* 1977 *E, I, F, W;*
1978 *I*
Mair, N.G.R. (*Edinburgh U*) 1951 *F, W, I, E*
Marshall, J.C. (*London Scottish*) 1954 *F, NZ,*
I, E, W
Maxwell, J.M. (*Langholm*) 1957 *I*
Michie, E.J.S. (*Aberdeen U, Aberdeen*
GSFP) 1954 *F, NZ, I, E;* 1955 *W, I, E;* 1956
F, W, I, E; 1957 *F, W, I, E*
Millican, J.G. (*Edinburgh U*) 1973 *W, I, E*
Milne, I.G. (*Heriot's FP, Harlequins*) 1979 *I,*
F, NZ; 1980 *I, F;* 1981 *NZ 1, 2, R, A;* 1982
E, I, F, W, A 1, 2; 1983 *I, F, W, E, NZ;* 1984
W, E, I, F, A; 1985 *F, W, E;* 1986 *F, W, E, I,*
R
Mitchell, G.W.E. (*Edinburgh Wands*) 1967
NZ; 1968 *F, W*
Morgan, D.W. (*Stewart's-Melville FP*) 1973
W, I, E, P; 1974 *I, F;* 1975 *I, F, W, E, NZ, A;*
1976 *F, W;* 1977 *I, F, W;* 1978 *I, F, W, E*
Muir, D.E. (*Heriot's FP*) 1950 *F, W, I, E;* 1952
W, I, E
Munnoch, N.M. (*Watsonians*) 1952 *F, W, I*
Munro, S. (*Ayr, W of Scotland*) 1980 *I, F;* 1981
F, W, E, I, NZ 1, 2, R; 1984 *W*
Munro, W.H. (*Glasgow HSFP*) 1947 *I, E*
Murdoch, W.C.W. (*Hillhead HSFP*) 1935 *E,*
NZ; 1936 *W, I;* 1939 *E;* 1948 *F, W, I, E*
Murray, K.T. (*Hawick*) 1985 *I, F, W*

Neill, J.B. (*Edinburgh Acads*) 1963 *E;* 1964 *F,*
NZ, W, I, E; 1965 *F*
Nichol, J.A. (*Royal HSFP*) 1955 *W, I, E*

Oliver, G.K. (*Gala*) 1970 *A*
Orr, J.H. (*Edinburgh City Police*) 1947 *F, W*

Paterson, D.S. (*Gala*) 1969 *SA;* 1970 *I, E, A;*
1971 *F, W, I, E (2/1C);* 1972 *W*
Paxton, I.A.M. (*Selkirk*) 1981 *NZ 1, 2, R, A;*
1982 *E, I, F, W, A 1, 2;* 1983 *I, E, NZ;* 1984
W, E, I, F; 1985 *I(r), F, W, E;* 1986 *W, E, I,*
R
Paxton, R.E. (*Kelso*) 1982 *I, A 2, R*
Pender, N.E.K. (*Hawick*) 1977 *I;* 1978 *F, W,*
E
Pollock, J.A. (*Gosforth*) 1982 *W;* 1983 *E, NZ;*
1984 *E (r), I, F, R;* 1985 *F*

Rea, C.W.W. (*W of Scotland, Headingley*)
1968 *A;* 1969 *F, W, I, SA;* 1970 *F, W, I, A;*
1971 *F, W, E (2/1C)*
Relph, W.K.L. (*Stewart's Coll FP*) 1955 *F, W,*
I, E
Renwick, J.M. (*Hawick*) 1972 *F, W, E, NZ;*
1973 *F;* 1974 *W, E, I, F;* 1975 *I, F, W, E, NZ,*
A; 1976 *F, W, E (r);* 1977 *I, F, W;* 1978 *I, F,*
W, E, NZ; 1979 *W, E, I, F, NZ;* 1980 *I, F,*
W, E; 1981 *F, W, E, I, NZ 1, 2, R, A;* 1982
E, I, F, W; 1983 *I, F, W, E;* 1984 *R*
Robertson, I. (*London Scottish, Watsonians*)

1968 *E;* 1969 *E, SA;* 1970 *F, W, I, E, A*
Robertson, K.W. (*Melrose*) 1978 *NZ;* 1979 *W,*
E, I, F, NZ; 1980 *W, E;* 1981 *F, W, E, I, R,*
A; 1982 *E, I, F, A 1, 2;* 1983 *I, F, W, E;* 1984
E, I, F, R, A; 1985 *I, F, W, E;* 1986 *I*
Robertson, M.A. (*Gala*) 1958 *F*
Robson, A. (*Hawick*) 1954 *F;* 1955 *F, W, I, E;*
1956 *F, W, I, E;* 1957 *F, W, I, E;* 1958 *W, A,*
I, E; 1959 *F, W, I, E;* 1960 *F*
Rodd, J.A.T. (*United Services, RN, London*
Scottish) 1958 *F, W, A, I, E;* 1960 *F, W;* 1962
F; 1964 *F, NZ, W;* 1965 *F, W, I*
Rollo, D.M.D. (*Howe of Fife*) 1959 *E;* 1960 *F,*
W, I, E, SA; 1961 *F, SA, W, I, E;* 1962 *F, W,*
E; 1963 *E, W, I, E;* 1964 *F, NZ, W, I, E;*
1965 *F, W, I, E, SA;* 1966 *F, W, I, E, A;* 1967
F, W, E, NZ; 1968 *F, W, I*
Rose, D.M. (*Jed-Forest*) 1951 *F, W, I, E, SA;*
1953 *F, W*
Ross, G.T. (*Watsonians*) 1954 *NZ, I, E, W*
Ross, I.A. (*Hillhead HSFP*) 1951 *F, W, I, E*
Ross, K.I. (*Boroughmuir FP*) 1961 *SA, W, I,*
E; 1962 *F, W, I, E;* 1963 *F, W, E*
Rowan, N.A. (*Boroughmuir*) 1980 *W, E;* 1981
F, W, E, I; 1984 *R;* 1985 *I*
Rutherford, J.Y. (*Selkirk*) 1979 *W, E, I, F,*
NZ; 1980 *I, F, E;* 1981 *F, W, E, I, NZ 1, 2,*
A; 1982 *E, I, F, W, A 1, 2;* 1983 *E, NZ;* 1984
W, E, I, F, R; 1985 *I, F, W, E;* 1986 *F, W, E,*
I, R

Scotland, K.J.F. (*Heriot's FP, Cambridge U,*
Leicester) 1957 *F, W, I, E;* 1958 *E;* 1959 *F,*
W, I, E; 1960 *F, W, I, E;* 1961 *F, SA, W, I, E;*
1962 *F, W, I, E;* 1963 *F, W, I, E;* 1965 *F*
Scott, D.M. (*Langholm, Watsonians*) 1950 *I,*
E; 1951 *W, I, E, SA;* 1952 *F, W, I;* 1953 *F*
Scott, J.S. (*St Andrews U*) 1950 *E*
Shackleton, J.A.P. (*London Scottish*) 1959 *E;*
1963 *F, W;* 1964 *NZ, W;* 1965 *I, SA*
Sharp, G. (*Stewart's FP, Army*) 1960 *F;* 1964
F, NZ, W
Shedden, D. (*W of Scotland*) 1972 *NZ;* 1973 *F,*
W, I, E, P; 1976 *W, E, I;* 1977 *I, F, W;* 1978
I, F, W
Shillinglaw, R.B. (*Gala, Army*) 1960 *I, E, SA;*
1961 *F, SA*
Simmers, B.M. (*Glasgow Acads*) 1965 *F, W;*
1966 *A;* 1967 *F, W, I;* 1971 *F (r)*
Sloan, D.A. (*Edinburgh Acads, London*
Scottish) 1950 *F, W, E;* 1951 *W, I, E;* 1953 *F*
Smith, A.R. (*Cambridge U, Gosforth, Ebbw*
Vale, Edinburgh Acads) 1955 *W, I, E;* 1956
F, W, I, E; 1957 *W, I, E;* 1958 *F, W, A, I, E;*
1959 *F, W, I, E;* 1960 *F, W, I, E, SA;* 1961 *F,*
SA, W, I, E; 1962 *F, W, I, E*
Smith, D.W.C. (*London Scottish*) 1949 *F, W,*
I, E; 1950 *F, W, I;* 1953 *I*
Smith, G.K. (*Kelso*) 1957 *I, E;* 1958 *F, W, A;*
1959 *F, W, I, E;* 1960 *F, W, I, E;* 1961 *F, SA,*
W, I, E
Smith, I.S.G. (*London Scottish*) 1969 *SA;*
1970 *F, W, I, E;* 1971 *F, W, I*
Smith, M.A. (*London Scottish*) 1970 *W, I, E,*
A
Smith, T.J. (*Gala*) 1983 *E, NZ;* 1985 *I, F*
Sole, D.M.B. (*Bath*) 1986 *F, W*
Spence, K.M. (*Oxford U*) 1953 *I*
Stagg, P.K. (*Sale*) 1965 *F, W, E, SA;* 1966 *F,*
W, I, E, A; 1967 *F, W, I, E, NZ;* 1968 *F, W,*
I, E, A; 1969 *F, W, I (r), SA;* 1970 *F, W, I, E,*
A
Steele, W.C.C. (*Langholm, Bedford, RAF,*
London Scottish) 1969 *E;* 1971 *F, W, I, E*

(2/1C]); 1972 F, W, E, NZ; 1973 F, W, I, E; 1975 I, F, W, E, NZ (r); 1976 W, E, I; 1977 E

Steven, P.D. *(Heriot's FP)* 1984 A; 1985 F, W, E

Steven, R. *(Edinburgh Wands)* 1962 I

Stevenson, G.D. *(Hawick)* 1956 E; 1957 F; 1958 F, W, A, I, E; 1959 W, I, E; 1960 W, I, E, SA; 1961 F, SA, W, I, E; 1963 F, W, I; 1964 E; 1965 F

Stewart, C.E.B. *(Kelso)* 1960 W; 1961 F

Strachan, G.M. *(Jordanhill)* 1971 E(C) (r); 1973 W, I, E, P

Suddon, N. *(Hawick)* 1965 W, I, E, SA; 1966 A; 1968 E, A; 1969 F, W, I; 1970 I, E, A

Swan, J.S. *(Army, London Scottish, Leicester)* 1953 E; 1954 F, NZ, I, E, W; 1955 F, W, I, E; 1956 F, W, I, E; 1957 F, W; 1958 F

Swan, M.W. *(Oxford U, London Scottish)* 1958 F, W, A, I, E; 1959 F, W, I

Tait, J.G. *(Edinburgh Acads)* 1880 I; 1885 I

Taylor, R.C. *(Kelvinside-West)* 1951 W, I, E, SA

Telfer, C.M. *(Hawick)* 1968 A; 1969 F, W, I, E; 1972 F, W, E; 1973 W, I, E, P; 1974 W, E, I; 1975 A; 1976 F

Telfer, J.W. *(Melrose)* 1964 F, NZ, W, I, E; 1965 F, W, I; 1966 F, W, I, E; 1967 W, I, E; 1968 E, A; 1969 F, W, I, E, SA; 1970 F, W, I

Thomson, A.M. *(St Andrews U)* 1949 I

Thomson, B.E. *(Oxford U)* 1953 F, W, I

Thomson, I.H.M. *(Heriot's FP, Army)* 1951 W, I; 1952 F, W, I; 1953 I, E

Thomson, R.H. *(London Scottish)* 1960 I, E, SA; 1961 F, SA, W, I, E; 1963 F, W, I, E; 1964 F, NZ, W

Tomes, A.J. *(Hawick)* 1976 E, I; 1977 E; 1978 I, F, W, E, NZ; 1979 W, E, I, F, NZ; 1980 F, W, E; 1981 F, W, E, I, NZ 1, 2, R, A; 1982 E, I, F, W, A 1, 2; 1983 I, F, W; 1984 W, E, I, F, R, A; 1985 W, E

Tukalo, I. *(Selkirk)* 1985 I

Turk, A.S. *(Langholm)* 1971 E (r)

Turnbull, G.O. *(Hawick)* 1951 F, SA

Turner, J.W.C. *(Gala)* 1966 W, A; 1967 F, W, I, E, NZ; 1968 F, W, I, E, A; 1969 F; 1970 E, A; 1971 F, W, I, E (2/1C])

Valentine, A.R. *(RNAS, Anthorn)* 1953 F, W, I

Valentine, D.D. *(Hawick)* 1947 I, E

Waddell, G.H. *(London Scottish, Cambridge U)* 1957 E; 1958 F, W, A, I, E; 1959 F, W, I, E; 1960 I, E, SA; 1961 F; 1962 F, W, I, E

Walker, M. *(Oxford U)* 1952 F

Watherston, W.R.A. *(London Scottish)* 1963 F, W, I

Watson, W.S. *(Boroughmuir)* 1974 W, E, I, F; 1975 NZ; 1977 I, F, W; 1979 I, F

Watt, A.G.M. *(Edinburgh Acads)* 1947 F, W, I, A; 1948 F, W

Weatherstone, T.G. *(Stewart's Coll FP)* 1952 E; 1953 I; 1954 F, NZ, I, E, W; 1955 F; 1958 W, A, I, E; 1959 W, I, E

Welsh, R.B. *(Hawick)* 1967 I, E

White, D.B. *(Gala)* 1982 F, W, A 1, 2

White, D.M. *(Kelvinside Acads)* 1963 F, W, I, E

Whyte, D.J. *(Edinburgh Wands)* 1965 W, I, E, SA; 1966 F, W, I, E, A; 1967 F, W, I, E

Wilson, G.A. *(Oxford U)* 1949 F, W, E

Wilson, J.H. *(Watsonians)* 1953 I

Wilson, R. *(London Scottish)* 1976 E, I; 1977 E, I, F; 1978 I, F; 1981 R; 1983 I

Wilson, R.L. *(Gala)* 1951 F, W, I, E, SA; 1953 F, W, E

Wilson, S. *(Oxford U, London Scottish)* 1964 F, NZ, W, I, E; 1965 W, I, E, SA; 1966 F, W, I, A; 1967 F, W, I, E, NZ; 1968 F, W, I, E

Wright, R.W.J. *(Edinburgh Wands)* 1973 F

Wright, S.T.H. *(Stewart's Coll FP)* 1949 E

Wright, T. *(Hawick)* 1947 A

Wyllie, D.S. *(Stewart's-Melville FP)* 1984 A; 1985 W (r), E

Young, R.G. *(Watsonians)* 1970 W

Young, W.B. *(Cambridge U, London Scottish)* 1937 W, I, E; 1938 W, I, E; 1939 W, I, E; 1948 E

Wales

Ackerman, R.A. *(Newport, London Welsh)* 1980 NZ; 1981 E, S, A; 1982 I, F, E, S; 1983 S, I, F; 1984 S, I, F, E, A; 1985 S, I, F, E, Fi

Anthony, L. *(Neath)* 1948 E, S, F

Ashton, C. *(Aberavon)* 1959 E, S, I; 1960 E, S, I; 1962 I

Bebb, D.I.E. *(Carmarthen TC, Swansea)* 1959 E, S, I, F; 1960 E, S, I, F, SA; 1961 E, S, I, F; 1962 E, S, F, I; 1963 E, F, NZ; 1964 E, S, F, SA; 1965 E, S, I, F; 1966 F, A; 1967 S, I, F, E

Beckingham, G. *(Cardiff)* 1953 E, S; 1958 F

Bennett, P. *(Llanelli)* 1969 F (r); 1970 SA, S, F; 1972 S (r), NZ; 1973 E, S, I, F, A; 1974 S, I, F, E; 1975 S (r), I; 1976 E, S, I, F; 1977 I, F, E, S; 1978 E, S, I, F

Bergiers, R.T.E. *(Cardiff Coll of Ed, Llanelli)* 1972 E, S, F, NZ; 1973 E, S, I, F, A; 1974 E; 1975 I

Bevan, G. *(Llanelli)* 1947 E

Bevan, J.C. *(Cardiff, Cardiff Coll of Ed)* 1971 E, S, I, F; 1972 E, S, F, NZ; 1973 E, S

Bevan, J.D. *(Aberavon)* 1975 F, E, S, A

Bishop, D.J. *(Pontypool)* 1984 A

Blyth, L. *(Swansea)* 1951 SA; 1952 E, S

Blyth, W.R. *(Swansea)* 1974 E; 1975 S (r); 1980 F, E, S, I

Bowen, B. *(South Wales Police)* 1983 R; 1984 S; 1985 Fi; 1986 E, S, I, F

Brace, D.O. *(Llanelli, Oxford U)* 1956 E, S, I, F; 1957 E; 1960 S, I, F; 1961 I

Braddock, K.J. *(Newbridge)* 1966 A; 1967 S, I

Bradshaw, K. *(Bridgend)* 1964 E, S, I, F, SA; 1966 E, S, I, F

Brewer, T.J. *(Newport)* 1950 E; 1955 E, S

Britton, G. *(Newport)* 1961 S

Brown, M. *(Pontypool)* 1983 R; 1986 E, S

Burcher, D.H. *(Newport)* 1977 I, F, E, S

Burgess, R.C. *(Ebbw Vale)* 1977 I, F, E, S; 1981 I, F; 1982 F, E, S

Burnett, R. *(Newport)* 1953 E

Butler, E.T. *(Pontypool)* 1980 F, E, S, I, NZ (r); 1982 S; 1983 E, S, I, F, R; 1984 S, I, F, E, A

Cale, W.R. *(Newbridge, Pontypool)* 1949 E, S, I; 1950 E, S, I, F

Cleaver, W.B. *(Cardiff)* 1947 E, S, F, I, A; 1948 E, S, F; 1949 I; 1950 E, S, I, F

Clegg, B.G. *(Swansea)* 1979 F

Cobner, T.J. *(Pontypool)* 1974 S, I, F, E; 1975 F, E, S, I, A; 1976 E, S; 1977 F, E, S; 1978 E, S, I, F, A I

Coleman, E. *(Newport)* 1949 E, S, I

Coles, F.C. *(Pontypool)* 1960 S, I, F

Collins, J. *(Aberavon)* 1958 A, E, S, F; 1959 E, S, I; 1960 E; 1961 F

Cook, T. *(Cardiff)* 1949 S, I

Coslett, K. *(Aberavon)* 1962 E, S, F

Cresswell, B. *(Newport)* 1960 E, S, I, F

Cunningham, L.J. *(Aberavon)* 1960 E, S, I, F; 1962 E, S, I, F; 1963 NZ; 1964 E, S, I, F, SA

Dacey, M. *(Swansea)* 1983 E, S, I, F, R; 1984 S, I, F, E, A

Daniel, L.T.D. *(Newport)* 1970 S

Daniels, P.C.T. *(Cardiff)* 1981 A; 1982 I

David, T.P. *(Llanelli, Pontypridd)* 1973 F, A; 1976 I, F

Davidge, G.D. *(Newport)* 1959 F; 1960 S, I, F, SA; 1961 E, S, I; 1962 F

Davies, C.H.A. *(Llanelli, Cardiff)* 1957 I; 1958 A, E, S, I; 1960 SA; 1961 E

Davies, C.L. *(Cardiff)* 1956 E, S, I

Davies, C. *(Cardiff)* 1947 S, F, E, A; 1948 E, S, F, I; 1949 F; 1950 E, S, I, F; 1951 E, S, I

Davies, D.B. *(Llanelli)* 1962 I; 1963 E, S

Davies, D.J. *(Neath)* 1962 I

Davies, D.M *(Somerset Police)* 1950 E, S, I, F; 1951 E, S, I, F, SA; 1952 E, S, I, F; 1953 I, F, NZ; 1954 E

Davies, E. *(Aberavon)* 1947 A; 1948 I

Davies, G. *(Cambridge U, Pontypridd)* 1947 S, A; 1948 E, S, F, I; 1949 E, S, F; 1951 E, S

Davies, H. *(Bridgend)* 1984 S, I, F

Davies, H.J. *(Cambridge U, Aberavon)* 1959 E, S

Davies, J. *(Neath)* 1985 E, Fi; 1986 E, S, I, F

Davies, L. *(Llanelli)* 1954 F, S; 1955 I

Davies, L. *(Bridgend)* 1966 E, S, I

Davies, M. *(Swansea)* 1981 A; 1982 I; 1985 Fi

Davies, N.G. *(London Welsh)* 1955 E

Davies, P.T. *(Llanelli)* 1985 E, Fi; 1986 E, S, I, F

Davies, R.H. *(Oxford U, London Welsh)* 1957 S, I, F; 1958 A; 1962 E, S

Davies, T.J. *(Devonport Services, Swansea, Llanelli)* 1953 E, S, I, F; 1957 E, S, I, F; 1958 A, E, S, F; 1959 E, S, I, F; 1960 E, SA; 1961 E, S, F

Davies, T.G.R. *(Cardiff, London Welsh)* 1966 A; 1967 S, I, F, E; 1968 E, S; 1969 S, I, F, NZ 1, 2, A; 1971 E, S, I, F; 1972 E, S, F, NZ; 1973 E, S, I, F, A; 1974 S, F, E; 1975 F, E, S, I; 1976 E, S, I, F; 1977 I, F, E, S; 1978 E, S, I, A 1, 2

Davies, T.M. *(London Welsh, Swansea)* 1969 S, I, F, E, NZ 1, 2; 1970 SA, S, E, I, F; 1971 E, S, I, F; 1972 E, S, F, NZ; 1973 E, S, I, F, A; 1974 S, I, F, E; 1975 F, E, S, I, A; 1976 E, S, I, F

Davies, W.G. *(Cardiff)* 1978 A 1, 2, NZ; 1979 S, I, F, E; 1980 F, E, S, NZ; 1981 E, S, A; 1982 I, F, E, S; 1985 S, I, F

Davis, C.E. *(Newbridge)* 1978 A 2; 1981 E, S

Dawes, S.J. *(London Welsh)* 1964 I, F, SA; 1965 E, S, I, F; 1966 A; 1968 I, F; 1969 E, NZ 2, A; 1970 SA, S, E, I, F; 1971 E, S, I, F

Devereux, D. (*Neath*) 1958 *A, E, S*
Devereux, J.A. (*South Glamorgan Institute, Bridgend*) 1986 *E, S, I, F*
Donovan, A.J. (*Swansea*) 1978 *A 2;* 1981 *I (r), A;* 1982 *E, S*
Donovan, R. (*South Wales Police*) 1983 *F (r)*
Douglas, M.H.J. (*Llanelli*) 1984 *S, I, F*

Edwards, A.B. (*London Welsh, Army*) 1955 *E, S*
Edwards, B. (*Newport*) 1951 *I*
Edwards, G.O. (*Cardiff, Cardiff Coll of Ed*) 1967 *F, E, NZ;* 1968 *E, S, I, F;* 1969 *S, I, F, E, NZ 1, 2, A;* 1970 *SA, S, E, I, F;* 1971 *E, S, I, F;* 1972 *E, S, F, NZ;* 1973 *E, S, I, F, A;* 1974 *S, I, F, E;* 1975 *F, E, S, I, A;* 1976 *E, S, I, F;* 1977 *I, F, E, S;* 1978 *E, S, I, F*
Eidman, I.H. (*Cardiff*) 1983 *S, R;* 1984 *I, F, E, A;* 1985 *S, I, Fi;* 1986 *E, S, I, F*
Evans, C. (*Pontypool*) 1960 *E*
Evans, D.P. (*Llanelli*) 1960 *SA*
Evans, G. (*Cardiff*) 1947 *E, S, F, I, A;* 1948 *E, S, F, I;* 1949 *E, S, I*
Evans, G. (*Maesteg*) 1981 *S (r), I, F, A;* 1982 *I, F, E, S;* 1983 *F, R*
Evans, G.L. (*Newport*) 1977 *F (r);* 1978 *F, A 2 (r)*
Evans, J.D. (*Cardiff*) 1958 *I, F*
Evans, P. (*Llanelli*) 1951 *E, F*
Evans, R. (*Bridgend*) 1963 *S, I, F*
Evans, R.T. (*Newport*) 1947 *F, I;* 1950 *E, S, F;* 1951 *E, S, I, F*
Evans, S. (*Swansea*) 1985 *F, E*
Evans, T.G. (*London Welsh*) 1970 *SA, S, E, I;* 1972 *E, S, F*
Evans, T.P. (*Swansea*) 1975 *F, E, S, I, A;* 1976 *E, S, I, F;* 1977 *I*
Evans, V. (*Neath*) 1954 *I, F, S*
Evans, W. (*Llanelli*) 1958 *A*
Evans, W.J. (*Pontypool*) 1947 *S*
Evans, W.R. (*Bridgend*) 1958 *A, E, S, I, F;* 1960 *SA;* 1961 *E, S, I, F;* 1962 *E, S, I*

Faulkner, A.G. (*Pontypool*) 1975 *F, E, S, I, A;* 1976 *E, S, I, F;* 1978 *E, S, I, F, A 1, 2, NZ;* 1979 *S, I, F*
Faull, J. (*Swansea*) 1957 *I, F;* 1958 *A, E, S, I, F;* 1959 *E, S, I;* 1960 *E, F*
Fenwick, S.P. (*Bridgend*) 1975 *F, E, S, A;* 1976 *E, S, I, F;* 1977 *I, F, E, S;* 1978 *E, S, I, F, A 1, 2, NZ;* 1979 *S, I, F, E;* 1980 *F, E, S, I, NZ;* 1981 *E, S*
Finlayson, A.A.J. (*Cardiff*) 1974 *I, F, E*
Ford, I. (*Newport*) 1959 *E, S*
Forward, A. (*Pontypool, Monmouth Police*) 1951 *S, SA;* 1952 *E, S, I, F*

Gale, N.R. (*Swansea, Llanelli*) 1960 *I;* 1963 *E, S, I, NZ;* 1964 *E, S, I, F, SA;* 1965 *E, S, I, F;* 1966 *E, S, I, F, A;* 1967 *E, NZ;* 1968 *E;* 1969 *NZ 1 (r), 2, A*
Gallacher, I.S. (*Llanelli*) 1970 *F*
Giles, R. (*Aberavon*) 1983 *R;* 1985 *Fi (r)*
Gore, W. (*Newbridge*) 1947 *S, F, I*
Gravell, R.W.R. (*Llanelli*) 1975 *F, E, S, I, A;* 1976 *E, S, I, F;* 1978 *E, S, I, F, A 1, 2, NZ;* 1979 *S, I;* 1981 *I, F;* 1982 *F, E, S*
Gray, A.J. (*London Welsh*) 1968 *E, S*
Greenslade, D. (*Newport*) 1962 *S*
Greville, H. (*Llanelli*) 1947 *A*
Griffiths, C. (*Llanelli*) 1979 *E (r)*
Griffiths, G.M. (*Cardiff*) 1953 *E, S, I, F, NZ;* 1954 *I, F, S;* 1955 *I, F;* 1957 *E, S*
Gwilliam, J.A. (*Cambridge U, Newport*) 1947 *A;* 1948 *I;* 1949 *E, S, I, F;* 1950 *E, S, I, F;*

1951 *E, S, I, SA;* 1952 *E, S, I, F;* 1953 *E, I, F, NZ;* 1954 *E*

Hadley, A.M. (*Cardiff*) 1983 *R;* 1984 *S, I, F, E;* 1985 *F, E, Fi;* 1986 *E, S, I, F*
Hall, I. (*Aberavon*) 1967 *NZ;* 1970 *SA, S, E;* 1971 *S;* 1974 *S, I, F*
Harris, D.J.E. (*Pontypridd, Cardiff*) 1959 *I, F;* 1960 *S, I, F, SA;* 1961 *E, S*
Hayward, D. (*Newbridge*) 1949 *E, F;* 1950 *E, S, I, F;* 1951 *E, S, I, F, SA;* 1952 *E, S, I, F*
Hayward, D.J. (*Cardiff*) 1963 *E, NZ;* 1964 *S, I, F, SA*
Hodgson, G.T.R. (*Neath*) 1962 *I;* 1963 *E, S, I, F, NZ;* 1964 *E, S, I, F, SA;* 1966 *S, I, F;* 1967 *I*
Holmes, T.D. (*Cardiff*) 1978 *A 2, NZ;* 1979 *S, I, F, E;* 1980 *F, E, S, I, NZ;* 1981 *A;* 1982 *I, F, E;* 1983 *E, S, I, F;* 1984 *E;* 1985 *S, I, F, E, Fi*
Hopkins, K. (*Cardiff*) 1985 *E*
Hopkins, R. (*Maesteg*) 1970 *E (r)*
Howells, G. (*Llanelli*) 1957 *E, S, I, F*
Hughes, D. (*Newbridge*) 1967 *NZ;* 1969 *NZ 2;* 1970 *SA, S, E, I*
Hughes, K. (*Cambridge U, London Welsh*) 1970 *I;* 1973 *A;* 1974 *S*
Hullin, W. (*Cardiff*) 1967 *S*
Hurrell, J. (*Newport*) 1959 *F*

James, B. (*Bridgend*) 1968 *E*
James, C.R. (*Llanelli*) 1958 *A, F*
James, M. (*Cardiff*) 1947 *A;* 1948 *E, S, F, I*
James, W.J. (*Aberavon*) 1983 *E, S, I, F, R;* 1984 *S;* 1985 *S, I, F, E, Fi;* 1986 *E, S, I, F*
Jarrett, K.S. (*Newport*) 1967 *E;* 1968 *E, S;* 1969 *S, I, F, E, NZ 1, 2, A*
Jeffery, J.J. (*Cardiff Coll of Ed, Newport*) 1967 *NZ*
Jenkins, L. (*Monmouth TC, Newport*) 1954 *I;* 1956 *E, S, I, F*
John, B. (*Llanelli, Cardiff*) 1966 *A;* 1967 *S, NZ;* 1968 *E, S, I, F;* 1969 *S, I, F, E, NZ 1, 2, A;* 1970 *SA, S, E, I;* 1971 *E, S, I, F;* 1972 *E, S, F*
John, E.R. (*Neath*) 1950 *E, S, I, F;* 1951 *E, S, I, F, SA;* 1952 *E, S, I, F;* 1953 *E, S, I, F, NZ;* 1954 *E*
John, G. (*St Luke's Coll, Exeter*) 1954 *E, F*
Johnson, W.D. (*Swansea*) 1953 *E*
Jones, B.J. (*Newport*) 1960 *I, F*
Jones, B.L. (*Devonport Services, Llanelli*) 1950 *E, S, I, F;* 1951 *E, S, SA;* 1952 *E, I, F*
Jones, D. (*Swansea*) 1947 *E, F, I;* 1949 *E, S, I, F*
Jones, D. (*Llanelli*) 1948 *E*
Jones, D.K. (*Llanelli, Cardiff*) 1962 *E, S, F, I;* 1963 *E, F, NZ;* 1964 *S, SA;* 1966 *E, S, I, F*
Jones, G. (*Ebbw Vale*) 1963 *S, I, F*
Jones, I.C. (*London Welsh*) 1968 *I*
Jones, K.D. (*Cardiff*) 1960 *SA;* 1961 *E, S, I;* 1962 *E, F;* 1963 *E, S, I, NZ*
Jones, K.J. (*Newport*) 1947 *E, S, F, I, A;* 1948 *E, S, F, I;* 1949 *E, S, I, F;* 1950 *E, S, I, F;* 1951 *E, S, I, F, SA;* 1952 *E, S, I, F;* 1953 *E, S, I, F, NZ;* 1954 *I, F, S;* 1955 *E, S, I, F;* 1956 *S, I, F;* 1957 *S*
Jones, R.E. (*Coventry*) 1967 *F;* 1968 *S, I, F*
Jones, R. N. (*Swansea*) 1986 *E, S, I, F*
Jones, S.T. (*Pontypool*) 1983 *S, I, F, R;* 1984 *S*
Jones, W.K. (*Cardiff*) 1967 *NZ;* 1968 *E, S, I, F*
Judd, S. (*Cardiff*) 1953 *E, S, I, F, NZ;* 1954 *E, F, S;* 1955 *E, S*

Keen, L. (*Aberavon*) 1980 *F, E, S, I*
Knill, F.M.D. (*Cardiff*) 1976 *F (r)*

Lane, S.M. (*Cardiff*) 1978 *A 1 (r), 2;* 1979 *I(r);* 1980 *S, I*
Leleu, J. (*London Welsh, Swansea*) 1959 *E, S;* 1960 *F, SA*
Lewis, A.J. (*Ebbw Vale*) 1970 *F;* 1971 *E, I, F;* 1972 *E, F;* 1973 *E, S, I, F*
Lewis, A.R. (*Abertillery*) 1966 *E, S, I, F, A;* 1967 *I*
Lewis, G.W. (*Richmond*) 1960 *E, S*
Lewis, J.R. (*South Glamorgan Institute, Cardiff*) 1981 *E, S, I, F;* 1982 *F, E, S*
Lewis, P.I. (*Llanelli*) 1984 *A;* 1985 *S, I, F, E*
Llewellyn, P.D. (*Swansea*) 1973 *I, F, A;* 1974 *S, E*
Llewelyn, D.B. (*Newport, Llanelli*) 1970 *SA, S, E, I, F;* 1971 *E, S, I, F;* 1972 *E, S, F, NZ*
Lloyd, D.J. (*Bridgend*) 1966 *E, S, I, F, A;* 1967 *S, I, F, E;* 1968 *S, I, F;* 1969 *S, I, F, E, NZ 1, A;* 1970 *F;* 1972 *E, S, F;* 1973 *E, S*
Lloyd, T. (*Maesteg*) 1953 *I, F*

Maddocks, K. (*Neath*) 1957 *E*
Main, D.R. (*London Welsh*) 1959 *E, S, I, F*
Mainwaring, H.J. (*Swansea*) 1961 *F*
Mainwaring, W.T. (*Aberavon*) 1967 *S, I, F, E, NZ;* 1968 *E*
Major, W. (*Maesteg*) 1949 *F;* 1950 *S*
Mantle, J.T. (*Loughborough Colls, Newport*) 1964 *E, SA*
Martin, A.J. (*Aberavon*) 1973 *A;* 1974 *S, I;* 1975 *F, E, S, I, A;* 1976 *E, S, I, F;* 1977 *I, F, E, S;* 1978 *E, S, I, F, A 1, 2, NZ;* 1979 *S, I, F, E;* 1980 *F, E, S, I, NZ;* 1981 *I, F*
Mathias, R. (*Llanelli*) 1970 *F*
Matthews, J. (*Cardiff*) 1947 *E, A;* 1948 *E, S, F;* 1949 *E, S, I, F;* 1950 *E, S, I, F;* 1951 *E, S, I, F*
Meredith, A. (*Devonport Services*) 1949 *E, S, I*
Meredith, B.V. (*St Luke's Coll, London Welsh, Newport*) 1954 *I, F, S;* 1955 *E, S, I, F;* 1956 *E, S, I, F;* 1957 *E, S, I, F;* 1958 *A, E, S, I;* 1959 *E, S, I, F;* 1960 *E, S, F, SA;* 1961 *E, S, I;* 1962 *E, S, F, I*
Meredith, C.C. (*Neath*) 1953 *S, NZ;* 1954 *E, I, F, S;* 1955 *E, S, I, F;* 1956 *E, I;* 1957 *E, S*
Michaelson, R.C.B. (*Aberavon, Cambridge U*) 1963 *E*
Morgan, C.H. (*Llanelli*) 1957 *I, F*
Morgan, C.I. (*Cardiff*) 1951 *I, F, SA;* 1952 *E, S, I;* 1953 *S, I, F, NZ;* 1954 *E, I, S;* 1955 *S, I, F;* 1956 *E, S, I, F;* 1957 *E, S, I, F;* 1958 *E, S, I, F*
Morgan, D.R. (*Llanelli*) 1962 *E, S, F, I;* 1963 *E, S, I, F, NZ*
Morgan, H.J. (*Abertillery*) 1958 *E, S, I, F;* 1959 *I, F;* 1960 *E;* 1961 *E, S, I, F;* 1962 *E, F, I;* 1963 *S, I, F;* 1965 *E, S, I, F;* 1966 *E, S, I, F, A*
Morgan, H.P. (*Newport*) 1956 *E, S, I, F*
Morgan, N. (*Newport*) 1960 *S, I, F*
Morgan, P. (*Aberavon*) 1961 *E, S, F*
Morgan, P.J. (*Llanelli*) 1980 *S (r), I, NZ (r);* 1981 *I*
Morgan, R. (*Newport*) 1984 *S*
Moriarty, R.D. (*Swansea*) 1981 *A;* 1982 *I, F, E, S;* 1983 *E;* 1984 *S, I, F, E;* 1985 *S, I, F*
Moriarty, W.P. (*Swansea*) 1986 *I, F*
Morris, H.T. (*Cardiff*) 1951 *F;* 1955 *I, F*
Morris, M.S. (*South Wales Police*) 1985 *S, I, F*
Morris, W.D. (*Neath*) 1967 *F, E;* 1968 *E, S, I,*

F; 1969 S, I, F, E, NZ 1, 2, A; 1970 SA, S, E, I, F; 1971 E, S, I, F; 1972 E, S, F, NZ; 1973 E, S, I, A; 1974 S, I, F, E
Morris, W.J. (*Newport*) 1965 S; 1966 F
Morris, W.J. (*Pontypool*) 1963 S, I

Nash, D. (*Ebbw Vale*) 1960 SA; 1961 E, S, I, F; 1962 F
Nicholas, D.L. (*Llanelli*) 1981 E, S, I, F
Nicholls, H. (*Cardiff*) 1958 I
Norris, C.H. (*Cardiff*) 1963 F; 1966 F
Norster, R.L. (*Cardiff*) 1982 S; 1983 E, S, I, F; 1984 S, I, F, E, A; 1985 S, I, F, E, Fi

O'Connor, A. (*Aberavon*) 1960 SA; 1961 E, S; 1962 F, I
O'Connor, R. (*Aberavon*) 1957 E
O'Shea, J.P. (*Cardiff*) 1967 S, I; 1968 S, I, F
Owen, G. (*Newport*) 1955 I, F; 1956 E, S, I, F

Pask, A.E.I. (*Abertillery*) 1961 F; 1962 E, S, F, I; 1963 E, S, I, F, NZ; 1964 E, S, I, F, SA; 1965 E, S, I, F; 1966 S, I, F, E, A; 1967 S, I, F
Payne, G.W. (*Army, Pontypridd*) 1960 E, S, I
Pearce, G.P. (*Bridgend*) 1981 I, F; 1982 I (r)
Perkins, S.J. (*Pontypool*) 1983 S, I, F, R; 1984 S, I, F, E, A; 1985 S, I, F, E, Fi; 1986 E, S, I, F
Perrins, V.C. (*Newport*) 1970 SA, S
Phillips, A.J. (*Cardiff*) 1979 E; 1980 F, E, S, I, NZ; 1981 E, S, I, F, A; 1982 I, F, E, S
Phillips, H. (*Swansea*) 1952 F
Pickering, D.F. (*Llanelli*) 1983 E, S, I, F, R; 1984 S, I, F, E, A; 1985 S, I, F, E, Fi; 1986 E, S, I, F
Powell, G. (*Ebbw Vale*) 1957 I, F
Price, B. (*Newport*) 1961 I, F; 1962 E, S; 1963 E, S, F, NZ; 1964 E, S, I, F, SA; 1965 E, S, I, F; 1966 E, S, I, F, A; 1967 S, I, F, E; 1969 S, I, F, NZ 1, 2, A
Price, G. (*Pontypool*) 1975 F, E, S, I, A; 1976 E, S, I, F; 1977 I, F, E, S; 1978 E, S, I, F, A 1, 2, NZ; 1979 S, I, F, E; 1980 F, E, S, I, NZ; 1981 E, S, I, F, A; 1982 I, F, E, S; 1983 E, I, F
Price, M.J. (*Pontypool, RAF*) 1959 E, S, I, F; 1960 E, S, I, F; 1962 E
Price, T.G. (*Llanelli*) 1965 E, S, I, F; 1966 E, A; 1967 S, F
Priday, A.J. (*Cardiff*) 1958 I; 1961 I
Prosser, R. (*Pontypool*) 1956 S, F; 1957 E, S, I, F; 1958 A, S, I, F; 1959 E, S, I, F; 1960 E, S, I, F, SA; 1961 I, F
Prothero, G.J. (*Bridgend*) 1964 S, I, F; 1965 E, S, I, F; 1966 E, S, I, F

Quinnell, D.L. (*Llanelli*) 1972 F (r), NZ; 1973 E, S, A; 1974 S, F; 1975 E (r); 1977 I (r), F, E, S; 1978 E, S, I, F, A 1, NZ; 1979 S, I, F, E; 1980 NZ

Raybould, W.H. (*London Welsh, Cambridge U, Newport*) 1967 S, I, F, E, NZ; 1968 I, F; 1970 SA, E, I, F (r)
Rees, A. (*Maesteg*) 1962 E, S, F
Rees, B.I. (*London Welsh*) 1967 S, I, F
Rees, C.F.W. (*London Welsh*) 1974 I; 1975 A; 1978 NZ; 1981 F; 1982 I, F, E, S; 1983 E, S, I, F
Rees, D. (*Swansea*) 1968 S, I, F
Rees, H.E. (*Neath*) 1979 S, I, F, E; 1980 F, E, S, I, NZ; 1983 E, S, I, F
Rees, P. (*Llanelli*) 1947 F, I
Rees, P.M. (*Newport*) 1961 E, S, I; 1964 I

Richards, B. (*Swansea*) 1960 F
Richards, D.S. (*Swansea*) 1979 F, E; 1980 F, E, S, I, NZ; 1981 E, S, I, F; 1982 I, F; 1983 E, S, I, R (r)
Richards, K. (*Bridgend*) 1960 SA; 1961 E, S, I, F
Richards, M.C.R. (*Cardiff*) 1968 I, F; 1969 S, I, F, E, NZ 1, 2, A
Richards, R. (*Cross Keys*) 1956 I
Richardson, S.J. (*Aberavon*) 1978 A 2 (r); 1979 E
Ring, M.G. (*Cardiff*) 1983 E; 1984 A; 1985 S, I, F
Ringer, P. (*Ebbw Vale, Llanelli*) 1978 NZ; 1979 S, I, F, E; 1980 F, E, NZ
Roberts, C. (*Neath*) 1958 I, F
Roberts, G.J. (*Cardiff*) 1985 F (r), E
Roberts, H.M. (*Cardiff*) 1960 SA; 1961 E, S, I, F; 1962 S, F; 1963 I
Roberts, M.G. (*London Welsh*) 1971 E, S, F; 1973 I, F; 1975 S; 1979 E
Robins, J.D. (*Birkenhead Park*) 1950 E, S, I, F; 1951 E, S, I, F; 1953 E, I, F
Robins, R.J. (*Pontypridd*) 1953 S; 1954 F, S; 1955 E, S, I, F; 1956 E, F; 1957 E, S, I, F
Robinson, I.R. (*Cardiff*) 1974 F, E
Rowlands, D.C.T. (*Pontypool*) 1963 E, S, I, F, NZ; 1964 E, S, I, F, SA; 1965 E, S, I, F
Rowlands, G. (*RAF, Cardiff*) 1953 NZ; 1954 E, F; 1956 F
Rowlands, K.A. (*Cardiff*) 1962 F, I; 1963 I; 1965 I, F

Shanklin, J.L. (*London Welsh*) 1970 F; 1972 NZ; 1973 I, F
Shaw, G. (*Neath*) 1972 NZ; 1973 E, S, I, F, A; 1974 S, I, F, E; 1977 I, F
Shaw, T.W. (*Newbridge*) 1983 R
Shell, R.C. (*Aberavon*) 1973 A (r)
Sparks, B. (*Neath*) 1954 I; 1955 E, F; 1956 E, S, I; 1957 S
Squire, J. (*Newport, Pontypool*) 1977 I, F; 1978 E, S, I, F, A 1, NZ; 1979 S, I, F, E; 1980 F, E, S, I, NZ; 1981 E, S, I, F, A; 1982 I, F, E; 1983 E, S, I, F
Stephens, I. (*Bridgend*) 1981 E, S, I, F, A; 1982 I, F, E, S; 1984 I, F, E, A
Stephens, J.R.G. (*Neath*) 1947 E, S, F, I; 1948 I; 1949 E, S, I, F; 1951 F, SA; 1952 E, S, I, F; 1953 E, S, I, F, NZ; 1954 E, I; 1955 E, S, I, F; 1956 S, I, F; 1957 E, S, I, F
Stone, P. (*Llanelli*) 1949 F
Sutton, S. (*Pontypool*) 1982 F, E

Tamplin, W.E. (*Cardiff*) 1947 S, F, I, A; 1948 E, S, F
Taylor, J. (*London Welsh*) 1967 S, I, F, E, NZ; 1968 I, F; 1969 S, I, F, E, NZ 1, A; 1970 F; 1971 E, S, I, F; 1972 E, S, F, NZ; 1973 E, S, I, F
Thomas, A. (*Newport*) 1963 NZ; 1964 E
Thomas, A.G. (*Swansea, Cardiff*) 1952 E, S, I, F; 1953 S, I, F; 1954 E, I, F; 1955 S, I, F
Thomas, B. (*Neath, Cambridge U*) 1963 E, S, I, F, NZ; 1964 E, S, I, F, SA; 1965 E; 1966 E, S, I; 1967 NZ; 1969 S, I, F, E, NZ 1, 2
Thomas, D. (*Aberavon*) 1961 I
Thomas, D. (*Llanelli*) 1954 I
Thomas, M.C. (*Newport, Devonport Services*) 1949 F; 1950 E, S, I, F; 1951 E, S, I, F, SA; 1952 E, S, I, F; 1953 F; 1956 E, S, I, F; 1957 E, S; 1958 E, S, I, F; 1959 I, F
Thomas, R.C. (*Swansea*) 1949 F; 1952 I, F; 1953 S, I, F, NZ; 1954 E, I, F, S; 1955 S, I;

1956 E, S, I; 1957 E; 1958 A, E, S, I, F; 1959 E, S, I, F
Thomas, W.D. (*Llanelli*) 1966 A; 1968 S, I, F; 1969 E, NZ 2, A; 1970 SA, S, E, I, F; 1971 E, S, I, F; 1972 E, S, F, NZ; 1973 E, S, I, F; 1974 E
Thorburn, P.H. (*Neath*) 1985 F, E, Fi; 1986 E, S, I, F
Titley, M.H. (*Bridgend, Swansea*) 1983 R; 1984 S, I, F, E, A; 1985 S, I, Fi; 1986 F
Trott, R.F. (*Cardiff*) 1948 E, S, F, I; 1949 E, S, I, F

Uzzell, J. (*Newport*) 1963 NZ; 1965 E, S, I, F

Waldron, R. (*Neath*) 1965 E, S, I, F
Wanbon, R. (*Aberavon*) 1968 E
Warlow, J. (*Llanelli*) 1962 I
Waters, D.R. (*Newport*) 1986 E, S, I, F
Watkins, D. (*Newport*) 1963 E, S, I, F, NZ; 1964 E, S, I, F, SA; 1965 E, S, I, F; 1966 E, S, I, F; 1967 I, F, E
Watkins, M.J. (*Newport*) 1984 I, F, E, A
Watkins, S.J. (*Newport, Cardiff*) 1964 S, I, F; 1965 E, S, I, F; 1966 E, S, I, F; 1967 S, I, F, E, NZ; 1968 E, S; 1969 S, I, F, E, NZ 1; 1970 E, I
Watkins, W. (*Newport*) 1959 F
Weaver, D. (*Swansea*) 1964 E
Wells, G. (*Cardiff*) 1955 E, S; 1957 I, F; 1958 A, E, S
Wheel, G.A.D. (*Swansea*) 1974 I, E (r); 1975 F, E, I, A; 1976 E, S, I, F; 1977 I, E, S; 1978 E, S, I, F, A 1, 2, NZ; 1979 S, I; 1980 F, E, S, I; 1981 E, S, I, F, A; 1982 I
Wheeler, P.J. (*Aberavon*) 1967 NZ; 1968 E
Whitefoot, J. (*Cardiff*) 1984 A (r); 1985 S, I, F, E, Fi; 1986 E, S, I, F
Williams, B.L. (*Cardiff*) 1947 E, S, F, I, A; 1948 E, S, F, I; 1949 E, S, I; 1951 I, SA; 1952 S; 1953 E, S, I, F, NZ; 1954 S; 1955 E
Williams, C. (*Aberavon, Swansea*) 1977 E, S; 1980 F, E, S, I, NZ; 1983 E
Williams, C.D. (*Cardiff, Neath*) 1955 F; 1956 F
Williams, D. (*Ebbw Vale*) 1963 E, S, I, F; 1964 E, S, I, F, SA; 1965 E, S, I, F; 1966 E, S, I, A; 1967 F, E, NZ; 1968 E; 1969 S, I, F, E, NZ 1, 2, A; 1970 SA, S, E, I; 1971 E, S, I, F
Williams, D.B. (*Newport, Swansea*) 1978 A 1; 1981 E, S
Williams, G. (*London Welsh*) 1950 I, F; 1951 E, S, I, F, SA; 1952 E, S, I, F; 1953 NZ; 1954 E
Williams, G. (*Bridgend*) 1981 I, F; 1982 E (r), S
Williams, G.P. (*Bridgend*) 1980 NZ; 1981 E, S, A; 1982 I
Williams, J.J. (*Llanelli*) 1973 F (r), A; 1974 S, I, F, E; 1975 F, E, S, I, A; 1976 E, S, I, F; 1977 I, F, E, S; 1978 E, S, I, F, A 1, 2, NZ; 1979 S, I, F, E
Williams, J.P.R. (*London Welsh, Bridgend*) 1969 S, I, F, E, NZ 1, 2, A; 1970 SA, S, E, I, F; 1971 E, S, I, F; 1972 E, S, F, NZ; 1973 E, S, I, F, A; 1974 S, I, F; 1975 F, E, S, I, A; 1976 E, S, I, F; 1977 I, F, E, S; 1978 E, S, I, F, A 1, 2, NZ; 1979 S, I, F, E; 1980 NZ; 1981 E, S
Williams, L. (*Cardiff*) 1957 S, I, F; 1958 E, S, I, F; 1959 E, S, I; 1961 F; 1962 E, S
Williams, L. (*Llanelli, Cardiff*) 1947 E, S, F, I, A; 1948 I; 1949 E
Williams, O. (*Llanelli*) 1947 E, S, A; 1948 E, S, F, I

Williams, R. (*Llanelli*) 1954 *S;* 1957 *F;* 1958 *A*

Williams, R.H. (*Llanelli*) 1954 *I, F, S;* 1955 *S, I, F;* 1956 *E, S, I;* 1957 *E, S, I, F;* 1958 *A, E, S, I, F;* 1959 *E, S, I, F;* 1960 *E*

Williams, S. (*Llanelli*) 1947 *E, S, F, I;* 1948 *S, F*

Williams, W.A. (*Newport*) 1952 *I, F;* 1953 *E*

Williams, W.O.G. (*Swansea, Devonport*

Services) 1951 *F, SA;* 1952 *E, S, I, F;* 1953 *E, S, I, F, NZ;* 1954 *E, I, F, S;* 1955 *E, S, I, F;* 1956 *E, S, I*

Williams, W.P.J. (*Neath*) 1974 *I, F*

Willis, W.R. (*Cardiff*) 1950 *E, S, I, F;* 1951 *E, S, I, F, SA;* 1952 *E, S;* 1953 *S, NZ;* 1954 *E, I, F, S;* 1955 *E, S, I, F*

Wiltshire, M.L. (*Aberavon*) 1967 *NZ;* 1968 *E, S, F*

Windsor, R.W. (*Pontypool*) 1973 *A;* 1974 *S, I, F, E;* 1975 *F, E, S, I, A;* 1976 *E, S, I, F;* 1977 *I, F, E, S;* 1978 *E, S, I, F, A 1, 2, NZ;* 1979 *S, I, F*

Young, J. (*Harrogate, RAF, London Welsh*) 1968 *S, I, F;* 1969 *S, I, F, E, NZ 1;* 1970 *E, I, F;* 1971 *E, S, I, F;* 1972 *E, S, F, NZ;* 1973 *E, S, I, F*

British Isles

Figures in brackets indicate the number of Internationals played on each tour. No figure in brackets denotes only one match played.

Ackerman, R.A. (*London Welsh, Wales*) 1983 *NZ (2[1r])*

Arneil, R.J. (*Edinburgh Acads, Scotland*) 1968 *SA (4)*

Ashcroft, A. (*Waterloo, England*) 1959 *A, NZ*

Bainbridge, S.J. (*Gosforth, England*) 1983 *NZ (2)*

Baird, G.R.T. (*Kelso, Scotland*) 1983 *NZ (4)*

Baker, D.G.S. (*Old Merchant Taylors, England*) 1955 *SA (2)*

Beattie, J.R. (*Glasgow Acads, Scotland*) 1983 *NZ (r)*

Beaumont, W.B. (*Fylde, England*) 1977 *NZ (3);* 1980 *SA (4)*

Bebb, D.I.E. (*Swansea, Wales*) 1962 *SA (2);* 1966 *A (2), NZ (4)*

Bennett, P. (*Llanelli, Wales*) 1974 *SA (4);* 1977 *NZ (4)*

Bevan, J.C. (*Cardiff Coll of Ed, Cardiff, Wales*) 1971 *NZ*

Black, A.W. (*Edinburgh U, Scotland*) 1950 *NZ (2)*

Bresnihan, F.P.K. (*UC Dublin, Ireland*) 1968 *SA (3)*

Brophy, N.H. (*UC Dublin, Ireland*) 1962 *SA (2)*

Brown, G.L. (*W of Scotland, Scotland*) 1971 *NZ (2);* 1974 *SA (3);* 1977 *NZ (3)*

Budge, G.M. (*Edinburgh Wands, Scotland*) 1950 *NZ*

Burcher, D.H. (*Newport, Wales*) 1977 *NZ*

Butterfield, J. (*Northampton, England*) 1955 *SA (4)*

Calder, J.H. (*Stewart's-Melville FP, Scotland*) 1983 *NZ*

Cameron, A. (*Glasgow HSFP, Scotland*) 1955 *SA (2)*

Campbell, S.O. (*Old Belvedere, Ireland*) 1980 *SA (3[1r]);* 1983 *NZ (4)*

Campbell-Lamerton, M.J. (*Halifax, Army, Scotland*) 1962 *SA (4);* 1966 *A (2), NZ (2)*

Carleton, J. (*Orrell, England*) 1980 *SA (3);* 1983 *NZ (3)*

Cleaver, W.B. (*Cardiff, Wales*) 1950 *NZ (3)*

Clifford, T. (*Young Munster, Ireland*) 1950 *NZ (3), A (2)*

Cobner, T.J. (*Pontypool, Wales*) 1977 *NZ (3)*

Colclough, M.J. (*Angoulême, England*) 1980 *SA (4);* 1983 *NZ (4)*

Connell, G.C. (*Trinity Acads, Scotland*) 1968 *SA*

Cotton, F.E. (*Loughborough Colls, Coventry, England*) 1974 *SA (4);* 1977 *NZ (3)*

Coulman, M.J. (*Moseley, England*) 1968 *SA*

Cowan, R.C. (*Selkirk, Scotland*) 1962 *SA*

Davies, C. (*Cardiff, Wales*) 1950 *NZ*

Davies, D.M. (*Somerset Police, Wales*) 1950 *NZ (2), A*

Davies, T.G.R. (*Cardiff, London Welsh, Wales*) 1968 *SA;* 1971 *NZ (4)*

Davies, T.J. (*Llanelli, Wales*) 1959 *NZ (2)*

Davies, T.M. (*London Welsh, Swansea, Wales*) 1971 *NZ (4);* 1974 *SA (4)*

Davies, W.G. (*Cardiff, Wales*) 1980 *SA*

Davies, W.P.C. (*Harlequins, England*) 1955 *SA (3)*

Dawes, S.J. (*London Welsh, Wales*) 1971 *NZ (4)*

Dawson, A.R. (*Wanderers, Ireland*) 1959 *A (2), NZ (4)*

Dixon, P.J. (*Harlequins, England*) 1971 *NZ (3)*

Dodge, P.W. (*Leicester, England*) 1980 *SA (2)*

Doyle, M.G. (*Blackrock Coll, Ireland*) 1968 *SA*

Duckham, D.J. (*Coventry, England*) 1971 *NZ (3)*

Duggan, W.P. (*Blackrock Coll, Ireland*) 1977 *NZ (4)*

Edwards, G.O. (*Cardiff, Wales*) 1968 *SA (2);* 1971 *NZ (4);* 1974 *SA (4)*

Evans, G. (*Maesteg, Wales*) 1983 *NZ (2)*

Evans, G.L. (*Newport, Wales*) 1977 *NZ (3)*

Evans, R.T. (*Newport, Wales*) 1950 *NZ (4), A (2)*

Evans, T.P. (*Swansea, Wales*) 1977 *NZ*

Evans, W.R. (*Cardiff, Wales*) 1959 *A, NZ (3)*

Faull, J. (*Swansea, Wales*) 1959 *A, NZ (3)*

Fenwick, S.P. (*Bridgend, Wales*) 1977 *NZ (4)*

Fitzgerald, C.F. (*St Mary's Coll, Ireland*) 1983 *NZ (4)*

Gibson, C.M.H. (*Cambridge U, NIFC, Ireland*) 1966 *NZ (4);* 1968 *SA (4[1r]);* 1971 *NZ (4)*

Gravell, R.W.R. (*Llanelli, Wales*) 1980 *SA (4[1r])*

Greenwood, J.T. (*Dunfermline, Scotland*) 1955 *SA (4)*

Griffiths, G.M. (*Cardiff, Wales*) 1955 *SA (3)*

Hay, B.H. (*Boroughmuir, Scotland*) 1980 *SA (3)*

Hayward, D.J. (*Newbridge, Wales*) 1950 *NZ (3)*

Henderson, N.J. (*Queen's U, Belfast, NIFC, Ireland*) 1950 *NZ*

Hewitt, D. (*Queen's U, Belfast, Instonians, Ireland*) 1959 *A (2), NZ (3);* 1962 *SA*

Higgins, R. (*Liverpool, England*) 1955 *SA*

Hinshelwood, A.J.W. (*London Scottish, Scotland*) 1966 *NZ (2);* 1968 *SA*

Holmes, T.D. (*Cardiff, Wales*) 1983 *NZ*

Hopkins, R. (*Maesteg, Wales*) 1971 *NZ (r)*

Horrocks-Taylor, J.P. (*Leicester, England*) 1959 *NZ*

Horton, A.L. (*Blackheath, England*) 1968 *SA (3)*

Irvine, A.R. (*Heriot's FP, Scotland*) 1974 *SA (2);* 1977 *NZ (4);* 1980 *SA (3)*

Irwin, D.G. (*Instonians, Ireland*) 1983 *NZ (3)*

Jackson, P.B. (*Coventry, England*) 1959 *A (2), NZ (3)*

Jeeps, R.E.G. (*Northampton, England*) 1955 *SA (4);* 1959 *A (2), NZ (3);* 1962 *SA (4)*

John, B. (*Cardiff, Wales*) 1968 *SA;* 1971 *NZ (4)*

John, E.R. (*Neath, Wales*) 1950 *NZ (4), A (2)*

Jones, B.L. (*Devonport Services, Llanelli, Wales*) 1950 *NZ, A (2)*

Jones, D.K. (*Llanelli, Cardiff, Wales*) 1962 *SA (3);* 1966 *A (2), NZ*

Jones, K.D. (*Cardiff, Wales*) 1962 *SA (4)*

Jones, K.J. (*Newport, Wales*) 1950 *NZ (3)*

Jones, S.T. (*Pontypool, Wales*) 1983 *NZ (3)*

Keane, M.I. (*Lansdowne, Ireland*) 1977 *NZ*

Kennedy, K.W. (*CIYMS, London Irish, Ireland*) 1966 *A (2), NZ (2)*

Kiernan, M.J. (*Dolphin, Ireland*) 1983 *NZ (3)*

Kiernan, T.J. (*Cork Constitution, Ireland*) 1962 *SA;* 1968 *SA (4)*

Kininmonth, P.W. (*Oxford U, Richmond, Scotland*) 1950 *NZ (3)*

Kyle, J.W. (*Queen's U, Belfast, NIFC, Ireland*) 1950 *NZ (4), A (2)*

Laidlaw, F.A.L. (*Melrose, Scotland*) 1966 *NZ (2)*

Laidlaw, R.J. (*Jed-Forest, Scotland*) 1983 *NZ (4[1r])*

Lamont, R.A. (*Instonians, Ireland*) 1966 *NZ (4)*

Lane, M.F. (*UC Cork, Ireland*) 1950 *NZ, A*

Larter, P.J. (*Northampton, RAF, England*) 1968 *SA*

Lewis, A.R. (*Abertillery, Wales*) 1966 *NZ (3)*

Lynch, J.F. (*St Mary's Coll, Ireland*) 1971 *NZ (4)*

McBride, W.J. (*Ballymena, Ireland*) 1962 *SA (2);* 1966 *NZ (3);* 1968 *SA (4);* 1971 *NZ (4);* 1974 *SA (4)*

Macdonald, R. (*Edinburgh U, Scotland*) 1950 *NZ, A*

McFadyean, C.W. (*Moseley, England*) 1966 *NZ (4)*

McGeechan, I.R. (*Headingley, Scotland*) 1974 *SA (4);* 1977 *NZ (4[1r])*

McKay, J.W. (*Queen's U, Belfast, Ireland*) 1950 *NZ (4), A (2)*

McLauchlan, J. (*Jordanhill, Scotland*) 1971
NZ (4); 1974 SA (4)
McLeod, H.F. (*Hawick, Scotland*) 1959 A (2),
NZ (4)
McLoughlin, R.J. (*Gosforth, Blackrock Coll,
Ireland*) 1966 A (2), NZ
MacNeill, H.P. (*Oxford U, Ireland*) 1983 NZ
(3[1r])
Marques, R.W.D. (*Harlequins, England*)
1959 A, NZ
Martin, A.J. (*Aberavon, Wales*) 1977 NZ
Matthews, J. (*Cardiff, Wales*) 1950 NZ (4), A
(2)
Meredith, B.V. (*Newport, Wales*) 1955 SA
(4); 1962 SA (4)
Meredith, C.C. (*Neath, Wales*) 1955 SA (4)
Millar, S. (*Ballymena, Ireland*) 1959 A (2),
NZ; 1962 SA (4); 1968 SA (2)
Milliken, R.A. (*Bangor, Ireland*) 1974 SA (4)
Morgan, C.I. (*Cardiff, Wales*) 1955 SA (4)
Morgan, D.W. (*Stewart's-Melville FP,
Scotland*) 1977 NZ (2[1r])
Morgan, H.J. (*Abertillery, Wales*) 1959 NZ
(2); 1962 SA (2)
Mulcahy, W.A. (*U C Dublin, Ireland*) 1959 A,
NZ; 1962 SA (4)
Mullen, K.D. (*Old Belvedere, Ireland*) 1950
NZ (2), A
Mulligan, A.A. (*Wanderers, London Irish,
Ireland*) 1959 NZ
Murphy, N.A.A. (*Cork Constitution, Ireland*)
1959 A, NZ (3); 1966 A (2), NZ (2)

Neary, A. (*Broughton Park, England*) 1977
NZ
Nelson, J.E. (*Malone, Ireland*) 1950 NZ (2),
A (2)
Norris, C.H. (*Cardiff, Wales*) 1966 NZ (3)
Norster, R.L. (*Cardiff, Wales*) 1983 NZ (2)

O'Donnell, R.C. (*St Mary's Coll, Ireland*)
1980 SA
O'Driscoll, J.B. (*London Irish, Ireland*) 1980
SA (4); 1983 NZ (2)
O'Reilly, A.J.F. (*Old Belvedere, Ireland*)
1955 SA (4); 1959 A (2), NZ (4)
Orr, P.A. (*Old Wesley, Ireland*) 1977 NZ
O'Shea, J.P. (*Cardiff, Wales*) 1968 SA

Pask, A.E.I. (*Abertillery, Wales*) 1962 SA (3);
1966 A (2), NZ (3)
Patterson, C.S. (*Instonians, Ireland*) 1980 SA
(3)
Patterson, W.M. (*Sale, England*) 1959 NZ
Paxton, I.A.M. (*Selkirk, Scotland*) 1983 NZ
(4)
Pedlow, A.C. (*CIYMS, Ireland*) 1955 SA (2)
Preece, I. (*Coventry, England*) 1950 NZ
Price, B. (*Newport, Wales*) 1966 A (2), NZ (2)
Price, G. (*Pontypool, Wales*) 1977 NZ (4);
1980 SA (4); 1983 NZ (4)

Price, M.J. (*Pontypool, Wales*) 1959 A (2),
NZ (3)
Prosser, T.R. (*Pontypool, Wales*) 1959 NZ
Pullin, J.V. (*Bristol, England*) 1968 SA (3);
1971 NZ (4)

Quinnell, D.L. (*Llanelli, Wales*) 1971 NZ;
1977 NZ (2); 1980 SA (2)

Ralston, C.W. (*Richmond, England*) 1974 SA
Rees, H.E. (*Neath, Wales*) 1977 NZ
Reid, T.E. (*Garryowen, Ireland*) 1955 SA (2)
Renwick, J.M. (*Hawick, Scotland*) 1980 SA
Richards, D.S. (*Swansea, Wales*) 1980 SA
Richards, M.C.R. (*Cardiff, Wales*) 1968 SA
(3)
Rimmer, G. (*Waterloo, England*) 1950 NZ
Ringland, T.M. (*Ballymena, Ireland*) 1983
NZ
Risman, A.B.W. (*Loughborough Colls,
England*) 1959 A (2), NZ (2)
Robbie, J.C. (*Greystones, Ireland*) 1980 SA
Robins, J.D. (*Birkenhead Park, Wales*) 1950
NZ (3), A (2)
Robins, R.J. (*Pontypridd, Wales*) 1955 SA (4)
Rogers, D.P. (*Bedford, England*) 1962 SA (2)
Rowlands, K.A. (*Cardiff, Wales*) 1962 SA (3)
Rutherford, D. (*Gloucester, England*) 1966 A
Rutherford, J.Y. (*Selkirk, Scotland*) 1983 NZ

Savage, K.F. (*Northampton, England*) 1968
SA (4)
Scotland, K.J.F. (*Cambridge U, Heriot's FP,
Scotland*) 1959 A (2), NZ (3)
Sharp, R.A.W. (*Oxford U, Redruth,
England*) 1962 SA (2)
Slattery, J.F. (*Blackrock Coll, Ireland*) 1974
SA (4)
Slemen, M.A.C. (*Liverpool, England*) 1980
SA
Smith, A.R. (*Edinburgh Wands, London
Scottish, Scotland*) 1962 SA (3)
Smith, D.W.C. (*London Scottish, Scotland*)
1950 A
Smith, G.K. (*Kelso, Scotland*) 1959 A (2), NZ
(2)
Squire, J. (*Newport, Pontypool, Wales*) 1977
NZ; 1980 SA (4); 1983 NZ
Squires, P.J. (*Harrogate, England*) 1977 NZ
Stagg, P.K. (*Oxford U, Sale, Scotland*) 1968
SA (3)
Steele, W.C.C. (*Bedford, RAF, Scotland*)
1974 SA (2)
Stephens, I. (*Bridgend, Wales*) 1983 NZ
Stephens, J.R.G. (*Neath, Wales*) 1950
A (2)

Taylor, J. (*London Welsh, Wales*) 1971 NZ (4)
Taylor, R.B. (*Northampton, England*) 1968
SA (4)

Telfer, J.W. (*Melrose, Scotland*) 1966 A (2),
NZ (3); 1968 SA (3)
Thomas, M.C. (*Devonport Services, Newport,
Wales*) 1950 NZ (2), A; 1959 NZ
Thomas, R.C.C. (*Swansea, Wales*) 1955 SA
(2)
Thomas, W.D. (*Llanelli, Wales*) 1966 NZ (2);
1968 SA (2[1r]); 1971 NZ (2)
Thompson, R.H. (*Instonians, London Irish,
Ireland*) 1955 SA (3)
Tucker, C.C. (*Shannon, Ireland*) 1980 SA (2)
Turner, J.W.C. (*Gala, Scotland*) 1968 SA (4)

Uttley, R.M. (*Gosforth, England*) 1974 SA
(4)

Waddell, G.H. (*Cambridge U, London
Scottish, Scotland*) 1962 SA (2)
Ward, A.J.P. (*Garryowen, Ireland*) 1980 SA
Watkins, D. (*Newport, Wales*) 1966 A (2), NZ
(4)
Watkins, S.J. (*Newport, Wales*) 1966 A (2),
NZ
Weston, M.P. (*Richmond, Durham City,
England*) 1962 SA (4); 1966 A (2)
Wheeler, P.J. (*Leicester, England*) 1977 NZ
(3); 1980 SA (4)
Willcox, J.G. (*Oxford U, Harlequins,
England*) 1962 SA (3)
Williams, B.L. (*Cardiff, Wales*) 1950 A (2),
NZ (3)
Williams, C. (*Swansea, Wales*) 1980 SA (4)
Williams, D. (*Ebbw Vale, Wales*) 1966 A (2),
NZ (3)
Williams, D.B. (*Cardiff, Wales*) 1977 NZ (3)
Williams, J.J. (*Llanelli, Wales*) 1974 SA (4);
1977 NZ (3)
Williams, J.P.R. (*London Welsh, Wales*) 1971
NZ (4); 1974 SA (4)
Williams, R.H. (*Llanelli, Wales*) 1955 SA (4);
1959 A (2), NZ (4)
Williams, W.O.G. (*Swansea, Wales*) 1955 SA
(4)
Willis, W.R. (*Cardiff, Wales*) 1950 NZ, A (2)
Windsor, R.W. (*Pontypool, Wales*) 1974 SA
(4); 1977 NZ
Winterbottom, P.J. (*Headingley, England*)
1983 NZ (4)
Wilson, S. (*London Scottish, Scotland*) 1966
A, NZ (4)
Wood, B.G.M. (*Garryowen, Ireland*) 1959
NZ (2)
Woodward, C.R. (*Leicester, England*) 1980
SA (2)

Young, J. (*Harrogate, RAF, Wales*) 1968 SA
Young, J.R.C. (*Oxford U, Harlequins,
England*) 1959 NZ
Young, R.M. (*Queen's U, Belfast, Collegians,
Ireland*) 1966 A (2), NZ; 1968 SA

France

Club abbreviations: *PUC*, Paris Université
Club; *RCF*, Racing Club de France; *SF*, Stade
Français. Matches against all countries are
listed even though not all are recognized as
full Internationals.

Abadie, A. (*Pau*) 1964 *I*
Abadie, A. (*Graulhet*) 1965 *R*; 1967 *SA 1, 3, 4,
NZ*; 1968 *S, I*

Abadie, L. (*Tarbes*) 1963 *R*
Aguerre, R. (*Biarritz*) 1979 *S*
Aguirre, J.-M. (*Bagnères*) 1971 *A 2*; 1972 *S*;
1973 *W, I, J, R*; 1974 *I, W, Arg 2, R, SA 1*;
1976 *W (r), E, US, A 2, R*; 1977 *W, E, S, I,
Arg 1, 2, NZ 1 2, R*; 1978 *E, S, I, W, R*; 1979
I, W, E, S, NZ 1, 2, R; 1980 *W, I*
Albaladejo, P. (*Dax*) 1954 *E, It*; 1960 *W, I, It,
R*; 1961 *S, SA, E, W, I, NZ 1, 2, A*; 1962 *S,
E, W, I*; 1963 *S, I, E, W, It*; 1964 *S, NZ, W,*

It, I, SA, Fi
Alvarez, A. (*Tyrosse*) 1945 *B 2*; 1946 *B, I,
W*; 1947 *S, I, W, E*; 1948 *I, A, S, W, E*; 1949
I, E, W; 1951 *S, E, W*
Amestoy, J.-B. (*Mont-de-Marsan*) 1964 *NZ,
E*
Arcalis, R. (*Brive*) 1950 *S, I*; 1951 *I, E, W*
Arino, M. (*Agen*) 1962 *R*
Aristouy, P. (*Pau*) 1948 *S*; 1949 *Arg 2*; 1950 *S,
I, E, W*

Arnaudet, M. (*Lourdes*) 1964 *I*; 1967 *It*, *W*

Arrieta, J. (*SF*) 1953 *E*, *W*

Astre, R. (*Béziers*) 1971 *R*; 1972 *I 1*; 1973 *E* (*r*); 1975 *E*, *S*, *I*, *SA 1, 2, Arg 2*; 1976 *A 2, R*

Averous, J.-L. (*La Voulte*) 1975 *S*, *I*, *SA 1, 2*; 1976 *I*, *W*, *E*, *US*, *A 1, 2, R*; 1977 *W*, *E*, *S*, *I*, *Arg 1, R*; 1978 *E*, *S*, *I*; 1979 *NZ 1, 2*; 1980 *E*, *S*; 1981 *A 2*

Azarete, J.-L. (*Dax, St Jean-de-Luz*) 1969 *W*, *R*; 1970 *S*, *I*, *W*, *R*; 1971 *S*, *I*, *E*, *SA 1, 2, A 1*; 1972 *E*, *W*, *I 2*, *A 1, R*; 1973 *NZ*, *W*, *I*, *R*; 1974 *I*, *R*, *SA 1, 2*; 1975 *W*

Badin, C. (*Chalon*) 1973 *W*, *I*; 1975 *Arg 1*

Baladie, G. (*Agen*) 1945 *B 1, 2, W*; 1946 *B*, *I*, *NZA*

Barrau, M. (*Beaumont, Toulouse*) 1971 *S*, *E*, *W*; 1972 *E*, *W*, *A 1, 2*; 1973 *S*, *NZ*, *E*, *I*, *J*, *R*; 1974 *I*, *S*

Barrière, R. (*Béziers*) 1960 *R*

Barthe, J. (*Lourdes*) 1954 *Arg 1, 2*; 1955 *S*; 1956 *I*, *W*, *It*, *E*, *Cz*; 1957 *S*, *I*, *E*, *W*, *R 1, 2*; 1958 *S*, *E*, *A*, *W*, *It*, *I*, *SA 1, 2*; 1959 *S*, *E*, *It*, *W*

Basauri, R. (*Albi*) 1954 *Arg 1*

Basquet, G. (*Agen*) 1945 *W*; 1946 *B*, *I*, *NZA*, *W*; 1947 *S*, *I*, *W*, *E*; 1948 *I*, *A*, *S*, *W*, *E*; 1949 *S*, *I*, *E*, *W*, *Arg 1*; 1950 *S*, *I*, *E*, *W*; 1951 *S*, *I*, *E*, *W*, *Arg 1*; 1952 *S*, *I*, *SA*, *W*, *E*, *It*

Bastiat, J.-P. (*Dax*) 1969 *R*; 1970 *S*, *I*, *W*; 1971 *S*, *I*, *SA 2*; 1972 *S*, *A 1*; 1973 *E*; 1974 *Arg 1, 2, SA 2*; 1975 *W*, *Arg 1, 2, R*; 1976 *S*, *I*, *W*, *A 1, 2, R*; 1977 *W*, *E*, *S*, *I*; 1978 *E*, *S*, *I*, *W*

Baudry, N. (*Montferrand*) 1949 *S*, *I*, *W*, *Arg 1, 2*

Baulon, R. (*Vienne, Bayonne*) 1954 *S*, *NZ*, *W*, *E*, *It*; 1955 *I*, *E*, *W*, *It*; 1956 *S*, *I*, *W*, *It*, *E*, *Cz*; 1957 *S*, *I*, *It*

Baux, J.-P. (*Lannemezan*) 1968 *NZ 1, 2, SA 1, 2*

Bayardon, J. (*Chalon*) 1964 *S*, *NZ*, *E*

Bégu, J. (*Dax*) 1982 *Arg 2 (r)*; 1984 *E*, *S*

Béguerie, C. (*Agen*) 1979 *NZ 1*

Belascain, C. (*Bayonne*) 1977 *R*; 1978 *E*, *S*, *I*, *W*, *R*; 1979 *I*, *W*, *E*, *S*; 1982 *W*, *E*, *S*, *I*; 1983 *E*, *S*, *I*, *W*

Belletante, G. (*Nantes*) 1951 *I*, *E*, *W*

Bénésis, R. (*Narbonne*) 1969 *W*, *R*; 1970 *S*, *I*, *W*, *E*, *R*; 1971 *S*, *I*, *E*, *W*, *A 2*; 1972 *S*, *I 1, 2*, *E*, *W*, *A 1, R*; 1973 *NZ*, *E*, *W*, *I*, *J*, *R*; 1974 *I*, *W*, *E*, *S*

Benetière, J. (*Roanne*) 1954 *It*, *Arg 1*

Berbizier, P. (*Lourdes*) 1981 *S*, *I*, *W*, *E*, *NZ 1, 2*; 1982 *I*, *R*; 1983 *S*, *I*; 1984 *S (r)*, *NZ 1, 2*; 1985 *Arg 1, 2, J 1, 2*; 1986 *S*, *I*, *W*, *E*, *R*

Berejnoi, J.-C. (*Tulle*) 1963 *R*; 1964 *S*, *W*, *It*, *I*, *SA*, *Fi*, *R*; 1965 *S*, *I*, *E*, *W*, *It*, *R*; 1966 *S*, *I*, *E*, *W*, *It*, *R*; 1967 *S*, *A*, *E*, *It*, *W*, *I*, *R*

Berges-Cau, R (*Lourdes*) 1976 *E (r)*

Bergougnan, Y. (*Toulouse*) 1945 *B 1, W*; 1946 *B*, *I*, *NZA*, *W*; 1947 *S*, *I*, *W*, *E*; 1948 *S*, *W*, *E*; 1949 *S*, *E*, *Arg 1, 2*

Bernard, R. (*Bergerac*) 1951 *S*, *I*, *E*, *W*

Berot, J.-L. (*Toulouse*) 1968 *NZ 3*, *A*; 1969 *S*, *I*; 1970 *E*, *R*; 1971 *S*, *I*, *E*, *W*, *SA 1, 2, A 1, 2*, *R*; 1972 *I 1*, *E*, *W*, *A 1*; 1974 *I*

Bertrand, P. (*Bourg*) 1951 *I*, *E*, *W*; 1953 *S*, *I*, *E*, *W*, *It*

Bertranne, R. (*Bagnères*) 1971 *E*, *W*, *SA 2, A 1, 2*; 1972 *S*, *I 1*; 1973 *NZ*, *E*, *J*, *R*; 1974 *I*, *W*, *E*, *S*, *Arg 1, 2, R*, *SA 1, 2*; 1975 *W*, *E*, *S*, *I*, *SA 1, 2, Arg 1, 2, R*; 1976 *S*, *I*, *W*, *E*, *US*, *A 1, 2, R*; 1977 *W*, *E*, *S*, *I*, *Arg 1, 2, NZ 1, 2, R*; 1978 *E*, *S*, *I*, *W*, *R*; 1979 *I*, *W*, *E*, *S*, *R*; 1980

W, *E*, *S*, *I*, *SA*, *R*; 1981 *S*, *I*, *W*, *E*, *R*, *NZ 1, 2*

Besson, P. (*Brive*) 1963 *S*, *I*, *E*; 1965 *R*; 1968 *SA 1*

Bianchi, J. (*Toulon*) 1985 *J 2*

Bichendaritz, J. (*Biarritz*) 1954 *It*, *Arg 1, 2*

Bidart, L. (*La Rochelle*) 1953 *W*

Biemouret, P. (*Agen*) 1969 *E*, *W*; 1970 *I*, *W*, *E*; 1971 *W*, *SA 1, 2, A 1*; 1972 *E*, *W*, *I 2*, *A 2*, *R*; 1973 *S*, *NZ*, *E*, *W*, *I*

Bienès, R. (*Cognac*) 1950 *S*, *I*, *E*, *W*; 1951 *S*, *I*, *E*, *W*; 1952 *S*, *I*, *SA*, *W*, *E*, *It*; 1953 *S*, *I*, *E*; 1954 *S*, *I*, *NZ*, *W*, *E*, *Arg 1, 2*; 1956 *S*, *I*, *W*, *It*, *E*

Bilbao, L. (*St Jean de Luz*) 1978 *I*; 1979 *I*

Billière, M. (*Toulouse*) 1968 *NZ 3*

Blanco, S. (*Biarritz*) 1980 *SA*, *R*; 1981 *S*, *W*, *E*, *A 1, 2, R*, *NZ 1, 2*; 1982 *W*, *E*, *S*, *I*, *R*, *Arg 1, 2*; 1983 *E*, *S*, *I*, *W*; 1984 *I*, *W*, *E*, *S*, *NZ 1, 2, R*; 1985 *E*, *S*, *I*, *W*, *Arg 1, J 1*; 1986 *S*, *I*, *W*, *E*, *R*

Boffelli, V. (*Aurillac*) 1971 *A 2, R*; 1972 *S*, *I 1*; 1973 *J*, *R*; 1974 *I*, *W*, *E*, *S*, *Arg 1, 2, R*, *SA 1, 2*; 1975 *W*, *S*, *I*

Bonal, J.-M. (*Toulouse*) 1968 *E*, *W*, *Cz*, *NZ 2, 3, SA 1, 2*; 1969 *S*, *I*, *E*, *R*; 1970 *W*, *E*

Boniface, A. (*Mont-de-Marsan*) 1954 *I*, *NZ*, *W*, *E*, *It*, *Arg 1, 2*; 1955 *S*, *I*; 1956 *S*, *I*, *W*, *It*, *Cz*; 1957 *S*, *I*, *W*, *R 2*; 1958 *S*, *E*; 1959 *E*; 1961 *NZ 1, 3, A*, *R*; 1962 *E*, *W*, *I*, *It*, *R*; 1963 *S*, *I*, *E*, *W*, *It*, *R*; 1964 *S*, *NZ*, *E*, *W*, *It*; 1965 *W*, *It*, *R*; 1966 *S*, *I*, *E*, *W*

Boniface, G. (*Mont-de-Marsan*) 1960 *W*, *I*, *It*, *R*, *Arg 1, 2, 3*; 1961 *S*, *SA*, *E*, *W*, *It*, *I*, *NZ 1, 2, 3, R*; 1962 *R*; 1963 *S*, *I*, *E*, *W*, *It*, *R*; 1964 *S*; 1965 *S*, *I*, *E*, *W*, *It*, *R*; 1966 *S*, *I*, *E*, *W*

Bonneval, E. (*Toulouse*) 1984 *NZ 2 (r)*; 1985 *W*, *Arg 1, 2, J 2*; 1986 *W*, *E*, *R*

Bonnus, F. (*Toulon*) 1950 *S*, *I*, *E*, *W*

Bontemps, D. (*La Rochelle*) 1968 *SA 2*

Bordenave, L. (*Toulon*) 1948 *A*, *S*, *W*, *E*; 1949 *S*

Bouguyon, G. (*Grenoble*) 1961 *SA*, *E*, *W*, *It*, *I*, *NZ 1, 2, 3, A*

Boujet, C. (*Grenoble*) 1968 *NZ 2*, *A (r)*, *SA 1*

Bouquet, J. (*Bourgoin, Vienne*) 1954 *S*; 1955 *E*; 1956 *S*, *I*, *W*, *It*, *E*, *Cz*; 1957 *S*, *E*, *W*, *R 2*; 1958 *S*, *E*; 1959 *S*, *It*, *W*, *I*; 1960 *S*, *E*, *W*, *I*, *R*; 1961 *S*, *SA*, *E*, *W*, *It*, *I*, *R*; 1962 *S*, *E*, *W*, *I*

Bourdeu, J.R. (*Lourdes*) 1952 *S*, *I*, *SA*, *W*, *E*, *It*; 1953 *S*, *I*, *E*

Bourgarel, R. (*Toulouse*) 1969 *R*; 1970 *S*, *I*, *E*, *R*; 1971 *W*, *SA 1, 2*; 1973 *S*

Brejassou, R. (*Tarbes*) 1952 *S*, *I*, *SA*, *W*, *E*; 1953 *W*, *E*; 1954 *S*, *I*, *NZ*; 1955 *S*, *I*, *E*, *W*, *It*

Brethes, R. (*St Sever*) 1960 *Arg 2*

Brun, G. (*Vienne*) 1950 *E*, *W*; 1951 *S*, *E*, *W*; 1952 *S*, *I*, *SA*, *W*, *E*, *It*; 1953 *E*, *W*, *It*

Brunet, Y. (*Perpignan*) 1975 *SA 1*; 1977 *Arg 1*

Buchet, E. (*Nice*) 1980 *R*; 1982 *E*, *R (r)*, *Arg 1, 2*

Buonomo, Y. (*Béziers*) 1971 *A 2, R*; 1972 *I 1*

Bustaffa, D. (*Carcassonne*) 1977 *Arg 1, 2, NZ 1, 2*; 1978 *W*, *R*; 1980 *W*, *E*, *S*, *SA*, *R*

Buzy, E. (*Lourdes*) 1946 *NZA*, *W*; 1947 *S*, *I*, *W*, *E*; 1948 *I*, *A*, *S*, *W*, *E*; 1949 *S*, *I*, *E*, *W*, *Arg 1, 2*

Cabanier, J.-M. (*Montauban*) 1963 *R*; 1964 *S*, *Fi*; 1965 *S*, *I*, *W*, *It*, *R*; 1966 *S*, *I*, *E*, *W*, *It*, *R*; 1967 *S*, *A*, *E*, *It*, *W*, *I*, *SA 1, 3, NZ*, *R*; 1968 *S*, *I*

Cabrol, H. (*Béziers*) 1972 *A 1 (r), 2*; 1973 *J*; 1974 *SA 2*

Calvo, G. (*Lourdes*) 1961 *NZ 1, 3*

Camberabero, D. (*La Voulte*) 1982 *R*, *Arg 1, 2*; 1983 *E*, *W*; 1985 *J 1, 2*

Camberabero, G. (*La Voulte*) 1961 *NZ 3*; 1962 *R*; 1964 *R*; 1967 *A*, *E*, *It*, *W*, *I*, *SA 1, 3, 4*; 1968 *S*, *E*, *W*

Camberabero, L. (*La Voulte*) 1964 *R*; 1965 *S*, *I*; 1966 *E*, *W*; 1967 *A*, *E*, *It*, *W*, *I*; 1968 *S*, *E*, *W*

Campaes, A. (*Lourdes*) 1965 *W*; 1967 *NZ*; 1968 *S*, *I*, *E*, *W*, *Cz*, *NZ 1, 2, A*; 1969 *S*, *W*; 1972 *R*; 1973 *NZ*

Cantoni, J. (*Béziers*) 1970 *W*, *R*; 1971 *S*, *I*, *E*, *W*, *SA 1, 2, A 1, R*; 1972 *I 1*; 1973 *S*, *NZ*, *W*, *I*; 1975 *W (r)*

Capdouze, J. (*Pau*) 1964 *SA*, *Fi*, *R*; 1965 *S*, *I*, *E*

Capendeguy, J.-M. (*Bègles*) 1967 *NZ*, *R*

Capitani, P. (*Toulon*) 1954 *Arg 1, 2*

Carabignac, J. (*Agen*) 1951 *S*, *I*; 1952 *SA*, *W*, *E*; 1953 *S*, *I*

Caron, L. (*Lyon, Castres*) 1947 *E*; 1948 *I*, *A*, *W*, *E*; 1949 *S*, *I*, *E*, *W*, *Arg 1*

Carpentier, M. (*Lourdes*) 1980 *E*, *SA*, *R*; 1981 *S*, *I*, *A 1*; 1982 *E*, *S*

Carrère, C. (*Toulon*) 1966 *R*; 1967 *S*, *A*, *E*, *W*, *I*, *SA 1, 3, 4, NZ*, *R*; 1968 *S*, *I*, *E*, *W*, *Cz*, *NZ 3, A*, *R*; 1969 *S*, *I*; 1970 *I*, *E*; 1971 *E*, *W*

Carrère, J. (*Vichy, Toulon*) 1956 *S*; 1957 *E*, *W*, *R 2*; 1958 *S*, *SA 1, 2*; 1959 *I*

Carrère, R. (*Mont-de-Marsan*) 1953 *E*, *It*

Casaux, L. (*Tarbes*) 1959 *I*, *It*; 1962 *S*

Cassagne, G. (*Bourgoin*) 1985 *J 1 (r)*

Cassagne, P. (*Pau*) 1957 *It*

Cassiède, M. (*Dax*) 1961 *NZ 3, A*, *R*

Caussade, A. (*Lourdes*) 1978 *R*; 1979 *I*, *W*, *E*, *NZ 1, 2, R*; 1980 *W*, *E*, *S*; 1981 *S (r)*, *I*

Cazals, P. (*Mont-de-Marsan*) 1961 *NZ 1, A*, *R*

Cazenave, F. (*RCF*) 1950 *E*; 1952 *S*; 1954 *I*, *NZ*, *W*, *E*

Celaya, M. (*Biarritz, SBUC*) 1953 *E*, *W*, *It*; 1954 *I*, *E*, *It*, *Arg 1, 2*; 1955 *S*, *I*, *E*, *W*, *It*; 1956 *S*, *I*, *W*, *It*, *E*, *Cz*; 1957 *S*, *I*, *E*, *W*, *R 2*; 1958 *S*, *E*, *A*, *W*, *It*; 1959 *S*, *E*; 1960 *S*, *E*, *W*, *I*, *R*, *Arg 1, 2, 3*; 1961 *S*, *SA*, *E*, *W*, *It*, *I*, *NZ 1, 2, 3, A*, *R*

Cester, E. (*TOEC, Valence*) 1966 *S*, *I*, *E*; 1967 *W*; 1968 *S*, *I*, *E*, *W*, *Cz*, *NZ 1, 3, A*, *SA 1, 2, R*; 1969 *S*, *I*, *E*, *W*; 1970 *S*, *I*, *W*, *E*; 1971 *A 1*; 1972 *R*; 1973 *S*, *NZ*, *W*, *I*, *J*, *R*; 1974 *I*, *W*, *E*, *S*

Chabowski, H. (*Nice*) 1985 *Arg 2*

Chadebech, P. (*Brive*) 1982 *R*, *Arg 1, 2*; 1986 *S*, *I*, *R*

Champ, E. (*Toulon*) 1985 *Arg 1, 2, J 1, 2*; 1986 *I*, *W*, *F*

Charvet, D. (*Toulouse*) 1985 *J 2*; 1986 *W*, *E*, *R*

Chenevay, C. (*Grenoble*) 1968 *SA 1*

Chevallier, B. (*Montferrand*) 1952 *S*, *I*, *SA*, *W*, *E*, *It*; 1953 *E*, *W*, *It*; 1954 *S*, *I*, *NZ*, *W*, *Arg 1*; 1955 *S*, *I*, *E*, *W*, *It*; 1956 *S*, *I*, *W*, *It*, *E*, *Cz*; 1957 *S*

Chiberry, J. (*Chambéry*) 1955 *It*

Cholley, G. (*Castres*) 1975 *E*, *S*, *I*, *SA 1, 2, Arg 1, 2, R*; 1976 *S*, *I*, *W*, *E*, *A 1, 2, R*; 1977 *W*, *E*, *S*, *I*, *Arg 1, 2, NZ 1, 2, R*; 1978 *E*, *S*, *I*, *W*, *R*; 1979 *I*, *S*

Cimarosti, J. (*Castres*) 1976 *US (r)*

Claverie, H. (*Lourdes*) 1954 *NZ*, *W*

Clemente, M. (*Oloron*) 1978 *R*; 1980 *S*, *I*

Codorniou, D. (*Narbonne*) 1979 *NZ 1, 2, R*; 1980 *W*, *E*, *S*, *I*; 1981 *S*, *W*, *E*, *A 2*; 1983 *E*, *S*, *I*, *W*, *A 1, 2, R*; 1984 *I*, *W*, *E*, *S*, *NZ 1, 2, R*; 1985 *E*, *S*, *I*, *W*, *Arg 1, 2, J 1*

Colombier, J. (*St Junien*) 1952 *SA*, *W*, *E*

Colomine, G. (*Narbonne*) 1979 *NZ 1*

Condom, J. (*Boucau*) 1982 *R;* 1983 *E, S, I, W, A 1, 2, R;* 1984 *I, W, E, S, NZ 1, 2, R;* 1985 *E, S, I, W, Arg 1, 2, J 1;* 1986 *S, I, W, E, R*

Costantino, J. (*Montferrand*) 1973 *R*

Costes, F. (*Montferrand*) 1979 *E, S, NZ 1, 2, R;* 1980 *W, I*

Crampagne, J. (*Bègles*) 1967 *SA 4*

Crancee, R. (*Lourdes*) 1960 *Arg 3;* 1961 *S*

Crauste, M. (*RCF, Lourdes*) 1957 *R 1, 2;* 1958 *S, E, A, W, It, I;* 1959 *E, It, W, I;* 1960 *S, E, W, I, It, R, Arg 1, 3;* 1961 *S, SA, E, W, It, I, NZ 1, 2, 3, A, R;* 1962 *S, E, W, I, It, R;* 1963 *S, I, E, W, It, R;* 1964 *S, NZ, E, W, It, I, SA, Fi, R;* 1965 *S, I, E, W, It, R;* 1966 *S, I, E, W, It*

Cremaschi, M. (*Lourdes*) 1980 *R;* 1981 *R, NZ 1, 2;* 1982 *W, S;* 1983 *A 1, 2, R;* 1984 *I, W*

Cristina, J. (*Montferrand*) 1979 *R*

Danos, P. (*Toulon, Béziers*) 1954 *Arg 1, 2;* 1957 *R 2;* 1958 *S, E, W, It, I, SA 1, 2;* 1959 *S, E, It, W, I;* 1960 *S, E*

Darbos, P. (*Dax*) 1969 *R*

Darracq, R. (*Dax*) 1957 *It*

Darrieussecq, A. (*Biarritz*) 1973 *E*

Darrieussecq, J. (*Mont-de-Marsan*) 1953 *It*

Darrouy, C. (*Mont-de-Marsan*) 1957 *I, E, W, It, R 1;* 1959 *E;* 1961 *R;* 1963 *S, I, E, W, It;* 1964 *NZ, E, W, It, I, SA, Fi, R;* 1965 *S, I, E, It, R;* 1966 *S, I, E, W, It, R;* 1967 *S, A, E, It, W, I, SA 1, 2, 4*

Dauga, B. (*Mont-de-Marsan*) 1964 *S, NZ, E, W, It, I, SA, Fi, R;* 1965 *S, I, E, W, It, R;* 1966 *S, I, E, W, It, R;* 1967 *S, A, E, It, W, I, SA 1, 2, 3, 4, NZ, R;* 1968 *S, I, NZ 1, 2, 3, A, SA 1, 2, R;* 1969 *S, I, E, R;* 1970 *S, I, W, E, R;* 1971 *S, I, E, W, SA 1, 2, A 1, 2, R;* 1972 *S, I 1, W*

Dauger, J. (*Bayonne*) 1945 *B 1, 2;* 1953 *S*

Dedieu, P. (*Béziers*) 1963 *E, It;* 1964 *W, It, I, SA, Fi, R;* 1965 *S, I, E, W*

De Gregorio, J. (*Grenoble*) 1960 *S, E, W, I, It, R, Arg 1, 2;* 1961 *S, SA, E, W, It, I;* 1962 *S, E, W;* 1963 *S, W, It;* 1964 *NZ, E*

Dehez, J.-L. (*Agen*) 1967 *SA 2;* 1969 *R*

Delage, C. (*Agen*) 1983 *S, I;* 1985 *J 1 (r)*

Delaigue, G. (*Toulon*) 1973 *J, R*

Desclaux, F. (*RCF*) 1949 *Arg 1, 2;* 1953 *It*

Desnoyer, L. (*Brive*) 1974 *R*

Detrez, P.-E. (*Nîmes*) 1983 *A 2 (r);* 1985 *J 1, 2*

Dintrans, P. (*Tarbes*) 1979 *NZ 1, 2, R;* 1980 *E, S, I, SA, R;* 1981 *S, I, W, E, A 1, 2, R, NZ 1, 2;* 1982 *W, E, S, I, R, Arg 1, 2;* 1983 *E, W, A 1, 2, R;* 1984 *I, W, E, S, NZ 1, 2, R;* 1985 *E, S, I, W, Arg 1, 2, J 1*

Dizabo, P. (*Tyrosse*) 1948 *A, S, E;* 1949 *S, I, E, W, Arg 2;* 1950 *S, I;* 1960 *Arg 1, 2, 3*

Domec, H. (*Lourdes*) 1953 *W, It;* 1954 *S, I, NZ, W, E, It;* 1955 *S, I, E, W;* 1956 *I, W, It;* 1958 *E, A, W, It, I*

Domenech, A. (*Vichy, Brive*) 1954 *W, E, It;* 1955 *S, I, E, W;* 1956 *S, I, W, It, E, Cz;* 1957 *S, I, E, W, It, R 1, 2;* 1958 *S, E, It;* 1959 *It;* 1960 *S, E, W, I, It, R, Arg 1, 2, 3;* 1961 *S, SA, E, W, It, I, NZ 1, 2, 3, A, R;* 1962 *S, E, W, I, It, R;* 1963 *W, It*

Dospital, P. (*Bayonne*) 1977 *R;* 1980 *I;* 1981 *S, I, W, E;* 1982 *I, R, Arg 1, 2;* 1983 *E, S, I, W;* 1984 *E, S, NZ 1, 2, R;* 1985 *E, S, I, W, Arg 1*

Dourthe, C. (*Dax*) 1966 *R;* 1967 *S, A, E, W, I, SA 1, 2, 3, NZ;* 1968 *W, NZ 3, SA 1, 2;* 1969 *W;* 1971 *SA 2 (r), R;* 1972 *I 1, 2, A 1, 2, R;* 1973 *S, NZ, W, I, J;* 1974 *I, Arg 1, 2, SA 1, 2;*

1975 *W, E, S*

Droitecourt, M. (*Montferrand*) 1972 *R;* 1973 *NZ (r), E;* 1974 *E, S, Arg 1, SA 2;* 1975 *SA 1, 2, Arg 1, 2, R;* 1976 *S, I, W, A 1;* 1977 *Arg 2*

Dubertrand, A. (*Montferrand*) 1971 *A 2, R;* 1972 *I 2;* 1974 *I, W, E, SA 2;* 1975 *Arg 1, 2, R;* 1976 *S, US*

Dubois, D. (*Bègles*) 1971 *S*

Dubroca, D. (*Agen*) 1979 *NZ 2;* 1981 *NZ 2 (r);* 1982 *E, S;* 1984 *W, E, S;* 1985 *Arg 2, J 1, 2;* 1986 *S, I, W, E, R*

Dufau, G. (*RCF*) 1948 *I, A;* 1949 *I, W;* 1950 *S, E, W;* 1951 *S, I, E, W;* 1952 *SA, W;* 1953 *S, I, E, W;* 1954 *S, I, NZ, W, E, It;* 1955 *S, I, E, W, It;* 1956 *S, I, W, It;* 1957 *S, I, E, W, It, R 1*

Duffaut, Y. (*Agen*) 1954 *Arg 1, 2*

Duhard, Y. (*Bagnères*) 1980 *E*

Dupont, J.-L. (*Agen*) 1983 *S*

Duprat, B. (*Bayonne*) 1966 *E, W, It, R;* 1967 *S, A, E, SA 2, 3;* 1968 *S, I;* 1972 *E, W, I 2, A 1*

Dupuy, J. (*Tarbes*) 1956 *S, I, W, It, E, Cz;* 1957 *S, I, E, W, It, R 2;* 1958 *S, E, SA 1, 2;* 1959 *S, E, It, W, I;* 1960 *W, I, It, Arg 1, 3;* 1961 *S, SA, E, NZ 2, R;* 1962 *S, E, W, I, It;* 1963 *W, It, R;* 1964 *S*

Dutin, B. (*Mont-de-Marsan*) 1968 *NZ 2, A, SA 2, R*

Dutrain, H. (*Toulouse*) 1945 *W;* 1946 *B, I;* 1947 *E;* 1949 *I, E, W, Arg 1*

Echave, L. (*Agen*) 1961 *S*

Elissalde, J.-P. (*La Rochelle*) 1980 *SA, R;* 1981 *A 1, 2, R*

Erbani, D. (*Agen*) 1981 *A 1, 2, NZ 1, 2;* 1982 *Arg 1, 2;* 1983 *S (r), I, W, A 1, 2, R;* 1984 *W, E, R;* 1985 *E, W (r), Arg 1;* 1986 *S, I, F, E, R*

Escommier, M. (*Montelimar*) 1955 *It*

Esponda, J.-M. (*RCF*) 1967 *SA 1, 2, R;* 1968 *NZ 1, 2, SA 2, R;* 1969 *S, I (r), E*

Estève, A. (*Béziers*) 1971 *SA 1;* 1972 *I 1, 2, E, W, A 2, R;* 1973 *S, NZ, E, I;* 1974 *I, W, E, S, R, SA 1, 2;* 1975 *W, E*

Estève, P. (*Narbonne*) 1982 *R, Arg 1, 2;* 1983 *E, S, I, W, A 1, 2, R;* 1984 *I, W, E, S, NZ 1, 2, R;* 1985 *E, S, I, W;* 1986 *S, I*

Etchenique, J. (*Biarritz*) 1974 *R, SA 1;* 1975 *E, Arg 2*

Etcheverry, M. (*Pau*) 1971 *S, I*

Fabre, J. (*Toulouse*) 1963 *S, I, E, W, It;* 1964 *S, NZ, E*

Fabre, M. (*Béziers*) 1981 *A 1, R, NZ 1, 2;* 1982 *I, R;* 1985 *J 1, 2*

Fauvel, J.-P. (*Tulle*) 1980 *R*

Ferrien, R. (*Tarbes*) 1950 *S, I, E, W*

Fite, R. (*Brive*) 1963 *W, It*

Fort, L. (*Agen*) 1967 *It, W, I, SA 1, 2, 3, 4*

Foures, H. (*Toulouse*) 1951 *S, I, E, W*

Fournet, F. (*Montferrand*) 1950 *W*

Fouroux, J. (*La Voulte*) 1972 *I 2, R;* 1974 *W, E, Arg 1, 2, R, SA 1, 2;* 1975 *W, Arg 1, R;* 1976 *S, I, W, E, US, A 1;* 1977 *W, E, S, I, Arg 1, 2, NZ 1, 2, R*

Furcade, R. (*Perpignan*) 1952 *S*

Gabernet, S. (*Toulouse*) 1980 *E, S;* 1981 *S, I, W, E, A 1, 2, R, NZ 1, 2;* 1982 *I;* 1983 *A 2, R*

Gachassin, J. (*Lourdes*) 1961 *S, I;* 1963 *R;* 1964 *S, NZ, E, W, It, I, SA, Fi, R;* 1965 *S, I, E, W, It, R;* 1966 *S, I, E, W, I, NZ;* 1968 *I, E;* 1969 *S, I*

Gallion, J. (*Toulon*) 1978 *E, S, I, W;* 1979 *I,*

W, E, S, NZ 2, R; 1980 *W, E, S, I;* 1983 *A 1, 2, R;* 1984 *I, W, E, S, R;* 1985 *E, S, I, W*

Galy, J. (*Perpignan*) 1953 *W*

Garuet, J.-P. (*Lourdes*) 1983 *A 1, 2, R;* 1984 *I, NZ 1, 2, R;* 1985 *E, S, I, W, Arg 1;* 1986 *S, I, W, E, R*

Gasc, J. (*Graulhet*) 1977 *NZ 2*

Gasparotto, G. (*Montferrand*) 1976 *A 2, R*

Gauby, G. (*Perpignan*) 1956 *Cz*

Gensanne, R. (*Béziers*) 1962 *S, E, W, I, It, R;* 1963 *S*

Gourdon, J.-F. (*RCF, Bagnères*) 1974 *S, Arg 1, 2, R, SA 1, 2;* 1975 *W, E, S, I, R;* 1976 *S, I, W, E;* 1978 *E, S;* 1979 *W, E, S, R;* 1980 *I*

Gratton, J. (*Agen*) 1984 *NZ 2, R;* 1985 *E, S, I, W, Arg 1, 2, J 1, 2;* 1986 *S*

Greffe, M. (*Grenoble*) 1968 *W, Cz, NZ 1, 2, SA 1*

Gruarin, A. (*Toulon*) 1964 *W, It, I, SA, Fi, R;* 1965 *S, I, E, W, It;* 1966 *S, I, E, W, It, R;* 1967 *S, A, E, It, W, I, NZ;* 1968 *S, I*

Guilbert, A. (*Toulon*) 1975 *E, S, I, SA 1, 2;* 1976 *A 1;* 1977 *Arg 1, 2, NZ 1, 2, R;* 1979 *I, W, E*

Guilleux, P. (*Agen*) 1952 *SA, It*

Haget, A. (*PUC*) 1953 *E;* 1954 *I, NZ, E, Arg 2;* 1955 *E, W, It;* 1957 *I, E, It, R 1;* 1958 *It, SA 2*

Haget, F. (*Agen, Biarritz*) 1974 *Arg 1, 2;* 1975 *SA 2, Arg 1, 2, R;* 1976 *S;* 1978 *S, I, W, R;* 1979 *I, W, E, S, NZ 1, 2, R;* 1980 *W, S, I;* 1984 *S, NZ 1, 2, R;* 1985 *E, S, I;* 1986 *S, I, W, E, R*

Harize, D. (*Cahors, Toulouse*) 1975 *SA 1, 2;* 1976 *A 1, 2, R;* 1977 *W, E, S, I*

Hauser, M. (*Lourdes*) 1969 *E*

Herice, D. (*Bègles*) 1950 *I*

Herrero, A. (*Toulon*) 1963 *R;* 1964 *NZ, E, W, It, I, SA, Fi, R;* 1965 *S, I, E, W;* 1966 *W, It, R;* 1967 *S, A, E, It, I, R*

Herrero, B. (*Nice*) 1983 *I*

Hiquet, J.-C. (*Agen*) 1964 *E*

Hoche, M. (*PUC*) 1957 *I, E, W, It, R 1*

Hortoland, J.-P. (*Béziers*) 1971 *A 2*

Imbernon, J.-F. (*Perpignan*) 1976 *I, W, E, US, A 1;* 1977 *W, E, S, I, Arg 1, 2, NZ 1, 2;* 1978 *E, R;* 1979 *I;* 1981 *S, I, W, E;* 1982 *I;* 1983 *I, W*

Iraçabal, J. (*Bayonne*) 1968 *NZ 1, 2, SA 1;* 1969 *S, I, W, R;* 1970 *S, I, W, E, R;* 1971 *W, SA 1, 2, A 1;* 1972 *E, W, I 2, A 2, R;* 1973 *S, NZ, E, W, I, J;* 1974 *I, W, E, S, Arg 1, 2, SA 2 (r)*

Janeczek, T. (*Tarbes*) 1982 *Arg 1, 2*

Jeanjean, P. (*Toulon*) 1948 *I*

Joinel, J.-L. (*Brive*) 1977 *NZ 1;* 1978 *R;* 1979 *I, W, E, S, NZ 1, 2, R;* 1980 *W, E, S, I, SA;* 1981 *S, I, W, E, R, NZ 1, 2;* 1982 *E, S, I, R;* 1983 *E, S, I, W, A 1, 2, R;* 1984 *I, W, E, S, NZ 1, 2;* 1985 *S, I, W, Arg 2;* 1986 *S, I, W, E, R*

Jol, M. (*Biarritz*) 1947 *S, I, W, E;* 1949 *S, I, E, W, Arg 1, 2*

Junquas, L. (*Tyrosse*) 1945 *B 1, 2, W;* 1946 *B, I, NZ A;* 1947 *S, I, W, E;* 1948 *S, W*

Kaczorowski, D. (*Le Creusot*) 1974 *I (r)*

Kaempf, A. (*St Jean-de-Luz*) 1946 *B*

Labadie, P. (*Bayonne*) 1952 *S, I, SA, W, E, It;* 1953 *S, I, It;* 1954 *S, I, NZ, W, E, Arg 2;*

1955 *S, I, E, W;* 1956 *I;* 1957 *I*

Labarthete, R. (*Pau*) 1952 *S*

Labazuy, A. (*Lourdes*) 1952 *I;* 1954 *S, W;* 1956 *E;* 1958 *A, W, I;* 1959 *S, E, It, W*

Laborde, C. (*RCF*) 1962 *It, R;* 1963 *R;* 1964 *SA;* 1965 *E*

Lacans, P. (*Béziers*) 1980 *SA;* 1981 *W, E, A 2, R;* 1982 *W*

Lacaussade, R. (*Bègles*) 1948 *A, S*

Lacaze, C. (*Lourdes, Angoulême*) 1961 *NZ 2, 3, A, R;* 1962 *E, W, I, It;* 1963 *W, R;* 1964 *S, NZ, E;* 1965 *It, R;* 1966 *S, I, E, W, It, R;* 1967 *S, E, SA 1, 3, 4, R;* 1968 *S, E, W, Cz, NZ 1;* 1969 *E*

Lacaze, P. (*Lourdes*) 1958 *SA 1, 2;* 1959 *S, E, It, W, I*

Lacome, M. (*Pau*) 1960 *Arg 2*

Lacrampe, F. (*Béziers*) 1949 *Arg 2*

Lacroix, P. (*Mont-de-Marsan, Agen*) 1958 *A;* 1960 *W, I, It, R, Arg 1, 2, 3;* 1961 *S, SA, E, W, I, NZ 1, 2, 3, A, R;* 1962 *S, E, W, I, R;* 1963 *S, I, E, W*

Lafarge, Y. (*Montferrand*) 1978 *R;* 1979 *NZ 1;* 1981 *I (r)*

Lafond, J.-B. (*RCF*) 1983 *A 1;* 1985 *Arg 1, 2, J 1, 2;* 1986 *S, I, W, E, R*

Lagisquet, P. (*Bayonne*) 1983 *A 1, 2, R;* 1984 *I, W, NZ 1, 2;* 1986 *R (r)*

Lagrange, J.-C. (*RCF*) 1966 *It*

Laporte, G. (*Graulhet*) 1981 *I, W, E, R, NZ 1, 2;* 1986 *W, E, R*

Larreguy, P. (*Bayonne*) 1954 *It*

Larrue, H. (*Carmaux*) 1960 *W, I, It, R, Arg 1, 2, 3*

Lasâosa, P. (*Dax*) 1950 *I;* 1952 *S, I, E, It;* 1955 *It*

Lassegue, J. (*Toulouse*) 1946 *W;* 1947 *S, I, W;* 1948 *W;* 1949 *I, E, W, Arg 1*

Lasserre, J.-C. (*Dax*) 1963 *It;* 1964 *S, NZ, E, W, It, I, Fi;* 1965 *W, It, R;* 1966 *R;* 1967 *S*

Lasserre, M. (*Agen*) 1967 *SA 2, 3;* 1968 *E, W, Cz, NZ 3, A, SA 1, 2;* 1969 *S, I, E;* 1970 *E;* 1971 *E*

Laudouar, J. (*Soustons, SBUC*) 1961 *NZ 1, 2, R;* 1962 *I, R*

Lauga, P. (*Vichy*) 1950 *S, I, E, W*

Lavergne, P. (*Limoges*) 1950 *S*

Lavigne, B. (*Agen*) 1984 *R;* 1985 *E*

Lazies, H. (*Auch*) 1954 *Arg 2;* 1955 *It;* 1956 *E;* 1957 *S*

Le Bourhis, R. (*La Rochelle*) 1961 *R*

Lecointre, M. (*Nantes*) 1952 *It*

Le Droff, J. (*Auch*) 1963 *It, R;* 1964 *S, NZ, E;* 1970 *E, R;* 1971 *S, I*

Lefevre, R. (*Brive*) 1961 *NZ 2*

Lenient, J.-J. (*Vichy*) 1967 *R*

Lepatey, J. (*Mazamet*) 1954 *It;* 1955 *S, I, E, W*

Lescarboura, J.-P. (*Dax*) 1982 *W, E, S, I;* 1983 *A 1, 2, R;* 1984 *I, W, E, S, NZ 1, 2, R;* 1985 *E, S, I, W, Arg 1, 2*

Lira, M. (*La Voulte*) 1962 *R;* 1963 *I, E, W, It, R;* 1964 *W, It, I, SA;* 1965 *S, I, R*

Londios, J. (*Montauban*) 1967 *SA 3*

Lorieux, A. (*Grenoble*) 1981 *A 1, R, NZ 1, 2;* 1982 *W;* 1983 *A 2, R;* 1984 *I, W, E, Arg 1*

Lubrano, A. (*Béziers*) 1972 *A 2;* 1973 *S*

Lux, J.-P. (*Tyrosse, Dax*) 1967 *E, It, W, I, SA 1, 2, 3, 4, R;* 1968 *I, E, Cz, NZ 3, A, SA 1, 2;* 1969 *S, I, E;* 1970 *S, I, W, E, R;* 1971 *S, I, E, W, A 1, 2;* 1972 *S, I 1, 2, E, W, A 1, 2, R;* 1973 *S, NZ, E;* 1974 *I, W, E, S, Arg 1, 2;* 1975 *W*

Magois, H. (*La Rochelle*) 1968 *SA 1, 2, R*

Malbet, J.-C. (*Agen*) 1967 *SA 2, 4*

Maleig, A. (*Oloron*) 1979 *W, E, NZ 2;* 1980 *W, E, SA, R*

Malquier, Y. (*Narbonne*) 1979 *S*

Manterola, T. (*Lourdes*) 1955 *It;* 1957 *R 1*

Mantoulan, C. (*Pau*) 1959 *I*

Marchal, J.-F. (*Lourdes*) 1979 *S, R;* 1980 *W, S, I*

Marocco, P. (*Montferrand*) 1985 *J 2;* 1986 *S, I, W, E, R*

Marot, A. (*Brive*) 1969 *R;* 1970 *S, I, W;* 1971 *SA 1;* 1972 *I 2;* 1976 *A 1*

Marquesuzaà, A. (*RCF*) 1958 *It, SA 1, 2;* 1959 *S, E, It, W;* 1960 *S, E, Arg 1*

Marracq, H. (*Pau*) 1961 *R*

Martin, J.-L. (*Béziers*) 1971 *A 2, R;* 1972 *S, I 1*

Martin, L. (*Pau*) 1948 *I, A, S, W, E;* 1950 *S*

Martine, R. (*Lourdes*) 1952 *S, I, It;* 1953 *It;* 1954 *S, I, NZ, W, E, It, Arg 2;* 1955 *S, I, W;* 1958 *A, W, It, I, SA 1, 2;* 1960 *S, E, Arg 3;* 1961 *S, It*

Martinez, G. (*Toulouse*) 1982 *W, E, S, Arg 1, 2;* 1983 *E, W*

Mas, F. (*Béziers*) 1962 *R;* 1963 *S, I, E, W*

Maso, J. (*Perpignan, Narbonne*) 1966 *It, R;* 1967 *S;* 1968 *S, W, Cz, NZ 1, 2, 3, A, R;* 1969 *S, I, W;* 1971 *SA 1, 2, R;* 1972 *E, W, A 2;* 1973 *W, I, J, R*

Matheu, J. (*Agen*) 1945 *W;* 1946 *B, I, NZA, W;* 1947 *S, I, W, E;* 1948 *I, A, S, W, E;* 1949 *S, I, E, W, Arg 1, 2;* 1950 *E, W;* 1951 *S, I*

Mauduy, G. (*Périgueux*) 1957 *It, R 1, 2;* 1958 *S, E;* 1961 *W, R*

Mauran, J. (*Castres*) 1952 *SA, W, E, It;* 1953 *I, E*

Menthiller, Y. (*Romans*) 1964 *W, It, SA, R;* 1965 *E*

Mericq, A. (*Agen*) 1959 *I;* 1960 *S, E, W;* 1961 *I*

Merquey, J. (*Toulon*) 1950 *S, I, E, W*

Mesny, P. (*RCF*) 1979 *NZ 1, 2;* 1980 *SA, R;* 1981 *I, W (r), A 1, 2, R, NZ 1, 2;* 1982 *I, Arg 1, 2*

Meyer, S. (*Périgueux*) 1960 *S, E, It, R, Arg 2*

Meynard, J. (*Cognac*) 1954 *Arg 1;* 1956 *Cz*

Mias, L. (*Mazamet*) 1951 *S, I, E, W;* 1952 *I, SA, W, E, It;* 1953 *S, I, W, It;* 1954 *S, I, NZ, W;* 1957 *R 2;* 1958 *S, E, A, W, I, SA 1, 2;* 1959 *S, It, W, I*

Mir, J.-H. (*Lourdes*) 1967 *R;* 1968 *I*

Mir, J.-P. (*Lourdes*) 1967 *A*

Mommejat, B. (*Cahors*) 1958 *It, I, SA 1, 2;* 1959 *S, E, It, W, I;* 1960 *S, E, I, R;* 1962 *S, E, W, I, It, R;* 1963 *S, I, W*

Moncla, F. (*RCF, Pau*) 1956 *Cz;* 1957 *I, E, W, It, R 1;* 1958 *SA 1, 2;* 1959 *S, E, It, W, I;* 1960 *S, E, W, I, It, R, Arg 1, 2, 3;* 1961 *S, SA, E, W, It, I, NZ 1, 2, 3*

Monie, R. (*Perpignan*) 1956 *Cz;* 1957 *E*

Moraitis, B. (*Toulon*) 1969 *E, W*

Morel, A. (*Grenoble*) 1954 *Arg 2*

Mournet, A. (*Bagnères*) 1981 *A 1 (r)*

Murillo, G. (*Dijon*) 1954 *It, Arg 1*

Noble, J.-C. (*La Voulte*) 1968 *E, W, Cz, NZ 3, A, R*

Normand, A. (*Toulouse*) 1957 *R 1*

Novès, G. (*Toulouse*) 1977 *NZ 1, 2, R;* 1978 *W, R;* 1979 *I, W*

Olive, D. (*Montferrand*) 1951 *I;* 1952 *I*

Orso, J.-C. (*Nice*) 1982 *Arg 1, 2;* 1983 *E, S, A 1;* 1984 *E (r), S, NZ 1;* 1985 *I (r), W, J 1, 2*

Othats, J. (*Dax*) 1960 *Arg 2, 3*

Paco, A. (*Béziers*) 1974 *Arg 1, 2, R, SA 1, 2;* 1975 *W, E, Arg 1, 2, R;* 1976 *S, I, W, E, US, A 1, 2, R;* 1977 *W, E, S, I, NZ 1, 2, R;* 1978 *E, S, I, W, R;* 1979 *I, W, E, S;* 1980 *W*

Palmié, M. (*Béziers*) 1975 *SA 1, 2, Arg 1, 2, R;* 1976 *S, I, W, E, US;* 1977 *W, E, S, I, Arg 1, 2, NZ 1, 2, R;* 1978 *E, S, I, W*

Paparemborde, R. (*Pau*) 1975 *SA 1, 2, Arg 1, 2, R;* 1976 *S, I, W, E, US, A 1, 2, R;* 1977 *W, E, S, I, Arg 1, NZ 1, 2;* 1978 *E, S, I, W, R;* 1979 *I, W, E, S, NZ 1, 2, R;* 1980 *W, E, S, SA, R;* 1981 *S, I, W, E, A 1, 2, R, NZ 1, 2;* 1982 *W, I, R, Arg 1, 2;* 1983 *E, S, I, W*

Pardo, L. (*Bayonne*) 1980 *SA, R;* 1981 *S, I, W, E, A 1;* 1982 *W, E, S;* 1983 *A 1 (r);* 1985 *S, I, Arg 2*

Pargade, J.-H. (*Lyon*) 1953 *It*

Paries, L. (*Biarritz*) 1968 *SA 2, R;* 1970 *S, I, W;* 1975 *E, S, I*

Pascalin, P. (*Mont-de-Marsan*) 1950 *I, E, W;* 1951 *S, I, E, W*

Pauthe, G. (*Graulhet*) 1956 *E*

Pebeyre, E. (*Fumel, Brive*) 1945 *W;* 1946 *I, NZA, W;* 1947 *S, I, W, E*

Pebeyre, M. (*Vichy, Montferrand*) 1970 *E, R;* 1971 *I, SA 1, 2, A 1;* 1973 *W*

Pecune, J. (*Tarbes*) 1974 *W, E, S;* 1975 *Arg 1, 2, R;* 1976 *I, W, E, US*

Pedeutour, P. (*Bègles*) 1980 *I*

Peron, P. (*RCF*) 1975 *SA 1, 2*

Perrier, P. (*Bayonne*) 1982 *W, E, S, I (r)*

Pesteil, J.-P. (*Béziers*) 1975 *SA 1;* 1976 *A 2, R*

Phliponneau, J.-F. (*Montferrand*) 1973 *W, I*

Piazza, A. (*Montauban*) 1968 *NZ 1, A*

Picard, T. (*Montferrand*) 1985 *Arg 2, J 2;* 1986 *R (r)*

Pilon, J. (*Périgueux*) 1949 *E;* 1950 *E*

Piqué, J. (*Pau*) 1961 *NZ 2, 3, A;* 1962 *S, It;* 1964 *NZ, E, W, It, I, SA, Fi, R;* 1965 *S, I, E, W, It*

Plantefol, A. (*RCF*) 1967 *SA 2, 3, 4, NZ, R;* 1968 *E, W, Cz, NZ 2;* 1969 *E, W*

Plantey, S. (*RCF*) 1961 *A;* 1962 *It*

Pomathios, M. (*Agen, Lyon, Bourg*) 1948 *I, A, S, W, E;* 1949 *S, I, E, W, Arg 1, 2;* 1950 *S, I, W;* 1951 *S, I, E, W;* 1952 *W, E;* 1953 *S, I, W;* 1954 *S*

Porthault, A. (*RCF*) 1951 *S, E, W;* 1952 *I;* 1953 *S, I, It*

Prat, J. (*Lourdes*) 1945 *B 1, 2, W;* 1946 *B, I, NZA, W;* 1947 *S, I, W, E;* 1948 *I, A, S, W, E;* 1949 *S, I, E, W, Arg 1, 2;* 1950 *S, I, E, W;* 1951 *S, E, W;* 1952 *S, I, SA, W, E, It;* 1953 *I, E, W, It;* 1954 *S, I, NZ, W, E, It;* 1956 *S, I, E, W, It*

Prat, M. (*Lourdes*) 1951 *I;* 1952 *S, I, SA, E;* 1953 *S, I, E;* 1954 *I, NZ, W, E, It;* 1955 *S, I, E, W, It;* 1956 *I, W, It, Cz;* 1957 *S, I, W, It, R 1;* 1958 *A, W, I*

Prin-Clary, J. (*Cavaillon, Brive*) 1945 *B 1, 2, W;* 1946 *B, I, NZA, W;* 1947 *S, I, W*

Puget, N. (*Toulouse*) 1961 *It;* 1966 *S, I, It;* 1967 *SA 1, 3, 4, NZ;* 1968 *Cz, NZ 1, 2, SA 1, 2, R;* 1969 *E, R;* 1970 *W*

Quaglio, A. (*Mazamet*) 1957 *R 2;* 1958 *S, E, A, W, I, SA 1;* 1959 *S, E, It, W, I*

Quilis, A. (*Narbonne*) 1967 *SA 1, 4, NZ;* 1970 *R;* 1971 *I*

Rancoule, H. (*Lourdes, Toulon, Tarbes*) 1955 *E, W, It;* 1958 *A, W, It, I, SA 1;* 1959 *S, It;* 1960 *I, It, R, Arg 1, 2;* 1961 *SA, E, W, It, NZ 1, 2;* 1962 *S, E, W, I, It*

Razat, J.-P. (*Agen*) 1962 *R;* 1963 *S, I, R*
Rebujent, R. (*RCF*) 1963 *E*
Revallier, D. (*Graulhet*) 1981 *S, I, W, E, A 1, 2, R, NZ 1, 2;* 1982 *W, S, I, R, Arg 1*
Rives, J.-P. (*Toulouse, RCF*) 1975 *E, S, I, Arg 1, 2, R;* 1976 *S, I, W, E, US, A 1, 2, R;* 1977 *W, E, S, I, Arg 1, 2, R;* 1978 *E, S, I, W, R;* 1979 *I, W, E, S, NZ 1, 2, R;* 1980 *W, E, S, I, SA;* 1981 *S, I, W, E, A 2;* 1982 *W, E, S, I, R;* 1983 *E, S, I, W, A 1, 2, R;* 1984 *I, W, E, S*
Rodriguez, L. (*Mont-de-Marsan*) 1981 *A 1, 2, R, NZ 1, 2;* 1982 *W, E, S, I, R;* 1983 *E, S;* 1984 *I, NZ 1, 2, R;* 1985 *E, S, I, W, J 1, 2*
Rogé, L. (*Béziers*) 1952 *It;* 1953 *E, W, It;* 1954 *S, Arg 1, 2;* 1955 *S, I;* 1956 *W, It, E;* 1957 *S;* 1960 *S, E*
Rollet, J. (*Bayonne*) 1960 *Arg 3;* 1961 *NZ 3, A;* 1962 *It;* 1963 *I*
Romero, H. (*Montauban*) 1962 *S, E, W, I, It, R;* 1963 *E*
Romeu, J.-P. (*Montferrand*) 1972 *R;* 1973 *S, NZ, E, W, I, R;* 1974 *W, E, S, Arg 1, 2, R, SA 1, 2 (r);* 1975 *W, SA 2, Arg 1, 2, R;* 1976 *S, I, W, E, US;* 1977 *W, E, S, I, Arg 1, 2, NZ 1, 2, R*
Roques, A. (*Cahors*) 1958 *A, W, It, I, SA 1, 2;* 1959 *S, E, W, I;* 1960 *S, E, W, I, It, Arg 1, 2, 3;* 1961 *S, SA, E, W, It, I;* 1962 *S, E, W, I, It;* 1963 *S*
Roques, J.-C. (*Brive*) 1966 *S, I, It, R*
Rossignol, J.-C. (*Brive*) 1972 *A 2*
Rouan, J. (*Narbonne*) 1953 *S, I*
Roucaries, G. (*Perpignan*) 1956 *S*
Rougerie, J. (*Montferrand*) 1973 *J*
Rousset, G. (*Béziers*) 1975 *SA 1;* 1976 *US*
Ruiz, A. (*Tarbes*) 1968 *SA 2, R*
Rupert, J.-J. (*Tyrosse*) 1963 *R;* 1964 *S, Fi;* 1965 *E, W, It;* 1966 *S, I, E, W, It;* 1967 *It, R;* 1968 *S*

Saisset, O. (*Béziers*) 1971 *R;* 1972 *S, I 1, A 1, 2;* 1973 *S, NZ, E, W, I, J, R;* 1974 *I, Arg 2, SA 1, 2;* 1975 *W*
Salas, P. (*Narbonne*) 1979 *NZ 1, 2, R;* 1980 *W, E;* 1981 *A 1;* 1982 *Arg 2*

Sallefranque, M. (*Dax*) 1981 *A 2;* 1982 *W, E, S*
Salut, J. (*TOEC*) 1966 *R;* 1967 *S;* 1968 *I, E, Cz, NZ 1;* 1969 *I*
Sanac, A. (*Perpignan*) 1952 *It;* 1953 *S, I;* 1954 *E;* 1956 *Cz;* 1957 *S, I, E, W, It*
Sangalli, F. (*Narbonne*) 1975 *I, SA 1, 2;* 1976 *S, A 1, 2, R;* 1977 *W, E, S, I, Arg 1, 2, NZ 1, 2*
Sappa, M. (*Nice*) 1973 *J, R;* 1977 *R*
Saux, J.-P. (*Pau*) 1960 *W, It, Arg 1, 2;* 1961 *SA, E, W, It, I, NZ 1, 2, 3, A;* 1962 *S, E, W, I, It;* 1963 *S, I, E, It*
Savitsky, M. (*La Voulte*) 1969 *R*
Seguier, N. (*Béziers*) 1973 *J, R*
Sella, P. (*Agen*) 1982 *R, Arg 1, 2;* 1983 *E, S, I, W, A 1, 2, R;* 1984 *I, W, E, S, NZ 1, 2, R;* 1985 *E, S, I, W, Arg 1, 2, J 1;* 1986 *S, I, W, E, R*
Senal, G. (*Béziers*) 1974 *Arg 1, 2, R, SA 1, 2;* 1975 *W*
Sillières, J. (*Tarbes*) 1968 *R;* 1970 *S, I;* 1971 *S, I, E;* 1972 *E, W*
Siman, M. (*Montferrand*) 1948 *E;* 1949 *S;* 1950 *S, I, E, W*
Sitjar, M. (*Agen*) 1964 *W, It, I, R;* 1965 *It, R;* 1967 *A, I, It, W, I, SA 1, 2*
Skréla, J.-C. (*Toulouse*) 1971 *SA 2, A 1, 2;* 1972 *I 1 (r), 2, E, W, A 1;* 1973 *W, J, R;* 1974 *W, E, S, Arg 1, R;* 1975 *W (r), E, S, I, SA 1, 2, Arg 1, 2, R;* 1976 *S, I, W, E, US, A 1, 2, R;* 1977 *W, E, S, I, Arg 1, 2, NZ 1, 2, R;* 1978 *E, S, I, W*
Sorrondo, M. (*Montauban*) 1946 *NZ A;* 1947 *S, I, W, E;* 1948 *I*
Spanghero, C. (*Narbonne*) 1971 *E, W, SA 1, 2, A 1, 2;* 1972 *S, E, W, I 2, A 1, 2;* 1974 *I, W, E, S, R, SA 1;* 1975 *E, S, I*
Spanghero, W. (*Narbonne*) 1964 *SA, Fi, R;* 1965 *S, I, E, W, It, R;* 1966 *S, I, E, W, It, R;* 1967 *S, A, E, SA 1, 2, 3, 4, NZ;* 1968 *S, I, E, W, NZ 1, 2, 3, A, SA 1, 2, R;* 1969 *S, I, W;* 1970 *R;* 1971 *E, W, SA 1;* 1972 *E, I 2, A 1, 2, R;* 1973 *S, NZ, E, W, I*
Stener, G. (*PUC*) 1956 *S, I, E;* 1958 *SA 1, 2*
Sutra, G. (*Narbonne*) 1967 *SA 2;* 1969 *W;* 1970 *S, I*

Swierczinski, C. (*Bègles*) 1969 *E;* 1977 *Arg 2*

Taffary, M. (*RCF*) 1975 *W, E, S, I*
Tarricq, P. (*Lourdes*) 1958 *A, W, It, I*
Tignol, P. (*Toulouse*) 1953 *S, I*
Torreilles, S. (*Perpignan*) 1956 *S*
Trillo, J. (*Bègles*) 1967 *SA 3, 4, NZ, R;* 1968 *S, I, NZ 1, 2, 3, A;* 1969 *I, E, W, R;* 1970 *E, R;* 1971 *S, I, SA 1, 2, A 1, 2;* 1972 *S, A 1, 2, R;* 1973 *S, E*

Ugartemendia, J.-L. (*St Jean-de-Luz*) 1975 *S, I*

Vannier, M. (*RCF, Chalon*) 1953 *W;* 1954 *S, I, Arg 1, 2;* 1955 *S, I, E, W, It;* 1956 *S, I, W, It, E;* 1957 *S, I, E, W, It, R 1, 2;* 1958 *S, E, A, W, It, I;* 1960 *S, E, W, I, It, R, Arg 1, 3;* 1961 *SA, E, W, It, I, NZ 1, A*
Vaquerin, A. (*Béziers*) 1971 *R;* 1972 *S, I 1, A 1;* 1973 *S;* 1974 *W, E, S, Arg 1, 2, R, SA 1, 2;* 1975 *W, E, S, I;* 1976 *US, A 1 (r), 2, R;* 1977 *Arg 2;* 1979 *W, E;* 1980 *S, I*
Varenne, F. (*RCF*) 1952 *S*
Viard, G. (*Narbonne*) 1969 *W;* 1970 *S, R;* 1971 *S, I*
Vigier, R. (*Montferrand*) 1956 *S, W, It, E, Cz;* 1957 *S, E, W, It, R 1;* 1958 *S, E, A, W, It, I, SA 1, 2;* 1959 *S, E, It, W, I*
Vignes, C. (*RCF*) 1957 *R 1, 2;* 1958 *S, E*
Villepreux, P. (*Toulouse*) 1967 *It, I, SA 2, NZ;* 1968 *I, Cz, NZ 1, 2, 3, A;* 1969 *S, I, E, W, R;* 1970 *S, I, W, E, R;* 1971 *S, I, E, W, A 1, 2, R;* 1972 *S, I 1, 2, E, W, A 1, 2*
Viviès, B. (*Agen*) 1978 *E, S, I, W;* 1980 *SA, R;* 1981 *S, A 1;* 1983 *A 1 (r)*

Wolff, J.-P. (*Béziers*) 1980 *SA, R;* 1981 *A 2;* 1982 *E*

Yachvili, M. (*Tulle, Brive*) 1968 *E, W, Cz, NZ 3, A, R;* 1969 *S, I, R;* 1971 *E, SA 1, 2, A 1;* 1972 *R;* 1975 *SA 2*

Zago, F. (*Montauban*) 1963 *I, E*

Australia

Figures in brackets indicate the number of Internationals played on each tour. No figure in brackets denotes only one match played. On European tours in some cases countries opposed are listed individually.

Abrahams, A.M.F. (*New South Wales*) 1967 *NZ;* 1968 *NZ;* 1969 *W*
Adams, N.J. (*New South Wales*) 1955 *NZ*
Allan, T. (*New South Wales*) 1946 *NZ (2). M;* 1947 *NZ;* 1947-48 *(T) S, I, W, E, F;* 1949 *M (3), NZ (2)*
Austin, L.R. (*New South Wales*) 1963 *E*

Ballesty, J.P. (*New South Wales*) 1968 *NZ (2), F;* 1968-69 *(ST) I, S;* 1969 *W, SA (3)*
Bannon, D.P. (*New South Wales*) 1946 *M*
Barker, H.S. (*New South Wales*) 1952 *Fi (2), NZ (2);* 1953 *SA;* 1954 *Fi (2)*
Barry, M.J. (*Queensland*) 1971 *SA*
Batch, P.G. (*Queensland*) 1975-76 *(T) S, W,* E; 1976 *Fi (3);* 1976-77 *(ST) F (2);* 1978 *W (2), NZ (3);* 1979 *Arg*
Batterham, R.P. (*New South Wales*) 1967 *NZ;* 1970 *N*
Battishall, B.R. (*New South Wales*) 1973-74 *(ST) E*
Baxter, A.J. (*New South Wales*) 1949 *M (3), NZ (2);* 1951 *NZ (2);* 1952 *NZ (2)*
Baxter, T.J. (*Queensland*) 1958 *NZ*
Bell, K.R. (*Queensland*) 1968-69 *(ST) S*
Berne, J.E. (*New South Wales*) 1975-76 *(T) S*
Besomo, K.S. (*New South Wales*) 1979 *I*
Betts, T.N. (*Queensland*) 1951 *NZ (2);* 1954 *Fi*
Black, J.W. (*New South Wales*) 1985 *NZ*
Blomley, J. (*New South Wales*) 1949 *M (3), NZ (2);* 1950 *BI (2)*
Bosler, J.M. (*New South Wales*) 1953 *SA*
Bourke, T.K. (*Queensland*) 1947 *NZ*
Boyce, E.S. (*New South Wales*) 1962 *NZ (2);* 1964 *NZ (3);* 1965 *SA (2);* 1966-67 *(T) W, S, E, I, F;* 1967 *I*

Boyce, J.S. (*New South Wales*) 1962 *NZ (3);* 1963 *E, SA (4);* 1964 *NZ (2);* 1965 *SA (2)*
Boyd, A.F. McC. (*Queensland*) 1958 *M*
Brass, J.E. (*New South Wales*) 1966 *BI;* 1966-67 *(T) W, S, E, I, F;* 1967 *I, NZ;* 1968 *NZ, F;* 1968-69 *(ST) I, S*
Broad, E.G. (*Queensland*) 1949 *M*
Brockhoff, J.D. (*New South Wales*) 1949 *M (2), NZ (2);* 1950 *BI (2);* 1951 *NZ (2)*
Brown, B.R. (*Queensland*) 1972 *NZ (2)*
Brown, J.V. (*New South Wales*) 1956 *SA (2);* 1957 *NZ (2);* 1957-58 *(T) W, I, E, S, F*
Brown, R.C. (*New South Wales*) 1975 *E (2)*
Brown, S.W. (*New South Wales*) 1953 *SA (3)*
Buchan, A.J. (*New South Wales*) 1946 *NZ (2);* 1947 *NZ (2);* 1947-48 *(T) S, I, W, E, F;* 1949 *M*
Burke, C.T. (*New South Wales*) 1946 *NZ;* 1947 *NZ (2);* 1947-48 *(T), S, I, W, E, F;* 1949 *M (2), NZ (2);* 1950 *BI (2);* 1951 *NZ (3);* 1953 *SA (3);* 1954 *Fi;* 1955 *NZ (3);* 1956 *SA (2)*

Burke, M.P. (*New South Wales*) 1984 *(T) E (r), I*; 1985 *NZ*

Burnet, D.R. (*New South Wales*) 1972 *F (2), NZ (3), Fi*

Butler, O.F. (*New South Wales*) 1969 *SA (2)*; 1970 *S*; 1971 *SA (2)*; 1971-72 *(ST) F (2)*

Cameron, A.S. (*New South Wales*) 1951 *NZ (3)*; 1952 *Fi (2), NZ (2)*; 1953 *SA (4)*; 1954 *Fi (2)*; 1955 *NZ (3)*; 1956 *SA (2)*; 1957 *NZ*; 1957-58 *(T) I*

Campbell, W.A. (*Queensland*) 1984 *Fi*

Campese, D.I. (*Australian Capital Territory*) 1982 *NZ (3)*; 1983 *US, Arg (2), NZ*; 1983 *(ST) It, F (2)*; 1984 *Fi, NZ (3), (T) E, I, W, S*

Carberry, C.M. (*New South Wales, Queensland*) 1973 *Tg*; 1973-74 *(ST) E*; 1975-76 *(T) I, US*; 1976 *Fi (3)*; 1981 *F (2)*; 1981-82 *(T) I, W, S, E*

Cardy, A.M. (*New South Wales*) 1966 *BI (2)*; 1966-67 *(T) W, S, E, I, F*; 1968 *NZ (2)*

Carroll, J.C. (*New South Wales*) 1953 *SA*

Carroll, J.H. (*New South Wales*) 1958 *M (2), NZ (3)*; 1959 *BI (2)*

Carson, P.J. (*New South Wales*) 1979 *NZ*; 1980 *NZ*

Casey, T.V. (*New South Wales*) 1963 *SA (3)*; 1964 *NZ (3)*

Catchpole, K.W. (*New South Wales*) 1961 *Fi (3), SA (2), F*; 1962 *NZ (3)*; 1963 *SA (3)*; 1964 *NZ (3)*; 1965 *SA (2)*; 1966 *BI (2)*; 1966-67 *(T) W, S, E, I, F*; 1967 *I, NZ*; 1968 *NZ*

Cawsey, R.M. (*New South Wales*) 1949 *M, NZ (2)*

Chapman, G.A. (*New South Wales*) 1962 *NZ (3)*

Cleary, M.A. (*New South Wales*) 1961 *Fi (3), SA (2), F*

Clements, P. (*New South Wales*) 1982 *NZ*

Cocks, M.R. (*New South Wales, Queensland*) 1972 *F (2), NZ (2), Fi*; 1973 *Tg (2)*; 1973-74 *(ST) W, E*; 1975 *J*

Codey, D. (*New South Wales Country*) 1983 *Arg*; 1984 *(T) E, W, S*; 1985 *NZ*

Colbert, R. (*New South Wales*) 1952 *Fi, NZ (2)*; 1953 *SA (3)*

Cole, J.W. (*New South Wales*) 1968 *NZ (2), F*; 1968-69 *(ST) I, S*; 1969 *W, SA (4)*; 1970 *S*; 1971 *SA (3)*; 1971-72 *(ST) F (2)*; 1972 *NZ (3)*; 1973 *Tg (2)*; 1974 *NZ*

Connor, D.M. (*Queensland*) 1957-58 *(T) W, I, E, S, F*; 1958 *M (2), NZ (3)*; 1959 *BI (2)*

Cooke, G.M. (*Queensland*) 1932 *NZ (3)*; 1933 *SA (3)*; 1946 *NZ*; 1947 *NZ*; 1947-48 *(T) S, I, W, E, F*

Cooke, B.P. (*Queensland*) 1979 *I*

Coolican, J.E. (*New South Wales*) 1982 *NZ*; 1983 *(ST) It, F (2)*

Cornelsen, G. (*New South Wales*) 1974 *NZ (2)*; 1975 *J*; 1975-76 *(T) S, W, E*; 1976-77 *(ST) F (2)*; 1978 *W (2), NZ (3)*; 1979 *I (2), NZ, Arg (2)*; 1980 *NZ (3)*; 1981-82 *(T) I, W, S, E*

Cornes, J.R. (*Queensland*) 1972 *Fi*

Cornforth, R.G.W. (*New South Wales*) 1947 *NZ*; 1950 *BI*

Costello, P.P.S. (*Queensland*) 1950 *BI*

Cottrell, N.V. (*Queensland*) 1949 *M (3), NZ (2)*; 1950 *BI (2)*; 1951 *NZ (3)*; 1952 *Fi (2), NZ (2)*

Cox, B.P. (*New South Wales*) 1952 *Fi (2), NZ (2)*; 1954 *Fi*; 1955 *NZ*; 1956 *SA*; 1957 *NZ (2)*

Cox, M.H. (*New South Wales*) 1981-82 *(T) W, S*

Cox, P.A. (*New South Wales*) 1979 *Arg (2)*; 1980 *Fi, NZ (2)*; 1981-82 *(T) W (r), S*; 1982 *S (2), NZ (3)*; 1984 *Fi, NZ (3)*

Cremin, J.F. (*New South Wales*) 1946 *NZ (2)*; 1947 *NZ*

Crittle, C.P. (*New South Wales*) 1962 *NZ (2)*; 1963 *SA (3)*; 1964 *NZ (3)*; 1965 *SA (2)*; 1966 *BI (2)*; 1966-67 *(T) S, E, I*

Cross, J.R. (*New South Wales*) 1955 *NZ (3)*

Cross, K.A. (*New South Wales*) 1949 *M, NZ (2)*; 1950 *BI (2)*; 1951 *NZ (2)*; 1952 *NZ*; 1953 *SA (4)*; 1954 *Fi (2)*; 1955 *NZ*; 1956 *SA (2)*; 1957 *NZ (2)*

Crowe, P.J. (*New South Wales*) 1976-77 *(ST) F*; 1978 *W (2)*; 1979 *I, NZ, Arg*

Curley, T.G.P. (*New South Wales*) 1957 *NZ (2)*; 1957-58 *(T) W, I, E, S, F*; 1958 *M, NZ (3)*

Curran, D.J. (*New South Wales*) 1980 *NZ*; 1981 *F (2)*; 1981-82 *(T) W*; 1983 *Arg*

Cutler, S.A.G. (*New South Wales*) 1982 *NZ (r)*; 1984 *NZ (3)*; 1984 *(T) E, I, W, S*; 1985 *NZ*

D'Arcy, A.M. (*Queensland*) 1980 *Fi, NZ*; 1981 *F (2)*; 1981-82 *(T) I, W, S, E*; 1982 *S (2)*

Darveniza, P. (*New South Wales*) 1969 *W, SA (3)*

Davidson, R.A.L. (*New South Wales*) 1952 *Fi (2), NZ (2)*; 1953 *SA*; 1957 *NZ (2)*; 1957-58 *(T) W, I, E, S, F*; 1958 *M*

Davis, C.C. (*New South Wales*) 1949 *NZ*; 1951 *NZ (3)*

Davis, E.H. (*Victoria*) 1947-48 *(T) S, W*; 1949 *M (2)*

Davis, G.V. (*New South Wales*) 1963 *E, SA (4)*; 1964 *NZ (3)*; 1965 *SA*; 1966 *BI (2)*; 1966-67 *(T) W, S, E, I, F*; 1967 *I, NZ*; 1968 *NZ (2), F*; 1968-69 *(ST) I, S*; 1969 *W, SA (4)*; 1970 *S*; 1971 *SA (3)*; 1971-72 *(ST) F (2)*; 1972 *F (2), NZ (3)*

Davis, G.W.G. (*New South Wales*) 1955 *NZ (2)*

Davis, R.A. (*New South Wales*) 1974 *NZ (3)*

Dawson, W.L. (*New South Wales*) 1946 *NZ (2)*

Diett, L.J. (*New South Wales*) 1959 *BI (2)*

Donald, K.J. (*Queensland*) 1957 *NZ*; 1957-58 *(T) W, I, E, S*; 1958 *M (2), NZ (3)*

Douglas, J.A. (*Victoria*) 1962 *NZ (3)*

Dowse, J.H. (*New South Wales*) 1961 *Fi (2), SA (2)*

Dunn, P.K. (*New South Wales*) 1958 *NZ (3)*; 1959 *BI (2)*

Dunworth, D.A. (*Queensland*) 1971-72 *(ST) F (2)*; 1972 *F (2)*; 1976 *Fi*

Eastes, C.C. (*New South Wales*) 1946 *NZ (2)*; 1947 *NZ (2)*; 1949 *M (2)*

Ella, G.A. (*New South Wales*) 1982 *NZ (2)*; 1983 *(ST) F (2)*

Ella, G.J. (*New South Wales*) 1982 *S*; 1983 *(ST) It*

Ella, M.G. (*New South Wales*) 1980 *NZ (3)*; 1981 *F*; 1981-82 *(T) S, E*; 1982 *S, NZ (3)*; 1983 *US, Arg (2), NZ, (ST) It, F (2)*; 1984 *Fi, NZ (3), (T) E, I, W, S*

Ellem, M.A. (*New South Wales*) 1976 *Fi (r)*

Elliott, F.M. (*New South Wales*) 1957 *NZ*

Ellis, K.J. (*New South Wales*) 1958 *NZ (3)*; 1959 *BI (2)*

Ellwood, B.J. (*New South Wales*) 1958 *NZ (3)*; 1961 *Fi (2), SA, F*; 1962 *NZ (5)*; 1963 *SA (4)*; 1964 *NZ*; 1965 *SA (2)*; 1966 *BI*

Emanuel, D.M. (*New South Wales*) 1957 *NZ*, 1957-58 *(T) W, I, E, S, F*; 1958 *M (3)*

Emery, N.A. (*New South Wales*) 1947 *NZ*; 1947-48 *(T) S, I, W, E, F*; 1949 *M (2), NZ (2)*

Fairfax, R.L. (*New South Wales*) 1971-72 *(ST) F (2)*; 1972 *F (2), NZ, Fi*; 1973-74 *(ST) W, E*

Farr-Jones, N.C. (*New South Wales*) 1984 *(T) E, I, W, S*; 1985 *NZ*

Fay, G. (*New South Wales*) 1971 *SA*; 1972 *NZ (3)*; 1973 *Tg (2)*; 1973-74 *(ST) W, E*; 1974 *NZ (3)*; 1975 *E (2), J*; 1975-76 *(T) S, W, I, US*; 1978 *W (2), NZ (3)*; 1979 *I*

Fenwicke, P.T. (*New South Wales*) 1957 *NZ*; 1957-58 *(T) W, I, E*; 1959 *BI (2)*

Finnane, S.C. (*New South Wales*) 1975 *E, J (2)*; 1975-76 *(T) E*; 1978 *W (2)*

Fogarty, J.R. (*Queensland*) 1949 *M (2)*

Forbes, C.F. (*Queensland*) 1953 *SA (3)*; 1954 *Fi*; 1956 *SA (2)*

Ford, B. (*Queensland*) 1957 *NZ*

Forman, T.R. (*New South Wales*) 1968-69 *(ST) I, S*; 1969 *W, SA (4)*

Fox, O.G. (*New South Wales*) 1957-58 *(T) F*

Freedman, J.E. (*New South Wales*) 1962 *NZ (3)*; 1963 *SA*

Freeman, E. (*New South Wales*) 1946 *NZ (r), M*

Freney, M.E. (*Queensland*) 1972 *NZ (3)*; 1973 *Tg*; 1973-74 *(ST) W, E (r)*

Furness, D.C. (*New South Wales*) 1946 *M*

Gardner, W.C. (*New South Wales*) 1950 *BI*

Garner, R.L. (*New South Wales*) 1949 *NZ (2)*

Gelling, A.M. (*New South Wales*) 1972 *NZ, Fi*

Gibbs, P.R. (*Victoria*) 1966-67 *(T) S*

Gordon, K.M. (*New South Wales*) 1950 *BI (2)*

Gould, R.G. (*Queensland*) 1980 *NZ (3)*; 1981-82 *(T) I, W, S*; 1982 *S, NZ (3)*; 1983 *US, Arg, (ST) F (2)*; 1984 *NZ (3), (T) E, I, W, S*; 1985 *NZ*

Graham, R. (*New South Wales*) 1973 *Tg (2)*; 1973-74 *(ST) W, E*; 1974 *NZ (2)*; 1975 *E, J (2)*; 1975-76 *(T) S, W, I, US*; 1976 *Fi (3)*; 1976-77 *(ST) F (2)*

Gregory, S.C. (*Queensland*) 1968 *NZ, F*; 1968-69 *(ST) I, S*; 1969 *SA (2)*; 1971 *SA (2)*; 1971-72 *(ST) F (2)*; 1972 *F (2)*; 1973 *Tg (2)*; 1973-74 *(ST) W, E*

Grey, G.O. (*New South Wales*) 1972 *F (r), NZ (3), Fi (r)*

Grigg, P.C. (*Queensland*) 1980 *NZ*; 1982 *S, NZ (3)*; 1983 *Arg, NZ*; 1984 *Fi, (T) W, S*; 1985 *NZ*

Grimmond, D.N. (*New South Wales*) 1964 *NZ*

Gudsell, K.E. (*New South Wales*) 1951 *NZ (3)*

Guerassimoff, J. (*Queensland*) 1963 *SA (3)*; 1964 *NZ (3)*; 1965 *SA*; 1966 *BI (2)*; 1966-67 *(T) E, I, F*

Gunther, W.J. (*New South Wales*) 1957 *NZ*

Hall, D. (*Queensland*) 1980 *Fi, NZ (3)*; 1981 *F (2)*; 1982 *S (2), NZ (2)*; 1983 *US, Arg (2), NZ*; 1983 *(ST) It*

Hamilton, B.G. (*New South Wales*) 1946 *M*

Handy, C.B. (*Queensland*) 1978 *NZ*; 1979 *NZ, Arg (2)*; 1980 *NZ (2)*

Hanley, R.G. (*Queensland*) 1983 *US (r)*; 1983 *(ST) It (r)*

Hardcastle, P.A. (*New South Wales*) 1946 *NZ (2), M*; 1947 *NZ*; 1949 *M*

Harding, M.A. (*New South Wales*) 1983 *(ST) It*

Harvey, P.B. (*Queensland*) 1949 *M (2)*

Harvey, R.M. (*New South Wales*) 1957-58 *(T) F*; 1958 *M*

Hatherell, W.I. (*Queensland*) 1952 *Fi (2)*

Hauser, R.G. (*Queensland*) 1975 *J (2[1r])*; 1975-76 *(T) W (r), E, I, US*; 1976 *Fi (3)*; 1976-77 *(ST) F (2)*; 1978 *W (2)*; 1979 *I (2)*

Hawker, M.J. (*New South Wales*) 1980 *Fi, NZ (3)*; 1981 *F (2)*; 1981-82 *(T) I, W, E*; 1982 *S (2), NZ (3)*; 1983 *US, Arg (2), NZ, (ST) It, F (2)*; 1984 *NZ (3)*

Hawthorne, P.F. (*New South Wales*) 1962 *NZ (3)*; 1963 *E, SA (4)*; 1964 *NZ (2)*; 1965 *SA (2)*; 1966 *BI (2)*; 1966-67 *(T) W, E, I, F*; 1967 *I, NZ*

Heinrich, E.L. (*New South Wales*) 1961 *Fi (3), SA, F*; 1962 *NZ (3)*; 1963 *E, SA*

Henrich, V.W. (*New South Wales*) 1954 *Fi (2)*

Heming, R.J. (*New South Wales*) 1961 *Fi (2), SA (2), F*; 1962 *NZ (4)*; 1963 *SA (3)*; 1964 *NZ (3)*; 1965 *SA (2)*; 1966 *BI (2)*; 1966-67 *(T) W, F*

Hillhouse, D.W. (*Queensland*) 1975-76 *(T) S, E*; 1976 *Fi (3)*; 1976-77 *(ST) F (2)*; 1978 *W (2)*; 1983 *US, Arg (2), NZ*; 1983 *(ST) It, F (2)*

Hills, E.F. (*Victoria*) 1950 *BI (2)*

Hindmarsh, J.C. (*New South Wales*) 1975 *J*; 1975-76 *(T) S, W, US*; 1976 *Fi (3)*; 1976-77 *(ST) F (2)*

Hipwell, J.N.B. (*New South Wales*) 1968 *NZ (2[1r]), F*; 1968-69 *(ST) I, S*; 1969 *W, SA (4)*; 1970 *S*; 1971 *SA (2)*; 1971-72 *(ST) F (2)*; 1972 *F (2)*; 1973 *Tg*; 1973-74 *(ST) W, E*; 1974 *NZ (3)*; 1975 *E (2), J*; 1975-76 *(T) S, W*; 1978 *NZ (3)*; 1981 *F (2)*; 1981-82 *(T) I, W, E*

Holt, N.C. (*Queensland*) 1984 *Fi*

Honan, B.D. (*Queensland*) 1968 *NZ (2[1r]), F*; 1968-69 *(ST) I, S*; 1969 *SA (4)*

Honan, R.E. (*Queensland*) 1964 *NZ (2)*

Horsley, G.R. (*Queensland*) 1954 *Fi*

Horton, P.A. (*New South Wales*) 1974 *NZ (3)*; 1975 *E (2), J (2)*; 1975-76 *(T) S, W, E*; 1976-77 *(ST) F (2)*; 1978 *W (2), NZ (3)*; 1979 *NZ, Arg*

How, R.A. (*New South Wales*) 1967 *I*

Howard, J.L. (*New South Wales*) 1970 *S*; 1971 *SA, F (r)*; 1972 *NZ, F (r)*; 1973 *Tg (2)*; 1973-74 *(ST) W*

Howell, M.L. (*New South Wales*) 1946 *NZ (r)*; 1947 *NZ*; 1947-48 *(T) S, I, W*

Hughes, N. McL. (*New South Wales*) 1953 *SA (4)*; 1955 *NZ (3)*; 1956 *SA (2)*; 1957-58 *(T) W, I, E, S, F*

James, P.M. (*Queensland*) 1958 *M (2)*

Johnson, A.P. (*New South Wales*) 1946 *NZ, M*

Johnson, B.B. (*New South Wales*) 1952 *Fi (2), NZ (2)*; 1953 *SA (3)*; 1955 *NZ (2)*

Johnson, P.G. (*New South Wales*) 1959 *BI (2)*; 1961 *Fi (3), SA (2), F*; 1962 *NZ (5)*; 1963 *E, SA (4)*; 1964 *NZ (3)*; 1965 *SA (2)*; 1966 *BI (2)*; 1966-67 *(T) W, S, E, I, F*; 1967 *I, NZ*; 1968 *NZ (2), F*; 1968-69 *(ST) I, S*; 1970 *S*; 1971 *SA (2)*; 1971-72 *(ST) F (2)*

Jones, G.G. (*Queensland*) 1952 *Fi (2)*; 1953 *SA (4)*; 1954 *Fi (2)*; 1955 *NZ (3)*; 1956 *SA*

Jones, P.A. (*New South Wales*) 1963 *E, SA*

Kay, A.R. (*Victoria*) 1958 *NZ*; 1959 *BI*

Kearney, K.H. (*New South Wales*) 1947 *NZ (2)*; 1947-48 *(T) S, I, W, E, F*

Kelleher, R.J. (*Queensland*) 1969 *SA (2)*

Keller, D.H. (*New South Wales*) 1947 *NZ*; 1947-48 *(T) S, I, W, E, F*

Knight, M. (*New South Wales*) 1978 *W (2), NZ*

Knight, S.O. (*New South Wales*) 1969 *SA (2)*; 1970 *S*; 1971 *SA (3)*

Kraefft, D.F. (*New South Wales*) 1947 *NZ*; 1947-48 *(T) S, I, W, E, F*

Lambie, J.K. (*New South Wales*) 1974 *NZ (3)*; 1975-76 *(T) W*

Lane, T.A. (*Queensland*) 1985 *NZ*

Larkin, K.K. (*Queensland*) 1958 *M (2)*

Latimer, N.B. (*New South Wales*) 1957 *NZ*

Lawton, T.A. (*Queensland*) 1983 *(ST) F (2[1r])*; 1984 *Fi, NZ (3)*; 1984 *(T) E, I, W, S*; 1985 *NZ*

Lenehan, J.K. (*New South Wales*) 1957-58 *(T) W, E, S, F*; 1958 *M (3)*; 1959 *BI (2)*; 1961 *SA (2), F*; 1962 *NZ (4)*; 1965 *SA (2)*; 1966-67 *(T) W, S, E, I, F*; 1967 *I*

L'Estrange, R.D. (*Queensland*) 1971-72 *(ST) F (2)*; 1972 *NZ (3)*; 1973 *Tg (2)*; 1973-74 *(ST) W, E*; 1974 *NZ (3)*; 1975-76 *(T) S, W, I, US*

Lisle, R.J. (*New South Wales*) 1961 *Fi (3), SA*

Livermore, A.E. (*Queensland*) 1946 *NZ, M*

Loane, M.E. (*Queensland*) 1973 *Tg (2)*; 1974 *NZ*; 1975 *E (2), J*; 1975-76 *(T) E, I*; 1976 *Fi (3)*; 1976-77 *(ST) F (2)*; 1978 *W (2)*; 1979 *I (2), NZ, Arg (2)*; 1981 *F (2)*; 1981-82 *(T) I, W, S, E*; 1982 *S (2)*

Logan, D.L. (*New South Wales*) 1958 *M*

Lowth, D.R. (*New South Wales*) 1958 *NZ*

Lucas, P.W. (*New South Wales*) 1982 *NZ (3)*

Lynagh, M.P. (*Queensland*) 1984 *Fi*; 1984 *(T) E, I, W, S*; 1985 *NZ*

McBain, M.I. (*Queensland*) 1983 *(ST) It, F*

MacBride, J.W.T. (*New South Wales*) 1946 *NZ (2), M*; 1947 *NZ (2)*; 1947-48 *(T) S, I, W, E, F*

McCarthy, F.J.C. (*Queensland*) 1950 *BI*

McDermott, L.C. (*Queensland*) 1962 *NZ (2)*

McDonald, B.S. (*New South Wales*) 1969 *SA*; 1970 *S*

Macdougall, D.G. (*New South Wales*) 1961 *Fi, SA*

Macdougall, S.G. (*New South Wales, Australian Capital Territory*) 1971 *SA*; 1973-74 *(ST) E*; 1974 *NZ (3)*; 1975 *E (2)*; 1975-76 *(T) E*

McGill, A.N. (*New South Wales*) 1968 *NZ (2), F*; 1969 *W, SA (4)*; 1970 *S*; 1971 *SA (3)*; 1971-72 *(ST) F (2)*; 1972 *F (2), NZ (3)*; 1973 *Tg (2)*

McIntyre, A.J. (*Queensland*) 1982 *NZ (3)*; 1983 *(ST) F (2)*; 1984 *Fi, NZ (3)*; 1984 *(T) E, I, W, S*; 1985 *NZ*

McKid, W.A. (*New South Wales*) 1975-76 *(T) E*; 1976 *Fi*; 1978 *NZ (2)*; 1979 *I (2)*

McLean, J.J. (*Queensland*) 1971 *SA (2)*; 1971-72 *(ST) F (2)*; 1972 *F (2), NZ (3), Fi*; 1973-74 *(ST) W, E*; 1974 *NZ*

McLean, P.E. (*Queensland*) 1974 *NZ (3)*; 1975 *J (2)*; 1975-76 *(T) S, W, E, I*; 1976 *Fi (3)*; 1976-77 *(ST) F (2)*; 1978 *W (2), NZ*; 1979 *I (2), NZ, Arg (2)*; 1980 *Fi*; 1981 *F (2)*; 1981-82 *(T) I, W, S, E*; 1982 *S*

McLean, P.W. (*Queensland*) 1978 *NZ (3)*; 1979 *I (2), NZ, Arg (2)*; 1980 *Fi (r), NZ*; 1981-82 *(T) I, W, S, E*; 1982 *S (2)*

McLean, R.A. (*New South Wales*) 1971 *SA (3)*; 1971-72 *(ST) F (2)*

McLean, W.M. (*Queensland*) 1946 *NZ (2), M*; 1947 *NZ (2)*

McMaster, R.E. (*Queensland*) 1946 *NZ (2), M*; 1947 *NZ (2)*; 1947-48 *(T) I, W*

MacMillan, D.I. (*Queensland*) 1950 *BI (2)*

McMullen, K.V. (*New South Wales*) 1962 *NZ (2)*; 1963 *E, SA*

Magrath, E. (*New South Wales*) 1961 *Fi, SA, F*

Malouf, B.P. (*New South Wales*) 1982 *NZ*

Manning, R.C.S. (*Queensland*) 1967 *NZ*

Mansfield, B.W. (*New South Wales*) 1975 *J*

Marks, R.J.P. (*Queensland*) 1962 *NZ (2)*; 1963 *E, SA (3)*; 1964 *NZ (3)*; 1965 *SA (2)*; 1966-67 *(T) W, S, E, I, F*; 1967 *I*

Marshall, J.S. (*New South Wales*) 1949 *M*

Martin, M.C. (*New South Wales*) 1980 *Fi, NZ (2)*; 1981 *F (2)*; 1981-82 *(T) W (r)*

Mathers, M.J. (*New South Wales*) 1980 *Fi, NZ (r)*

Meadows, J.E.C. (*Victoria, Queensland*) 1974 *NZ*; 1975-76 *(T) S, W, I, US*; 1976 *Fi (2)*; 1976-77 *(ST) F (2)*; 1978 *NZ (3)*; 1979 *I (2)*; 1981-82 *(T) I, S, E*; 1982 *NZ (2)*; 1983 *US, Arg, NZ*

Meadows, R.W. (*New South Wales*) 1958 *M (3), NZ (3)*

Melrose, T.C. (*New South Wales*) 1978 *NZ*; 1979 *I (2), NZ, Arg (2)*

Miller, A.R. (*New South Wales*) 1952 *Fi (2), NZ (2)*; 1953 *SA (4)*; 1954 *Fi (2)*; 1955 *NZ (3)*; 1956 *SA (2)*; 1957 *NZ (2)*; 1957-58 *(T) W, E, S, F*; 1958 *M (3)*; 1959 *BI (2)*; 1961 *Fi (3), SA, F*; 1962 *NZ (2)*; 1966 *BI (2)*; 1966-67 *(T) W, S, I, F*; 1967 *I, NZ*

Miller, J.M. (*New South Wales*) 1962 *NZ*; 1963 *E, SA*; 1966-67 *(T) W, S, E*

Monaghan, L.E. (*New South Wales*) 1973-74 *(ST) E*; 1974 *NZ (3)*; 1975 *E (2)*; 1975-76 *(T) S, W, E, I, US*; 1976-77 *(ST) F*; 1978 *W (2), NZ*; 1979 *I (2)*

Moon, B.J. (*New South Wales*) 1978 *NZ (2)*; 1979 *I (2), NZ, Arg (2)*; 1980 *Fi, NZ (3)*; 1981 *F (2)*; 1981-82 *(T) I, W, S, E*; 1982 *S (2)*; 1983 *US, Arg (2), NZ*; 1983 *(ST) It, F (2)*; 1984 *Fi, NZ (3)*; 1984 *(T) E*

Mooney, T.P. (*Queensland*) 1954 *Fi (2)*

Morton, A.R. (*New South Wales*) 1957 *NZ (2)*; 1957-58 *(T) F*; 1958 *M (3)*; 1959 *BI (2)*

Mossop, R.P. (*New South Wales*) 1949 *NZ (2)*; 1950 *BI (2)*; 1951 *NZ*

Moutray, I.E. (*New South Wales*) 1963 *SA*

O'Connor, M.D. (*Australian Capital Territory, Queensland*) 1979 *Arg (2)*; 1980 *Fi, NZ (3)*; 1981 *F (2)*; 1981-82 *(T) I, E*; 1982 *S (2)*

O'Gorman, J.F. (*New South Wales*) 1961 *Fi, SA (2), F*; 1962 *NZ*; 1963 *E, SA (4)*; 1965 *SA (2)*; 1966-67 *(T) W, S, E, I, F*; 1967 *I*

O'Neill, D.J. (*Queensland*) 1964 *NZ (2)*

O'Neill, J.M. (*Queensland*) 1952 *NZ (2)*; 1956 *SA (2)*

Osborne, D.H. (*Victoria*) 1975 *E (2), J*

Outterside, R. (*New South Wales*) 1959 *BI (2)*

Parker, A.J. (*Queensland*) 1983 *Arg (2[1r]), NZ*

Pashley, J.J. (*New South Wales*) 1954 *Fi (2); 1958 M (3)*

Pearse, G.K. (*New South Wales*) 1975-76 *(T) W (r), I, US; 1976 Fi (3); 1978 NZ (3)*

Perrin, P.D. (*Queensland*) 1962 *NZ*

Phelps, R. (*New South Wales*) 1955 *NZ (2); 1956 SA (2); 1957 NZ (2); 1957-58 (T) W, I, E, S, F; 1958 M, NZ (3); 1961 Fi (3), SA (2), F; 1962 NZ (3)*

Phipps, J.A. (*New South Wales*) 1953 *SA (4); 1954 Fi (2); 1955 NZ (2); 1956 SA (2)*

Phipps, P.J. (*New South Wales*) 1955 *NZ*

Pilecki, S.J. (*Queensland*) 1978 *W (2), NZ (2); 1979 I (2), NZ, Arg (2); 1980 Fi, NZ (2); 1982 S (2); 1983 US, Arg (2), NZ*

Piper, B.J.C. (*New South Wales*) 1946 *NZ (2), M; 1947 NZ; 1947-48 (T) S, I, W, E, F; 1949 M (3)*

Poidevin, S.P. (*New South Wales*) 1980 *Fi, NZ (3); 1981 F (2); 1981-82 (T) I, W, S, E; 1982 NZ (3); 1983 US, Arg (2), NZ, (ST) It, F (2); 1984 Fi, NZ (3), (T) E, I, W, S; 1985 NZ*

Potter, R.T. (*Queensland*) 1961 *Fi*

Pope, A.M. (*Queensland*) 1968 *NZ (r)*

Potts, J.M. (*New South Wales*) 1957 *NZ (2); 1957-58 (T) W, I; 1959 BI*

Price, R.A. (*New South Wales*) 1974 *NZ (3); 1975 E (2), J (2); 1975-76 (T) US*

Primmer, C.J. (*Queensland*) 1951 *NZ (2)*

Proctor, I.J. (*New South Wales*) 1967 *NZ*

Prosser, R.B. (*New South Wales*) 1966-67 *(T) E, I; 1967 I, NZ; 1968 NZ (2), F; 1968-69 (ST) I, S; 1969 W, SA (4); 1971 SA (3); 1971-72 (ST) F (2); 1972 F (2), NZ (3), Fi*

Purcell, M.P. (*Queensland*) 1966-67 *(T) W, S; 1967 I*

Purkis, E.M. (*New South Wales*) 1957-58 *(T) S; 1958 M*

Rathie, D.S. (*Queensland*) 1972 *F (2)*

Reid, T.W. (*New South Wales*) 1961 *Fi (3), SA; 1962 NZ*

Reilly, N.P. (*Queensland*) 1968 *NZ (2), F; 1968-69 (ST) I, S; 1969 W, SA (4)*

Reynolds, R.J. (*New South Wales*) 1984 *Fi, NZ (3)*

Richards, G. (*New South Wales*) 1978 *NZ (2[1r]); 1981 F*

Richardson, G.C. (*Queensland*) 1971 *SA (3); 1972 NZ (2), Fi; 1973 Tg (2); 1973-74 (ST) W*

Roberts, B.T. (*New South Wales*) 1956 *SA*

Roberts, H.F. (*Queensland*) 1961 *Fi (2), SA, F*

Robertson, I.J. (*New South Wales*) 1975 *J (2)*

Roche, C. (*Queensland*) 1982 *S (2), NZ (3); 1983 US, Arg (2), NZ; 1983 (ST) It, F (2); 1984 Fi, NZ (3); 1984 (T) I*

Rodriguez, E.E. (*New South Wales*) 1984 *Fi, NZ (3); 1984 (T) E, I, W, S; 1985 NZ*

Rose, H.A. (*New South Wales*) 1967 *I, NZ; 1968 NZ (2), F; 1968-69 (ST) I, S; 1969 W, SA (4); 1970 S*

Rosenblum, R.G. (*New South Wales*) 1969 *SA (2); 1970 S*

Ross, W.S. (*Queensland*) 1979 *I (2), Arg; 1980 Fi, NZ (2); 1982 S (2); 1983 US, Arg (2), NZ*

Rothwell, P.R. (*New South Wales*) 1951 *NZ (3); 1952 Fi*

Rowles, P.G. (*New South Wales*) 1972 *Fi; 1973-74 (ST) E*

Roxburgh, J.R. (*New South Wales*) 1968 *NZ (2), F; 1969 W, SA (4); 1970 S*

Ruebner, G. (*New South Wales*) 1966 *BI (2)*

Ryan, J.R. (*New South Wales*) 1975 *J; 1975-76 (T) I, US; 1976 Fi (3)*

Ryan, K.J. (*Queensland*) 1957-58 *(T) E; 1958 M, NZ (3)*

Ryan, P.F. (*New South Wales*) 1963 *E, SA; 1966 BI (2)*

Sayle, J.L. (*New South Wales*) 1967 *NZ*

Schulte, B.G. (*Queensland*) 1946 *NZ, M*

Scott, P.R.I. (*New South Wales*) 1962 *NZ (2)*

Shambrook, G.G. (*Queensland*) 1976 *Fi (2)*

Shaw, A.A. (*Queensland*) 1973-74 *(ST) W, E; 1975 E (2), J; 1975-76 (T) S, W, E, I, US; 1976 Fi (3); 1976-77 (ST) F (2); 1978 W (2), NZ (3); 1979 I (2), NZ, Arg (2); 1980 Fi, NZ (3); 1981 F (2); 1981-82 (T) I, W, S; 1982 S (2)*

Shaw, G.A. (*New South Wales*) 1969 *W, SA (r); 1970 S; 1971 SA (3); 1971-72 (ST) F (2); 1973-74 (ST) W, E; 1974 NZ (3); 1975 E (2), J (2); 1975-76 (T) W, E, I, US; 1976 Fi (3); 1976-77 (ST) F (2); 1979 NZ*

Shehadie, N.M. (*New South Wales*) 1947 *NZ; 1947-48 (T) E, F; 1949 M (3), NZ (2); 1950 BI (2); 1951 NZ (3); 1952 Fi (2), NZ; 1953 SA (4); 1954 Fi (2); 1955 NZ (3); 1956 SA (2); 1957 NZ; 1957-58 (T) W, I*

Sheil, A.G.R. (*Queensland*) 1956 *SA*

Shepherd, D.J. (*Victoria*) 1964 *NZ; 1965 SA (2); 1966 BI (2)*

Skinner, A.J. (*New South Wales*) 1969 *W, SA; 1970 S*

Slack, A.G. (*Queensland*) 1978 *W (2), NZ (2); 1979 NZ, Arg (2); 1980 Fi; 1981-82 (T) I, W, S, E; 1982 S, NZ; 1983 US, Arg (2), NZ; 1983 (ST) It; 1984 Fi, NZ (3); 1984 (T) E, I, W, S*

Smith, P.V. (*New South Wales*) 1967 *NZ; 1968 NZ (2), F; 1968-69 (ST) I, S; 1969 W, SA*

Smith, R.A. (*New South Wales*) 1971 *SA (2); 1972 F (2), NZ (3[1r]), Fi; 1975 E (2), J (2); 1975-76 (T) S, W, E, I, US; 1976 Fi (3); 1976-77 (ST) F (2)*

Solomon, H.J. (*New South Wales*) 1949 *M, NZ; 1950 BI (2); 1951 NZ (2); 1952 Fi (2), NZ (2); 1953 SA (3); 1955 NZ*

Stapleton, E.T. (*New South Wales*) 1951 *NZ (3); 1952 Fi (2), NZ (2); 1953 SA (4); 1954 Fi; 1955 NZ (3); 1958 NZ*

Stegman, T.R. (*New South Wales*) 1973 *Tg (2)*

Stephens, O.G. (*New South Wales*) 1973 *Tg (2); 1973-74 (ST) W; 1974 NZ (2)*

Stewart, A.A. (*New South Wales*) 1979 *NZ, Arg (2)*

Stone, J.M. (*New South Wales*) 1946 *M, NZ*

Storey, N.J.D. (*New South Wales*) 1962 *NZ*

Strachan, D.J. (*New South Wales*) 1955 *NZ (2)*

Streeter, S.F. (*New South Wales*) 1978 *NZ*

Stumbles, B.D. (*New South Wales*) 1972 *NZ (3[1r]), Fi*

Sullivan, P.D. (*New South Wales*) 1971 *SA (3); 1971-72 (ST) F (2); 1972 F (2), NZ (2), Fi; 1973 Tg (2); 1973-74 (ST) W*

Summons, A.J. (*New South Wales*) 1957-58 *(T) W, I, E, S; 1958 M, NZ (3); 1959 BI (2)*

Sweeney, T.L. (*Queensland*) 1953 *SA*

Taafe, B.S. (*New South Wales*) 1969 *SA; 1972 F (2)*

Tate, M.J. (*New South Wales*) 1951 *NZ; 1952 Fi (2), NZ (2); 1953 SA; 1954 Fi (2)*

Taylor, D.A. (*Queensland*) 1968 *NZ (2), F; 1968-69 (ST) I, S*

Taylor, J.I. (*New South Wales*) 1971 *SA; 1972 F (2), Fi*

Teitzel, R.G. (*Queensland*) 1966-67 *(T) W, S, E, I, F; 1967 I, NZ*

Thompson, P.D. (*Queensland*) 1950 *BI*

Thompson, R.J. (*Western Australia*) 1971 *SA; 1971-72 (ST) F (r); 1972 Fi*

Thornett, J.E. (*New South Wales*) 1955 *NZ (3); 1956 SA (2); 1957-58 (T) W, I, S, F; 1958 M (2), NZ (2); 1959 BI (2); 1961 Fi (2), SA (2), F; 1962 NZ (4); 1963 E, SA (4); 1964 NZ (3); 1965 SA (2); 1966 BI (2); 1966-67 (T) F*

Thornett, R.N. (*New South Wales*) 1961 *Fi (3), SA (2), E; 1962 NZ (5)*

Tindall, E.N. (*New South Wales*) 1973 *Tg*

Tonkin, A.E.J. (*New South Wales*) 1947-48 *(T) S, I, W, E, F; 1950 BI*

Tooth, R.M. (*New South Wales*) 1951 *NZ (3); 1954 Fi (2); 1955 NZ (3); 1957 NZ (2)*

Trivett, R.K. (*Queensland*) 1966 *BI (2)*

Turnbull, A. (*Victoria*) 1961 *Fi*

Turnbull, R.V. (*New South Wales*) 1968-69 *(ST) I*

Tuynman, S.N. (*New South Wales*) 1983 *(ST) F (2); 1984 (T) E, I, W, S; 1985 NZ*

Tweedale, E. (*New South Wales*) 1946 *NZ (2); 1947 NZ; 1947-48 (T) S, I, E, F; 1949 M (3)*

Vaughan, D. (*New South Wales*) 1983 *US, Arg; 1983 (ST) It, F (2)*

Vaughan, G.N. (*Victoria*) 1957-58 *(T) E, S, F; 1958 M (3)*

Walker, A.K. (*New South Wales*) 1947 *NZ; 1947-48 (T) E, F; 1950 BI (2)*

Walker, L.R. (*New South Wales*) 1982 *NZ (2)*

Walsh, J.J. (*New South Wales*) 1953 *SA (4)*

Walsham, K.P. (*New South Wales*) 1962 *NZ; 1963 E*

Weatherstone, L.J. (*Australian Capital Territory*) 1975 *E (2), J (2); 1975-76 (T) S (r), E, I*

Wells, B.G. (*New South Wales*) 1958 *M*

White, J.P.L. (*New South Wales*) 1958 *NZ (3); 1961 Fi (3), SA (2), F; 1962 NZ (5); 1963 E, SA (4); 1964 NZ (3); 1965 SA (2)*

White, S.W. (*New South Wales*) 1956 *SA (2); 1957-58 (T) I, E, S; 1958 M (2)*

Williams, J.L. (*New South Wales*) 1963 *SA (3)*

Williams, S.A. (*New South Wales*) 1980 *Fi, NZ (2); 1981 F (2); 1981-82 (T) E; 1982 NZ (3); 1983 US, Arg (2[1r]), NZ, (ST) It, F (2); 1984 NZ (3), (T) E, I, W, S; 1985 NZ*

Wilson, B.J. (*New South Wales*) 1949 *NZ (2)*

Wilson, C.R. (*Queensland*) 1957 *NZ; 1958 NZ (3)*

Windon, C.J. (*New South Wales*) 1946 *NZ (2); 1947 NZ; 1947-48 (T) S, I, W, E, F; 1949 M (3), NZ (2); 1951 NZ (3); 1952 Fi (2), NZ (2)*

Windsor, J.C. (*Queensland*) 1947 *NZ*

Winning, K.C. (*Queensland*) 1951 *NZ*

Wood, R.N. (*Queensland*) 1972 *Fi*

Wright, K.J. (*New South Wales*) 1975 *E (2), J; 1975-76 (T) US; 1976-77 (ST) F (2); 1978 NZ (3)*

Yanz, K. (*New South Wales*) 1957-58 *(T) F*

Figures in brackets indicate the number of Internationals played on each tour. No figure in brackets denotes only one match played. On European tours in some cases countries opposed are listed individually.

Allen, F.R. (*Auckland*) 1946 A (2); 1947 A (2); 1949 SA (2)
Allen, N.H. (*Counties*) 1980 A; 1980 (ST) W
Anderson, A. (*Canterbury*) 1983 (ST) S, E; 1984 A (3)
Archer, W.R. (*Otago, Southland*) 1955 A (2); 1956 SA (2)
Arnold, D.A. (*Canterbury*) 1963-64 (T) I, W, E, F
Arnold, K.D. (*Waikato*) 1947 A (2)
Ashby, D.L. (*Southland*) 1958 A
Ashworth, B.G. (*Auckland*) 1978 A (2)
Ashworth, J.C. (*Canterbury*) 1978 A (3); 1980 A (3); 1981 SA (3); 1982 A (2); 1983 BI (4), A; 1984 F (2), A (3); 1985 E (2), A

Batty, G.B. (*Wellington, Bay of Plenty*) 1972-73 (T) W, S, E, I, F; 1973 E; 1974 A (2), (ST) I; 1975 S; 1976 SA (4); 1977 BI
Beatty, G.E. (*Taranaki*) 1950 BI
Bell, R.H. (*Otago*) 1951 A; 1952 A (2)
Bevan, V.D. (*Wellington*) 1949 A (2); 1950 BI (4)
Birtwistle, W.M. (*Canterbury*) 1965 SA (4); 1967-68 (T) E, W, S
Black, J.E. (*Canterbury*) 1977 (ST) F; 1979 A; 1980 A
Black, N.W. (*Auckland*) 1949 SA
Blake, A.W. (*Wairarapa*) 1949 A
Boggs, E.G. (*Auckland*) 1946 A; 1949 SA
Bond, J.G. (*Canterbury*) 1949 A
Bowden, N.J.G. (*Taranaki*) 1952 A
Bowers, R.G. (*Wellington*) 1953-54 (T) I, F
Braid, G.J. (*Bay of Plenty*) 1983 (ST) S, E
Bremner, S.G. (*Auckland, Canterbury*) 1952 A; 1956 SA
Briscoe, K.C. (*Taranaki*) 1959 BI; 1960 SA (4); 1963-64 (T) I, W, E, S
Brown, R.H. (*Taranaki*) 1955 A; 1956 SA (4); 1957 A (2); 1958 A (3); 1959 BI (2); 1961 F (3); 1962 A
Bruce, O.D. (*Canterbury*) 1976 SA (3); 1977 BI (3), (ST) F (2); 1978 A (2), (T) I, W, E, S
Bryers, R.F. (*King Country*) 1949 A
Budd, T.A. (*Southland*) 1946 A; 1949 A
Burgess, G.A.J. (*Auckland*) 1981 SA
Burgess, R.E. (*Manawatu*) 1971 BI (3); 1972 A; 1972-73 (T) W, I, F
Burke, P.S. (*Taranaki*) 1955 A; 1957 A (2)
Bush, W.K. (*Canterbury*) 1974 A (2); 1975 S; 1976 I, SA (2); 1977 BI (3[1ir]); 1978 (T) I, W; 1979 A
Buxton, J.B. (*Canterbury*) 1955 A; 1956 SA

Callesen, J.A. (*Manawatu*) 1974 A (3); 1975 S
Cameron, L.M. (*Manawatu*) 1980 A; 1981 SA (3[1ir]); 1981 (ST) R
Carrington, K.R. (*Auckland*) 1971 BI 3
Catley, E.H. (*Waikato*) 1946 A; 1947 A (2); 1949 SA (4)
Caulton, R.W. (*Wellington*) 1959 BI (3); 1960

SA (2); 1961 F; 1963 E (2); 1963-64 (T) I, W, E, S, F; 1964 A (3)
Cherrington, N.P. (*North Auckland*) 1950 BI
Christian, D.L. (*Auckland*) 1949 SA
Clamp, M. (*Wellington*) 1984 A (2)
Clark, D.W. (*Otago*) 1964 A (2)
Clark, W.H. (*Wellington*) 1953-54 (T) W, I, E, S; 1955 A (2); 1956 SA (3)
Clarke, D.B. (*Waikato*) 1956 SA (2); 1957 A (2); 1958 A (2); 1959 BI (4); 1960 SA (2); 1961 F (3); 1962 A (5); 1963 E (2); 1963-64 (T) I, W, E, S, F; 1964 A (2)
Clarke, I.J. (*Waikato*) 1953-54 (T) W; 1955 A (3); 1956 SA (4); 1957 A (2); 1958 A (2); 1959 BI (2); 1960 SA (2); 1961 F (3); 1962 A (3); 1963 E (2)
Cockerill, M.S. (*Taranaki*) 1951 A (3)
Codlin, B.W. (*Counties*) 1980 A (3)
Collins, J.L. (*Poverty Bay*) 1964 A; 1965 SA (2)
Connor, D.M. (*Auckland*) 1961 F (3); 1962 A (5); 1963 E (2); 1964 A (2)
Conway, R.J. (*Otago, Bay of Plenty*) 1959 BI (3); 1960 SA (3); 1965 SA (4)
Cossey, R.R. (*Counties*) 1958 A
Cottrell, W.D. (*Canterbury*) 1968 A (2), F (2); 1970 SA; 1971 BI (4)
Couch, M.B.R. (*Wairarapa*) 1947 A; 1949 A (2)
Coughlan, T.D. (*South Canterbury*) 1958 A
Creighton, J.N. (*Canterbury*) 1962 A
Crichton, S. (*Wellington*) 1983 (ST) S, E
Crowley, K.J. (*Taranaki*) 1985 E (2), A, Arg (2)
Crowley, P.J.B. (*Auckland*) 1949 SA (2); 1950 BI (4)
Cunningham, G.R. (*Auckland*) 1979 A, (ST) S, E; 1980 A (2)
Currie, C.J. (*Canterbury*) 1978 (T) I, W

Dalton, A.G. (*Counties*) 1977 (ST) F; 1978 A (3), (T) I, W, E, S; 1979 F (2), (ST) S; 1981 S (2), SA (3); 1981 (ST) R, F (2); 1982 A (3); 1983 BI (4), A; 1984 F (2), A (3); 1985 E (2), A
Dalton, R.A. (*Wellington*) 1947 A (2)
Dalzell, G.N. (*Canterbury*) 1953-54 (T) W, I, E, S, F
Davie, M.G. (*Canterbury*) 1983 (ST) E (r)
Davies, W.A. (*Auckland, Otago*) 1960 SA; 1962 A (2)
Davis, K. (*Auckland*) 1952 A; 1953-54 (T) W, I, E, S, F; 1955 A; 1958 A (3)
Davis, L.J. (*Canterbury*) 1976 I; 1977 BI (2)
Davis, W.L. (*Hawke's Bay*) 1967 A; 1967-68 (T) E, W, F, S; 1968 A (2), F; 1969 W (2); 1970 SA
Deans, R.M. (*Canterbury*) 1983 (ST) S, E; 1984 A (3[1ir])
Delamore, G.W. (*Wellington*) 1949 SA
Diack, E.S. (*Otago*) 1959 BI
Dick, M.J. (*Auckland*) 1963-64 (T) I, W, E, S, F; 1965 SA; 1966 BI; 1967 A; 1967-68 (T) E, W, F; 1969 W (2); 1970 SA (2)
Dixon, M.J. (*Canterbury*) 1953-54 (T) I, E, S, F; 1954 SA (4); 1957 A (2)
Dobson, R.L. (*Auckland*) 1949 A
Donald, A.J. (*Wanganui*) 1983 (ST) S, E; 1984 F (2), A (3)
Donaldson, M.W. (*Manawatu*) 1977 (ST) F

(2); 1978 A (3), (T) I, E, S; 1979 F (2), A, (ST) S (r); 1981 SA (r)
Dougan, J.P. (*Wellington*) 1972 A; 1973 E
Duff, R.H. (*Canterbury*) 1951 A (3); 1952 A (2); 1955 A (2); 1956 SA (4)
Duncan, M.G. (*Hawke's Bay*) 1971 BI (2[1ir])
Dunn, E. (*North Auckland*) 1979 A; 1979 (ST) S; 1981 S
Dunn, I.T.W. (*North Auckland*) 1983 BI (2), A
Dunn, J.M. (*Auckland*) 1946 A

Eastgate, B.P. (*Canterbury*) 1952 A (2); 1953-54 (T) S
Elliot, K.G. (*Wellington*) 1946 A (2)
Elsom, A.E.G. (*Canterbury*) 1952 A (2); 1953-54 (T) W; 1955 A (3)
Elvidge, R.R. (*Otago*) 1946 A (2); 1949 SA (4); 1950 BI (3)
Erceg, C.P. (*Auckland*) 1951 A (3); 1952 A
Eveleigh, K.A. (*Manawatu*) 1976 SA (2); 1977 BI (2)

Farrell, C.P. (*Auckland*) 1977 BI (2)
Fawcett, C.L. (*Auckland*) 1976 SA (2)
Finlay, B.E.L. (*Manawatu*) 1959 BI
Finlay, J. (*Manawatu*) 1946 A
Fitzgerald, J.T. (*Wellington*) 1952 A
Fitzpatrick, B.B.J. (*Wellington*) 1953-54 (T) W, I, F
Fleming, J.K. (*Wellington*) 1979 (ST) S, E; 1980 A (3)
Ford, B.R. (*Marlborough*) 1977 BI (2); 1978 (T) I; 1979 (ST) E
Fox, G. (*Auckland*) 1985 Arg (1)
Fraser, B.G. (*Wellington*) 1979 (ST) S, E; 1980 A, (ST) W; 1981 S (2), SA (3); 1981 (ST) R, F (2); 1982 A (3); 1983 BI (4), A, (ST) S, E; 1984 A
Frazer, H.F. (*Hawke's Bay*) 1946 A (2); 1947 A (2); 1949 SA
Furlong, B.D.M. (*Hawke's Bay*) 1970 SA

Gard, P.C. (*North Otago*) 1971 BI
Gardiner, A.J. (*Taranaki*) 1974 A
Gemmell, B. McL. (*Auckland*) 1974 A (2)
Gillespie, W.D. (*Otago*) 1958 A
Goddard, M.P. (*South Canterbury*) 1946 A; 1947 A; 1949 SA (2)
Going, S.M. (*North Auckland*) 1967 A; 1967-68 (T) F; 1968 F; 1969 W (2); 1970 SA (2[1ir]); 1971 BI (4); 1972 A (2); 1972-73 (T) W, S, E, I, F; 1973 E; 1974 (ST) I; 1975 S; 1976 I (r), SA (4); 1977 BI (2)
Graham, D.J. (*Canterbury*) 1958 A (2); 1960 SA (2); 1961 F (3); 1962 A (5); 1963 E (2); 1963-64 (T) I, W, E, S, F; 1964 A (3)
Graham, W.G. (*Otago*) 1979 F (r)
Grant, L.A. (*South Canterbury*) 1947 A (2); 1949 SA (2)
Gray, K.F. (*Wellington*) 1963-64 (T) I, W, E, S, F; 1964 A (3); 1965 SA (4); 1966 BI (4); 1967-68 (T) W, F, S; 1968 A, F (2); 1969 W (2)
Gray, W.N. (*Bay of Plenty*) 1955 A (2); 1956 SA (4)
Green, C.I. (*Canterbury*) 1983 (ST) S (r), E; 1984 A (3); 1985 E (2,), A, Arg (2)
Guy, R.A. (*North Auckland*) 1971 BI (4)

Haden, A.M. (*Auckland*) 1977 *BI (4), (ST) F (2)*; 1978 *A (3), (T) I, W, E, S*; 1979 *F (2), A, (ST) S, E*; 1980 *A (3), (ST) W*; 1981 *S, SA (3), (ST) R, F (2)*; 1982 *A (3)*; 1983 *BI (4), A*; 1984 *F (2)*; 1985 *Arg (2)*

Haig, J.S. (*Otago*) 1946 *A (2)*

Haig, L.S. (*Otago*) 1950 *BI (3)*; 1951 *A (3)*; 1953-54 *(T) W, E, S*

Hales, D.A. (*Canterbury*) 1972 *A (3)*; 1972-73 *(T) W*

Hammond, I.A. (*Marlborough*) 1952 *A*

Harris, P.C. (*Manawatu*) 1976 *SA*

Harvey, L.R. (*Otago*) 1949 *SA (4)*; 1950 *BI (4)*

Hazlett, E.J. (*Southland*) 1966 *BI (4)*; 1967 *A*; 1967-68 *(T) E*

Heeps, T.R. (*Wellington*) 1962 *A (5)*

Hemi, R.C. (*Waikato*) 1953-54 *(T) W, I, E, S, F*; 1955 *A (3)*; 1956 *SA (3)*; 1957 *A (2)*; 1959 *BI (3)*

Henderson, P. (*Wanganui*) 1949 *SA (4)*; 1950 *BI (3)*

Herewini, M.A. (*Auckland*) 1962 *A*; 1963-64 *(T) I, S, F*; 1965 *SA*; 1966 *BI (4)*; 1967 *A*

Hewson, A.R. (*Wellington*) 1981 *S (2), SA (3), (ST) R, F (2)*; 1982 *A (3)*; 1983 *BI (4), A*; 1984 *F (2), A*

Higginson, G. (*Canterbury, Hawke's Bay*) 1980 *(ST) W*; 1981 *S, SA*; 1982 *A (2)*; 1983 *A*

Hill, S.F. (*Canterbury*) 1955 *A*; 1956 *SA (3)*; 1957 *A (2)*; 1958 *A*; 1959 *BI (4)*

Hines, G.R. (*Waikato*) 1980 *A*

Hobbs, M.J.B. (*Canterbury*) 1983 *BI (4), A*; 1983 *(ST) S, E*; 1984 *F (2), A (3)*; 1985 *E (2), A, Arg (2)*

Hopkinson, A.E. (*Canterbury*) 1967-68 *(T) S*; 1968 *A, F (3)*; 1969 *W*; 1970 *SA (3)*

Horsley, R.H. (*Wellington*) 1960 *SA (3)*

Hotop, J. (*Canterbury*) 1952 *A (2)*; 1955 *A*

Hughes, A.M. (*Auckland*) 1949 *A (2)*; 1950 *BI (4)*

Hunter, B.A. (*Otago*) 1971 *BI (3)*

Hurst, I.A. (*Canterbury*) 1972-73 *(T) I, F*; 1973 *E*; 1974 *A (2)*

Irvine, I.B. (*North Auckland*) 1952 *A*

Irwin, M.W. (*Otago*) 1955 *A (2)*; 1956 *SA*; 1958 *A*; 1959 *BI (2)*; 1960 *SA*

Jaffray, J.L. (*Otago, South Canterbury*) 1972 *A*; 1975 *S*; 1976 *I, SA*; 1977 *BI*; 1979 *F (2)*

Jarden, R.A. (*Wellington*) 1951 *A (2)*; 1952 *A (2)*; 1953-54 *(T) W, I, E, S, F*; 1955 *A (3)*; 1956 *SA (4)*

Jefferd, A.C.R. (*East Coast*) 1981 *S (2), SA*

Johnstone, B.R. (*Auckland*) 1976 *SA*; 1977 *BI (2), (ST) F (2)*; 1978 *(T) I, W, E, S*; 1979 *F (2), (ST) S, E*

Johnstone, P. (*Otago*) 1949 *SA (2)*; 1950 *BI (4)*; 1951 *A (3)*

Jones, M.G. (*North Auckland*) 1973 *E*

Jones, P.F. (*North Auckland*) 1953-54 *(T) E, S*; 1955 *A (2)*; 1956 *SA (2)*; 1958 *A (3)*; 1959 *BI*; 1960 *SA*

Joseph, H.T. (*Canterbury*) 1971 *BI (2)*

Karam, J.F. (*Wellington, Horowhenua*) 1972-73 *(T) W, S, E, I, F*; 1974 *A (3), (ST) I*; 1975 *S*

Katene, T. (*Wellington*) 1955 *A*

Kearney, J.C. (*Otago*) 1947 *A*; 1949 *SA (3)*

Kelly, J.W. (*Auckland*) 1949 *A (2)*

Kember, G.F. (*Wellington*) 1970 *SA*

Ketels, R.C. (*Counties*) 1980 *(ST) W*; 1981 *S (2), (ST) R, F*

Kirk, D.E. (*Otago*) 1985 *E (2), A, Arg (1)*

Kirkpatrick, I.A. (*Canterbury, Poverty Bay*) 1967-68 *(T) F*; 1968 *A (2[1r]), F (3)*; 1969 *W (2)*; 1970 *SA (4)*; 1971 *BI (4)*; 1972 *A (3)*; 1972-73 *(T) W, E, I, F*; 1973 *E*; 1974 *A (3), (ST) I*; 1975 *S*; 1976 *I, SA (4)*; 1977 *BI (4)*

Kirton, E.W. (*Otago*) 1967-68 *(T) E, W, F, S*; 1968 *A (2), F (3)*; 1969 *W (2)*; 1970 *SA (2)*

Kirwan, J.J. (*Auckland*) 1984 *F (2)*; 1985 *E (2), A, Arg (2)*

Knight, G.A. (*Manawatu*) 1977 *(ST) F (2)*; 1978 *A (3), (T) E, S*; 1979 *F (2), A*; 1980 *A (3), (ST) W*; 1981 *S (2), SA (2)*; 1982 *A (3)*; 1983 *BI (4), A*; 1984 *F (2), A (3)*; 1985 *E (2), A*

Knight, L.G. (*Poverty Bay*) 1977 *BI (4), (ST) F (2)*

Koteka, P.T. (*Waikato*) 1981 *(ST) F*; 1982 *A (2)*

Kreft, A.J. (*Otago*) 1968 *A*

Laidlaw, C.R. (*Otago, Canterbury*) 1963-64 *(T) F*; 1964 *A*; 1965 *SA (4)*; 1966 *BI (4)*; 1967-68 *(T) E, W, S*; 1968 *A (2), F (2)*; 1970 *SA (3)*

Laidlaw, K.F. (*Southland*) 1960 *SA (3)*

Lambert, K.K. (*Manawatu*) 1973-73 *(T) S (r), E, I, F*; 1973 *F*; 1974 *(ST) I*; 1976 *SA (3)*; 1977 *BI (2)*

Le Lievre, J.M. (*Canterbury*) 1962 *A*

Lendrum, R.N. (*Counties*) 1973 *E*

Leslie, A.R. (*Wellington*) 1974 *A (3)*; 1974 *(ST) I*; 1975 *S*; 1976 *I, SA (4)*

Lineen, T.R. (*Auckland*) 1957 *A (2)*; 1958 *A (3)*; 1959 *BI (4)*; 1960 *SA (3)*

Lister, T.N. (*South Canterbury*) 1968 *A (2), F*; 1969 *W (2)*; 1970 *SA (2)*; 1971 *BI*

Little, P.F. (*Auckland*) 1961 *F (3)*; 1962 *A (3)*; 1963-64 *(T) I, W, E, S, F*

Loader, C.J. (*Wellington*) 1953-54 *(T) I, E, S, F*

Lochore, B.J. (*Wairarapa*) 1963-64 *(T) E, S*; 1965 *SA (4)*; 1966 *BI (4)*; 1967 *A*; 1967-68 *(T) E, W, F, S*; 1968 *A, F (2)*; 1969 *W (2)*; 1970 *SA (4)*; 1971 *BI*

Loveridge, D.S. (*Taranaki*) 1978 *(T) W*; 1979 *(ST) S, E*; 1980 *A (3), (ST) W*; 1981 *S (2), SA (3), (ST) R, F (2)*; 1982 *A (3)*; 1983 *BI (4), A*; 1985 *Arg (1)*

Lunn, W.A. (*Otago*) 1949 *A (2)*

Lynch, T.W. (*Canterbury*) 1951 *A (3)*

McAtamney, F.S. (*Otago*) 1956 *SA*

McCaw, W.A. (*Southland*) 1951 *A (3)*; 1953-54 *(T) W, F*

McCool, M.J. (*Wairarapa-Bush*) 1979 *A*

McCormick, W.F. (*Canterbury*) 1965 *SA*; 1967-68 *(T) E, W, F, S*; 1968 *A (2), F (3)*; 1969 *W (2)*; 1970 *SA (3)*; 1971 *BI*

McCullough, J.F. (*Taranaki*) 1959 *BI (3)*

Macdonald, H.H. (*Canterbury, North Auckland*) 1972-73 *(T) W, S, E, I, F*; 1973 *E*; 1974 *(ST) I*; 1975 *S*; 1976 *I, SA (3)*

McDowell, S. (*Auckland*) 1985 *Arg (2)*

McEldowney, J.T. (*Taranaki*) 1977 *BI (2)*

MacEwan, I.N. (*Wellington*) 1956 *SA*; 1957 *A (2)*; 1958 *A (3)*; 1959 *BI (3)*; 1960 *SA (4)*; 1961 *F (3)*; 1962 *A (4)*

McGrattan, B. (*Wellington*) 1983 *(ST) S, E*; 1985 *Arg (2)*

McHugh, M.J. (*Auckland*) 1946 *A (2)*; 1949 *SA*

McIntosh, D.N. (*Wellington*) 1956 *SA (2)*; 1957 *A (2)*

McKay, D.W. (*Auckland*) 1961 *F (3)*; 1963 *E (2)*

McKechnie, B.J. (*Southland*) 1977 *(ST) F (2)*; 1978 *A (2[1r]), (T) W (r), E, S*; 1979 *A*; 1981 *SA (r)*; 1981 *(ST) F*

McLachlan, J.S. (*Auckland*) 1974 *A*

McLaren, H.C. (*Waikato*) 1952 *A*

McLean, J.K. (*King Country, Auckland*) 1947 *A*; 1949 *A*

MacLeod, B.E. (*Counties*) 1964 *A (3)*; 1965 *SA (4)*; 1966 *BI (4)*; 1967-68 *(T) E, W, F, S*; 1968 *A (2), F (3)*; 1969 *W (2)*; 1970 *SA (2)*

McMullen, R.F. (*Auckland*) 1957 *A (2)*; 1958 *A (3)*; 1959 *BI (3)*; 1960 *SA (3)*

McNab, J.R. (*Otago*) 1949 *SA (3)*; 1950 *BI (3)*

McNaughton, A.M. (*Bay of Plenty*) 1971 *BI (3)*

McPhail, B.E. (*Canterbury*) 1959 *BI (2)*

MacRae, I.R. (*Hawke's Bay*) 1966 *BI (4)*; 1967 *A*; 1967-68 *(T) E, W, F, S*; 1968 *F (2)*; 1969 *W (2)*; 1970 *SA (4)*

McRae, J.A. (*Southland*) 1946 *A (2[1r])*

Mains, L.W. (*Otago*) 1971 *BI (3)*; 1976 *I*

Major, J. (*Taranaki*) 1967 *A*

Mason, D.F. (*Wellington*) 1947 *A (r)*

Matheson, J.D. (*Otago*) 1972 *A (3)*; 1972-73 *(T) W, S*

Meads, C.E. (*King Country*) 1957 *A (2)*; 1958 *A (3)*; 1959 *BI (3)*; 1960 *SA (4)*; 1961 *F (3)*; 1962 *A (4)*; 1963 *E (2)*; 1963-64 *(T) I, W, E, S, F*; 1964 *A (3)*; 1965 *SA (4)*; 1966 *BI (4)*; 1967 *A*; 1967-68 *(T) E, W, F, S*; 1968 *A (2), F (3)*; 1969 *W (2)*; 1970 *SA (4)*; 1971 *BI (4)*

Meads, S.T. (*King Country*) 1961 *F*; 1962 *A (2)*; 1963-64 *(T) I*; 1964 *A (3)*; 1965 *SA (4)*; 1966 *BI (4)*

Meates, K.F. (*Canterbury*) 1952 *A (2)*

Meates, W.A. (*Otago*) 1949 *SA (3)*; 1950 *BI (4)*

Mexted, G.G. (*Wellington*) 1950 *BI*

Mexted, M.G. (*Wellington*) 1979 *(ST) S, E*; 1980 *A (3), (ST) W*; 1981 *S (2), SA (3), (ST) R, F (2)*; 1982 *A (3)*; 1983 *BI (4), A*; 1983 *(ST) S, E*; 1984 *F (2), A (3)*; 1985 *E (2), A, Arg (2)*

Milner, H.P. (*Wanganui*) 1970 *SA*

Mitchell, T.W. (*Canterbury*) 1976 *SA (r)*

Moore, G.J.T. (*Otago*) 1949 *A*

Moreton, R.C. (*Canterbury*) 1962 *A (2)*; 1964 *A (3)*; 1965 *SA (2)*

Morgan, J.E. (*North Auckland*) 1974 *A, (ST) I*; 1976 *SA (3)*

Morris, T.J. (*Nelson Bays*) 1972 *A (3)*

Morrison, T.G. (*Otago*) 1973 *E (r)*

Morrissey, P.J. (*Canterbury*) 1962 *A (3)*

Mourie, G.N.K. (*Taranaki*) 1977 *BI (2), (ST) F (2)*; 1978 *(T) I, W, E, S*; 1979 *F (2), A, (ST) S, E*; 1980 *(ST) W*; 1981 *S (2), (ST) F (2)*; 1982 *A (3)*

Muller, B.L. (*Taranaki*) 1967 *A*; 1967-68 *(T) E, W, F*; 1968 *A, F*; 1969 *W*; 1970 *SA (3)*; 1971 *BI (4)*

Mumm, W.J. (*Buller*) 1949 *A*

Murdoch, K. (*Otago*) 1970 *SA*; 1972 *A*; 1972-73 *(T) W*

Murdoch, P.H. (*Auckland*) 1964 *A (2)*; 1965 *SA (3)*

Myers, R.G. (*Waikato*) 1978 *A*

Nathan, W.J. (*Auckland*) 1962 *A (5)*; 1963 *E (2)*; 1963-64 *(T) W, F*; 1966 *BI (4)*; 1967 *A*

Nelson, K.A. (*Otago*) 1962 *A (2)*
Nesbit, S.R. (*Auckland*) 1960 *SA (2)*
Norton, R.W. (*Canterbury*) 1971 *BI (4)*; 1972 *A (3)*; 1972-73 *(T) W, S, E, I, F*; 1973 *E*; 1974 *A (3)*, *(ST) I*; 1975 *S*; 1976 *I, SA (4)*; 1977 *BI (4)*

O'Callaghan, M.W. (*Manawatu*) 1968 *F (3)*
O'Callaghan, T.R. (*Wellington*) 1949 *A*
O'Donnell, D.H. (*Wellington*) 1949 *A*
Old, G.H. (*Manawatu*) 1981 *SA, (ST) R (r)*; 1982 *A (r)*
Oliver, D.O. (*Otago*) 1953-54 *(T) I, F*
Oliver, F.J. (*Southland, Otago, Manawatu*) 1976 *SA*; 1977 *BI (4)*, *(ST) F (2)*; 1978 *A (3)*, *(T) I, W, E, S*; 1979 *F (2)*; 1981 *SA*
Orr, R.W. (*Otago*) 1949 *A*
Osborne, W.M. (*Wanganui*) 1975 *S*; 1976 *SA (2[1r])*; 1977 *BI (4)*, *(ST) F (2[1r])*; 1978 *(T) I, W, E, S*; 1980 *(ST) W*; 1982 *A (2)*
O'Sullivan, T.P.A. (*Taranaki*) 1960 *SA*; 1961 *F*; 1962 *A (2)*

Parkinson, R.M. (*Poverty Bay*) 1972 *A (3)*; 1972-73 *(T) W, S, E*; 1973 *E*
Pickering, E.A.R. (*Waikato*) 1958 *A*; 1959 *BI (2)*
Pierce, M.J. (*Wellington*) 1985 *E (2), A, Arg (1)*
Pokere, S.T. (*Southland, Auckland*) 1981 *SA*; 1982 *A (3)*; 1983 *BI (4), A, (ST) S, E*; 1984 *F (2), A (2)*; 1985 *E (2), A*
Purvis, N.A. (*Otago*) 1976 *I*

Rangi, R.E. (*Auckland*) 1964 *A (2)*; 1965 *SA (4)*; 1966 *BI (4)*
Reid, A.R. (*Waikato*) 1952 *A*; 1956 *SA (2)*; 1957 *A (2)*
Reid, H.R. (*Bay of Plenty*) 1980 *A (2), (ST) W*; 1983 *(ST) S, E*; 1985 *Arg (2)*
Rhind, P.K. (*Canterbury*) 1946 *A (2)*
Rickit, H. (*Waikato*) 1981 *S (2)*
Robertson, B.J. (*Counties*) 1972 *A (2)*; 1972-73 *(T) S, E, I, F*; 1974 *A (3)*, *(ST) I*; 1976 *I, SA (4)*, *(ST) F (2)*; 1978 *A (3)*, *(T) W, E, S*; 1979 *F (2)*; 1980 *A (2)*, *(ST) W*; 1981 *S (2)*
Robertson, D.J. (*Otago*) 1974 *A (3)*, *(ST) I*; 1975 *S*; 1976 *I, SA (3)*; 1977 *BI*
Robinson, C.E. (*Southland*) 1951 *A (3)*; 1952 *A (2)*
Rollerson, D.L. (*Manawatu*) 1980 *(ST) W*; 1981 *S, SA (3)*, *(ST) R, F (2[1r])*
Roper, R.A. (*Taranaki*) 1949 *A*; 1950 *BI (4)*
Rowley, H.C.B. (*Wanganui*) 1949 *A*
Rutledge, L.M. (*Southland*) 1978 *A (3)*, *(T) I, W, E, S*; 1979 *F (2), A*; 1980 *A (3)*

Salmon, J.L.B. (*Wellington*) 1981 *(ST) R, F (2[1r])*
Savage, L.T. (*Canterbury*) 1949 *SA (3)*
Scott, R.W.H. (*Auckland*) 1946 *A (2)*; 1947 *A (2)*; 1949 *SA (4)*; 1950 *BI (4)*; 1953-54 *(T) W, I, E, S, F*
Scown, A.I. (*Taranaki*) 1972 *A (3)*; 1972-73 *(T) W (r), S*
Seear, G.A. (*Otago*) 1977 *(ST) F (2)*; 1978 *A (3)*, *(T) I, W, E, S*; 1979 *F (2), A*
Shaw, M.W. (*Manawatu*) 1980 *A (3[1r]), (ST) W*; 1981 *S (2), SA (2), (ST) R, F (2)*; 1982 *A (3)*; 1983 *BI (4), A, (ST) S, E*; 1984 *F (2), A*; 1985 *E (2), A, Arg (2)*

Shelford, F.K. (*Bay of Plenty*) 1981 *SA, (ST) R*; 1984 *A (2)*
Simpson, J.G. (*Auckland*) 1947 *A (2)*; 1949 *SA (4)*; 1950 *BI (3)*
Simpson, V. (*Canterbury*) 1985 *Arg (2)*
Sims, G.S. (*Otago*) 1972 *A*
Skeen, J.R. (*Auckland*) 1952 *A*
Skinner, K.L. (*Otago, Counties*) 1949 *SA (4)*; 1950 *BI (4)*; 1951 *A (3)*; 1952 *A (2)*; 1953-54 *(T) W, I, E, S, F*; 1956 *SA (2)*
Skudder, G.R. (*Waikato*) 1969 *W*
Sloane, P.H. (*North Auckland*) 1979 *(ST) E*
Smith, A.E. (*Taranaki*) 1969 *W (2)*; 1970 *SA*
Smith, B.W. (*Waikato*) 1984 *F (2), A*
Smith, I.S.T. (*Otago, North Otago*) 1964 *A (3)*; 1965 *SA (3)*; 1966 *BI (3)*
Smith, J.B. (*North Auckland*) 1946 *A*; 1947 *A*; 1949 *A (2)*
Smith, R.M. (*Canterbury*) 1955 *A*
Smith, W.R. (*Canterbury*) 1980 *A*; 1982 *A (3)*; 1983 *BI (2)*; 1983 *(ST) S, E*; 1984 *F (2), A (3)*; 1986 *E (2), A, Arg (1)*
Spiers, J.E. (*Counties*) 1979 *(ST) S, E*; 1981 *(ST) R, F (2)*
Steel, A.G. (*Canterbury*) 1966 *BI (4)*; 1967 *A*; 1967-68 *(T) F, S*; 1968 *A (2)*
Steele, L.B. (*Wellington*) 1951 *A (3)*
Stephens, O.G. (*Wellington*) 1968 *F*
Stevens, I.N. (*Wellington*) 1972-73 *(T) S, E*; 1974 *A*
Stewart, A.J. (*Canterbury, South Canterbury*) 1963 *E (2)*; 1963-64 *(T) W, E, S, F*; 1964 *A*
Stewart, K.W. (*Southland*) 1973 *E*; 1974 *A (3)*, *(ST) I*; 1975 *S*; 1976 *I, SA (2)*; 1979 *(ST) S, E*; 1981 *SA (2)*
Stone, A.M. (*Waikato*) 1981 *(ST) F (2)*; 1983 *BI (r)*; 1984 *A*
Strahan, S.C. (*Manawatu*) 1967 *A*; 1967-68 *(T) E, W, F, S*; 1968 *A (2), F (3)*; 1970 *SA (3)*; 1972 *A (3)*; 1973 *E*
Stuart, K.C. (*Canterbury*) 1955 *A*
Stuart, R.C. (*Canterbury*) 1949 *A (2)*; 1953-54 *(T) W, I, E, S, F*
Stuart, R.L. (*Hawke's Bay*) 1977 *(ST) F (r)*
Sutherland, A.R. (*Marlborough*) 1970 *SA (2)*; 1971 *BI*; 1972 *A (3)*; 1972-73 *(T) W, E, I, F*

Tanner, J.M. (*Auckland*) 1950 *BI*; 1951 *A (3)*; 1953-54 *(T) W*
Tanner, K.J. (*Canterbury*) 1974 *A (3)*, *(ST) I*; 1975 *S*; 1976 *I, SA*
Taylor, M.B. (*Waikato*) 1979 *F (2), A, (ST) S, E*; 1980 *A (2)*
Taylor, N.M. (*Bay of Plenty, Hawke's Bay*) 1977 *BI (2[1r]), (ST) F (2)*; 1978 *A (3)*, *(T) I*; 1982 *A*
Taylor, W.T. (*Canterbury*) 1983 *BI (4), A, (ST) S*; 1984 *F (2), A (2)*; 1985 *E (2), A, Arg (2)*
Tetzlaff, P.L. (*Auckland*) 1947 *A (2)*
Thimbleby, N.W. (*Hawke's Bay*) 1970 *SA*
Thomas, B.T. (*Auckland, Wellington*) 1962 *A*; 1964 *A*
Thorne, G.S. (*Auckland*) 1968 *A (2), F (3)*; 1969 *W*; 1970 *SA (4)*
Thornton, N.H. (*Auckland*) 1947 *A (2)*; 1949 *SA*
Townsend, L.J. (*Otago*) 1955 *A (2)*
Tremain, K.R. (*Canterbury, Hawke's Bay*) 1959 *BI (3)*; 1960 *SA (4)*; 1961 *F (2)*; 1962 *A (3)*; 1963 *E (2)*; 1963-64 *(T) I, W, E, S, F*; 1964 *A (3)*; 1965 *SA (4)*; 1966 *BI (4)*; 1967 *A*; 1967-68 *(T) E, W, S*; 1968 *A, F (3)*

Twigden, T.M. (*Auckland*) 1980 *A (2)*

Urbahn, R.J. (*Taranaki*) 1959 *BI (3)*
Urlich, R.A. (*Auckland*) 1970 *SA (2)*
Uttley, I.N. (*Wellington*) 1963 *E (2)*

Vincent, P.B. (*Canterbury*) 1956 *SA (2)*
Vodanovich, I.M.H. (*Wellington*) 1955 *A (3)*

Walsh, P.T. (*Counties*) 1955 *A (3)*; 1956 *SA (3)*; 1957 *A (2)*; 1958 *A (3)*; 1959 *BI*; 1963 *E*
Watt, B.A. (*Canterbury*) 1962 *A (2)*; 1963 *E (2)*; 1963-64 *(T) W, E, S*; 1964 *A*
Watt, J.R. (*Wellington*) 1958 *A*; 1960 *SA (4)*; 1961 *F (2)*; 1962 *A (2)*
Watts, M.G. (*Taranaki*) 1979 *F (2)*; 1980 *A (3[1r])*
Webb, D.S. (*North Auckland*) 1959 *BI*
Whetton, A.J. (*Auckland*) 1984 *A (2[2r])*; 1985 *A (r), Arg (1) (r)*
Whetton, G.W. (*Auckland*) 1981 *SA*; 1981 *(ST) R, F (2)*; 1982 *A*; 1983 *BI (4)*; 1984 *F (2), A (3)*; 1985 *E (2), A, Arg (2)*
Whineray, W.J. (*Canterbury, Waikato, Auckland*) 1957 *A (2)*; 1958 *A (3)*; 1959 *BI (4)*; 1960 *SA (4)*; 1961 *F (3)*; 1962 *A (5)*; 1963 *E (2)*; 1963-64 *(T) I, W, E, S, F*; 1965 *SA (4)*
White, H.L. (*Auckland*) 1953-54 *(T) I, E, F*; 1955 *A*
White, R.A. (*Poverty Bay*) 1949 *A (2)*; 1950 *BI (4)*; 1951 *A (3)*; 1952 *A (2)*; 1953-54 *(T) W, I, E, S, F*; 1955 *A (3)*; 1956 *SA (4)*
White, R.M. (*Wellington*) 1946 *A (2)*; 1947 *A (2)*
Whiting, G.J. (*King Country*) 1972 *A (2)*; 1972-73 *(T) S, E, I, F*
Whiting, P.J. (*Auckland*) 1971 *BI (3)*; 1972 *A (3)*; 1972-73 *(T) W, S, E, I, F*; 1974 *A (3)*, *(ST) I*; 1976 *I, SA (4)*
Williams, B.G. (*Auckland*) 1970 *SA (4)*; 1971 *BI (3)*; 1972 *A (3)*; 1972-73 *(T) W, S, E, I, F*; 1973 *E*; 1974 *A (3)*, *(ST) I*; 1975 *S*; 1976 *I, SA (4)*; 1977 *BI (4)*, *(ST) F*; 1978 *A (3)*, *(T) (r), W, E, S*
Williams, G.C. (*Wellington*) 1967-68 *(T) E, W, F, S*; 1968 *A*
Williment, M. (*Wellington*) 1964 *A*; 1965 *SA (3)*; 1966 *BI (4)*; 1967 *A*
Willocks, C. (*Otago*) 1946 *A (2)*; 1949 *SA (3)*
Wilson, B.W. (*Otago*) 1977 *BI (2)*; 1978 *A (3)*; 1979 *F (2), A*
Wilson, D.D. (*Canterbury*) 1953-54 *(T) E, S*
Wilson, H.W. (*Otago*) 1949 *A*; 1950 *BI*; 1951 *A (3)*
Wilson, N.L. (*Otago*) 1951 *A (3)*
Wilson, R.G. (*Canterbury*) 1979 *(ST) S, E*
Wilson, S.S. (*Wellington*) 1977 *(ST) F (2)*; 1978 *A (3)*, *(T) I, W, E, S*; 1979 *F (2), A, (ST) S, E*; 1980 *A, (ST) W*; 1981 *S (2), SA (3), (ST) R, F (2)*; 1982 *A (3)*; 1983 *BI (4), A, (ST) S, E*
Wolfe, T.N. (*Wellington, Taranaki*) 1961 *F (3)*; 1962 *A (2)*; 1963 *E*
Woodman, F.A. (*North Auckland*) 1981 *SA (2)*; 1981 *(ST) F*
Wyllie, A.J. (*Canterbury*) 1970 *SA (2)*; 1971 *BI (3)*; 1972-73 *(T) W, S, E, I, F*; 1973 *E*

Yates, V.M. (*North Auckland*) 1961 *F (3)*
Young, D. (*Canterbury*) 1956 *SA*; 1958 *A (3)*; 1960 *SA (4)*; 1961 *F (3)*; 1962 *A (4)*; 1963 *E (2)*; 1963-64 *(T) I, W, E, S, F*

Figures in brackets indicate the number of Internationals played on each tour. No figure in brackets denotes only one match played. On European tours in some cases countries opposed are listed individually.

Ackermann, D.S.P. (*Western Province*) 1955 *BI (3)*; 1956 *A (2), NZ (2)*; 1958 *F*

Allen, P.B. (*Eastern Province*) 1960 *S*

Antelme, M.J.G. (*Transvaal*) 1960 *NZ (4)*; 1960-61 *(T) F*

Baard, A.P. (*Western Province*) 1960-61 *(T) I*

Barnard, A.S. (*Eastern Province*) 1984 *S Am (2)*

Barnard, J.H. (*Transvaal*) 1964-65 *(ST) S;* 1965 *A (2), NZ (2)*

Barnard, R.W. (*Transvaal*) 1970 *NZ (r)*

Barnard, W.H.M. (*Northern Transvaal*) 1949 *NZ;* 1951-52 *(T) W*

Bates, A.J. (*Western Transvaal*) 1969-70 *(T) E;* 1970 *NZ (2)*; 1972 *E*

Bayvel, P.C.R. (*Transvaal*) 1974 *BI (2)*; 1974 *(ST) F (2)*; 1975 *F (2)*; 1976 *NZ (4)*

Beck, J.J. (*Western Province*) 1981 *NZ (2[2r]), US*

Bedford, T.P. (*Natal*) 1963 *A (4)*; 1964 *W, F;* 1964-65 *(ST) I;* 1965 *A (2)*; 1968 *BI (4)*; 1968-69 *(ST) F (2)*; 1969 *A (4)*; 1969-70 *(T) S, E, I, W;* 1971 *F (2)*

Bekker, H.J. (*Western Province*) 1981 *NZ (2)*

Bekker, H.P.J. (*Northern Transvaal*) 1951-52 *(T) E, F;* 1953 *A (4)*; 1955 *BI (3)*; 1956 *A (2), NZ (4)*

Bekker, M.J. (*Northern Transvaal*) 1960 *S*

Bekker, R.P. (*Northern Transvaal*) 1953 *A (2)*

Bestbier, A. (*Orange Free State*) 1974 *(ST) F (r)*

Bezuidenhoudt, C.E. (*Northern Transvaal*) 1962 *BI (3)*

Bezuidenhoudt, N.S.E. (*Northern Transvaal*) 1972 *E;* 1974 *BI (3)*; 1974 *(ST) F (2)*; 1975 *F (2)*; 1977 *Wld*

Blair, R. (*Western Province*) 1977 *Wld*

Bosch, G.R. (*Transvaal*) 1974 *BI, (ST) F (2)*; 1975 *F (2)*; 1976 *NZ (4)*

Botha, D.S. (*Northern Transvaal*) 1981 *NZ*

Botha, H.E. (*Northern Transvaal*) 1980 *S Am (2), BI (4), S Am (ST) (2), F;* 1981 *I (2), NZ (3), US;* 1982 *S Am (2)*

Botha, J.P.F. (*Northern Transvaal*) 1962 *BI (3)*

Botha, P.H. (*Transvaal*) 1965 *A (2)*

Brewis, J.D. (*Northern Transvaal*) 1949 *NZ (4)*; 1951-52 *(T) S, I, W, E, F;* 1953 *A*

Briers, T.P.D. (*Western Province*) 1955 *BI (4)*; 1956 *NZ (3)*

Brynard, G.S. (*Western Province*) 1965 *A, NZ (4)*; 1968 *BI (2)*

Buchler, J.U. (*Transvaal*) 1951-52 *(T) S, I, W, E, F;* 1953 *A (4)*; 1956 *A*

Burger, M.B. (*Northern Transvaal*) 1980 *BI (r), (ST) S Am;* 1981 *US (r)*

Burger, S.W.P. (*Western Province*) 1984 *E (2)*

Carelse, G. (*Eastern Province*) 1964 *W, F;* 1964-65 *(ST) I, S;* 1967 *F (3)*; 1968-69 *(ST) F (2)*; 1969 *A (4)*; 1969-70 *(T) S*

Carlson, R.A. (*Western Province*) 1972 *E*

Cilliers, G.D. (*Orange Free State*) 1963 *A (3)*

Claassen, J.T. (*Western Transvaal*) 1955 *BI*
(4); 1956 *A (2), NZ (4)*; 1958 *F (2)*; 1960 *S, NZ (3)*; 1960-61 *(T) W, I, E, S, F;* 1961 *I, A (2)*; 1962 *BI (4)*

Claassen, W. (*Natal*) 1981 *I (2), NZ (2), US;* 1982 *S Am (2)*

Cockrell, C.H. (*Western Province*) 1969-70 *(T) S, I, W*

Cockrell, R.J. (*Western Province*) 1974 *(ST) F (2)*; 1975 *F (2)*; 1976 *NZ (2)*; 1977 *Wld;* 1981 *NZ (3[1r]), US*

Coetzee, J.H.H. (*Western Province*) 1974 *BI;* 1975 *F (r)*; 1976 *NZ (4)*

Cronje, P.A. (*Transvaal*) 1971 *F (2), A (3)*; 1974 *BI (2)*

De Bruyn, J. (*Orange Free State*) 1974 *BI*

De Klerk, I. J. (*Transvaal*) 1969-70 *(T) E, I, W*

De Klerk, K.B.H. (*Transvaal*) 1974 *BI (3[1r])*; 1975 *F (2)*; 1976 *NZ (3[1r])*; 1980 *S Am (2), BI;* 1981 *I (2)*

Delport, W.H. (*Eastern Province*) 1951-52 *(T) S, I, W, E, F;* 1953 *A (4)*

De Villiers, D.J. (*Western Province*) 1962 *BI (2)*; 1964-65 *(ST) I;* 1965 *NZ (3)*; 1967 *F (4)*; 1968 *BI (4)*; 1968-69 *(ST) F (2)*; 1969 *A (2)*; 1969-70 *(T) E, I, W;* 1970 *NZ (4)*

De Villiers, H.O. (*Western Province*) 1967 *F (4)*; 1968-69 *(ST) F (2)*; 1969 *A (4)*; 1969-70 *(T) S, E, I, W*

De Vos, D.J.J. (*Western Province*) 1964-65 *(ST) S;* 1969 *A;* 1969-70 *(T) S*

De Waal, A.N. (*Western Province*) 1967 *F (4)*

De Wet, A.E. (*Western Province*) 1969 *A (2)*; 1969-70 *(T) E*

Dinkelmann, E.E. (*Northern Transvaal*) 1951-52 *(T) S, I, E, F;* 1953 *A (2)*

Dirksen, C.W. (*Northern Transvaal*) 1963 *A;* 1964 *W;* 1964-65 *(ST) I, S;* 1967 *F (4)*; 1968 *BI (2)*

Dryburgh, R.G. (*Western Province*) 1955 *BI (3)*; 1956 *A, NZ (2)*; 1960 *NZ (2)*

Du Plessis, C.J. (*Western Province*) 1982 *S Am (2)*; 1984 *E (2), S Am (2)*

Du Plessis, D.C. (*Northern Transvaal*) 1977 *Wld;* 1980 *S Am*

Du Plessis, F. (*Transvaal*) 1949 *NZ (3)*

Du Plessis, M. (*Western Province*) 1971 *A (3)*; 1974 *BI (2)*; 1974 *(ST) F (2)*; 1975 *F (2)*; 1976 *NZ (4)*; 1977 *Wld;* 1980 *S Am (2), BI (4), S Am (ST), F*

Du Plessis, M. (*Western Province*) 1984 *S Am (2)*

Du Plessis, P.G. (*Northern Transvaal*) 1972 *E*

Du Plessis, T.D. (*Northern Transvaal*) 1980 *S Am (2)*

Du Plessis, W. (*Western Province*) 1980 *S Am (2), BI (4), S Am (ST) (2), F;* 1981 *NZ (3)*; 1982 *S Am (2)*

Du Plooy, A.J.J. (*Eastern Province*) 1955 *BI*

Du Preez, F.C.H. (*Northern Transvaal*) 1960-61 *(T) E, S;* 1961 *A (2)*; 1962 *BI (4)*; 1963 *A;* 1964 *W, F;* 1964-65 *A (2), NZ (4)*; 1967 *F;* 1968 *BI (4)*; 1968-69 *(ST) F (2)*; 1969 *A (4)*; 1969-70 *(T) S, I, W;* 1970 *NZ (4)*; 1971 *F (2), A (3)*

Du Preez, J.G.H. (*Western Province*) 1956 *NZ*

Du Rand, J.A. (*Rhodesia, Northern Transvaal*) 1949 *NZ (2)*; 1951-52 *(T) S, I, W, E, F;* 1953 *A (4)*; 1955 *BI (4)*; 1956 *A (2), NZ (4)*

Du Toit, P. A. (*Northern Transvaal*) 1949 *NZ (3)*; 1951-52 *(T) S, I, W, E, F*

Du Toit, P.G. (*Western Province*) 1981 *NZ;* 1982 *S Am (2)*; 1984 *E (2)*

Du Toit, P.S. (*Western Province*) 1958 *F (2)*; 1960 *NZ (4)*; 1960-61 *(T) W, I, E, S, F;* 1961 *I, A (2)*

Duvenage, F.P. (*Griqualand West*) 1949 *NZ (2)*

Edwards, P. (*Northern Transvaal*) 1980 *S Am (2)*

Ellis, J.H. (*South West Africa*) 1965 *NZ (4)*; 1967 *F (4)*; 1968 *BI (4)*; 1968-69 *(ST) F (2)*; 1969 *A (4)*; 1969-70 *(T) S, I, W;* 1970 *NZ (4)*; 1971 *F (2), A (3)*; 1972 *E;* 1974 *BI (4), (ST) F (2)*; 1976 *NZ*

Engelbrecht, J.P. (*Western Province*) 1960 *S;* 1960-61 *(T) W, I, E, S, F;* 1961 *A (2)*; 1962 *BI (3)*; 1963 *A (2)*; 1964 *W, F;* 1964-65 *(ST) I, S;* 1965 *A (2), NZ (4)*; 1967 *F (4)*; 1968 *BI (2)*; 1968-69 *(ST) F (2)*; 1969 *A (2)*

Ferreira, P.S. (*Western Province*) 1984 *S Am (2)*

Fourie, C. (*Eastern Province*) 1974 *(ST) F (2)*; 1975 *F (2)*

Fourie, T.T. (*South-East Transvaal*) 1974 *BI*

Fourie, W.L. (*South-West Africa*) 1958 *F (2)*

Frederickson, C.A. (*Transvaal*) 1974 *BI;* 1980 *S Am (2)*

Froneman, D.C. (*Orange Free State*) 1977 *Wld*

Fry, S.P. (*Western Province*) 1951-52 *(T) S, I, W, E, F;* 1953 *A (4)*; 1955 *BI (4)*

Gainsford, J.L. (*Western Province*) 1960 *S, NZ (4)*; 1960-61 *(T) W, I, E, S, F;* 1961 *A (2)*; 1962 *BI (4)*; 1963 *A (4)*; 1964 *W, F;* 1964-65 *(ST) I, S;* 1965 *A (2), NZ (4)*; 1967 *F (3)*

Geel, P.J. (*Orange Free State*) 1949 *NZ*

Geffin, A. (*Transvaal*) 1949 *NZ (4)*; 1951-52 *(T) S, I, W*

Geldenhuys, S.B. (*Northern Transvaal*) 1981 *NZ (2), US;* 1982 *S Am (2)*

Gentles, T.A. (*Western Province*) 1955 *BI (3)*; 1956 *NZ (2)*; 1958 *F*

Geraghty, E.M. (*Border*) 1949 *NZ*

Gerber, D.M. (*Eastern Province*) 1980 *S Am (ST) (2), F;* 1981 *I (2), NZ (3), US;* 1982 *S Am (2)*; 1984 *E (2), S Am (2)*

Gerber, M.C. (*Eastern Province*) 1958 *F (2)*; 1960 *S*

Gericke, F.W. (*Transvaal*) 1960 *S*

Germishuys, J.S. (*Orange Free State, Transvaal*) 1974 *BI;* 1976 *NZ (4)*; 1977 *Wld;* 1980 *S Am (2), BI (4), S Am (ST) (2), F;* 1981 *I (2), NZ (2), US*

Goosen, C.P. (*Orange Free State*) 1965 *NZ*

Greenwood, C.M. (*Western Province*) 1961 *I*

Greyling, P.J.F. (*Orange Free State*) 1967 *F (4)*; 1968 *BI;* 1968-69 *(ST) F (2)*; 1969 *A (4)*; 1969-70 *(T) S, E, I, W;* 1970 *NZ (4)*; 1971 *F (2), A (3)*; 1972 *E*

Grobler, C.J. (*Orange Free State*) 1974 *BI;* 1975 *F (2)*

Heunis, J.W. (*Northern Transvaal*) 1981 *NZ (r), US;* 1982 *S Am (2)*; 1984 *E (2), S Am (2)*

Hill, R.A. (*Rhodesia*) 1960-61 *(T) W, I;* 1961 *I, A (2)*; 1962 *BI;* 1963 *A*

Hoffman, R.S. (*Boland*) 1953 *A*

Holton, D.N. (*Eastern Province*) 1960 *S*
Hopwood, D.J. (*Western Province*) 1960 *S*, *NZ (2)*; 1960-61 *(T) W, E, S, F*; 1961 *I, A (2)*; 1962 *BI (4)*; 1963 *A (3)*; 1964 *W, F*; 1964-65 *(ST) S*; 1965 *NZ (2)*
Howe, B.F. (*Border*) 1956 *NZ (2)*

Jansen, E. (*Orange Free State*) 1981 *NZ*
Jansen, J.S. (*Orange Free State*) 1970 *NZ (4)*; 1971 *F (2), A (3)*; 1972 *E*
Johnstone, P.G.A. (*Western Province*) 1951-52 *(T) S, I, W, E, F*; 1956 *A, NZ (3)*
Jordaan, R.P. (*Northern Transvaal*) 1949 *NZ (4)*

Kahts, W.J.H. (*Northern Transvaal*) 1980 *BI (3)*, *S Am (ST) (2), F*; 1981 *I (2), NZ*; 1982 *S Am (2)*
Kaminer, J. (*Transvaal*) 1958 *F*
Kenyon, B.J. (*Border*) 1949 *NZ*
Kirkpatrick, A.I. (*Griqualand West*) 1953 *A*; 1956 *NZ*; 1958 *F*; 1960 *S, NZ (4)*; 1960-61 *(T) W, I, E, S, F*
Koch, A.C. (*Boland*) 1949 *NZ (3)*; 1951-52 *(T) S, I, W, E, F*; 1953 *A (3)*; 1955 *BI (4)*; 1956 *A, NZ (2)*; 1958 *F (2)*; 1960 *NZ (2)*
Koch, H.W. (*Western Province*) 1949 *NZ (4)*
Kotze, G.J.M. (*Western Province*) 1967 *F (4)*
Krantz, E.F.W. (*Orange Free State*) 1976 *NZ*; 1981 *I*
Kritzinger, J.L. (*Transvaal*) 1974 *BI (2)*; 1974 *(ST) F (2)*; 1975 *F (2)*; 1976 *NZ*
Kroon, C.M. (*Eastern Province*) 1955 *BI*
Kuhn, S.P. (*Transvaal*) 1960 *NZ (2)*; 1960-61 *(T) W, I, E, S, F*; 1961 *I, A (2)*; 1962 *BI (4)*; 1963 *A (3)*; 1964-65 *(ST) I, S*

Lategan, M.T. (*Western Province*) 1949 *NZ (4)*; 1951-52 *(T) S, I, W, E, F*; 1953 *A (2)*
Lawless, M.J. (*Western Province*) 1964 *F*; 1969-70 *(T) E (r), I, W*
Le Roux, M. (*Orange Free State*) 1980 *BI (4)*, *S Am (ST) (2), F*; 1981 *I*
Lochner, G.P. 'Butch' (*Western Province*) 1955 *BI*; 1956 *A (2), NZ (4)*; 1958 *F (2)*
Lockyear, R.J. (*Griqualand West*) 1960 *NZ (4)*; 1960-61 *(T) I, F*
Lourens, M.J. (*Northern Transvaal*) 1968 *BI (3)*
Louw, M.J. (*Transvaal*) 1971 *A (2)*
Louw, R.J. (*Western Province*) 1980 *S Am (2)*, *BI (4), S Am (ST) (2), F*; 1981 *I (2), NZ (2)*; 1982 *S Am (2)*; 1984 *E (2), S Am (2)*

MacDonald, A.W. (*Rhodesia*) 1965 *A, NZ (4)*
Macdonald, D.A. (*Western Province*) 1974 *BI*
Malan, A.S. (*Transvaal*) 1960 *NZ (4)*; 1960-61 *(T) W, I, E, S, F*; 1962 *BI*; 1963 *A (3)*; 1964 *W*; 1964-65 *(ST) I, S*
Malan, E. (*Northern Transvaal*) 1980 *BI (2[1r])*
Malan, G.F. (*Western Province*) 1958 *F*; 1960 *NZ (3)*; 1960-61 *(T) E, S, F*; 1962 *BI (3)*; 1963 *A (3)*; 1964 *W*; 1965 *A (2), NZ (2)*
Malan, P. (*Transvaal*) 1949 *NZ*
Mallett, N.V.H. (*Western Province*) 1984 *S Am (2)*
Mans, W.J. (*Western Province*) 1964-65 *(ST) I, S*
Marais, F.P. (*Boland*) 1949 *NZ (2)*; 1951-52 *(T) S*; 1953 *A (2)*
Marais, J.F.K. (*Western Province*) 1963 *A*; 1964 *W, F*; 1964-65 *(ST) I, S*; 1965 *A*; 1968 *BI (4)*; 1968-69 *(ST) F (2)*; 1969 *A (4)*; 1969-

70 *(T) S, E, I, W*; 1970 *NZ (4)*; 1971 *F (2), A (3)*; 1974 *BI (4)*; 1974 *(ST) F (2)*
McCallum, I.D. (*Western Province*) 1970 *NZ (4)*; 1971 *F (2), A (3)*; 1974 *BI (2)*
McCallum, R.J. (*Western Province*) 1974 *BI*
Montini, P.E. (*Western Province*) 1956 *A (2)*
Moolman, L.C. (*Northern Transvaal*) 1977 *Wld*; 1980 *S Am (2), BI (4), S Am (ST) (2), F*; 1981 *I (2), NZ (3), US*; 1982 *S Am (2)*; 1984 *S Am*
Mordt, R.H. (*Zimbabwe-Rhodesia, Northern Transvaal*) 1980 *S Am (2), BI (4), S Am (ST) (2), F*; 1981 *I, NZ (3), US*; 1982 *S Am (2)*; 1984 *S Am (2)*
Moss, C. (*Natal*) 1949 *NZ (4)*
Muller, G.H. (*Western Province*) 1969 *A (2)*; 1969-70 *(T) S, W*; 1970 *NZ (4)*; 1971 *F (2)*; 1972 *E*; 1974 *BI (3)*
Muller, H.S.V. (*Transvaal*) 1949 *NZ (4)*; 1951-52 *(T) S, I, W, E, F*; 1953 *A (4)*
Myburgh, J.L. (*Northern Transvaal*) 1962 *BI*; 1963 *A*; 1964 *W, F*; 1968 *BI (3)*; 1968-69 *(ST) F (2)*; 1969 *A (4)*; 1969-70 *(T) E, I, W*; 1970 *NZ (2)*

Naude, J.P. (*Western Province*) 1963 *A*; 1965 *A (2), NZ (3)*; 1967 *F (4)*; 1968 *BI (4)*
Neethling, J.B. (*Western Province*) 1967 *F (4)*; 1968 *BI*; 1969-70 *(T) S*; 1970 *NZ (2)*
Nel, J.A. (*Transvaal*) 1960 *NZ (2)*; 1963 *A (2)*; 1965 *A, NZ (4)*; 1970 *NZ (2)*
Nel, J.J. (*Western Province*) 1956 *A (2), NZ (4)*; 1958 *F (2)*
Nimb, C.F. (*Western Province*) 1961 *I*
Nomis, S.H. (*Transvaal*) 1967 *F*; 1968 *BI (4)*; 1968-69 *(ST) F (2)*; 1969 *A (4)*; 1969-70 *(T) S, E, I, W*; 1970 *NZ (4)*; 1971 *F (2), A (3)*; 1972 *E*

Ochse, J.K. (*Western Province*) 1951-52 *(T) I, W, E, F*; 1953 *A (3)*
Oelofse, J.S.A. (*Transvaal*) 1953 *A (4)*
Olivier, E. (*Western Province*) 1967 *F (4)*; 1968 *BI (4)*; 1968-69 *(ST) F (2)*; 1969 *A (4)*; 1969-70 *(T), S, E*
Oosthuizen, J.J. (*Western Province*) 1974 *BI, (ST) F (2)*; 1975 *F (2)*; 1976 *NZ (4)*
Oosthuizen, O.W. (*Northern Transvaal, Transvaal*) 1981 *I (2[1r]), NZ (2), US*; 1982 *S Am (2)*; 1984 *E (2)*
Oxlee, K. (*Natal*) 1960 *NZ (4)*; 1960-61 *(T) W, I, S*; 1961 *A (2)*; 1962 *BI (4)*; 1963 *A (3)*; 1964 *W*; 1965 *NZ (2)*

Parker, W.H. (*Eastern Province*) 1965 *A (2)*
Pelser, H.J.M. (*Transvaal*) 1958 *F*; 1960 *NZ (4)*; 1960-61 *(T) W, I, F*; 1961 *I, A (2)*
Pfaff, B.D. (*Western Province*) 1956 *A*
Pickard, J.A.J. (*Western Province*) 1953 *A (2)*; 1956 *NZ*; 1958 *F*
Pienaar, Z.M.J. (*Orange Free State*) 1980 *S Am (r), BI (4), S Am (ST) (2), F*; 1981 *I (2), NZ (3)*
Pitzer, G. (*Northern Transvaal*) 1967 *F (4)*; 1968 *BI (4)*; 1968-69 *(ST) F (2)*; 1969 *A (2)*
Pope, C.F. (*Western Province*) 1974 *BI (4)*; 1975 *F (2)*; 1976 *NZ (4)*
Potgieter, H.L. (*Orange Free State*) 1977 *Wld*
Prentis, R.B. (*Transvaal*) 1980 *S Am (2), BI (4), S Am (ST) (2), F*; 1981 *I (2)*
Prinsloo, J. (*Transvaal*) 1958 *F (2)*
Prinsloo, J. (*Northern Transvaal*) 1963 *A*
Putter, D.J. (*Western Transvaal*) 1963 *A (3)*

Ras, W.J. de Wet (*Orange Free State*) 1976 *NZ (r)*; 1980 *S Am (r)*
Rens, I.J. (*Transvaal*) 1953 *A (2)*
Retief, D.F. (*Northern Transvaal*) 1955 *BI (3)*; 1956 *A (2), NZ (4)*
Riley, N. (*Eastern Transvaal*) 1963 *A*
Robertson, I.W. (*Rhodesia*) 1974 *(ST) F (2)*; 1976 *NZ (3)*
Rogers, C.D. (*Transvaal*) 1984 *E (2), S Am (2)*
Rosenberg, W. (*Transvaal*) 1955 *BI (3)*; 1956 *NZ*; 1958 *F*
Rossouw, D.H. (*Western Province*) 1953 *A (2)*
Roux, F. du T. (*Western Province*) 1960-61 *(T) W*; 1961 *A (2)*; 1962 *BI (4)*; 1963 *A*; 1965 *A (2), NZ (4)*; 1968 *BI (2)*; 1968-69 *(ST) F (2)*; 1969-70 *(T) I*; 1970 *NZ (4)*
Roux, O.A. (*Northern Transvaal*) 1969-70 *(T) S, E, I, W*; 1972 *E*; 1974 *BI (2)*

Sauermann, J.T. (*Transvaal*) 1971 *F (2), A*; 1972 *E*; 1974 *BI*
Schlebusch, J.J.J. (*Orange Free State*) 1974 *BI (2)*; 1975 *F*
Schmidt, L.U. (*Northern Transvaal*) 1958 *F*; 1962 *BI*
Schoeman, J. (*Western Province*) 1963 *A (2)*; 1964-65 *(ST) I, S*; 1965 *A, NZ (2)*
Serfontein, D.J. (*Western Province*) 1980 *BI (4), S Am (ST) (2), F*; 1981 *I (2), NZ (3), US*; 1982 *S Am (2)*; 1984 *E (2), S Am (2)*
Sinclair, D.J. (*Transvaal*) 1955 *BI (4)*
Skene, A.L. (*Western Province*) 1958 *F*
Smith, C.M. (*Orange Free State*) 1963 *A (2)*; 1964 *W, F*; 1965 *A (2), NZ*
Smith, D.J. (*Zimbabwe-Rhodesia*) 1980 *BI (4)*
Snyman, D.S.L. (*Western Province*) 1972 *E*; 1974 *BI (2[1r])*; 1974 *(ST) F (2)*; 1975 *F (2)*; 1976 *NZ (2)*; 1977 *Wld*
Snyman, J.C.P. (*Orange Free State*) 1974 *BI (3)*
Sonnekus, G.H.H. (*Orange Free State*) 1974 *BI*; 1984 *E (2)*
Spies, J.J. (*Northern Transvaal*) 1970 *NZ (4)*
Stander, J.C.J. (*Orange Free State*) 1974 *BI (r)*; 1976 *NZ (4)*
Stapelberg, W.P. (*Northern Transvaal*) 1974 *(ST) F (2)*
Starke, J.J. (*Western Province*) 1956 *NZ*
Steenekamp, J.G.A. (*Transvaal*) 1958 *F*
Stewart, D.A. (*Western Province*) 1960 *S*; 1960-61 *(T) E, S, F*; 1961 *I*; 1963 *A (3)*; 1964 *W, F*; 1964-65 *(ST) I*
Stofberg, M.T.S. (*Orange Free State, Northern Transvaal, Western Province*) 1976 *NZ (2)*; 1977 *Wld*; 1980 *S Am (2), BI (4), S Am (ST) (2), F*; 1981 *I (2), NZ (2), US*; 1982 *S Am (2)*; 1984 *E (2)*
Strauss, J.A. (*Western Province*) 1984 *S Am (2)*
Strauss, J.H.P. (*Transvaal*) 1976 *NZ (2)*; 1980 *S Am*
Strydom, C.F. (*Orange Free State*) 1955 *BI*; 1956 *A (2), NZ (2)*; 1958 *F*
Strydom, L.J. (*Northern Transvaal*) 1949 *NZ (2)*
Suter, M.R. (*Natal*) 1964-65 *(ST) I, S*
Swart, J.J.N. (*South West Africa*) 1955 *BI*

Taylor, O.B. (*Natal*) 1962 *BI*
Tobias, E.G. (*SARF, Boland*) 1981 *I (2)*; 1984 *E (2), S Am (2)*
Truter, J.T. (*Natal*) 1963 *A*; 1964 *F*; 1965 *A*

Twigge, R.J. (*Northern Transvaal*) 1960 *S*

Van Aswegen, H.J. (*Western Province*) 1981 *NZ*

Van Den Berg, D.S. (*Natal*) 1975 *F (2)*; 1976 *NZ (2)*

Van Der Merwe, A.J. (*Boland*) 1955 *BI (3)*; 1956 *A (2)*, *NZ (4)*; 1958 *F*; 1960 *S*, *NZ*

Van Der Merwe, B.S. (*Northern Transvaal*) 1949 *NZ*

Van Der Merwe, H.S. (*Northern Transvaal*) 1960 *NZ*; 1963 *A (3)*; 1964 *F*

Van Der Merwe, J.P. (*Western Province*) 1969-70 *(T) W*

Van Der Merwe, P.R. (*South Western Districts*) 1981 *NZ (2)*, *US*

Van Der Schyff, J.H. (*Griqualand West*) 1949 *NZ (4)*; 1955 *BI*

Van Der Watt, A.E. (*Western Province*) 1969-70 *(T) S (r)*, *E*, *I*

Van Heerden, J.L. (*Northern Transvaal, Transvaal*) 1974 *BI (2)*; 1974 *(ST) F (2)*; 1975 *F (2)*; 1976 *NZ (4)*; 1977 *Wld*; 1980 *BI (3)*, *S Am (ST) (2)*, *F*

Van Jaarsveld, C.J. (*Transvaal*) 1949 *NZ*

Van Jaarsveldt, D.C. (*Rhodesia*) 1960 *S*

Van Schoor, R.A.M. (*Rhodesia*) 1949 *NZ (3)*;

1951-52 *(T) S, I, W, E, F*; 1953 *A (4)*

Van Vollenhoven, K.T. (*Northern Transvaal*) 1955 *BI (4)*; 1956 *A (2)*, *NZ*

Van Wyk, C.J. (*Transvaal*) 1951-52 *(T) S, I, W, E, F*; 1953 *A (4)*; 1955 *BI*

Van Wyk, J.F.B. (*Northern Transvaal*) 1970 *NZ (4)*; 1971 *F (2)*, *A (3)*; 1972 *E*; 1974 *BI (3)*; 1976 *NZ (2)*

Van Zyl, B.P. (*Western Province*) 1961 *I*

Van Zyl, C.G.P. (*Orange Free State*) 1965 *NZ (4)*

Van Zyl, G.H. (*Western Province*) 1958 *F*; 1960 *S*, *NZ (4)*; 1960-61 *(T) W, I, E, S, F*; 1961 *I*, *A (2)*; 1962 *BI (3)*

Van Zyl, H.J. (*Transvaal*) 1960 *NZ (4)*; 1960-61 *(T) I, E, S*; 1961 *I*, *A (2)*

Van Zyl, P.J. (*Boland*) 1961 *I*

Veldsman, P.E. (*Western Province*) 1977 *Wld*

Viljoen, J.F. (*Griqualand West*) 1971 *F (2)*, *A (3)*; 1972 *E*

Viljoen, J.T. (*Natal*) 1971 *A (3)*

Villet, J.V. (*Western Province*) 1984 *E (2)*

Visagie, P.J. (*Griqualand West*) 1967 *F (4)*; 1968 *BI (4)*; 1968-69 *(ST) F (2)*; 1969 *A (4)*; 1969-70 *(T) S, E*; 1970 *NZ (4)*; 1971 *F (2)*, *A (3)*

Visagie, R.G. (*Orange Free State*) 1984 *E (2)*,

S Am (2)

Visser, J. de V. (*Western Province*) 1981 *NZ*, *US*

Viviers, S.S. (*Orange Free State*) 1956 *A (2)*, *NZ (3)*

Vogel, M.L. (*Orange Free State*) 1974 *BI (r)*

Wagenaar, C. (*Northern Transvaal*) 1977 *Wld*

Wahl, J.J. (*Western Province*) 1949 *NZ*

Walker, H.N. (*Orange Free State*) 1953 *A*; 1956 *A*, *NZ (2)*

Walton, D.C. (*Natal*) 1964 *F*; 1964-65 *(ST) S*; 1965 *NZ (2)*; 1969 *A (2)*; 1969-70 *(T) E*

Whipp, P.J.M. (*Western Province*) 1974 *BI (2)*; 1975 *F*; 1976 *NZ (3)*; 1980 *S Am (2)*

Williams, A.P. (*Western Province*) 1984 *E (2)*

Williams, J.G. (*Northern Transvaal*) 1971 *F (2)*, *A (3)*; 1972 *E*; 1974 *BI (3)*, *(ST) F (2)*; 1976 *NZ (2)*

Wilson, L.G. (*Western Province*) 1960 *NZ (2)*; 1960-61 *(T) W, I, E, F*; 1961 *I*, *A (2)*; 1962 *BI (4)*; 1963 *A (4)*; 1964 *W*, *F*; 1964-65 *(ST) I*, *S*; 1965 *A (2)*, *NZ (4)*

Wolmarans, B.J. (*Orange Free State*) 1977 *Wld*

Wyness, M.R.K. (*Western Province*) 1962 *BI (4)*; 1963 *A*

John Pullin, England hooker (forty two caps), appeared seven times for the Lions.

Record Cap-Holders
up to 30th April 1986

England

43	A. Neary
42	J.V. Pullin
41	P.J. Wheeler
36	D.J. Duckham
34	D.P. Rogers
34	W.B. Beaumont
34	J.P. Scott
32	P.W. Dodge
31	W.W. Wakefield
31	F.E. Cotton
31	M.A.C. Slemen
30	E. Evans
29	R. Cove-Smith
29	C.R. Jacobs
29	M.P. Weston
29	P.J. Squires
28	J. Butterfield
28	S.J. Smith
27	A.T. Voyce
27	J.S. Tucker
27	G.S. Pearce
26	J. Carleton
25	C.N. Lowe
25	J.D. Currie
25	M.S. Phillips
25	C.B. Stevens
25	W.H. Hare
25	M.J. Colclough
24	R.E.G. Jeeps
24	P.J. Larter
24	A.G. Ripley
23	J. MacG.K. Kendall-Carpenter
23	R.W.D. Marques
23	R.M. Uttley
22	W.J.A. Davies
22	P.E. Judd
22	C.W. Ralston
22	P.J. Dixon
22	J.G.G. Birkett
21	H.G. Periton
21	C.R. Woodward
20	P.B. Jackson
20	N.E. Horton

Ireland

69	C.M.H. Gibson
63	W.J. McBride
61	J.F. Slattery

54 T.J. Kiernan	**Scotland**	21 W.B. Welsh
51 M.I. Keane	52 J.M. Renwick	21 P.W. Kininmonth
50 P.A. Orr	51 A.R. Irvine	21 A.J.W. Hinshelwood
46 J.W. Kyle	50 A.B. Carmichael	21 D.W. Morgan
45 K.W. Kennedy	44 A.F. McHarg	21 W. Cuthbertson
42 G.V. Stephenson	44 C.T. Deans	21 J.R. Beattie
41 N.A.A. Murphy	43 J.McLauchlan	20 C. Reid
41 W.P. Duggan	41 A.J. Tomes	20 D.S. Davies
40 N.J. Henderson	40 H.F. McLeod	20 J.C. Dykes
40 R.J.McLoughlin	40 D.M.D. Rollo	20 W.R. Logan
37 S. Millar	37 J.MacD. Bannerman	20 J.C. Dawson
35 J.R. Kavanagh	37 J.Y. Rutherford	20 J.T. Greenwood
35 W.A. Mulcahy	36 R.J. Laidlaw	20 J.W.C. Turner
34 E.O'D. Davy	33 I.G. Milne	20 N.A. MacEwan
30 A.C. Pedlow	33 K.W. Robertson	
30 G.T. Hamlet	33 A.R. Smith	**Wales**
30 W.E. Crawford	32 I.S. Smith	55 J.P.R. Williams
30 J.D. Clinch	32 F.A.L. Laidlaw	53 G.O. Edwards
29 J.L. Farrell	32 I.R. McGeechan	46 T.G.R. Davies
29 B.G.M. Wood	32 D.G. Leslie	44 K.J. Jones
29 A.J.F. O'Reilly	31 N.S. Bruce	41 G. Price
28 M. Sugden	31 I.H.P. Laughland	38 T.M. Davies
28 J.S. McCarthy	30 G.L. Brown	36 D. Williams
27 A.M. Magee	29 W.I.D. Elliot	35 R.M. Owen
27 A.R. Dawson	28 W.M. Simmers	34 B.V. Meredith
27 M.G. Molloy	28 P.K. Stagg	34 D.I.E. Bebb
27 J.J. Moloney	27 J.W.Y. Kemp	34 W.D. Morris
26 J.C. Walsh	27 K.J.F. Scotland	34 A.J. Martin
26 R.M. Young	27 P.C. Brown	33 W.J. Bancroft
26 J.B. O'Driscoll	27 D.I. Johnston	32 B. Price
25 G.R. Beamish	27 J.H. Calder	32 J.R.G. Stephens
25 K.D. Mullen	26 D. Drysdale	32 G.A.D. Wheel
25 F.P.K. Bresnihan	26 J.C. McCallum	30 J.J. Williams
25 A.T.A. Duggan	26 G.P.S. Macpherson	30 S.P. Fenwick
25 B.J. McGann	25 W.E. Maclagan	29 W.J. Trew
25 T.O. Grace	25 J.B. Nelson	29 C.I. Morgan
25 S.A. McKinney	25 J.P. Fisher	29 P. Bennett
25 H.P. MacNeill	25 J.W. Telfer	29 J. Squire
25 C.F. Fitzgerald	25 G.R.T. Baird	28 R.W. Windsor
24 J.A.E. Siggins	25 I.A.M. Paxton	27 A.J. Gould
23 A. Tedford	24 G.D. Stevenson	27 W.C. Powell
23 J.W. McKay	24 M.A. Biggar	27 M.C. Thomas
22 F. Gardiner	24 J. Aitken	27 H.J. Morgan
22 J.A. O'Meara	23 M.C. Morrison	26 R.C.C. Thomas
22 A.A. Mulligan	23 J.A. Beattie	26 A.E.I. Pask
22 M.K. Flynn	23 M.J. Campbell-Lamerton	26 S.J. Watkins
22 A.H. Ensor	23 J.N.M. Frame	26 J. Taylor
22 S.O. Campbell	23 W.C.C. Steele	25 G. Travers
22 D.G. Lenihan	23 B.H. Hay	25 H. Tanner
21 C.E. Allen	22 D.R. Bedell-Sivright	25 B. John
21 R. Roe	22 A. Robson	25 N.R. Gale
21 P.O.'Callaghan	22 S. Wilson	25 W.D. Thomas
21 T.M. Ringland	22 R.J. Arneil	24 E. Gwyn Nicholls
20 J.C. Parke	21 R.G. MacMillan	24 R.T. Gabe
20 J.McVicker	21 W.P. Scott	24 D.J. Lloyd
20 C.J. Hanrahan	21 W.E. Kyle	24 T.D. Holmes
20 D.J. O'Brien	21 J.M.B. Scott	23 J.J. Hodges
20 N.H. Brophy	21 J.R. Paterson	23 E.C. Davey
20 M.G. Doyle		

Above *Jim Renwick, Scotland's most capped player with fifty two appearances, has only recently retired from playing for Hawick.* Right *Gareth Edwards is Wales' most capped scrum-half with fifty three appearances (plus ten for the British Lions).*

23	J.A. Gwilliam	45	J.-L. Joinel	25	R. Biénès
23	R.H. Williams	43	M. Crauste	25	E. Ribère
23	J. Young	42	W. Spanghero	25	M. Prat
23	D.L. Quinnell	40	J.-P. Lux	25	L. Mias
23	R.W.R. Gravell	38	J. Prat	25	J. Gachassin
22	T.R. Prosser	38	S. Blanco	25	J.-P. Bastiat
22	B.L. Williams	35	M. Celaya	25	A. Paco
22	W.O.G. Williams	34	A. Boniface	25	F. Haget
22	S.J. Dawes	34	A. Domenech	24	P. Albaladejo
21	T.J. Davies	34	J.-C. Skréla	24	C. Lacaze
21	E.M. Jenkins	34	P. Dintrans	24	R. Bénésis
21	B. Thomas	33	G. Dufau	24	J. Trillo
21	W.R. Willis	30	M. Vannier	23	A. Roques
21	D. Watkins	30	E. Cester	23	G. Boniface
21	W.G. Davies	29	P. Villepreux	23	C. Carrère
21	R.A. Ackerman	28	C. Darrouy	23	G. Cholley
20	W. Llewellyn	28	J. Dupuy	23	J. Gallion
20	A.F. Harding	28	C. Dourthe	22	M. Pomathios
20	J. Webb	28	J. Iraçabal	22	J.-P. Romeu
20	A. Skym	28	J.-M. Aguirre	21	M. Communeau
		28	P. Sella	21	F. Moncla
		27	A. Cassayet	21	J.-L. Azarète
France		27	J. Bouquet	20	B. Chevallier
52	R. Bertranne	26	G. Basquet	20	P. Lacroix
50	B. Dauga	26	D. Codorniou	20	C. Spanghero
47	J.-P. Rives	26	J. Condom	20	J.-L. Averous
46	R. Paparemborde	25	A. Jauréguy	20	P. Berbizier

Australia

42	P.G. Johnson
41	A.R. Miller
39	G.V. Davis
37	J.E. Thornett
36	J.N.B. Hipwell
36	A.A. Shaw
31	B.J. Moon
30	N.M. Shehadie
30	P.E. McLean
29	S.P. Poidevin
28	M.E. Loane
27	K.W. Catchpole
27	G.A. Shaw
27	A.G. Slack
26	C.T. Burke
25	R.B. Prosser
25	G. Cornelsen
25	M.G. Ella
24	J.K. Lenehan
24	J.P.L. White
24	J.W. Cole
24	G. Fay
24	M.J. Hawker
24	S.A. Williams
23	R. Phelps
22	R.A. Smith
22	J.E.C. Meadows
22	R.G. Gould
21	E.T. Bonis
21	P.F. Hawthorne
21	R.J. Heming
21	A.N. McGill
20	A.S. Cameron
20	B.J. Ellwood
20	C.J. Windon

New Zealand

55	C.E. Meads
41	A.M. Haden
39	I.A. Kirkpatrick
38	K.R. Tremain
38	B.G. Williams
35	A.G. Dalton
34	B.J. Robertson
34	S.S. Wilson
34	G.A. Knight
34	M.G. Mexted
32	W.J. Whineray
31	D.B. Clarke
29	S.M. Going
29	M.W. Shaw
27	R.W. Norton
25	B.J. Lochore
24	B.E. McLeod
24	K.F. Gray
24	I.J. Clarke

24	D.S. Loveridge
24	J.C. Ashworth
23	R.A. White
23	B.G. Fraser
22	D.J. Graham
22	D. Young
21	G.N.K. Mourie
20	K.L. Skinner
20	C.R. Laidlaw
20	I.N. MacEwan
20	P.J. Whiting

South Africa

38	F.C.H. Du Preez
38	J.H. Ellis
35	J.F.K. Marais
33	J.P. Engelbrecht
33	J.L. Gainsford
28	J.T. Claassen
27	F.du T. Roux
27	L.G. Wilson
25	T.P. Bedford
25	D.J.de Villiers
25	P.J.F. Greyling
25	S.H. Nomis
25	P.J. Visagie
22	D.J. Hopwood
22	A.C. Koch
22	M. Du Plessis
21	J.A.du Rand
21	M.T.S. Stofberg
20	L.C. Moolman

World

The table includes all recognized International matches. British Isles appearances are in brackets after players concerned.

69	C.M.H. Gibson (*Ireland*)	(12)
63	W.J. McBride (*Ireland*)	(17)
61	J.F. Slattery (*Ireland*)	(4)
55	C.E. Meads (*New Zealand*)	
55	J.P.R. Williams (*Wales*)	(8)
54	T.J. Kiernan (*Ireland*)	(5)
53	G.O. Edwards (*Wales*)	(10)
52	R.Bertranne (*France*)	
52	J.M. Renwick (*Scotland*)	(1)
51	M.I. Keane (*Ireland*)	(1)
51	A.R. Irvine (*Scotland*)	(9)
50	B. Dauga (*France*)	
50	A.B. Carmichael (*Scotland*)	
50	P.A. Orr (*Ireland*)	(1)
49	J.-P. Rives (*France*)	
46	J.W. Kyle (*Ireland*)	(6)
46	T.G.R. Davies (*Wales*)	(5)
45	K.W. Kennedy (*Ireland*)	(4)
44	K.J. Jones (*Wales*)	(3)

44	A.F. McHarg (*Scotland*)	
44	C.T. Deans (*Scotland*)	
43	J. McLauchlan (*Scotland*)	(8)
43	A. Neary (*England*)	(1)
43	M. Crauste (*France*)	
44	R. Paparemborde (*France*)	
42	W. Spanghero (*France*)	
42	J.V. Pullin (*England*)	
42	G.V. Stephenson (*Ireland*)	
41	N.A.A. Murphy (*Ireland*)	(8)
41	G. Price (*Wales*)	(12)
41	P.J. Wheeler (*England*)	(7)
41	A.M. Haden (*New Zealand*)	
41	W.P. Duggan (*Ireland*)	(4)
40	N.J. Henderson (*Ireland*)	(1)
40	H.F. McLeod (*Scotland*)	(6)
40	D.M.D. Rollo (*Scotland*)	
40	R.J. McLoughlin (*Ireland*)	(3)
40	J.-P. Lux (*France*)	

Australia's leading cap-winners, in recognized Internationals, are P.G. Johnson and G.V. Davis, 39 caps each. A.R. Miller won 41 Australian caps, but only 31 in recognized Internationals.

The following list includes appearances by home countries' players for British Isles teams (the Lions) in International matches against New Zealand, Australia and South Africa (up to 30th April 1986). The number of Lions' caps is recorded in brackets.

81	(12)	C.M.H. Gibson (*Ireland*)
80	(17)	W.J. McBride (*Ireland*)
65	(4)	J.F. Slattery (*Ireland*)
63	(10)	G.O. Edwards (*Wales*)
63	(8)	J.P.R. Williams (*Wales*)
59	(5)	T.J. Kiernan (*Ireland*)
59	(9)	A.R. Irvine (*Scotland*)
55		C.E. Meads (*New Zealand*)
53	(12)	G. Price (*Wales*)
52	(6)	J.W. Kyle (*Ireland*)
52		R. Bertranne (*France*)
52	(1)	M.I. Keane (*Ireland*)
52	(1)	J.M. Renwick (*Scotland*)
51	(5)	T.G.R. Davies (*Wales*)
51	(8)	J. McLauchlan (*Scotland*)
51	(1)	P.A. Orr (*Ireland*)
50		B. Dauga (*France*)
50		A.B. Carmichael (*Scotland*)
49	(8)	N.A.A. Murphy (*Ireland*)
49	(4)	K.W. Kennedy (*Ireland*)
49	(7)	J.V. Pullin (*England*)
49		J.-P. Rives (*France*)
48	(7)	P.J. Wheeler (*England*)
47	(3)	K.J. Jones (*Wales*)
46	(9)	S. Millar (*Ireland*)
46	(6)	H.F. McLeod (*Scotland*)
46	(8)	T.M. Davies (*Wales*)
45	(4)	W.P. Duggan (*Ireland*)
45		J.-L. Joinel (*France*)
44		A.F. McHarg (*Scotland*)

44	(1)	A. Neary (*England*)
44		R. Paparemborde (*France*)
44		C.T. Deans (*Scotland*)
43		M. Crauste (*France*)
43	(3)	R.J. McLoughlin (*Ireland*)
42	(8)	B.V. Meredith (*Wales*)
42	(8)	D.I.E. Bebb (*Wales*)
42		W. Spanghero (*France*)
41		G.V. Stephenson (*Ireland*)
41	(1)	N.J. Henderson (*Ireland*)
41	(6)	W.A. Mulcahy (*Ireland*)
41	(5)	D. Williams (*Wales*)
41		A.M. Haden (*New Zealand*)
40		D.M.D. Rollo (*Scotland*)
40		J.-P. Lux (*France*)
40	(8)	I.R. McGeechan (*Scotland*)

Leading Lions cap-winners are W.J. McBride 17, R.E.G. Jeeps (*England*) 13, C.M.H. Gibson 12, G. Price 12, and A.J.F. O'Reilly (*Ireland*), R.H. Williams (*Wales*) and G.O. Edwards 10 each, up to 30th April 1986.

Referees

Up to 30th April 1986, in matches involving IB countries, British Isles and for which caps were awarded.

23	K.D. Kelleher (*Ireland*)
23	D.G. Walters (*Wales*)
22	M. Joseph (*Wales*)
21	R.C. Williams (*Ireland*)
19	A.M. Hosie (*Scotland*)
18	M.J. Dowling (*Ireland*)
18	J.R. West (*Ireland*)
17	D.P. D'Arcy (*Ireland*)
17	F. Palmade (*France*)
17	A.E. Freethy (*Wales*)
16	B.S. Cumberlege (*England*)
15	C.H. Gadney (*England*)
14	I. David (*Wales*)
14	Dr I.R. Vanderfield (*Australia*)
13	J.P. Murphy (*New Zealand*)
13	D.I.H. Burnett (*Ireland*)
13	T.H. Vile (*Wales*)
13	N.R. Sanson (*Scotland*)
13	C. Norling (*Wales*)
13	R.G. Byres (*Australia*)
12	R.F. Johnson (*England*)
11	Air Cdre G.C. Lamb (*England*)
11	M.A. Allan (*Scotland*)
11	A.I. Dickie (*Scotland*)
11	N.H. Lambert (*Ireland*)
10	T.N. Pearce (*England*)

Mike Gibson (British Lions and Ireland) in action for the Lions against Border in East London (South Africa), 17th July 1974. He is the world record holder with sixty nine caps.

1986-87

Five Nations Championship – 1986-87

17th January 1987	England v. Scotland	Twickenham
	Wales v. Ireland	Cardiff
7th February 1987	Ireland v. England	Dublin
	France v. Wales	Paris
21st February 1987	England v. France	Twickenham
	Scotland v. Ireland	Murrayfield
7th March 1987	France v. Scotland	Paris
	Wales v. England	Cardiff
21st March 1987	Ireland v. France	Dublin
	Scotland v. Wales	Murrayfield

Japan Tour to England and Scotland

17th Sept. 1986	v. South of Scotland	In the South
20th Sept. 1986	v. North of Scotland	Aberdeen
23rd Sept. 1986	v. Edinburgh	Edinburgh
27th Sept. 1986	v. SCOTLAND XV	Murrayfield
1st Oct. 1986	v. Leicestershire	Leicester
4th Oct. 1986	v. Cornwall	Redruth
7th Oct. 1986	v. Combined English Students	Gloucester
11th Oct. 1986	v. ENGLAND XV	Twickenham

No All-Blacks in Paris

When New Zealand's All-Blacks tour France in autumn 1986 they will play no matches in Paris. The two Tests will be in Toulouse and Nantes.

22nd Oct. 1986	Regional Selection	Strasbourg
25th Oct. 1986	Regional Selection	Clermont-Ferrand
29th Oct. 1986	Regional Selection	Toulon
1st Nov. 1986	Regional Selection	Perpignan
4th Nov. 1986	Regional Selection	Bayonne
8th Nov. 1986	First International	Toulouse
11th Nov. 1986	French Barbarians	La Rochelle
15th Nov. 1986	Second International	Nantes

Thorn EMI Divisional Championship (England)

6th December 1986	London v. Midlands	London Area
6th December 1986	North v. South & South-West	North
13th December 1986	North v. Midlands	North
13th December 1986	South & South-West v. London	South & South-West
20th December 1986	London v. North	London Area
20th December 1986	Midlands v. South & South-West	Midlands

John Player Special Cup (England) 1986-87

27th September 1986	First Round
25th October 1986	Second Round
24th January 1987	Third Round
14th February 1987	Fourth Round
28th February 1987	Quarter-finals
28th March 1987	Semi-finals
25th April 1987	Final (at Twickenham)

Scottish Inter-District Championship 1986-87

26th November 1986	Edinburgh v. Glasgow	Edinburgh
29th November 1986	Glasgow v. South	Glasgow
	Anglo-Scots v. North & Midlands	England
6th December 1986	North & Midlands v. South	North & Midlands
13th December 1986	North & Midlands v. Edinburgh	North & Midlands
	South v. Anglo-Scots	South
20th December 1986	Edinburgh v. Anglo-Scots	Edinburgh
	Glasgow v. North & Midlands	Glasgow
27th December 1986	Anglo-Scots v. Glasgow	England
	South v. Edinburgh	South
3rd January 1987	International Trial	Murrayfield

Irish Inter-Provincial Championship 1986-87

25th October 1986	Connacht v. Leinster	Connacht
25th October 1986	Munster v. Ulster	Munster
8th November 1986	Leinster v. Munster	Dublin
8th November 1986	Ulster v. Connacht	Belfast
22nd November 1986	Munster v. Connacht	Munster
22nd November 1986	Ulster v. Leinster	Belfast

Schweppes Welsh Challenge Cup 1986-87

20th September 1986	First Preliminary Round
18th October 1986	Second Preliminary Round
15th November 1986	First Round Proper
20th December 1986	Second Round Proper
24th January 1987	Third Round Proper
21st February 1987	Fourth Round Proper
28th March 1987	Semi-finals (on neutral grounds)
2nd May 1987	Final (at National Ground, Cardiff)

The French Championship 1986-87

Qualifying 'Poules'

Poule 1
Toulouse, Graulhet, Montferrand, Béziers, Narbonne, Brive, Nice, Grenoble, Aurillac, Romans

Poule 2
Agen, Toulon, Perpignan, Biarritz, Nîmes, Racing Club de France, Lourdes, Bayonne, Valence, Pau

Poule 3
Tarbes, Oloron, Hagetmau, Dax, Mont-de-Marsan, Boucau, Bagnères, Tyrosse, Bègles, Angoulême

Poule 4
Le Creusot, La Voulte, Bourgoin, Hyères, Tulle, Carcassonne, Castres, Voiron, Saint-Gaudens, Albi

Other Important Dates for 1986-87

25th October 1986	Wales 'B' v. France 'B'	Pontypridd
1st November 1986	Ireland v. Romania (full International)	Lansdowne Road, Dublin
6th December 1986	Italy 'B' v. Scotland 'B'	Italy
9th December 1986	Oxford v. Cambridge	Twickenham
7th February 1987	Scotland 'B' v. France 'B'	Murrayfield

Acknowledgements

Our sincere thanks to Colin Elsey (Colorsport) for his help and excellent photographs. Also to Robert Kitson (Hayters), J. F. Jeavons-Fellows (North Midlands RFU), *The Daily Telegraph* Manchester Office, Guy Burden (Assistant Secretary, Bisley Office Equipment Southern Merit Table), Nick Cain *(Rugby World & Post)*, the *Western Morning News* (Plymouth), R. M. Hickey and Bryn Thomas of Aberavon RFC (whose help with Welsh matters has been invaluable).

Photographs
We would like to thank the following for providing photographic material for use in the book:

J. D. Fitzgerald: page 155
John Frimann (Dansk Rugby Union): page 59
Tricia Moore: page 47
Roy Peters: pages 48 and 49
Rugby World & Post: page 43
All other photographs were supplied by Colorsport.